D0025313

Curriculum

An Introduction to the Field

SECOND EDITION

Edited by

JAMES R. GRESS

The University of Toledo

•

With the Assistance of

DAVID E. PURPEL

University of North Carolina,
Greensboro

McCutchan Publishing Corporation
P.O. Box 774
Berkeley, California 94701

Library of Congress catalog card number 88–60451
ISBN 0–8211–0617–1

Printed in the United States of America

Contents

Preface

For many, the curriculum is a plan for schooling. For some, the curriculum is the program of study, activity, and guidance that the school plans and implements. For some, curriculum is the experience of each student in school. In any case, schooling is essential to the continuing American revolution. The processes for planning, implementing, and evaluating the curriculum are an important part of "an ongoing constitutional convention." The curriculum is clearly a significant arena for sorting our public values and priorities in making public policy. The curriculum is our most important public policy.

As a field of professional practice and scholarly inquiry, curriculum has a rich tradition and varied perspective. Perspectives of curriculum practice and theory are unfortunately unclear, however, to many teachers and other school professionals. The significance of curriculum is too little appreciated by graduate education students, whose study often includes little exposure to this field. The import of curriculum is little known by otherwise informed professionals outside education and by the public.

This text identifies the principal issues of school curriculum and the curriculum field, their historical roots and philosophical frameworks. The text presents alternative perspectives for addressing curriculum as plan for and experience of schooling and as process and product of change. The text includes overviews of issues of practice and inquiry in six parts. It also includes thirty-one edited selections from the curriculum literature accumulated in nearly a century of practice and inquiry.

As in the first edition, the overviews and reading selections are organized around sets of issues that are focal points in curriculum. The number of sets has been reorganized from seven in the first edition to six in the second. In both first and second editions, four sets of issues address definition and history; philosophical frameworks; curriculum implementation, evaluation, and change; and theory and research. In addition, three sets of issues addressed separately in the first edition are combined in the second, including planning and design, curriculum arenas and participants, and the nature and formulation of objectives. Finally, a set of issues addressing the hidden curriculum is new in this second edition. The overviews of each set of issues are printed in their entirety at the beginning of the respective parts of the new edition.

Part One of the text examines alternative definitions of curriculum and traces emergence of a field of practice and inquiry. It reviews some early contributions to the curriculum field and sketches the unprecedented change of the past quarter-century. Part One identifies the field's principal themes and the variations that have marked its history.

In Part Two, alternative philosophical frameworks for addressing curriculum issues are identified. Philosophical assumptions underlying alternative frameworks are identified and compared. Relationships between curriculum and values are explored.

Curriculum planning and design are addressed in Part Three. Prescriptive and descriptive planning models are presented, and the issues of planning arena and participants are addressed. Some relationships between school and society are clarified here. Part Three also summarizes alternative curriculum designs and presents a traditional conception for design. Finally, it presents a critique of traditional planning and design.

Part Four addresses the hidden curriculum. Discrepancy between curriculum as plan and curriculum as experience of schooling is clarified and documented. Possible discrepancy between values and curriculum is also examined. The hidden curriculums of work, of the textbook, and of the foundations of schooling are explored, and relationships among schooling, politics, and language are made explicit.

Curriculum implementation, evaluation, and change are examined in Part Five. It elaborates components and variations in curriculum implementation and variables associated with them. It also details alternative sets of principles for curriculum evaluation. Part Five examines determinants of curriculum change and stability as identified in both recent and earlier treatments of the field.

In Part Six, alternative conceptual and methodological structures for curriculum theory and research are identified and discussed. Paradigms for curriculum theory are examined, and relationships between theory and practice are suggested.

In each part of the text, the overview of issues is complemented by classic selections from the field's literature. The overviews provide unity and coherence for the reader. The reading selections provide alternative approaches to the issues identified and samples of the field's rich tradition and varied perspective. The text is addressed to three groups: to teachers and other school personnel, whose professional understanding is critical to schooling in a democracy; to graduate students in curriculum and related areas of professional education, who inherit particular responsibility in the field; and to professionals outside education and the public, whose stake in curriculum and schooling is perhaps underestimated.

ACKNOWLEDGMENTS

Several special contributions to this second edition need acknowledgment. I wish to thank the University of Toledo for sabbatical leave to complete work on the manuscript. Particular thanks are expressed to Mrs. Eva Hulisz, whose skill and patience were tested in many drafts of the manuscript, and to the secretarial and clerical staff in UT's College of Education and Allied Professions, whose cooperation and support for all my projects cannot be overestimated. I wish to thank McCutchan editors Sylvia E. Stein and Kim Sharrar as well.

As with the first edition, special thanks are due Professor David Purpel, who encouraged work on a second edition, suggested some new reading selections, commented extensively on readings and overview drafts, challenged my thinking, and provided much insight, particularly in Part Two on curriculum frameworks. Special thanks are also due Lucia Carter Taylor for being my friend and for helping me to address my own hidden curriculum.

Finally, appreciation is expressed to those whose written contributions to the field of curriculum, particularly in the past decade, have continued to stimulate my interest, to enhance the field, and to ensure the vitality of American public schooling.

James R. Gress

The University of Toledo
October 1987

PART ONE

Definition and Perspective

In the first century of its development, the field of curriculum has evolved rich and varied perspectives. The diversity of viewpoints espoused, together with the insightful analyses on all sides of issues, make the curriculum field an exciting microcosm of the ongoing constitutional convention that is American schooling. A major purpose of this text is to illustrate the diversity of thought and practice in the field of curriculum today and to provide a framework and context within which to synthesize this diversity.

Part One explores definitions of the term curriculum and distinguishes between it and other key schooling terms. Part One then overviews the field's history and concludes with comments about the future.

THE PROBLEM OF DEFINITION

Typically, introductory treatments of this sort begin with a definition of key terms. In this case, an attempt at definition is particularly appropriate and useful because much of one's understanding of the problems and issues treated in subsequent parts of the text will be colored by one's way of defining curriculum and vice versa. The attempt at definition reveals immediately some of the fundamental controversy in the field.

In a rather comprehensive treatment of the question of definition, Tanner and Tanner (1980, pp. 6–30) identify six categories of definitions of curriculum. A reading of their treatment reveals some twenty-odd definitions proposed by individual curriculum authorities. Table 1.1 displays the categories of definition identified by the Tanners and provides illustrative example definitions of each. The table also identifies questions associated with particular definitions.

It is apparent in Table 1.1 that, in settling upon a definition of curriculum, several questions need to be addressed:

1. What is the relationship of organized knowledge to learning?
2. What is the relationship between classical knowledge and modern studies?
3. Does the curriculum focus only on the learner's intellectucal development?
4. What is the relationship between learning in school and learning in other contexts?
5. What is the relationship between school curriculum and culture?
6. How are the methods of disciplined inquiry related to problem solving?
7. What is the school's relationship to change?
8. Which learning functions does the school best serve?
9. How are the means of learning related to the ends of learning?
10. What is the relationship between curriculum and instruction?
11. How is learning like, and different from, other social enterprises?

Answers to questions such as these may vary from one person to another. Indeed, variation is a vital component of discourse and practice in the field. However, all those who want to understand curriculum need to frame some answer to each of these questions.

In Selection 1.1, Oliver also cites several definitions of curriculum found in the literature. Oliver then utilizes an inductive exercise to formulate his own definition of curriculum. He discusses a curriculum as a program of studies, as a program of activities, and as a program of guidance.

Oliver's principal focus is curriculum improvement. In order to discuss improvement, however, it is first necessary to identify and define what will be improved. Any of the programs he discusses might be a focus of efforts at improvement. By discussing improvement, then, Oliver illustrates further complexity of definition. One may or may not agree with the definition of curriculum Oliver finally proposes, but Oliver's exercises can clarify some of the consequences of settling on one or another definition of curriculum.

DIFFERENCES IN DEFINITION

Wiles and Bondi (1984, pp. 5–7) trace differences in curriculum definition historically. Derived from the Latin *currere*, to run the course, the traditional definition of curriculum is "course of study." Associated with conservative positions, this traditional definition focuses on subject matter to be learned. A break with that tradition came in 1935. A second definition of curriculum focused on the socializing function of the school. By the 1950s, this second definition had been refined to denote planned experiences of the school. Other definitions of curriculum include its relationship to all dimensions of human growth and development, in school and out.

Differences in definition of curriculum may be linked to at least two important considerations. First, curriculum is linked to formal learning in schools. However, learning also occurs outside schools, and learning in school may be informal as well as formal. A definition of curriculum as experience, for example, may or may not link curriculum only with learning in school. Considerations of hidden curriculum look at informal, rather than formal, learning.

Second, when recognizing formal learning in school, definitions of curriculum may differ along a continuum of considerations from intention or recommendation, at one end, to outcome or actual learning, at the other end. Learning in schools is part of a complex and dynamic institutional arrangement. Defining curriculum, however, usually involves focusing on one part of that dynamic, on one point along the institutional continuum.

Another consideration that can account for differences in definition is the complexity of the elements of learning in school. This consideration acknowledges various curriculum elements in the school learning process, including goals and objectives, subject matter content, instructional activities and materials, teacher and learner behaviors, and assessment strategies. A given school curriculum may or may not contain some or all of these elements. Thus, definitions of curriculum may differ from one curriculum to another.

In addition, differences in curriculum definition may occur as attention to the identified elements of the learning process shifts from time to time. At one time, for example, attention to curriculum elements may be limited to goals and objectives, subject matter content, or learner behaviors. At another time, or in another place, attention may include instructional materials or assessment strategies.

Finally, all definitions of curriculum and the questions that can be raised in this regard are questions of values. The nature and ramifications of the values questions involved are explored at length in Part

Table 1.1 **Definition of Curriculum**

Tanners' Category	*Example Definitions*	*Some Problems*
Cumulative tradition of organized knowledge	Body of subjects set out by teachers for students to cover	What should this body of subject matter include?
	The permanent studies such as grammar, reading, logic and rhetoric, mathematics, and the greatest books of the Western World	How is this to be related to modern studies and the changing state of knowledge?
		How does the school address the physical, social, emotional, and moral needs of the learner?
	Disciplined study in the language arts, mathematics, sciences, history, and foreign language	What is the significance of such knowledge to the learner's life?
	The conceptual and syntactical structures of the disciplines	How are interdisciplinary problems to be addressed?
Modes of thought	The increasingly wide range of possible modes of thinking about human experiences	How are modes of thought related to individual problem-solving situations?
Race experience	The total culture of a society, the common elements that make a society more than an aggregation of individuals	
	A sequence of potential experiences	How does the learner learn to adapt to

	set up by the school for the purposes of disciplining the learner in group ways of thinking and acting	the changing conditions of the society itself?
		How does the learner relate specialized knowledge to personal or social needs?
Experience	All the experiences the learner has under the guidance of the school	Which experiences are unique to school?
	The total experience with which the school deals in educating young people	Are undesirable experiences the province of the school?
	All the learning of students that is planned by and directed by the school to attain its educational objectives	How are the outcomes of student experience important?
	All the activities provided by the school	
	The life and program of the school . . . an enterprise in guided living	How are these different from similar enterprises, such as family?
	The experiences in which pupils are expected to engage in schools and the sequence of these experiences	What is the relationship between in-class activities?
	A vital interaction of people and things in a free-wheeling setting	
	A methodological inquiry exploring the range of ways in which the elements of teacher, student, subjects, and milieu can be seen	What is the relationship between means and ends?

Table 1.1 *continued*

Tanners' Category	*Example Definitions*	*Some Problems*
Plan	A plan for learning	How are such plans alike or different from others (e.g., lesson plan)?
	A document designed as a point-of-departure for instructional planning	
	Those planning endeavors that take place prior to instruction	
Ends or Outcomes	All planned learning outcomes for which the school is responsible	How is curriculum to be distinguished from instruction?
	A structured series of intended learning outcomes	
Production System	That series of things that learners must do and experience by way of developing abilities to do things well that make up the affairs of adult life	Which of these things should be undertaken specifically by the school?
	A production process that leads to a measurable product called terminal behavior	Is the child only an adult-in-the-making?
	Planned learning outcomes represented by lists of quantifiable or behavioral objectives	What are the differences between the school and the factory?

Can unmeasurable outcomes be included?

Is learning simply the sum of identifiable parts?

Two of this text. How one links curriculum to learning, freezes attention on the institutional dynamic within which curriculum is identified, and gives attention to elements of school curriculum are, in part, matters of values or priorities. For example, one may attach more value to race experience and the questions it raises than to organized knowledge. Or one may see the learned curriculum as bottom line, and another may see written curriculum as more important. Or school objectives may be considered more important than learning activities. In each case, differences in values or priorities are expressed.

OTHER APPROACHES TO DEFINITION

There are other approaches to defining the term curriculum. Schubert (1986), for example, discusses images, or characterizations, of curriculum rather than definitions. His categories of images are not unlike the Tanners' categories of definition or Glatthorn's types of curriculums. Schubert identifies and describes curriculum, alternatively, as content or subject matter, as program of planned activities, as intended learning outcomes, as cultural reproduction, as experience, as discrete tasks and concepts, as agenda for social reconstruction, and as *currere* (pp. 26–33).

One may also distinguish between curriculum, on the one hand, and related terms, such as instruction or teaching, on the other. Because the distinction is only conceptual, there is danger of separating in practice things that are highly interrelated. Thus, the *raison d'être* of curriculum is instruction . . . and vice versa. Instruction is influenced by curriculum and, in turn, both are related to such other schooling phenomena as teaching and administration. Nevertheless, some attempt at distinction in defining curriculum, instruction, teaching, and other dimensions of schooling will be useful.

Beauchamp (1981, pp. 6–9) identifies three contexts within which the term curriculum may be used. First, "an individual . . . may legitimately speak of a curriculum." Then, he points out that "a second legitimate use of the term . . . is to refer to a *curriculum system* as . . . the system within which decisions are made about what the curriculum will be and how it will be implemented." Finally, he states, "a third legitimate use of the term . . . is to identify a *field of study*," that is, the field of curriculum. Beauchamp emphasizes the establishment of precise meanings for each.

However, Tanner and Tanner (1975, pp. 6–9, 42–47) argue against a single definition of curriculum or, at least, against any of the definitions identified thus far. Their argument is threefold. First, they point out that "the conflicting definitions [of curriculum] may serve to keep inquiry fluid and may help illuminate philosophical differences that are the sources of conflict." Differing definitions of curriculum, differing frameworks for curriculum, differing curriculum planning and design rationales, differing views of the hidden curriculum, differing implementation and evaluation systems, and differing modes of curriculum inquiry reflect differing philosophical positions held by proponents of one position or another. The field of curriculum is rich with such differences.

Tanner and Tanner (1975) also point out that curriculum, like other fields, is a human enterprise. As such, it is conditioned, in part, by the historical and cultural circumstances in which it is found. Definitions of curriculum, therefore, may vary at different times and for different persons. Tanner and Tanner argue that the definition of curriculum should be sufficiently broad in its scope to accommodate the several views that may be held in the field. A definition of curriculum is, then, a beginning rather than an ending point.

SOME HISTORICAL PERSPECTIVE

Differences in definitions of curriculum also illustrate important historical shifts in thinking in the field of curriculum. The twenty-sixth NSSE yearbook (Rugg, 1926) illustrates one major shift in thinking about curriculum. This work distinguishes between "subject-matter to be taught" and "ways of responding or reacting" (p. 18), that is, between intent and actuality in thinking about a curriculum. Curriculum study is a reservoir of such shifts, and some understanding of the emergence of the field lends important perspective.

In Selection 1.2, Hollis Caswell, an important figure in the evolution of curriculum thinking and practice, highlights some past developments in curriculum both in colleges and universities and in the public schools. Caswell (in Robison, 1966) observes that the marriage of the college curriculum worker and the elementary and secondary curriculum supervisor has contributed greatly to the field in the past, and it continues to enhance its vitality through organizations such as the Association for Supervision and Curriculum Development.

Caswell identifies and discusses three overriding issues with respect to the school's curriculum: purpose, continuity, and balance. He notes that these issues are critical in the field, both in practice and in inquiry, and that it is a unique role of those in the curriculum field to address such issues. The importance of that role is underscored by continuing short-sighted shifts in the thinking of many about curriculum. These shifts are a result, in part, of oversimplified or reactionary movements in society and in professional education itself. Shifts in thinking about curriculum that have taken place since the original publication of this selection argue well for Caswell's thesis.

Caswell focuses much of his discussion on two matters of central concern in curriculum: (1) the problem of goals, purposes, objectives, or aims of schooling and (2) the problem of sequence, articulation, coherence, and continuity. These matters have received varying degrees of attention as the field has emerged, and they continue to be important issues. Both matters are addressed at length in Part Three of this text.

Caswell associates the emergence of a field of professional work and study with the contributions of key persons as well as with key issues and problems. He makes specific reference to Frank McMurry, Franklin Bobbitt, W. W. Charters, and Harold Rugg. An examination of the contributions of these and others to the curriculum field can add further perspective to the emergence of the field and its central issues.

EARLY CONTRIBUTIONS TO CURRICULUM

In Selection 1.3, Kliebard traces the early history of the curriculum field as it evolved in pursuit of change. Kliebard attributes the vitality of that pursuit to several factors, including a growing high school student population, the expansion of knowledge, change from a rural to an urban society, and a significant influx of immigrants.

Kliebard also attributes the vitality of the pursuit of change in American education at the turn of the twentieth century to the strength of personalities like William Torrey Harris, Charles W. Eliot, Nicholas Murray Butler, G. Stanley Hall, and, later, John Dewey, John Franklin Bobbitt, Werrett Wallace Charters, and David Snedden. Kliebard demonstrates how the early debate among these educational statesmen within special committees of the National Education Association, a prominent school forum in the 1890s and early 1900s, shaped the early direction of the emerging curriculum field.

Seguel's (1966) study of the formative years of the curriculum field from its beginnings in the National Herbart Society, the embryo of the National Society for the Study of Education, to its institutionalization at Teachers College under Hollis Caswell lends additional perspective to the history of the field. Using the biographies and the writings of selected prominent curriculum authorities in five periods of the field's early evolution, Seguel's work highlights many of the major issues that have defined the province of the field.

Beginning with the students of Johann Herbart, teaching technique and other curriculum issues were taken out of the realm of conventional wisdom and placed in the realm of professional discourse. In addition, the student and the teacher were brought "out into the center of the educational stage, . . . relegating the theorist and the administrator to the wings in the role of supporting cast" (Seguel, 1966, pp. 43–44). The Herbartians addressed the issues of systematizing teaching and learning and of efficiency in education. They also raised the issue of relationships between the structure of organized knowledge, on the one hand, and the psychological structures of the learner's mind, on the other. They addressed the moral aim of education, an issue to the present. The issues addressed by the early Herbartians were also one basis for John Dewey's contributions to the curriculum field.

As Seguel points out, John Dewey's impact on American education was felt in all areas, including the young field of curriculum. Dewey's criticisms of the Herbartians' ideas served as a catalyst for transforming their work to fit the unique American social context that absorbed so much of Dewey's own attention. Dewey's challenges to the Herbartians "gave the profession an enlarged vision of the potential of education in American culture" (Seguel, 1966, p. 63). Seguel's discussion of these challenges is summarized here in the following four questions that continue to be significant for the curriculum field:

1. How can knowledge be used to enrich and improve human life? What role does the school play in this process?
2. How can the school focus on the experimental and instrumental nature of knowledge?
3. How can the school be organized to enhance the continuity of individual growth and development?
4. How can the teacher's primary role in curriculum decision making be most effectively related to institutional control?

That Dewey formulated such basic questions early on is one indication of the scope of his contributions to curriculum and to American educational thought and practice.

Seguel's analysis includes the work of Franklin Bobbitt and Werrett Wallace Charters in the 1920s. Bobbitt often is characterized as the "father of curriculum." Both Bobbitt and Charters put more emphasis on planning for classroom instruction (curriculum making) than the

Herbartians did and more emphasis on organizational questions than on other issues in the field. Their contributions illustrate the interconnectedness of school administration and curriculum (Bobbitt, 1918, 1924; Charters, 1923).

Bobbitt and Charters also focused attention on the perennial issue of the needs of the individual student versus those of society as bases for educational objectives. As Seguel (1966, pp. 102–103) summarizes it:

> The first position (Charters') accepted society as it was and emphasized the importance of the individual. The second position (Bobbitt's) sought to improve the society and located the individual in a social context. Both positions were to be espoused by later students of the curriculum.

Through the principles of curriculum planning they introduced, Bobbitt and Charters were influential in translating principles of industrial production in currency in their time into a model for the selection and organization of content for the curriculum. In doing so, they attempted to formulate curriculum-planning processes that are useful for accommodating changing values within society. The model they developed has been challenged more than once since their time, particularly its industrial orientation, but the basic ingredients of the model continue in use today, and the search for ways to reflect changing value systems in a school's curriculum is still a major problem in the field.

The work of Harold Rugg represents both a shift of orientation in the field and a major synthesis of curriculum thought in the 1920s and 1930s. Rugg brought attention to the culture gap between the school and American society during his time. The twenty-sixth National Society for the Study of Education yearbook, which Rugg (1926) edited, was based on a survey of curriculum making up to that time. Rugg's work prompted the curriculum field to look for relationships between education and the social sciences and to identify foundations of education. Rugg provides a comprehensive focus that never forgets that curriculum inquiry is barren unless based on the insights of the disciplines, particularly the social sciences.

The early evolution of the curriculum field climaxed in its institutionalization at Teachers College under Hollis L. Caswell, who brought to curriculum a school administrator's perspective and vast experience in statewide curriculum planning. Caswell's leadership in such state curriculum projects as those in Alabama, Florida, Mississippi, and Virginia was well known. The field study movement he personified represented a marriage of the organization and planning interests of the administrator and those of the university curriculum specialist.

Caswell was a driving force in the founding of the Society for Curriculum Study, which was a major forum of dialog in the field in the 1930s and 1940s. Later, this society merged with the National Education Association's Department of Supervisors and Directors of Instruction to become the Association for Supervision and Curriculum Development. The association continues to be a common meeting ground for curriculum specialists at all levels of schooling.

This summary of Seguel's analysis overlooks many important aspects of her work. However, it introduces the variety of philosophical and technical issues that continue to constitute curriculum's purview, and it illustrates a continual shifting of focuses that characterizes the field. In Seguel's (1966, p. 184) own words:

> These early theorists sensed the need to visualize or theorize, if you will, about the relationship between values and the actual instructional process. Interestingly enough, the emphasis of such theorizing has seemed to oscillate, overconcentrated at one point in values, at another in instruction. A good clear statement of educational values would be met with the cry for attention to the means to carry them out. Technical attention would be given to instruction, and another theorist would show how sterile such atttention really was. If the period is looked at as a whole, this shifting pattern of interest in either values or instruction, philosophies or techniques, becomes apparent. The positive note here is that the field of curriculum making, historically considered, offers precisely that formulation which, if developed, should steady these shifts and make it possible for the curriculum maker to realize the full potential of his field.

CONTEMPORARY CURRICULUM CONTRIBUTIONS

To set into perspective the major divisions in the curriculum field since World War II, a work to parallel Seguel's might identify and analyze the work and contributions of Ralph Tyler (1949) and his traditional offspring, the empiricist views of Beauchamp (1981) and Walker (1973), and the positions of such reconceptualists as Macdonald (in Pinar, 1975) and Giroux (1985). These contributions, as they distinguish important distinctions in curriculum theory and research, are discussed and illustrated in Part Six (also see McClure, 1971). Here, attention is given briefly to the general nature of current divisions in the field and the issues they highlight.

There is little doubt that the Tyler (1949) rationale identified four questions that have been the focus of much attention in the field since their publication:

1. What educational purposes shall the school seek to obtain?
2. What educational experiences can be provided that are likely to attain these purposes?
3. How can these educational experiences be effectively organized?
4. How can we determine whether these purposes are being attained?

In addition, rational attempts to deal with such curriculum questions were influenced by development of the taxonomies of educational objectives (Bloom et al., 1956; Krathwohl, 1964).

Further developments in the field in the 1950s were elaborations of other elements of the Tyler work. But inquiry is not static; a field's problems are probably not susceptible to a *final* solution, rational or otherwise. Indeed, it was the status quo of the field and the overly rational approaches in curriculum that, in part, prompted the upheaval of new forces in the field in the sixties. The emergence of new social forces confronted the schools; their accompanying problems confronted the field of curriculum.

For a time, rationality of a different kind was offered as a key to solving these problems. The college and university scholars in the academic disciplines, most notably in mathematics and the natural sciences, emerged center stage. The field of curriculum focused attention on—or was overshadowed by—questions about the structure of the disciplines of knowledge and the nature of scholarly inquiry.

Treatment of these issues replaced questions about the nature and development of the elementary and secondary school learner, about the role of the teacher in the learning process, and about the relationships between changing social values and the school's curriculum—questions that had been at the center of attention in curriculum at various times in the past. A conference of scholars at Wood's Hole, Massachusetts, had devoted attention to questions of the learner's readiness, intuition, and motivation (Bruner, 1960), but much of that attention to the learner was overlooked in the flurry of subsequent activity and educational innovation that focused primarily on subject matter.

The 1970s and 1980s have witnessed a return to the issues identified by Dewey and by Rugg, issues of child growth and development, the experiential nature of knowledge, and the school's relationship to social change. Developments in the field of curriculum in this period are mapped, in part, by Macdonald (1971) and, later, by Pinar (1978).

In the past quarter-century, empiricists like Beauchamp (1981) have called for the construction of a scientific theory of curriculum, that is, descriptive theory. They have identified the principal elements of such a theory based, primarily, on the methods of the social scientist. Empiricists like Johnson (1967) have attempted to identify curriculum variables and to describe their relationships to one another.

Walker (1973) has also focused on the need for empirical research in curriculum. He advocated the development of descriptive theory to explain central phenomena in the field, for example, the relationships between goals and objectives, the scope and balance of subject matter, or the sequence of learning. He points up the lack of such study in the professional literature. He has identified and discussed misconceptions about empirical research that, in his view, have constrained greater commitment to it by curriculum specialists.

Walker's concern with the dearth of empirical findings in curriculum reflects Goodlad's (1969, p. 368) earlier concern. Goodlad also expressed apprehension that "Curriculum researchers appear to be hung up on a limited repertoire of methodologies . . . [and that] the field of curriculum . . . has not yet struck out boldly in an effort to employ, adapt, and invent methodologies suited to the peculiar character of the problems at hand" (pp. 367–68). If a particular approach produces limited results, perhaps another is in order.

In the past-quarter century, Pinar (1975) and others have advocated a reconceptualization of the curriculum field. Begun as a critique of the curriculum field, a field preoccupied with technical concerns, Pinar's work turned its attention to reconceptualization of experience and a consequent personal emancipation. For example, curriculum experts like Apple (1979, 1983) have demonstrated how schools, teachers, classrooms, and textbooks reinforce values positions that tend to perpetuate discrimination against some social groups. For some, the hidden curriculum becomes a political as well as an educational issue.

The reconceptualist movement has included historical critique of the field (Kliebard, 1970, 1979) and aesthetic critique of curriculum language (Huebner, 1984; in Pinar, 1975). The movement has also enhanced the existentialist thinking of Greene (1971). More recently, reconceptualization has evolved a critical praxis. Giroux (1985), for example, examines the cultural politics of the hidden curriculum by simultaneous attention to politics, schooling, and language. His examination of curriculum language does not stop, however, with greater understanding of the hidden curriculum. Giroux advocates sociopolitical change in schooling and curriculum consistent with stated social ideals, and he charges students and teachers with responsibility for change.

In a recent sketch of the history of the curriculum field, Tyler (1981) describes the field's continuing concern with what subjects should be taught in school and how. Tyler also describes the impact of population shifts and of a changing knowledge base. Tyler examines three additional elements in the evolution of the field: (1) the universal of curriculum content despite the American tradition of local control of schools, (2) the role of research, including the well-known Eight Year Study, and (3) the unprecedented expenditure of federal monies on school reform in the post-Sputnik era. He concludes his sketch with an argument that there are differing curriculum responsibilities within different areas. Perhaps the most important area for curriculum change has been the federal arena.

The unprecedented federal involvement in schooling and curriculum in the past quarter-century is one of two significant developments examined by Boyd (1978, reprinted in Sykes and Schaffarzick, 1979). The other development he examines in Selection 1.4, referring to it as "the professionalization of reform."

Thus, in the past twenty-five years, the field of curriculum has become increasingly sophisticated professionally and somewhat isolated from the local community. To some extent, developments that have led to the current state of affairs have already begun to be reversed. In any case, Boyd's examination in Selection 1.4 here gives useful perspective to changes in the curriculum field as it has matured in the most recent past.

Although no constitutional provision establishes federal authority or responsibility for schools, the enormity of curriculum change supported by the U.S. Congress and a host of federal agencies, as well as by the federal judiciary in a wide range of school litigation, has clearly established a national arena for curriculum policy-making. At the same time, the education of the young, once shared with the school by the family, church, a variety of youth groups, and others, increasingly has become a responsibility assumed more and more by school professionals as it has been abdicated by other institutional groups.

In Selection 1.5, Gress characterizes developments in the curriculum field as "variations on themes." He identifies some elements of the frameworks within which curriculum thought has evolved and cites use of a dialectic model for continuing necessary synthesis in the field.

Gress also asserts that theoretical development in the field cannot be carried forth meaningfully apart from sociopolitical considerations. He suggests that both theory building and practice in the field could benefit substantially from broader input and involvement of several constituent groups, especially teachers. Throughout, he stresses the values dimensions of the curriculum field.

Developments in the field of curriculum rely, to a great extent, on choices of ideological frameworks, especially values positions. Alternatives are explored in Part Two of this text. Developments also rely on the contributions of the constituent groups that participate in theory and practice. These issues are further explored in Part Five.

CONCLUSION

During its first century, the field of curriculum has been a microcosm of the challenges and achievements of America's experiment in public education. Moreover, the curriculum field and American public education have reflected the dynamic of change in our society as a whole during the twentieth century.

As we approach the year 2000, we can speculate about the challenges to confront schools and curriculum in the next century. Changing demographics of the school student population (Feistritzer, 1985; Hodgkinson, 1985) and the role and place of the United States in a changing world economy (Naisbitt, 1982) suggest new challenges to traditional school commitments to universal schooling, development of basic skills, reinforcement of the democratic ethic, development of the whole child, home-school partnership in education, excellence, and equal opportunity. These commitments had been bolstered in each succeeding decade of challenge in a changing society by the curriculum and the field of professional theory and practice that has evolved around it.

Apple (1983) has identified continuing challenges for curriculum in its content, form, and the decision-making processes that shape it. These challenges will involve literacy, basic skills, school preparation for the workplace, mathematics and science, computers, cultural diversity, ecology, and world peace. The challenges will raise issues of content rigidity, especially in urban schools, a widening gap of curriculum differentiation between the haves and have-nots, quality of content and instructional materials, and reduced curricular diversity, among others. The challenges will come from business, industry, organized labor, increasingly powerful state education agencies, a "deskilled" teaching force, a polarizing society, and the economic community.

We can also speculate that the school curriculum will respond to these challenges as effectively as it has in the past. We can point out that increased challenge is, in part, a result of past success. We can observe that the school's perennial critics have persisted so vocally, in one view, because the school and its curriculum have responded so effectively to past challenge. Our society expects so much from its schools because, in the past, its schools have met its expectations. The other view, of course, is that the school has not responded adequately to its critics.

Part of our optimism for the future is the rich diversity of thought and practice that constitutes the curriculum field as it approaches a new century...diversity in definition, alternative philosophical frameworks, models of planning and design, increasing understanding of the hidden curriculum, increasingly sophisticated understanding of change, and refined conceptualization of theory and research. It is this diversity of curriculum thought and practice that this text examines and illustrates.

REFERENCES

Apple, Michael W. *Ideology and Curriculum*. London: Routledge and Kegan Paul, 1979.

Apple, Michael W. *Education and Power*. London: Routledge and Kegan Paul, 1983.

Apple, Michael W. "Curriculum in the Year 2000: Tensions and Possibilities," *Phi Delta Kappan* 64:321–26, January, 1983.

Beauchamp, George A. *Curriculum Theory*. Itasca, Ill.: F.E. Peacock, 1961; 1968; 1975; 1981.

Bloom, Benjamin S., et al. (eds.). *Taxonomy of Educational Objectives, Handbook I: Cognitive Domain*. New York: Longmans, Green, 1956.

Bobbitt, John Franklin. *The Curriculum*. Boston: Houghton Mifflin, 1918.

Bobbitt, John Franklin. *How to Make a Curriculum*. Boston: Houghton Mifflin, 1924.

Boyd, William L. "The Changing Politics of Curriculum Policy-Making for American Schools," *Review of Educational Research* 48:577–628, Fall, 1978.

Boyd, William L. "The Politics of Curriculum Change and Stability," *Educational Researcher* 79:12–18, February, 1979.

Bruner, Jerome. *The Process of Education*. Cambridge, Mass.: Harvard University Press, 1960.

Charters, Werrett Wallace. *Curriculum Construction*. New York: Macmillan, 1923.

Feistritzer, C. Emily. *Cheating Our Children*. Washington, D.C.: National Center for Education Information, 1985.

Giroux, Henry. "Critical Pedagogy, Cultural Politics and the Discourse of Experience," *Journal of Education* 167: 22–41, 1985.

Glatthorn, Alan A. (ed.). *Curriculum Renewal*. Alexandria, Va.: ASCD, 1987.

Goodlad, John I. "Curriculum: State of the Field," *Review of Educational Research* 39: 367–88, June, 1969.

Greene, Maxine. "Curriculum and Consciousness," *Teachers College Record* 73: 253–69, December, 1971.

Gress, James R. "Curriculum: Variations on Themes," *Theory Into Practice* 15: 98–106, April, 1976.

Hodgkinson, Harold L. *All One System: Demographics of Education — Kindergarten through Graduate School*. Washington, D.C.: Institute for Educational Leadership, 1985.

Huebner, Dwayne. "The Search for Religious Metaphors in the Language of Education," *Phenomenology and Pedagogy* 2: 112–23, October, 1984.

Johnson, Mauritz, Jr. "Definitions and Models in Curriculum Theory," *Educational Theory* 17:127–40, Spring, 1967.

Kliebard, Herbert M. "Reappraisal: The Tyler Rationale," *School Review* 78:259–72, February, 1970.

Kliebard, Herbert M. "The Drive for Curriculum Change in the United States, 1890–1958: I—The Ideological Roots of Curriculum as a Field of Specialization," *Journal of Curriculum Studies* 4:191–202, July–September, 1979.

Krathwohl, David R., et al. (eds.). *Taxonomy of Educational Objectives*. Handbook II: *Affective Domain*. New York: David McKay, 1964.

Macdonald, James B. "Curriculum Theory," *Journal of Educational Research* 64:196–200, January, 1971.

McClure, Robert M. (ed.). *The Curriculum: Retrospect and Prospect*. Seventieth Yearbook of the National Society for the Study of Education, Part I. Chicago: University of Chicago Press, 1971.

Naisbitt, John. *Megatrends*. New York: Warner Books, 1982.

Oliver, Albert I. *Curriculum Improvement: A Guide to Problems, Principles and Procedures*. New York: Dodd, Mead, 1965.

Pinar, William (ed.). *Curriculum Theorizing*. Berkeley: McCutchan, 1975.

Pinar, William. "Notes on the Curriculum Theory," *Journal of Educational Research* 7:5–12, April, 1978.

Robison, Helen F. (ed.). *Precedents and Promise in the Curriculum Field*. New York: Teachers College Press, 1966.

Rugg, Harold (ed.). *The Foundations Aid Technique of Curriculum Construction*. Twenty-sixth Yearbook of the National Society for the Study of Education, Parts I and II. Bloomington, Ill.: Public School Publishing Company, 1926.

Schubert, William H. *Curriculum: Perspective, Paradigm and Possibility*. New York: Macmillan, 1986.

Seguel, Mary Louise. *The Curriculum Field: Its Formative Years*. New York: Teachers College Press, 1966.

Sykes, Gary, and Jon Schaffarzick (eds.). *Value Conflicts and Curriculum Issues*. Berkeley: McCutchan, 1979.

Tanner, Daniel, and Laurel N. Tanner. *Curriculum Development: Theory into Practice*. New York: Macmillan, 1975; 1980.

Tyler, Ralph W. *Basic Principles of Curriculum and Instruction*. Chicago: University of Chicago Press, 1949.

Tyler, Ralph W. "Curriculum Development Since 1900," *Educational Leadership* 39:598–601, May, 1981.

Walker, Decker F. "What Curriculum Research?" *Journal of Curriculum Studies* 5:58–72, May, 1973.

Wiles, Jon, and Joseph C. Bondi. *Curriculum Development, a Guide to Practice*. Columbus, Ohio: Bell and Howell, 1979; 1984.

Selection 1.1

What Is the Meaning of Curriculum?

Albert I. Oliver

THE PROBLEM OF DEFINITION

Below are recent quotations from actual sources, all using the same word, "curriculum," and each meaning something different by the word.

"Yer out!" screams a synchronized formation of prospective umpires, and up goes fists to prove it. Hand signals, like proper stance, voice control, interpretation of the rules and the handling of tough situations, are all part of the school's curriculum.[1]

After an extensive survey of its curriculum, Yale's committee has issued several proposals. It points out that students have become so involved in extracurricular pursuits that they have come to favor the football over the pencil. The report continues by setting up an elaborate system under which activities would be safely submerged in the academic curriculum.[2]

There is widespread dissatisfaction among physics teachers over the present curriculum.[3]

A curriculum is something to be felt rather than something to be seen. The transplanting of the structural aspects of a promising (elsewhere) program tends to overlook the fact that the true blueprint is in the minds and hearts of the teachers.[Spears, 1950, p. 27]

The curriculum is a cultural yardstick.[4]

SOURCE. *Curriculum Improvement: A Guide to Problems, Principles, and Procedures* (New York: Dodd, Mead, 1965), pp. 3-18.

Are these different meanings for "curriculum" really important or are they niggling? Problem 1 will show that they actually represent different dimensions of educational thinking and practice. It will also be suggested that through a developmental consideration of terminology one can clarify his own position with relation to many of the perplexing problems schools face today. No attempt will be made . . . to impose an arbitrary definition of "curriculum"; rather, you will be asked to study various interpretations and to arrive at a tentative definition. As you consider the problems in this text, "curriculum" may become a more meaningful term. In a sense, the search is for a *concept* of curriculum rather than for a formal definition; for an *emerging* concept rather than for a predetermined one.

DEVELOPING YOUR OWN CONCEPT

What will be *your* emerging concept of curriculum? Write down, before doing any further reading or discussion, your present *operational definition* of "curriculum." An operational definition is called for because teachers and administrators sometimes lack understanding of how to put ideas into operation. In education classes or at education conferences the statement is glibly made that "the curriculum is the total of all the school-directed experiences." On the job, however, a much narrower concept may prevail. Consider arguments over "extra pay for extra duty." Whether one holds a narrow or a broad concept of curriculum can determine what responsibilities are "extra." In making your additional definition, you should also consider the demands of some taxpayers that "unnecessary frills" be cut out of the curriculum. Again, the decision as to what is "unnecessary" will depend on the concept of curriculum.

The very diversity of curriculum practices, programs, and interpretations throughout the United States makes it difficult to explain just what a curriculum is. At this point there is merit in going to the literature to see how the term is used. Each of you should try three things:

1. Copy from at least four sources (textbooks, encyclopedias, dictionaries) the exact wording of the definition for "curriculum." These might be considered definitions from authority.

2. Read articles in at least three different educational journals. Note how the word "curriculum" is used or implied in these articles. These might be considered definitions "from the field." To which authoritative interpretation does each article apparently subscribe?

3. If your own definition has changed, restate it.

Since this . . . subscribes to a cooperative approach to curriculum development, it is suggested that the members of the study group pool their definitions. The range would look something like this, from the broad to the narrow:

Curriculum is
- all the experiences the child has regardless of when or how they take place.
- all the experiences the learner has under the guidance of the school.
- all the courses which a school offers.
- the systematic arrangement of certain courses designed for certain pupil purposes, e.g., "college-preparatory curriculum."
- courses offered within a certain subject field, e.g., "the science curriculum," "the language arts curriculum."
- the program in a specialized professional school, e.g., "the two-year curriculum in nursing."
- those courses taken by an individual, e.g., John and Peter may both be college-preparatory, but John's curriculum might be different in that he takes French instead of Spanish or that he has a different teacher in English.

In a sense the first idea, that a curriculum is one's life experience, is the *child's* curriculum. It is not a manageable concept from the point of view of organized education. A more practical outlook is expressed in the second statement that the *school* curriculum is that part of an individual's day for which the school has direct responsibility. However, educators are becoming ever more aware that out-of-school experiences can supplement the in-school experience. Thus the curriculum worker will seek both to utilize and to influence nonschool living.

For those who envision the curriculum as "experiences for the learners," it must be recognized that there are always planned experiences which may have learning potential but which do not come under the practical interpretation of curriculum responsibility. For example, a child might fall in a classroom and skin his knee badly enough to require medical attention. This incident may teach the youngster more about safety and first aid than a whole course, but it would be absurd to expect the school to add Toe-stubbing-and-knee-skinning to its offerings. However, it must be pointed out that a teacher who has the concepts of curriculum that this . . . seeks to develop would be quick to utilize this unplanned experience as a learning device, not only for the injured child but also for the rest of the group. From such fortuitous events can come the aspects of flexibility so desirable in a good educational program.

We are now ready to examine a threefold interpretation of "curriculum," followed by a look at some dimensions of "curriculum improvement."

THE EDUCATIONAL PROGRAM

In order to come closer to the essence of our subject we may tentatively consider as a synonym for "curriculum" the term "the educational program." The educational program consists of three basic elements: (1) the program of studies, (2) the program of activities, (3) the program of guidance. The following outline points out some of the distinguishing characteristics of these elements:

Element	*Characteristic*	*Time Emphasis*
Program of studies	Human experience	Past
Program of activities	Pupil experience	Present
Program of guidance	Counseling service	Past, present, future

These elements will be considered in more detail in later problems dealing with the educational program. A brief interpretation of each will be presented here, since this threefold view of curriculum is fundamental to an emerging concept of curriculum improvement.

Program of Studies

What is the nature of the program-of-studies element of the curriculum? If one says to the principal of a school, "I would like to see the curriculum," the chances are that he will proffer an outline which reveals essentially only *this* aspect of the educational program. It probably will be a listing of the subjects offered, as in the following "Orange Book" prepared for the Newton (Massachusetts) Senior High School:

CURRICULUM III

This Curriculum is for pupils who want a general education and who do not desire highly specialized training in trade or business. All electives are chosen in consultation with a guidance counselor. A "work experience" program is available to seniors in this Curriculum.

Grade X Subjects	*Credits*	*Periods per week*
English 2 (131, 134)	5	4
Science (631, 633)	5	4
Introduction to Business (724, 725)	5	4
Industrial Crafts (boys) (760)	2½	4
Home Economics X (girls) (751)	2½	4
World History (431, 434)	5	4
Physical Education (002, 003)	1	2
Elective, music or art	1	2
Grade XI Subjects	*Credits*	*Periods per week*
English 3 (132, 135)	5	4
Science (632, 634)	5	4
U.S. History (432, 435)	5	4
Home Construction (boys) (762)	2½	4
Physical Education (002, 003)	1	2
1 or more electives	5 to 10	4 to 8
Grade XII Subjects	*Credits*	*Periods per week*
English 4 (133, 136)	5	4
Society and the Home XII (756)	5	4
Problems of Democracy (433, 436)	5	4
Physical Education (002, 003)	1	2
1 or more electives	5 to 10	4 to 8

Other headings found in similar student handbooks present course titles and units given under such headings as Commercial Curricula (Secretarial, Clerical, Bookkeeping), Industrial Education, Distributive Education, General Curriculum, and College Preparatory Curriculum.

The areas of study identified for most elementary schools are similar throughout the country, since there is belief in a "common curriculum" rather than in the diversification found at the secondary level. A basic elementary school program of studies includes:

The Language Arts (communicating), reading, writing, spelling, written language, oral language, listening, literature
Arithmetic (understanding quantitative relationships)
Science (investigating the natural environment)
Health and Physical Education (maintaining a healthy life)
Social Studies (studying relationships among people)
Music and Art (enriching living)

The chief variation in the learning areas included is that some elementary schools are introducing modern foreign languages.

These course listings indicate that the emphasis is upon exploration of the culture, a sort of "Cook's Tour" of the past. No one would dispute the statement that a basic function of the school is to transmit the cultural heritage to the young; the crucial issue is "which heritage?" The cultural heritage of mankind is great and our store of knowledge is growing at a tremendous rate. It all cannot be transmitted; the school must serve as an agency, not only to select, but also to interpret, apply, and organize in some coherent fashion.

The cultural heritage is usually grouped into broad areas for certain uses. For example, "mathematics" is a label given to man's accumulated and accepted ways of dealing with quantitative aspects of his environment. "English" (for our North American culture) is a collection of the accepted rules for oral and written communication, with examples of that communication (literature).

As valuable as the program of studies is in the educational program, curriculum workers must think beyond this element and must help laymen (and even their fellow educators) to think beyond it.

Program of Activities

Many educators see in the program of activities a way to vitalize the curriculum. Their analysis of the problems of the program of studies, coupled with examples of failure of many pupils to "learn" the cultural background, has led them to ask if a curriculum should contain more than selected *content.* One study that strongly suggested the need for a broader concept of curriculum was the Regent's Inquiry into the system of "Regents'" examinations given in high schools in New York State. It revealed, relative to an investigation of pupils' citizenship growth, that (1) the attitudes which students hold have no relation to the quantity of work in social studies classes; (2) students do not seem to be greatly affected by the program of instruction in the social studies (Wilson, 1938, chap. IX).

This survey and others led to the belief that the educational program should include actual *pupil* experiences as contrasted to cultural experience. This broader view of curriculum recognizes that the school is not concerned only with having every child learn a body knowledge, but, rather, that he experience a method of facing life. A child may learn civics from his teacher, but he learns citizenship from his playmates!

Recognition of the part played by the program of activities in the educational program pervades all levels of the schooling "ladder," but with an interesting shift of emphasis. In the elementary school the activity concept tends to be incorporated into the daily program.

Sometimes within a class the child is associated with a smaller group for the purpose of constructing a project, enacting a skit, making a report, judging the work of others, or conducting a discussion. On an individual basis, he may "show-and-tell" something within his own experience. Although the class schedule may indicate that the subject matter is arithmetic, a visitor is likely to find groups working on activities which will develop number concepts. In short, he may find that many times the program of studies and the program of activities are blended.

At the same time the elementary school program plans and provides for school activities outside the realm of formal subjects. These activities include student government and service groups, clubs, school patrols, assemblies, and recreation (including athletics).

If the curriculum worker now visits a secondary school, he will discover a less integrated program of activities. He may find the program of studies so firmly entrenched that activities other than *reading, remembering,* and *reciting* are dubbed "extracurricular," a term which connotes a lack of prestige as well as a limited interpretation of curriculum. Here, again, we see that the meaning of curriculum is more important than a mere dictionary definition. One might well speculate on the significance of the shift of thinking in some modern educational quarters as evidenced by the tendency to move from the term "extracurricular" to "co-curricular" and then to "extra-class." It should be apparent even this early in your study of curriculum improvement that the desired concept for the program of activities is that it be "curricular."

In many secondary schools a specific "activity period" is designated. This may be a daily part of the schedule or it may appear only once or twice a week. Some activities by their very nature take place after school but are still a part of the planned educational program. Some idea of the scope of these activities may be had by a look at Activities at Urbana (Illinois) Junior High School:

Student Council
All-School Dances
Athletics and Intramurals
Service Clubs
Assemblies
Interest Clubs such as:

Art, Astronomy, Audubon Club, Bicycle Club, Camping, Chess, Collections, Creative Writing, Current Events, Dancing, Dramatics, Foreign Cars, Girls' Glee Club, Golf, Handicrafts (Leather and Plastics), History, Homemaking (Boys' and Girls'), Jewelry Making, Language Clubs (English, French, German, Spanish), Library, Mathematics Club, Model Building (Airplanes, Boats, Cars, Ships), Photography Club, Projectionists Club, Radio Club, Reading, Science, and Travel.

At the college level cleavage between the programs of studies and activities is even greater. Here, "program of activities" refers essentially to the campus life of the students. Indeed, a university may have a Dean for the College for Women who is responsible for academic (program of studies) affairs and a Dean of Women who concerns herself with the students' nonacademic life. Except for his possible personal interest in some activity such as dramatics or music, the typical college professor knows little about the extra-class events of his or other students. The professors are specialists in cultural heritage. The colleges are aware, however, of the "whole student" concept and have been giving increased attention to a student's high school activities in their admission policies. The college specialist for the program of activities is a Dean of Student Affairs. Thus, although the programs of studies and activities are not well blended, there are elements of both in the over-all curriculum concept in higher education. A thought-provoking illustration of the use of activities as part of the college curriculum comes from Bowling Green College which offered a course on dating. An interesting outcome has been that those taking that course get better grades in their academic courses—presumably because they have become better adjusted socially!

As will be discussed more fully . . . , the educator's philosophy will affect the emphasis he gives to this phase of the educational program. Is the purpose of the school to (1) transmit the cultural heritage? (2) bring about social change? (3) or both? The answer to that question will make a significant difference in the kind of program developed.

Program of Guidance

Learning is an individual matter, yet many of an individual's problems center in interpersonal and group situations. Overall curriculum design, even though it includes the two elements described above, may lose sight of each individual. How can the curriculum become "personalized"? Assuming that no individual will "take" the entire educational program, how can the opportunities it affords best be utilized by each student?

An answer to these and similar questions lies in "guidance." Guidance is a service; it is a point of view; it is an integrative force for the individual and for the educational program. As a distinct part of the educational program it is relatively new, having been started in Boston in the early 1920s, chiefly as job placement. Now the concept has expanded to become a composite of personnel services. Today, more and more educators consider the guidance program an integral part of the total educational program. It reflects an extension of school services beyond formal academic education.

After its initial role as "job placement," guidance was viewed as "help in time of need." However, this concept did not take into consideration its preventative aspects. Today, guidance is concerned primarily with prevention rather than cure. In secondary education certain people are usually identified as counselors, although increasing effort is being made to explore the role of the classroom teacher in guidance. Elementary schools are beginning to designate teacher-counselors from their staffs. This movement was highlighted by the 1955 Yearbook of the Association for Supervision and Curriculum Development, *Guidance IN the Curriculum.* There is a place for programs of guidance and for counseling services, but *all* curriculum workers must recognize that there are as many problems of growing up as there are pupils and that what works with one will not necessarily work with another. Thus, guidance affords an opportunity to build individuality into the curriculum. Better than the program of studies (which emphasizes the past), better than the program of activities (which emphasizes the present), guidance cuts across time barriers. It draws upon the past, but usually the past of a particular individual. It recognizes the present, for that is when the problems or the symptoms of problems are arising. It looks to the future, since its ultimate goal is to help the pupil become increasingly able to face his own problems and to make his own decisions.

The Tucson (Arizona) Public Schools guidance and counseling services have eight general objectives. Note how these tie together the other phases of the curriculum:

1. To assist in making the educational process more personal, giving individual help to each child in accordance with his needs.
2. To bring about satisfactory mutual adjustments of the school and the child.
3. To help students make desirable personal adjustments with self and others.
4. To assist young people to discover their vocational, physical, educational, and social possibilities.
5. To help students recognize their moral responsibilities.
6. To provide the student with experiences in the practice of making decisions.
7. To provide teachers with background information for better understanding of students.
8. To provide leadership for in-service education for teachers to help them use the guidance program effectively.

The Unity of Elements in the Educational Program

To gain an emerging concept of curriculum, then, you are urged to consider the educational program as made up of at least three fundamental elements—program of studies, program of activities, and program of guidance. Much of this can be planned or structured in advance. In fact, curriculum improvement is essentially making plans and getting people ready to accept those plans for use with a certain student body. This *can* lead to rigidity. This *can* mean the submergence of individuality. This *can* produce a cult of conformity. To avoid these and other undesirable results, one should keep in mind that the ultimate in curriculum improvement is *concern for the individual.*

The comprehensiveness of the curriculum concept is well revealed in the following excerpt from the Kansas *Curriculum Guide for Elementary Schools* (1958 Revision):

WHAT IS THE CURRICULUM?

Basically the curriculum is what happens to children in school as a result of what teachers do. It includes all of the experiences of children for which the school should accept responsibility. It is the program used by the school as a means of accomplishing its purposes.

Direct teaching in the classroom is a part of the curriculum. School activities—such as clubs, sports, students councils and the like—are also parts of the curriculum, since these presumably have been planned by the school to help achieve certain educational objectives. School services—such as libraries, health services, guidance, and counseling—are, in a like manner, parts of the curriculum. Even the climate of interpersonal relationships prevailing in a school at a given time is a part of the curriculum, since it is an important conditioning factor in the learning and adjustment of children for which the school should accept responsibility.

A curriculum planner, then, is one who seeks to *create conditions* that will improve learning. All this leads inevitably to consideration of the physical plant. For example, in Abington Township (Pennsylvania) the preliminary planning for an intermediate high school to house grades 9 and 10 was based upon taking curriculum know-how and translating it into bricks and mortar. In the introduction to one of the preliminary reports Superintendent O. H. English observed, "The new intermediate high school is being planned and built around people and the best ways of educating them. After the architects have folded away their drawing boards, and each contractor has crossed the final T's of his contractual obligations, the job of teaching and learning begins. But the job has already begun! Who will be taught, what will be taught, by whom, and how, have been determined to a significant degree by the nature and design of the building facilities. That is why we began planning our building with people and learning in mind."

NOTES

1. Caption to a picture in *Sports Illustrated* describing a school for baseball umpires.

2. Editorial in *The Pennsylvania News,* an undergraduate newspaper at the University of Pennsylvania.

3. Report from the Physical Science Study Committee established by the National Science Foundation.

4. G. Robert Koopman in an address to the 35th Annual Convention of the Council for Exceptional Children.

REFERENCES

Spears, Harold. *The High School for Today*. New York: American Book Co., 1950.

Wilson, Howard. *Education for Citizenship. Report of the Regent's Inquiry*. New York: McGraw-Hill, 1938.

Selection 1.2

Emergence of the Curriculum as a Field of Professional Work and Study

Hollis L. Caswell

The curriculum has been a subject of study and innovation since the beginning of organized education. Innumerable historical events and persons have contributed to its present form and content. Names such as Comenius, Pestalozzi, Herbart, Froebel, Horace Mann, and William T. Harris are reminders that serious thought about the curriculum and extensive efforts to achieve new and better forms have been an ever-present characteristic of Western education.

Emergence of the curriculum as a distinctive field of professional activity occurred around 1920. In 1918 Professor Franklin Bobbitt of the University of Chicago published the first general book on the subject. In 1920 in Los Angeles he directed the first city system-wide program of curriculum revision. Earlier, supervisors and administrators had written courses of study on a piecemeal basis. Preparation of supervisory personnel to write curricula was a secondary goal in courses on supervision, such as the one given by Professor Frank McMurry at Teachers College, Columbia University. Professor Bobbitt took the major step of dealing with the curriculum in all subjects and grades on a unified and comprehensive basis.

In 1922 Denver inaugurated a system-wide program of curriculum revision. About that time Winnetka, Illinois, launched a series of intensive research studies that laid the basis for its distinctive

SOURCE. In *Precedents and Promise in the Curriculum Field,* ed. Helen F. Robison (New York: Teachers College Press, 1966), pp. 1-11.

curriculum approach emphasizing individual pupil progress. The next large-scale, system-wide revision program to attract nationwide attention was in St. Louis. In 1925 a major effort was initiated there involving the work of several hundred teachers and the assistance of a large group of specialists as consultants. Within two years new courses of study were prepared in all elementary and secondary school subjects.

During this period of activity in city school systems two further developments helped establish the curriculum as a field of professional study. First, several major books on the subject were published. Of special importance in the early years of the movement was a comprehensive analysis by W. W. Charters of The Ohio State University, published in 1923 under the title *Curriculum Construction.* Second, curriculum laboratories were organized. The first was at Teachers College, Columbia University, and was established in 1926 under the direction of Herbert Bruner with Florence Stratemeyer as associate.

Thus curriculum revision became a matter of wide interest. Study and field activity rapidly expanded. In 1926, the National Society for the Study of Education published a major review of the movement, devoting both parts of its yearbook to the subject. The report was prepared by a distinguished committee under the chairmanship of Harold Rugg. This book gives the best presently available account of the early development of the organized curriculum movement. By 1930, state departments of education had become seriously interested in comprehensive programs of curriculum improvement. The first such programs were in South Dakota and Alabama. The most widely known and generally influential one was in Virginia. Within the decade many states undertook programs. Also during the 1930s the Eight-Year Study of the Progressive Education Association stimulated curriculum revision.

State curriculum programs took the lead in making a highly important redefinition of the meaning of the curriculum. Whereas earlier work accepted the traditional concept of the curriculum as consisting of a group of courses of study, leaders of state programs came to view the curriculum operationally, considering it to be composed of the experiences pupils actually had under the guidance of the school. Earlier, efforts were directed primarily to writing consistent, good documents. When they were published, it became the responsibility of the supervisory staff to get classroom teachers to follow them. It soon became evident that this was no simple task. Elaborate arrangements for the preparation of courses of study by committees composed of representatives of classroom teachers were designed, and extensive plans were made for installation of the resulting courses of study by supervisors and principals. But even so, leaders in state curriculum programs became aware that these revised courses of study did not as a rule lead to changes in classroom practice. Courses of study gathered dust on shelves. It became increasingly clear that revision of the curriculum should have the central purpose of modifying instruction, and that curriculum programs must utilize many means to achieve this end in addition to writing courses of study. The Florida state curriculum program in 1930 was the first to adopt as its central purpose the improvement of instruction and to start its work with an in-service study program for all teachers in the state. The Virginia program greatly extended this approach. General acceptance of this pragmatic emphasis came quite quickly.

Two events were of special importance. One was the organization at Teachers College, Columbia University, of the Department of Curriculum and Teaching in 1937. This largely grew out of the insight of Jesse H. Newlon, who, as Superintendent of Schools, had been instrumental in initiating the curriculum program in Denver in 1922. The Department of Curriculum and Teaching drew together work and staff from seven older departments to deal at all school and college levels with what had previously been classified as curriculum, supervision, general methods, materials of teaching, and in-service education. The other event of great importance was the establishment of the Association for Supervision and Curriculum Development. Curriculum workers had previously belonged to the Society for Curriculum Study, and supervisory personnel to the Department of Supervisors and Directors of Instruction. The new association brought all together in a working group and set instructional improvements as a common goal.

Paralleling this development was a gradual shift in administrative organization in state and city school systems to insure a unified and consistent curriculum, extending from the kindergarten through the high school. In 1930 the State Superintendent in Virginia organized all curriculum and supervisory personnel in a single administrative unit under the direction of a major officer. Gradually other systems began to change so that by the close of the decade there was wide acceptance of the concept that all work relating to the curriculum and instruction should be unified under the guidance of a single administrator.

CRITICISM AND PERSISTENCE OF THE MOVEMENT

In its beginning the curriculum movement, like all new approaches in education, had its critics and from time to time it has experienced rough going. In 1934 William C. Bagley, in his book entitled *Education and Emergent Man,* wrote a section headed, "The Golden Decade: Curriculum Experts, Curriculum Committees, Curriculum Chaos." He stated, following discussion of developments from 1912 to 1920:

> Then came a series of events that resulted in a state of confusion which persists at the time of the present writing. Several persons began to make the study of the total school curriculum problem their special field—which is a large order for any one person to undertake. It was not long before the reconstruction of curricula became the educational fashion. . . . The movement spread rapidly . . . and by 1933 there were no fewer than 35,000 different curricula on file in the curriculum laboratory of Teachers College, Columbia University . . . (p. 140).

Bagley was by no means alone in his criticism of curriculum revision by local school systems. Many saw the curriculum as such a broad and indefinite area of study that no individual could develop expertness in it. Others felt that only subject matter specialists had significant contributions to make. Many considered the work of classroom teachers in curriculum planning so naive as not to merit attention in a serious educational endeavor. Yet the movement thrived. More and more school systems accepted it as essential that they have a system-wide, organized curriculum program; more and more schools of education included courses on the curriculum in their offerings; more and more books and articles and research studies were written about curriculum development.

The movement has now persisted for nearly a half century. During this time many educational practices have come and gone—and some have even had a rebirth. Ability grouping was considered a panacea by many during the late twenties. Yet under the impact of extensive research it practically disappeared from the educational scene until its recent resurrection in the hope that it would foster academic excellence. The Platoon School was a widely popular plan of curriculum and school organization in many of our large cities for years. A national association fostered its development. Yet it is gone, with hardly a vestige remaining. The activity curriculum had a large group of ardent followers among both educators and laymen. It would now be a courageous person who proposed to a community that its schools follow this plan. These and other educational practices have developed and disappeared during the period that the curriculum movement has spread from one school system to another.

Why is this the case? Why have curriculum activity, study, and research persisted? In answering this question we can clarify and rededicate ourselves to the areas of study which the curriculum should encompass and to the kinds of competence curriculum workers should possess.

MATTERS OF CENTRAL CONCERN

Within the limits of this paper it is possible to sketch only briefly some of the central concerns of the curriculum as it has emerged as a recognized field of professional activity and study. There are a number of basic educational problems that I believe are the central responsibility of curriculum workers, for they alone are in a position to resolve them effectively. This is the reason, as I see it, that the curriculum as an area of study has persisted in programs of professional education, and why school systems have increasingly devoted personnel and money to curriculum work. By way of illustration, I shall discuss briefly three problem areas that have been persistent concerns through most or all of the curriculum movement.

Goals, purposes, objectives, or aims of education—terms which I shall use synonymously in this discussion—represent one major area of curriculum concern. This is not to imply by any means that these are exclusively the concern of curriculum workers. It is from goals, purposes, or aims that education achieves direction. If goals are lacking in clarity, breadth, or consistency the educational program will lack these same qualities. No educational worker should be unconcerned about goals, for in every activity from planning a school building to teaching a class, goals are implicit, recognized or not. A central concern of philosophers is values, and values provide the basis for selecting goals. But goals of education as stated by philosophers are general in nature. They suggest the direction education should take but leave a great gap which must be filled if teachers and students are to have meaningful guidance for day-by-day activities. The fundamental problem facing curriculum specialists is to establish a consistent relationship between general goals, on the one hand, and specific objectives that guide teaching, on the other.

Good teaching requires a strong sense of purpose. If the student is to have maximum opportunity to achieve the general goals of education, the teacher must understand how each specific objective fits into a configuration of purposes which, in time, tie into a coordinated developmental sequence. To define and formulate goals of education so that they are truly operational guides to teaching is a difficult task and one that should always be central in curriculum work. Unless this is well done the educational program will lack consistency and cumulative effect.

The Los Angeles curriculum program in 1920 was the first instance in which an effort was made to formulate a series of teaching objectives in the various subjects that were developmental in nature and contributed consistently to centrally-held educational goals. The St. Louis program in 1926 went further in a thorough treatment of this problem. During this period substantial research studies such as Billings' (1929) on generalizations basic to the social studies and reports such as those from Winnetka provided useful information.

For many years the translation of aims of education into operational guides for teaching was recognized as a central curriculum problem. Of late it has received much less attention. This is of critical importance when you consider the nature of our times. We are in a period in which values are being questioned, in which teaching practice has undergone great change, in which a vast array of new content has arisen, in which the demands of society upon schools have increased with each passing year, and in which goals of education are a major source of controversy. It is my judgment that curriculum workers neglect a principal responsibility when they fail to give major attention to research and practice that help clarify the goals education should serve, that interpret these goals into specific objectives which serve as operationally effective guides to teaching, and that foster consistency among the various phases of the curriculum.

The next major area of concern to which I direct your attention is the problem commonly referred to as assuring sound sequence or continuity in the curriculum. This problem was foreshadowed by the work of certain national committees following 1910. Reports of these committees reflected general concern among professional educators about the disjointed way in which the curriculum was organized. I refer especially to the Committee on Economy of Time established in 1911, which made four reports over a period of eight years, and to work on articulation. A strong feeling existed that the educational program was not organized to achieve the greatest cumulative effect in pupil achievement and the most economical learning. One of the most important elements contributing to this concern was the fact that the curriculums at the elementary and secondary school levels and in the various subjects were planned with little reference to each other. There was great concern also about the gap between high school and college work.

Early curriculum programs made a direct attack on this problem at the school level by a deductive procedure for deriving objectives for each unit of instruction in each grade and each subject from general aims of education. It was believed that through such a procedure the problem would be solved for the school program because continuity would be assured from the first grade through high school and consistency of objectives for different subjects would be established.

After a decade of work it became apparent that other factors than aims were involved in developing a curriculum that provided the desired articulation or sequential relationships. Personal and social problems, the developmental characteristics of pupils, the essential interrelationships of facts, methods of work, and concepts in various subject matter fields, and the influence of out-of-school situations on school experience were recognized as additional important factors. Consequently in the 1930s the problem of articulation was defined more broadly as the problem of sequence. Various plans were devised and put to trial to assure a curriculum sequence that effectively took into account these several factors. Fusion of subjects was tried, sequences of large units of work were developed, the social-functions approach with emphasis on persistent problems of living was devised, and the core curriculum plan was created. None of these attempts to devise a new and more effective procedure for defining sequence met with outstanding success. Gradually the problem came to be described as one of providing continuity in the curriculum, a definition that brought the problem closer to classroom practice. It continued to be studied by curriculum workers, but no significantly new and more satisfactory methods have been developed by which appropriate emphasis can be given in curriculum planning to the three basic factors involved: (1) the potentialities of the learner and his already acquired interests, attitudes, and knowledge, (2) personal and social problems wherein learnings become dynamic, meaningful, and useful, and (3) the organization of knowledge so that the learner gains in power and depth of understanding, and masters methods of work that provide him the most reliable means that he can command to meet new situations.

At the present time the dominant influence is the same as operated during the period from 1890 to 1920. Once again national committees are devising new programs in subject matter fields for the secondary school. As in the earlier period we are now starting at the top and working down. Already considerable curriculum revision at the elementary school level is done more with the idea of building down from the high school program than because studies of elementary-aged children indicate the changes are desirable. Even so, the full impact of this trend has not yet been felt. Another likeness is that present revision is carried forward primarily by subject specialists from graduate faculties of universities. Still another likeness is that work in the various subjects is done with little regard for what the total curriculum should encompass. This piecemeal approach led to the fragmented program that was considered a major weakness in earlier years.

Continuity is now of even greater importance than in the past.

With the tremendous increase in knowledge, specialization has become even greater. Yet, important advances in knowledge which are of great general social significance occur very frequently where fields cross; in other words, interdisciplinary relationships are of increasing importance. Thus the challenging concerns of the great group of subject specialists move further away from using the knowledge in their fields to help solve the problems nonspecialists encounter in daily life. Concern for general education wanes, and we begin preparing mathematicians, physicists, and chemists in the elementary school. The problems of the citizen, the homemaker, the person with leisure time, and youth unable to get jobs swamp our society; but these problems are given short shrift by many of those who exert great influence on the curriculum of American schools today.

In the period following 1910 academic scholars such as James Harvey Robinson, Alfred North Whitehead, and Charles Beard, as well as professional students of education, recognized the weaknesses of the fragmented curriculum that had resulted from subject matter committees building from the top down with little if any concern for developmental characteristics of students and for those general life situations in which knowledge functions. There is no reason that a curriculum so designed today will have any more felicitous results. In fact, Dr. Alvin Weinberg, Director of the Oak Ridge National Laboratory, this past summer characterized the work of national committees in the new mathematics and the sciences as dangerous, calling the curriculum plans they have developed "puristic monsters." The root of the problem, he holds, is control by university specialists whose central concern is purity of concept, which leads to remoteness from everyday life (*New York Times,* August 6, 1965). This is the same criticism made earlier by James Harvey Robinson and the others to whom I have just referred.

This problem of developing a truly sequential curriculum must be approached with a view of the total educational offering. Those who solve it must see across subject and grade and school boundaries. They must be able to build a whole of educational experience that is larger than the sum of its parts because of the mutual support and interrelationship of the parts. Only general curriculum workers are in a position to discharge this responsibility. Others must of course contribute, but no one else has the freedom from vested interest to look impartially at the competing claims of various groups of specialists and to balance these interests in terms of the best service to students and society.

A third major area of study that is a distinctive responsibility of general curriculum workers is that of balance in the educational offering. The curriculum through the years has developed by a process of accretion. As new fields have arisen their proponents have had to fight hard to secure a place for them in the school offering. The result has been that the curriculum is largely a patchwork. The emphasis given to various studies is determined substantially by historical accident and by the relative strength of the competing supporters of various subjects.

The only way out of this difficulty is to employ a procedure that provides for an impartial review of the educational potentialities of all fields of study at each level of instruction, and that formulates a guiding set of priorities. These priorities should not be determined by special interest group pressures, legislative action, or the particular likes and dislikes of teachers but rather by analysis of the comparative contribution of each to the growth of individual students and to social well-being. Knowledge of developmental psychology, of national goals, of the potential contribution of various subjects, and of the teaching-learning process must be brought together in consistent criteria applied to determine such a set of priorities and to formulate a plan of curriculum organization.

Subject specialists should have an important part in this process, for they can best identify the potentialities of their fields for student growth. But much more is needed. The specialist in developmental psychology, in goals of education, and in teaching-learning procedures should also be involved. It is the task of the general curriculum worker to bring together the knowledge of these specialists in a manner which will afford a reasoned basis for determining *how much of what* shall be included in the curriculum at various levels of study. The outcome desired is a curriculum design which provides a reasoned balance of emphasis upon various areas of study for given students.

General curriculum workers should now take hold of this problem with much greater vigor. They should attack the study of design at the level to which the Educational Policies Commission had brought it in *Education for All American Youth*; they should examine carefully the work of subject committees of recent years to discover those ideas and techniques which hold significance for designing a consistent, balanced total program; they should study field programs such as the one in North Carolina where practitioners have gone forward in developing an outstanding program in occupational preparation along with a strengthened academic offering. From these sources and from analyses of national conditions and the needs and problems of children and youth, they should project new and improved curriculum designs. If the general curriculum worker does not deal with balance and priorities, nobody else will, and we shall continue to have a curriculum in our schools that is a patchwork, rather than one planned on the basis of a broad and fundamental view of the kind of education our nation and our people need in the kind of world in which we now live.

SOME GENERAL CONCLUSIONS

Viewing the emergence of the organized curriculum movement with present perspective, there are several general conclusions that I offer for your consideration:

1. The organized curriculum movement has the central purpose of avoiding a fragmented, out-of-date curriculum that is shaped by competing special interest groups. It seeks to develop instead a program which supports common objectives throughout and which is characterized by a balanced emphasis on the several areas of study and various types of pupil activities. It seeks also to guide pupils into experiences that are appropriate to their developmental characteristics, challenging to their interests, and which relate constructively to significant social conditions and needs.
2. The persistence of important professional problems that are studied systematically only by general curriculum workers has made the curriculum a field of established professional importance.
3. During the course of the curriculum movement, the extension of the concept of curriculum development from writing courses of study to that of affording new and more educationally desirable experiences for students has had a profound effect on the scope and activities of curriculum programs. It has led to general acceptance of the idea that classroom teachers generally must take a major part in curriculum programs since change in practice depends upon their ability and willingness to modify existing teaching procedures.
4. Comprehensive curriculum programs—especially since the early ones such as at Denver and St. Louis—have not generally made optimum use of subject specialists. As a result activities and subject matter that are most educationally desirable often have not been included in the curriculum.
5. The plans of organization of a large proportion of curriculum programs have been too narrow and rigid to encompass the

varied pupil activities and subject matter essential to meet the wide range of aptitudes and abilities in a school serving all the people. The result has been that important educational needs of both students and society have been neglected. A curriculum that challenges the abilities and meets the needs of a student who has the promise of becoming a productive, creative scholar in an academic field, and which also provides for a pupil with below average verbal ability who has the promise of becoming a responsible and efficient worker in one of the skilled trades, must provide wide scope and great flexibility in organization.

6. We have not defined with sufficient preciseness the areas of study which are encompassed in the curriculum as a field of professional work, nor developed through research and carefully evaluated practice an adequate body of knowledge which clearly demonstrates the significance of the field.
7. A major source of strength in the curriculum movement has been a persistent concern for improvement of the process of curriculum change. From activity and job analysis, contract plans, and fusion of subjects into broad fields, through analysis of social life into areas of living, and other approaches, the central concern has been to develop a process which would lead to the actual improvement of learning experiences for students. Thus the movement has been characterized both by persistence of a dominant purpose and flexibility of method.

In conclusion, I have undertaken through this analysis of the emergence of the curriculum movement to show that those who work on the curriculum have a highly important professional responsibility to discharge. The modern curriculum movement has survived doubts; it has gone through troubled times. The greatest test lies just ahead. If the movement is to continue and grow in strength and effectiveness, it will require wisdom, hard work, and readiness to seek new and better means of enlisting the cooperative action of all those who have an interest in the curriculum. Above all it will require a level of professional dedication that imbues curriculum workers with the courage to insist that their voices be heard in the councils of those groups that shape the future of our educational system.

REFERENCES

Bagley, William C. *Education and Emergent Man*. New York: Thomas Nelson and Sons, 1934.

Billings, Neal. *A Determination of Generalizations Basic to the Social Studies Curriculum*. Baltimore, Md.: Warwick and York, 1929.

Selection 1.3

The Drive for Curriculum Change in the United States, 1890–1920. Part I — The Ideological Roots of Curriculum as a Field of Specialization

Herbert M. Kliebard

In a period of some seventy years organized curriculum development in the United States evolved from the preoccupation of a handful of educational statesmen operating within a relatively cloistered setting to the concern of a virtual army of specialists and a matter of urgent national concern. The course of such a transformation was far from orderly with different issues and different mechanisms for curriculum change emerging in response to those issues. Rather than a clear-cut development in regular stages, one finds a mosaic of competing curriculum ideologies and curriculum development patterns. The purpose of this paper, then, is not to represent curriculum development as evolving from primitive beginnings to ever more sophisticated practices, but simply to convey something of the range of activity that has characterized organized curriculum development in the United States during the period of 1890 to 1959 and to interpret these practices in the light of prevailing curriculum ideologies.

Beginning in the 1890s, concern about the rapidly expanding secondary-school population led the National Education Association to appoint a series of committees to deal with this issue. The reports of these committees unleashed a storm of controversy regarding the nature and function of schooling and, particularly, the extent to which the curriculum

---

SOURCE. Reprinted in an abridged form, with permission of the author and publisher, from *Journal of Curriculum Studies* 11:3 (1979): 191–202.

had to be reformed in the light of changes in American society. . . . From modest beginnings the curriculum reform enterprise grew into a national preoccupation replete with a trained corps of committed reformers, professional journals, and advanced degree programs in universities. After Sputnik, curriculum reform merged with a massive federally sponsored program of curricular change tied to national defence.

SPECIAL COMMITTEES OF THE NATIONAL EDUCATION ASSOCIATION

Systematic thinking about curriculum probably began as soon as there was systematic thought about education generally. The period of the 1890s, however, provides a starting point for the consideration of systematic curriculum development in the United States, since it was a period of unusual general ferment in education. It is difficult to pinpoint exactly what stimulated this ferment, but a number of events may have contributed to it. In 1889, a vigorous and widely known Commissioner of Education was appointed. A respected philosopher and editor of the *Journal of Speculative Philosophy*, as well as the former superintendent of the St. Louis school system, William Torrey Harris was to have the longest reign as Commissioner of Education, a period in which he participated actively in the debates over competing curricular ideologies. The year 1890 marked the beginning of a forty-year period when the high-school population doubled every decade. To many, this burgeoning high-school population implied a mandate for curricular reform. Moreover, the sheer growth of knowledge in the nineteenth century contributed to a challenge to the hegemony of the traditional subjects in the school curriculum not only by the natural sciences and modern foreign languages, but the social sciences as well.

Added to these events was a growing public consciousness of the transformation in American society from a predominantly rural country of small towns and villages to an urban, industrial nation. But it was not simply the technological and demographic changes that were visible. These changes had produced an awareness, at least among some, that many of the nineteenth-century institutions were no longer operating as effectively as they had in the past and needed to be reformed or redirected. The situation became even more complicated, according to some reformers, by the increasing waves of immigrants, particularly from Southern and Eastern Europe. Indeed, to many reformers, the Americanization of immigrants was to become a special function of the schools in the decades ahead.

In the 1890s the forum for national discussion of education was provided by the National Education Association (NEA). The published proceedings of their conferences during this period reveal not only hot debate of the most pressing educational issues of the time, but the inclusion as active participants of the most prestigious figures in the education profession and the academic world generally — William Torrey Harris, the Commissioner of Education, Charles W. Eliot, president of Harvard University, Nicholas Murray Butler, professor of philosophy at Columbia University and later its president, G. Stanley Hall, a prominent psychologist and president of Clark University, as well as leading school superintendents and the principals of major high schools. By all accounts, the debates at NEA conferences were at the least exciting and sometimes acrimonious.

Some of the most lively debates revolved around the relationship between secondary schools and colleges, and it was an issue in this relationship that led to formation of the Committee of Ten, a commission that was to deal with some of the most pressing curricular matters of the day. The issue was the wide diversity that existed with respect to what constituted an appropriate high-school program for college admission. Most colleges required Latin for admission, but the persistence of a requirement in Greek was more contentious, since Latin was often elected by high-school students who were not preparing to go to college. The need to elect Greek as early as the second year of high school presented a dilemma for students and for the administrators responsible for school programs. Complicating this situation was the fact that requirements within these subjects, the particular works to be studied, varied considerably from one college to another. Although the recommendations of the Committee of Ten were to have far greater ramifications than this particular issue, it was the demand for greater uniformity in college-entrance requirements and, therefore, of the curriculum that led the NEA in 1892 to allocate $2500 for the formation of the Committee of Ten and the publication of its recommendations.

The man chosen to head the committee was the president of Harvard University, Charles W. Eliot. Eliot had emerged as a leader in educational reform, not just in higher education where he strongly urged adoption of the elective system, but in elementary and secondary schools as well. He was active in the New England Association of Colleges and Preparatory Schools and had addressed the NEA Department of Superintendence on several previous occasions. In 1892 he had discussed, "Shortening and enriching the grammar school course," and in this address he made a series of recommendations about the elementary-school curriculum that revealed an intimate knowledge of typical programs and the characteristic ways of teaching certain subjects. He proposed, for example, a reduction in the amount of arithmetic taught, arguing for the earlier introduction of algebra and geometry. He also thought that the study of a foreign language could be introduced as early as the fourth or fifth grade as part of general language study. And he objected to geography being taught "chiefly as a memory study from books and flat atlases and [where] much time is given to committing to memory masses of facts which cannot be retained, and which are of little value if retained" (Eliot, 1961b, p. 49). Anticipating the objection to these and other recommendations that students of elementary-school age may not be capable of undertaking the advanced subjects that he was proposing, Eliot argued, "It is a curious fact that we Americans habitually underestimate the capacity of pupils at almost every stage of education from the primary school through the university. . . . It seems to me probable that the proportion of grammar school children incapable of pursuing geometry, algebra and a foreign language would turn out to be much smaller than we now imagine. (Eliot, 1961b, pp. 52–53).

It was this optimism about human intellectual capacities that was behind some of the recommendations that were to emerge from the Committee of Ten rather than essential conservatism or the failure to account for individual differences that the critics of the time as well as many later interpreters alleged. Ideologically, Eliot was a mental disciplinarian and, as such, he was committed to the development of the powers of the mind as the central function of schooling. Although differences in intellectual capacities were recognized by mental disciplinarians, they were not considered so significant as to warrant different programmes of study for different identifiable groups within the school population. Only in the gross popularizations of the day (including, unfortunately, those used in many normal schools) and in latter-day caricatures of the theory was the mind actually depicted as a muscle to be developed through vigorous exercise. The essence of mental discipline as a curriculum theory was its stress on the formal aspects of school subjects as opposed to their content; mental disciplinarians were more interested in the effect on the mind of studying a school subject than they were in what knowledge was gained through the study of that subject. The form that different subjects took, it was assumed, had varying effects on habits of thought. Eliot, however, differed from most mental disciplinarians of the day in that he did not attribute any permanent special disciplinary value to traditional subjects, such as Latin or Greek, as opposed to, say, modern foreign languages. If a subject were capable of sustained study at all, it had potential disciplinary value, particularly if that subject were of interest to the student; hence, Eliot's advocacy of the elective system not just in higher education, but in high school and upper elementary grades.

Under Eliot's direction, the Committee of Ten proceeded expeditiously to the publication of its Report. He had organized the Committee into nine conferences, three around the traditional subjects of the day — Latin, Greek, and mathematics — and six around modern subjects — English, natural history, geography, physical science, modern foreign languages, and the social studies — history, civil government, and political economy. The conferences convened on 28 December 1892 to take up a series of eleven questions that Eliot had proposed for their consideration. The questions covered such mundane issues as at what point the various subjects should be introduced, how long they should be studied, and what topics should be covered. In addition, Eliot asked the various conferences to consider whether the subject should "be treated differently for pupils who are going to college, for those who are going to a scientific school, and for those who, presumably, are going to neither" (National Education Association, 1893, p. 6). He was thus asking the participants to consider the question of curriculum differentiation, particularly that based on the criterion of whether or not a student intended to go to college. Eliot, as chairman of the Committee, assembled and interpreted the reports of the individual conferences.

A major feature of the report when it was issued in 1893 was four suggestive "programmes" or courses of study, each recommended as acceptable for college admission. Although the choice among these four courses of study — classical, Latin-scientific, modern languages, and English — probably did not go as far as Eliot would have liked in the direction of electivism, the programmes did represent a considerable broadening of what was typically acceptable for college admission. The modern languages and the English courses of study, for example, had no absolute requirement in either Latin or Greek. Even the classical programme recommended beginning Greek in the third year of high school rather than the second, thus postponing what had been a critical decision for high-school students and abbreviating the requirement, a recommendation that raised the ire of professors of Greek at Harvard. While this reform, as well as others recommended by the Committee, may be regarded as moderate, the overall effect was distinctly liberating, for although the charge of the Committee was, in a sense, to create uniformity as to college entrance requirements, they addressed the problem by suggesting a considerable broadening of the concept of what should be an acceptable programme for college admission.

With respect to the critical question of distinctive tracks for different segments of the high-school population, the Committee was unequivocal. They unanimously rejected the notion of a different course of study for college-entrance and non-college-entrance groups. In fact, they went so far as to reject the notion of college preparation as a major function of the secondary school. "The secondary schools of the United States, taken as a whole," the report said, "do not exist for the purpose of preparing boys and girls for colleges. Only an insignificant percentage of the graduates of these schools go to colleges or scientific schools" (National Education Association, 1893, p. 51). Although they did declare at one point that in the training of teachers and in providing instruction "the two programmes called, respectively, modern languages and English must *in practice* be distinctly inferior to the other two" (p. 48, emphasis added), they were careful to qualify this distinction by the phrase, "under existing conditions" (p. 48). Here, they were undoubtedly referring to the greater experience with the classical and Latin-scientific courses of study and possibly to a superior corps of teachers in those programmes, but they were being careful to avoid not only a distinction between college-entrance programmes and programmes "for life" but also the implication that there was anything *inherently* inferior to the modern languages and English courses of study.

Of almost equal significance to the report itself was the nature of the reaction to it, both the immediate one and its overall place in the mythology of the curriculum field. At the meeting where the report was presented to the National Council of the National Education Association, G. Stanley Hall voiced certain criticisms that have, to some degree, become part of the conventional wisdom about the Committee of Ten. In particular, Hall was critical of the notion that all students should be taught subjects in essentially the same way. In his massive book, *Adolescence*, published in 1904, Hall expanded and elaborated his criticism. He referred to the recommendation that the same subjects be taught to all students regardless of their probable destination as "Masterpiece of college policy," thus encouraging the widely accepted interpretation of the Committee of Ten Report as imposing college domination on the high-school curriculum (Hall, 1904, p. 510). Hall went on to accuse the Committee of ignoring "the great army of incapables" that was presumably inhabiting the schools. In obvious contrast to Eliot's optimism about the capacities of students, Hall's tendency was to emphasize and even exaggerate differences in human intellectual capacity and in so doing make these differences the basis of an argument in favor of curriculum differentiation. Hall was also critical of the principle that "all subjects are of equal educational value if taught equally well," although the Committee was asserting this principle only in the limited sense of subjects being of equal value insofar as college admission was concerned. Finally, Hall argued that "only mischief" had been created by the notion "that fitting for college is essentially the same as fitting for life" (p. 510). In making this accusation, Hall was subtly reversing what the Committee had actually recommended. The Committee of Ten's argument was that education was for "life" and that colleges should accept this education for life as appropriate for college admission. Hall was accusing the Committee of developing a college-entrance curriculum and then calling it an education for life.

In replying to Hall's charges, Eliot reasserted the basic assumptions of the Committee of Ten and in particular the notion that the school is a place "in which training for power and general cultivation are the fundamental ideas," and not, as Hall assumed, a place for the "training in special means of obtaining a predestined sort of livelihood" (Eliot, 1961a, p. 153). Eliot, in raising the issue of educational predestination, demonstrated his sensitivity to the way in which a sorting and labeling process in schooling and an unequal distribution of knowledge can have a profound effect on life chances. Eliot's position was that under the guise of attending to differences in intellectual capacities of students, the social and vocational roles that these students will one day occupy are predetermined. Readers of Hall's book, Eliot argued, "will refuse to believe that the American public intends to have its children sorted before their teens into clerks, watchmakers, lithographers, telegraph operators, masons, teamsters, farm laborers, and so forth, and treated differently in their schools according to these prophecies of their appropriate life careers. Who are to make these prophecies?" (p. 153). But, in spite of Eliot's rebuttal, Hall's interpretation of the Committee of Ten's infliction of a college-entrance curriculum on the entire high-school population was incorporated into educational textbooks as early as 1909 and became accepted dogma in the curriculum field (Brown, 1909, p. 58). The notion of college domination of the curriculum, presumably imposed by a benighted or self-seeking Committee, was to fit nicely into an emerging ideology that put its greatest emphasis on fitting students for the practical and social duties of life as opposed to intellectual attainments.

THE EMERGENCE OF THE CURRICULUM FIELD

Curriculum reform by way of NEA-appointed committees flourished until the early twentieth century. A Committee of Fifteen reported on the co-ordination of elementary-school studies in 1895, unleashing a searing conflict between Commissioner Harris and the American Herbartians; the Report of the Committee on College Entrance Requirements was issued in 1899; and the Committee on Economy of Time in Education reported in 1913. But by the early twentieth century, the spirit of science was infusing the educational world. The debates that the various committee reports generated were lively, to be sure, but increasingly it seemed that the sure hand of science was needed to guide curriculum reform. No one exemplified this spirit of scientific curriculum making more than John Franklin Bobbitt. Bobbitt was awarded his Ph.D. from Hall's Clark University in 1909 and began a long and productive career at the University of Chicago. Although his appointment was in the area of educational administration, his abiding interest was in curriculum development, and in just a few years he became the prototype of the modern curriculum specialist.

Bobbitt burst forth on the national educational scene with a lengthy article in the Twelfth Yearbook of the National Society for the Study of Education with the unpromising title, "Some General Principles of Management Applied to the Problems of City-School Systems" (Bobbitt, 1913). In it, he developed a theme he had introduced a year before in his article, "The Elimination of Waste in Education" (Bobbitt, 1912). Elimination of waste through increased efficiency had become a popular cause, and Bobbitt was one of the first to draw an analogy between the efficiency achieved in business and industry and the efficiency that could be achieved in the curriculum. In drawing this analogy, Bobbitt drew principally on the work of the father of the scientific management movement, Frederick Winslow Taylor, obviously proceeding on the assumption that, just as the application of scientific precision had achieved increased efficiency in industry, so could the application of those same principles achieve success in the curriculum. In his major work, *The Principles of Scientific Management*, Taylor set forth the ideas that would guide increase in production through science. Taylor was, for example, quite explicit as to the steps to be taken in order to produce efficiency for any given task:

> *First.* Find, say, ten or fifteen different men (preferably in as many separate establishments and different parts of the country) who are especially skillful in doing the particular work to be analyzed.
> *Second.* Study the exact series of elementary operations or motions which each of these men uses in doing the work which is being investigated, as well as the implements each man uses.
> *Third.* Study with a stop-watch the time required to make each of these elementary movements and then select the quickest way of doing each element of the work.
> *Fourth.* Eliminate all false movements, slow movements, and useless movements.
> *Fifth.* After doing away with all unnecessary movements, collect into one series the quickest and best movements as well as the best implements. [1911, pp. 117–18]

During his early career Bobbitt devoted himself to the task of translating Taylor's procedures into curriculum making. From such management procedures Bobbitt and like-minded contemporaries such as Werrett W. Charters and David Snedden were able to extract the basic principles on which a "scientific curriculum" could be based. The endpoints of the curriculum should no longer be described in vague or global terms. They had to be stated in advance and described with precision. These outcomes should represent small units of work, each with a definite standard attached. The means toward the achievement of these units should be judged by the criterion of efficiency in reaching the desired outcome with all waste motions eliminated. Curriculum development became an effort to standardize the means by which predetermined specific outcomes might be achieved. Success was judged by the extent to which the actual outcomes matched the predictions. By developing such a production metaphor Bobbitt provided the educational world with a lens through which the curriculum development process could be viewed. It permitted certain features of the process to be seen, filtered out others, and exaggerated still more.

Of critical importance was the process by which the outcomes of the curriculum would be determined. Outcomes would no longer be formulated; they would be *discovered*. Just as natural scientists and scientific managers "discover" the secrets of nature and of efficient production, so would the "scientific curriculum maker" discover what features of human activity should be stated as the objectives of the curriculum.

> The curriculum-discoverer will first be an analyst of human nature and of human affairs. His task at this point is not at all concerned with "the studies" — later he will draw up appropriate studies as *means*, but he will not analyze the tools to be used in a piece of work as a mode of discovering the objectives of that work. His first task rather, in ascertaining the education appropriate for any special class, is to discover the total range of habits, skills, abilities, forms of thought, valuations, ambitions, etc., that its members need for the effective performance of their vocational labors; likewise the total range needed for their civic activities; their health activities; their recreations; their language; their parental, religious, and general social activities. The program of analysis will be no narrow one. It will be as wide as life itself. As it thus finds all the things that make up the mosaic of full-formed human life, it discovers the full range of educational objectives. [Bobbitt, 1918, p. 43]

Charters, one of the foremost exponents of the emerging enterprise of scientific curriculum making, conducted a formidable array of studies in widely divergent areas to demonstrate the universality of the technique. Charters applied the new science to curriculum development in secretarial work, pharmacy, librarianship, veterinary medicine, teacher training, and to being a woman (with the development of the curriculum for Stephens College of Columbia, Missouri, a women's college) (Charters, 1921 and

1926). A leading sociologist of education, Charles C. Peters, proposed a version of Taylor's scientific management for the task of developing a curriculum in religious education. Just as Taylor began by assembling the best workmen in a given field, Peters declared that, "We shall need to pick out a hundred, or a thousand *best Christians* and study their characteristics. We shall need to observe their habits, their ideals, their beliefs, their attitudes, etc., and compare these so as to ascertain what ones are common to all, or nearly all (and hence essential to Christianity), and what ones are merely accidental or personal" (Peters, 1921, p. 375). In Christian education as in education generally, Peters argued, "objectives must be isolated through a scientific sociological study, not set up by the *a prior* methods of philosophy." Thus did eternal value questions of human conduct become amenable to an objective scientific procedure for determining objectives.

The implications of the application of scientific precision to the curriculum planning process by Bobbitt and his contemporaries were enormous. First, a standard procedure for stating the objectives of the curriculum was instituted, a procedure that came to be called *activity analysis* or sometimes *job analysis*. Using this procedure, the actual activities of human beings, broken down into minute units and idealized, would become the objectives. Thus would be created, presumably, a close relationship between what was studied in school and the activities of life. Second, the subjects of study would no longer be the central feature of the curriculum; they became relegated to the status of the *means* by which objectives drawn from life activities and stated with precision would be achieved. Finally, the scope of the curriculum would be indefinitely widened. No longer would the curriculum be directed principally toward intellectual development or, as the mental disciplinarians believed, improving the powers of the mind. The scope of the curriculum would be as broad as life itself, preparing the youth of the country for all the duties of life, not simply those involving intellectual and cultural pursuits. In short, the emergence of the curriculum field as a distinct field of specialization within education was associated with a revolution in the way curriculum development was perceived.

Strangely enough, the revolution in curriculum development evoked more NEA committee reports, including one of the most respected and most frequently cited in the curriculum literature. The continued reverence in which the report of the Commission on the Reorganization of Secondary Education (1918) is held within curriculum studies is indicative of the persistence of the social efficiency doctrine it reflects. Popularly known as the *Cardinal Principles* Report (or sometimes incorrectly as the Seven

Cardinal Principles).* The *Cardinal Principles of Secondary Education* was a personal triumph for the former mathematics teacher at Brooklyn Manual Training High School, Clarence Kingsley, who was its main author. The report referred to profound changes in American life "within the past few decades" (Commission on the Reorganization of Secondary Education, 1918, p. 7), changes which "call for extensive modification in secondary education" (p. 8). In order to ascertain the curricular implications of the changes, the report endorsed the new scientific approach, taking the position that "to determine the objectives that should guide education in a democracy it is necessary to analyze the activities of the individual" (p. 9). It is not surprising, therefore, that the seven aims they enunciated actually represent categories of human activity: (1) health; (2) command of fundamental processes; (3) worthy home membership; (4) vocation; (5) citizenship; (6) worthy use of leisure; (7) ethical character (pp. 10–11). Along with each of the aims was a series of recommendations as to how they should be carried out; for example, under (4), worthy home membership, the report recommends, "The majority of girls who enter wage-earning occupations directly from the high school remain in them for only a few years, after which home-making becomes their lifelong occupation. For them the high-school period offers the only assured opportunity for that lifelong occupation, and it is during this period that they are most likely to form their ideals of life's duties and responsibilities" (p. 12).

The *Cardinal Principles* report was a moderate statement of the social efficiency ideology. David Snedden (1919), for example, thought it to be "almost hopelessly academic." Yet the deficiencies of scientific curriculum making are clearly exhibited. Under the guise of a value-neutral "scientific" approach to the objectives of the curriculum, curriculum discoverers would go out into the world to record the activities that take place. After suitably idealizing them, these activities would become the objectives. The scientific curriculum makers were simply taking the world as it is (or, more correctly, the world as they saw it) and assuming that this was the world as it ought to be. Since women, for example, were presumably engaging in home making as their "lifelong occupation," they should be trained to do that well. The issue of a self-fulfilling prophecy seems not to have arisen. And contrary to Eliot's earlier warning about the dangers inherent in basing the curriculum on a prophecy about one's future status and thereby encouraging early "bifurcation," the doctrine of social efficiency urged precise predictions as to one's future social and vocational

* Although the most widely quoted section of the report is the "main aims of education," the entire 32-page document actually constitutes the "cardinal principles," not just the seven aims.)

role and the careful adapting of the curriculum to fit the person to that role. So was one prepared for the duties of life.

Apart from this fundamental confusion as to the world as it is and the world as it ought to be, the *Cardinal Principles* report embodied another prominent feature of the social efficiency ideology. The value of school subjects was no longer to be found in the subjects themselves; their value, indeed their very existence as school subjects, was made contingent on their contribution to the achievement of the objectives scientifically drawn from "life." As the report put it, "Each subject now taught in high schools is in need of extensive reorganization in order that it may contribute more effectively to the objectives outlined herein, and the place of that subject in secondary education should depend upon the value of such contribution" (Commission on the Reorganization of Secondary Education, 1918, p. 16). Thus would history, through some process of contortion, contribute to "citizenship," civic education and literature, to "worthy use of leisure." But certain subjects — geometry, foreign languages, physics — surely must have had difficulty demonstrating their instrumental value to the duties of life.

An interesting sidelight on the development of the social efficiency ideology applied to curriculum can be seen in the role of the transcendent figure in American education, John Dewey. Although never a full-fledged Herbartian, Dewey became a member of the Herbart Club in 1892 and participated in many of the national debates on educational policy including, of course, those on curricular matters. At various times, he took issue with William Torrey Harris, attacked some of the most cherished Herbatian concepts, and was critical of certain features of the child-study movement as exemplified by G. Stanley Hall. Dewey's reputation grew enormously, as a result of his work from 1896 to 1904 with the famous Laboratory School at the University of Chicago and through the publication of articles in professional journals and widely read books such as *School and Society* (1899), *How We Think* (1910), and *Democracy and Education* (1916). He succeeded Charles W. Eliot as honorary president of the Progressive Education Association, which was formed in 1919, and ultimately came to be known as the father of a vague entity called progressive education.

Although the social efficiency reformers — Franklin Bobbitt, W.W. Charters, David Snedden, and the like — are also often characterized as "progressives," Dewey differed sharply from them on the most fundamental issues in education generally and on curriculum development in particular. One of Bobbitt's central principles was that, "Education is primarily for adult life, not for child life. Its fundamental responsibility is to prepare for the fifty years of adulthood, not for the twenty years of childhood and youth," (Bobbitt, 1924, p. 8). In sharp contrast, Dewey argued that, "education . . . is a process of living and not a preparation for future living" (Dewey, 1964, p. 430). Although Bobbitt, Charters, and Snedden believed that the ends of education were to be drawn from "life activities" with education being the means of performing those activities well, and that "to set up any end outside of education, as furnishing its goal and standard, is to deprive the educational process of much of its meaning, and tends to make us rely upon false and external stimuli in dealing with the child" (Dewey, 1964, pp. 434–35). One of the hallmarks of the socially efficient curriculum was that it prepared definitely and specifically for a particular occupational and social role; Dewey took the position that such a conception of education was not only undemocratic in the sense argued earlier by Eliot, but that "an attempt to train for too specific a mode of efficiency defeats its own purpose. When the occupation changes its methods, such individuals are left behind with even less ability to readjust themselves than if they had a less definite training" (Dewey, 1916, p. 140). In fact, Dewey took the lead in opposing the expanding role of vocational education in the curriculum. (See, for example, Wirth, 1974.) Ironically, although Dewey is so closely identified with American education in the first half of the twentieth century, his actual influence was insignificant when compared to that of the social efficiency curriculum reformers. Of supreme irony is the fact that when, in the early 1950s, social efficiency applied to the curriculum became a *cause célèbre* and academic critics were charging anti-intellectualism in American education, Dewey's name increasingly became associated with the position he so vigorously opposed.

REFORM THROUGH SPECIALIZATION AND STANDARDIZATION

Our review took as its starting point the educational ferment in the last decade of the nineteenth century that led the NEA to appoint a select commission to review the issues and present its recommendations. Perhaps it was the very moderation of the reforms embodied in the Report of the Committee of Ten that led to the bitter controvery surrounding its recommendations. Powerful critics, such as G. Stanley Hall, felt that the profound changes that had been wrought in American life required a more drastic restructuring of the school curriculum than Eliot's committee proposed, particularly with respect to the new population of high-school students allegedly unsuited to the programmes of study that had become established in American secondary schools.

The sense of a pressing need to reform the curriculum of American schools in the light of change grew even more urgent in the first two decades of the twentieth century, culminating, as we have seen, in the identification of curriculum as a specialized field of study, characterized by certain ideological presuppositions and a *modus operandi* known as activity analysis. Although a clear choice existed between the kind of reform that was embodied in the work of John Dewey and that of the social efficiency reformers such as Franklin Bobbitt and David Snedden, the emerging curriculum field clearly preferred the scientific precision and utilitarian payoff that social efficiency promised, and the impact of an ideological position drawing its modes of operation and criteria of success from the management of industry has had a lasting, though largely unrecognized, impact on curriculum thinking in the United States.

. . .

REFERENCES

Bobbitt, F. "Elimination of Waste in Education." *The Elementary School Teacher* 12:6 (February 1912).

Bobbitt, F. "Some General Principles of Management Applied to the Problems of City-School Systems." In the Twelfth Yearbook of the National Society for the Study of Education, Part I. Chicago: National Society for the Study of Education, 1913.

Bobbitt, F. *The Curriculum*. Boston: Houghton Mifflin Co., 1918.

Bobbitt, F. *How to Make a Curriculum*. New York: The MacMillian Co., 1924.

Brown, J.F. *The American High School*. New York: The MacMillian Co., 1909.

Charters, W.W. "The Reorganization of Women's Education," *Educational Review* 62: 3 (October 1921).

Charters, W.W. "Curriculum for Women," *University of Illinois Bulletin* 23: 27 (March 8, 1926).

Commission on the Reorganization of Secondary Education. *Cardinal Principles of Secondary Education*. United States Bureau of Education Bulletin No. 35. Washington, D.C.: United States Bureau of Education, 1918.

Dewey, J. *Democracy and Education*. New York: The MacMillian Co., 1916.

Dewey, J. "My Pedagogic Creed." In R.G. Archambault (ed.), *John Dewey on Education*. New York: Random House, 1964. (Originally published as a pamphlet by E.L. Kellogg and Co. in 1897.

Eliot, C.W. "The Fundamental Assumptions in the Report of the Committee of Ten." In E.A. Krug, *Charles W. Eliot and Popular Education*. New York: Teachers College Press, 1961. (a)

Eliot, C.W. "Shortening and Enriching the Grammar School Course." In E.A. Krug (ed.), *Charles W. Eliot and Popular Education*. New York: Teachers College Press, 1961. (b)

Hall, G.S. *Adolescence*. New York: Appleton & Co., 1904.

National Education Association. *Report of the Committee on Secondary School Studies*. Washington, D.C.: Government Printing Office, 1893.

Peters, C.C. "Notes on Methods of Isolating Scientifically the Objectives of Religious Education," *Pedagogical Seminary* 28: 4 (December 1921).

Snedden, D. "The Cardinal Principles of Secondary Education," *Schools and Society* 9: 227 (May 3, 1919).

Taylor, F.W. *The Principles of Scientific Management*. New York: Harper and Brothers Publishers, 1911.

Wirth, A.G. "Philosophical Issues in the Vocational-Liberal Studies Controversy (1900–1917): John Dewey vs. The Social Efficiency Philosophers," *Studies in Philosophy and Education* 8: 5 (Winter 1974): 169–182.

Selection 1.4

The Politics of Curriculum Change and Stability[1]

William Lowe Boyd

The business of trying to change or reform the public schools of America has become just that: from a hobby for "do-gooders" and a vocation for muckraking journalists, the pursuit of educational innovation and reform has emerged as a big business involving a broad array of public and private foundations and R&D organizations. Yet, after more than two decades of systematic efforts at reform — from the new curriculum materials of the 1960s to more recent federally sponsored innovation projects — recent research (e.g., Goodlad and others, 1970; Berman and McLaughlin, 1976) has revealed that, contrary to numerous claims, little really has changed. We thus are left with the problem of understanding the paradox of how there could be so little change when there seemed to be so much evidence of momentous change.

The most succinct explanation is that it turns out that all too often innovative policies which were *enacted* were only partially *implemented* at best. As we shall see, this fact has profound implications for curriculum policy-making, innovation strategies, and the "business" of reform. But the vitally important distinction between policy-making and policy implementation does not tell the whole story. Inherent in the educational policy-making process itself are contradictory pressures that restrain edu-

---

SOURCE. Reprinted with permission of the American Educational Research Association from *Educational Researcher* 79 (February 1979): 12–18.

cational change. Indeed, policymakers are confronted with the dilemma of the schools being asked to preserve and to change society simultaneously. And whether they attempt to preserve or reshape society, curriculum policymakers are inescapably involved in a political act, for their positions will have some bearing upon "who gets what, when, and how" now and in the future.[2]

Currently, the accelerated pace of social change has exacerbated the tension between pressures for societal maintenance and for societal change, and, with the upsurge of ethnic and minority consciousness and the pursuit of equality, curriculum policy-making has been dramatically politicized. In this context, we clearly need a better understanding of the character of curriculum policy-making and the circumstances under which the curriculum changes or remains constant.

SOCIAL CHANGE AND INCREMENTAL AND NONINCREMENTAL CURRICULUM POLICY-MAKING

If there is one proposition about curriculum politics that is clear, it is that the school curriculum becomes an issue in communities and societies that are undergoing significant change (Iannaccone, 1967; Coleman, 1965). Such change calls into question the adequacy or appropriateness of existing curricula. For example, as Kirst and Walker (1971) note, national political tensions, generally arising from one or another kind of change, inevitably seem to make themselves felt in curriculum policy debates. Yet, if the most notable and spectacular curriculum politics are associated with crisis and the problems of managing change, Kirst and Walker suggest that curriculum policy-making usually proceeds quietly and *incrementally*, with value conflicts "resolved through low profile politics." In other words, curriculum policy-making, rather than being characterized by dramatic crisis policy-making, or by the often prescribed but seldom realized model of *rational* decision-making, generally is characterized by the modest and mundane strategy of *disjointed incrementalism*, for example, acceptance of the broad outlines of the existing situation with only marginal changes contemplated and serial analysis and piecemeal alterations rather than a single comprehensive attack on the policy problem (Braybrooke and Lindblom, 1963).

However, this aspect of Kirst and Walker's (1971) analysis becomes confusing when they later say that "*Crises occur at such short intervals* in the history of American education — immigration, the great Red scare, war, depression, war again, Sputnik, racial violence, war again — *that crisis policy-making is normal and normal policy-making exceptional*" (p.

198, emphasis added). This observation is striking and insightful, but where does it leave us in terms of understanding the curriculum policy-making process?

The conventional, informed view of educational policy-making — curricular or otherwise — is that it is characterized by incrementalism, perhaps even more so than policy-making in most other organizations and institutions (Elboim-Dror, 1970). The strong tendency toward incrementalism in educational policy-making can be seen to have a number of sources. Many analysts have called attention to the fact that education's dependence on, and vulnerability to, its societal environment causes the public schools to have to serve multiple and sometimes conflicting goals. New goals are acquired even while the established goals are retained. Expectations for the role of the schools seem to expand continuously. The school is asked to be an engine for progress and reform, but at the same time is always expected to maintain society. Thus, by a process of accretion, goals proliferate and increasingly compete with one another for scarce resources. The result is an ever more cumbersome context and structure for decision-making, making incremental policy-making increasingly likely.

Yet, *nonincremental* or innovative curriculum policies nevertheless emerge with surprising frequency. Kirst and Walker imply that innovative policies have emerged frequently because they have been elicited by the surprisingly frequent crises our nation has experienced. In turn, this suggests that the *key* curriculum politics we need to understand are those surrounding crisis policy-making, for the curriculum policy decisions made then presumably will be only incrementally modified until the next crisis.

However, this is a troublesome conclusion. As Elboim-Dror (1970) notes, the incrementalism of educational policy-making "might be satisfactory for an organization that only tries to adjust itself to a stable and slowly changing environment, but it does not suit a rapidly changing and demanding environment pressing for innovation and change from within. If education is to meet successfully its many demanding tasks and missions, it will have to find new and more dynamic decision strategies" (p. 247). And so it has: *education in fact has found such a strategy*, and this strategy, which has been called the "professionalization of reform," has contributed substantially to the increased complexity and politicization of curriculum policy-making. But, at the same time that the "professionalization of reform" fosters nonincremental policy-making, a number of significant restraints on policy innovation impede and transform innovative policy initiatives. Thus, to understand contemporary curriculum politics one must look beyond crisis policy-making, for a focus on it alone is incomplete and misleading.

THE PROFESSIONALIZATION OF REFORM

Significantly, the nationally sponsored curriculum reform movement was underway *before* the Sputnik crisis lent a sense of urgency to the venture. Indeed, it is characteristic of the evolving policy-making process that many innovative policies have emerged under *noncrisis* conditions. Contrary to the theory of incrementalism, Moynihan (1973) suggests that some innovative policies arise through the recognition that existing policies are failing, that "marginal changes, 'tireless tinkering,' will no longer do." This kind of recognition may also be tied, Moynihan proposes, to the "institutionalization" in and about the federal government of the use of social scientists as professional policy advisors. However, given the extreme modesty of the analytical and predictive capabilities of contemporary social scientists, in the face of the awesome complexities of social policy problems, the most intriguing explanation Moynihan (1969, pp. 21–37) offers for the increasing emergence of innovative policies in *noncrisis* situations is what he calls "the professionalization of reform."

Moynihan (1969) argues that whereas in the past efforts to reform societal institutions generally arose due to discontent and pressures that had built up in the public external to the institutions, by midcentury the process of reform had acquired a degree of institutionalization and expertise such that it began to take on the characteristics of an enterprise with "a self-starting capacity of its own." "Increasingly, efforts to change the American social system for the better arose from initiatives undertaken by persons whose profession was to do just that" (Moynihan, 1969, p. 23). Moynihan (1969) says that this development first became evident when President Kennedy's election "brought to Washington as officeholders, or consultants, or just friends, a striking echelon of persons whose profession might justifiably be described as knowing what ails societies and whose art is to get treatment underway before the patient is especially aware of anything noteworthy taking place" (p. 23).

Thus, with the professionalization of reform came a cadre of full-time social critics and advocates for change, devoted to *raising or creating issues* and sometimes, according to Moynihan, succeeding in creating *crises* as well, as in the case of the urban unrest brought on (aggravated?) by the strategy of maximum feasible participation of the poor in federally sponsored reform programs. While a more complete, and charitable, interpretation of the professionalization of reform would acknowledge that professionals positioned in national organizations and agencies have an important responsibility to attend to, and anticipate, national needs — and may have accomplished much good (as well as some ill) in so doing — it nevertheless is hard to deny that the generally liberal-activist ideology of these professionals, in combination with their self-interest in career advancement and the maintenance and enhancement needs of their organizations, must influence their policy recommendations. Indeed, as Moynihan (1973) notes, speaking of the various councils of advisors serving the President, they "tend to measure their success by the number of things they get started" (p. 546).

The "professionalization of reform" helps us to understand the growth and nature of the national network concerned with the "business of curriculum reform, as well as its penchant for policy innovations, many of which become controversial. Thus, just as Moynihan (1969) proposes that "the war on poverty was not declared at the behest of the poor; it was declared in their interest by persons confident of their own judgment in such matters" (p. 25), so too, Hottois and Milner (1975) find evidence that the initiative for introducing sex education in most instances came from educators, *contrary* to educators' claims that such instruction was being added to the curriculum in response to public demands. In turn, the origin of the whole national movement came from a professional sex education "establishment," which was convinced that such instruction was needed, and which actively propagated the idea and showed local educators how to "finesse" the public relations problems involved in introducing it. For example, just as Moynihan spoke of "getting the treatment underway before the patient is especially aware," Hottois and Milner (1975) note that "Some proponents argued that since sex education occurred in classrooms in most schools prior to the existence of any formal program, it was educationally sound, completely honest, and politically astute to claim that the programs were not really new. Thus, the proper strategy was to emphasize that sex education was really being expanded and improved rather than initiated" (p. 40).

While the introduction of sex education frequently may have constituted a particularly blatant example of the professionalization of curriculum reform, there are other interesting and provocative examples worth noting. For instance, it is unlikely that public school educators often began teaching the scientific theory of evolution due to popular demand for it. In fact, just the opposite frequently has been the case, with the only visible public opinion on the matter running strongly *against* the teaching of the theory, due to fundamentalist religious objections to it. Of course, as Nelkin (1976) notes, most scientists scarcely would think that the question of whether to teach evolution is a matter to be decided on religious or democratic grounds. From their point of view, evolution is a scientifically validated theory and its inclusion in biology courses is both imperative and a matter only to be decided on the basis of scientific evidence and expertise. Just as the professionals generally have taken the lead in adding evolution to the curriculum, it also is likely that they usually have taken the initiative in introducing the new social studies, including the controversial *Man: A Course of Study* (MACOS) (Nelkin, 1976).

In short, the professionalization of reform has introduced an extraordinary, dynamic, and controversial new force into the social and educational policy-making process. Convinced of their expertise and prerogatives, armed with "solutions looking for problems," supported by federal and foundation funding, and stimulated by the discovery, as a result of the civil rights movement, of whole new classes of disadvantaged students and forms of discrimination (for example, non-English-speaking students, handicapped students, sex discrimination), the professional reformers energetically pursue their visions of equal educational opportunity and a better and more just society. A key means of this pursuit, and one of the most important aspects of this development, clearly is the "litigation explosion." Although not confined to educational affairs, this phenomenon has been extraordinarily salient and influential in these affairs, frequently and heavily affecting the nature of the public school curriculum (cf. van Geel, 1976).

While it is likely that much good has come out of these efforts, the discussion so far should be sufficient to suggest why from some points of view the professionalization of reform is a mixed blessing. Not only has it increased the pace of disturbing changes, but, with the assistance of the law, it increasingly has imposed the cosmopolitan and secular values of the professional reformers on the people of "middle America."

CONSTRAINTS ON POLICY INNOVATION

On the other side of the coin are the various constraints on policy innovation that inhibit change or *even the consideration* of certain kinds of alternatives. The importance of these constraints is such that they require a search well beyond the dramatic domain of crisis policy-making in our quest for a complete understanding of curriculum politics.

Viewed as a group, all of the constraints on policy innovation can be seen to be related to the maintenance needs of society, communities, organizations, and individuals. While the literature on the subject tends to focus on either the institutional level or the individual level, in reality, individuals make choices with regard to innovations in the context of the structure of incentives created by the institutions within which they find themselves. Thus, "professional reformers" housed in action/innovation-oriented organizations maximize their advancement by being innovative. But within the perverse structure of incentives in the quasi-monopolistic, nonprofit bureaucracy of the public schools, the costs of innovation for administrators and teachers often, or even generally, appear to outweigh the benefits (Michaelsen, 1977). Yet, public schools do adopt innovations. However, as Pincus (1974) suggests, "private firms are more likely to adopt innovations that promote economic efficiency, whereas [public] schools are more likely to adopt innovations that promote bureaucratic and social stability" (p. 119).

Nondecision-Making

Some of the most potent of these constraints on policy innovation emanate from the fascinating realm of *nondecision-making*. In an oft-cited article, Backrach and Baratz (1962) argue that there are two faces of power — one manifest in actual political disputes and their resolution, and the other expressed covertly through the ability of powerful interests to control the agenda of decision-making and prevent the discussion of "unsafe" or "undesirable" issues. The suppression of possible issues or alternatives can result from them actually being vetoed in *nonpublic* deliberations or, even more effectively, by the creation by powerful interests (past and present) of a "mobilization of bias" in terms of widespread and pervasive values and beliefs — throughout an organization, community, region, or society — that delimits what it is "safe" to do and what "should not" be done.

Nondecision-making and the mobilization of bias, by keeping potential issues and alternatives from being discussed or, in some cases, even recognized, are formidable barriers to change. The strength of local, regional, and ethnocultural mobilizations of bias mandate that professional reformers often have to work hard at "consciousness raising" to get their reform proposals taken seriously. For example, as Tyler (1974) notes in reviewing the educational issues attacked by the federal government during the 1960s, such as segregation and the problems of the disadvantaged: ". . . in most cases, they were not even recognized as problems on the local level until the Congressional debates and the availability of federal funds brought them to local attention" (p. 185). In matters such as the segregation issue, it took years of effort to get the initial federal action started.

A graphic example of the problems associated with the mobilization of bias — in terms of the WASPish myth of the culturally homogeneous, unitary community and its educational corollary that all students should be treated alike — is found in the frequent "invisibility" of culturally different students (Waserstein, 1975). A similar kind of problem has often existed in regard to the various classes of students with special physical, emotional, or learning problems, whose needs sometimes are ignored or who sometimes are misclassified and then effectively consigned to oblivion. Budoff (1975), for example, describes the extraordinary efforts that were required by a coalition of concerned citizens and child advocates to get the Boston Public Schools to treat these kinds of students properly. A conclusion that emerges time and again from accounts such as this is that, because of the combination of cultural blinders and insufficient educational resources, special classes of students, whose needs are expensive and troublesome to meet, are likely to remain neglected in many school systems unless the systems are compelled, by some legal means, to behave otherwise. Thus, a substantial part of the litigation explosion in education has beeen necessitated by this cold reality.

The Zone of Tolerance, Vulnerability, and Conflict Avoidance

Within the boundaries set by the mobilization of bias in a given community, and the predominant community values and expectations concerning the public schools, there exists a "zone of tolerance" within which local educators are free to exercise professional leadership. When educators exceed the boundaries of the zone of tolerance (which may be broad or narrow and clearly or poorly defined), they come into conflict with values dear to the particular community and face the likelihood of controversy and opposition. However, educators are strongly inclined to avoid conflict and hence are cautious about testing the boundaries of the zone of tolerance. Thus, this cautiousness inhibits innovation in the curriculum as well as in other aspects of the educational enterprise.

Conflict avoidance tends to be a salient orientation in the minds of school administrators because it is a leading theme in the ideology of their profession, because it is reinforced through the nature of the typical recruitment and socialization process they go through, and because of their frequently keen sense of political vulnerability (Boyd, 1976). This sense of vulnerability, along with the paucity of incentives for risk-taking within the nonprofit, quasi-monopolistic structure of the public schools, tends to make school administrators and teachers reluctant to incur the psychic costs and risks of innovation and possible controversy.

Research indicates that the latitude or discretion granted to local educators varies primarily according to the *type of community* and, even within communities, according to the *type of issue or policy question* that is faced (Boyd, 1976). For instance, speaking in broad generalities, rural school districts and districts located in the "sun belt" of the United States tend to have relatively conservative constituencies. These conservative constituencies are more sensitive and restrictive about the content of courses, such as social studies, literature, and biology, which touch core cultural values; but in all but the most cosmopolitan districts, educators have less freedom of action in these kinds of courses than in the more abstract and value-free subjects such as mathematics. At the same time, however, the method of teaching abstract skills such as mathematics and reading is sometimes a matter of public controversy, especially in conservative communities.

Noninstruction

There is evidence that community socioeconomic status may influence the content and mode of instruction of politically and culturally sensitive courses. In a study of high school civic education in three Boston suburban communities — one upper-middle class, one lower-middle class, and one working class — Litt (1963) found differences among political themes in civics texts, attitudes of community leaders concerning the proper orientation of the community school's civic education program, and in the effects of the civics courses on student political attitudes. Significantly, the differences in political themes emphasized were nearly identical with the preferences of the community leaders.

In an interesting article that relates to Litt's research, Zeigler and Peak (1970) have discussed the political significance of *unrealistic* civic education, that is, instruction that de-emphasizes or neglects the central role of conflict and its resolution in the political process. They contend that such apolitical civic education is common, cite considerable research to support this contention, and argue that unrealistic civic education fosters a conservative orientation in the public that contributes to the maintenance of the *status quo*. Building on the notion of nondecision-making, they propose that high school civic education is unrealistic due to *noninstruction*, that is, "not because of what is said, but more because of what is *not* said" (p. 126). However, contrary to Litt's findings, they suspect that the cause of unrealistic civic education is less the result of the influence of community elites than it is of the *conservative* characteristics of the recruitment and socialization processes of the education professions.

The Politics of Controversy and Nonpublication

Teachers have long recognized that educators can get into a great deal of trouble by teaching controversial matters. But even when educators have substantial public support and are willing to take the "heat" that may be generated by venturing into sensitive areas, those who are offended, even if only a small minority, sometimes can exploit the situation to gain their ends through a "politics of controversy." In other words, as Block and van Geel (1975) put it, ". . . if one can merely make the program 'controversial' there is a good chance both politicians and bureaucrats will back off from it."

The politics of controversy has perhaps its greatest impact on education by causing textbook publishers to go to great lengths to try to avoid inclusion of potentially controversial material in their publications. With very large investments at stake in the production of new textbooks, most publishers feel they cannot take the risks of controversy.

The effects of *overt* censorship and *prior* censorship, or *nonpublication*, on the curriculum might not be quite so bad if teachers and school systems commonly produced their own basic or supplementary curriculum materials. Sadly, as Kirst and Walker (1971) have noted, the vast majority of teachers and systems are almost entirely dependent on the available published materials. The consequence is that although most curriculum decisions ultimately are made at the local school district level, the choices usually are restricted to the available alternatives prepared, and generally precensored, by external groups.

. . .

Noncompliance and Nonimplementation

Unhappily, for reformers, it turns out that it is one thing to get innovative schemes accepted and launched and quite another to get them implemented successfully. Though this might seem obvious, it really was not until the generally meager results of the "Great Society" and "War on Poverty" reform efforts of the 1960s prompted a close examination of what was actually going on at the sites of innovative projects that the full and extraordinary significance of the implementation problem became clear.

One of the best documented examples we have of the complex politics of implementation is found in studies of Title I of ESEA (for example, Murphy, 1971; Hughes and Hughes, 1972). As van Geel (1976) has noted, if all the statutory requirements, regulations, and guidelines of Title I had been fully enforced, it would have resulted in a virtual revolution in educational programming at the local level. But, a host of political and organizational problems blunted the intent of Title I.

Of course, depending on one's point of view and the issue at hand, the *looseness* in the federal system that enables evasion and noncompliance may be a good thing. One of the goals of our founding fathers, of course, was to build into our governmental structure "checks and balances" that would prevent the abuse of centralized authority and promote the need for persuasion, cooperation, and compromise. The structured necessity for this kind of dialogue, though it may prolong the agony of change on one level, on another level ameliorates possible destructive tensions and facilitates meeting the simultaneous need to maintain society while changing it. The difficulty for educational reformers, however, is that they sometimes wonder if they are succeeding in changing schooling at all, for the problem of the looseness of the federal system is exacerbated by the peculiar "loose coupling" of ends, means, and authority in the educational system. This state of affairs makes enforcement, supervision, and evaluation of educational programs, whether traditional or innovative, quite difficult and obscures accountability for educational outcomes.

But the failures of public schooling, and efforts to reform it in the 1960s, increasingly have led to calls for accountability. However, there are a host of technical and political problems inherent in all educational accountability schemes so far devised. Indeed, the magnitude of these problems is such that it ironically is proving quite difficult to implement the very schemes designed in part to circumvent the implementation problem.

Perhaps the most disturbing of a great many disturbing revelations to educational reformers in the past decade has been the discovery of the extent to which nonimplementation of educational innovations occurs *even* when local school district authorities and teachers seem favorably disposed toward them. In other words, beyond active and conscious noncompliance, there is the equally important problem of how to successfully and fully translate innovative ideas into practice among nominally compliant educators who, nevertheless, normally have few tangible incentives for innovative behavior. As the authors of *Behind the Classroom Door* concluded, on the basis of observations in 158 classrooms in 67 schools: ". . . some of the highly recommended and publicized innovations of the past decade or so were dimly conceived and, at best, partially implemented in the schools claiming them. The novel features seemed to be blunted in the effort to twist the innovation into familiar conceptual frames or established patterns of schooling" (Goodlad et al., 1970, p. 72). These conclusions have been substantiated by the large, systematic study of federally supported innovation programs conducted by the Rand Corporation. The Rand researchers found that nonimplementation was common and that the most that could be hoped for was a process of *mutual adaptation* in which both the practices in a given school and the innovative project being attempted were modified by one another (Berman and McLaughlin, 1976).

CONCLUSION

Having briefly surveyed the ethereal world of the "professional reformers" and the subterranean world of "nondecision-making" and its cousins, we are now in a better position to assess the extent to which curriculum policy-making is characterized by incrementalism — or, alternatively, the extent to which "crisis policy-making is normal and normal policy-making exceptional." Although analysts typically have concluded that educational policy-making is preponderantly incremental, there is a very real sense in which the ambivalence that Kirst and Walker (1971) display on the subject is justified. When one examines the nature of curriculum policy-making closely, there is a paradoxical appearance of incremental and nonincremental policy-making going on simultaneously. Beyond the frequency with which nonincremental policy-making occurs due to closely spaced national crises, the "professionalization of reform" and the growth of the business sector concerned with this enterprise have greatly increased the incidence of innovative policy-making. But the paradoxical simultaneity of incremental and nonincremental policy-making also is the result of the complexity of policy-making within our federal system. Thus, we often have both kinds of policy-making going on simultaneously, with local policy-makers usually maintaining the status quo or slowly deciding to adopt innovative curriculum ideas developed and advocated at higher levels.

Yet, since many of the curriculum policy decisions at higher levels come down in the form of mandates, the local policy-makers — and ultimately the teaching personnel delivering the educational services — also are occupied with deciding the extent to which, and the speed with which, they will comply with these mandates. Thus, the impact of nonincremental policy-making, whether due to the stimulation of crises or the efforts of professional reformers, is heavily tempered by the numerous constraints on policy innovation. Indeed, nonincremental policy thrusts are far more than incrementally modified by the snares and hazards of the implementation process. This process amounts to a continuation of the policy-making process through the politics of administration.

In sum, the puzzling simultaneity of incrementalism and nonincrementalism in the policy-making process can be seen as two sides of the same coin. On one side is the complex apparatus of organizations and agencies involved with curriculum policy-making at the national level, a set of machines lubricated by professionals attentive to potential crises and devoted to heroic visions, nonincremental reform, and their own career advancement. On the other side is the labyrinthine, "loosely coupled" system by which education is governed at the subnational levels and ultimately delivered at the local level. The extraordinary complexity and massive inertia of this loosely linked system easily can transform heroic ventures into pedestrian projects. Thus, along with the high human and monetary costs of curriculum change, these characteristics — in part reflecting societal, organizational, and individual maintenance needs — ensure that real change will take place slowly.[3]

Moreover, it is essential to note that recent far-reaching changes in the structure of authority over curriculum policy-making seem likely to increase the probability of incremental, rather than nonincremental, policy-making. In his comprehensive treatment of this subject, van Geel (1976) calls attention to the increased involvement in policy-making of the courts, state and federal agencies, and teachers' unions. He concludes that the curriculum policy-making system is now more complex, legalized, centralized and bureaucratized and includes more veto points. These characteristics, plus their tendency to become more pronounced and to reinforce one another, seem likely to make nonincremental curriculum policy-making increasingly difficult. While we can expect the professional reformers to continue their valiant efforts in behalf of innovative policy-making, they increasingly may become entrapped in the very machinery they helped to create.

It is hard to escape the conclusion that the "business" of reform has grown and proceeded according to a principle of "top-down," externally imposed innovation that is sadly out of tune with the realities involved in changing American public education. If the public were not now demanding results, it might be possible for the professional reformers to continue "business as usual," assisted, as LaNoue (1971) has noted, by an "educational research establishment, with its built-in incentive to discover failure which justifies ever more research" (p. 305). But, the public is now far less tolerant of this sort of thing, though this is what the public may continue to get, like it or not. However, if we are really serious about reforming public education, it appears that we must strike at the heart of the problem, namely the perverse structure of incentives that discourages innovation and provides few rewards for excellence within the nonprofit, monopolistic milieu of the public schools (cf., Michaelsen, 1977). Assured of a captive clientele — at least insofar as the birth rate permits — and utilizing a "lockstep" reward system based on seniority rather than merit, the public schools scarcely provide a climate conducive to risk-taking, experimentation, and responsiveness to consumers. Indeed, it is remarkable that many public schools perform as well as they do, considering their basic reward structure.[4]

. . .

NOTES

1. This is a revised and much abridged version of a paper commissioned by the Curriculum Development Task Force of the National Institute of Education, U.S. Department of Health, Education, and Welfare. The original paper appears in the *Review of Educational Research* 42:4 (Fall 1978) and was reprinted in Gary Sykes and John Schaffarzick (eds.), *Value conflicts and curriculum issues: Lessons from research and experience*. Berkeley, Calif.: McCutchan Publishing Co., 1979.

2. The quotation is Laswell's (1936) succinct statement of the focus of political science.

3. For insightful discussions amplifying these problems in curriculum change, see Cuban (1976) and McKinney and Westbury (1975).

4. Research is needed on what might be called the "secondary" reward structure of public schools, that is, the extent to which and circumstances under which quasi-intrinsic motivations, flowing, for example, from school or community traditions, skilled leadership, or the "professionalism" of educators, produce a level of faculty performance beyond what might be expected simply from the basic "lockstep" reward structure.

REFERENCES

Backrach, P., and M.S. Baratz. "Two Faces of Power," *American Political Science Review* 56 (1962): 947–52.

Berman, P., and M.W. McLaughlin. "Implementation of Educational Innovation," *The Educational Forum* 40 (1976): 345–70.

Block, A., and T. van Geel, "State of Arizona Curriculum Law." In T. van Geel with assistance of A. Block, *Authority to Control the School Curriculum: An Assessment of Rights in Conflict*. A study completed under a grant from the National Institute of Education, 1975, ERIC Document No. ED 125070.

Boyd, W.L. "The Public, the Professionals, and Educational Policy-making: Who Governs?" *Teachers College Record* 77 (1976): 568–70.

Braybrooke, D., and C.E. Lindblom. *A Strategy of Decision*. New York: The Free Press, 1963.

Budoff, M. "Engendering Change in Special Education Practices," *Harvard Educational Review* 45 (1975): 507–26.

Coleman, J.S. (ed.) *Education and Political Development*. Princeton, New Jersey: Princeton University Press, 1965.

Cuban, L. "Determinants of Curriculum Change and Stability, 1870–1970." Paper prepared for the N.I.E. Curriculum Development Task Force. Arlington, Virginia, October 15, 1976.

Elboim-Dror, R. "Some Characteristics of the Education Policy Formation System," *Policy Sciences* 1 (1970): 231–53.

Goodlad, J.I., M.F. Klein, and associates. *Behind the Classroom Door*. Columbus, Ohio: Charles Jones, 1970.

Hottois, J., and N.A. Milner. *The Sex Education Controversy*. Lexington, Massachusetts: D.C. Heath, 1975.

Hughes, J.F., and A.O. Hughes. *Equal Education*. Bloomington: Indiana University Press, 1972.

Iannaccone, L. *Politics in Education*. New York: Center for Applied Research in Education, 1967.

Kirst, M.W., and D.F. Walker. "An Analysis of Curriculum Policy-making," *Review of Educational Research* 41 (1971): 479–509.

LaNoue, G.R. "The Politics of Education," *Teachers College Record* 73:2 (1971): 304–19.

Laswell, H.D. *Politics: Who Gets What, When and How*? New York: McGraw-Hill, 1936.

Litt, E. "Civic Education, Community Norms, and Political Indoctrination," *American Sociological Review* 28 (1963): 69–75.

McKinney, W.L., and I. Westbury. "Stability and Change: The Public Schools of Gary, Indiana," 1940–70. In W.A. Reid and D.F. Walker (eds.), *Case Studies in Curriculum Change*. London: Routledge and Kegan Paul, 1975.

Michaelsen, J.B. "Revision, Bureaucracy, and School Reform: A Critique of Katz," *School Review* 85 (1977): 229–46.

Moynihan, D.P. *Maximum Feasible Misunderstanding*. New York: The Free Press, 1969.

Moynihan, D.P. *The Politics of a Guaranteed Income*. New York: Random House, 1973.

Murphy, J.T. "Title I of ESEA: The Politics of Implementing Federal Education Reform," *Harvard Educational Review* 41 (1971): 35–63.

Nelkin, D. "The Science-Textbook Controversies," *Scientific American* 234:4 (1976): 33–39.

Pincus, J. "Incentives for Innovation in the Public Schools," *Review of Educational Research* 44 (1974): 113–44.

Tyler, R.W. "The Federal Role in Education," *The Public Interest* 34 (Winter 1974): 154–87.

van Geel, T. *Authority to Control the School Program*. Lexington, Massachusetts: D.C. Heath, 1976.

van Geel, T. "Parental Preferences and the Politics of Spending Public Educational Funds," *Teachers College Record* 79 (1978) 339–63.

Waserstein, A. "Organizing for Bilingual Education: One Community's Experience," *Inequality in Education* 19 (February 1975) 23–30.

Zeigler, L.H., and W. Peak. "The Political Functions of the Educational System," *Sociology of Education* (Spring 1970): 115–42.

Selection 1.5

Curriculum: Variations on Themes

James R. Gress

The celebration of the bicentennial anniversary of the American political revolution affords an opportunity to consider another uniquely American revolution, our system of schooling for the early and middle childhood years. The public elementary school symbolizes the greatest part of our schooling enterprise; but the kindergarten, the primary school, the middle school, and more recently, an array of early childhood schools are a part of it as well. A look at the evolution of their curriculums can refresh our perspective of these institutions, identify reasons for our present position, and suggest some future directions.

The curriculum is viewed here as a plan for schooling which embodies our philosophy and goals. It is an intellectual statement intended to guide formal learning. However, the curriculum's *raison d'etre* is the ultimate quality of schooling it stimulates. Therefore, a complete consideration of the curriculum must concern itself not only with the intellectual syntheses which underlie its design but also with the socio-political realities which affect its engineering.

CONTINUING CHANGE

The proposition that formal schooling for our young, like other social institutions, has in the past and continues to reflect significant change provides a useful point-of-departure for examining some of

---

SOURCE. *Theory Into Practice* 15 (April 1976), pp. 98-106.

the diversity of our thinking about our schooling and its curriculum. To begin, therefore, let us recall some of the more recent developments related to the public school in America generally and then turn our attention to the evolution of its curriculum in particular.

Even a casual recollection of just the past ten years reveals the variety and amount of change in our thinking about almost every aspect of public schooling. For example, the frenzied efforts to find enough "warm bodies" to teach in every school classroom have now given way in some quarters to nightmares about "teacher surpluses," and the impact of the end of the post-WW II "baby boom" has seriously questioned our previously expansionistic assumptions about other aspects of schooling as well. In another vein, the consequences of court decisions like *Serrano v. Priest, Horace Mann League v. United States, Keyes v. School District No. 1, Denver,* and *Rodriquez v. San Antonio School District* have torn at the very political, fiscal, and social fiber of the schools. And the sacred traditions of "local control" have been unquestionably obliterated, in part, by massive federal appropriations for schools; NDEA 1958 and ESEA 1965 are only some hallmarks. Perennially with us, the "accountability movement" has continued to manifest itself in ever new ways—PPBS, voucher systems, performance contracting, behavioral objectives, and, perhaps, alternative schooling.

Change is everywhere around us. In another area, NEA leaders now spend almost more time fighting for collective bargaining than they once spent berating the "unionism" of the AFT and, having entered the political arena, are preparing to spend through NEA-PAC more money on a 1976 presidential endorsement than they once spent on instructional activities. Professional dialogue has shifted from educational parks to magnet schools—and back again. The rise and fall of the Ocean Hill-Brownsville experiment and the change from "separate but equal" to court-ordered bussing illustrate other shifts. And the schools' horizons have been dotted by instructional innovations from i.t.a. to an "alphabet soup" of elementary science programs, from sex education and black studies to computer-assisted instruction, and from the structure of the disciplines to the quality of the human environment.

Changing directions has always been characteristic of professional education. In a comprehensive and systematic survey of the literature and contemporary practice forty years ago, Zirbes (1935, p. 37) concluded "that there is an increasing momentum of educational change, and that, unless those who are entrusted with educational responsibilities reckon with these forces intelligently, education will indeed be disrupted." One might wonder today, for example, how the eventual need to replace literally thousands of aging school buildings in inner cities and rural areas alike may in the future impact our traditional concept of school as a "place." Certainly change is an essential ingredient in all educational thinking and practice. How it can impact them is not always as clear.

An essential difference, however, between change in 1976 and change in the 1930s or in 1776 would seem to be the Tofflerian vertigo brought on by the increasing acceleration of change. The present value crisis in American society is not a product of change or even of the rate of change. Rather, it appears that an increasingly accelerating change confuses the predictability of human experience and mortally threatens the stability of our very existence. In spite of this, it seems more useful to try to examine the nature of the revolution itself rather than to bemoan our present dizziness. To this end, we turn to the central issue in schooling, its curriculum.

CURRICULUM DESIGNS: TYPES AND TRENDS

The revolution, or evolution, of curriculums for early and middle childhood education in the United States has its roots in the social and political experience of Western culture and owes its philosophical debt to the Greeks, to Comenius, to Pestallozi and Froebel, to Locke and Rousseau, to Herbart and to Dewey. Its extant designs reflect the work of those whose more recent contributions history has yet to judge—the McMurrys, Bobbitt and Charters, Rugg and Caswell; and even more recently, Herrick, Stratemeyer, Taba, and a host of our own contemporaries.[1] Their work has resulted in the last hundred years or less in several alternative curriculum designs for the elementary school, each utilizing a particular point-of-departure in its construction and each reflecting a particular viewpoint.

In their recent volume, Saylor and Alexander (1974, pp. 198-240) have presented a comprehensive survey of curriculum movements in the United States and their resultant designs. The designs they have categorized include those focused on specific competencies, designs organized around the separate subjects as well as the disciplines of knowledge, those which emphasize social activities and problems, those which focus on learning processes and skills and those designs constructed from identified individual learner needs and interests. Such a classification identifies alternative approaches to curriculum design which have been proposed, and these authors' discussion of the features, strengths and weaknesses of the various types of designs suggests some of the overlapping relationships as well as contradictions among them. For example, one can find essentially the same rationale for a competency-based curriculum whether one consults Franklin Bobbitt (1918) or Popham and Baker (1970). What differs in this instance as in the case of a school subjects design *à la* Herbart (McMurry, 1895) versus that of Alpren (1967) is, in part, the historical circumstance within which each authority advocated a design. In order to gain some additional perspective about the relationships between and among designs, therefore, it is appropriate to consider them in an evolutionary context.

Vandenberg (1971) has used the Hegelian dialectic to formulate a model of the evolution of educational thought in the United States which may be useful for sorting some of these additional relationships. Vandenberg's model displays a pendulum of thinking over time which incorporates the "actions and reactions" in this evolution of thought but, more importantly, the syntheses of thinking which have generally characterized it. As Vandenberg points out:

> The "syntheses"—mental discipline, Herbartianism, child-centered progressive education, and life-adjustment—represent mainstream educational thinking because they encompassed insights contained in earlier points of view within frameworks of new emphases. The "antitheses"—child study, the scientific movement, reconstructionism, academic excellence—represent oppositional points of view that have been important and fruitful by way of stimulating controversy and remembering facets of schooling that were forgotten or neglected by overcommitted adherents to mainstream views, but remain tangential to education as a cumulative field of study because of their lack of *capacity to build on what has gone before.* [P. 36; emphasis added]

Thus, while categories or types of curriculums such as those developed by Saylor and Alexander identify the designs which have been a part of the experience of the American elementary school and its institutional offspring, Vandenberg's analysis is further useful for suggesting at least one criterion that may be used to focus on the most important trends in design and to characterize this evolution as movement along a major continuum of thought.

The mainstream syntheses of thought he has identified parallel three major curriculum designs: (1) the separate school subjects model, (2) the progressive model centered on the needs and interests of students, and (3) the life-adjustment model. Viewed along a continuum, the evolution of these models may be characterized as a gradual bringing into focus within the elementary school curriculum the nature of the relationships between the possible sources of curriculum: organized knowledge, the developmental needs of children and what Stratemeyer (1957), for example, called "persistent life situations."

Vandenberg's continuum also demonstrates a shifting away from the logico-deductive organization of the accumulated knowledge of human experience and a shifting toward the psycho-inductive nature of individual learning in curriculum design. But the reactionary movements of the past, as well as the almost erratic shifts of focus in our more recent curriculum experience, also suggest that we have yet collectively to achieve a satisfactory resolution of the apparent conflict in the three essential sources of curriculum. Vocal proponents of academic rationalism and behaviorism, of humanism and of social reconstructionism of several varieties (see, for example, Eisner and Vallance, 1974) are all still with us. Before suggesting where we may be headed in this regard, however, a brief look at analyses of the decline of three principal curriculum design movements may suggest some of the reasons for our lack of complete synthesis and call our attention to a relationship between intellectual and socio-political developments.

THWARTED EFFORTS

Harold Rugg's comprehensive statement in the 26th NSSE Yearbook (1926) includes an analysis of our earliest experience in the development of the elementary school curriculum (Part I, pp. 17-32). He concluded that, from the beginning, our schools have tended to lag behind developments in the larger society, and (more importantly here) he attributed the "culture lag" phenomenon to our tendency to isolate schooling from living, to the disciplinary orientation of the professors who dominated public schooling and to the entrenchment of authors and publishers in the curriculum. Kirst and Walker's more recent analysis (1971) would suggest that part of what Rugg found to be true about curriculum movements in the past still persists: they either fail to consider political realities or they deliberately serve special interests.

Toward a more recent end of the historical continuum of curriculum evolution is the experience of the 1950s and 1960s. McClure's analysis (1971, pp. 45-75) of curriculum developments in this period concludes that there are two jobs yet to be done: nurturing the truly positive contributions made in the past and engaging in a massive "work in" to bring these contributions into the over-all conduct of schooling. In the same work, Sand (pp. 219-244) cites shifts in student power, community power and teacher power as important determinants of continuing curriculum change, and Schaefer (pp. 3-25) recalls Cremin's words in calling for "a new tough-minded progressivism that is at the same time consonant with the best in our tradition and appropriate to contemporary needs." Such analyses reaffirm our position that the curriculum of the elementary school has yet to achieve an acceptable intellectual synthesis of conflicting sources and that earlier attempts at synthesis were ultimately thwarted, in addition, in socio-political arenas.

Perhaps an era of special promise for the elementary school as well as for the curriculum synthesis toward which it has moved can be found in Progressive Education. Taking its cues from Dewey's comprehensive philosophical analyses, the Progressive movement perhaps came closest to a resolution of the curriculum's basic intellectual and political issues. Yet Progressivism, too, fell victim to many of the same fallacies already identified, as Cremin's classic work (1961, pp. 347-53) concludes. Cremin attributed Progressivism's decline to internal strife and fragmentation, to a negativism and protest which overshadowed more positive forces, to unrealistic demands on the public school teacher, to simplistic and wholesale attempts to replicate its early successes, to a generally more conservative social reaction and to its divorce from the lay public which it ultimately needed to serve. Again, our progress was interrupted, in part, by our failure as professional educators to collectively understand our direction and to keep in touch with the greater society. A persuasive vision of what the curriculum might be and how schooling for the early and middle childhood years might effectively proceed has not yet been realized.

INSIGHTS?

What conclusions might be drawn from this brief survey of the evolution of the curriculum in the American elementary school? What implications for its future development and the development of other forms of schooling for the early and middle childhood years might be isolated? Probably several. No attempt will be made here to identify them all or to suggest "a final solution" to these problems for at least two reasons. First, any one solution seems antithetical to the most appropriate method of intellectual inquiry, being both historically premature and also inconsistent with our pluralistic traditions. Secondly, it would be presumptuous to make such an attempt within the confines of these few pages. However, some strands of thought might be woven together here to suggest general directions.

Changing focuses in the elementary school curriculum might be characterized somewhat simply as shifting emphases on subject matter, the individual and the society, that is, as "variations on themes."

But individual movements and the curriculum proposals they have nurtured rightfully deserve Taba's criticism (1962, pp. 414-415) that "the problem of balance is unresolved. Only the stakes have changed" and her observation that our "tendency to rationalize a curriculum pattern in terms of a single principle . . . is in effect a gross oversimplification which has many undesirable consequences. One is a kind of myopia in developing and implementing curriculum designs." But as Vandenberg's analysis demonstrates, at least the mainstream of educational thinking and curriculum evolution has represented a gradual synthesis of the three principal emphases in design in a way which reflects earlier developments and which brings the importance of each into ever clearer focus. It remains for us, then, to continue this synthesis.

Tyler's approach (1949) to the sources of curriculum, to lay them all out side by side, as it were, though perhaps simplistically eclectic and overly rational, at least reminded us that in the final analysis we must deal with all three. The question is not, however: Which is the most important? The question is: How is each important? Dewey (1902, pp. 3-4) offered a key:

> Profound differences in theory are never gratuitous or invented. They grow out of conflicting elements in a genuine problem—a problem which is genuine just because the elements, taken as they stand, are conflicting. Any significant problem involves conditions that for the moment contradict each other. Solution comes only by getting away from the meaning of terms that is already fixed upon and coming to see conditions from another point of view, and hence in a fresh light. But this reconstruction means travail of thought. Easier than thinking with surrender of already formed ideas and detachment from facts already learned is just to stick by what is already said, looking about for something with which to buttress it against attack.

Extant curriculum designs do share at least one common element. Each represents an individual's particular "interest," that of its creator. And each suggests what appeared to be most important to its advocate. Each not only embodies a set of design features and principles but also represents the way some individual thought and felt about priorities in schools. Each curriculum design becomes the former, in large part, as a result of the latter. This fact can provide some clues for reconciling otherwise conflicting designs. It is possible to think of every curriculum design as a specific example of the generic case of an "individual needs and interests" design. Reconciling conflicting intellectual premises may be, in part, a matter of asking: For whom is the design intended? For example, if intended for the professional scholar, then a disciplines design is probably very appropriate—not because it focuses on the structure of disciplines *per se* but because that is, in current jargon, where the scholar's "head is at." If the design, on the other hand, is intended to guide the learning of young children, then the curriculum must likewise adequately consider the child's developmental progress.

As to the place of social considerations in curriculum design, Dewey (1915, pp. 23-40) points out that the interaction between the child and his or her environment is "naturally" directed by the group and the situation, that the social situation is itself a reference for action and the individual's need for group membership is intrinsic to the disposition of all persons. By starting with reference to an individual, therefore, a curriculum design will necessarily deal with social problems as well as with organized subject matter. Our problem is not a choice among possibly conflicting value systems in curriculum design but a method of utilizing all in ways which adequately account for and explain each for some individual.

At a second level, our attention needs also to be directed to engineering curriculums—planning, implementing, and evaluating them—in ways which provide for the necessary socio-political linkages which appear to have been largely overlooked in the past. A curriculum cannot be imposed by any one individual or group upon others since its ultimate success in guiding classroom instruction must take into account the thinking and actions of others as well as our own. The school classroom and the classroom teacher are important linkages in this respect. We will return to the role of the teacher later.

Beyond the classroom, the major socio-political focus for our continuing attention is the school community itself. Curriculum engineering is not a purely rational activity. It is very much a political process.[2] Professional educators appear to be guilty of a charge Adler (1965) levelled at professional philosophers, namely, that of so technologicalizing the inquiry as to remove it from the everyday experience of all persons. Schooling is not the exclusive cult of professional educators. The curriculum is the domain of more than theorists, school supervisors, and curriculum consultants. The American elementary school and its curriculum is a social enterprise whose continuing health depends, in part, on its ability to relate to the entire community.

The body politic is our best safeguard against the distortions of special interest groups, including our own. Curriculum is, in the final analysis, a question of values. And values are everybody's business. This is not to say that curriculum design is a simple matter of identifying the "lowest common denominators" in our society. Rather, it is to say that solely elitist ideals are irrelevant to an institution which encompasses all of society. Elementary schooling is not the university, nor should it be. And those fortunate enough to be counted among an elite, whether by wisdom or wit, need not protect our own flanks by imposing our ideas on others. Indeed, our very positions, in the universities and in the public schools, carry with them a special obligation *to listen* as well as to share our perspectives with those outside them. Thomas Merton once wrote, "If I give you my truth but fail to receive your truth in return, then there can be no truth between us" (1961, p. 81). Our experience suggests that in the past we often have been busier dispensing truth rather than sharing it. We have often been lost in a flurry of peripheral curriculum changes because we have failed, in part, to stop and ask others where we are going.

DIRECTIONS

Our attention needs to be directed, then, at two complementary and parallel levels. First, a continuing synthesis of the mainstream ideas of curriculum must move forward. We need to keep our attention directed to where schooling for our young is headed. We have paid an enormous price as a society for the distortions and excesses such as those which grew out of Progressive Education and which tended, on the one hand, to pervert the clearer thinking of Dewey and, on the other, to ignore totally the contributions to be made by other points-of-view. Our more recent curriculum experience has been little more than a series of reactionary spasms. And the general chaos has been further exacerbated by an accelerated change and the articulated and unarticulated intuitions of those who have either sensed that something was amiss or have offered oversimplified analyses and consequent solutions, the most radical and yet symptomatic of which has been the proposal to "junk the whole system" (Illich, 1970).

One lesson is clear, an emergent curriculum synthesis must account both for the insights of various points of view and at the same time impact the quality of elementary schooling. Keeping the system of intellectual dialogue open within the profession as well as between the profession and the greater academic and social communities may itself accomplish, in part, the synthesis we seek.

We need also to devote continuing attention to cementing the necessary relationships between the elementary school and society at large. Earlier, it was noted that America itself is in the midst of a division over basic values. To hold the schools alone culpable for all the perceived "evils" in American society as it approaches its two-hundredth anniversary is really too easy in addition to the most serious implications of an acceptance of such blame. And to assume that our social ills might be remedied if we can somehow manage to put the schools back "in order" again ignores the interdependent nature of all social institutions. On the other hand, to reject any responsibility of schooling to play some role in the solution of our social crises seems equally antagonistic and only heats the counter-productive rhetoric of "accountability." Schooling in the early and middle childhood years is the one institution in our culture, as in others, which can serve as a mechanism for simplifying the experience of the young in a complex society, for providing an "idealized" model of that maturing society, and for broadening and balancing both the experiences of the young and, ultimately, the environments of the society itself (Dewey, 1915, pp. 10-22). But this traditional purpose can easily be lost in the throes of change. Keeping the broader perspective intact necessitates a continuing re-examination of purposes. Curriculum, which should be the heart and soul of the schooling enterprise, provides a vehicle for such examination, and the most effective system of curriculum engineering is necessarily one which involves keeping in touch with all elements of society. Curriculum is perhaps the most important social policy we make. It, therefore, deserves the fullest use of the democratic process which is the truest decision-making structure in the American polity.

THE CLASSROOM TEACHER: LINK OR BARRIER?

Once a curriculum is planned, its implementation is perhaps almost solely dependent on the classroom teacher. Our brief analyses of earlier curriculum movements remind us of the importance of the classroom teacher in this regard. For example, a reawakening to that importance was perhaps one of the more painful lessons of our recent toying with "teacher-proof" curriculums. Some of us thought that desirable changes in schooling could be brought about through the engineering of national curriculums which reflected the insights of the "best and brightest" among us. Among the things we have failed to recognize in our past efforts, however, is that classroom teachers are thinking persons whose own intellectual accomplishments may be constrained more by the parochialism of their professors than by any native inferiority. The thinking in which most classroom teachers engage is perhaps different in kind from that which presumably occupies scholars. But this difference need not prompt a kind of hierarchy which values very little the contributions of the classroom teacher to curriculum thought. Learning is not really a mass enterprise which can somehow be manipulated on a wholesale basis—even by an enlightened elite. In the most basic way, education is the accumulated experience of individuals. And, in school, the most important link between the individual child and the quality of his or her learning is the teacher—much maligned, abused and used—but still the single most important resource of formal schooling.

Inservice teacher education is clearly outside the scope of this article, but some attention must be directed to the necessity of establishing communication between the thousands of practicing professionals who are a key to achieving intellectual synthesis in curriculum and to translating it into what goes on in our schools. In a very real sense, differences in curriculums—at least from the point of view of their implementation—lie in differences among teachers about what is important to achieve in the classroom. Discrepancies between curriculum as "a plan," on the one hand, and as "the experience of students," on the other, can be greatly minimized if greater attention can be given to the critical link between the two, the classroom teacher.

At a typical summer conference for teachers, John Goodlad recounted his travels around the United States to visit (at the enthusiastic invitations of school administrators and their teachers) the presumably "nongraded" schools in vogue at the time. He described the new physical plants and the new arrays of instructional technology and materials, yet concluded regrettably that he had not seen a "nongraded" school—at least he and the practitioners apparently hadn't been talking about the same thing. We hadn't got "the idea."

The elementary curriculum has been described as "variations on themes," yet somehow the basic chords have eluded our ears as our intensity for keeping up with all the latest "hits" has overshadowed our ability to appreciate messages. Silberman (1970), like Dewey (1915), called it "mindlessness." To be sure, the words are there, but not yet set to the composer's music. The composer is all of us, not each of us. And the classroom teachers are a great part of us. Unless the massive inservice programs which appear on the horizon attend to every classroom teacher's need *to think about* what he or she is doing, then we shall all be doomed to endlessly replaying old recordings. To be sure such thinking will need to be based on a wealth of actual classroom teaching experience, and such theorizing will need to adequately explain such experience in ways that are more intellectually honest than the "arm chair" prescriptions which have characterized much of teacher education in the past. Intellectual synthesis must, nonetheless, continue to be at the core of all of our activity, teacher's and professor's alike. And such synthesis will most fruitfully proceed in a system of open exchange between the two and with the public as well.

. . .

CONCLUSION

As we celebrate the Bicentennial, then, let us also celebrate the progress of the American elementary school and the unique revolution of ideas and practices which have come to shape curriculum for the early and middle childhood years. But let us temper our celebration with reflection. Democracy will survive; it is endemic to the human spirit. Whether the American system will survive, however, is still open to question. Education will survive for learning is human life itself. How effectively early and middle childhood education will allow our young to participate in the continuing American revolution will depend, in part, on the ability of the curriculum to accommodate changing intellectual and socio-political forces. Some may "hold these truths to be self-evident." All of us should reflect upon them from time to time, and this occasion seemed an appropriate one to do so.

NOTES

1. Seguel's work (1966) illuminates the contributions of the earliest of these authorities. Some setting into perspective of the principal contributions of the past thirty years or so may now be in order.

2. Decker Walker's embryo model (1971) suggests some provocative research lines in this respect.

REFERENCES

Adler, Mortimer, J. *The Conditions of Philosophy*. New York: Atheneum, 1965.

Alpren, Morton (ed.) *The Subject Curriculum, Grades K-12*. Columbus, Ohio: Charles E. Merrill, 1967.

Bobbitt, Franklin. *The Curriculum*. Boston: Houghton Mifflin, 1918.

Cremin, Lawrence. *The Transformation of the School*. New York: Random House, 1961.

Dewey, John. *The Child and the Curriculum*. Chicago: University of Chicago Press, 1902.

Dewey, John. *Democracy and Education*. New York: Macmillan, 1915.

Eisner, Elliot W., and Elizabeth Vallance. *Conflicting Conceptions of Curriculum*. Berkeley, Calif.: McCutchan, 1974.

Illich, Ivan. *Deschooling Society*. New York: Harper and Row, 1970.

Kirst, Michael W., and Decker F. Walker. "An Analysis of Curriculum Policy-making," *Review of Educational Research* 41 (Fall 1971): 479–509.

McClure, Robert M. (ed.) *The Curriculum: Retrospect and Prospect*. Seventieth Yearbook of the National Society for the Study of Education. Part I. Chicago: University of Chicago Press, 1971.

McMurry, Charles. *A Course of Study for the Eight Grades of the Common Schools, Including a Handbook of Practical Suggestions to Teachers*. Bloomington, Ill.: Public School Publishing, 1895.

Merton, Thomas. "A Letter to Pablo Antonio Cuadra Concerning Giants." In *Emblems of a Season of Fury*. Norfolk, Conn.: New Directions, 1961.

Popham, W. James, and Eva L. Baker. *Systematic Instruction*. Englewood Cliffs, N.J.: Prentice-Hall, 1970.

Rugg, Harold, and William Withers. *Social Foundations of Education*. Englewood Cliffs, N.J.: Prentice-Hall, 1955.

Saylor, J. Galen, and William and M. Alexander. *Planning Curriculum for Schools*. New York: Holt, Rinehart, and Winston, 1974.

Seguel, Mary Louise. *The Curriculum Field: Its Formative Years*. New York: Teachers College Press, 1966.

Silberman, Charles E. *Crisis in the Classroom*. New York: Random House, 1970.

Stratemeyer, Florence, et al. *Developing a Curriculum for Modern Living*. 2d ed. New York: Teachers College Press, 1957.

Taba, Hilda. *Curriculum Development: Theory and Practice*. New York: Harcourt, Brace, and World, 1962.

Tyler, Ralph. *Basic Principles of Curriculum and Instruction*. Chicago: University of Chicago Press, 1949.

Vandenberg, Donald. *Being and Education: An Essay in Existential Phenomenology*. Englewood Cliffs, N.J.: Prentice-Hall, 1971.

Walker, Decker F. "A Naturalistic Model for Curriculum Development," *School Review* 80 (November 1971): 51–65.

Zirbes, Laura. *Curriculum Trends*. Washington, D.C.: Association for Childhood Education, 1935.

PART TWO

Frameworks for Curriculum

In order to address issues in the field of curriculum systematically and meaningfully, one must understand some of the alternative frameworks available for the task. These frameworks are sets of assumptions one makes about the nature of man and woman, about knowledge, and about values. There are several frameworks within which a variety of curriculum issues may be addressed. Each framework makes explicit fundamental philosophical assumptions that address the following questions:

Being

1. Who is man/woman?
2. Why does he/she exist?
3. What is his/her relationship to his/her environment?

Knowing

4. What is knowledge?
5. How does man/woman know?...learn?
6. What is truth?
7. What is experience? How is it related to knowledge?

Valuing

8. How do human beings live together?
9. What values does the school teach?
10. What knowledge is of most worth?

One's responses to these questions, and to others like them, constitute a statement of basic curriculum assumptions. These assumptions are a framework for addressing curriculum issues such as the purposes and objectives for schooling, the worth of knowledge, curriculum design, and planning, implementation, and evaluation strategies.

In particular, assumptions about the nature and value of knowledge and how it is acquired have key implications for curriculum, and these assumptions may be used to compare and contrast frameworks. As Broudy (1982, p. 574) has reminded us, these assumptions have "preoccupied educators from the beginning of formal schooling." Broudy has also identified possible responses to Spencer's well-known query, "What knowledge is of most worth?" including success, money, publicity, competence, and happiness. The selections in Part Two explore alternative responses.

English (in ASCD, 1983, pp. 1–17) has classified contemporary curriculum issues as ideological, technical, and operational; each classification has theoretical and practical dimensions. The selections in Part Two address the ideological issues.

CURRICULUM FRAMEWORKS AND PHILOSOPHIES OF EDUCATION

The term framework is used deliberately here. It is used in lieu of the term philosophy of education because of the relationship between school curriculum and philosophies of education. Although it is true that a school's curriculum addresses fundamental philosophical questions, like the ones previously identified, it is also true that curriculums do not correspond precisely with sets of assumptions that constitute formal philosophies of education.

Identifying assumptions made explicit by formal philosophies of education is useful here not because it then makes explicit the criteria for determining in which philosophy of education a given curriculum may be rooted, but because it illustrates the range of alternative assumptions. Table 2.1 illustrates assumptions made explicit in major educational philosophies. In addition, Table 2.1 illustrates a range of psychological and ethical assumptions perhaps implicit in curriculum frameworks.

Most school curriculums are based on the whole range of available assumptions. School curriculums accommodate a variety of philosophical frameworks in our pluralistic society. Inherent conflict is offset by changing emphases and priorities. Frameworks are collections of philosophical assumptions, sometimes made explicit, sometimes not, often conflicting, nearly always fluid. Frameworks are less formal than traditionally identified philosophies, varying somewhat from individual to individual, interest group to interest group, time to time, and place to place. Frameworks can also be less comprehensive than formal philosophies, and they may evolve as one's thinking about the issues they address evolves.

Two problems face those who attempt to categorize and analyze curriculum frameworks. One is the problem of labels; the other is the problem of overlap. In examining frameworks, it may be confusing to concentrate only on labels for each of the alternatives identified. Such an approach assumes a one-to-one correspondence between a given set of assumptions and a given label. This is very often an erroneous assumption because a framework may be labeled in different ways, depending, very often, on the person labeling it. What one labels romanticism, another calls radicalism. Radicalism may mean one thing to one person and something else to another. What is important here is that one can identify differences in alternative frameworks, however they are labeled.

The problem of framework overlap involves a lack of mutual exclusivity of frameworks. The problem is not one of labeling two identical sets of assumptions differently. The problem is two frameworks' sharing a number of common assumptions but being different in one or more additional assumptions. Not every framework necessarily addresses exactly the same set of assumptions and not all the assumptions in the one will be identical with those in the other. However, all frameworks address particular attention to what Spencer called the knowledge of most worth.

ALTERNATIVE FRAMEWORKS

The selections included in Part Two represent alternative and significant curriculum frameworks competing for acceptance. They not only provide prescriptive notions of what curriculum ought to be but also indicate the psychological, philosophical, and ethical assumptions that underlie their educational goals. In addition, some frameworks reflect various modes for categorizing and analyzing curriculum frameworks generally. The reader is urged to study and compare not only

Table 2.1 **Five Major Educational Philosophies**

	Perennialism	*Idealism*	*Realism*	*Experimentalism*	*Existentialism*
Reality, ontology	A world of reason and god	A world of mind	A world of things	A world of experience	A world of existing
Truth (knowledge), epistemology	Reason and revelation	Consistency of ideas	Correspondence and sensation (as we see it)	What works, what is	Personal, subjective choice
Goodness, axiology	Rationality	Imitation of ideal self, person to be emulated	Laws of nature	The public test	Freedom
Teaching reality	Disciplinary subjects and doctrine	Subject of the mind—literary, philosophical	Subjects of physical world—math, science	Subject matter of social experiences—social studies	Subject matter of choice—art, ethics, philosophy
Teaching truth	Discipline of the mind via drill	Teaching ideas via lecture, discussion	Teaching for mastery of information—demonstrate, recite	Problem solving, project method	Arousing personal responses—questioning
Teaching goodness (values)	Disciplining behavior (to reason)	Imitating heroes and other exemplars' sequences	Training in rules of conduct	Making group decisions	Awakening self to responsibility

Why schools exist	To reveal reasons and God's will	To sharpen the mind and intellectual processes	To reveal the order of the world and universe	To discover and expand the society we live in, to share experiences	To aid children in knowing themselves and their place in society
What should be taught	Eternal truths	Wisdom of the ages	Laws of physical reality	Group inquiry into social problem areas, social science, method and subject together	Unregimented topic
Role of the teacher	Interprets, tells	Reports, person to be emulated	Displays, imparts knowledge	Aids, consults	Questions, assists student in personal journey
Role of the student	Passive reception	Receives, memorizes	Manipulates, passive participation	Active participation, contributes	Determines own rules
School's attitude toward change	Truth is eternal, no real change	Truth to be preserved, antichange	Always coming toward perfection, orderly change	Change is ever present, a process	Change is necessary at all times

Source: Jon Wiles and Joseph C. Bondi, *Curriculum Development: A Guide to Practice* (Columbus, Ohio: Bell and Howell, 1984), pp. 54–55.

the selections here but also those cited by others (see, for example, Tanner and Tanner, 1980, pp. 103–131).

Developmental Frameworks

In Selection 2.1, Kohlberg and Mayer begin with a specific curriculum issue: the question of objectives in early childhood education. In order to address that specific question, they identify and characterize three types of frameworks—romantic frameworks, cultural transmission frameworks, and progressive frameworks. In each case, the authors sort out the psychological, or ontological, epistemological, and ethical-value assumptions that underlie the frameworks.

In addition, they argue a case favoring assumptions in a progressive framework in comparison to assumptions within the other two frameworks. Thus, these authors have surveyed a good part of the territory of alternative curriculum frameworks and made a case for one of them. The knowledge of most worth, in their view, is a developmental issue.

Kohlberg and Mayer also discuss in some detail the cognitive-developmental psychology, the interactionist epistemology, and the developmental-philosophical ethics that characterize progressive frameworks. In order to do so, they utilize formulations of that framework in the words of Dewey (1902, 1938) as well as the more contemporary formulation of Piaget (1960) and others.

Interest and experience are key concepts in a progressive framework for curriculum. Dewey's curriculum framework is elaborated in many of his writings (in particular, Dewey, 1902, 1916). The framework Dewey initially formulated has often been misunderstood and, at times, made simplistic tricks. However, in Selection 2.2, Dewey himself points out that it is understanding of interest and experience with references to curriculum that allows method to be more than tricks.

Dewey's understanding of the relationship between scholarship and instruction leads him to conclude that the learner's interest is the most important curriculum criterion. The knowledge of most worth is that dictated by a child's prior experience and understanding, that is, interest. It is the learner's interest that should guide curriculum and teaching, as it already guides learning.

Dewey points out that, for many, the curriculum is determined by social and logical considerations without reference to the individual learner. Methods of instruction, on the other hand, are determined on the basis of psychological considerations, that is, how to make the child in school learn something toward which he or she may have no natural disposition. However, curriculum and methods are not separate phenomena, only separate considerations of a single phenomenon: learning.

The logical structure of knowledge is something imposed on it among a community of scholars at various points in its accumulation. The accumulation of knowledge, however, is driven by the learning needs of individual scholars.

Cultural Transmission Frameworks

In responding to the NEA's Committee of Fifteen, Dewey (1897, pp. 356–357) examines the false dualism between "the curriculum, or subject matter of instruction, and the method (of instruction) . . . between mental operation, on one hand, and intellectual content on the other." In Selection 2.3, Phenix also examines a false dualism that holds there are "two disparate realms of method . . . the methods of professional scholarship and research, and . . . the methods of instruction." Phenix argues that the methods of scholarship in the disciplines are also the methods of instruction, and he concludes, albeit differently from Dewey, that the disciplines must dictate curriculum.

Phenix argues that the worth of knowledge is the degree to which it is disciplined and, thus, instructive. According to this framework, the school's curriculum should reflect the fact that education is a recapitulation of the collective inquiry from which the disciplines were established. Further, the nature of the disciplines is given, not chosen.

It will be helpful here to point out that discipline, when used to identify a body of knowledge, refers to its specific rigor. This rigor is knowledge's conceptual and syntactical structures. Conceptual structure defines a discipline in terms of the principal concepts and generalizations that focus on inquiry and discourse. Syntactical structure defines a discipline in terms of the principal methods that direct inquiry and research. According to Phenix, the degree to which a body of knowledge is disciplined can be determined by the criteria of analytic simplification, synthetic coordination, and dynamism. These same criteria are the bases for determining the instructiveness of a body of knowledge.

Phenix concludes that the disciplines of knowledge are the alternative perspectives and methods produced by the culture for understanding reality and, indeed, for making sense of one's own existence. Inasmuch as they may constitute tools for working at fundamental learning tasks that are within the province of schooling to foster, the disciplines are a useful basis for designing school curriculums and need to be transmitted from generation to generation. Phenix's viewpoint was widely cited during the period in which the structure of the disciplines was the dominant grounding for the school curriculum (see also Ford and Pugno, 1964; King and Brownell, 1966).

Phenix, in Selection 2.3, sets forth basic premises for the disciplines of knowledge as a curriculum framework. The disciplines of knowledge framework is one example of conservative frameworks. There have been numerous variations of a conservative framework. Although Spencer (1860), for example, challenged much of the conservative tradition in centuries of curriculum thought before him, he himself offered an essentially conservative framework. A more recent version of a conservative framework is the *Paideia Proposal* (Adler, 1982).

The grounding of curriculum in contemporary social needs was also prompted historically within a conservative framework. Examples of this kind of study include activity analysis (see, e.g., Charters, 1923) and the identification of common problems of living or persistent life situations (see Stratemeyer et al., 1957). Both examples attempt to identify adult behaviors or skills required for coping with existing cultural conditions. Another example (Smith, in Herrick and Tyler, 1950, pp. 3–16) argues that a curriculum must be derived within a framework that focuses on cultural forces rather than cultural conditions.

Romantic Frameworks

Selection 2.4 offers a romantic framework for curriculum, one Lamm calls radical. Lamm reasserts the importance of making explicit the assumptions of a framework for subsequent curriculum discourse and for the theories of instruction. His examination of a radical framework focuses, in particular, on epistemological dimensions. He begins by identifying three conceptions of the purpose of instruction and, more generally, of the goal of schooling and the objectives of a school curriculum. These conceptions focus on socialization and training, on acculturation, and on individuation or self-actualization.

Diversity and a definition of radical as mood are important concepts in Lamm's analysis. He defines mood by contrasting it with method and with a coherent set of assumptions with which he claims it differs. However, he clarifies fairly systematically the assumptions of a romantic framework, and he uses the romantic framework to formulate understandings of motivation, learning, and teaching.

Lamm explores three views of the value of knowledge, its purpose in our lives, and the process by which it is acquired. The first view emphasizes the social utility of knowledge. It views learning in terms of the effectiveness of the learner's socialization. According to this view, the most worthwhile knowledge is that which allows a learner to fit in with existing social arrangements. The second view asserts that knowledge is valuable for its own sake. It views learning as acculturation, a process by which the learner becomes civilized. Here Lamm discusses the place of the disciplines as they were presented by Phenix.

Lamm's own view of the worth of knowledge sees learning and curriculum in terms of a process of individuation. His view emphasizes individual self-actualization, becoming one's potential. Lamm elaborates self-actualization in its components of creativity, subjectivity, and self-awareness. Knowledge is worthwhile to the extent that it facilitates the learner's sense of well-being necessary to create. Knowledge is valuable to the extent that it is meaningful in the life of the individual learner and that it promotes the self-awareness that is understanding of self and the world.

The selections by Kohlberg and Mayer, Dewey, Phenix, and Lamm illustrate developmental, cultural transmission, and romantic frameworks for curriculum. Additional illustrations the reader may find valuable include work by Dewey (1902, 1916), Hutchins and Adler (1972), Bloom (1981), Counts (1932), Freire (1978), and Greene (1971, 1973). The reader should keep in mind that these additional illustrations of frameworks, and others, may not fit neatly into the developmental, cultural transmission, and romantic categories.

TRANSCENDING OLD CATEGORIES

Macdonald's transcendental framework in Selection 2.5 goes beyond the view of knowledge advocated by the radical. This view of the value of knowledge begins with a dialectic of experience analogous to the dualisms discussed in the selections by Phenix and Dewey. The dualisms of the conservative and progressive visions of curriculum parallel the nature of experience in Macdonald's cultural transmission and developmental ideologies. The romantic vision parallels Macdonald's romantic ideology, with an important exception. For Macdonald, romantic and radical are not synonymous. Rather, he views what he calls a radical ideology as a variation of the developmental ideology, that is, as a variation of the progressive vision. Both radical and developmental are dialectics, one emphasizing social reality and the other inner experience. However, both are dialectics and not dualisms.

The transcendental ideology goes beyond the other dialectics; Macdonald represents it as a dual dialectic, a dialectic not only between social reality and inner experience but also within inner experience itself. A transcendental framework values the emergence of a spirituality within inner consciousness, not only a dialectic with what is outside self but a detachment from it as well. The transcendental values a self-acceptance that is centered. Centering goes beyond consciousness and self-actualization in the recognition of a power beyond self. It is, somewhat simplistically, self-actualization that is not self-centered.

No one framework may be adequate for addressing all curriculum issues or for dealing with any one issue completely. Anyone engaged in serious inquiry or practice must examine issues on the basis of a number of alternative assumptions about the nature of man, knowledge, and values before settling on any one approach to an issue or upon the set of assumptions implicit in that particular approach. That examination has the advantage both of bringing rigor to the field and of assisting the individual scholar or practitioner in better understanding the advantages and liabilities of current frameworks and in evolving new ones.

Finally, the choice of framework for addressing a particular curriculum issue may depend, in part, upon the level of schooling. Thus, the set of assumptions for curriculum issues related to the elementary school may not match assumptions for similar issues in the university or the junior high school.

CURRICULUM AND VALUES

School curriculums mirror values assumptions and priorities in their frameworks. What are values? The literature on values yields extensive discussion of the formulation and uses of values, of the origins and kinds of values, and of the relationships of values to culture and to individual human behavior. This discussion, however, gives few precise definitions of values. It appears to be easier to give specific examples of values than to state generally what values are. Dictionary definitions of values revolve, to a great extent, around the notion of relative worth.

What is at issue with respect to values in a curriculum framework is the relative worth of conceptualizations of the purpose of schooling, the relative worth of alternative bases upon which issues like purposes of schooling might be decided, or the relative worth of specific statements of purpose. Whatever else values are, or are not, they are reflected in choices of objectives for schooling, in choices of curriculum content and design, and in choices of instructional materials and activities. Values are also inherent in the content of a particular curriculum.

In his summary discussion of relationships between values and a curriculum, Beauchamp (1981, p. 91) states:

> Values and value judgments permeate curriculum decisions. The primary problem of curriculum is to decide what shall be taught in schools. This is a value question in itself. . . . In the process of choosing what shall be taught in schools, a host of additional value judgments must be made.

Thus, not only is a curriculum an expression of values, but one's general orientation to the curriculum, one's choice of a curriculum design, and one's focus in curriculum inquiry are expressions of values as well.

In attempting to construct a conceptual system for the field of curriculum, Goodlad and Richter (1966) identify some major questions in the field and some means for addressing them. They note that, wherever one begins in this regard, the choice of a beginning point is itself an expression of values. If a conceptualization of the issues is itself an expression of values, is there any way to deal with the issues involved that is independent of values? Goodlad and Richter (1966, p. 9) offer an initial insight:

> A conceptual system is not value-free. To accept curriculum practice (for example) as one beginning point is to express a value. But once having posed the problems and issues according to an initial set of values, a conceptual, system should facilitate the application of alternative values positions to each commonplace of the system.

To put the point another way, one must begin one's consideration of the relative value of alternative curriculum frameworks from some value position. One must recognize that such a beginning is a value position itself. Such a recognition then can allow one to consider alternative positions, and that consideration, in turn, can lead one to modify the original position or, at the very least, to clarify it and to understand how and why it is at odds with some others.

In this regard, Tanner and Tanner (1975, pp. 53–59) bemoan that, in most curriculum planning they have observed, curriculums are changed "as expedient and opportunistic responses to the dominant sociopolitical forces rather than stemming from a rationale based on sound theory and conceptual research" (p. 53). Implicit in the Tanners' observation is their own expression of the values from which a curriculum ought to be derived. It might reasonably be inferred that these authors place great value on curriculum elements that reflect rational study (conceptual research) and a philosophical position with which they would tend to agree (sound theory).

CONCLUSION

Curriculum issues are addressed, either implicitly or explicitly, within philosophical frameworks. These frameworks are statements of the assumptions about the nature and meaning of man, knowledge, and values. There are several frameworks available for use. Sets of assumptions about man, knowledge, and values identify conservative, progressive, romantic, and other frameworks in the field of curriculum.

Curriculum frameworks are statements of value positions from which inquiry and practice in the field are initiated. A number of frameworks exist that can provide direction. Some may argue for a continuing synthesis of ideas to constitute a more comprehensive framework for curriculum than may yet be available in any of those investigated here. Any currently available framework will probably be lacking in some respects where only a limited number of dimensions of reality are considered or where the perspective on any dimension is narrow. As Schwab (1971, p. 500) puts it:

> The very coexistence [in this case, of alternative frameworks] . . . points to an inadequacy of each and to the problem posed by this inadequacy. Each omits what another includes . . . Each . . . draws on a view . . . which differs from the views . . . drawn upon by the other[s]. . . . Again, the coexistence . . . points to an incompletion of each.

In the meantime, it remains for the curriculum field to utilize available frameworks.

Use of any framework to address given curriculum issues includes a statement of values. The choice of framework itself is a statement of values. One needs to make values explicit at the outset of discourse and practice. A continuing synthesis of thinking within individual disciplines, partly as a result of systematic application to current curriculum issues, is necessary and perhaps inevitable. However, making values and other framework assumptions explicit is rarely complete.

The curriculum field must rely, then, on incomplete frameworks. However, this fact compels greater, rather than lesser, rigor in the conduct of inquiry and practice.

REFERENCES

Adler, Mortimer J. *The Paideia Proposal.* New York: Macmillan, 1982.

Association for Supervision and Curriculum Development. *Fundamental Curriculum Decisions.* Alexandria, Va.: Association for Supervision and Curriculum Development, 1983.

Beauchamp, George A. *Curriculum Theory.* Itasca, Ill.: F.E. Peacock, 1961; 1968; 1975; 1981.

Bloom, Benjamin S. *All Our Children Learning.* New York: McGraw-Hill, 1981.

Broudy, Harry S. "What Knowledge Is of Most Worth?" *Elementary School Journal* 82:574–78, May, 1982.

Charters, W.W. *Curriculum Construction.* New York: Macmillan, 1923.

Counts, George S. *Dare the School Build a New Social Order?* New York: John Day, 1932.

Dewey, John. "The Psychological Aspect of the School Curriculum," *Educational Review* 14:356–69, April, 1897.

Dewey, John. *The Child and the Curriculum.* Chicago: University of Chicago Press, 1902.

Dewey, John. *Democracy and Education.* New York: Macmillan, 1916.

Dewey, John. *Experience and Education.* New York: Macmillan, 1938.

Ford, G. W., and Lawrence Pugno (eds.). *The Structure of Knowledge and the Curriculum.* Chicago: Rand McNally, 1964.

Freire, Paolo. *Pedagogy in Process.* New York: Seabury, 1978.

Goodlad, John I., and Maurice N. Richter, Jr. *The Development of a Conceptual System for Dealing with Problems of Curriculum and Instruction.* Los Angeles: Institute for Development of Educational Activities, University of California, 1966.

Greene, Maxine. "Curriculum and Consciousness," *Teachers College Record* 73:253–69, December, 1971.

Greene, Maxine. *Teacher as Stranger.* New York: Wadsworth, 1973.

Herrick, Virgil E., and Ralph W. Tyler (eds.). *Toward Improved Curriculum Theory.* Chicago: University of Chicago Press, 1950.

Hutchins, Robert Maynard, and Mortimer J. Adler (eds.). *The Great Ideas Today.* Chicago: Encyclopaedia Britannica, 1972.

King, Arthur R., Jr., and John A. Brownell. *The Curriculum and the Disciplines of Knowledge.* New York: John Wiley, 1966.

Kohlberg, Lawrence, and Rochelle Mayer. "Development as the Aim of Education," *Harvard Educational Review* 42:449–96, November, 1972.

Passow, A. Harry (ed.). *Curriculum Crossroads.* New York: Teachers College Press, 1962.

Piaget, Jean. *The Child's Conception of the World.* New York: Humanities Press, 1929; 1960.

Pinar, William (ed.). *Heightened Consciousness, Cultural Revolution and Curriculum Theory.* Berkeley: McCutchan, 1974.

Purpel, David E., and Maurice Belanger (eds.). *Curriculum and Cultural Revolution.* Berkeley: McCutchan, 1972.

Schwab, Joseph J. "The Practical: Art of the Eclectic," *School Review* 79: 493–542, April, 1971.

Spencer, Herbert. *Education: Intellectual, Moral, Physical.* New York: A.L. Burt, 1860.

Stratemeyer, Florence, et al. *Developing a Curriculum for Modern Living* (2nd ed.). New York: Teachers College Press, 1957.

Tanner, Daniel, and Laurel N. Tanner. *Curriculum Development: Theory into Practice.* New York: Macmillan, 1975; 1980.

Wiles, Jon, and Joseph C. Bondi. *Curriculum Development, a Guide to Practice.* Columbus, Ohio: Bell and Howell, 1979; 1984.

Selection 2.1

Development as the Aim of Education

Lawrence Kohlberg and *Rochelle Mayer*

The most important issue confronting educators and educational theorists is the choice of ends for the educational process. Without clear and rational educational goals, it becomes impossible to decide which educational programs achieve objectives of general import and which teach incidental facts and attitudes of dubious worth. While there has been a vast amount of research comparing the effects of various educational methods and programs on various outcome measures, there has been very little empirical research designed to clarify the worth of these outcome measures themselves. After a deluge of studies in the sixties examining the effects of programs on I.Q. and achievement tests, and drawing policy conclusions, researchers finally began to ask the question, "What is the justification for using I.Q. tests or achievement tests to evaluate programs in the first place?"

The present paper examines such fundamental issues and considers the strategies by which research facts can help generate and substantiate educational objectives and measures of educational outcomes.

This presentation begins by making explicit how a cognitive-

SOURCE. Reprinted in an abridged version from *Harvard Educational Review* 42 (November 1972), pp. 449-496.

developmental *psychological* theory can be translated into a rational and viable progressive *educational ideology, i.e.,* a set of concepts defining desirable aims, content, and methods of education. We contrast the progressive ideology with the "romantic" and the "cultural transmission" schools of thought, with respect to underlying psychological, epistemological, and ethical assumptions. . . . We claim that the cognitive-developmental or progressive approach can satisfactorily handle these issues because it combines a psychological theory of development with a rational ethical philosophy of development. . . .

Subsequently, we look at the ways in which these ideologies form the basis for contemporary educational policy. . . . We conclude that the available research lends little support for either of these alternative educational strategies. More specifically:

1. The current prevalent definition of the aims of education, in terms of academic achievement supplemented by a concern for mental health, cannot be justified empirically or logically.
2. The overwhelming emphasis of educational psychology on methods of instruction and tests and measurements which presuppose a "value-neutral" psychology is misplaced.
3. An alternative notion that the aim of the schools should be the stimulation of human development is a scientifically, ethically, and practically viable conception which provides the framework for a new kind of educational psychology.

THREE STREAMS OF EDUCATIONAL IDEOLOGY

There have been three broad streams in the development of Western educational ideology. While their detailed statements vary from generation to generation, each stream exhibits a continuity based upon particular assumptions of psychological development.

Romanticism

The first stream of thought, the "romantic," commences with Rousseau and is currently represented by Freud's and Gesell's followers. A.S. Neill's Summerhill represents an example of a school based on these principles. Romantics hold that what comes from within the child is the most important aspect of development; therefore the pedagogical environment should be permissive enough to allow the inner "good" (abilities and social virtues) to unfold and the inner "bad" to come under control. Thus teaching the child the ideas and attitudes of others through rote or drill would result in meaningless learning and the suppression of inner spontaneous tendencies of positive value.

Romantics stress the biological metaphors of "health" and "growth" in equating optimal physical development with bodily health and optimal mental development with mental health. To label this ideology "romantic" is not to accuse it of being unscientific; rather it is to recognize that the nineteenth century discovery of the natural development of the child was part of a larger romantic philosophy, an ethic and epistemology involving a discovery of the natural and the inner self.

With regard to childhood, this philosophy involved not only an awareness that the child possessed an inner self but also a valuing of childhood, to which the orgins of the self could be traced. The adult, through taking the child's point of view, could experience otherwise inaccessible elements of truth, goodness, and reality.

As stated by G. H. Mead (1936, p. 61): "The romantic comes back to the existence of the self as the primary fact. That is what gives the standard to values. What the Romantic period revealed was not simply a past but a past as the point of view from which to come back at the self. . . . It is this self-conscious setting-up of the past again that constitutes the origin of romanticism." . . .

Cultural Transmission

The origins of the cultural transmission ideology are rooted in the classical academic tradition of Western education. Traditional educators believe that their primary task is the transmission to the present generation of bodies of information and of rules or values collected in the past; they believe that the educator's job is the direct instruction of such information and rules. The important emphasis, however, is not in the sanctity of the past, but on the view that educating consists of transmitting knowledge, skills, and social and moral rules of the culture. Knowledge and rules of the culture may be rapidly changing or they may be static. In either case, however, it is assumed that education is the transmission of the culturally given.

More modern or innovative variations of the cultural transmission view are represented by educational technology and behavior modification.[2] Like traditional education, these approaches assume that knowledge and values—first located in the culture—are afterwards internalized by children through the imitation of adult behavior models, or through explicit instruction and reward and punishment. Accordingly, the educational technologist evaluates the individual's success in terms of his ability to incorporate the responses he has been taught and to respond favorably to the demands of the system. Although the technologist stresses the child as an individual learner, learning at his own pace, he, like the traditionalist, assumes that what is learned and what is valued in education is a culturally given body of knowledge and rules.

. . .

In contrast to the child-centered romantic school, the cultural transmission school is society-centered. It defines educational ends as the internalization of the values and knowledge of the culture. The cultural transmission school focuses on the child's need to learn the discipline of the social order, while the romantic stresses the child's freedom. The cultural transmission view emphasizes the common and established, the romantic view stresses the unique, the novel, and the personal.

Progressivism

The third stream of educational ideology which is still best termed "progressive," following Dewey (1938), developed as part of the pragmatic functional-genetic philosophies of the late nineteenth and early twentieth centuries. As an educational ideology, progressivism holds that education should nourish the child's natural interaction with a developing society or environment. Unlike the romantics, the progressives do not assume that development is the unfolding of an innate pattern or that the primary aim of education is to create an unconflicted environment able to foster healthy development. Instead, they define development as a progression through invariant ordered sequential stages. The educational goal is the eventual attainment of a higher level or stage of development in adulthood, not merely the healthy functioning of the child at a present level. In 1895, Dewey and McLellan suggested the following notion of education for attainment of a higher stage:

> Only knowledge of the order and connection of the stages in the development of the psychical functions can insure the full maturing of the psychical powers. Education is the work of supplying the conditions which will enable the psychical functions, as they successively arise, to mature and pass into higher functions in the freest and fullest manner (p. 207).

In the progressive view, this aim requires an educational environment that actively stimulates development through the presentation of resolvable but genuine problems or conflicts. For progressives, the organizing and developing force in the child's experience is the child's active thinking, and thinking is stimulated by the problematic, by cognitive conflict. Educative experience makes the child think–think in ways which organize both cognition and emotion. Although both the cultural transmission and the progressive views emphasize "knowledge," only the latter sees the acquisition of "knowledge" as *an active change in patterns of thinking* brought about by experiential problem-solving situations. Similarly, both views emphasize "morality," but the progressive sees the acquisition of morality as an active change in patterns of response to problematic social situations rather than the learning of culturally accepted rules.

The progressive educator stresses the essential links between cognitive and moral development; he assumes that moral development is not purely affective, and that cognitive development is a necessary though not sufficient condition for moral development. The development of logical and critical thought, central to cognitive education, finds its larger meaning in a broad set of moral values. The progressive also points out that moral development arises from social interaction in situations of social conflict. Morality is neither the internalization of established cultural values nor the unfolding of spontaneous impulses and emotions; it is justice, the reciprocity between the individual and others in his social environment.

PSYCHOLOGICAL THEORIES UNDERLYING EDUCATIONAL IDEOLOGIES

We have described three schools of thought describing the general ends and means of education. Central to each of these educational ideologies is a distinctive educational psychology, a distinctive psychological theory of development (Kohlberg, 1968). Underlying the romantic ideology is a maturationist theory of development; underlying the cultural transmission ideology is an associationistic-learning or environmental-contingency theory of development; and underlying the progressive ideology is a cognitive-developmental or interactionist theory of development.

The three psychological theories described represent three basic metaphors of development (Langer, 1969). The romantic model views the development of the mind through the metaphor of organic growth, the physical growth of a plant or animal. In this metaphor, the environment affects development by providing necessary nourishment for the naturally growing organism. Maturationist psychologists elaborating the romantic metaphor conceive of cognitive development as unfolding through prepatterned stages. They have usually assumed not only that cognitive development unfolds but that individual variations in rate of cognitive development are largely inborn. Emotional development is also believed to unfold through hereditary stages, such as the Freudian psychosexual stages, but is thought to be vulnerable to fixation and frustration by the environment. For the maturationist, although both cognitive and social-emotional development unfold, they are two different things. Since social-emotional development is an unfolding of something biologically given and is not based on knowledge of the social world, it does not depend upon cognitive growth.

The cultural transmission model views the development of the mind through the metaphor of the machine. The machine may be the wax on which the environment transcribes its markings, it may be the telephone switchboard through which environmental stimulus-energies are transmitted, or it may be the computer in which bits of information from the environment are stored, retrieved, and recombined. In any case, the environment is seen as "input," as information or energy more or less directly transmitted to, and accumulated in, the organism. The organism in turn emits "output" behavior. Underlying the mechanistic metaphor is the associationistic, stimulus-response or environmentalist psychological theory, which can be traced from John Locke to Thorndike to B. F. Skinner. This psychology views both specific concepts and general cognitive structures as reflections of structures that exist outside the child in the physical and social world. The structure of the child's concepts or of his behavior is viewed as the result of the association of discrete stimuli with one another, with the child's responses, and with his experiences of pleasure and pain. Cognitive development is the result of guided learning and teaching. Consequently, cognitive education requires a careful statement of desirable behavior patterns described in terms of specific responses. Implied here is the idea that the child's behavior can be shaped by immediate repetition and elaboration of the correct response, and by association with feedback or reward.

The cognitive-developmental metaphor is not material, it is dialectical; it is a model of the progression of ideas in discourse and conversation. The dialectical metaphor was first elaborated by Plato, given new meaning by Hegel, and finally stripped of its metaphysical claims by John Dewey and Jean Piaget, to form a psychological method. In the dialectical metaphor, a core of universal ideas are redefined and reorganized as their implications are played out in experience and as they are confronted by their opposites in argument and discourse. These reorganizations define qualitative levels of thought, levels of increased epistemic adequacy. The child is not a plant or a machine; he is a philosopher or a scientist-poet. The dialectical metaphor of progressive education is supported by a cognitive-developmental or interactional psychological theory. Discarding the dichotomy between maturation and environmentally determined learning, Piaget and Dewey claim that mature thought emerges through a process of development that is neither direct biological maturation nor direct learning, but rather a reorganization of psychological structures resulting from organism-environment interactions. Basic mental structure is the product of the patterning of interaction between the organism and the environment, rather than a direct reflection of either innate neurological patterns or external environmental patterns.

. . .

EPISTEMOLOGICAL COMPONENTS OF EDUCATIONAL IDEOLOGIES

We have considered the various psychological theories as parts of educational ideologies. Associated with these theories are differing epistemologies or philosophies of science, specifying what is knowledge, *i.e.*, what are observable facts and how can these facts be interpreted. Differences in epistemology, just as differences in actual theory, generate different strategies for defining objectives.

Romantic educational ideology springs not only from a maturational psychology, but from an existentialist or phenomenological epistemology, defining knowledge and reality as referring to the immediate inner experience of the self. Knowledge or truth in the romantic epistemology is self-awareness or self-insight, a form of truth with emotional as well as intellectual components. As this form of truth extends beyond the self, it is through sympathetic understanding of humans and natural beings as other "selves."

In contrast, cultural transmission ideologies of education tend to involve epistemologies which stress knowledge as that which is repetitive and "objective," that which can be pointed to in sense-experience and measurement and which can be culturally shared and tested.

The progressive ideology, in turn, derives from a functional or pragmatic epistemology which equates knowledge with neither inner experience nor outer sense-reality, but with an equilibrated or resolved relationship between an inquiring human actor and a problematic situation. For the progressive epistemology, the immediate or introspective experience of the child does not have ultimate truth or reality. The meaning and truth of the child's experience depends upon its relationship to the situations in which he is acting. At the same time, the progressive epistemology does not attempt to reduce psychological experience to observable responses in reaction to observable stimuli or situations. Rather, it attempts to functionally coordinate the external meaning of the child's experiences as *behavior* with its internal meaning as it appears to the observer.

With regard to educational objectives, these differences in epistemology generate differences with respect to three issues. The first issue concerns whether to focus objectives on internal states or external behavior. In this respect, cultural transmission and romantic ideologies represent opposite poles. The cultural transmission view evaluates educational change from children's performances, not from their feelings or thoughts. Social growth is defined by the conformity of behavior to particular cultural standards such as honesty and industriousness. These skill and trait terms are found in both common-sense evaluations of school grades and report cards, and in "objective" educational psychological measurement. Behaviorist ideologies systematize this focus by rigorously eliminating references to internal or subjective experience as "non-scientific." Skinner (1971) says:

> We can follow the path taken by physics and biology by turning directly to the relation between behavior and the environment and neglecting . . . states of mind. . . . We do not need to try to discover what personalities, states of mind, feelings, . . . intentions—or other prerequisites of autonomous man really are in order to get on with a scientific analysis of behavior (p. 15).

In contrast, the romantic view emphasizes inner feelings and states. Supported by the field of psychotherapy, romantics maintain that skills, achievements, and performances are not satisfying in themselves, but are only a means to inner awareness, happiness, or mental health. They hold that an educator or therapist who ignores the child's inner states in the name of science does so at his peril, since it is these which are most real to the child.

The progressive or cognitive-developmental view attempts to integrate both behavior and internal states in a functional epistemology of mind. It takes inner experience seriously by attempting to observe thought process rather than language behavior and by observing valuing processes rather than reinforced behavior. In doing so, however, it combines interviews, behavioral tests, and naturalistic observation methods in mental assessment. The cognitive-developmental approach stresses the need to examine mental competence or mental structure as opposed to examining only performance, but it employs a functional rather than an introspective approach to the observation of mental structure. An example is Piaget's systematic and reproducible observations of the preverbal infant's thought-structure of space, time, and causality. In short, the cognitive-developmental approach does not select a focus on inner experience or on outer behavior objectives by epistemological fiat, but uses a functional methodology to coordinate the two through empirical study.

A second issue in the definition of educational objectives involves whether to emphasize immediate experience and behavior or long-term consequences in the child's development. The progressive ideology centers on education as it relates to the child's experience, but attempts to observe or assess experience in functional terms rather than by immediate self-projection into the child's place. As a result the progressive distinguishes between *humanitarian* criteria of the quality of the child's experience and *educative* criteria of quality of experience, in terms of long-term developmental consequences. According to Dewey (1938):

> Some experiences are miseducative. Any experience is miseducative that has the effect of arresting or distorting the growth of further experience. . . . An experience may be immediately enjoyable and yet promote the formation of a slack and careless attitude . . . [which] operates to modify the quality of subsequent experiences so as to prevent a person from getting out of them what they have to give. . . . Just as no man lives or dies to himself, so no experience lives or dies to itself. Wholly independent of desire or intent, every experience lives on in further experiences. Hence the central problem of an education based on experience is to select the kind of present experiences that live fruitfully and creatively in subsequent experience (pp. 25-28).

Dewey maintains that an educational experience which stimulates development is one which arouses interest, enjoyment, and challenge in the immediate experience of the student. The reverse is not necessarily the case; immediate interest and enjoyment does not always indicate that an educational experience stimulates long-range development. Interest and involvement is a necessary but not sufficient condition for education as development. For romantics, especially of the "humanistic psychology" variety, having a novel, intense, and complex experience is *self-development* or self-actualization. For progressives, a more objective test of the effects of the experience on later behavior is required before deciding that the experience is developmental. The progressive views the child's enjoyment and interest as a basic and legitimate criterion of education, but views it as a humanitarian rather than an educational criterion. The progressive holds that education must meet humanitarian criteria, but argues that a concern for the enjoyment and liberty of the child is not in itself equivalent to a concern for his development.

Psychologically, the distinction between humanitarian and developmental criteria is the distinction between the short-term value of the child's immediate experience and the long-term value of that experience as it relates to development. According to the progressive view, this question of the relation of the immediate to the long-term is an empirical rather than a philosophic question. As an example, a characteristic behaviorist strategy is to demonstrate the reversibility of learning by performing an experiment in which a preschooler is reinforced for interacting with other children rather than withdrawing in a corner. This is followed by a reversal of the experiment, demonstrating that when the reinforcement is removed the child again becomes withdrawn. From the progressive or cognitive-developmental perspective, if behavior changes are of this reversible character they cannot define genuine educational objectives. The progressive approach maintains that the worth of an educational effect is decided by its effects upon later behavior and development. Thus, in the progressive view, the basic problems of choosing and validating educational ends can only be solved by longitudinal studies of the effects of educational experience.

The third basic issue is whether the aims of education should be universal as opposed to unique or individual. This issue has an epistemological aspect because romantics have often defined educational goals in terms of the expression or development of a unique self or identity; "objectivist" epistemologies deny that such concepts are accessible to clear observation and definition. In contrast, cultural transmission approaches characteristically focus on measures of individual differences in general dimensions of achievement, or social behavior dimensions on which any individual can be ranked. The progressive, like the romantic, questions the significance of defining behavior relative to some population norm external to the individual. Searching for the "objective" in human experience, the progressive seeks universal qualitative states or sequences in development. Movement from one stage to the next is significant because it is a sequence in the individual's own development, not just a population average or norm. At the same time, insofar as the sequence is a universally observed development it is not unique to the individual in question.

In summary, the cognitive-developmental approach derives from a functional or pragmatic epistemology which attempts to integrate the dichotomies of the inner versus the outer, the immediate versus the remote in time, the unique versus the general. The cognitive-developmental approach focuses on an empirical search for continuities between inner states and outer behavior and between immediate reaction and remote outcome. While focusing on the child's experience, the progressive ideology defines such experience in terms of universal and empirically observable sequences of development.

ETHICAL VALUE POSITIONS UNDERLYING EDUCATIONAL IDEOLOGIES

When psychologists like Dewey, Skinner, Neill and Montessori actually engage in innovative education, they develop a theory which is not a mere statement of psychological principle, it is an ideology. This is not because of the dogmatic, non-scientific attitude they have as psychologists, but because prescription of educational practice cannot be derived from psychological theory or science alone. In addition to theoretical assumptions about how children learn or develop (the psychological theory component) educational ideologies include value assumptions about what is educationally good or worthwhile. To call a pattern of educational thought an ideology is to indicate it is a fairly systematic combination of a theory about psychological and social fact with a set of value principles.

The Fallacy of Value Neutrality

A "value-neutral" position, based only on facts about child development or about methods of education, cannot in itself directly contribute to educational practice. Factual statements about what the processes of learning and development *are* cannot be directly translated into statements about what children's learning and development *ought to be* without introduction of some value-principles.

In "value-neutral" research, learning does not necessarily imply movement to a stage of greater cognitive or ethical adequacy. As an example, acquisition of a cognitively arbitrary or erroneous concept (*e.g.*, it is best to put a marble in the hole) is considered learning in the same general sense as is acquisition of a capacity for logical inference. Such studies do not relate learning to some justifiable notion of knowledge, truth, or cognitive adequacy. Values are defined relative to a particular culture. Thus, morality is equivalent to conformity to, or internalization of, the particular standards to the child's group or culture. As an example, Berkowitz (1964) writes: "Moral values are evaluations of actions generally believed by the members of a given society to be either 'right' or 'wrong'" (p. 44).

Such "value-free" research cannot be translated into prescriptions for practice without importing a set of value-assumptions having no relation to psychology itself. The effort to remain "value-free" or "non-ideological" and yet prescribe educational goals usually has followed the basic model of counselling or consulting. In the *value-free consulting model,* the client (whether student or school) defines educational ends and the psychologist can then advise about means of education without losing his value-neutrality or imposing his values. Outside education, the value-free consulting model not only provides the basic model for counselling and psychotherapy, where the client is an individual, but also for industrial psychology, where the client is a social system. In both therapy and industrial psychology the consultant is paid by the client and the financial contract defines whose values are to be chosen. The educator or educational psychologist, however, has more than one client. What the child wants, what parents want, and what the larger community wants are often at odds with one another.

An even more fundamental problem for the "value-free" consulting model is the logical impossibility of making a dichotomy between value-free means and value-loaded ends. Skinner (1971, p. 17) claims that "a behavior technology is ethically neutral. Both the villain and the saint can use it. There is nothing in a methodology that determines the values governing its use." But consider the use of torture on the rack as a behavior technology for learning which could be used by saint and villain alike. On technological grounds Skinner advises against punishment, but this does not solve the ethical issue.

Dewey's logical analysis and our present historical awareness of the value consequences of adopting new technologies have made us realize that choices of means, in the last analysis, also imply choices of ends. Advice about means and methods involves value considerations and cannot be made purely on a basis of "facts." Concrete, positive reinforcement is not an ethically neutral means. To advise the use of concrete reinforcement is to advise that a certain kind of character, motivated by concrete reinforcement, is the end of education. Not only can advice about means not be separated from choice of ends, but there is no way for an educational consultant to avoid harboring his own criteria for choosing ends. The "value-neutral" consulting model equates value-neutrality with acceptance of value-relativity, *i.e.,* acceptance of whatever the values of the client are. But the educator or educational psychologist cannot be neutral in this sense either.

Values and the Cultural Transmission Ideology

In an effort to cope with the dilemmas inherent in value-neutral prescription, many psychologists tend to move to a cultural transmission ideology, based on the value premise of *social relativity.* Social relativity assumes some consistent set of values characteristic of the culture, nation, or system as a whole. While these values may be arbitrary and may vary from one social system to another, there is at least some consensus about them. This approach says, "Since values are relative and arbitrary, we might as well take the given values of the society as our starting point and advocate 'adjustment' to the culture or achievement in it as the educational end." The social relativist basis of the Bereiter-Engelmann system, for example, is stated as follows:

> In order to use the term cultural deprivation, it is necessary to assume some point of reference. . . . The standards of the American public schools represent one such point of reference. . . . There are standards of knowledge and ability which are consistently held to be valuable in the schools, and any child in the schools who falls short of these standards by reason of his particular cultural background may be said to be culturally deprived (1966, p. 24).

The Bereiter-Engelmann preschool model takes as its standard of value "the standard of the American public schools." It recognizes that this standard is arbitrary and that the kinds of learning prized by the American public schools may not be the most worthy; but it accepts this arbitrariness because it assumes that "all values are relative," that there is no ultimate standard of worth for learning and development.

Unlike Bereiter and Engelmann, many social relativist educators do not simply accept the standards of the school and culture and attempt to maximize conformity to them. Rather, they are likely to elaborate or create standards for a school or society based on value premises derived from what we shall call "the psychologist's fallacy." According to many philosophical analysts, the effort to derive statements of *ought* (or value) directly from statements of *is* (or fact) is a logical fallacy termed the "naturalistic fallacy" (Kohlberg, 1971). The psychologist's fallacy is a form of the naturalistic fallacy. As practiced by psychologists, the naturalistic fallacy is the direct derivation of statements about what human nature, human values, and human desires ought to be from psychological statements about what they are. Typically, this derivation slides over the distinction between what is desired and what is desirable.

The following statement from B. F. Skinner (1971) offers a good example of the psychologist's fallacy:

> Good things are positive reinforcers. Physics and biology study things without reference to their values, but the reinforcing effects of things are the province of behavior science, which, to the extent that it concerns itself with operant reinforcement, is a science of values. Things are good (positively reinforcing) presumably because of the contingencies of survival under which the species evolved. It is part of the genetic endowment called 'human nature' to be reinforced in particular ways by particular things. . . . The effective reinforcers are matters of observation and no one can dispute them (p. 104).

In this statement, Skinner equates or derives a value word (good) from a fact word (positive reinforcement). The equation is questionable; we wonder whether obtaining positive reinforcement really is good. The psychologist's fallacy or the naturalistic fallacy is a fallacy because we can always ask the further question, "Why is that good?" or "By what standard is that good?" Skinner does not attempt to deal with this further question, called the "open question" by philosophers. He also defines good as "cultural survival." The postulation of cultural survival as an ultimate value raises the open question too. We may ask, "Why should the Nazi culture (or the American culture) survive?" The reason Skinner is not concerned with answering the open question about survival is because he is a cultural relativist, believing that any non-factual reasoning about what is good or about the validity of moral principles is meaningless. He says:

> What a given group of people calls good is a fact, it is what members of the group find reinforcing as a result of their genetic endowment and the natural and social contingencies to which they have been exposed. Each culture has its own set of goods, and what is good in one culture may not be good in another (p. 128).

The Fallacy of Value-Relativism

Behind Skinner's value-relativism, then, lie the related notions that: 1) all valid inferences or principles are factual or scientific; 2) valid statements about values must be statements about facts of valuing; and 3) what people actually value differs. The fact that people do value different things only becomes an argument for the notion that value are relative if one accepts the first two assumptions listed. Both assumptions are believed by many philosophers to be mistaken because they represent forms of the fact-value confusion already described as the naturalistic fallacy. Confusing discourse about values, the relativist believes that when ethical judgment is not empirical science, it is not rational. This equation of science with rationality arises because the relativist does not correctly understand philosophical modes of inquiry. In modern conceptions, philosophy is the clarification of concepts for the purpose of critical evaluation of beliefs and standards. The kinds of beliefs which primarily concern philosophy are normative beliefs or standards, beliefs about what ought to be rather than about what is. These include standards of the right or good (ethics), of the true (epistemology), and of the beautiful (esthetics). In science, the critical evaluation of factual beliefs is limited to criteria of causal explanation and prediction; a "scientific" critical evaluation of normative beliefs is limited to treating them as a class of facts. Philosophy, by contrast, seeks rational justification and criticism of normative beliefs, based on considerations additional to their predictive or causal explanatory power. There is fairly widespread agreement among philosophers that criteria for the validity of ethical judgments can be established independent of "scientific" or predictive criteria. Since patterns for the rational statement and justification of normative beliefs, or "oughts," are not identical with patterns of scientific statement and justification, philosophers can reject both Skinner's notion of a strictly "scientific" ethics and Skinner's notion that whatever is not "scientific" is relative. The open question, "Why is reinforcement or cultural survival good?," is meaningful because there are patterns of ethical justification which are ignored by Skinner's relativistic science.

Distinguishing criteria of moral judgment from criteria of scientific judgment, most philosophers accept the "methodological non-relativism" of moral judgment just as they accept the methodological non-relativism of scientific judgment (Brandt, 1956). This ethical non-relativism is based on appeal to principles for making moral judgments, just as scientific non-relativism is based on appeal to principles of scientific method or of scientific judgment.

In summary, cultural transmission ideologies rest on the value premise of social relativism—the doctrine that values are relative to, and based upon, the standards of the particular culture and cannot be questioned or further justified. Cultural transmission ideologies of the "scientific" variety, like Skinner's, do not recognize moral principles since they equate what is desirable with what is observable by science, or with what is desired. Philosophers are not in agreement on the exact formulation of valid moral principles though they agree that such formulations center around notions like "the greatest welfare" or "justice as equity." They also do not agree on choice of priorities between principles such as "justice" and "the greatest welfare." Most philosophers do agree, however, that moral evaluations must be rooted in, or justified by, reference to such a realm of principles. Most also maintain that certain values or principles ought to be universal and that these principles are distinct from the rules of any given culture. A principle is a universalizeable, impartial mode of deciding or judging, not a concrete cultural rule. "Thou shalt not commit adultery" is a rule for specific behavior in specific situations in a monogamous society. By contrast, Kant's Categorical Imperative—act only as you would be willing that everyone should act in the same situation—is a principle. It is a guide for choosing among behaviors, not a prescription for behavior. As such it is free from culturally-defined content; it both transcends and subsumes particular social laws. Hence it has universal applicability.

In regard to values, Skinner's cultural transmission ideology is little different from other, older ideologies based on social relativism and on subjective forms of hedonism, *e.g.*, social Darwinsim and Benthamite utilitarianism. As an educational ideology, however, Skinner's relativistic behavior technology has one feature which distinguishes it from older forms of social utilitarianism. This is its denial that rational concern for social utility is itself a matter of moral character or moral principle to be transmitted to the young. In Skinner's view, moral character concepts which go beyond responsiveness to social reinforcement and control rely on "prescientific" concepts of free will. Stated in different terms, the concept of moral education is irrelevant to Skinner; he is not concerned with teaching to the children of his society the value-principles which he himself adopts. The culture designer is a *psychologist-king,* a value relativist, who somehow makes a free, rational decision to devote himself to controlling individual behavior more effectively in the service of cultural survival. In Skinner's scheme there is no plan to make the controlled controllers, or to educate psychologist-kings.

Values and the Romantic Ideology

At first sight the value premises of the romantic ideology appear to be the polar opposites of Skinner's cultural transmission ideology. Opposed to social control and survival is individual freedom, freedom for the child to be himself. For example, A. S. Neill (1960) says:

> How can happiness be bestowed? My own answer is: Abolish authority. Let the child be himself. Don't push him around. Don't teach him. Don't lecture him. Don't elevate him. Don't force him to do anything (p. 297).

As we have pointed out, the romantic ideology rests on a psychology which conceives of the child as having a spontaneously growing mind. In addition, however, it rests on the ethical postulate that "the guardians of the young should merit the proud title of the defenders of the happiness and rights of children" (G. S. Hall, 1901, p. 24). The current popularity of the romantic ideology in "free school," "de-school," and "open school" movements is related to increased adult respect for the rights of children. Bereiter (1972) carries this orientation to an extreme conclusion:

> Teachers are looking for a way to get out of playing God. . . . The same humanistic ethos that tells them what qualities the next generation should have also tells them that they have no right to manipulate other people or impose their goals upon them. The fact is that there are no morally safe goals for teachers any more. Only processes are safe. When it comes to goals, everything is in doubt. . . . A common expression, often thrown at me, when I have argued for what I believed children should be taught, is "Who are we to say what this child should learn." The basic moral problem . . . is inherent in education itself. If you are engaged in education, you are engaged in an effort to influence the course of the child's development . . . it is to determine what kinds of people they turn out to be. It is to create human beings, it is, therefore, to play God (pp. 26-27).

This line of thought leads Bereiter to conclude:

> The Godlike role of teachers in setting goals for the development of children is no longer morally tenable. A shift to informal modes of education does not remove the difficulty. This paper, then, questions the assumption that education, itself, is a good undertaking and considers the possibilities of a world in which values other than educational ones, come to the fore (p. 25).

According to Bereiter, then, a humanistic ethical concern for the child's rights must go beyond romantic free schools, beyond deschooling, to the abandonment of an explicit concern for education. Bereiter contrasts the modern "humanistic ethic," and its concern for the child's rights, with the earlier "liberal" concern for human rights which held education and the common school as the foundation of a free society. This earlier concern Bereiter sees expressed most cogently in Dewey's progressivism.

The historical shift in the conception of children's rights and human rights leading Bereiter to reject Dewey's position is essentially a shift from the liberal grounding of children's rights in ethical principles to the modern humanistic grounding of children's rights in the doctrine of ethical relativity.

Bereiter is led to question the moral legitimacy of education because he equates a regard for the child's liberty with a belief in ethical relativity, rather than recognizing that liberty and justice are universal ethical principles. "The teacher may try to play it safe by sticking to the middle of the road and only aiming to teach what is generally approved, but there are not enough universally endorsed values (if, indeed, there are any) to form the basis of an education" (Bereiter, 1972, p. 27). Here, he confuses an ethical position of tolerance or respect for the child's freedom with a belief in ethical relativity, not recognizing that respect for the child's liberty derives from a principle of justice rather than from a belief that all moral values are arbitrary. Respect for the child's liberty means awarding him the maximum liberty compatible with the liberty of others (and of himself when older), not refusal to deal with his values and behavior. The assumption of individual relativity of values underlying modern romantic statements of the child's liberty is also reflected in the following quote from Neill (1960):

> Well, we set out to make a school in which we should allow children freedom to be themselves. In order to do this, we had to renounce all discipline, all direction, all suggestion, all moral training, all religious instruction. We have been called brave, but it did not require courage. All it required was what we had—a complete belief in the child as a good, not an evil, being. For almost forty years, this belief in the goodness of the child has never wavered; it rather has become a final faith (p. 4).

For Neill, as for many free school advocates, value relativity does not involve what it did for Bereiter—a questioning of all conceptions of what is good in children and good for them. Neill's statement that the child is "good" is a completely non-relativist conception. It does not, however, refer to an ethical or moral principle or standard used to direct the child's education. Instead, just as in Skinner's cultural transmission ideology, the conception of the good is derived from what we have termed the psychologist's fallacy. Neill's faith in the "goodness of the child" is the belief that what children *do* want, when left to themselves, can be equated with what they *should* want from an ethical standpoint. In one way this faith is a belief that children are wired so as to act and develop compatibly with ethical norms. In another sense, however, it is an ethical postulation that decisions about what is right for children should be derived from what children do desire—that whatever children do is right.

This position begs the open question, "Why is freedom to be oneself good; by what standard is it a good thing?"

The question is raised by Dewey as follows (1938):

> The objection made [to identifying the educative process with growing or developing] is that growth might take many different directions: a man, for example, who starts out on a career of burglary may grow in that direction . . . into a highly expert burglar. Hence it is argued that "growth" is not enough; we must also specify the direction in which growth takes place, the end toward which it tends (p. 75).

In Neill's view it is not clear whether there is a standard of development, *i.e.*, some standard of goodness which children who grow up freely all meet, or whether children who grow up freely are good only by their own standards, even if they are thieves or villains by some other ethical standards. To the extent that there is a nonrelativist criterion employed by Neill, it does not derive from, nor is it justified by, the ethical principles of philosophy. Rather, it is derived from matters of psychological fact about "mental health" and "happiness."

> The merits of Summerhill are the merits of healthy free children whose lives are unspoiled by fear and hate (Neill, 1960, p. 4).
>
> The aim of education, in fact, the aim of life is to work joyfully and to find happiness (Neill, 1960, p. 297).

Freedom, then, is not justified as an ethical principle but as a matter of psychological fact, leading to "mental health and happiness." These are ultimate terms, as are the terms "maximizing reinforcement" and "cultural survival" for Skinner. For other romantic educators the ultimate value terms are also psychological, *e.g.*, "self-realization," "self-actualization," and "spontaneity." These are defined as "basic human tendencies" and are taken as good in themselves rather than being subject to the scrutiny of moral philosophy.

We have attempted to show that romantic libertarian ideologies are grounded on value-relativism and reliance on the psychologist's fallacy, just as are cultural-transmission ideologies, which see education as behavior control in the service of cultural survival. As a result of these shared premises, both romantic and cultural-transmission ideologies tend to generate a kind of elitism. In the case of Skinner, this elitism is reflected in the vision of the psychologist as a culture-designer, who "educates others" to conform to culture and maintain it but not to develop the values and knowledge which would be required for culture-designing. In the case of the romantic, the elitism is reflected in a refusal to impose intellectual and ethical values of libertarianism, equal justice, intellectual inquiry, and social reconstructionism on the child, even though these values are held to be the most important ones:

> . . . Summerhill is a place in which people who have the innate ability and wish to be scholars will be scholars; while those who are only fit to sweep the streets will sweep the streets. But we have not produced a street cleaner so far. Nor do I write this snobbishly, for I would rather see a school produce a happy street cleaner than a neurotic scholar (Neill, 1960, pp. 4-5).

In summary, in spite of their libertarian and non-indoctrinative emphases, romantic ideologies also have a tendency to be elitist or partonizing. Recalling the role of Dostoievsky's Grand Inquisitor, they see education as a process which only intends the child to be happy and adjusted rather than one which confronts the child with the ethical and intellectual problems and principles which the educator himself confronts. Skinner and Neill agree it is better for the child to be a happy pig than an unhappy Socrates. We may question, however, whether they have the right to withhold that choice.

Value Postulates of Progressivism

Progressive ideology, in turn, rests on the value postulates of ethical liberalism.[3] This position rejects traditional standards and value-relativism in favor of ethical universals. Further, it recognizes that value universals are ethical principles formulated and justified by the method of philosophy, not simply by the method of psychology. The ethical liberal position favors the active stimulation of the development of these principles in children. These principles are presented through a process of critical questioning which creates an awareness of the ground and limits of rational assent; they also are seen as relevant to universal trends in the child's own social and moral development. The liberal recognition of principles as *principles* clears them from confusion with psychological facts. To be concerned about children's happiness is an ethical imperative for the educator without regard to "mental health," "positive reinforcement," or other psychological terms used by educators who commit the "psychologist's fallacy." Rational ethical principles, not the values of parents or culture, are the final value-arbiters in defining educational aims. Such principles may call for consultation with parents, community, and children in formulating aims, but they do not warrant making them final judges of aims.

The liberal school recognizes that ethical principles determine the ends as well as the means of education. There is great concern not only to make schools more just, *i.e.*, to provide equality of educational opportunity and to allow freedom of belief but also to educate so that free and just people emerge from the schools.

Accordingly, liberals also conscientiously engage in moral education. It is here that the progressive and romantic diverge, in spite of a common concern for the liberty and rights of the child. For the romantic, liberty means non-interference. For the liberal, the principle of respect for liberty is itself defined as a moral aim of education. Not only are the rights of the child to be respected by the teacher, but the child's development is to be stimulated so that he may come to respect and defend his own rights and the rights of others.

Recognition of concern for liberty as a principle leads to an explicit, libertarian conception of moral education. According to Dewey and McLellan (1895),

> Summing up, we may say that every teacher requires a sound knowledge of ethical and psychological principles. . . . Only psychology and ethics can take education out of the rule-of-thumb stage and elevate the school to a vital, effective institution in the *greatest of all constructions—the building of a free and powerful character* (p. 207).

In the liberal view, educational concern for the development of a "free character" is rooted in the principle of liberty. For the romantic or relativist libertarian this means that "everyone has their own bag," which may or may not include liberty; and to actively stimulate the development of regard for liberty or a free character in the child is as much an imposition on the child as any other educational intervention. The progressive libertarians differ on this point. They advocate a strong rather than a weak application of liberal principles to education. Consistent application of ethical principles to education means that education *should* stimulate the development of ethical principles in students.

In regard to ethical values, the progressive ideology adds the postulates of *development* and *democracy* to the postulates of liberalism. The notion of educational democracy is one in which justice between teacher and child means joining in a community in which value decisions are made on a shared and equitable basis, rather than non-interference with the child's value-decisions. Because ethical principles function as principles, the progressive ideology is "democratic" in a sense that romantic and cultural transmission ideologies are not.

In discussing Skinner we pointed to a fundamental problem in the relation between the ideology of the relativist educator and that of the student. Traditional education did not find it a problem to reconcile the role of teacher and the role of student. Both were members of a common culture and the task of the teacher was to transmit that culture and its values to the student. In contrast, modern psychologists advocating cultural transmission ideologies do not hold this position. As social relativists they do not really believe in a common culture; instead they are in the position of transmitting values which are different both from those they believe in and those believed in by the student. At the extreme, as we mentioned earlier, Skinner proposes an ideology for ethically relative psychologist-kings or culture designers who control others. Clearly there is a contradiction between the ideology for the psychologist-king and the ideology for the child.

Romantic or radical ideologies are also unable to solve this problem. The romantic adopts what he assumes are the child's values, or takes as his value premise what is "natural" in the child rather than endorsing the culture's values. But while the adult believes in the child's freedom and creativity and wants a free, more natural society, the child neither fully comprehends nor necessarily adheres to the adult's beliefs. In addition, the romantic must strive to give the child freedom to grow even though such freedom may lead the child to become a reactionary. Like the behavior modifier, then, the romantic has an ideology, but it is different from the one which the student is supposed to develop.

The progressive is non-elitist because he attempts to get all children to develop in the direction of recognizing the principles he holds. But is this not indoctrinative? Here we need to clarify the postulates of development and democracy as they guide education.

For the progressive, the problem of offering a non-indoctrinative education which is based on ethical and epistemological principles is partially resolved by a conception that these principles represent developmentally advanced or mature states of reasoning, judgment, and action. Because there are culturally universal stages or sequences of moral development (Kohlberg and Turiel, 1971), stimulation of the child's development to the next step in a natural direction is equivalent to a long range goal of teaching ethical principles.

Because the development of these principles is natural they are not imposed on the child—he chooses them himself. A similar developmental approach is taken toward intellectual values. Intellectual education in the progressive view is not merely a transmission of information and intellectual skills, it is the communication of patterns and methods of "scientific" reflection and inquiry. These patterns correspond to higher stages of logical reasoning, Piaget's formal operations. According to the progressive, there is an important analogy between scientific and ethical patterns of judgment or problem solving, and there are overlapping rationales for intellectual and ethical education. In exposing the child to opportunities for reflective scientific inquiry, the teacher is guided by the principles of scientific method which the teacher himself accepts as the basis of rational reflection. Reference to such principles is non-indoctrinative if these principles are not presented as formulae to be learned ready-made or as rote patterns grounded in authority. Rather, they are part of a process of reflection by the student and teacher. A similar approach guides the process of reflection on ethical or value problems.

The problem of indoctrination is also resolved for the progressive by the concept of democracy. A concern for the child's freedom from indoctrination is part of a concern for the child's freedom to make decisions and act meaningfully. Freedom, in this context, means democracy, *i.e.,* power and participation in a social system which recognizes basic equal rights. It is impossible for teachers not to engage in value-judgments and decisions. A concern for the liberty of the child does not create a school in which the teacher is value-neutral and any pretense of it creates "the hidden curriculum" (Kohlberg, 1969). But it can create a school in which the teacher's value-judgments and decisions involve the students democratically.

. . .

STRATEGIES FOR DEFINING EDUCATIONAL OBJECTIVES AND EVALUATING EDUCATIONAL EXPERIENCE

We have considered the core psychological and philosophical assumptions of the three major streams of educational ideology. Now we shall consider these assumptions as they have been used to define objectives in early education.

There appear to be three fundamental strategies for defining educational objectives, which we call "the bag of virtues" or "desirable trait" strategy, the "industrial psychology" or "prediction of success" strategy and the "developmental-philosophic" strategy. These strategies tend to be linked, respectively, with the romantic, the cultural transmission, and the progressive educational ideologies.

The romantic tends to define educational objectives in terms of a "bag of virtues"—a set of traits characterizing an ideal healthy or fully-functioning personality. Such definitions of objectives are justified by a psychiatric theory of a spontaneous, creative, or self-confident personality. This standard of value springs from the romantic form of the psychologist's fallacy. Statements of value (desirability of a character-trait) are derived from psychological propositions of fact, *e.g.*, that a given trait is believed to represent psychological "illness" or "health."

The cultural transmission ideology defines immediate objectives in terms of standards of knowledge and behavior learned in school. It defines the long-range objective as eventual power and status in the social system (*e.g.*, income, success). In Skinner's terms, the objective is to maximize the reinforcement each individual receives from the system, while maintaining the system. In defining objectives, this focus on prediction of later success is common to those whose interest lies in maintaining the system in its present form and those whose interest lies in equalizing opportunity for success in the system.

Within the cultural transmission school there is a second strategy for elaborating objectives which we have called the "industrial psychology" approach (Kohlberg, 1972). Psychologically, this strategy is more explicitly atheoretical than the "bag of virtues" approach; with regard to values it is more socially relativistic. Adopting the stance of the value-free consultant, it evaluates a behavior in terms of its usefulness as a means of the student's or the system's ends, and focuses on the empirical prediction of later successes. In practice, this approach has focused heavily on tests and measurements of achievement as they predict or relate to later success in the educational or social system.

The third strategy, the developmental-philosophic, is linked to the progressive ideology. The progressive believes that a liberal conception of education pursuing intrinsically worthy aims or state is the best one for everyone. Such a conception of objectives must have a psychological component. The progressive defines the psychologically valuable in developmental terms. Implied in the term "development" is the notion that a more developed psychological state is more valuable or adequate than a less developed state.

The developmental-philosophic strategy attempts to clarify, specify, and justify the concept of adequacy implicit in the concept of development. It does so through: a) elaborating a formal psychological theory of development—the cognitive-developmental theory; b) elaborating a formal ethical and epistemological theory of truth and worth linked to the psychological theory; c) relating both of these to the facts of development in a specific area; and d) describing empirical sequences of development worth cultivating.

. . .

SUMMARY AND CONCLUSIONS

The present paper essentially recapitulates the progressive position first formulated by John Dewey. This position has been clarified psychologically by the work of Piaget and his followers; its philosophic premises have been advanced by the work of modern analytic philosophers like Hare, Rawls, and Peters. The progressive view of education makes the following claims:

1. That the aims of education may be identified with development, both intellectual and moral.
2. That education so conceived supplies the conditions for passing through an order of connected stages.
3. That such a developmental definition of educational aims and process requires both the method of philosophy or ethics and the method of psychology or science. The justification of education as development requires a philosophic statement explaining why a higher stage is a better or a more adequate stage. In addition, before one can define a set of educational goals based on a philosophical statement of ethical, scientific, or logical principles one must be able to translate it into a statement about psychological stages of development.
4. This, in turn, implies that the understanding of logical and ethical principles is a central aim of education. This understanding is the philosophic counterpart of the psychological statement that the aim of education is the development of the individual through cognitive and moral stages. It is characteristic of higher cognitive and moral stages that the child himself constructs logical and ethical principles; these, in turn, are elaborated by science and philosophy.
5. A notion of education as attainment of higher stages of development, involving an understanding of principles, was central to "aristocratic" Platonic doctrines of liberal education. This conception is also central to Dewey's notion of a democratic education. This democratic educational end for all humans must be "the development of a free and powerful character." Nothing less than democratic education will prepare free people for factual and moral choices which they will inevitably confront in society. The democratic educator must be guided by a set of psychological and ethical principles which he openly presents to his students, inviting criticism as well as understanding. The alternative is the "educator-king," such as the behavior-modifier

with an ideology of controlling behavior, or the teacher-psychiatrist with an ideology of "improving" students' mental health. Neither exposes his ideology to the students, allowing them to evaluate its merit for themselves.

6. A notion of education for development and education for principles is liberal, democratic, and non-indoctrinative. It relies on open methods of stimulation through a sequence of stages, in a direction of movement which is universal for all children. In this sense, it is natural.

The progressive position appears idealistic rather than pragmatic, industrial-vocational, or adjustment-orientated, as is often charged by critics of progressivism who view it as ignoring "excellence." But Dewey's idealism is supported by Piagetian psychological findings which indicate that all children, not only well-born college students, are "philosophers" intent on organizing their lives into universal patterns of meaning. It is supported by findings that most students seem to move forward in developmentally oriented educational programs. Furthermore, the idealism of the developmental position is compatible with the notion that the child is involved in a process of both academic and vocational education. Dewey denied that educational experience stimulating intellectual and moral development could be equated with academic schooling. He claimed that practical or vocational education as well as academic education could contribute to cognitive and moral development; it should be for all children, not only for the poor or the "slow." Our educational system currently faces a choice between two forms of injustice, the first an imposition of an arbitrary academic education on all, the second a division into a superior academic track and an inferior vocational track. The developmental conception remains the only rationale for solving these injustices, and for providing the basis for a truly democratic educational process.

NOTES

1. The position presented in this paper was elaborated in a different form in *Proceedings of the Conference on Psychology and the Process of Schooling in the Next Decade: Alternative conceptions.* Washington, D.C.: U.S. Office of Education, 1971. This paper, itself, is an abridged version of a chapter in a forthcoming book by the authors, *Early Education, A Cognitive Developmental View.* Chicago: Dryden Press (in preparation).

2. The romantic-maturationist position also has "conservative" and "radical" wings. Emphasizing "adaptation to reality," psychoanalytic educators like

A. Freud (1937) and Bettelheim (1970) stress mental health as ego-control, while radicals stress spontaneity, creativity, etc.

3. There are two main schools of ethical liberalism. The more naturalistic or utilitarian one is represented in the works of J. S. Mill, Sidgewick, Dewey, and Tufts. The other is represented in the works of Locke, Kant, and Rawls. A modern statement of the liberal ethical tradition in relation to education is provided by R. S. Peters (1968).

REFERENCES

Bereiter, C. "Moral Alternatives to Education," *Interchange* 3:1 (1972): 25–41.

Bereiter, C., and S. Engelmann. *Teaching Disadvantaged Children in Preschool.* Englewood Cliffs, N.J.: Prentice-Hall, 1966.

Berkowitz, L. *Development of Motives and Values in a Child.* New York: Basic Books, 1964.

Bettelheim, B. "On Moral Education." In T. Sizer (ed.), *Moral Education.* Cambridge, Mass.: Harvard University Press, 1970.

Brandt, R.B. *Ethical Theory.* Englewood Cliffs, N.J.: Prentice-Hall, 1956.

Dewey, J. *Experience and Education.* New York: Collier, 1963 — originally written in 1938.

Dewey, J., and J. McLellan. "The Psychology of Number." In R. Archambault (ed.), *John Dewey on Education: Selected Writings.* New York: Random House, 1964 — originally written in 1895.

Freud, A. *The Ego and the Mechanisms of Defense.* London: Hogarth Press, 1937.

Hall, G.S. "The Ideal School Based on Child Study," *The Forum* 32 (1901).

Kohlberg, L. "Early Education: A Cognitive-Developmental View," *Child Development* 39 (December 1968): 1013–62.

Kohlberg, L. "Stage and Sequence: The Cognitive-Developmental Approach to Socialization." In D. Goslin (ed.), *Handbook of Socialization Theory and Research.* New York: Rand McNally, 1969.

Kohlberg, L. "The Moral Atmosphere of the School." Paper delivered at Association for Supervision and Curriculum Development Conference on the "Unstudied Curriculum." Washington, D.C., January 9, 1969. Printed in A.A.S.C. Yearbook, 1970.

Kohlberg, L. "From Is to Ought: How to Commit the Naturalistic Fallacy and Get Away With It in the Study of Moral Development." In T. Mischel (ed.), *Cognitive Development and Epistemology.* New York: Academic Press, 1971.

Kohlberg, L. "The Contribution of Developmental Psychology to Education: Examples from Moral Education," *The Educational Psychologist* 10 (Winter 1972): 2–14.

Kohlberg, L., and E. Turiel. "Moral Development and Moral Education." In G. Lesser (ed.), *Psychology and Educational Practice.* Chicago: Scott Foresman, 1971.

Langer, J. *Theories of Development.* New York: Holt, Rinehart, and Winston, 1969.

Mead, G.H. *Movements of Thought in the Nineteenth Century*. Chicago: University of Chicago Press, 1936.

Neill, A.S. *Summerhill*. New York: Hart, 1960.

Peters, R.S., *Ethics and Education*. Chicago: Scott Foresman, 1968.

Skinner, B.F. *Beyond Freedom and Dignity*. New York: Knopf, 1971.

Selection 2.2

The Psychological Aspect of the School Curriculum

John Dewey

There is a rough and ready way, in current pedagogical writing, of discriminating between the consideration of the curriculum or subject matter of instruction and the method. The former is taken to be objective in character, determined by social and logical considerations without any particular reference to the nature of the individual. It is supposed that we can discuss and define geography, mathematics, language, and the like as studies of the school course, without having recourse to principles that flow from the psychology of the individual. The standpoint of method is taken when we have to reckon with the adaptation of this objective given material to the processes, interests, and powers of the individual. The study is there ready-made; method inquires how the facts and truths supplied may be most easily and fruitfully assimilated by the pupil.

Taken as a convenient working distinction, no great harm is likely to arise from this parceling out of the two phases of instruction. When pressed, however, into a rigid principle, and made the basis for further inferences, or when regarded as a criterion by reference to which other educational questions may be decided, the view is open to grave objections.

On the philosophic side it sets up a dualism that, to my own mind, is indefensible; and that, from any point of view, is questionable. Moreover,

SOURCE. From John Dewey, "The Psychological Aspect of the School Curriculum," *Educational Review* 14 (April 1897): 356–69. Reprinted with permission of the Society for the Advancement of Education.

many of the writers who hold this distinction on the practical or pedagogical side would certainly be the last to admit it if it were presented to them as a philosophic matter. The dualism is one between mental operation on one side, and intellectual content on the other — between mind and the material with which it operates; or, more technically, between subject and object in experience. The philosophic presupposition is that there is somehow a gap or chasm between the workings of the mind and the subject matter on which it works. In taking it for granted that the subject matter may be selected, defined, and arranged without any reference to psychological consideration (that is, apart from the nature and mode of action of the individual), it is assumed that the facts and principles exist in an independent and external way, without organic relation to the methods and functions of mind. I do not see how those who refuse to accept this doctrine as good philosophy can possibly be content with the same doctrine when it presents itself in an educational garb.

This dualism reduces the psychological factor in education to an empty gymnastic. It makes it a mere formal training of certain distinct powers called perception, memory, judgment, which are assumed to exist and operate by themselves, without organic reference to the subject matter. I do not know that it has been pointed out that the view taken by Dr. Harris in the Report of the Committee of Fifteen regarding the comparative worthlessness of the psychological basis in fixing educational values is a necessary consequence of the dualism under discussion. If the subject matter exists by itself on one side, then the mental processes have a like isolation on the other. The only way successfully to question this condemnation of the psychological standpoint is to deny that there is, as a matter of fact, any such separation between the subject matter of experience and the mental operations involved in dealing with it.

The doctrine, if logically carried out in practice, is even less attractive than on the strictly theoretical side. The material, the stuff to be learned, is, from this point of view, inevitably something external, and therefore indifferent. There can be no native and intrinsic tendency of the mind toward it, nor can it have any essential quality that stimulates and calls out the mental powers. No wonder the upholders of this distinction are inclined to question the value of interest in instruction, and to throw all the emphasis on the dead lift of effort. The externality of the material makes it more or less repulsive to the mind. The pupil, if left to himself, would, on this assumption, necessarily engage himself in something else. It requires a sheer effort of will power to carry the mind over from its own intrinsic workings and interests to this outside stuff.

On the other side, the mental operation being assumed to go on without any intrinsic connection with the material, the question of method is degraded to a very low plane. Of necessity it is concerned simply with the various devices that have been found empirically useful, or that the ingenuity of the individual teacher may invent. There is nothing fundamental or philosophical that may be used as a standard in deciding points in method. It is simply a question of discovering the temporary expedients and tricks that will reduce the natural friction between the mind and the external material. No wonder, once more, that those who hold even unconsciously to this dualism (when they do not find the theory of effort to work practically) seek an ally in the doctrine of interest interpreted to mean the amusing, and hold that the actual work of instruction is how to make studies that have no intrinsic interest interesting — how, that is, to clothe them with factitious attraction, so that the mind may swallow the repulsive dose unaware.

The fact that this dualistic assumption gives material on one hand such an external and indifferent character, while on the other it makes method trivial and arbitrary, is certainly a reason for questioning it. I propose, accordingly, in the following pages, to examine this presupposition, with a view to showing that, as a matter of fact, psychological considerations (those that have to deal with the structures and powers of the individual) enter not only into the discussion of method, but also into that of subject matter.

The general tone of Dr. Harris's criticism of my monograph on *Interest as related to will* is so friendly and appreciative that it would be hypercritical and controversial for me to carry on the discussion longer without raising some deeper problem. I am convinced that much of the existing difference of opinion as regards not only the place of interest in education but the meaning and worth of correlation is due to failure to raise the more fundamental question that I have just proposed; and that the thing needed in the present state of discussion is, as it were, to flank these two questions by making articulate the silent presupposition that has been so largely taken for granted.

What, then, do we mean by a study in the curriculum? What does it stand for? What fixes the place that it occupies in the school work? What furnishes it its end? What gives it its limitations? By what standard do we measure its value? The ordinary schoolteacher is not, of course, called on to raise such questions. He has certain subjects given to him. The curriculum is, as we say, laid out, and the individual teacher has to do the best he can with the studies as he finds them. But those who are concerned theoretically with the nature of education, or those who have to do practically with the organization of the course of study — those who "lay out" the course — cannot afford to ignore these questions.

On the whole, the most philosophic answer that has as yet been given to these questions in America is that worked out by Dr. Harris in his deservedly famous St. Louis reports, and more recently formulated by him in the Report of the Committee of Fifteen, as well as in the articles that he has written opposing the Herbartian conception of correlation. In substance, we are told that a study is the gathering up and arranging of the facts and principles relating to some typical aspect of social life, or which afford a fundamental tool in maintaining that social life; that the standard for selecting and placing a study is the worth that it has in adapting the pupil to the needs of the civilization into which he is born.

I do not question this statement, so far as it goes on the positive side. The objectional point is the negative inference that this social determination is exclusive of the psychological one. The social definition is necessary, but is the psychological one less pressing? Supposing we ask, for example, how a given study plays the part assigned to it in social life? What is it that gives it its function? How does the study operate in performing this function? Suppose we say not simply that geography does, as a matter of fact, occupy a certain important position in interpreting to the child the structure and processes of the civilization into which he is born; suppose that, in addition, we want to know how geography performs this task. What is it that intrinsically adapts it to this and gives it a claim to do something that no other study or group of studies can well perform? Can we answer this question without entering into the psychological domain? Are we not inquiring, in effect, what geography is on the psychological side—what it is, that is to say, as a mode or form of experience?[1]

Moreover, we must ask how the given study manages to do the work given it before we can get any basis on which to select the material of instruction in general; and much more before we can select the material for pupils of a certain age or of a certain social environment. We must take into account the distinction between a study as a logical whole and the same study considered as a psychological whole. From the logical standpoint, the study is the body or system of facts that are regarded as valid, and that are held together by certain internal principles of relation and explanation. The logical standpoint assumes the facts to be already discovered, already sorted out, classified, and systematized. It deals with the subject matter on the objective standpoint. Its only concern is whether the facts are really facts, and whether the theories of explanation and interpretation used will hold water. From the psychological standpoint, we are concerned with the study as a mode or form of living individual experience. Geography is not only a set of facts and principles, which may be classified and discussed by themselves; it is also a way in which some actual individual feels and thinks the world. It must be the latter before it can be the former. It becomes the former only as the culmination or completed outgrowth of the latter. Only when the individual has passed through a certain amount of experience, which he vitally realizes on his own account, is he prepared to take the objective and logical point of view, capable of standing off and analyzing the facts and principles involved.

Now, the primary point of concern in education is beyond question with the subject as a special mode of personal experience, rather than with the subject as a body of wrought-out facts and scientifically tested principles. To the child, simply because he is a child, geography is not, and cannot be, what it is to the one who writes the scientific treatise on geography. *The latter has had exactly the experience that it is the problem of instruction to induce on the part of the former*. To identify geography as it is to the pupil of seven or fifteen with geography as it is to Humboldt or Ritter is a flagrant case of putting the cart before the horse. With the child, instruction must take the standpoint not of the accomplished results, but of the crude beginnings. We must discover what there is lying within the child's present sphere of experience (or within the scope of experiences that he can easily get) that deserves to be called geographical. It is not the question of *how* to teach the child geography, but first of all the question of *what* geography is for the child.

There is no fixed body of facts which, in itself, is eternally set off and labeled geography, natural history, and physics. Exactly the same objective reality will be one or other, or none of these three, according to the interest and intellectual attitude from which it is surveyed. Take a square mile of territory, for example; if we view it from one interest, we may have trigonometry; from another standpoint we should label the facts regarding it botany; from still another, geology; from another, mineralogy; from another, geography; from still another standpoint it would become historical material. There is absolutely nothing in the fact, as an objective fact, that places it under any one head. Only as we ask what kind of an experience is going on, what attitude some individual is actually assuming, what purpose or end some individual has in view, do we find a basis for selecting and arranging the facts under the label of any particular study.

Even in the most logical and objective consideration, we do not, therefore, really escape from the psychological point of view. We do not get away from all reference to the person having an experience, and from the point of how and why he has it. We are simply taking the psychology of the adult (that is to say, of the one who has already gone through a certain series of experiences), of one who has, therefore, a certain background and course of growth, and substituting the mature and developed interest of such a person for the crude and more or less blind tendency that the child has. If we act on this distinction in our educational work, it means that we substitute the adult's consciousness for the child's consciousness.

I repeat, therefore, that the first question regarding any subject of study is the psychological one, What is that study, considered as a form of living, immediate, personal experience? What is the interest in that experience? What is the motive or stimulus to it? How does it act and react with reference to other forms of experience? How does it gradually differentiate itself from others? And how does it function so as to give them additional definiteness and richness of meaning? We must ask these questions not only with reference to the child in general, but with reference to the specific child—the child of a certain age, of a certain degree of attainment, and of specific home and neigborhood contacts.

Until we ask such questions, the consideration of the school curriculum is arbitrary and partial, because we have not the ultimate criterion for decision before us. The problem is not simply what facts a child is capable of grasping or what facts can be made interesting to him, but what experience does he himself have in a given direction. The subject must be differentiated out of that experience in accordance with its own laws. Unless we know what these laws are, what are the intrinsic stimuli, modes of operation, and functions of a certain form of experience, we are practically helpless in dealing with it. We may follow routine or we may follow abstract logical consideration, but we have no decisive educational criterion. It is the problem of psychology to answer these questions; and when we get them answered, we shall know how to clarify, build up, and put in order the content of experience, so that in time it will grow to include the systematic body of facts that the adult's consciousness already possesses.

This is a distinctly practical question—a question that concerns the actual work of the schoolroom and not simply the professorial chair. On the whole, I believe that the crying evil in instruction today is that the subject matter of the curriculum, both as a whole and in its various stages, is selected and determined on the objective or logical basis instead of on the psychological. The humble pedagogue stands with his mouth and his hands wide open, waiting to receive from the abstract scientific writers the complete system that the latter, after centuries of experience and toilsome reflection, have elaborated. Receiving in this trustful way the ready-made "subject," he proceeds to hand it over in an equally ready-made way to the pupil. The intervening medium of communication is simply certain external attachments in the way of devices and tricks called "methods" and certain sugar coatings in the way of extrinsic inducements termed "arousing of interest."

All this procedure overlooks the point that the first pedagogical question is, How, out of the crude native experience that the child already has, the complete and systematic knowledge of the adult consciousness is gradually and systematically worked out. The first question is, How experience grows; not, What experience the adult has succeeded in getting together during his development from childhood to maturity. The scientific writer, having a background of original experience, and having passed through the whole period of growth, may safely assume them and not get lost; the subject matter standing to him in its proper perspective and relation. But when this adult material is handed over ready-made to the child, the perspective is ignored, the subject is forced into false and arbitrary relations, the intrinsic interest is not appealed to, and the experience that the child already has, which might be made a vital instrument of learning, is left unutilized and to degenerate.

The genuine course of procedure may be stated as follows:

We have first to fix attention on the child to find out what kind of experience is appropriate to him at the particular period selected; to discover, if possible, what it is that constitutes the special feature of the child's experience at this time; and why it is that his experience takes this form rather than another. This means that we observe in detail what experiences have most meaning and value to him, and what attitude he assumes toward them. We search for the point, or focus, of interest in these experiences. We ask where they get their hold on him and how they make their appeal to him. We endeavor by observation and reflection to see what tastes and powers of the child are active in securing these experiences. We ask what habits are being formed; what ends and aims are being proposed. We inquire what the stimuli are and what responses the child is making. We ask what impulses are struggling for expression; in what characteristic ways they find an outlet; and what results inure to the child through their manifestation.

All this is a psychological inquiry. It may be summed up, if I am permitted to use the word, under the head of "interest." Our study is to find out what the actual interests of the child are; or, stated on the objective side, what it is in the world of objects and persons that attracts and holds the child's attention, and that constitutes for him the significance and worth of his life. This does not mean that these interests, when discovered, give the ultimate standard for school work, or that they have any final regulative value. It means that the final standard cannot be discovered or used until this preliminary inquiry is gone through with. Only by asking and answering such questions do we find out where the child really is; what he is capable of doing; what he can do to the greatest advantage and with the least waste of time and strength, mental and physical. We find here our indicators or pointers as to the range of facts and ideas legitimate to the child. While we do not get the absolute rule for the selection of subject matter, we do most positively get the key to such selection. More than this, we here have revealed to us the resources and allies on which the taecher may count in the work of instruction. These native existing interests, impulses, and experiences are all the leverage that the teacher has to work with. He must connect with them or fail utterly. Indeed, the very words leverage and connection suggest a more external relation than actually exists. The new material cannot be attached to these experiences or hung on them from without, but must be differentiated from them internally. The child will never realize a fact or possess an idea that does not grow out of this equipment of experiences and interests that he already has. The problem of instruction, therefore, is how to induce this growth.

The phenomena of interest, then, are to be studied as symptoms. Only through what the child does can we know what he is. That which enables us to translate the outward doing over into its inner meaning is the ability to read it in terms of interest. If we know the interest the child has, we know not simply what he externally does, but why he does it; where its connection with his own being can be found. Wherever we have interest we have signs of dawning power. Wherever we have phenomena of a lack of interest, wherever we have repulsion, we have sure tokens that the child is not able to function freely, is not able to control and direct his own experience as he would; or, if I may use what Dr. Harris calls a "glib and technical term," does not "*express himself*" easily and freely. Once more, these phenomena of interest are not final. They do not say to the teacher: We are your final end, and all your energies are to be devoted to cultivating us just as we are. Nonetheless, they are indices and instruments; they are the only clues that the instructor can possibly have to what experiences are such really, and not simply in name. They reveal the general standpoint from which any subject must be presented in order to lay hold on the child. The problem of the teacher is to read the superficial manifestations over into their underlying sources. Even "bad" interests, like that of destruction, are the signs of some inner power that must be discovered and utilized.

In the second place, in saying that these psychical phenomena afford opportunities, give clues, and furnish leverages, we are virtually saying that they set problems. They need to be interpreted. They have the value of signs, and, like all signs, must be interpreted into the realities for which they stand. Now it is the province of the subject matter on its logical and objective side to help us in this work of translation. We see the meaning of the beginning through reading it in terms of its outcome; of the crude in terms of the mature. We see, for example, what the first babbling instincts and impulses mean by contemplating the articulate structure of language as an instrument of social communication, of logical thought, and of artistic expression. We see what the interest of the child in counting and measuring represents, by viewing the developed system of arithmetic and geometry. The original phenomena are prophecy. To realize the full scope of the prophecy, its promise and potency, we must look at it not in its isolation, but in its fulfillment.

This doctrine is misconceived when taken to mean that these accomplished results of the adult experience may be made a substitute for the child's experience, or may be directly inserted into his consciousness through the medium of instruction, or, by any external device whatsoever, grafted on him. Their value is not that of furnishing the immediate material or subject matter of instruction, any more than the phenomena of interest furnish the final standards and goals of instruction. The function of this ordered and arranged experience is strictly interpretative or mediatory. We must bear it in mind in order to appreciate, to place, the value of the child's interests as he manifests them.

Thus we come, in the third place, to the selection and determination of the material of instruction, and to its adaptation to the process of learning. This involves the interaction of two points of view just considered. It is working back and forth from one to the other. The transitory and more or less superficial phenomena of child life must be viewed through their full fruitage. The objective attainments of the adult consciousness must be taken out of their abstract and logical quality and appreciated as living experiences of the concrete individual. Then we may see what both subject matter and method of instruction stand for. The subject matter is the present experience of the child, taken in the light of what it may lead to. The method is the subject matter rendered into the actual life experience of some individual. The final problem of instruction is thus the reconstruction of the individual's experience, through the medium of what is seen to be involved in that experience as its matured outgrowth.

We have two counterpart errors: one is the appeal to the child's momentary and more or less transitory interest, as if it were final and complete, instead of a sign of nascent power; as if it were an end instead of an instrument; as if it furnished an ideal instead of setting a problem. The other is taking the studies from the scientific standpoint, and regarding them as affording the subject matter of the curriculum. As the phenomena of interest need to be controlled by reference to their fullest possibility, so the scientific content of the studies needs to be made over by being "psychologized," seen as what some concrete individual may experience in virtue of his own impulses, interests, and powers. It is the element of control that takes us out of the region of arbitrary tricks and devices into the domain of orderly method. It is the making over and psychological translation of the studies that renders them a genuine part of the *Lehrstoff* of the pupil. It is because of the necessity of this operation, the transfiguring of the dead objective facts by seeing them as thoughts and feelings and acts of some individual, that we are justified in saying that there is a psychological aspect to the curriculum.

In applying this to the actual studies that make up the present curriculum, no one would deny, I suppose, that language, literature, history, and art, being manifestations of human nature, cannot be understood in their entirety, nor yet fully utilized in the work of instruction, until they are regarded as such manifestation. But we must go a point further, and recognize that in education we are not concerned with the language that has been spoken, the literature that has been created, the history that has been lived, but with them only as they become a part of what an individual reports, expresses, and lives. Even in the sciences, where we appear to be dealing with matters that are more remote from the individual, we need to remember that educationally our business is not with science as a body of fixed facts and truths, but with it as a method and attitude of experience. Science in the sense in which we can find it stated in books, or set forth in lectures, is not the subject matter of instruction. Anything that can be found in these forms is simply an index and instrument. It sets before us our goal — the attitude of kind and mind of experience that we wish to induce; when it is read over, into psychological terms, it helps us reach our goal; but without the psychological rendering, it is inert, mechanical, and deadening.

Because the actual, as distinct from the abstract or possible, subject is a mode of personal experience, not simply an ordered collection of facts and principles, the curriculum as a whole, and every study in detail, has a psychological side whose neglect and denial lead to confusion in pedagogic theory; and in educational practice to the dead following of historic precedent and routine, or else to the substitution of the abstract and the formal for the vital and personal.

NOTES

1. I note that many critics have objected to the title of the book, *The Psychology of Number*, on the ground that, as one objector put it, "Psychology is the science of mind, and hence this title virtually reads, 'The science of the mind of number,' which is absurd." Do these critics mean that quantity, number, and so on are not modes of experience? That they are not specific intellectual attitudes and operations? Do they deny that from the educational, as distinct from the scientific standpoint, the consideration of number as a mode of experience, as a mental attitude and process of functioning, is more important than the definition of a number from a purely objective standpoint?

Selection 2.3

The Disciplines as Curriculum Content

Philip H. Phenix

In 1956 I published a paper entitled "Key Concepts and the Crisis in Learning," in which I developed the thesis that economy and efficiency in learning, in a time of vast proliferation of knowledge, can best be achieved by attending to the "key concepts" in the several fields of learning. Since that time many important developments in curriculum studies have taken place along somewhat similar lines.

In recent years various study commissions have been at work reorganizing the subject matter of some of the major fields of learning; the Teacher Education and Professional Standards commissions have worked for *rapprochement* between academic scholars and specialists in education; and leading investigators like Jerome Bruner have dealt with the importance of structure for the mastery of knowledge. The present discussion seeks to develop some of these same themes, with special reference to the idea of the disciplines.

My thesis, briefly, is that *all* curriculum content should be drawn from the disciplines, or, to put it another way, that *only* knowledge contained in the disciplines is appropriate to the curriculum.

SOURCE. In *Curriculum Crossroads,* ed. A. Harry Passow (New York: Teachers College Press, 1962), pp. 57-65.

Exposition of this position requires first that we consider what is meant by a discipline. The word "discipline" is derived from the Latin word *discipulus,* which means a disciple, that is, one who receives instruction from another. *Discipulus* in turn stems from the verb *discere,* to learn. Etymologically, then, a discipline may be construed as knowledge the special property of which is its appropriateness for teaching and its availability for learning. A discipline is knowledge organized for instruction.

Basic to my theme is this affirmation: the distinguishing mark of any discipline is that the knowledge which comprises it is instructive—that it is peculiarly suited for teaching and learning. Implicit in this assertion is the recognition that there are kinds of knowledge which are not found within a discipline. Such nondisciplined knowledge is unsuitable for teaching and learning. It is not instructive. Given this understanding of what a discipline is, it follows at once that all teaching should be disciplined, that it is undesirable to have any instruction in matters which fall beyond the the disciplines. This means that psychological needs, social problems, and any of a variety of patterns of material based on other than discipline content are not appropriate to the determination of what is taught—though obviously such nondisciplinary considerations *are* essential to decision about the *distribution* of discipline knowledge within the curriculum as a whole.

DISPARATE METHODS

The position here taken is at odds with the one taken by many people both in the field of education and in the several disciplines. The common assumption of these people is that the disciplines are in the realm of pure knowledge—of specialized professional scholarship and research—and that ordinary education is a different sort of enterprise. The disciplines have a life of their own, it is held, and knowledge in them is not directly available for the purposes of instruction, but to be suitable for education must be translated and transformed so as to become useful and meaningful to ordinary learners. Thus, the argument goes, for the curriculum we should draw upon life situations, problems, projects and the like, for the primary *content* of instruction, using the knowledge supplied by the disciplines as auxiliary material to be employed as required by the basic instructional process. The person is supposed to learn primarily from experience as it comes naturally and not as it is artificially conceptualized and organized in the academic fields.

Correspondingly, under this customary view, there are two disparate realms of method; there are methods of professional scholarship and research, and there are methods of instruction. There is a specialized logic of the disciplines and there is a largely unrelated psycho-logic of teaching and learning. From this division arises the well-known bifurcation between the academic scholars and the professional educators. The former pride themselves on their erudition and despise or neglect pedagogy, while the latter busily pursue the problems of teaching and learning, often with little understanding or concern for the standards of rigorous scholarship.

This dualism is destructive both to scholarship and to education. It presupposes a concept of the academic disciplines which has no relation to the instructiveness of the knowledge contained therein and a concept of teaching and learning disconnected from the essential structure of the products of disciplined inquiry. We need to recover the essential meaning of a discipline as a body of instructive knowledge. So understood, the disciplines will be seen as the clue to good teaching and learning, and instructiveness will be seen as the mark of a good discipline. Furthermore, scholars will learn once more to measure their success by their ability to teach, and teachers will again be judged by the depth of their understanding, and the academics and the educationists will dwell together in peace, if indeed any such distinction will any longer be required!

It is wrong to suppose that the more profound scholarly inquiry is the further removed it is from suitability for teaching purposes. On the contrary, profundity is in proportion to illuminative quality. The esoteric knowledge that is often described as profound is more aptly termed obscure. The characteristic feature of disciplined intelligence is that difficulties and confusions are overcome and understanding of the subject is thereby facilitated. In short, the test for quality in knowledge is its communicability. Knowledge which is hard to teach is for that reason inferior. Knowledge which readily enlightens the learner's understanding is superior.

Now what is it that makes knowledge instructive? How does undisciplined understanding differ from disciplined understanding? There are three fundamental features, all of which contribute to the availability of knowledge for instruction and thus provide measures for degree and quality of discipline. These are (1) analytic simplification; (2) synthetic coordination; and (3) dynamism. Let us consider each criterion in turn.

Analytic Simplification

The primal essential for effective teaching is simplification. All intelligibility rests on a radical reduction in the multiplicity of impressions which impringe on the senses and the imagination. The infant begins life with the booming, buzzing confusion of which James spoke, and his learning consists in the growing ability to sort and select, that is, to simplify. The lower animals have built-in simplifiers in the instinctive mechanisms. Human beings have a much more interesting and powerful apparatus of simplification, through intelligence. The index of intelligence is, of course, the power of symbolization. Symbols—preeminently but not exclusively those of language—are means of marking out useful and memorable features of experience for special notice. All significant words are such markers. Thus, the word "hand" designates a *kind* of object, to which an indefinite number of particular objects (hands) correspond. The point for emphasis is that a symbol—for example, a word—allows human beings drastically to reduce the complexity of their experience by subsuming an indefinite wealth of particulars under a single concept.

The secret of human learning is in generalization, that is, in transcending the multifariousness of raw experience. All thinking requires conceptualization. Concepts are classes of particulars. They are selections from the inchoate mass of impressions of certain features of things which enable them to be treated as a class rather than one by one. Thought proceeds by a process of rigorous selection, emphasis, and suppression of data. A person is intelligent to the degree that he actively discriminates in his entertainment of stimuli. In our pursuit of the full, rich life we may forget that the key to felicity and wisdom lies as much or more in our power of excluding as in receiving impressions. Our humanness rests on a wise asceticism, not on indiscriminate hospitality to every message impinging on us from the world about us.

This simplification of experience through the use of symbols may be called analytic. The sorting out of classes of things is the process of analysis. It proceeds by the discrimination of similarities and differences, whereby entities may be divided and arranged in orderly fashion. Analysis is possible only because the human mind is able to abstract, that is, to discern properties, qualities, or forms of things. Every concept is an abstraction—a drawing out of certain features of a class of things for purposes of generalization and grouping. The function of abstraction is to simplify—to reduce the complexity of unanalyzed experience by selecting certain shared properties of kinds of things and neglecting their other features.

It is commonly assumed that abstract thinking is difficult and complicated. This assumption betrays a misunderstanding of what abstraction is. Analytic abstraction is a way of thinking which aims at ease of comprehension and reduction of complexity. For this reason all learning—all growth in understanding—takes place through the use of simplifying concepts. It is the key to effectiveness of instruction.

All this bears directly on the question of the place of the disciplines in teaching and learning. A discipline is essentially nothing more than an extension of ordinary conceptualization. It is a conceptual system whose office is to gather together a large group of cognitive elements into a common framework of ideas. That is, its goal is the simplification of understanding. This is the function of the techniques, models, and theories which are characteristic of any discipline. They economize thought by showing how diverse and apparently disparate elements of experience can be subsumed under common interpretive and explanatory schemes.

Thus, contrary to the popular assumption, knowledge does not become more and more complicated as one goes deeper into a discipline. If it is a real discipline and not merely a field for the display of erudition, the further one goes in it the more pervasive are the simplicities which analysis reveals. For example, how grand and liberating is the simplicity afforded by the atomic theory of matter as one seeks to comprehend the endless complexity of the world of material substances! Again, how much simpler Copernicus made the understanding of the apparent motions of the stars and planets, and how much easier Darwin made the comprehension of the varieties of living things!

The test of a good discipline is whether or not it simplifies understanding. When a field of study only adds new burdens and multiplies complexities, it is not properly called a discipline. Likewise, when a real discipline in certain directions begins to spawn concepts and theories which on balance are a burden and hindrance to insight, in those areas it degenerates into undisciplined thinking.

One of the greatest barriers to progress in learning is the failure to catch the vision of simplicity which the disciplines promise. When students (and their teachers) consider the movement from elementary to advanced stages in a subject as requiring the taking on of more and more burdens of knowledge, of ever-increasing complexity, just as physically one becomes with exercise capable of carrying increasingly heavy loads, it is little wonder that they so often resist instruction and postpone learning as long as possible. If, on the other hand, it can be made clear that, like Christian in Bunyan's allegory, the academic pilgrimage aims at release from the burdens of merely accumulated experience and leads to intellectual salvation through the insightful and revelatory concepts and theories contained in the traditions of the disciplines, how eager students become to learn and how ready to exchange their hampering ignorance for liberating understanding!

Synthetic Coordination

Let us now turn, more briefly, to the second feature of a discipline which makes knowledge in it instructive, namely, *synthetic coordination.* A discipline is a conceptual structure whose function is not only to simplify understanding but also to reveal significant patterns and relationships. Analysis is not an end in itself; it is the basis of synthesis. By synthesis is meant the construction of new wholes, the coordination of elements into significant coherent structures. Disciplined thinking is *organized thinking.* Differences and distinctions are recognized within an ordered framework which permits synoptic vision.

Such synthetic coordination is not opposed in tendency to analytic simplifications; both are aspects of a common process of intelligible ordering. The perception of meaningful differences is possible only against some common measure. Thus, the notion of parts within an ordered whole involves both the differentiation which is presupposed by the idea of parts and the unity which is implied by the idea of a whole. A discipline is a synthetic structure of concepts made possible by the discrimination of similarities through analysis. It is a hierarchy of ideas ordered as a unity-in-difference.

It is only in this sense that disciplined knowledge can be called complex. The simplifications of abstraction make possible the construction of cognitive complexes—i.e., the weaving together of ideas into coherent wholes. Concepts are no longer entertained in isolation, but are seen in their interconnections and relationships.

What occurs in disciplined thinking is a reconstruction of experience. The brute multiplicity of primordial experience is simplified by conceptual abstraction, and these abstractions are then synthesized into more and more comprehensive patterns of coordination. In this way naive experience is transformed from a meaningless hodgepodge of impressions into a relatively meaningful pattern of understanding.

Herein lies the great pedagogical virtue of a discipline. Whatever is taught within a discipline framework draws strength and interest from its membership within a family of ideas. Each new idea is illuminated by ideas previously acquired. A discipline is a community of concepts. Just as human beings cannot thrive in isolation, but require the support of other persons in mutual association, so do isolated ideas wither and die, while ideas comprehended within the unity of a discipline tend to remain vivid and powerful within the understanding.

Dynamism

The third quality of knowledge in a discipline I have called its *dynamism*. By this is meant the power of leading on to further understandings. A discipline is a *living* body of knowledge, containing within itself a principle of growth. Its concepts do not merely simplify and coordinate; they also invite further analysis and synthesis. A discipline contains a *lure to discovery*. Its ideas excite the imagination to further exploration. Its concepts suggest new constructs which provide larger generalizations and reconstituted modes of coordination.

James B. Conant has pointed to this dynamism as a distinguishing feature of scientific knowledge. Science is an enterprise in which fruitfulness is the mark of a good conceptual scheme. Theories which merely coordinate and organize a given body of data but do not stimulate further experimentation and inquiry are scientifically unimportant. This principle may also be taken as definitive for any discipline. Instructiveness is proportionate to fruitfulness. Knowledge which only organizes the data of experience but does not excite further questions and inquiries is relatively undisciplined knowledge. Disciplined ideas not only constitute families of concepts, but these families beget progeny. They have generative power. This is why they are instructive. They lead on and out: they educate.

DISCIPLINED AND NONDISCIPLINED KNOWLEDGE

There is, of course, no sharp dividing line between disciplined and nondisciplined knowledge. There are on the one extreme isolated bits of information which are not within any organized discipline, and on the other extreme there are precisely articulated theoretical structures which are readily recognized as disciplined according to the meaning developed above. In between are bodies of knowledge which have all degrees of discipline. Perhaps it would be well also to speak of weak disciplines and strong disciplines, the difference being in the degree to which their contents satisfy the three criteria for instructiveness earlier stated. Thus, mathematics, with powerful analytic tools and the dynamic for endless fruitful elaborations, by the present criteria would appear to be a stronger discipline than most present-day political science, which (from my limited knowledge of it) seems to have relatively few unifying concepts and theoretical schemes permitting wide synthesis and creative expansion. Again, I would rate comparative linguistics which seems to possess a powerful and productive set of concepts as a stronger discipline than aesthetics, which still operates largely in terms of individual subjective judgments about particular objects, one by one.

A distinction may also be useful between a discipline and an area of study. Not all areas of study are disciplines, since not all of them display analytic, synthetic, and dynamic qualities. Thus, it seems to me that "education" is an area of study rather than a discipline. Within this area disciplined learning is possible. For example, I think a good case can be made for a discipline of curriculum, or of educational psychology, or of educational philosophy—though I would not wish to rate these disciplines as to strength. Similarly, "business" and "social studies" appear to be areas of study rather than disciplines. Not everyone who cries "discipline, discipline" shall enter the kingdom of learning, but only those who can show analytic simplification, synthetic coordination, and dynamism in their knowledge schemes.

My theme has been that the curriculum should consist entirely of knowledge which comes from the disciplines, for the reason that the disciplines reveal knowledge in its teachable forms. We should not try to teach anything which has not been found actually instructive through the labors of hosts of dedicated inquirers. Education should be conceived as a *guided recapitulation of the processes of inquiry which gave rise to the fruitful bodies of organized knowledge comprising the established disciplines.*

In this brief analysis there has been no time to consider the problem of levels. I do not intend to suggest that the whole conceptual apparatus of a discipline should be brought to bear on teaching at every level of education. There are elementary and advanced stages of disciplined inquiry. The great simplicities, the comprehensive syntheses, and the powerful dynamisms usually belong to the more advanced stages. Nevertheless, from the very earliest years on up, it is only discipline knowledge which should be taught in the curriculum. Every discipline has in it beginning concepts and more developed concepts, all of which belong to the discipline authentically and properly. There is no place in the curriculum for ideas which are regarded as suitable for teaching because of the supposed nature, needs, and interests of the learner, but which do not belong within the regular structure of the disciplines, for the disciplines are in their essential nature bodies of knowledge organized for the most effective instruction.

This view asserts the identity of the psycho-logic of teaching and learning with the logic of the disciplines, contrary to many of the current theories of the teaching-learning process. Or, it might be more generally acceptable among educators to say that the view measures the logic (and the authenticity) of a discipline by its instructiveness.

REALISTIC AND NOMINALISTIC VIEWS OF KNOWLEDGE

In closing, one further point can only be indicated here, without development or detailed defense. The priority and primacy of the disciplines in education are greatly buttressed by a realistic view of knowledge, as opposed to a nominalistic one. In realism it is asserted that concepts and theories disclose the real nature of things, while in nominalism it is affirmed that the structure of thought is a matter of human convention. Academic and educational nominalists believe that experience can be categorized and concepts organized in endless ways, according to the inclination and decision and for the convenience of individuals and societies. Furthermore, it is held, scholars can choose their own special ways of organizing knowledge and educators can choose other ways, the differences corresponding to the disparity in purposes in the two groups. Thus arise the supposed contrasts between the logic of the disciplines and the psycho-logic of the educative process.

Such nominalism is rejected in the realistic view here proposed. From a realistic standpoint nominalism is epistemologically impious and pedagogically disastrous, a source of internecine strife and intellectual estrangement. There is a logos of being which it is the office of reason to discover. The structure of things is revealed, not invented, and it is the business of inquiry to open that structure to general understanding through the formation of appropriate concepts and theories. Truth is rich and varied, but it is not arbitrary. The nature of things is *given,* not chosen, and if man is to gain insight he must employ the right concepts and methods. Only by obedience to the truth thus discovered can he learn or teach.

In short, authentic disciplines are at one and the same time approximations to the given orders of reality and disclosures of the paths by which persons may come to realize truth in their own being; which is simply to say that the disciplines are the sole proper source of the curriculum.

I think it is the special province of people in the schools of education to see clearly the relationship between disciplined knowledge on the one hand and the tasks of teaching and learning on the other, and the interrelations between the fields of knowledge within the curriculum as a whole. In the light of these visions, educators can help the disciplines to be truer to their own essential nature and instruction to find once again its proper resource.

Selection 2.4

The Status of Knowledge in the Radical Concept of Education

Zvi Lamm

Curriculum planning is an area where epistemological and psychological beliefs and opinions meet: Beliefs about the nature of knowledge and its purpose in the life of individuals and society on the one hand, and beliefs about the process by which the individual acquires knowledge and the conditions on which this process depends, on the other. Instruction can only be defined in relation to a conception of knowledge, since instruction is education by means of knowledge. Not all education stands in need of knowledge. Education can take place by means of interpersonal relations, or by means of individual explorations in the immediate environment. When education uses knowledge as a *means* it becomes instruction. Decisions made about the nature of knowledge and the process of its acquisition determine the nature of instruction. Different decisions with regard to these two aspects—the epistemological and the psychological—give rise to different patterns of instruction. Epistemological and psychological choices in this field are so decisive that patterns of instruction derived from the various choices possible are phenomena which have nothing in common apart from their common name—instruction. From the different patterns of instruction created by specific epistemological and psychological choices, distinct strategies of curriculum planning are derived. What are these patterns?

SOURCE. In *Curriculum and the Cultural Revolution,* eds. David E. Purpel and Maurice Belanger (Berkeley, Calif.: McCutchan, 1972), pp. 124-42.

By the time epistemological conceptions originating in philosophical theories emerge in methods of instruction and the principles of curriculum planning, they have been transformed. This is why attempts at a systematic classification of the philosophical conceptions of cognition and knowledge are not applicative to an exposition of instruction. While theories of instruction are doubtless connected to accepted epistemological theories, the connection is not a systematic one subject to the laws of logical consistency, and the discovery of a relation between a specific epistemological theory and a specific theory of education is, at best, no more than an intellectual exercise.[1] For this reason, the classification of epistemological approaches we intend to present here will be drawn directly from theories of instruction, i.e., after the transformation undergone as a result of adaptation to the needs of the school.[2]

The explicit or implicit epistemological components in theories of instruction may be described with the assistance of the following three formulae:

1. Knowledge is meant for use.
2. Knowledge has intrinsic value.
3. Knowledge is a means in the process of individuation.

The first formula is characteristic of the conception of instruction as a technique of socialization (in the narrowest sense of the word). The basic assumption here is that the functioning of an individual in society depends on his knowing specific things, understanding specific things, valuing specific things, being able to do specific things, and believing specific things. According to this conception knowledge consists of information, comprehension, skills, and beliefs which are accepted in the society the student will live in when he grows up. The validity of this type of knowledge is determined by its utility.

The concept of utility in this context is not necessarily a narrow one: a knowledge of *Hamlet* or of the baroque may be useful in a specific society, though not in the same sense that a knowledge of commercial arithmetic or personal hygiene are said to be useful. Familiarity with certain types of literature, or certain types of sport, may be required of people wishing to belong to certain social groups and their knowledge of these subjects will thus become very useful indeed. Once the teaching of *Hamlet,* commercial arithmetic, or personal hygiene is justified by the argument of utility, it makes no difference if the knowledge acquired is used in solving concrete problems, attaining well-being, gaining privileges, or for any other end. It makes no difference because instruction which is guided by this epistemological principle crystallizes in the end into a single pattern of behavior. Characteristic of this pattern of behavior is an emphasis on the philosophical-educational concept of *training* which gives birth to the technique of instruction called by J. Piaget *the receptive method.*[3] The concept of *training* refers to a process mainly concerned with the practicing of skills according to models of roles, the concept of receptiveness refers to a technique for its implementation.

When instruction is conceived as a technique of socialization, the status of knowledge is that of a model of behavior to be imitated, where behavior is interpreted in the widest possible sense to include thoughts, feelings, imagination, actions, habits, etc. What the student is expected to learn is how to reconstruct expected models of behavior.

The second formula, "Knowledge has intrinsic value," is characteristic of the conception of instruction as a technique of acculturation. Acculturation is the process by which the individual becomes a member of a specific society. In its narrow technical sense, this concept is today used to refer to the transition from one society to another, as in the case of immigrants from traditional cultures making the transition to modern cultures. In its broader meaning, acculturation is the universal process which is undergone by every child born to woman, and which transforms merely biological beings into civilized or "cultured" beings, who have acquired the ways of behaving evolved during the course of the history of the societies into which they were born. The concept of culture is used in two ways. The first is the way in which it is used by anthropologists, and is interchangeable with the term society as used by sociologists. In this sense culture is a neutral concept with no connotation of value, signifying the totality of patterns of behavior and organization by whose means various collectives solve their problems. In its second sense the concept of culture is a value concept referring to an ongoing process of improvement undergone by individuals, groups, and societies on their way to perfection. Their progress in this direction is the criterion for their classification, since according to this conception there are some groups and individuals who are more cultured than others. What is implied by defining a group or an individual as "more cultured" is that they are more human than others. Culture is the means by which biological beings are transformed into human beings. Knowledge is here conceived as the product of the most human of human beings, and at the same time as the means by which all people are transformed into human beings. The status of knowledge in education undertaken in this spirit is not utilitarian or instrumental, but ritual. Wisdom and morality, feeling and imagination, reverence, loyalty, and similar human characteristics are thought of as being stored in the knowledge which the human race transmits from one generation to another. By means of this knowledge these characteristics are reestablished in generation after generation of human beings, who remain human by virtue of their presence. Two concepts mediate between this conception of knowledge and the school. One is discipline and the other is character. From the point of view of content, knowledge is allowed to be in a state of constant change, but change is not arbitrary. It is controlled by systems of principles and laws which direct it. These systems, the disciplines, are the constant elements in knowledge which make change possible. (See Phenix, 1962.) Education by and for knowledge means the subjection of the mind of the student to the authority of the disciplines.[4] This holds too for the second mediating concept, character. Character is the product of individual submission to the yoke of principles. Individual initiation into a world of principles, laws, and disciplines in the realms of both intellect and morality is what is meant by education when it is conceived as a technique of acculturation. Man does not acquire knowledge in order to be better off, but in order to be better. (See Eliot, 1948, chap. 6.) This knowledge has no purpose beyond the cultivation of human qualities, and it is valuable for its own sake, i.e., its value is intrinsic. The phychological component in this approach differs from the psychological component in the previous approach. Individuals cannot be induced to accept the authority of principles simply by means of practice. Principles are designed for use in situations for which the individual has not been trained as well as for use in situations with which he is familiar. To be able to use principles effectively in unfamiliar situations the individual must first have internalized them, transformed them into a facet of his own personality. Internalization and not conditioning is therefore the psychological concept which is most representative of this approach to education.

Despite the differences between the two approaches outlined above, they have one common denominator. In both, instruction is regarded as a bridge between knowledge (however interpreted) and the learner. In both, instruction mediates between knowledge, which is a phenomenon defined by inherent laws (models of behavior or disciplines), and the learner who is regarded as lacking in something until he acquires knowledge as given. This common denominator accounts for the fact that in most schools the two conceptions exist side by side: the disciplinary and the instrumental approach, techniques of internalization and techniques of conditioning.

The third approach, characterized by the formula "Knowledge is a means in the process of individuation," differs from both the first and the second in that it does not share their common denominator. In both previous approaches instruction is designed to bridge the gap between student and knowledge where knowledge is regarded by both as the hard and given element in the equation. Knowledge can be programmed for the purposes of instruction; it can be manipulated to a certain extent in order to adapt it to the level of development reached by the student, but only on condition that the structure of knowledge inherent in the disciplines or the models of behavior is not damaged by these manipulations. If it is desired to bridge a gap between two phenomena, one of which is hard and given, it is inevitable that the other will bear the brunt of whatever manipulation is necessary. No wonder that where the end is socialization or acculturation, education is based mainly on manipulating the student. The third approach regards the student as the hard element in the equation which may not be manipulated, and knowledge as the soft element which can (and must) be adapted to the needs of the student. This is the core of the radical approach to knowledge in education.

The principle of individuation is defined as a process "on which depends the breaking up of the general into the particular, into single beings or individuals" (Jacobi, 1965, p. 13). The meaning attributed to this concept by psychologists operating with it today is closely associated with the meaning of the concept of *self-actualization.* Individuation is a process in which the individual actualizes his unique personality and crystallizes his unique identity. The source of energy and the structural basis for the drive to actualize human potentialities is present within human beings and is not imposed from outside. A. Maslow, one of the outstanding representatives of this philosophical-anthropological approach in psychology, has described the principle of individuation in the following terms (1959, p. 130):

> Man demonstrates *in his own nature* a pressure toward fuller and fuller Being, more and more perfect actualization of his humanness in exactly the same naturalistic, scientific sense that an acorn may be said to be "pressing toward" being an oak tree, or that a tiger can be observed to "push toward" tigerish, or a horse toward being equine. Man is not molded or shaped into humanness or

taught to be human. The role of the environment is ultimately to permit him or help him to actualize *his own* potentialities, not its potentialities. The environment does not give him potentialities and capacities; he has them in inchoate or embryonic form, just exactly as he has embryonic arms and legs.

The assumption underlying these words requires that education (and also instruction) be given a different interpretation from the one implied in the two previous approaches. We do not learn humanity by acquiring social roles or by internalizing the principles, values, and norms of a specific culture. Humanity is a given datum present in human beings, and education is the process designed to enable the individual to actualize his own humanity, which is unique to him as an individual different from others. We thus arrive at a further assumption. The imparting of knowledge whether as a means of socialization or as a means of acculturation is a process designed to make people alike (or at least to mold them according to patterns of given social roles or cultural groups). Society with its patterns and mechanisms and culture with its values and norms are designed to serve as common denominators for individuals who are different from one another. The differences among people make it necessary to adapt the means of imparting knowledge, but as far as ends are concerned, all people are considered equal. Knowledge must be imparted differently to gifted children and to ordinary children, but the role which it is expected to play is the same for both. In this sense, the difference between people is something which has to be overcome in order to include everyone in the common denominator which is given in society (according to those whose end is socialization) or in culture (according to those whose end is acculturation).

According to the radical conception of education, diversity is not an obstacle to be overcome but a basic premise defining the humanity of human beings. H. Read, one of the representatives of modern radicalism in education, explains this point as follows (1944, pp. 16-17):

This diversity is not a biological accident. It is the dialectical basis of natural selection, of human evolution. Any attempt, therefore, whether by education or coercion, to eliminate the differences between persons would frustrate the natural dissemination and growth of the human race. It is possible and even "scientific" to hold that we should attempt to control this growth just as we have controlled the growth of species like the horse and the sheep. But such control could only be effectively exercised if we had an agreed aim in view. We breed horses for strength or speed, sheep for a finer fleece. But it is a godlike assumption to breed the human race for any predetermined quality, and the idea has only entered the minds of totalitarian philosophers like Plato and Hegel, or been the policy of extreme fanatists who have attempted to put the ideals of such philosophers into practice.

The human in man is not something which he receives from outside himself, but something which is inherent in him and which is manifested in ways which are not standard but personal. To be human does not mean to be like someone or something; to be human always means to be distinct, to be unique. Diversity is a necessary condition both for the actualization of the human in the individual and for the survival of the human race.

In any consideration of the problem of knowledge and its place in education the assumptions discussed above create great difficulties. In the conception of instruction as a technique of socialization the place of knowledge is clear: it is a kind of catalogue of patterns of behavior. In the conception of instruction as an instrument of acculturation the place of knowledge is also clear: it is human wisdom and experience crystallized and organized in principles and values. According to both these conceptions knowledge is both the means and the model for molding the personalities of the young. But what is knowledge and what is its function in an education whose guiding assumption is that the developmental model for the individual lies within, inside the developing person himself?

This question defines the theoretical difficulty but does not exhaust it. Development must be defined as taking place "from within" without doing away with the necessity for external factors to support and assist the process. Development can be attributed to internal factors which are actualized only in interaction with external factors. In this case, too, the place of knowledge in education is clear: it consists of those factors outside the individual in interaction with which he actualizes his developmental potential. However, this solution (adopted by those who regard instruction as a means of acculturation) is likely to conflict with the recognition of diversity as a quality which defines the human. If the interaction between developmental potential and knowledge ends by advancing conformity, similarity, and uniformity, then it will have helped to bring about that state of affairs feared by Read: the frustration of the growth and dissemination of the human race, let alone the frustration of the developmental potential of the individual person. In a more concrete form, this problem may be presented thus: intellectual development, according to this conception, depends on the intellectual potential which is present in the individual, but which will not be actualized unless he is brought into interaction with areas of knowledge outside himself, e.g., mathematics or history. But mathematics is a *relatively* stable system of thought, and so is history, or at least so are the ways of thinking about and evaluating historical events habitual in various historical schools. What is to be expected when the individual learner comes into interaction with these areas of knowledge? It is to be expected that he will gradually adapt himself to the ways of thinking characteristic of the mathematical and historical disciplines. This adaptation means that the individual student will, in his ways of thinking, become like those who studied history and mathematics before him. This similarity means the elimination of the uniqueness and the narrowing down of the diversity which the radical conception defined as basic conditions for the actualization of human being. And this is the core of the difficulty in defining the status of knowledge in education in the spirit of the radical conception.

Publications composed in the radical spirit may be classified into a number of categories. The broadest of these is the category dealing with criticism of existing schools and education (for example, Holt, 1964, and Goodman, 1964). A second category consists of attempts to establish alternative theories of education and instruction (for example, Read, 1944; Sanford, 1963; Leonard, 1968; Soderquist, 1964). A third category describes attempts to put radical theories into practice (Sudbury Valley School District, 1970; Barth, 1969). In each of these categories it is possible to discern the theoretical sources sustaining the radical approach to modern education. One of these sources is the social radicalism centering around anarchistic ideologies whose representatives include B. Russell, H. Read, P. Goodman, and Ivan Ilich. A second source of modern educational radicalism is to be found among existentialist thinkers, especially among those who have attempted to establish psychological theories on existentialist foundations, such as A. Maslow (1962), C. Rogers (1969), and many others whose names are associated with the *Journal of Humanistic Psychology*. The third source which sustains the radical approach to modern education is to be found in the Freudian "left," represented by H. Marcuse, W. Reich, E. Fromm, and others. (See Robinson, 1969.)

Radicalism is neither a method nor a program, and it cannot be defined or described in the way that a philosophical method or a psychological school can be defined or described. Radicalism is a mood[5] which gives rise on the one hand to criticism of education as it exists, and on the other hand to ideas about alternative ways of education. The connection between these ideas is not necessarily one of logical consistency. Ideas which may appear to be conflicting or contradictory are united by virtue of the mood which embraces and which gave birth to them. The tenets of anarchistic ideology, the themes of existentialist philosophy, and the implications of psychoanalysis were not miraculously transformed into a coherent system of thought by means of some radical principle or other: on the contrary, critical thinking which preceded them adopted from these systems a number of assumptions, conclusions, and ideas which suited its needs, although they did not combine to form a system capable of withstanding close logical scrutiny. There is thus no reason to expect a systematic, well-founded and conclusive answer to the difficulties experienced in defining the status of knowledge in the radical conception of education from its proponents. Their answer is given in terms of the discovery of and commitment to an alternative. What is the nature of this alternative?

Unlike the status of knowledge as defined by the dominant socializatory and acculturative trends in the institutionalized education of our society, the radical approach to education regards knowledge as a means designed to further three main processes:

1. The intensification of creativity
2. The intensification of subjectivity
3. The intensification of self-awareness.

CREATIVITY

The promotion of creativity is a fashionable slogan in education today. It is popular not only in radical circles but also with many of the high priests of tradition and routine in education. Even those who regard education as a means of socialization bring forward arguments of their own in support of creativity as an educational goal: modern science, technology, and society, all need people who are willing and able to innovate, invent, and change (see Torrance, 1970). Like any other idea in education, the idea of creativity derives its meaning from the context in which it is presented. Creativity in the spirit of socialization differs from creativity in the spirit of acculturation. In the latter, creativity is associated with the concept of method (see Ryle, 1949). The concept of creativity proposed by the radicals is rooted in the conception of the educative process as a process of individuation by means of self-actualization. E. Fromm (1959, p. 163) describes this idea in the following terms:

Well-being I would describe as the ability to be creative, to be aware, and to respond; to be independent and fully active, and by this very fact to be one with the world. To be concerned with *being*, not with *having*; to experience joy in the very act of living—and to consider living creatively as the only meaning of life. Well-being is not an assumption in the mind of a person. It is expressed in his whole body, in the way he walks, in the tonus of his muscles.

Creativity as described by Fromm and others (see Sanford, 1968) is a condition of well-being, and well-being is the aim of life. Creativity is not desired because it is a condition of creation, although it ensures that creation will take place. Creativity is a mode of life, an individual mode which prevents human life from being emptied of meaning.

We are not concerned here with the psychological description of creativity, but with its epistemological implications. What are the implications of this interpretation of creativity for the status of knowledge in the life of the individual and especially in the process of instruction? Knowledge is here conceived as the raw material designed to enable the individual to actualize his drive to create. This statement is not in itself sufficient to characterize the radical view of knowledge and creativity. Whenever knowledge and creativity are considered together, knowledge is seen as the object of creativity. What characterizes the radical view is the rejection of the inherent prescriptive structure of knowledge. It is not the laws according to which knowledge is organized which dictate the permissible limits of its manipulation, but the characteristics of the creative person which determine the type, the scope, the direction, and the nature of the manipulations possible.

The background against which this view grew up may be identified without too much difficulty. The rapid changes in knowledge, the expectations of further changes, the speed with which one theory succeeds another in the various areas of research, in short the dynamics of modern science, all went to strengthen a belief in experimentation, in daring, in independence of conventions and authorities. In this atmosphere it was possible for an epistemological position to crystallize which gave the creative spirit of the individual person priority over the principles of knowledge evolved over generations of creation.

Changes in modern science, however, while no doubt assisting the attitude towards knowledge described above to take shape, were not in themselves sufficient for its crystallization. Another factor which came into play in the radical mood was the identification of knowledge with culture and the evaluation of culture as a mechanism of repression.

For the individual to enjoy a state of well-being he must be liberated from the culture which enslaves him by means of knowledge and repression. (See Read, 1963; Henry, 1963; Cooper, 1968.)

> A large part of education will always be devoted to the formation of a person, which will make the individual "clean about the house" and socially presentable, and will teach him, not what is but what may be regarded as, real; all human societies are at all times far more interested in instructing their members in the techniques of not looking, of overlooking and of looking the other way than in sharpening their observation, increasing their alertness and fostering their love of truth. [Neumann, 1969, p. 38].

Creativity in relation to knowledge is regarded by radicals in education as an act of liberation from culture with its patterns and authority. In this sense it is a necessary condition for the well-being of the individual, who is enabled to actualize himself by manipulating knowledge without enslaving his being to the repressive mechanisms operated by culture through knowledge.

SUBJECTIVITY

Subjectivity as the attitude of the individual toward knowledge is in this context identical to meaningfulness. Knowledge exists in the learner when it is meaningful in his life. When it is not meaningful it leads to the dehumanization of its possessor. He becomes its tool and instrument and takes no responsibility for what he knows. It is the subjectivity of knowledge which gives it its validity.

Van Cleve Morris (1966, pp. 121-23) argues:

> Knowledge is always in part subjective. That is, for anything to be true, it must first pass into and be taken hold of by some subjective consciousness. It must be *chosen*, i.e., appropriated, before it can be true for that consciousness. Knowledge is not something purely objective and laid out to be learned (at bottom, knowledge *becomes* knowledge only when a subjectivity takes hold of it and puts it into his own life). In this sense, then, the individual may be said to be responsible for his own knowledge . . . school subjects are only tools for the realization of subjectivity.

The choice in favor of subjectivity is an epistemological choice par excellence, clearly influenced by existentialist philosophy. Even so, however, educational radicalism is not a logical extension and systematic development of existentialist epistemology. The concept of subjectivity in the radical mood is sustained by a further source which has nothing to do with a rational examination of the nature of knowledge. The assumption of subjectivity frees the teacher from the necessity of manipulating his students. The opposite assumption—that knowledge is objective or has intrinsic value—obliges the teacher to "mold," to "structure," to "direct," etc., the mind of the student, for without this assistance there can be no certainty that he will ever arrive at a comprehension of the principles underlying the disciplines or the values implicit in knowledge. The moment the teacher recognizes subjectivity as the test of meaning he grants the student the status of the hard factor in education, and knowledge becomes the soft factor which must be adapted to meet his requirements. At the same time he also abolishes the authority implicitly granted knowledge in traditional conceptions of education, and with it his own authority as the one who imparts knowledge. Subjectivity in the radical conception of education is an assumption which facilitates a student-centered education, based on the interests of the student and the needs of his development, and committed toward him.

SELF-AWARENESS

Knowledge serves education as a means in establishing the ability of the individual to understand the world and himself by exercising his reason. In Western societies, rationalism, in the spirit of acculturation, is regarded as a basic value. Unfortunately, however, the road from rationalism to rationalization is short and extremely slippery. Rationalization is a defense mechanism which far from furthering the reasoning powers of the individual sabotages them severely. The individual may be endangered in two ways by the cultivation of his intellect. The first of these is the deformation of his personality to such an extent that it becomes an instrument subservient to the knowledge imparted to him. This is the case with many scientists and research workers whose human experience has been so impoverished that they have become part of their own scientific apparatus. While this process may be regarded as the price to be paid for the achievements of mankind in revealing the secrets of nature, it is also possible to cast doubt on the value of the contributions to knowledge made by personalities so deformed. The second danger is more serious and lacks even the advantage of contributing knowledge. People whose lives are completely subjugated to reason may end up by being incapable of using their reason at all. This is what has happened to hundreds of thousands of people whose imaginations, emotions, and perceptions, the controls vital to the regulation of reason, have so far decayed that they are dependent for their functioning on stereotypes and other arbitrary concepts internalized at one or another stage of their lives, and cannot look at the world without them. Knowledge can be a very dangerous instrument in the hands of education because it tends to become a center of authority giving rise to a heteronomic attitude in the individual toward it.

The passionate desire to liberate mankind which is characteristic of the radical mood is revealed in the sensitivity of the radicals to the danger of men's minds being enslaved and their liberty lost to the despotism of knowledge which has been accumulated and structured by previous generations. The educational problem which presents itself here is how to impart knowledge to a person so that he will control it and not it him. The way to achieve this goal is by promoting the self-awareness of the individual. Self-awareness in this context has a twofold meaning. In the first place it is designed to play a hygienic role in the mental life of the individual. This idea is derived from psychoanalysts and is essentially an attempt to prevent suppression and repression thus doing away with the need for defense mechanisms, including rationalization. In the second place, self-awareness is the product and the distinguishing characteristic of individuation. On this interpretation self-awareness is not a means but the supreme goal of education.

According to W. A. Weisskopf (1969):

> Individuation is the process which leads to the split between consciousness and the unconscious. A tendency toward individuation is at work in man, something which drives man to become aware of himself. The result is a separation of self and world. The same tendency may have created being out of non-being, life out of an organic nature, and consciousness out of life. The source and the ground of this tendency is unknown and can only be "explained" by theology and metaphysics. Whatever its origin, it is a definite ontological datum. Consciousness, the last phenomenon in this evolution, consists in the transcending of the given situation. Man is the living being which "is" and at the same time knows that he is. Therefore he asks the ontological question (Heidegger), the question of the meaning of his existence, of the whence and whither. The striving for a meaning is a direct consequence of transcending being through consciousness.
>
> Conscious transcendence includes not only knowledge of what actually is but also the knowledge of alternative potentialities. However, the finite nature of man requires choices between alternative possibilities.

According to this view self-awareness is on the one hand a process of detachment, of the emergence of the identity of the individual as a separate being, of his emergence as an autonomous creature. On the other hand, self-awareness is the basis of life which is always the product of a choice between alternatives. The alternative which is chosen makes all the others impossible. Self-awareness is a recognition of the limitations of the possibilities present in human life and the acceptance by the individual of responsibility for his own decisions. By means of self-awareness the individual accepts the reality principle on the one hand and responsibility for his life on the other.

N. Sandford translates this idea into the language of teaching:

> The teacher's role is not only to provide external, logical challenges to the opinions a student proffers in class, but also to turn the student's scrutiny inward upon himself in search of the sources of his beliefs. He ought to be encouraged to think, for example, in classes of history, politics, anthropology, economics, and sociology, how his character has been shaped by western culture, by his social class, and by the town he came from. A teacher of literature may insist that his students understand fictional characters before judging them; this requires a student's ego to identify, at least for the purposes of understanding, with personalities quite alien to his—in short, to develop a measure of tolerance. [Sutich, 1969, pp. 862-63]

The epistemological meaning of knowledge from the point of view of awareness as a goal of education is that of a sample of alternatives assisting the student who comes into contact with them to become aware of himself.

Creativity as a mode of life, subjectivity as a test of the validity of knowledge, and self-awareness as its goal are the dimensions of knowledge in the radical conception of education. Taken together, they give knowledge a new status in instruction, differing from any other in the history of education. This status is essentially an instrumental one—knowledge is an instrument—but not in the same sense that it is an instrument in instruction regarded as socialization. In the radical interpretation knowledge is not an instrument to train the young to take part in social life, nor to place them in defined social roles (although occupation with knowledge trains them for this too) but an instrument which is designed mainly to further the process of their emergence as unique individuals, i.e., their individuation.

Educational instrumentality is also attributed to knowledge in the conception of instruction as a technique of acculturation. While mathematics, literature, history, philosophy, etc., are regarded as having intrinsic value, these areas of knowledge are also regarded as instruments by means of which the characteristics of the learner are formed and molded. Radicals, too, see knowledge as an instrument in the process of the emergence of the individual, but they reject the ritualistic-intrinsic attitude toward it. The value of knowledge is measured by its ability to provide the young learner with opportunities for self-actualization. Since people who learn are different from one another, it may be assumed that opportunities for self-actualization will be provided in different areas of knowledge for different people.

The psychological-didactic approach postulated from this epistemological position may be reduced to one central principle: self-regulation.

The concept of self-regulation is more characteristic than any other of the uniqueness of radical thought in education. The radical position can be distinguished from all other educational theories by means of this master concept which grants new meaning to several basic concepts defining instruction.

The first of these concepts is that of motivation. In most theories of instruction (and of educational psychology) motivation is regarded as a means which must be activated in order for the student to learn. The principle of self-regulation renounces manipulations of the student's motivation on the assumption that the drive to activity is an inborn human characteristic and as long as this primary motivation is allowed to remain alive it will lead to exploratory behavior in an environment where the necessary conditions for learning are created. Most schools however use secondary motivations—achievement motivation, social motivation, motivation stemming from a sense of duty. The common denominator of all these motivations is that before learning what he is supposed to learn at school, the student has already learned that all learning is a nuisance. A nuisance which must be borne in order to get ahead of others in the competitive procedures enshrined in the vast majority of classrooms, or win the approval of parents and teachers, or escape the pangs of the punishing conscience. J. Holt (1964), one of the representatives of radicalism who is also closely involved in the practical work of education, argues that:

> We destroy the disinterested (I do *not* mean *un*interested) love of learning in children, which is so strong when they are small, by encouraging and compelling them to work for petty and contemptible rewards—gold stars, or papers marked 100 and tacked to the wall, or A's on report cards, or honor rolls, or dean's lists, or Phi Beta Kappa keys—in short, for the ignoble satisfaction of feeling that they are better than someone else. We encourage them to feel that the end and aim of all they do in school is nothing more than to get a good mark on a test, or to impress someone with what they seem to know. We kill, not only their curiosity, but their feeling that it is a good and admirable thing to be curious, so that by the age of ten most of them will not ask questions, and will show a good deal of scorn for the few who do. [P. 168]

Self-regulation means a choice in favor of primary motivations, in favor of activity motivated by curiosity and not by competition, the need to belong or a sense of duty.

The second concept which derives new meaning from self-regulation is learning. Learning is a process which leads to changes in the behavior of the learner. It is not however a single uniform process. Conditioning changes behavior, identification changes behavior, and self-exploratory activity changes behavior, too. These three processes are different in kind and different in their products. Behavior formed by habit differs from behavior chosen in accordance with an internalized principle, and both differ from creative behavior. Different types of learning may be classified into two groups: learning which exploits the potential present in the learner and learning which enriches this potential. The products of the first type of learning are behaviors which are to some extent fixed. The success of this type of learning is measured by the fact that no further change takes place in the area of the learned behavior. Since all development is also change, this means that learning of this type is designed to put a stop to development in the area of learning. In this sense learning of this type exploits existing developmental potential. The second type of learning is designed to encourage developmental potential, i.e., to ensure the possibility of further change. The criterion for the success of this type of learning is not what the student has learned, but what he is still able to learn and is actually learning on the basis of what he has already learned. (See Leonard, 1968.) This second type of learning can only take place on condition that it answers the primary needs of the student, his curiosity, his drive to activity, and reinforces them. Such learning depends on the self-regulation of the student. According to Holt (1964, p. 179) "We cannot have real learning in school if we think it is our duty and our right to tell children what they must learn. We cannot know at any moment, what particular bit of knowledge or understanding a child needs most, will most strengthen and best fit his model of reality. Only he can do this. He may not do it very well, but he can do it a hundred times better than we can."

The third and last concept deriving new meaning from self-regulation and complementing the others, is that of leadership in instruction. In traditional instruction the role of leader is exclusively assigned to the teacher, because this type of instruction is built on the assumption (usually not explicit) that in the process of their schooling students develop a resistance to learning. The teacher is thus required to lead, i.e., to direct the wills of his students. In the process of this direction, what almost inevitably happens is that the wills of the students are deflected from learning toward satisfying the expectations of the teacher-leader. Traditional instruction has no answer to this problem even when deploring its results. In the view of radical educators, the teacher has a different role to play. He is called upon to organize the environment of his students in such a way that it will provide sufficient stimuli to engage them in interaction with it. The interaction of the individual with his environment is a necessary condition for learning, and if the interaction takes place through self-regulation, self-motivation, and learning for its own sake, it ensures the enrichment of developmental potential and leads to self-actualization and eventually to individuation: to the emergence of an autonomous and authentic individual person.

In the radical conception of education the status of knowledge in instruction is that of one of the components in the total learning environment. The interaction of the individual with his environment is the mechanism which enables him to develop his abilities and characteristics. When this interaction is *directed* by education, *directed* development of the individual's abilities and characteristics takes place, i.e., a molding or structuring of his personality. The model for this molding or structuring is the personality type preferred by a given culture or society. The anarchistic element in educational radicalism rejects this model because it rejects existing cultures and existing societies. The existentialist element in radicalism rejects this model because it rejects all predetermined models for man. (See Sartre, 1966, p. 755.) The psychoanalytic element in radicalism rejects this model because it regards it as the product of repression, by means of which man is distorted by society. This is the basis for the rejection of direction by educational radicalism and its expectation that the interaction created between the young person and his environment will support his development without forcing it into patterns and molds. The status of knowledge in this view is no different from the status of objects, interpersonal relations, and other possible factors in the environment: it is an object through which the learner explores his environment and especially himself. The specific strategy adopted by radicals in education with regard to curriculum planning arises from this conception of the status of knowledge in instruction. Curriculum planning in the radical conception means organizing the environment. This is a subject, however, which cannot be dealt with within the framework of this discussion.

Can it be argued that the epistemological and psychological components of modern radicalism in education constitute a closed and coherent system? Do its assumptions provide grounds for answering the questions to which the process of instruction gives rise in these areas?

These questions can only be answered by another question: have closed coherent systems proved more productive for educational theory and practice than moods which lacked strict systems but were sensitive to real problems not recognized by prevailing systems precisely because they were closed?

NOTES

1. An attempt to discover the epistemological components in the various conceptions of instruction has been made, and with a great measure of success, by I. Scheffler (1965).

In this essay the author analyzes the meaning of philosophical texts which illuminate the epistemological points of view of theories of instruction. The direction of his inquiry is therefore from philosophical sources to the theories of instruction. An understanding of instruction necessitates, too, an inquiry in the opposite direction: from instructional practices to the theories of instruction and theories of knowledge. An inquiry of this nature reveals the transformation undergone by epistemological assumptions on their way from philosophical theories to theories of instruction and finally to instructional practices. Another example of an analysis of the epistemological components in instructional theories before they are transformed is J. T. Fox (1969).

2. The same is true for theories of learning which undergo a similar transformation. A proper understanding of the concepts of condition, motivation, internalization, etc., in their original psychological context may thus contribute little to the understanding of their usage in the context of educational practice.

3. Although Piaget (1971, pp. 66–67) deals with this method when describing the schools of the eastern European people's republics, the characteristics of this method can be found everywhere. "The first of these [ideological] inspirations tends to present mental life as being the product of the combination of two essential factors: the biological factor and social life. The organic factor provides for the existence of the conditions for learning: the laws of primary 'conditioning' (in the Pavlovian sense) and those of the second system of sign-forming, or the system of language. Social life, on the other hand, provides the totality of practical rules and bodies of knowledge arrived at collectively and passed on from one generation to the next."

Similar descriptions of this kind of teaching are given by many of the radical critics of the prevailing school.

Paulo Freire (1971, p. 58) has labeled this pattern of instruction as the banking concept of education: "Education thus becomes an act of depositing in which the students are depositories and the teacher is the depositor."

Neil Postman and Charles Weingartner (1969, p. 32) describe this kind of teaching as being based on the "vaccination theory" of education, "and if you have 'had' it you are immune and need not take it again."

4. This does not mean that all the knowledge imparted by such teaching stems from disciplines, rather that teaching in this epistemological framework is

regarded primarily as a technique for training the pupil in the principles of organized knowledge, i.e., in disciplines.

5. I have borrowed the concept *mood* from K. D. Benne (1967). Benne distinguishes between the therapeutic mood, prophetic-revolutionary mood, and liberal-optimistic mood.

REFERENCES

Barth, B.S. "Open Education, Assumptions About Learning and Knowledge," *Journal of Education Philosophy and Theory* 1 (1969): 29–39.

Benne, K.D. *Education for Tragedy*. Lexington: University of Kentucky Press, 1967.

Cooper, D. (ed.). *The Dialectics of Liberation*. Baltimore, Md.: Penguin, 1968.

Eliot, T.S. *Notes Toward the Definition of Culture*. London: Faber and Faber, 1948.

Fox, J.T. "Epistemology, Psychology and Their Relevance for Education in Bruner and Dewey," *Educational Theory* 19 (Winter 1969): 58–79.

Freire, Paulo. *Pedagogy of the Oppressed*. New York: Herder and Herder, 1971.

Fromm, E. "Values, Psychology and Human Existence." In A. Maslow and P.A. Sorokin (eds.), *New Knowledge in Human Values*. New York: Harper and Row, 1959.

Goodman, P. *Compulsory Mis-Education and the Community of Scholars*. New York: Vintage, 1964.

Henry, Jules. *Culture Against Man*. New York: Random House, 1963.

Holt, John. *How Children Fail*. New York: Dell, 1964.

Jacobi, J. *The Way of Individuation*. New York: Harcourt, Brace and World, 1965.

Leonard, G.B. *Education and Ecstasy*. New York: Dell, 1968.

Maslow, Abraham. "Psychological Data and Value Theory." In A. Maslow and P.A. Sorokin (eds.), *New Knowledge in Human Values*. New York: Harper and Row, 1959.

Maslow, Abraham. *Toward a Psychology of Being*. Princeton, N.J.: Von Nostrand, 1962.

Morris, Van Cleve. *Existentialism in Education*. New York: Harper and Row, 1966.

Neumann, Erich. *Depth Psychology and a New Ethic*. London: Hodder and Stoughton, 1969.

Phenix, Philip H. "The Disciplines as Curriculum Context." In A. Harry Passow (ed.), *Curriculum Crossroads*, pp. 57–65. New York: Teachers College Press, 1962.

Piaget, J. *Science of Education and the Psychology of the Child*. New York: Viking Press, 1971.

Postman, Neil, and Charles Weingartner. *Teaching as a Subversive Activity*. New York: Dell Publishing Co., 1969.

Read, Herbert. *The Education of Free Men*. London Freedom Press, 1944.

Read, Herbert. *To Hell with Culture*. New York: Schocken Books, 1963.

Robinson, P.A. *The Freudian Left*. New York: Harper and Row, 1969.
Rogers, C. *Freedom to Learn*. Columbus, Ohio: Merrill, 1969.
Ryle, G. *The Concept of Mind*. London: Hutchinson, 1949.
Sanford, N. "Education for Individual Development," *American Journal of Orthopsychiatry* 38: 5 (October 1963).
Sartre, J.P. *Being and Nothingness*. New York: Washington Square Press, 1966.
Scheffler, I. "Philosophical Models of Teaching," *Harvard Educational Review* 35 (Spring 1965): 131–43.
Soderquist, H.O. *The Person and Education*. Columbus, Ohio: Merrill, 1964.
Sudbury Valley School District. *The Crisis in American Education, An Analysis and a Proposal*. Sudbury Valley School Press, 1970.
Sutich, A.S., et al. (eds.), *Readings in Humanistic Psychology*. New York: Free Press, 1969.
Torrance, E.P. "Achieving Socialization without Sacrificing Creativity," *The Journal of Creative Behavior* 4: 3 (1970): 183–89.
Weisskopf, W.A. "Existential Crisis and the Unconscious." In A.S. Sutich et al. (eds.), *Readings in Humanistic Psychology*. New York: Free Press, 1969.

Selection 2.5

A Transcendental Developmental Ideology of Education

James B. Macdonald

The title was prompted by the recent Kohlberg and Mayer (1972) article entitled "Development as an Aim of Education." They talk about three ideologies: romantic, developmental, and cultural transmission. It is clear to me that there are at least two other potential ideologies that I am calling radical and transcendental developmental. I shall attempt to step off from Kohlberg and Mayer's framework to discuss briefly the radical ideology and to develop what I believe to be a transcendental developmental ideology. It is my contention that the radical and transcendental ideologies are the most potentially useful in the modern world.

The elements or components of ideologies as described by Kohlberg and Mayer are psychological theories, epistemological components, and ethical value positions. These correspond roughly with the philosopher's concern for ontological, epistemological, and axiological considerations. Essentially this amounts to a statement of the nature of man, the nature of knowledge, and the nature of values.

The romantic ideology Kohlberg and Mayer perceive is fundamentally concerned with human nature and the unfolding or maturation of the individual. Knowledge in this ideology is said to be existential or phenomenological, and it refers directly to the inner experience of the self. Truth is self-knowledge and extends to others by sympathetic understanding of other selves. The ethical theory of

SOURCE. In *Heightened Consciousness, Cultural Revolution, and Curriculum Theory,* ed. William Pinar (Berkeley, Calif.: McCutchan, 1974), pp. 85-116.

the romantic is based upon the freedom of the individual to be himself, assuming that individuals, when free, are essentially good unless society makes them otherwise.

The cultural transmission ideology is grounded in behaviorist psychology. Essentially the individual is shaped by his environmental experiences in terms of the associations and stimulus-response sets he encounters and acquires. Knowledge is the outer reality, the "objective" world, that can be found in sense experience and culturally shared. Value theory is either an ethically neutral stance or a social relativism that accepts the present cultural values for which there would appear to be consensus.

Between these two, in the sense that it is neither a model of inner experience or outer experience but a dialectic between inner and outer, lies developmental ideology. The transaction itself creates reality which is neither an inner nor an outer phenomenon, but something else. Dewey's method of intelligence and the cognitive-developmental work of Piaget with its concern for inner structures and outer structures encountered in interaction are the psychological models for this ideology. Knowledge is equated with a resolved relationship between inner experience and outer reality. Truth is pragmatic in that it depends upon its relationship to the situation in which we find ourselves. Values are based upon ethical universals derived philosophically, and they serve as developmental means and ends. Thus rational ethical principles, not the actual values of the child or the culture, serve as arbiters for defining aims.

Analysis of these ideologies suggests that the following elements are the critical aspects of ideology. Figure 2.5-1 illustrates this.

Figure 2.5-1 is of course highly simplistic, but it illustrates the inner and outer aspects of ideology and the dominant directions of the critical flow of the human encounter. Thus, the romantic conception is mainly from inner to outer, the cultural transmission from outer to inner, and the developmental is dialectical.

Kohlberg and Mayer assume that the radical position is equivalent to the romantic, or at least they use these terms interchangeably at times. This I believe to be in error. It is in error, that is, if radical is meant to imply political radicalism of a Marxian persuasion.

The political radical is committed to a dialectical model, as is the developmental. However, as the work of Paulo Freire (1970, p. 186) shows, it has a fundamentally different interpretation of the dialectic.

The developmental and radical models look identical only on the surface, for the radical model is weighted on the side of social realities. The developmental model is weighted on the side of inner cognitive structures. The progressive position assumed that democracy was the ideal social reality and continued its analysis of the interaction process with that assumption in mind. The radical model, on the other hand, is essentially based upon an analysis of why democratic ideas are not realized, thus emphasizing environmental structures.

We still do not generally recognize this radical thrust in curriculum thinking, but the growing edge of writing in the past five or ten years leans toward a resurgence of romanticism and a renewal of past reconstructionist terms of the radical tradition. Neither is, I believe, the same as its predecessor, and I shall try to use historical perspective to validate both assertions.

The political view of curriculum that appears to provide the most

FIGURE 2.5-1. Elements in Educational Ideology

(A) Romantic

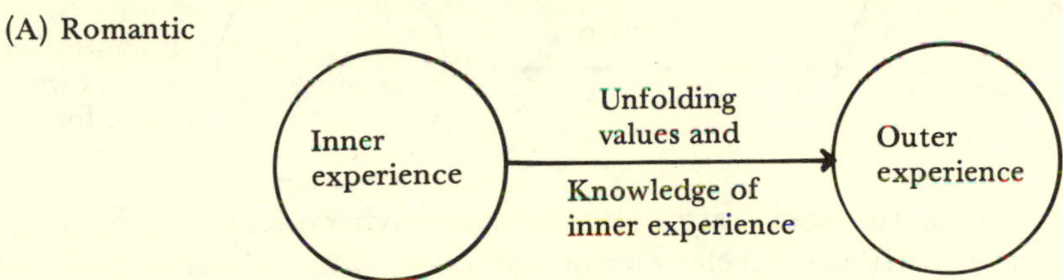

(B) Cultural transmission

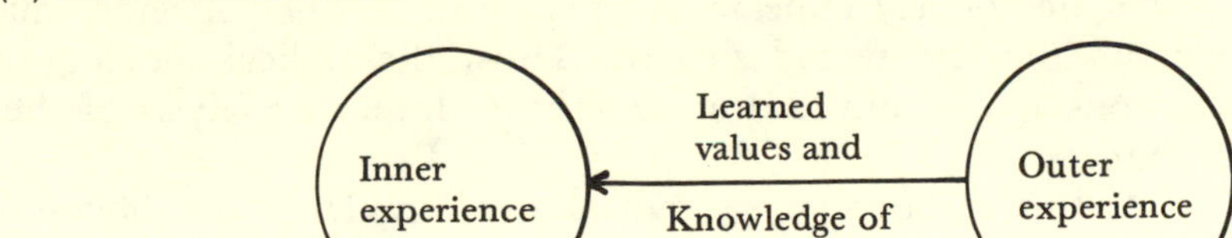

(C) Developmental

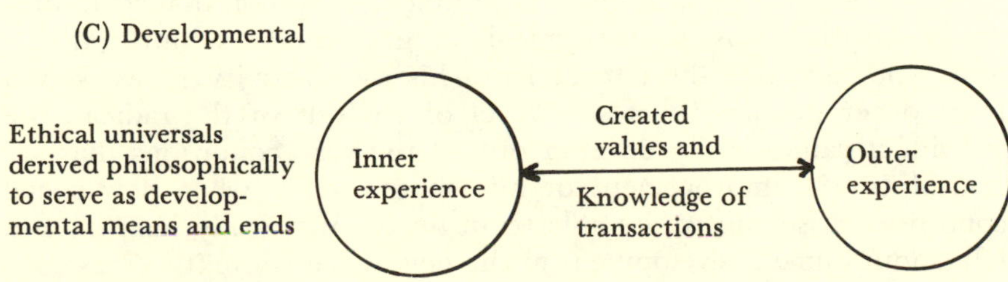

satisfying analysis is Marxian in orientation. There are classical and Neo-Marxian differences of opinion that are of great interest and impact. However, I shall try to generalize the radical position as an ideology in terms of what Kohlberg and Mayer left out.

The radical point of view takes off from the essential proposition that the critical element in human life is the way people live together. It further posits that the way people live together is determined essentially by the structure of our economic arrangements, the ownership of means of production, and the distribution of goods and services through the possession of power.

FIGURE 2.5-2. Model of Praxis

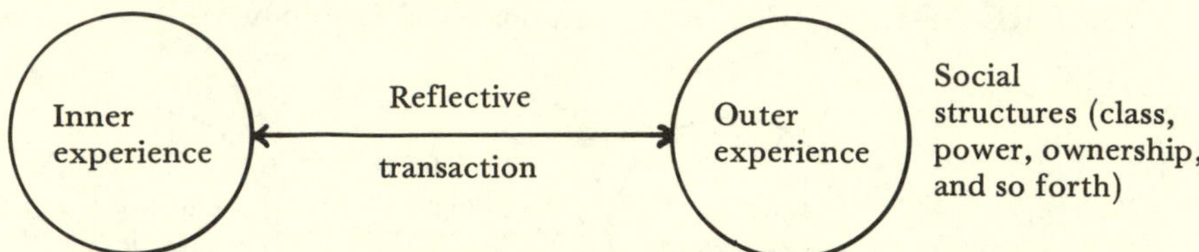

It is the social structures of the environment that provide the radical with his developmental impetus, rather than the biological structures of development in the individual that are so important for the liberal or progressive. This is not to say that either group ignores the other, but it is to say that the democratic ideal of the liberal as the social condition best able to foster individual development leaves much to be desired in terms of its usefulness for a historical analysis of why democracy appears to operate in a rather different manner than its rhetoric would suggest. Thus, the radical ideology raises questions that could lead us to another level of analysis of the curriculum.

At this level of analysis, radical ideology claims that liberal developmental ideology and romantic ideology are embedded in the present system. That is, the emphasis upon the individual and his unfolding or developing necessitates an acceptance of the social structures as status quo in order to identify in any empirical manner the development of the individual. Thus, developmental theory is culture and society bound, and it is bound to the kind of a system that structures human relationships in hierarchical dominance and submission patterns and alienates the person from his own activity in work and from other people. Given the level of analysis of the radical, the individual cannot fully develop out of the very conditions that are central to the improvement of human life. Only when new social conditions arise will we be able to begin to empirically identify and talk about human development in the new social context.

At this level of questions a radical curriculum thinker might ask:

1. How are the patterns of human relationships found in the broader society revealed in schools?
2. What function does the school have in the system, and how does this affect practices?
3. Why is there unequal opportunity to learn in schools, at least in terms of race and social class?
4. Why are textbooks biased in terms of race and sex, and why is history nonauthentic or biased?
5. Do schools provide for unequal access to knowledge by the way they operate?
6. How should we structure human relationships in school?

There are, of course, radical answers to such questions. However, questions tend to frame the answers we get, and the critical point here is that educational problems become quite different when one looks at them from a radical perspective.

My problem with the radical or political view of curriculum is not its level of analysis or the questions it asks, per se; instead, it is the feeling I have that it is also one step behind the world. Thus, I feel that, as McLuhan once said, we are traveling down a superhighway at faster and faster speeds looking out the rearview mirror. Kohlberg and Mayer's three ideologies are "over the hill," so to speak, but the political view is in the mirror. It does provide us with some idea of how straight the road is ahead provided our speed does not exceed our reaction time. What we need is some way to look beyond, if only a few feet.

The radical view of education in its political manifestations does provide us with a historical analysis—as well as with concepts for analyzing contemporary phenomena. Yet I find this historical view limiting in its materialistic focus, and I suspect that it is grounded fundamentally in the Industrial Revolution and reflects the same linear rationality and conceptualizing that characterizes the rise of science and technology. It is a "social science" of human relations and a "science" of history. Like all history, this is a special reading of the past that helped make sense out of the nineteenth-century present. The world today is not the same, and a different reading of history is needed to help make sense of our contemporary world.

The radical-political perspective as a base for curriculum thinking does not adequately allow for the tacit dimension of culture: it is a hierarchical historical view that has outlived its usefulness both in terms of the emerging structure of the environment and of the psyches of people today. I propose that the structure of the world environment today must be approached through the existence of a nuclear, electronic-computerized, multimedia technology rather than the more linear, single-media machine world. Further, I would propose that concomitant psychological structures in individuals must be viewed in a different perspective. I would like to reflect briefly upon these two ideas and then project some new questions for curriculum thinking.

Our present technology and our present world population have restricted our political options in ways we could not have readily foreseen. We are faced with such problems as energy crises that threaten the very survival of members of our population. Short of detechnologizing society, we are faced with the fact that political action that in any way threatens our fundamental technological cultural base is no longer a viable alternative unless we are willing, in the name of ideals, to inflict untold suffering and the threat of extinction on millions of human beings. Freedom to stop the workings of "the system" via revolution of some sort is no longer simply a threat to the power factions in our society; it is indeed a threat to all human beings.

I believe we have entered a new hierarchical level with our electronic world. This passage may have seemed gradual, but its impact has essentially been to produce a difference in kind (instead of in degree) in the condition of human existence. The institutionalization of nuclear and electronic technology, though dependent upon what its industrial predecessor has contributed, is an operating pattern, a cultural milieu that has never existed before.

The sense of powerlessness and impotence we feel is not a sign of alienation in the traditional Marxian sense. It is a true reflection of the state of the human beings to the extent that we transfer psychological states grounded in a premodern society. With an industrial psychological outlook we are indeed powerless when we consider our destructive nuclear capacity and our dependence upon computers and power sources to simply maintain our existence. No longer are we dominated by the owners of the tools of work; they are also dominated by the need for survival and power sources.

We have in effect created our first man-made gods in material form. We have created a human condition that, should it collapse by disaster or human direction, would destroy rich and poor alike. Now all people must serve the technical "gods" in some nonthreatening way in order to insure social and perhaps personal survival. Political action and political analysis of the human condition is now too limited a perspective with which to view our conditions of existence.

They can threaten our very survival if used by people having an outmoded attitudinal structure. Precisely because radicals have been so busy pushing and tugging at the means of production and distribution, they do not see that they share the same technological world view—what liberals love, radicals hate, and both are equally possessed by technology.

A key phenomenon in understanding this transition is television. It is incomprehensible to me how people raised as children is a non-television world can miss the fact that the youth of today have been and are being dramatically affected by this overriding multimedia impact on their lives. To grow up with television is to grow up in an obviously mediated world.

Curriculum thinking should be grounded in cultural realities. One may see cultural realities in terms of a relativistic perspective or in long-range developmental terms. In my own developmental speculation I see the present and future technological domination of man as a step in the road toward human evolution. It is my personal myth that today's technology is yesterday's magic. Further, it is my intuitive feeling that technology is in effect an externalization of the hidden consciousness of human potential. Technology, in other words, is a necessary development for human beings in that it is the means of externalizing the potential that lies within. Humanity will eventually transcend technology by turning inward, the only viable alternative that allows a human being to continue to experience oneself in the world as a creative and vital element. Out of this will come the rediscovery of human potential.

SOCIAL SIGNALS OF TRANSCENDENCE

We are not completely without sociological validation of a transcendent ideology. Peter Berger (1969, p. 103), for example, has presented a sociological analysis of human behavior that is relevant. Berger suggests that the one major implication of modern relativistic sociology is that it relativizes the relativizers as well. That is, taking a relativistic position also puts the relativists in the historical position of having their doctrine relativized.

He suggests that we examine the behavior of people and look empirically, using sociological methods, for what he calls signals of transcendence. In so doing, Berger finds as a beginning hypothesis that there are at least four such signals, that is, prototypical human gestures: the propensity for order and the automatic assurance of the adult to the child that everything is all right (that is, you can trust the world); the existence of play; the existence of hope; and the existence of damnation. Berger finds these gestures difficult to explain without some sense of transcendence. The propensity to order and have faith and trust in the meaning of things, playing, hoping, and the sense of indignation that some human actions lie beyond the acceptable are all unnecessary and inexplicable if everything is simply relative and realistic. Humor is also difficult to explain in such a context.

Thus, humans have both the propensity to play and laugh as if we need not be serious and the propensity to trust, order, and damn with a seriousness that transcends everyday political and economic concern. The case for nothing but social reality and psychological development, he feels, must be proved by the proponents of those views, not by those who see signals of transcendence.

The doors of human conception opened and ushered in the technological revolution. Political thinking is a rational social adjunct to a conceptual culture. Now we are facing the opening of the doors of perception in human experience, not as the minor mystical phenomena that have appeared throughout history, but as a large-scale movement of consciousness on the part of our young. A multimedia world is perceptual, not linear, in the utilization of concepts, but patterned concepts are received upon impact as perceptual experience. The psychological attitude born in this culture is a psychology of individuation, not individualism or socialism.

The human race is beginning to take another major step into the unknown source of its imagination, that same source that has created technology and all of the cultural trappings we possess. The signs are apparent in today's world and in the history of human *being*. In a very real sense it is as if we are coming to know that what we have imagined and conceptualized resides within us as potential, rather than having to be made into conceptual and material form.

Think for a moment about the mysteries of human experiences rather than our achievements. How can people walk on coals as hot as 2500 degrees without visible signs of burning on either their feet or clothing? What explains the various forms of extrasensory perception? How can people dream the future? What are teleportation, telekinesis, and similar experiences? What is a mystical experience?

You may write them off as empirically unfounded, just as Julius Caesar would have written off the technological world of today as utter impossibility. But the testimony of human history in terms of witnessing and personal experience cannot be ignored, for it is out of this very source of the unknown that whatever we have achieved has emerged. There is no reason to suspect that we have realized our human potential, and there is reasonable evidence that we may be rapidly approaching a new level of psychological and cultural growth from which dramatically new understandings of human potential will emerge.

It is my best guess that the next step, already begun, is an inward journey that will manifest itself by discovery, through perception and imagery, of human potential only slightly realized until now, and an outer journey for new communal life stages that are pluralistic and limited to small groups (tribes?) of people. The new communities will, of necessity, not threaten the technological superstructure that supports life, but they will seek pluralistic life styles within the superstructure.

A TRANSCENDENTAL DEVELOPMENTAL IDEOLOGY

A transcendental ideology seems to be necessary because I find the source of value positions to be inadequate in the other four. It is never clear on what basis or by what source the values of objective neutrality, social relativism, or ethical principle are derived. In other words, I find all four ideologies unclear in their ontological and phenomenological grounding.

There are two directions I could take at this point: the transcendental or the hermeneutic. I am not now equipped to pursue the latter course. From what I do know of this line of analysis, it seems to result in a cultural relativism that I find unacceptable at present. I will leave this door ajar for further study, however. What follows is fundamentally addressed to critical problems I see in the four ideologies described earlier.

My position is best approached through the concept of a dual dialectical process. A dialectic exists not only between the individual and his environment but also within the individual himself. Figure 2.5-3 will help to illustrate what I mean.

The relatively closed portions of Figure 2.5-3 represent the explicit knowledge systems of the individual and the situational context within which he acts. This represents a position similar to that held by radical ideologists, as far as it goes. Thus, I would agree that human activity is in part created by the reflective transaction of human consciousness in situational contexts.

It is clear, however, that, within the limits of the closed part, there can be no access to values or ethical principles that do not arise out of a utilitarian reflection upon the objective historical or personal consequences of human activity. Without positing a method of reflective intelligence based upon an analysis of the consequences of human activity, there could be no assessment of "good" other than a

FIGURE 2.5-3. A Dual Dialectic

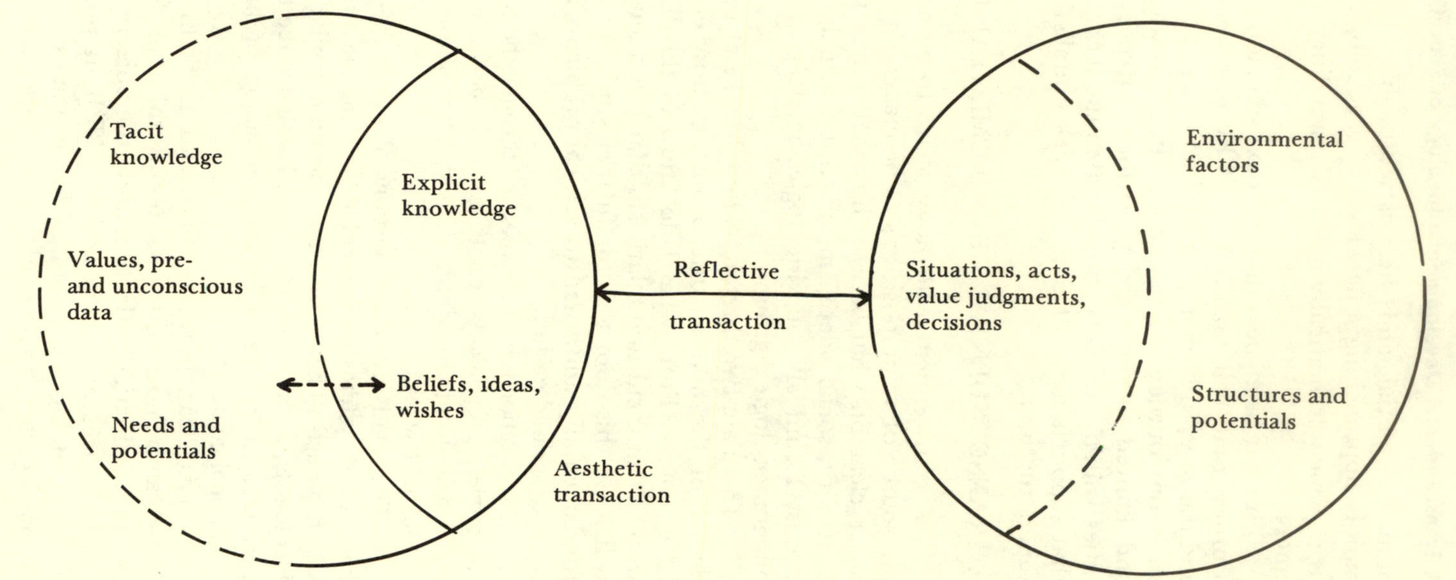

bare survival adjustment to reality, much in the manner of most other animals.

Utilitarianism as a source of values is, however, a relatively unsatisfactory position. It does not allow for or account for phenomena in human experience that have been readily apparent to persons throughout history and in contemporary society. Central to this discontent is the cognitive orientation of reflection as the method of intelligence and the only source of analysis for human activity. Thus, an a priori valuing of rationality is necessary in utilitarianism. Where does it come from?

That this gives only a partial account of human being is indicated by the second dialectic, between the explicit awareness of the individual and the nonexplicit nature of the individual. The self, in other words, is composed of both conscious awareness and unconscious data at any given time.

Values, I believe, are articulated in the lives of people by the dual dialectic of reflecting upon the consequence of an action and sounding the depths of our inner selves. Only a process something like this can explain why "what works is not always good." Some dual dialectic is also needed to explain the existence of reason, or aesthetic rationality, to counterbalance purely technological rationality.

The self as a concept has suffered at the hands of everyone from behaviorists to analytical philosophers. I find this interesting but neither the empirical reductionism of behaviorists nor the analysis of common usage convince me that there could not be an agency where phenomenological experience would permit the analyst to analyze and the behaviorist to behaviorize. Neither come to grips with what allows them to perform at all. I find the concept of self as an experiencing agency to be useful for this purpose, and I would suggest that a self is no less mystical than a culture or a society since all three can only be structured as hypothetical constructs by some languaging agency.

The inner dialectic of the self is a critical element if we are to advance the position that culture is in any way created by human being. The possibility of value may well be limited in alternatives by the individual-biological-social dialectic, but the validation of values would seem to demand some source other than explicit and rational knowledge.

Herbert Marcuse (1969, p. 91; 1964) seemed to recognize a need for something similar—a new sensibility as well as a raised level of critical consciousness—in the idea of aesthetic rationality. Aesthetic rationality, Marcuse suggested, can serve as a sort of gauge for a free society. He found a source for the form that a new society could take in the area of sensibility. Marcuse would argue, however, that sensibility is formed from the conditions of the social structure as well as from the explicit and rational data of the world. He would further argue that sensibility and rationality can only be transformed by engaging in praxis, the collective practice of creating an environment.

It is not clear where this leaves Marcuse. On the one hand, he appears to assume some biological base for sensibility; and, on the other hand, he appears to see new sensibility as emerging from new social conditions. I strongly suspect that Marcuse has, at least as a sensibility of his own, a basic idea of the "good man" grounded in his biology. If freed, it could redirect the formation of a rational world.

The importance here of Marcuse's position is the recognition of an area of sensibility or aesthetic rationality. The dual dialectic of inner aesthetic and technical rationality and outer individual and social condition is implicit in his statements. The difference between our views would apparently be the poverty of sources of aesthetic rationality that he appears to accept and the necessity of treating sensibility only in the context of the construction of new social environments. I propose that there are phenomenologically identifiable sources of aesthetic rationality not accounted for by Marcuse, and phenomenologically identifiable methods of creating individual perceptual environments and enlarging human sensibility that do not depend upon praxis as he defines it.

The problem of the source and validation of values is thus not adequately resolved in the ideologies described by Kohlberg and Mayer or by the radical position. We are left essentially with values that are either picked up culturally by association or conditioned in us behavioristically, emergent from our biological nature, or derived from cognitive reflection upon experience (individually or historically).

None of these approaches can account for the emergence, validation, and source of all values without ignoring a sizable segment of our own cultural history and personal experience. Values I would submit, as with knowledge, are personal, developed from a dual dialectical process that represents development in a hierarchical structure that surpasses one's biology, culture, or society.

Psychological theory, if there must be such an adjunct to educational ideology, must also be seen as a focus upon the question of human being. That is, narrow empirical or developmental views lead us away from our ontological ground of being rather than causing us to come to grips with human nature. They must also be grounded in something beyond their own conceptions. Thus, psychological theory must be grounded in existence and utilize the methods of phenomenology if it hopes to cope with being.

I have found much of value in the works of C. G. Jung (1959, p. 544) and William James (1958, p. 396; see Wild, 1970, p. 420). The sense of their works for me lies in their apparent willingness to cope with all forms of psychological manifestation in human activity and to discipline their inquiries through observation and phenomenological methodology. I am less concerned with their conceptualizations than their orientation and methodology, although their concepts have been useful in many instances.

Jung was concerned with metaphysics throughout both his practical work and his theoretical writing. His biography is a rare experience in reading; it tells us that he was a fascinating, introspective, and idiosyncratic individual, but, more important, it shows how he used his personality in his work. He is perhaps a modern paradigm of man's unified struggle for meaning, using his own personality and culture and methodologically disciplining that inner struggle and cultural potential to probe the nature of human being.

As an analytical psychologist, he never developed a theory of child development. He felt that the ideas of Freud and Adler were perfectly usable with the young. Instead, he focused on the process of individuation, and it is the implications of this concept that contribute to the transcendental ideology of education.

Jung worked most often with people who were successful in life, but who, upon reaching middle age, found that life lacked meaning. He felt that the tasks of the first half of life were best symbolized by the myth of the hero. What concerned him was, as Anthony Storr says, what happened when the hero emancipated himself from the past, proved his (Adlerian) power, and gained his (Freudian) mate?

This led Jung and his patients to a search for values, and for Jung the supreme value was that of integration, of "wholeness." Thus, the conscious attitude of integration is one of acceptance, of ceasing to do violence to one's own nature by repressing or overdeveloping any part of it. This Jung called a "religious" attitude, although not necessarily related to any recognizable creed.

Then, the second half of life became a spiritual quest. He believed, contrary to Freud, that the concept of God was a "psyche aptitude" of human nature appearing everywhere in culture and history. He further believed that only by recognizing some higher authority than the ego could people detach themselves sufficiently from sexuality, the will to power, and other compulsions. If man had no spiritual inner experience, he would make a God of something else, whether sex, power, or even rationality. The God Jung discovered through his work was the sense of "wholeness," the undiscovered self.

The problem of alienation for Jung was an alienation from the ground of his being. Thereby it created loneliness, and his life lacked meaning and significance. Loneliness did not, he felt, come from having no people around; it came from being out of touch with oneself and thus being unable to communicate things that seem important or from holding views that others deem inadvisable.

Concepts that Jung used to express his views such as "archetypes," the "collective unconscious," his psychological typology of "introversion-extroversion," are more or less useful as the case may be. They are not central to my own thinking except to point toward an inner potential that the person must come to experience.

Of perhaps greater use is Jung's concept of the psyche being self-regulating. That, for Jung, was a psychology of "individuation" based upon the idea that the person is self-regulating when he has attained a balance and integration in his potentialities. Self-regulation strives toward unity, toward the integration of inner and outer realities in a meaningful wholeness.

James, on the other hand, was a self-proclaimed supernaturalist, in contrast to a naturalistic perspective of what he called a "crass" or pluralistic nature. He was, I suspect, as American as "apple pie" in his generally optimistic, searching, pluralistic, pragmatic, and radical empirical bent. Yet he was an unusual person for a psychologist because he had an insatiable curiosity about all the phenomena of human personal experience, and an aversion to closed or absolute meanings.

James felt as at home examining extrasensory perception or religious experiences as the more mundane aspects of attention, perception, cognition, and so forth. Jung refers to James's earlier work in a number of instances, but James probably died before he was well acquainted with Jung's work.

The lesson that James leaves us is similar to Jung's in that his openness and methodology reflect an attitude toward psychology that is especially useful for our purposes. What James brings to our thought is a more critical use of the dialectic between inner implicit and outer explicit reality. By acceptance of the inner realm as a source of meaning, James only intends that we test it in our lives, that we accept it as phenomenological fact but verify it for ourselves by its meaning for us in our human activity. It is, in other words, a dialectic of self-reflection of the commerce between our inner and explicit consciousness, and its verification for us (as in the case of psychoanalysis) does not necessarily invalidate or validate concretely the experiences of others or limit the potential of human beings.

Thus, for James, Jung's concepts might well be what James called "overbeliefs." What he would agree to is the critical acceptance of human experiences seemingly arising from within but central to the understanding of humanness. Thus, he could say (1958, p. 388), "Disregarding overbeliefs, and confining ourselves to what is common and generic, we have in the *fact that the conscious* person is continuous with a wider self through which . . . *experiences* come, a positive content of experience which, it seems to me, is *literally and objectively true as far as it goes.*"

He concludes his work in religious experiences with his expression of his own overbelief, sounding somewhat like Carlos Castaneda and his adventures with Don Juan. "The whole drift of my education goes to persuade me that the world of our present consciousness is only one out of many worlds of consciousness that exist, and that those other worlds must contain experiences which have a meaning for life also; and that although in the main their experiences and those of this world keep discrete, yet the two become continuous at certain points, and higher energies filter in" (p. 391).

Components of Epistemology

The epistemological components of a transcendental ideology are grounded in the concept of personal knowledge. Thus, knowledge is not simply things and relationships that are real in the outer world and waiting to be discovered, but it is a process of personalizing the outer world through the inner potential of the human being as it interacts with outer reality.

At this level I am speaking not of idiosyncratic individual worlds, although these are important, but I am referring to the idea that the created culture of human life is a common set of personal constructs. Personal in the sense that all cognitive constructs are grounded in individual personal meaning and that our shared culture, as well as language usages, serves as a pragmatic survival device. This outer necessity does not change the fundamental nature of knowledge.

The work of Michael Polanyi (1967, p. 99) is instructive at this point. He develops the idea of the tacit dimension of knowledge. By this I take him to mean that any explicit knowing is grounded in a tacit knowing that makes sense out of explicit statements. Thus, Polanyi begins with what he calls the fact "that we can know more than we can tell."

It is necessary to understand what one knows in order to make sense of it. Polanyi refers to this as a process of "indwelling." Understanding, however, is tacit in that understanding may only be inferred from the explicit knowledge we possess. This process of tacit knowing exists in both practical and formal knowledge structures, and in aesthetic and scientific realms.

As Polanyi remarks (1967, p. 20), "The skill of a driver cannot be replaced by a thorough schooling in the theory of the motorcar: The knowledge I have of my own body differs altogether from the knowledge of its physiology; and the rules of rhyming and prosody do not tell me what a poem told me, without any knowledge of its rules." And, a mathematical theory can be constructed only by relying on prior tacit knowing and can function as a theory within an act of knowing, which consists in our attending from it to the previously established experience on which it bears.

Many of our present educational problems seem more understandable if we accept the tacit dimension of knowing. It is useful, for example, to consider the problem of school achievement among culturally different populations as fundamentally a problem of tacit knowing.

In Polanyi's terms, explicit knowledge use requires an act of commitment that cannot be formalized since "you cannot express a commitment noncommitally." The lack of commitment among culturally different students has been referred to as motivation and attention or value problems. Essentially it can be thought of as the absence of a tacit knowing which makes sense of (helps the student understand) the meaning of the explicit knowledge he is encountering. In mundane terms he lacks the experiential background for the tasks. He has not interiorized experiences that make sense of his school tasks. Thus, he is unable to *understand* and *commit* himself to the enterprise.

On a more general level, the problems of testing take on a more understandable quality when seen in the light of tacit knowledge. The sense of injustice and unfairness encountered frequently among students in reference to tests is helpfully explained when one accepts the idea that "we can know more than we can tell" and that it is possible not to understand the meaning or direction of tests and err because the tacit awareness we bring to a test situation may well not match the tacit assumption of the test maker.

A positive side to this problem may be seen in the use of humor. Much of our humor in the form of stories is grounded in the development of a story line that arouses a tacit understanding in the listener and is revealed to be in error when the punch line is delivered. The punch line is frequently "funny" because the listener quickly realizes that the tacit base in the story has been juxtaposed to his own tacit knowledge. A good humorist is a past master of utilizing the tacit dimension.

An epistemology must further come to grips with the so-called hard knowledge of our culture. It seems doubtful if any knowledge is "harder" than modern physics, and it is instructive to note epistemological implications found in the knowledge of modern physical science.

According to Arthur Koestler (1972, p. 158) modern physics has entered a phase of epistemology whereby modern physicists are ever more receptive to the possibility of the seemingly impossible. In a way one might say, at least in relation to the subatomic or supergalactic dimension, that physicists have literally gone out of their senses.

According to Koestler, Werner Heisenberg, in the field of quantum physics, has remarked that "atoms are not things . . . when we get down to the atomic level, the objective world of space and time no longer exists, and the mathematical symbols of theoretical physics refer merely to possibilities, not to facts." The Principle of Uncertainty or Indeterminacy, credited to Heisenberg, demonstrates that the more accurately a physicist is able to determine the velocity of an electron, the less able he is to determine its location (and the reverse).

Further, matter as entity behaves as waves or particles, but on mutually exclusive terms. This concept of complementarity means that two mutually exclusive frames of reference are complementary. Both are needed to provide an exhaustive view of phenomena.

As Sir James Jeans said (1937, p. 172), "Today there is a wide measure of agreement, which on the physical side of science approaches almost to unanimity, the stream of knowledge is heading toward a nonmechanical reality; the universe begins to look more like a great thought than like a great machine."

The story of neutrinos is perhaps the most bewildering. Neutrinos, it appears, have virtually no physical properties and apparently pass through solid bodies as if they were empty space. Koestler further tells how V. A. Firsoff described neutrons as existing in a different kind of space, governed by different laws.

There is, of course, much more to modern physical theory, but it is a journey that I am ill prepared to take. I can only relate what reporters in this field seem to feel the knowledge implications are. In essence, the materialistic cause-effect world has collapsed as explanation of newly perceived phenomena. These phenomena appear to operate in a different dimension of reality and are referred to by many in mentalistic rather than materialistic terms.

Koestler, in his work, sees a convergence between physical theory and the data of extrasensory perception. At least the findings and theories of modern physicists are no less "unusual" and tend to be partially integratable with such things as precognition and psychokinesis. Fundamentally, he feels they reveal a basic polarity in matter which he describes as causal self-assertive tendency and an acausal integration tendency to function as a part of a larger whole. He ends his essay (1972, p. 140) with "the limitation of our biological equipment may condemn us to the role of Peeping Toms at the keyhole of eternity. But at least let us take the stuffing out of the keyhole, which blocks even our limited view."

An article by Bilanvik and Sudarshan (1969) further illustrates the incredible potential of emerging physical theory. They remark that there is an unwritten precept in modern physics that "anything which is not prohibited is compulsory." They then go on to attempt to demonstrate that in terms of relativity theory there is no contradictory reason why "negative energy particles" traveling "backward in time" cannot exist. In the process they posit the existence of what they name "transcendent" tachyons.

An epistemology that does not recognize tacit knowledge components, or the fantastic possibilities and implications of our most advanced fields of inquiry, is simply weighted down with the baggage of philosophical and materialistic biases. How, what, and why are far more open questions than we are often led to believe, and the possibilities of accessibility to knowledge from "hidden" inner sources operating on acausal, or integrative, or serial and synchronistic bases point directly toward the awareness of another ground of knowledge in human being.

Centering as the Aim of Education

The aim of education should be a centering of the person in the world. Mary Caroline Richards (1962, p. 159) has expressed this idea beautifully. Much of what I have to say is at least consonant with her views, if not directly adapted from them.

Centering does not mean mental health. Though I have no quarrel with the intentions of people who want everyone to be mentally healthy, the term is too ridden with a psychologism that limits our perspective about human beings. It appears as a statistical concept, and those who are mentally healthy may in fact be "other-directed" persons, having little sense of a core or center.

Further, centering does not mean self-actualization, for that process, at least as I interpret it, is filled with assumptions about personality development that seem arbitrary and somewhat closed to me. One's personality, I would feel, is better thought of as something to be used to find a centering rather than something to be developed. Our efforts are better spent helping personalities as we find them ground their selves in a center of their being.

The idea of centering may be found in a wide variety of sources throughout history and the contemporary world. It is essentially what William James called a religious experience, although here it seems more appropriate to refer to the *spiritual.*

It is important that centering be recognized as a process that may occur in a religious context, but it is not dependent upon any sect or creed, whether Eastern Zen or Western Christianity, for its validation. It is a human experience facilitated in many ways by a religious attitude when this attitude encompasses the search to find our inner being or to complete one's awareness of wholeness and meaning as a person.

The work of some psychologists is important in helping us recognize the existence of inner potential, but the science of psychology, with its methodological and assumptive base, can only point toward the existence of the experience of centering. It cannot deal directly with it.

The "back door" or "front door" of human being, whichever suits your purpose, must be unlocked and left ajar if centering is to occur. The process draws its power and energy from sources that are not completely explicable. The naming of these sources of energy is not terribly helpful, even though one word that occurs frequently in relation to this experience is God. But God is not known; He is not understood; He is used. Thus, centering occurs through the use of spiritual resources, whatever one wishes to call them.

Spiritual energy does not shape the explicit knowledge of the person in absolute or noncultural ways. Centering takes place within the culture of the individual, and the process of centering utilizes the data of an individual's culture, what he explicitly knows through social praxis. The variety of religions, mystics, spiritualists, and other manifestations found throughout history fundamentally tells us that inner resources and strength can be made available and used but not what verbal form or perceptual reality this potential takes.

Centering as the aim of education calls for the completion of the person or the creation of meaning that utilizes all the potential given to each person. It in no way conflicts with the accumulated knowledge of a culture; it merely places this knowledge in the base or ground from which it grows. As such, centering is the fundamental process of human being that makes sense out of our perceptions and cognitions of reality.

It is important we do not turn away from examining the idea of centering simply because it is connected with spirituality. This term simply is the best one available in the attempt to refocus our fundamental educational concerns, even though it is fraught with heavy cultural biases in our society.

The data of spiritual literature when related to the axiological, psychological, social, and epistemological components I have alluded to make it quite difficult for us to reject the possibilities of centering. It appears to me that we are witnessing a period of discovery and transition leading toward a convergence of phenomena very much like centering. I, personally, am satisfied with the particular term.

What kinds of questions can we now ask about curriculum in view of the developmental aim of centering?

1. What kinds of activity are encouraged that provide for opening up perceptual experiences?
2. What kinds of activity facilitate the process of sensitizing people to others, to inner vibrations?
3. What kinds of activity provide experiences for developing close-knit community relationships?
4. What kinds of activity encourage and facilitate religious experiences?
5. What kinds of activity facilitate the development of patterned meaning structures?
6. What ways can we organize knowledge to enlarge human potential through meaning?
7. How can we facilitate the development of inner strength and power in human beings?

CURRICULUM CONTENT

Let me take a mundane example of the implications of the perspective of centering on the so-called discipline by focusing upon mathematics. Then we can reflect on more speculative but less mundane matters.

It is apparent that the substance of the culture we call discipline may be used to create new knowledge to be passed on, to provide substantive content within social roles to attack social problems, or to enlarge individual human potential.

If we were fundamentally concerned about enlarging human potential, we would view mathematics as a way of conceptualizing or thinking and creating a special kind of meaning system. Being able to think mathematically would result in the development of a human potential that could not be gained through any other avenue. Mathematics, in other words, could be seen as a special world perspective, not as a single view but one of a number of potential cultural views for opening up individuals to their potential.

This is counterposed to, though not mutually exclusive from, either the language use of mathematics for creating science, or pure mathematics, or the functional uses of computation. Teaching mathematics "for its own sake" means for the sake of enlarging the human potential of individuals in a way that is unique.

The importance of this perspective may be referred back to the developmental point of view provided by Kohlberg and Mayer. If we accept Dewey's concept of providing experiences that both interest people and contribute to their long-range development, it is clearly essential that the kind of long-range development be identifiable. Is the long-range development to be seen in terms of the discipline of mathematics? Or is it to be viewed in terms of its social usefulness to the individual in society? Or is it to be oriented toward the development of potential patterns of meaning for individuals?

Though, as I said, these ends are not mutually exclusive, they are functionally different in the sense that, when we make educative value judgments about the kinds and patterns of experiences people encounter, we create a situation which in practice reflects one of these orientations as a primary view of the goal of development.

What is problematical about mathematics? If we assume, for lack of a better term, that a desirable mathematical problem for an individual is one which he sees as problematic and which promises to contribute to his long-range development, does it make any difference how we help him to create experiences that will meet both criteria in terms of one or another of the possible long-range perspectives? I think that it clearly does make a fundamental difference in the way we create curriculum environments and the manner in which we enter into instructional practices.

It is very difficult for me to see exactly what kinds of experiences would facilitate the long-range development of meaning perspective through mathematics. I can only alert mathematicians or mathematical thinkers to this task. But I think that I can clearly see some things we presently do that do not contribute directly to this end.

It makes no sense to me from this view, for example, to have a highly sequenced, logically programmed mathematics curriculum.

The kind of mathematics and when it is encountered must be based upon a far more sensitive awareness of the meaning systems of individuals. Further, it makes little sense to structure the great majority of learning tasks in a convergent manner. It would appear to me that "playing" with numbers in a much freer kind of problem situation would be far more valuable.

Nor does it make much sense to "package" mathematics textbooks and other materials around narrow tasks, skills, or computations. It would be far better to set out to create mathematics as a set of problem situations that can be entered at different levels by different persons who can then branch out, if they wish, into geometry, algebra, calculus, or what have you. Thus, the emphasis upon individuated entrance in mathematical meaning systems, open and playful encounters, and highly diverse materials built around a problem situation that can go in a variety of directions sounds much more satisfying to me.

Ecology is an emerging social concern that has a corollary in the centering process. It takes a unitary view of the world. Thus, the inner unity of the centering process has an outer reality in the concern for a unitary world built upon an understanding of ecology. It appears that any sane attempt to educate the young must deal substantively with the impact of man and technology on his own living environment, and there appears to be little hope that we can simply solve our ecological problems with the next generation of technological developments. Ecological problem solutions call for the same value search and commitment growing from the inner knowledge of what we are and what we can be. There is a need to transcend the linear and technical problem-solving approaches of the past if we are to survive our ecological crises. Thus, a global view of the interrelationships of human structures and activities must be a central aspect of any curriculum which purports to have a transcendent developmental view.

This section on content can be concluded with one last reflection that I owe to Charity James, with whom I worked for a year at Goldsmith College at the University of London. If we were intent upon developing human potential, we would realize that we live in a highly verbal, conceptual culture. We would further realize, as Lawrence Kubie (1963) has pointed out, that we tend to pay a high price in potential for this human achievement. The price is fundamentally related to the dialectic of our explicit and inner selves, and it is focused upon the withering away of portions of our creative potential. This is not new, but what is rarely noted is that the emphasis upon nonverbal or body language, hidden culture, or the arts, is not crucial in this matter.

What we seem to lose is our ability to gain access to ourselves and our creative potential through the process of visualization. We have in fact created a negative concept called hallucinations to guard against the very use of some of the visualizing potential. We seem not to trust ourselves.

Dreams are, I suppose, a human example of the process of visualization, yet dreams are rarely in our control. What I speak of is the power to control and create visualization, to bring to our vision things not present to our senses. To have visions is not the same as to create them.

A somewhat dramatic illustration of the human potential for visualization is provided by Colin Wilson (1972, p. 289) in his biography of Abraham Maslow. Wilson was lecturing in one of Maslow's classes when he remarked that in the act of masturbation it is possible by imagination to carry on a sexual activity where the mental act needs no object.

Maslow objected and pointed out that monkeys also masturbate. Wilson responded with the question of whether Maslow (whose early work was in the primate laboratory at Wisconsin) had ever seen a male monkey masturbate in total isolation, without the stimulus of a female monkey somewhere in the vicinity. Maslow remarked that he had not. Thus, Wilson illustrated the capacity of the human being to make a physical response via visualization as if to reality.

The Processes in Curriculum

Centering is the aim of a transcendental ideology. As such, it is a process one enters into. Thus, the question of the objective of a transcendental curriculum must be seen in process terms also. But processes are not ends in themselves. The ends are infinitely varied and unknowable in any finite sense with reference to a given individual. Processes, rather, refer to the engagement of the individual in human activity, which facilitates the process of centering.

For the sake of clarity an analogy may be made at this point to Dewey's developmental ideology. That is, if centering is viewed as the long-range developmental goal of curriculum, then process and content may be seen in terms of this goal. Content is selected in terms of the readiness and interest level of the students, primarily by the person involved coming to know what their immediate concerns are that are related to cultural substance. The essential component remains the processes or activities or events that occur. There are a number of possible processes that would facilitate centering.

Pattern making. This critical process reflects itself in the need to transform reality symbolically, to create order in search of meaning, and it is fundamental for locating oneself in time and space and for providing cognitive awareness that may facilitate centering. The pattern-making process must be distinguished clearly from the transmission of preformed patterns to the individual. Although cultural substance can never be formless by definition, the emphasis placed upon the nature of the individual encounter is critical. Thus, pattern making would emphasize the creative and personal ordering of cultural data as the individual engaged in activity.

Playing. The attitude and activity of play is a critical aspect of the pattern-making process. Play in this sense refers to playing with ideas, things, and other people. To engage in the encounter with cultural substance in a playful manner provides the individual with a self-regulating potentiality. Playfulness is at the service of the individual and frees persons to order and create without the necessity of constant attention and direction of the adult world. Thus, the process of "playing" would seem to be necessary to facilitate pattern making and to provide for self-regulation of activity.

Meditative thinking. "Why" is the fundamental thought question for a transcendental ideology, why in the sense of examining the fundamental meaning of things. Technical or calculative thinking, so central to our society, is built into the very pores of our social skin. To facilitate centering in the individual we must encourage meditative thinking. Rather than fostering the activity of thought in a functional, utilitarian way, a problem-solving process, we must foster what Martin Heidegger (1966, p. 93) called a "releasement toward things" and an "openness to the mystery." Thus, nothing can be accepted simply on its own terms in its social utility. Rather, we must encourage the young to say both yes and no to culture and probe the ground from which our culture arises, through meditative thinking.

Imagining. Another way of approaching pattern making, play, and meditative thinking comes through the activity of imagining—imagining as a process in contrast to verbalizing. Our verbal culture and language culture and language forms, as useful and necessary as they are, have also become the dominant form of thinking and expressing ourselves. The danger of this one-sided verbal emphasis is the constant externalizing of meaning, of coming to name the object and manipulate external reality. Imagining on the contrary provides an internal referent for the external world. The work of Rudolf Steiner (1968) and the Waldorf Schools provides considerable insight into this process. Steiner emphasizes the technique of presenting knowledge to the child first through his own imagination and only later following up with empirical observation. In essence the individual first forms his own images of encounters as he listens or actively creates. Thus, imagination as the ability to picture in the mind what is not present to the senses is a perceptual power that involves the whole person, that puts him in contact with the ground of his being.

The aesthetic principle. It is clear that the guidance of much of the arrangement of physical facilities, interpersonal relations, and individual expression must come from what Herbert Read (1956, p. 308) called the aesthetic principle. Read called the guidance of human education by the aesthetic principle the natural form of education. The preadolescent education of individuals, Read argued, should move from feeling to drama, sensation to visual and plastic design, intuition to dance and music, and thought to craft. Then, from the play of children emerging from their feelings, sensations, intuitions, and thinking, the individual could gradually grow toward cultural art forms guided by the aesthetic principle. Thus, the activities of dramatization, designing, dancing, playing music, and making or crafting are important in a transcendent ideology.

The body and our biology. Physical education, Alan Watts (1972) has said, is "the fundamental discipline of life." Watts, however, did not mean the games and skills of the traditional curriculum. Rather, he meant coming to grips with our own biological being and all that it means. Thus, he was able to propose that learning to husband plants and animals for food, how to cook, how to make clothes and build houses, how to dance and breathe, how to do yoga for finding one's true center, and how to make love were examples of this discipline. Although we rarely admit to a mind-body separation on a philosophical level, it is clear by the way we educate the young that we do not consider the biological aspects of the person to be relevant to the real business of education. Thus, the emphasis upon cognitive-verbal learning not only separates us from our inner resources but it divorces us from our biological organism. To be at home in our bodies is critical for human centering, and it would seem to me that far more attention should be paid to this phenomenon. It is interesting that the field of biofeedback is growing today. Thus, the use of machines to provide a conscious awareness of bodily functions, such as heartbeats or brain waves, may help to develop an integrated knowledge of the phenomena of our existence. It is perfectly reasonable to propose that the school curriculum processes may come to provide us with avenues for knowing ourselves as biological entities. Again, I would not claim biological and body knowledge as an end in itself. What I would say is that, in the centering of the human being, the awareness of "who I am" and "what my biological and physical potential are" are necessary avenues for the long-range development of the centering process.

The education of perception. This is the final area that needs exploring here. I refer to perception in the sense of William James's many other worlds of consciousness that exist aside from our present one, rather than in the sense of a functional psychological mechanism. The most impressive and exciting recent work in this area comes from an anthropologist—Carlos Castaneda's fascinating trilogy (e.g., 1969), in which he relates his experiences with the old Indian medicine man. I am not sure what the implications of this work are, but I am sure that the creation of altered states of consciousness is a human potential that is important to the process of centering.

THE TEACHER IN THE PROCESS

The developmental ideology of Dewey, Piaget, and others, as described by Kohlberg and Mayer perceives the teacher to be a person who comes to know the students but who also makes judgments about the long-range implications of experiences on the development of the children. So far as this goes, then, it is not incompatible with a transcendental developmental ideology. A transcendental ideology would, however, define this process in a different manner.

The teacher from a transcendental point of view is also in process. That is, the developmental aim of centering is as valid and important to the person of the teacher as it is to the child. Thus, the teacher does not "stand back" in a judgmental stance in the same manner. Rather, the teacher is immersed in the process of centering from her own point of view. Thus, the relationships between students and teachers are mutually responsive to the aim of centering.

The key distinction between these two developmental ideologies is the fundamental difference between knowing and understanding. In a secular or psychological developmental ideology, knowing the child, knowing his developmental status, and knowing the long-range developmental goals are essentially explicit cognitive acts. They are dependent upon being once removed from the children in a judgmental stance. This implies a maturity that is static in its essence, an end point which only the teacher has access to and only the teacher has arrived at. Thus, the predominant rationality of the teacher is still a technical process of planning, manipulating, and calculating, even though the intentions and relationships are, for example, more humane, perhaps, than those found in cultural transmission ideology. A transcendental ideology would shift the predominant rationality toward the aesthetic, intuitive, and spontaneous in the mutual process of centering.

Children learning and teachers teaching are fundamentally dependent upon the tacit dimensions. Explicit awareness or knowledge of each other and of teaching or learning tasks is embedded in a tacit realm that provides the ground for understanding, for making activity meaningful. Teachers cannot be said to understand children simply because they possess a considerable amount of explicit knowledge about them. Understanding is a deeper concept. It demands a sort of indwelling in the other, a touching of the sources of the other. Understanding others is not a "useful" procedure in the sense that knowing is, in that it does not provide the basis for planning, manipulating, and calculating. Understanding provides the ground for relating, for being fully there in the presence and as a presence to the other, for what Huebner called a continuance of the joint pilgrimage. The explicit knowledge of child development or of specific children may facilitate our understanding of them if it is internalized and integrated into our inner self. It is, however, only one avenue toward understanding.

There is another path, much harder but more direct. This is the process of locating one's center in relation to the other: to "see" one's self and the other in relation to our centers of being; to touch and be touched by another in terms of something fundamental to our shared existence.

This act of relationship, called understanding, is only known after the fact. "*Now*, I understand!" It is an act of listening, but not to the explicit content that a person is expressing. Rather, it is "tuning in" to the "vibrations" of bodily rhythms, feeling tone, inward expressions of a person's attempts to integrate and to maintain his integrity as a whole person.

Explicit content may facilitate this process, but often it creates a cognitive dissonance, an interference with really listening to the center of the person. We can easily be led away from this center by the way in which the other's explicitness reflects upon our own needs for centering. This interference raises barriers in ourselves to understanding, and shuts down our own expression of our being. So much of the explicit expression of cognition is really no more than dignified "cocktail chatter." Whether it is the weather, religion, sex education, politics, another person's foibles and problems, or the latest gossip does not matter.

Dialogue is different. Explicit cognitive expressions are oriented in dialogue toward creating something from the inner resources of two or more people. It is entered into with the intent of listening, and listening beneath the surface. The hope is that out of the explicit dialogue the creative inner workings of the participants will be freed and combined. Short of dialogue, even the expression of ideas, of philosophical or religious truths, of psychological insights, is often in the service of the cognitive ego of the participants. Dialogue does not just occur in a face-to-face relation; it can take place for the person through reading a book, or even, heaven forbid, listening to a talk on curriculum theory. Inner verbal and visual activities are possible without direct interaction.

Problem solving as a vehicle for progressive interactive method in this context, on the other hand, necessitates the introduction of social power structures in order to facilitate activity. Thus, when development is based upon a problem-solving schema, the orientation of activity is externalized, and it necessitates the organization of human activity into a social power structure. It further implies that development is a process of mastering the outer world through solutions by problem-solving methods of intelligence. When centering is the main process in relationships, problems are not always solved. As centering evolves, some problems disappear, still others become redefined, and some are solved in a sense of bringing to bear unity of self through thought, feeling, and action.

Psychoanalysis, one supposes, is a recognition of the phenomena of inner meaning in each person. Yet, as valuable as the process may be, the difference in the ability of psychologists to help others lies mainly in their ability to listen and understand, not in terms of their cognitive developmental theories but in interpreting the explicit data of the other as symbolic or in getting individuals to solve their own problems. The successful psychoanalyst is probably one who listens and reveals his own centeredness, who helps the patient gather his own inner resources for centering by being and revealing, by listening and responding, by offering and receiving.

Implicit understanding is to poetry as explicit knowledge is to science. The explicitness of science is in contrast to the unity and expressiveness of poetry. Science "adds up"; poetry integrates. It is becoming less clear to scientists whether explicit knowledge even "adds up," not at least until we have made a poem of the other in our own being. When we make a poem of the other in ourselves, we do not trap either in categories and classes. When we understand each other, we create a shared poem of our existence. Understanding is the crystallization of our aesthetic knowing; explicit knowledge is its rational handmaiden. To know a child is to describe his characteristics; to understand him is to be able to write a poem that captures his essence.

The teacher in such a process is, therefore, engaged in the art of living. The task of both student and teacher is the development of their own centering through contact with culture and society, bringing as much of their whole selves as they can to bear upon the process. There is no specifiable set of techniques or of rules or of carefully defined teaching roles. It is primarily a willingness to "let go" and to immerse oneself in the process of living with others in a creative and spontaneous manner, having faith in ourselves, others, and the culture we exist in as a medium for developing our own centering.

In concluding, I would like to clear up one possible misconception about the processes of curriculum and teaching leading toward centering in the educational ideology of transcendence. These processes are not haphazard; nor do they operate upon the romantic notion of the natural unfolding of the child. I quote from Mary Caroline Richards (1962, pp. 101-2):

> It is a terrible thing when a teacher gives the impression that he does not care what the child does. It is false and it is unfaithful. The child hopes that an adult will have more sense and more heart than that. The teacher therefore seeks to understand what the child hungers for in the life of his imagination, his mind, his senses, his motion, his will. This means that he (thc teacher) does not take things at their face value, but sees elements in relation to a lifetime process of deep inner structure.

REFERENCES

Berger, Peter. *A Rumor of Angels*. Garden City, N.Y.: Doubleday, 1969.

Bilanvik, Olexa-Myron, and E.C. George Sudarshan. "Particles Beyond the Light Barrier," *Physics Today* (May 1969).

Castaneda, Carols. *Journeys with Don Juan*. New York: Simon and Schuster, 1969.

Freire, Paulo. *Pedagogy of the Oppressed*. New York: Herder and Herder, 1970.

Heidegger, Martin. *Discourse on Thinking*. New York: Harper Torchbook, 1966.

James, William. *Varieties of Religious Experiences*. New York: New American Library, 1958.

Jeans, Sir James. *The Mysterious Universe*. Cambridge, Eng.: Cambridge University Press, 1937.

Jung, C.G. *The Basic Writings of C.G. Jung*. Ed. V.S. DeLazlo. New York: Modern Library, 1959.

Koestler, Arthur. *The Roots of Coincidence*. New York: Random House, 1972.

Kohlberg, L., and Rochelle Mayer. "Development as the Aim of Education," *Harvard Educational Review* 42: 4 (November 1972): 449–96.

Kubie, Lawrence. "Protecting Preconscious Functions." In *Nurturing Individual Potential*. Washington, D.C.: Association for Supervision and Curriculum Development, 1963.

Marcuse, Herbert. *An Essay on Liberation*. Boston: Beacon Press, 1969.

Polanyi, Michael. *The Tacit Dimensions*. Garden City, N.Y.: Doubleday Anchor Books, 1967.

Read, Herbert. *Education Through Art*. London: Faber and Faber, 1956.

Richards, Mary Caroline. *Centering*. Middletown, Conn.: Wesleyan University Press, 1962.

Watts, Alan. *In My Own Way*. New York: Pantheon, 1972.

Wilson, Colin. *New Pathways in Psychology*. New York: Taplinger, 1972. New York: Taplinger, 1972.

PART THREE

Curriculum Planning and Design

Curriculum planning has been a subject of professional discussion, practice, and inquiry in the United States at least since Franklin Bobbitt (1924) introduced a science of curriculum making in the early part of this century. His model of curriculum planning, and the model of his contemporary, W. W. Charters (1923), have survived and dominated a half-century's thought and practice in one form or another. The basic elements of their work underlie Tyler's (1949) classic formulation. However, in the last two decades, a growing critique has challenged the domination of curriculum as science.

Curriculum design refers to the characteristics or features of curriculum as a product of planning. There are a great many design proposals extant in the professional literature. One may be distinguished from another on the basis of the nature and organization of its elements—objectives, subject matter content, learning experiences, evaluation scheme. Groups of designs may be identified on the basis of common elements. Similar curriculum designs have similar strengths and limitations.

CURRICULUM PLANNING

Much of the literature in the field of curriculum has dealt exclusively with curriculum planning. The kinds of issues traditionally addressed in that literature are illustrated in fifty-eight early positions taken by the National Society for the Study of Education (NSSE) Committee on the Technique of Curriculum-Making (Rugg, 1926, pp. 9–28). These issues include educational goals and objectives, subject matter in curriculum, conditions for learning, curriculum design, and the issues of curriculum planning—its arena and its participants.

Prescriptive Planning Models

In general, the literature of curriculum planning is prescriptive. Its chief purpose has been to advocate useful principles to guide the work of those engaged in planning curriculums. The literature has changed little since the early work of Bobbitt and Charters and the subsequent work of Caswell and Campbell (1935). The same principles survive through four editions of the work of Saylor and Alexander (1954, 1966, 1974, 1981) and in most of the current texts in wide use in the field even today.

Much of this literature uses a rational, or technical, approach to constructing prescriptions for curriculum planning (Miller and Seller, 1985, pp. 204–31). The approaches begin with needs assessments for selecting objectives. The objectives selected serve as the basis for identifying and organizing learning experiences and for evaluating their effectiveness. This predominant planning model is, of course, the Tyler rationale. Tyler (1949) prescribed basic principles of curriculum and instruction in terms of four questions:

1. What educational purposes should the school seek to attain?
2. How can learning experiences that are likely to be useful in attaining these objectives be selected?
3. How can learning experiences for effective instruction be organized?
4. How can the effectiveness of learning experiences be evaluated?

Other prescriptive models include those of Taba (1962), Weinstein and Fantini (1970), Gagné and Briggs (1979), and Robinson, Ross, and White (1980). These latter models begin, respectively, with inquiry and thinking processes, learner needs, behavioral learning theory, and cognition and problem solving. However, like Tyler, they address the four questions he identified.

Tyler has restated his rationale for curriculum planning in Selection 3.1. Tyler begins his restatement with the question of a need to construct or reconstruct a curriculum, pointing out that curriculum planning is undertaken in response to a perceived problem situation. Thus, curriculum planning is, to a great extent, systematic problem solving aimed at a particular institutional problem, namely, guiding learning in schools.

The problem-solving model Tyler proposes in his rationale for curriculum planning begins with needs assessment to identify factors that have precipitated a problem situation and to isolate data about them to aid in problem solving. The factors include students, social or cultural variables, the learning process, organized knowledge, and, perhaps, the planning process itself. Tyler's own thinking about factors potentially related to curriculum problems was refined in a statement (Tyler, 1976) in which he urged greater attention to the active role of the student in the learning process and a more comprehensive assessment of student learning outside schools.

Tyler recognizes that the identification of factors related to a given curriculum problem and the use of new data to solve a problem cannot take place in isolation. Schooling is a complex institution, and its curriculum resists isolated or unilateral attempts at change. Curriculum, as institutional policy, is subject to a number of internal and external forces that need to be recognized and accommodated in some way in the curriculum-planning process.

In their analysis of curriculum policy making, Kirst and Walker (1971, pp. 488–98) identify a number of external influences on curriculum, including (1) groups that establish minimum standards, (2) groups or individuals who generate alternative curriculum models or proposals, and (3) groups that lobby for particular curriculum components or changes.

Included in the first group are accrediting agencies, state education agencies, standardized testing services, and various professional associations. The second group is composed of textbook publishers, commercial and noncommercial producers of curriculum materials, private foundations, the federal government, noneducation professional associations, university professors, and other professional educators. The third group includes those with vested interests in schools and in the curriculum, such as the U.S. Chamber of Commerce, the John Birch Society, the American Civil Liberties Union, the Council for Basic Education, and the AFL-CIO.

Kirst and Walker (1971, pp. 498–504) also note that local school boards and their professional staffs are minimally effective in influencing curriculum. This observation focuses even more attention on external influencers as curriculum planners attempt to execute their responsibilities.

A Descriptive Planning Model

Some attention has been given to the study of curriculum planning where the emphasis has been on describing the dynamics of curriculum planning as a scientific phenomenon. The central question addressed is "How does curriculum planning occur?" rather than "How should curriculum planning be done?" Empirical methods have been used to describe the nature of the decision-making process in curriculum planning. One purpose of such descriptive study of the dynamics of curriculum planning can be the refining of useful prescriptive formulations. Walker describes a naturalistic model of curriculum planning in Selection 3.2. In contrast to the traditional model, Walker's analysis focuses not on what ought to happen in the planning process, but on what does happen.

In Selection 3.2, Walker utilizes a quasi-political conceptualization of curriculum planning to detail his analysis. The main elements of the descriptive model he formulates are platform, design, and deliberation. Platform is described as the explicit and implicit value systems of curriculum planners. Curriculum design is the result of a complex decision-making process. Hence, understanding a curriculum's design requires understanding the deliberation process that produced it.

Juxtaposition of Walker's naturalistic model of curriculum development and the traditional Tyler model for planning offers some useful comparisons of prescriptive and descriptive approaches to problem solving and points to an underlying tension in curriculum thinking and practice. Both the prescriptive and descriptive approaches can add useful insights to one's understanding of curriculum planning and other curriculum issues.

The original Tyler approach assumes that curriculum planning is highly rational and that a consensus of planning participants relies only on an appropriate laying out of the facts (Tyler, 1949, p. 34). Walker's conception of platform and deliberation clearly recognizes the importance of a rational behavior in curriculum planning, but his model assumes neither a probability of prior consensus nor an evolution of consensus based entirely on rational considerations.

A comparison of the two approaches underscores a realization that curriculum planning always takes place in a particular context. In curriculum planning, some choices are excluded because of the particular platforms interacting in a given planning situation. In addition, thoughtful considerations of the constraints of local resources for curriculum planning necessarily balance one's vision of the most desirable choices with a sober recognition of the possible choices as well.

ARENAS AND PARTICIPANTS

As part of his conceptualization of curriculum engineering processes, including curriculum planning, Beauchamp (1981, p. 146) constructed a model of a curriculum system. Table 3.1 identifies the input, output, and content processes for systems maintenance. The maintenance elements identify the principal issues of curriculum engineering.

The issues include the choices about both the arena and the participants for curriculum planning. Curriculum is planned in a number of arenas. On a continuum, these community arenas range from the national arena to an individual school arena. The identification of arenas also includes the state and school district. One may want to consider interstate arenas as well. The question here is, "In what arena(s) should a curriculum be planned?"

Arguments might be advanced, both pro and con, for different arenas. For example, a need for adequate expertise and resources may dictate that the planning process be carried out in a national arena, while a need for local accountability requires that planning be done within a school district arena.

Table 3.1 **Model of a Curriculum System**

Input	*Content and Process for System Maintenance*	*Output*
Educational foundations Community characteristics Personalities of persons involved Curriculum experience The subject matters from disciplines and other subjects Social and cultural values	Choice of arena for curriculum process Selection of personnel Selection and execution of working procedures determining curriculum goals selection of curriculum design planning and writing Establishing implementation procedures Establishing procedures for appraising and revising the curriculum	A curriculum Increased knowledge by participants Changed attitudes Commitment to act

Taken from George A. Beauchamp, *Curriculum Theory*. 4th ed. (Itasca, Ill.: F. E. Peacock Publishers, Inc., 1981), p. 146.

The locus of influence and control of public schools in the United States has shifted from time to time. For example, Zeigler et al. (1977) have identified four phases of control of school policy, including curriculum. In the first phase before 1900, the principal determiners of school policy were the members of boards of education, whose high level of interaction with fairly small local constituencies provided direct links between a community and its school's curriculum. In the early part of this century, a second phase of influence and control was characterized by centralization and professionalization. Curriculum decisions, like other school policies, increasingly became the domain of school superintendents and experts produced by schools of education. Following World War II, characteristics of centralization and professionalization of curriculum planning were overshadowed by a nationalization of influence and control in curriculum, as in other school policy-making areas. In this period, the influence and control of academics and federal bureaucrats so dominated school decision making that, according to Zeigler et al. (1977, p. 537), "the notion of lay control through school boards [became] obsolete."

In the last quarter-century or so, a shift of the locus of control toward the national arena has continued. Although the authors of our Constitution did not spell out a role for the federal government in education or, more specifically, in schooling, the unprecedented federal expenditures for schools since Lyndon Johnson's presidency and the unprecedented federal litigation involving schools since *Brown* vs. *Board of Education* have made schooling very much a federal enterprise, removing curriculum decision making even further from the local community.

The 1980s have witnessed a resurgence of national commissions and studies aimed at influencing the purpose and content of the curriculum. Beginning with the National Commission on Excellence in Education (1983), numerous national reports call for changes in school curriculum (Adler, 1982; Boyer, 1983; CEEB, 1983; ECS, 1983; NSF, 1983; Twentieth Century Fund, 1983). In addition, studies like that directed by Goodlad (1984) provide extensive descriptive data to support calls for curriculum change.

Perhaps curriculum control in the federal or national arena has been a logical next step in the move away from the local arena begun with the statewide curriculum planning of the 1930s and 1940s and the emergence of the professional school elite described by Boyd (1979). Perhaps the movement has begun to reverse itself in the 1980s as the federal block grants to states have replaced the plethora of individual federal entitlement programs that preceded them.

In the United States, schooling traditionally has been an individual state function. In most instances, the financing and control of public schooling has been delegated to local boards of education. The role of the state, usually exercised through its state education agency, generally has been that of coordinator in providing guidelines, endorsing statewide consensus, and acting as a clearinghouse and consultant in matters of statewide concern.

State influence and the importance of the state education agency as a locus of curriculum activity have varied in the past, and they are to continue to do so. During the 1930s and 1940s, a notable emphasis on curriculum engineering in the state arena was achieved. Harap (1937, pp. 1–3) reported statewide affairs under way at that time in thirty-two states. Caswell's (1930, pp. 16–23) description of the Alabama Curriculum Program details an exemplary episode in this period. In many states, the activity of education agencies and even state legislatures has again become a focus of important curriculum and other school-related acitivities as shifting power structures and renewed interest in teacher education have evolved.

Traditionally, most curriculum activity has been within local school district arenas. Most professional educators, at some point in their careers, have been associated with a school district curriculum committee—charged with articulating objectives, organizing subject matter content, selecting instructional materials or activities, and designing evaluation strategies. And most of those involved in such curriculum activities can identify some of the characteristics of such activities and the relative constraints of a district arena.

In an article now over a half-century old, Bobbitt in Selection 3.3 has outlined some obstacles to curriculum planning in the school district arena and some consequent principles of action. Shifts away from local influence and control of curriculum have put these obstacles in new contexts. Nevertheless, the treatment Bobbitt presents can afford useful insights even today.

To be sure, the curriculum field has been afforded many insights in the last fifty years, and one need not agree with Bobbitt's particular biases in addressing the issues he raises. Nevertheless, the issues Bobbitt raises in Selection 3.3 continue to be real ones, and they can be used to formulate questions:

1. In what context is the question of a school district's purposes and funtions to be considered?
2. How can local school districts broaden the perspectives of those involved in local curriculum activities?

3. What resources are at a local district's disposal in constructing curriculum objectives?
4. What resources are at a local district's disposal in addressing other curriculum matters, such as content, instructional materials and activities, evaluation?
5. In what ways can a local curriculum decision-making body be related to other community-wide issues and concerns?

Questions about curriculum arenas overlap questions about participants in curriculum engineering processes. For example, if it were decided that the proper arena for curriculum planning is the state, then the participants in the planning activities may be selected either because of their statewide authority and visibility or because, collectively, they represented identified statewide constituencies. Conversely, the identification of a certain group of individuals as participants in curriculum planning is predicated on at least an implicit assumption about the locus of activity or arena. For example, the previously described nationalization of curriculum was accompanied by the center-stage emergence of academics, especially in the natural sciences, in policy-making. Nevertheless, curriculum in any arena is usually undertaken by participants selected from identifiable categories of potential participants. These categories include curriculum experts, school administrators, teachers, and laypersons. Verduin (1967) has constructed a "curriculum improvement continuum" that identifies various participant categories (see Figure 3.1).

Historically, curriculum planning has been the domain of professional educators, and it even may be seen by some as an exclusive cult of curriculum authorities and school administrators. But curriculum planning may involve a number of other persons as well. Changing balances of power within, and outside, the educational community underscore the importance of these others. They include, within the school, teachers, students, and other professionals. Outside the

Figure 3.1 **The Curriculum Improvement Continuum**

Outside Experts		Outside Experts and Selected Staff		Central Office Personnel and Selected Staff		Cooperative Efforts of Staff
	Outside Experts and Administration		Central Office Personnel		Administration and Selected Staff	

Source: John Verduin, *Cooperative Curriculum Improvement* (Englewood Cliffs, N.J.: Prentice-Hall, 1967), p. 15.

school, additional participants in curriculum planning may include parents, other laypersons, professional experts of one kind or another, and, most recently, politicians.

Verduin concluded his work by noting a power struggle among groups asserting various prerogatives in curriculum decision making. Note should be made here of the classroom teacher's involvement in this regard. The importance of teacher participation has been underscored by many. In Selection 2.2, Dewey (1897, p. 359) points out that the "ordinary schoolteacher is not, of course, called on to raise such (curriculum) questions." Dewey (1897, p. 194) points out "that every member of the school system, from the first-grade teacher to the principal of the high school, must have some share in the exercise of educational power," including curriculum. McNeil (1985, p. 132) identifies four components of the role of the teacher:

1. Adapting learning opportunities to individual differences;
2. Developing learning opportunities;
3. Developing learning centers;
4. Relating curriculum to teaching.

Beyond the question of which groups of experts and other professional educators to include, however, is the question of the participation of laypersons in these activities. One can argue that because, ultimately, it is the right of parents to educate their children, parents and other members of the lay citizenry should determine through their participation in curriculum activities what is taught in our schools, why and how it is taught, and how well the schools meet stated objectives or serve identified interests.

Gress (1983) documents the reciprocal relationship between education and community. Noting a historical trend toward professionalization and centralization of school decision making in the last quarter-century, in particular, he notes a recent trend toward wider citizen participation in educational policy-making, especially at state and local levels. Reviewing the literature of school-community intervention programs, Gress then details elements of a school-community change program focused on improved schooling and improved community participation in decision making by strengthening school-community relationships.

The elements of an argument for citizen participation in curriculum planning, then, are based on a need for broad citizen participation in public institutions, including public schools, and a concomitant need for open and informed communication among all those affected by the institution. In a more recent analysis of citizen participation, English (ASCD, 1980, pp. 1–18) has identified elements of school-community relationships. Following a description of factors that prompt school-community conflict, English assesses several methods of community involvement in curriculum planning.

With respect to the responsibility for education entrusted to schools, Commager (1976) has pointed out that we have perhaps lost sight of the Athenian ideal of *paideia*, the proposition that the education of the young is not the exclusive domain of schools. Schools have taken on more, and more exclusive, responsibility for education, assuming responsibility previously shared with the family, the church, the labor union, the scouting movement, and so on, as these institutions have either lost credibility or abdicated shared responsibility with schools. We need, argues Commager, to return to *paideia*, the view that the education of the young is not only the most important activity in any society, but the very purpose for the existence of society.

CURRICULUM DESIGN AND OBJECTIVES

As used by Herrick (in Herrick and Tyler, 1950, p. 37), "Curriculum design is a statement of the pattern of relationships which exist among the elements of a curriculum as they are used to make one consistent set of decisions about the nature of the curriculum of the child. . . ." The distinctive features of a curriculum are its individual elements—objectives, subject matter, learning activities, and so on—and the overall emphasis(es) produced by their organization.

Beauchamp (1981, pp. 114–16, 130–31) identifies and describes several elements of a curriculum that can further clarify the concept of curriculum design:

> A commonly included feature is an outline of the culture content to be taught . . . arranged sequentially by grades, or levels, according to the administrative organization of the school. . . . Another component . . . is a statement of goals and/or specific objectives . . . A third ingredient that may be included . . . is a statement that sets forth the purposes for creation of the curriculum and that stipulates ways in which the curriculum is to be used. . . . A fourth possible item . . . one that is rarely included, is an appraisal scheme. . . . Most curriculums . . . include what may be termed instructional guides . . . [i.e.,] directions to teachers pertaining to methods.

In the latter respect, a curriculum may include specific instructional elements such as learning activities or experiences, materials and other instructional resources, or even teaching strategies. The formulation of objectives has often been problematic.

A quarter-century ago, Ammons (1962) discussed further the definition, function, and use of educational objectives, and she identified some problems in this area. She argued that statements of objectives should provide necessary points of reference in curriculum design but that assumptions about the actual use, and usefulness, of such statements are not supported by fact. She asserted that most statements of objectives found in curriculums are not really designed to serve the functions of classroom teachers.

Formulation and use of curriculum objectives has been facilitated by development of the taxonomy of educational objectives (Bloom et al., 1956; Krathwohl et al., 1964). The taxonomy includes a number of categories of objectives within each of its three main parts—the cognitive, the psychomotor, and the affective domains. Bloom and his colleagues (1956, p. 7) introduce the three domains as follows:

> Our original plans called for a complete taxonomy in three major parts—the cognitive, the affective, and the psycho-motor domains. . . . The cognitive domain. . . . includes those objectives which deal with the recall or reorganization of knowledge and the development of intellectual abilities and skills. This is the domain. . . . in which most of the work in curriculum development has taken place and where the clearest definitions of objectives are to be found.

A second part of the taxonomy is the affective domain. It includes objectives that describe changes in interest, attitudes, values, and the development of appreciations and adequate adjustment. A third domain is the psycho-motor skill area. The taxonomy of objectives utilizes these three domains to classify objectives ranging, in each domain, from the relatively simple to the relatively complex.

Selection 3.4 by Krathwohl includes an outline of the classification systems constructed for the cognitive and affective domains. Little progress has been made in the development of a parallel classification for objectives in the psychomotor domain. Krathwohl begins by observing that terms commonly used in constructing statements of objectives lack specificity with respect to intended evaluation. Krathwohl then describes the taxonomy for classifying objectives developed by Bloom, himself, and others.

Krathwohl also discusses potential strengths and uses of the taxonomy. These include focusing attention on student (learner) behaviors, specifying particular learning outcomes, choosing appropriate learning experiences in curriculum design and in actual instruction, ensuring comprehensiveness and balance in a curriculum's design, understanding relationships among curriculum elements, constructing evaluation schema, facilitating evaluation experiments, programing instruction, and clarifying the meanings and uses of curriculum terminology.

ALTERNATIVE CURRICULUM DESIGNS

Almost forty years ago, Smith and colleagues (1950, pp. 372–531) identified three pure type curriculum designs: the subject curriculum, the core curriculum, and the activity curriculum. The first is "an organization of the content . . . into bodies of knowledge which are taught in complete isolation from one another" (p. 377). The second is a program whose "structure . . . is fixed by the broad social problems or by themes of social living" (p. 420). The third is an "educational program . . . to be shaped by the interests and purposes of those to be educated" (p. 468). To these three designs, Taba (1962, pp. 382–412) adds the broad field curriculum and the social processes/life functions curriculum.The former is a "combining [of] several . . . areas [subjects] into larger fields . . . toward lining up essential principles," and the latter results from "organizing . . . around the activities of mankind . . . to provide a patterned relationship between the content of curriculum and life." (p. 393).

Particular curriculum designs, then, result from a variety of organizing patterns, and each has a particular focus: bodies of knowledge, essential principles, social problems or themes, human activities, or individual interests. With respect to the elementary school, Foshay (in Shane, 1953, pp. 104–30) has traced curriculum design trends through the post–World War II era. Alberty's statement (in Henry, 1953, pp. 118–40) provides parallel analysis for the secondary school. The work of Dressel (1971) reviews the patterns of thinking about various college and university curriculums, and the work by Reynolds (1970) represents a first step in studying curriculums of the community or junior college.

Differences in curriculum designs are largely a matter of the organization and consequent focus of subject matter. Some treatments of curriculum design, especially with respect to elementary and secondary schools, have distinguished designs on the basis of *how* the subject matter is to be delivered (instruction) as well as on the basis of *what* subject matter is to be delivered (curriculum). For example, Eisner and Vallance (1974, pp. 1–18) classified and discussed five focuses in curriculum design that result, in part, from conflicting conceptions of general curriculum problems. Those five focuses respectively emphasize development of cognitive processes, use of technology, personal self-actualization, social reconstruction/relevance, and enhancement of academic rationalism. Alternatively, McNeil's more recent work (1985, pp. 3–81) classifies curriculum designs as humanistic, social reconstructist, technological, and academic. In both classifications, attention to instructional issues tends to overlap attention to curriculum issues.

Saylor and Alexander (1974) completed what is probably the most comprehensive study of alternative curriculum designs. They identified five general categories of designs by focus: specific competencies designs, disciplines or separate subjects designs, social activities and problems designs, process skills designs, and individual needs and interests designs (pp. 189–244). The authors presented the historical context for the evolution of specific designs in each category and briefly discussed emergent designs. Table 3.2 summarizes Saylor and Alexander's (1974, pp. 198–240) discussion of the characteristic features, strengths, and limitations of curriculum designs in each of the five categories.

In Selection 3.5, Taba develops a classical conceptual framework for curriculum design questions that identifies and relates elements of any curriculum. Taba underscores two principal deficiencies of extant curriculum design models. The first deficiency is an observed tendency of most curriculum design prescriptions to rest on a single principle or consideration. Taba points out that different principles of organization may come into play with respect to the several elements of most curriculums so that "one important characteristic of [an] adequate curriculum [design]" is that it "rest on multiple criteria and consider a multiplicity of factors" (Taba, 1962, p. 414). Thus, according to Taba, issues of curriculum design are not resolved by a simplistic choice among several valid principles, but rather by appropriate uses of several principles simultaneously. The second deficiency of many curriculum designs Taba identifies is "the confusion about which principles or considerations apply at which points of curriculum development" (p. 415). In illustrating some of the differences involved, Taba introduces and explicates concepts of scope and sequence in curriculum design and presents elements of actual designs to illustrate questions empirically.

Models for analyzing curriculum designs such as the one formulated by Taba will be useful for conceptualizing problems in this area. Certainly, such models illustrate much of the complexity and confusion in an area where rhetoric often is substituted for systematic analysis.

Table 3.2 **Generic Curriculum Designs: Features, Strengths, and Limitations**

Category	*Characteristic Features*	*Strengths*	*Limitations*
Designs focused on specific competencies	Assumes direct relationships among objectives, learning activity, and performance Desired performances often are stipulated as behavioral objectives Specifies objectives as first curriculum planning step Learning activites are designed to achieve each objective	Traditional designs not relevant to needs of life Focus on teaching students to perform the activities and demonstrate the ideals determined by analysis of human needs and activities as significant for direct training Both student and teacher performance can be effectively determined Specific job training utilizes to the fullest that learning results from experience, and the more meaningful and significant the experience, the more that is learned	Performance can be contrived, falsified, especially when it becomes a basis for marks Has much utility for some objectives but is futile for others
Designs focused on disciplines/subjects	Relative orderliness . . . neatly divided into subjects, which themselves frequently are subdivided . . . corresponding to school grades and even marking and reporting periods	It is convenient to use structure of knowledge (i.e., disciplines) as basis for structuring a curriculum The kinds and amounts of knowledge and its	Subjects have been created to meet curriculum needs that are not matched by disciplinary content Lack of direct relation of the organized subject

	Entrenched in the high school by Carnegie unit system . . . with the original definition (1909) of a unit of credit as the study of a subject . . . for one period a day throughout the school year Many subjects utilize inherent structures of corresponding disciplines, but the structure of other subjects created for practical reasons is left unclear	availability for school use are major determinants of the curriculum Emphasis on structure will help each student achieve his or her optimum intellectual development	matter to the problems and interests of the learner
Designs focused on social activities and problems	Includes designs focused on social functions, the individual's areas of living, or persistent life problems, and social reconstruction Organizing element is a strand or cluster of social activities and/or problems Extremist view eliminates need for schooling altogether	Designs can contribute directly to the needs of society for continuing improvement Relevant to student needs; therefore, of great significance and interest to students Can utilize resources of entire community in learning experiences	Not a basis for an entire curriculum Needs to be supplemented with opportunities to develop specific competencies and to pursue individual interests
Designs focused on process skills	Content becomes a vehicle for developing processes, such as those that constitute problem solving	The most significant goal of schooling is the development of lifelong learning skills and interests	Designs have tended to focus on only one portion of a curriculum plan

Table 3.2 *continued*

Category	*Characteristic Features*	*Strengths*	*Limitations*
	Basic pattern is set by processes not unique to a given field (e.g., observing, classifying, hypothesizing, decision making) Some focus on processes in the affective domain (e.g., valuing) as well as in the cognitive domain	Design affords maximum carryover into life processes and skills Adaptable to a number of areas of study Facilities of development of continuous progress education	
Designs focused on individual needs and interests	Uses experience of learner as starting point Highly flexible, with built-in-provisions for development and modification to conform to the needs and interests of particular learners Involves learner in curriculum planning Based on understanding of principles of child growth Basis for curriculums in many "free" or "alternative" schools Provision of options for individual students	More relevant for learners than other designs High degree of motivation inherent; therefore, high learner success Facilities individual achievement	Possible neglect of social goals Misinterpretation of meaning of "interests"

CRITIQUE OF PLANNING MODELS

In Part Three, we have examined both curriculum planning and design. In Selection 3.6, Macdonald and Purpel offer a critique of the dominant model of curriculum planning and an alternative vision of what curriculum planning might be. They elaborate the alternative by making explicit their own framework for curriculum planning as the term framework was used in Part Two of this text.

The authors offer a critique of the Tyler rationale in terms used by a number of others (e.g., Kliebard, 1970), specifically, its technical and engineering emphasis and its implicit acceptance of the political and social status quo, lack of sensitivity to cultural diversity, exclusive reliance on expert or elite perspectives, and the absence of both an explicit statement of framework and any method for specifying framework. Macdonald and Purpel offer further critique on methodological, aesthetic, and religious criteria.

Macdonald and Purpel then argue the need for framework in a curriculum-planning model, something they, like Walker (1971), call platform. The authors argue that platform provides a means for accounting for the political, aesthetic, and moral dimensions of life and, thus, of education. In explicating their position, they use the framework of transcendence elaborated in Selection 2.5 by Macdonald in Part Two. The authors also make explicit ingredients of their own curriculum-planning platform, giving particular attention to religious, or spiritual, dimensions, making liberation the goal of education.

Finally, these authors spell out a number of principles of the nature of the curriculum-planning process, as they see it, its participants and its decision making.

CONCLUSION

Planning curriculums for schools has been a major focus of study for curriculum theoreticians and practitioners for well over a half century. Much of the field's professional literature supports the dominance of a single model of curriculum planning. That model, generalized from the early work of the field's founders and the later work of their disciples and intellectual offspring, prescribes systematic steps for curriculum planning.

Some attempts have been made to study curriculum planning empirically. For the most part, a political framework has been used as a basis for describing curriculum-planning phenomena.

An area of study and practice parallel in magnitude to curriculum planning is curriculum design. Planning includes the steps and procedures utilized to produce a curriculum; it refers to the process. Design is concerned with the features of the curriculum produced; it refers to the product.

A curriculum may include a number of elements—objectives, subject matter, activities, materials, evaluation schemes, and the like. How these elements are formulated and organized, in particular, the focus of subject matter organization, bears on the design of a curriculum. Several alternative designs have been identified and categorized in different ways in the literature.

As one considers the necessary scope and sequence of a curriculum for an elementary or secondary school, or for baccalaureate or professional schooling, the relative strengths and deficiencies of alternative designs may become apparent. An acceptable curriculum for schooling at any level probably incorporates elements of a number of designs. For this reason, among others, curriculum planning and design will continue to be important areas of study and practice in the field.

REFERENCES

Adler, Mortimer J. *The Paideia Proposal.* New York: Macmillan, 1982.

Ammons, Margaret. "The Definition, Function, and Use of Educational Objectives," *Elementary School Journal* 62:432–36, May, 1962.

Association for Supervision and Curriculum Development. *Community and Curriculum*. Alexandria, Va. Ill.: ASCD, 1980.

Beauchamp, George A. *Curriculum Theory.* Itasca, Ill.: F.E. Peacock, 1961; 1968; 1975; 1981.

Bloom, Benjamin S., et al. *Taxonomy of Educational Objectives, Handbook I: Cognitive Domain*. New York: Longmans, Green, 1956.

Bobbitt, John Franklin. *How to Make a Curriculum*. Boston: Houghton Mifflin, 1924.

Bobbitt, John Franklin. "Difficulties to be Met in Local Curriculum Making," *Elementary School Journal* 25:653–63, May, 1925.

Boyd, William L. "The Politics of Curriculum Change and Stability," *Educational Researcher* 79:12–18, February, 1979.

Boyer, Ernest L. *High School.* New York: Harper and Row, 1983.

Caswell, Hollis L. "The Alabama Curriculum Program," *Peabody Journal of Education* 8:16–23, July, 1930.

Caswell, Hollis L., and Doak S. Campbell. *Curriculum Development.* New York: American Books Company, 1935.

Charters, Werrett Wallace. *Curriculum Construction*. New York: Macmillan, 1923.

College Entrance Examination Board. *Academic Preparation for College: What Students Need to Know and Be Able to Do*. New York: College Entrance Examination Board, 1983.

Commager, Henry Steele. *The People and Their Schools*. Bloomington, Ind.: Phi Delta Kappa Educational Foundation, 1976.

Dewey, John. "The Psychological Aspect of the School Curriculum," *Educational Review* 14:356–69, April, 1897.

Dressel, Paul L. *College and University Curriculum*. Berkeley: McCutchan, 1971.

Education Commission of the States. *Action for Excellence*. Denver: Education Commission of the States, 1983.

Eisner, Elliott W., and Elizabeth Vallance (eds.). *Conflicting Conceptions of Curriculum*. Berkeley: McCutchan, 1974.

Gagné, Robert M., and L. J. Briggs. *Principles of Instructional Design*. New York: Holt, Rinehart and Winston, 1979.

Goodlad, John I. *A Place Called School*. Hightstown, N.J.: McGraw-Hill, 1984.

Gress, James R. "A Study of Community Impact and School Improvement," *Action in Teacher Education* 5: 11–16, Spring–Summer, 1983.

Harap, Henry (ed.). *The Changing Curriculum*. New York: Appleton-Century-Crofts, 1937.

Herrick, Virgil E., and Ralph W. Tyler (eds.). *Toward Improved Curriculum Theory*. Chicago: University of Chicago Press, 1950.

Henry, Nelson B. (ed.). *Adapting the Secondary School Program to the Needs of Youth*. Fifty-second Yearbook of the National Society for the Study of Education, Part I. Chicago: University of Chicago Press, 1953.

Kirst, Michael W., and Decker F. Walker. "An Analysis of Curriculum Policy Making." *Review of Educational Research* 41: 479–509, June, 1971.

Kliebard, Herbert M. "Reappraisal: The Tyler Rationale," *School Review* 78:259–72, February, 1970.

Krathwohl, David R., et al. (eds.). *Taxonomy of Educational Objectives*, Handbook II: *Affective Domain*. New York: David McKay, 1964.

Lindvall, C. M. (ed.). *Defining Educational Objectives*. Pittsburgh: University of Pittsburgh Press, 1964.

Macdonald, James B., and David E. Purpel. "Curriculum and Planning: Visions and Metaphors," *Journal of Curriculum and Supervision* 2:178–92, Winter, 1987.

McNeil, John D. *Curriculum: A Comprehensive Introduction*. Boston: Little, Brown, 1977; 1981; 1985.

Miller, John P., and Wayne Seller. *Curriculum: Perspectives and Practice*. New York: Longman, 1985.

National Commission on Excellence in Education. *A Nation at Risk*. Washington, D.C.: National Commission on Excellence in Education, 1983.

National Science Foundation. *Educating Americans for the 21st Century*. Washington, D.C.: NSF, 1983.

Pinar, William (ed.). *Heightened Consciousness, Cultural Revolution, and Curriculum Theory*. Berkeley: McCutchan, 1974.

Reynolds, James J. *The Comprehensive Junior College Curriculum*. Berkeley: McCutchan, 1970.

Robinson, F., et al. *Curriculum Development for Improved Instruction*. Toronto: Ontario Institute for Studies in Education, 1985.

Rugg, Harold (ed.). *The Foundations Aid Technique of Curriculum Construction*. Twenty-sixth Yearbook of the National Society for the Study of Education, Parts I and II. Bloomington, Ill.: Public School Publishing Company, 1926.

Saylor, J. Galen, and William M. Alexander. *Curriculum Planning for Better Teaching and Learning*. New York: Holt, Rinehart and Winston, 1954; 1966; 1974; 1981.

Schaffarzick, Jon, and David H. Hampson (eds.). *Strategies for Curriculum Development*. Berkeley: McCutchan. 1975.

Shane, Harold G. (ed.). *The American Elementary School*. Thirtieth John Dewey Society Yearbook. New York: Harper and Row, 1953.

Smith, B. Othanel, et al. *Fundamentals of Curriculum Development*. Yonkers-on-Hudson, N.Y.: World Book, 1950; 1957.

Taba, Hilda. *Curriculum Development: Theory and Practice*. New York: Harcourt, Brace and World, 1962.

Twentieth Century Fund. *Report of the Task Force on Federal Elementary and Secondary Education Policy*. New York: Twentieth Century Fund, 1983.

Tyler, Ralph W. *Basic Principles of Curriculum and Instruction*. Chicago: University of Chicago Press, 1949.

Verduin, John R., Jr. *Cooperative Curriculum Improvement*. Englewood Cliffs, N.J.: Prentice-Hall, 1967.

Walker, Decker F. "A Naturalistic Model for Curriculum Development," *School Review* 80:51–65, October, 1971.

Weinstein, Gerald, and Mario D. Fantini (eds.). *Toward Humanistic Education: A Curriculum of Affect*. New York: Praeger, 1970.

Zeigler, L. Harmon, et al. "How School Control Was Wrested from the People," *Phi Delta Kappan* 58:534–39, March, 1977.

Selection 3.1

Specific Approaches to Curriculum Development

Ralph W. Tyler

The term "curriculum" is used in several different ways in current educational literature. In its most limited sense, it is an outline of a course of study. At the other extreme, the curriculum is considered to be everything that transpires in the planning, teaching, and learning in an educational institution. In this chapter the term will be used to include the plans for an educational program. The term "curriculum development," then, will refer to developing the plans for an educational program, including the identification and selection of educational objectives, the selection of learning experiences, the organization of the learning experiences, and the evaluation of the educational program.

Approaches to curriculum development are likely to vary with different kinds of educational institutions: those used in professional schools are not usually like those used in liberal arts colleges, and those appropriate for colleges may not be feasible in elementary schools. The focus of this chapter is on approaches to curriculum development in American public elementary and secondary schools.

The term "approach" also has a variety of meanings in contemporary educational discourse. Here it will be used to include the

SOURCE. In *Strategies for Curriculum Development,* eds. Jon Schaffarzick and David H. Hampson (Berkeley, Calif.: McCutchan, 1975), pp. 17-33.

various aspects of the development process, including the assumptions, the purposes, the criteria, the procedures, and the participants in curriculum development projects.

The content of this chapter is derived from my experience in curriculum development beginning in Nebraska in 1925. Although many of the projects in which I have been involved have been in colleges or professional schools, a considerable part of my activities has been with elementary and secondary schools, for example, the Eight Year Study with high schools and the Neighborhood Education Center involving four elementary schools in an inner-city, "disadvantaged" area.

THE NATURE OF CURRICULUM DEVELOPMENT

Curriculum development is a practical enterprise, not a theoretical study. It endeavors to design a system to achieve an educational end and is not primarily attempting to explain an existential phenomenon. The system must be designed to operate effectively in a society where a number of constraints are present, and with human beings who have purposes, preferences, and dynamic mechanisms in operation. Hence, an essential early step in curriculum development is to examine and analyze significant conditions that influence the construction and operation of the curriculum.

PRIMARY ANALYSIS

One important factor for early analysis is the need or problem that has led to the decision to construct or reconstruct a curriculum. For example, the many recent attempts to develop new curricula for disadvantaged children have been largely stimulated both by the recognition that children from low-income families, especially minorities, are making little progress in their academic work and by the pressure on the schools exerted by active minority groups. The several national curriculum development projects in science and mathematics were mainly promoted by scientists and mathematicians who pointed to the out-of-date content that they found in high school textbooks and who were concerned by the small percent of high school students taking advanced courses in science and mathematics.

The current interest in building new curricula for "career education" appears to derive from several needs or problems that are now recognized. One problem is the large-scale lack of understanding on the part of children and youth of the modern world of work. Another is the increasing alienation of youth from the adult society including lack of plans or planning for their occupations. A third is the current high level of unemployment of youth between the ages of sixteen and twenty-one, and a fourth is the lack of vocational courses in the high school for job areas that are experiencing increasing demand.

Most curriculum approaches do not involve a systematic analysis of the needs or problems that have stimulated the interest in a given curriculum project. As a result, it is likely that some of the curriculum development efforts will not adequately provide for the needs or solve the problems, or the local schools will not adopt the new curricula because they do not appear to be responsive to the problems that are recognized locally. For example, the most expensive curriculum development project undertaken to that time was the high school physics course produced by the Physical Science Study Committee.* In spite of the large expenditures both in development and in teacher institutes to help physics teachers understand and utilize the materials, schools using them today as the committee intended them to be used are in a distinct minority. Part of this ineffectiveness can be attributed to other factors, but one obvious error made by PSSC was its failure to work with local schools sufficiently to know what problems and difficulties they were having in physics courses and to see that the new physics curriculum would furnish a way of solving some of these problems or overcoming some of their difficulties.

Far too often the following questions are asked: "How can we get the schools to change?" or "Why aren't the schools innovative?" The school ought not change for the sake of change nor innovate for the sake of innovation. The school has a mission which it performs more or less well. Where it believes it is succeeding in its mission, it sees no reason to change. Where it encounters problems or discovers it is

---

*The Physical Science Study Committee, chaired by Jerold Zacharias of the Massachusetts Institute of Technology, obtained in 1959 the first grant from the National Science Foundation to produce a new high school physics course.

failing in its mission, the school is usually interested in doing something likely to solve the problem. The schools accepted the diagnosis of physicists that the content of high school physics textbooks was out of date, and they welcomed the efforts of PSSC to produce authentic, up-to-date material. They did not, however, recognize the necessity for a new kind of learning experience and a new kind of teaching strategy. Hence, as Goodlad and his colleagues (1974) found in their observations of a sample of PSSC classrooms, the PSSC materials were being utilized in the same way that previous textbooks had been used. It is doubtful, furthermore, whether many high schools considered the relatively small enrollment in advanced physics classes as a serious problem. Had they done so, they might have helped the Physical Science Study Committee analyze possible causes for this enrollment situation and develop more effective plans than were represented by the PSSC course. It is interesting that neither the PSSC nor Project Physics has stopped the downward trend in enrollment in high school physics classes.

Another important facet of analyzing the problem is to identify the particular category of students who are having difficulties with the present curriculum or for whom no satisfactory learning system is available. In the field of primary reading, for example, 75 to 80 percent of American children achieve the skills required to comprehend typical newspaper items and children's stories by age thirteen. However, 20 to 25 percent do not learn to read adequately. These children are usually found in the inner cities and in very rural areas. They commonly come from low-income families where the parents have had little education. Designing a more effective reading curriculum for these categories of children is a different task than the effort to develop a curriculum to be used for all primary children.

Similarly, an analysis of the problem of the individualization of learning reveals certain categories of children who devise their own individual sequence of learning and proceed at their own rate while others require a curriculum specifically designed to enable them to learn and to progress sequentially. It is an inefficient use of resources to design an individualized curriculum for those who develop one for themselves.

It is still early enough for major curriculum development projects in career education to analyze the problems more fully before designing curricula to deal with them. The proponents of some of these are, nevertheless, telling the community, and especially low-income parents, that the new curriculum when in operation will largely guarantee the employment of graduates who do not go on to postsecondary schools. An analysis of the problem would have shown that it is not primarily the lack of occupational skills that prevents the large-scale employment of seventeen-year-olds. Most employing institutions will not hire youth under age twenty-one no matter how skilled they may be. If this be true, the implication for the design of curricula for occupational skill training would connect it directly with employment, possibly through cooperative education or through postsecondary technical training. The main point I wish to make is that curriculum development projects must begin with an analysis of the needs or problems that have stimulated the decision to develop a new or revised curriculum.

Related to the analysis of the relevant problems, the approach should examine the contemporary educational environments, including the home, the peer group, the larger community, and the school, in order to identify dynamic factors that influence the problem and the constraints that must be considered in designing an effective curriculum. For example, an analysis of the large environment of young children in a slum neighborhood might reveal a pervasive negative attitude toward the school and schooling that strongly influences the children's work in school; thus many of them consider their time in school not only as irrelevant but boring, unhappy, and often painful. A curriculum that assumes that the students want to learn what the school has to teach will be ineffective. Some way of influencing the out-of-school environment is necessary, or a curriculum must be designed with highly potent internal rewards.

Particular attention should be given to teachers when one is considering the positive and negative dynamic factors that must be taken into account in the curriculum development project. A curriculum designed as a complete, almost teacher-proof, learning system will not usually be acceptable to teachers in any field in which they feel confident that they can teach and do not dislike the teaching role. The curriculum preferred and more likely to be used by teachers is one with components from which the teacher can make selections and/or adaptations in terms of what he perceives to be necessary for the conditions under which he works and what he believes best utilizes his skill, ingenuity, and personal style. A rigid learning system that permits or requires very little artistry on the part of the teacher is likely to be accepted only when the teacher dislikes the teaching task—as in routine drill in spelling, handwriting, or computation—or feels that he does not have the competence to teach it well. The curriculum development plan will, in most cases, need to include means for working with teachers to assure that the curriculum meets their needs and that they can handle their roles effectively.

One of the limiting factors requiring attention in many curriculum projects is the conscious or unconscious assumption on the part of the school that it is fully as much a sorting institution as it is an educational one. In the past these two functions largely went together. Many children from families with educated parents went to school with some notion of what they were expected to learn and how to go about learning it. This made it possible for them to be guided by the existing curriculum, including textbooks and other learning materials, and to use them successfully. A number of students, on the other hand, did not understand the purposes or the learning tasks they were assigned and saw no connection between the curriculum and those things that were important to them. The class activities and the learning materials neither caught their attention nor stimulated their efforts. Normal school practice was to assign high marks to those who found meaning and satisfaction in the curriculum and low marks to those who did not carry on the learning tasks successfully. Thus "good students" were encouraged to continue their education while "poor students" were discouraged and dropped out or were pushed out.

It has been common in the past to place responsibility for failure on the quality of students rather than on the adequacy of the curriculum, and, since the society did not appear to suffer when "poor students" did not learn, the school was not attacked for sorting them out. Now, however, an uneducated person is a costly liability to American society, and the schools are expected to educate all children. It is also widely recognized that every child who has no serious physical handicap is capable of learning the kinds of behavior emphasized by the schools.

This change in expectation necessitates not only new orientation on the part of many teachers but also new understanding and skills. In curriculum development it requires the formulation of learning objectives that are understood both by teachers and students and believed by both to be desirable and attainable. An approach that seeks to develop a curriculum that will be meaningful and helpful to students who have not learned much heretofore involves working with such children and their teachers to clarify meaningful educational goals and to find learning experiences that stimulate the children's attention and interest and that they can carry through successfully.

Some constraints arise from the traditional role of the public schools in America. In the past children and youth learned outside of school most of what was required to be a constructive adult. They gradually were inducted into adult life because the barriers separating them from adults were neither many nor rigid. By the time they were fifteen or sixteen they had participated with adults in most of life's arenas: home, work, church, playing field, and social and civic activities. But the school was expected to expand the horizon of children by opening up the resources of scholarship, which went far beyond the firsthand experience in the community. The school was not to be a substitute for direct experience but a means of enlarging it. Reading, writing, history, geography, literature, mathematics, science—these were subjects that could open up a vast world of experiences, ideas, and knowledge that could free young people from the limitation of their parochial environment. Hence, teachers were sought who had had scholarly preparation. Now, a bachelor's degree is a minimum requirement for teacher certification in all states. Scholarly interests and background are assets for much teaching, but they are a constraint when teachers are expected to provide vocational guidance relating to occupations that are foreign to academic college programs. Ginzberg's study of career guidance (1971) shows its inadequacy in the typical American high school. A scholarly teacher is unlikely to know much about blue-collar jobs and to be a role model for them; he is also likely to have low esteem for such jobs and to communicate this to his students. Such a constraint needs to be considered in planning career education curricula in order to determine what is possible in a school and what will have to be learned elsewhere.

Although I have used career education as an extreme example of a constraint that must be recognized in the typical teaching staff, most curriculum development projects will find that teachers or other school personnel have not yet acquired the attitudes, understanding, or skills necessary to guide some of the desirable learning experiences. Where such constraints are identified, they need to be dealt with by providing for necessary teacher education, by allocating the learning activities to other institutions or individuals, or by eliminating them from the curriculum.

When the education or preparation of teachers, administrators, parents, or others is an essential part of the curriculum plan, the feasibility in terms of the efficient allocation of resources for this task is frequently overlooked. In Israel, for example, the Science Teaching Center developed a new science curriculum that required extensive further education of teachers in order for them to guide the learning of their students. After the materials were developed, the expenditures for the teacher education program were estimated. Much to the consternation of the project staff, it was found that the cost of educating Israel's high school science teachers to use the new course would require all of the in-service education funds of the Ministry of Education for ten years. And there was, in the meantime, great demand for curriculum development in the field of social studies. The total requirements, including personnel, equipment and supplies, consultations, and the further education of teachers, should be carefully estimated when a major curriculum project is undertaken. In the past many, if not most, such projects have failed to come to full fruition because the practical requirements could not be met.

RATIONALE FOR CURRICULUM BUILDING

After identifying the needs or problems to which the curriculum development project should be responsive and the constraints under which the curriculum must operate, the curriculum builders have a clearer picture of the requirements the curriculum will have to satisfy, and it is then possible to work on the several components of the total project. To guide these activities a rationale is helpful, if not essential. Various rationales are described in the currect educational literature, and several of them have been used successfully. However, I prefer the one outlined in my syllabus, *Basic Principles of Curriculum and Instruction* (Tyler, 1949) because it is comprehensive and has been employed effectively in a number of curriculum projects.

In this rationale, four major tasks serve as the focuses of curriculum construction: the selection and definition of the learning objectives; the selection and creation of appropriate learning experiences; the organization of the learning experiences to achieve a maximum cumulative effect; and the evaluation of the curriculum to furnish a continuing basis for necessary revisions and desirable improvements. In the case of projects that seek to construct the total school curriculum, the selection and definition of the learning objectives will commonly be attacked first, but a project that deals with only one subject or curriculum area may begin with the evaluation of an earlier curriculum, and then move to objectives, learning experiences, and organization. In some cases, as in building a curriculum in the field of literature, the first step may be the selection of literary works that appear to offer a variety of new experiences for students and then to consider what can be learned from the reading of these materials that is important for the students. Whichever of the four major tasks is undertaken first, the complete development project will involve them all, often moving to and fro among them several times as ideas emerge that are checked and rechecked among the several components of the curriculum.

Selecting and Defining Objectives

Curriculum building is not a process based on precise rules, but involves artistic design as well as critical analysis, human judgments, and empirical testing. In selecting objectives, for example, curriculum makers need current data and future estimates about opportunities and problems in various sectors of society—occupational, sociocivic, home and family, recreational. These data should be accurate and reliable, but the interpretations drawn from them as to what students can learn that enables them to respond to the opportunities or help solve the problems are judgments that are not precise and become more dependable only as they are tested in actual curriculum practice. Similarly, information about the interests of particular students, their abilities, and their problems should be accurate and reliable, but the interpretations drawn from them as to what these students can learn that will broaden their interests as well as satisfy them, that will furnish a more comprehensive set of abilities as well as build on those already acquired, and that will enable them to deal successfully with their problems are judgments that become more dependable as they are tested in the operation of the curriculum. Even more matters of human judgment are the decisions concerning what students can learn of significance from a given subject-matter field—its concepts, generalizations, questions for inquiry, methods of inquiry, skills, attitudes, and facts. When it comes to the enhanced emotional responses that can be learned from the study of literature and other arts, human judgments and the results of actual curriculum practices are the major bases for selecting objectives.

Recognizing the importance in selecting objectives of human judgments based on experience as well as relevant data systematically collected and analyzed, I recommend the procedure of group deliberation as described by Joseph J. Schwab in his "The Arts of the Practical" (1971) and illustrated in some detail by Seymour Fox at the AERA Convention in 1971. Suggestions and judgments of teachers, subject-matter specialists, curriculum specialists, psychologists, sociologists, and specialists in human development can be considered and their probable consequences deliberated in ways that lead to constructive decisions that form the basis of initial objectives to be tested for their attainability and their effects in real curriculum projects.

This procedure of deliberation is also helpful in defining the level of generalization on which to focus an objective. Since 1910 American curriculum practice has alternated between two extremes: learning objectives stated so generally that they failed to clarify the kind of behavior the student was to be helped to learn; and objectives that are so specific that they fail to provide for the level of generalization of behavior of which human beings are capable. To state that an objective of arithmetic is to teach students to "think" is obviously too general to guide the selection of learning experiences, the activities of the student or of the teacher, but to formulate more than 3,000 objectives of arithmetic as E. L. Thorndike (1922) did more than fifty years ago is to caricature human learning. Children can, for example, acquire the "idea" of addition and learn to add with a score of illustrative examples without practicing on each of the one hundred combinations of one-digit numbers taken two at a time. When I wrote in 1931 of the need for stating objectives in terms of behavior, I made definite reference to the fact that an objective could be clearly defined in terms of generalized behavior if the students involved were able to generalize at that level. An objective can be clear without being specific.

During the Second World War, when large numbers of workers had to be trained quickly to carry on specific tasks like soldering electronic circuitry, the training directors emphasized specific objectives. After the war this was carried over into education without scrutinizing the difference between objectives appropriate for very short training programs for specific jobs and long-term educational programs in schools. In making judgments about the level of generality to be the focus of a given educational objective, one should use the process of deliberation carried on by the types of groups suggested above.

The syllabus mentioned earlier comments on the use of the school's educational philosophy as a screen or set of criteria for selecting objectives, particularly for distinguishing the more important from the less important ones. The syllabus also points out the way in which knowledge of the psychology of learning can be used to estimate the probability of attaining a given objective under the conditions found in a particular school. It is obvious that the effort to develop learning experiences for an objective that has small likelihood of being attained will be wasted.

The selection and definition of objectives for a curriculum are a complex but necessary—and continuing—task. It is continuing both as the rest of the curriculum tasks are carried on and after the curriculum is operating because new external conditions and experiences with the curriculum in the school will be providing new information and the bases for new judgments about objectives. A curriculum must be ever relevant in the best sense of that word.

Selecting and Creating Learning Experiences

Creating learning experiences is an even more artistic enterprise than the selection of objectives. It is true that certain conditions must be met for an experience to aid the student in reaching the objective. The student must, for example, carry on the behavior that is the learning objective in order to learn it. The learner must, furthermore, obtain satisfaction (reinforcement) from the desired behavior in order for it to become part of his repertoire of behavior. Opportunities for practicing the behavior and for feedback to inform the learner when his performance is not satisfactory so that he can try again are also conditions to be met by a set of learning experiences. But these are criteria largely used in appraising possible learning experiences, not means of creating them. Not all teachers or curriculum builders are able to create new and effective learning experiences. A procedure I have found useful is to ask each of those involved in the curriculum development project to suggest a few learning experiences that seem to him appropriate and then to use the deliberative process to review, criticize, and identify those offering promise enough for further development. The persons who, in this preliminary exercise, created some experiences that held up under deliberative review are then encouraged to produce more.

In creating learning experiences, it is important to use the perspective of the different kinds of students for whom they are designed. The initial activities should attract the attention of each student and seem worth doing because they can help him learn something he wants to learn, because they are interesting to do, or because persons he respects are doing them. These activities should also be well within his present ability to carry on successfully so that he can gain confidence in going on with further activities. Although practice is essential in learning, repetitive drill soon becomes boring, and the student does not give adequate attention to it. This effort to use the student's perspective is often overlooked in creating learning experiences. It is necessary to keep firmly in mind that human learners rarely, if ever, want to be "shaped" by others. Each one has purposes and interests of his own and utilizes much energy and effort to further his purposes and satisfy his interests. If a school activity is perceived as interesting and/or useful for his purposes, he enters into it energetically, whereas if it seems irrelevant or boring or painful, he avoids it, or limits his involvement as much as he can. I have found that observing and interviewing students when they are actively engaged in learning things they think important help me to develop initial outlines for experiences that will help these students learn things the school seeks to teach.

Another important principle to keep in mind is to make use of peer-group influences as far as they can be appropriately employed in the development of the desired objectives. Solitary activities are hard for children to carry on for long periods of time. Group projects and games, group discussions, group attacks on problems, and group planning of emotionally charged experiences are illustrations of activities that provide powerful learning experiences. A two-student group is a special case in which learning can be enhanced. The two may be of different ages in a tutoring relationship, of the same age in a cooperative endeavor, or of the same age in a competitive contest. When participants in a curriculum development project are encouraged to explore the many types of social learning, they usually are able to create a wider range of effective learning experiences than they produced before.

Learning experiences that facilitate transfer usually require explicit attention. Every educational program seeks to aid students in developing new ways of thinking, feeling, and acting that will be employed by them in the various appropriate situations they encounter in their lives. Education has been unsuccessful if the student does not transfer what he learns in school to his life outside. Because many things to be learned in school are new ways of viewing situations, new ways of attacking problems, new ways of understanding and explaining phenomena, new ways of responding emotionally to aesthetic experiences, new kinds of interests, and new social, intellectual, and communication skills, they are often in sharp contrast to the habits, ideas, and practices of many students. Without learning experiences that furnish help to apply these new things to life situations the student is encountering, he may not transfer school learning to his life outside the classroom. Hence, for every objective, the participants in curriculum development will find it helpful to consider the ways in which, and the conditions under which, the behavior being learned can appropriately be employed by the student outside the classroom. Thus, an important criterion for a set of learning experiences is the inclusion of a number that stimulate the student to use outside the school what he is learning in school. Too frequently the curriculum omits this important component.

Organizing Learning Experiences

The syllabus referred to earlier discusses the relatively minor changes in student behavior that result from single, isolated learning experiences. However, when they are organized so that each subsequent experience builds on what has been learned in earlier ones and so that the student can perceive the connection between what he is learning in one field and what he is learning in another, the cumulative effect in changes in the learner's behavior is greatly enhanced. The purpose guiding the task of organizing learning experiences in the curriculum is to seek to maximize their combined impact. In obtaining a larger cumulative effect, attention should be given both to the sequence of experiences within each field of learning, such as mathematics, social studies, and occupational planning, and the extent of integration among the fields. By integration is meant the learner's perception of meaningful connectives from one field to another so that what he learns day by day in the several fields will be part of his repertoire of behavior, and he can draw upon the learning in all the fields as he encounters situations or problems where they are appropriate.

To plan for sequence and integration, organizing elements such as concepts, skills, and values are helpful. This means, for example, that the curriculum makers identify major concepts that are useful in explaining and controlling phenomena and that are sufficiently complex and pervasive to enable the student to gain increasing depth of understanding and increasing breadth of application of them as he progresses from week to week and year to year in the curriculum. Some concepts may also be related to phenomena in other fields or problems that cut across several fields so that they are useful elements for aiding integration of learning.

Curriculum makers can also identify significant skills that are sufficiently complex and pervasive to serve as organizing elements to achieve sequence and integration. And, for objectives involving attitudes, appreciations, interests, and personal commitments, curriculum makers can identify important values that can serve as organizing elements.

The syllabus comments on the variety of organizing principles that are found in current curriculums. I doubt if there is a single organizing principle that is to be preferred because it clearly contributes to a greater cumulative effect of the learning experiences. The principles can generally be selected on the ground that they furnish a sequence or an integration that is meaningful and effective with the students and teachers who are expected to use them.

In addition to criteria, elements, and principles of organization, the curriculum makers must deal with the problem of the organizing structures, such as courses, units, topics, lessons, and their relative rigidity or flexibility. The recent debate on individualization of instruction furnishes an initial list of issues and criteria with regard to the size and definition of useful structures, while the debates on the open classroom fairly well outline the issues and criteria to guide in developing an appropriate balance between flexibility and rigidity.

Curriculum Evaluation

The term "evaluation" is used in several different ways in current educational publications, ranging from the inclusion of all information needed by decision makers in education to the other extreme in which it is restricted to the use of an objective testing program. I shall employ the term to include the process of comparing the ideas and assumptions involved in curriculum development with the realities to which they refer. Most of the planning, the monitoring, and the reporting of curriculum activities is guided by the conceptions the participants have about the persons, processes, and objects involved. Unless there is continuous checking to ascertain the probable validity of these notions, the curriculum development project will have little relation to the actual situations that are being encountered. Evaluation is this checking process.

The checking process should be applied at four different stages in curriculum development. When one or more ideas are proposed for developing a program, a set of materials, or an instructional device, evaluation should be undertaken to find out whether there is any evidence from earlier experiments or experience that indicates the probable effectiveness of the idea. In reviewing recent curriculum development projects, I am disappointed to see how frequently ideas are accepted that have been tried or tested in the past and found fallacious. It is unfortunate that so many of the project directors are newcomers to curriculum development and are unfamiliar with its detailed history because much wasted effort is likely to be avoided by evaluation at the idea stage.

Evaluation is also essential in the implementation stage. When a plan is presumably in operation an actual check of the school situations usually reveals a number of places reporting the plan is in operation when, in fact, it is not. In some cases this is due to a lack of understanding of the essential features of the plan, so that the implementation lacks salient conditions essential to the idea. In other cases those implementing the plan feel that it will not work, and so they establish a program that they think is better. There are even cases where an old procedure is continued while it is professed that the new idea is in operation. I found in the study of activity schools in New York City in 1942 that less than half the classrooms in these schools were actually carrying on activity programs.

Various techniques have been developed for sampling the actual implementation of educational programs. John Goodlad and his colleagues (1974) have devised a rather comprehensive schedule for his current study of schooling in the United States. Seymour Fox and his colleagues in the Hebrew University of Jerusalem have developed an analysis procedure that relates the actual operations to the purposes and guiding principles of the plan. In our study of activity schools we used a checklist of sixty-one items based on an analysis of the plan for these schools.

A third stage in which evaluation contributes to the effectiveness of the curriculum is during its actual operation, both in guiding its development during early trials and also in monitoring its continuing use. Placement tests, mastery tests, and diagnostic tests can keep students and teachers in touch with the actual learning process and can furnish information to guide them. An assessment program conducted once or twice a year can provide data that serve to alert the principal or the central administration regarding problems needing special attention. The sixty-eighth yearbook of the National Society for the Study of Education entitled *Evaluation: New Roles; New Means* (Tyler, 1969) describes some of these procedures.

Finally, evaluation needs to be conducted to find out the extent to which students are actually developing the patterns of behavior that the curriculum was designed to help them learn. Before curriculum makers had developed sophisticated achievement tests, this kind of evaluation was conducted with norm-referenced achievement tests that were not based on a sample of behavior that the students were expected to learn but only on those exercises which differentiated among pupils. This often meant that the exercises did not reflect what the curriculum was designed to help students learn, but involved behavior not in the curriculum, which sharply differentiated students who came from backgrounds where they experienced these things from students who did not. Because schools attempt to help all children learn, the exercises that sample what the children are really learning in school often do not differentiate sharply among them.

Curriculum makers have recently become more interested in using criterion-referenced tests rather than norm-referenced ones. They have also become aware of various other devices that indicate what students have learned. It seems likely that evaluation of the outcomes of new curricula will be increasingly valid.

CONCLUSION

The approach outlined in this chapter is pragmatic. It assumes limited resources for curriculum development and effective implementation. It seeks, therefore, to utilize available knowledge and experience at each step. A grand, comprehensive, total school curriculum is assumed to be impracticable to develop and implement with the resources available. Hence the first step is to identify serious difficulties or problems with the present curriculum that should be given primary attention. The second step is to outline explicitly the constraints under which a new curriculum must operate. To maximize the constructive participation in curriculum development a group procedure, including group deliberation, is suggested. The construction process itself is outlined in terms of four major tasks: selecting objectives, developing learning experiences, organizing learning experiences, and evaluation. This approach has been successful in my own experience, and I believe it has value for others.

REFERENCES

Ginzberg, Eli. *Career Guidance: Who Needs It, Who Provides It, Who Can Improve It*. New York: McGraw-Hill, 1971.

Goodlad, John I., M. Frances Klein, et al. *Looking Behind the Classroom Door*. Rev. ed. Worthington, Ohio: Charles A. Jones, 1974.

Schwab, Joseph J. "The Practical: Arts of Eclectic," *School Review* 79 (August 1971): 493–542.

Thorndike, E.L. *Psychology of Arithmetic*. New York: Macmillan, 1922.

Tyler, Ralph W. *Basic Principles of Curriculum and Instruction*. Chicago: University of Chicago Press, 1949.

Tyler, Ralph W. (ed.). *Evaluation: New Roles, New Means*. Sixty-eighth Yearbook of the National Society for the Study of Education. Part II. Chicago: University of Chicago Press, 1969.

Selection 3.2

A Naturalistic Model for Curriculum Development

Decker F. Walker

This paper[1] presents a model of curriculum development as it is practiced in modern curriculum projects. It is a naturalistic model in the sense that it was constructed to represent phenomena and relations observed in actual curriculum projects as faithfully as possible with a few terms and principles.[2]

The field of curriculum already can boast an outstandingly successful model of curriculum development based on the work of a generation of curriculum theorists from Franklin Bobbitt to Ralph W. Tyler. The formal elements of that model—the classical model—are the objective and the learning experience. Its logical operations are determining objectives, stating them in proper form, devising learning experiences, selecting and organizing learning experiences to attain given outcomes, and evaluating the outcomes of those experiences. This model has undergone fifty years of continuous development and use. It has facilitated the systematic study of education, and it has served as the basis for a respectable and growing educational technology.

For all its successes, however, this classical model seems not to have represented very well the most characteristic features of tradi-

SOURCE. *School Review* 80 (October 1971), pp. 51-65. Published by The University of Chicago Press.

tional educational practice.[3] In most cases when teachers or subject matter specialists work at curriculum development, the objectives they formulate are either a diversion from their work or an appendix to it, not an integral part of it. It may be that curriculum developers, to the extent that they deviate from the classical model, are wasting effort or, worse, misdirecting children's education. But it is also possible that the classical model neglects or distorts important aspects of contemporary practice in curriculum development. If so, a model of curriculum development frankly based on practice should illuminate novel facets of the curriculum development process, correct misconceptions about that process, and enable us to understand both the failures and the successes of the classical model.

THE NATURALISTIC MODEL

The model of the process of curriculum development to be presented here consists of three elements: the curriculum's *platform,* its *design,* and the *deliberation* associated with it.

The curriculum developer does not begin with a blank slate. He could not begin without some notion of what is possible and desirable educationally. The system of beliefs and values that the curriculum developer brings to his task and that guides the development of the curriculum is what I call the curriculum's *platform.* The word "platform" is meant to suggest both a political platform and something to stand on. The platform includes an idea of what is and a vision of what ought to be, and these guide the curriculum developer in determining what he should do to realize his vision.

The second formal element in the model, *deliberation,*[4] is aptly characterized by Schwab (1969) as follows:

> [Deliberation] . . . treats both ends and means and must treat them as mutually determining one another. It must try to identify, with respect to both, what facts may be relevant. It must try to ascertain the relevant facts in the concrete case. It must try to identify the desiderata in the case. It must generate alternative solutions. It must take every effort to trace the branching pathways of consequences which may flow from each alternative and affect desiderata. It must then weigh alternatives and their costs and consequences against one another, and choose, not the right alternative, for there *is* no such thing but the best one.

A curriculum's *design,*[5] like an automobile's design, is the set of abstract relationships embodied in the designed object. The design is the theoretically significant output of the curriculum development process. When it is embodied in a material form, a curriculum's design, like an automobile's design, presents itself to us as a single material entity, a Gestalt, which must then be represented in some schematic way if we are to deal with it analytically.

We are accustomed to speaking of curricula as if they were objects produced by curriculum projects. The trouble with this view is that the curriculum's effects must be ascribed to events, not materials. The materials are important because their features condition the events that affect those using the materials. The *curriculum's design*—the set of relationships embodied in the materials-in-use which are capable of affecting students—rather than the materials themselves are the important concerns of the curriculum specialist.

The trouble with the concept of design is that the curriculum's design is difficult to specify explicitly and precisely. A method is needed for representing the potentially effective features of a set of curriculum materials schematically so that design elements can be identified and treated analytically. One way to specify a curriculum's design is by the series of *decisions* that produce it. A curriculum's design would then be represented by the choices that enter into its creation. Just as an experienced architect could construct a model of a building from a complete record of the decisions made by the building's designer as well as from a set of blueprints, so a curriculum developer could substantially reconstruct a project's curriculum plan and materials from a record of the choices they made. It may seem awkward to represent a design as a series of decisions, but I hope to show that such a representation has many features that will appeal to both theorists and researchers.

In the development of any curriculum some design decisions will be made with forethought and after a consideration of alternatives. These decisions make up the curriculum's *explicit* design. But the curriculum developer adopts some courses of action automatically, without considering alternatives. In these cases it is awkward to speak of a decision, even though the result is the same as if a decision has been overtly made. These unconsidered choices make up the curriculum's *implicit* design.

A curriculum's implicit design can never be completely specified in this mode of representation because the number of decisions, implicit and explicit, that underlie a project's materials is impossibly large. This limitation is not serious, however, for with accurate records any question that can be asked about the implicit design can be answered. In framing the question the questioner must ask how a particular issue was decided, and this characterization of the issue defines the decision of interest. Theoretically, at least, records of the curriculum maker's behavior should reveal the course of action he chose at that point, even though he did not formulate the decision himself.

In this naturalistic model, then, the theoretically interesting output of the curriculum development process is not a collection of objects, not a list of objectives, not a set of learning experiences, but a set of design decisions. The process by which beliefs and information are used to make these decisions is *deliberation.* The main operations in curriculum deliberation are *formulating decision points, devising alternative choices* at these decision points, *considering arguments* for and against suggested decision points and decision alternatives, and, finally, *choosing* the most defensible alternative subject to acknowledged constraints.

THE DYNAMICS OF THE NATURALISTIC MODEL

The animating principle in curriculum deliberation is the desire for defensibility, for justifiability of decisions (Scheffler, 1958). The curriculum designer wants to be able to say he was constrained either by circumstances or by his principles to decide as he did. To be constrained by circumstances is the curriculum designer's strongest possible justification, for then he has no genuine choice. If every decision were dictated by circumstances beyond his control, however, he would have no freedom to remake the world as he wished it to be. But when all circumstantial constraints are considered the curriculum designer finds he still has options left. It is his commitment to making these remaining choices in a defensible way that leads him to search for additional principles which are not natural, but man-made. The curriculum developer expects that these *conventional* principles will be accepted not as facts of life but as expressions of a shared view of the way life can and should be. Taken together, these natural and conventional principles provide enough constraints to enable the decision maker to resolve consistently issues that arise and to justify his decisions on the ground that anyone who acknowledged his principles would choose as he chose.

Needless to say, the derivation of curriculum-making constraints from natural and conventional principles and the application of these constraints to decision making is a horribly complicated job. We should not be surprised, therefore, to find that curriculum deliberations are chaotic and confused. Alternatives are often formulated and defended before the issue has been clearly stated. Feelings run high. Personal preferences are expressed in the same breath with reasoned arguments. But we must not be misled into believing either that such confusion is worthless or that it is the inevitable consequence of deliberation. Deliberation is defined by logical, not social psychological criteria, and it may take many forms. The most common form in current practice is argumentation and debate by a group of people. But it could be done by one person, and no logical barrier stands in the way of its being performed by a computer.

The heart of the deliberative process is the justification of choices. This justification takes the form: "If you accept *this,* then you must choose *that.*" In justifying a choice we appeal to that which is already accepted in order to secure approval for our less-well-accepted choice. Those assumptions which the curriculum designer accepts and which serve as the basis for the justification of his choices constitute the curriculum's platform. Almost anything that is accepted as good, true, or beautiful can be part of a platform. Certainly beliefs about what exists and about what is possible are necessary parts of any platform. I call such beliefs *conceptions.* "We believe there is a learnable strategy for discovering one's unspoken notions, one's unstated ways of approaching things," states a conception of what is learnable (Bruner, 1966, p. 93).

Beliefs about what relations hold between existing entities, that is, beliefs about what is true, I call *theories.* "The teacher imparts attitudes toward a subject and, indeed, attitudes toward learning itself," states a theory of the development of attitudes toward learning (Bruner, 1966, p. 123).

Beliefs about what is educationally desirable, that is, beliefs about the good and the beautiful in education, I call aims. "We teach a subject not to produce little living libraries on that subject, but rather to get a student to think mathematically for himself, to consider matters as a historian does, to take part in the process of knowledge-getting," states an aim in general terms (Bruner, 1966, p. 72). Educational objectives are one form in which aims can be stated.

These three platform components—conceptions, theories, and aims—are sophisticated products of reflections on life and on education. However, a curriculum maker's actions are frequently based on less carefully conceptualized notions. Two kinds of less explicit but nevertheless powerful platform components are worth our attention: *images* and *procedures.* Images specify the desirable simply by indicating an entity or class of entities that is desirable without specifying why or in what way it is desirable.[6] Heroes are cultural images. So are outstanding works of art or admired scientific theories. Procedures specify courses of action or decision that are desirable without specifying why or in what way they are desirable. "Be honest" and "Minimize the time necessary to learn" are procedures since they specify a method of operation without specifying why or in what way that method is a good one.

Frequently the curriculum developer cannot decide among a set of alternatives either because all the alternatives are consistent with his platform or because none are, or because he does not have enough information to determine whether they are consistent with his platform. In these cases the curriculum designer must seek additional information in order to make a justifiable decision. Even when his platform principles make him confident that his choice is a good one, the responsible curriculum maker will often seek empirical confirmation of his beliefs. Data, while not part of the platform, can be a most persuasive basis for justification.

The curriculum designer may feel justified in a particular decision whenever he regards it as consistent with his platform and the information available to him. But judging the consistency of a decision alternative with a system of platform principles and a body of data is a complicated affair. Any decision is likely to fall under the purview of several platform principles and be judged more or less desirable in their separate lights. Also, the platform itself is likely to contain conflicting tendencies, if not outright contradictions, which only appear when the consequences of various principles are thoroughly worked out. For both these reasons and more a curriculum designer may change his platform as his work progresses.

In current practice, however, such changes seem to be relatively minor. For the most part they consist of elaborations of existing principles and adjudications of unanticipated conflicts. These minor alterations are preserved and kept consistent through the action of *precedent.* When a situation arises that is substantially the same as one already encountered, the curriculum designer need not laboriously justify the new situation in terms of platform principles; he can simply cite precedent. The application of precedent is such an important component of curriculum planning that I find it convenient to speak of the body of precedents evolved from the platform as *policy* and reserve the word platform for principles accepted from the start.

This completes the naturalistic model. The diagram in Figure 3.2-1 shows the major components of the model and their relationships. The platform is shown as the base on which further work rests. Platform principles together with whatever data the project collects are the raw material used in deliberation, in the course of which curriculum materials are designed. The design stands at the apex of

FIGURE 3.2-1. A Schematic Diagram of the Main Components of the Naturalistic Model

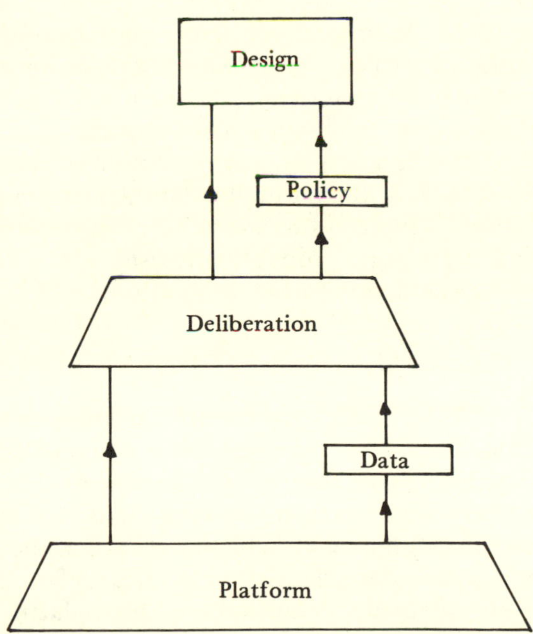

the structure to indicate both its status as the ultimate end of the process and its dependence upon the other components.

This model is primarily descriptive, whereas the classical model is prescriptive. This model is basically a temporal one: it postulates a beginning (the platform), an end (the design), and a process (deliberation) by means of which the beginning progresses to the end. In contrast, the classical model is a means-end model: it postulates a desired end (the objective), a means for attaining this end (the learning experience), and a process (evaluation) for determining whether the means does indeed bring about the end. The two models differ radically in the roles they assign to objectives and to evaluation in the process of curriculum development.

In the classical model objectives are essential, since, without an objective, learning experiences cannot be rationally selected and assessed. In the naturalistic model, on the other hand, objectives are only one means among others for guiding our search for better educational programs. Objectives are not a starting point in this model but a late development of the curriculum maker's platform.

Evaluation in the classical model is a self-corrective process for determining whether learning experiences lead to the attainment of given objectives.[7] Without it, all is speculation. In the naturalistic model this kind of evaluation is not *logically* necessary. Design decisions *can* be justified by reference to the platform only. However, the empirical data that evaluation can provide on the effects of design decisions can be compelling evidence in a justificatory argument. In other words, in the naturalistic model evaluation is a useful tool for justifying design decisions, even though it is quite possible and not nonsensical (although probably unwise) for a curriculum developer to neglect systematic formal evaluation.[8]

THE NATURALISTIC MODEL AND CURRICULUM RESEARCH

If the naturalistic model represents the process of curriculum development faithfully, then we must revise many of our ideas about the conduct and evaluation of curriculum projects. For example, the USOE's requirement that persons seeking funds for curriculum development state their objectives behaviorally when they submit their application makes no sense if, as I believe, a defensible set of objectives is the output of deliberation based on a platform. If detailed information about the applicant's plans is needed before a grant can be awarded, that information is more fully and easily communicated by a platform which includes conceptions, explanations, images, and procedures as well as general aims.

Some curriculum practices predicated on the naturalistic model differ substantially from current practices. I wish to focus attention here on the implications of this model for research in the field of curriculum.

This model must be more fully developed before it can dependably guide research. But this elaboration and development itself requires research. In particular, a large investment of intellectual labor is necessary to create research techniques that will permit the study of curriculum designs and their platforms and deliberations. Assuming that such techniques can be developed, the model could contribute to curriculum research in several distinct ways.

1. *The model itself contains propositions that need to be tested.* According to the model, curriculum designers have platforms which strongly influence their deliberation and their final design. Do curriculum development groups in fact share a greater body of common beliefs than one would expect of groups of similar composition? Do the curriculum developer's justifications appeal to this body of shared beliefs? Do curriculum-making groups with similar platforms conduct similar deliberations and produce similar curriculum designs?

2. *The model provides a conceptual basis for descriptive studies of curriculum development.* Despite a decade and a half of unprecedented activity in curriculum development we know very little about the methods of operation of curriculum development groups. In what ways have the platforms of the different groups operating within a subject-matter area differed? How have the platforms of groups in one subject field differed from those in the other fields? What platform elements are common to most contemporary curriculum projects? What kinds of issues arise in curriculum deliberations? How many alternatives does a curriculum development group typically examine in deciding a question? On what data sources do they draw in formulating and justifying decision points and decision alternatives? It is too late for us to ask these questions of the projects which are now having such a great influence over what children learn, but we can resolve to do better. Until we can answer such basic descriptive questions we cannot hope to make much headway on deeper questions in curriculum theory.

3. *The model provides a conceptual basis for studies of the effectiveness of various design elements.* Studies of the effectiveness of contrasting educational "treatments" have been notoriously sterile. Yet, if different curriculum designs do not produce different results, curriculum development is a futile enterprise. One of the most pressing empirical tasks in the field of curriculum is the rigorous

establishment of connections between curricular variables (i.e., design elements) and learning outcomes. At present we are in a position to say with some confidence that a physics course produces learning that would not have occurred had the student not taken a course in physics. Evaluation studies of the new curricula have given us evidence which shows that students who take physics courses which have somewhat different aims will have greater success achieving those aims emphasized in their course and less success with the aims emphasized in another course. But we need evidence that some of the subtler design features to which curriculum makers give so much thought have observable effects on students.

Many of the new courses in mathematics and science have students manipulate physical materials as a means of teaching abstract concepts and relations. Since these materials are relatively expensive, a systematic determination of the additional learning ascribable to this design feature would help to justify the costs of the materials. Furthermore, an understanding of the role of manipulation in facilitating learning would be of great scientific importance. An evaluation study would normally consider the curriculum as an undifferentiated "treatment." What is needed, however, is a determination of the effects of a single design element.

One possible approach to the difficult research problem of isolating the effect of a single design element might be to excise the element (in this case manipulation) from the curriculum's platform and deliberation in all cases where it can possibly be removed. When necessary, the omitted design element could be replaced by a reasonable but much less costly alternative.[9] (Thought experiments or imaginative visualization might serve as alternatives to manipulation of materials.) If small-scale intensive studies show no important differences in the learning of groups exposed to the design element and groups given a comparable curriculum without the design element, then the value of this element would be called into question. If differences are found, the nature and extent of these differences should be valuable clues to the learning process by means of which the design element produces its effects.

4. The model could facilitate curriculum research *by making it possible to formulate succinctly questions that have not received enough attention from curriculum specialists.* A model suggests certain questions for research simply because they are so easily framed in the model's terms. The classical model has encouraged studies of the best form for objectives and of the results of various ways of formulating objectives. The naturalistic model, because it

employs different terms, suggests other questions. Justification is an important component of the naturalistic model. But the same choice can be attacked and defended on many different grounds. Which grounds are appropriate? Which kinds of grounds should be accorded greater weight? Which in fact receive greater weight in curriculum developers' deliberations? The study of the logical and empirical foundations of the process of justifying curriculum decisions is an important and neglected problem in the field.

Another neglected problem in curriculum concerns the ordering of decisions. Considering some questions before others can make a tremendous difference in the final design. A curriculum devleoper in his early work can so restrict the scope of his remaining decisions as to inadvertently close off whole fields of options. Should the curriculum developer make the choices he regards as crucial at an early stage in his work? What are the consequences of bringing different kinds of questions into the deliberations at different points? What areas of decision are interrelated in such a manner that making decisions of one kind reduces options in related areas in ways other than through reduction of resources?

5. *The model should help to identify problems from other fields whose solution would facilitate curriculum development.* Curriculum designers rely explicitly and implicitly on natural and conventional principles in their platforms and their deliberations. Frequently these principles are not tested propositions. They are condensations of practical experience, conventional wisdom, speculative hypotheses, or simply hunches. Perhaps curriculum developers should avoid such "principles," but they do not. We have insufficient experience with curriculum development to assess the extent to which these unverified principles prove to be true, so we cannot say whether curriculum makers are wise to rely on such principles. But it seems that the recent wave of curriculum projects, by operating on hypothetical psychological principles about such phenomena as discovery learning, has stimulated psychologists to investigate some questions they had not raised before. A more systematic study of the platforms and deliberations of curriculum development groups should uncover more such principles in need of investigation by our colleagues in other fields.

An example of a principle that curriculum projects seem to employ implicitly, but which has received little disciplined attention, is the role of consistency of experience in attaining certain kinds of long term learning. A curriculum developer interested in fostering inquiry will avoid any suggestion of dogmatism or arbitrary closure in his curriculum plans and materials because he believes it will detract from the course's effectiveness in developing an inquiring approach to learning. He fears that one or two experiences inconsistent with this attitude would destroy weeks of effort spent demonstrating the value and usefulness of the inquiring mode. To my knowledge this problem has been neither formulated nor investigated by educational psychologists.

NOTES

1. This paper is based on an earlier paper entitled "An Empirical Model of the Process of Curriculum Development" presented at the 1970 Annual Meeting of the American Educational Research Association in Minneapolis.

2. The model is based on reports of projects such as William Wooton's (1965), Richard J. Merrill and David Ridgway's (1969), and Arnold Grobman's (1969); and on the author's first-hand observation and study of one project as reported in "Toward More Effective Curriculum Development Projects in Art" (*Studies in Art Education* [Winter 1970]), and in "A Case Study of the Process of Curriculum Development," mimeographed (Stanford University, July 1969).

3. The classical model is, of course, intended to be prescriptive rather than descriptive, but those who recommend it as a norm imply thereby that practice guided by the model does what ordinary practice does, only better. The following articles are only a small sample of the rather sizable literature on the shortcomings of the classical model when it is applied to the classroom teaching or traditional curriculum development efforts: J. Myron Atkin (1963), Elliot W. Eisner (1967), Phillip W. Jackson and Elizabeth Belford (1965), James B. Macdonald (1966).

4. Also see David P. Gauthier (1963) for an excellent philosophical treatment of deliberation.

5. The term "curriculum design" first explicated by Herrick (1950) and used to mean the major distinctive features of a curriculum is closely related to, but distinct from, the phrase "a curriculum's design" used here. My usage applies the latter term to the *complete set* of abstract relationships embodied in the curriculum materials, whereas Herrick's usage confines the former term to the *prominent* and *distinctive features* of what I have called the curriculum's design. The same ambiguity attends the use of the word design in other contexts. When we speak of the 1967 Valiant's design, for example, we can mean the entire design including all details, although we ordinarily mean only the distinctive and prominent features of the design.

6. The idea that vague notions can nevertheless be effective by virtue of being represented in a concrete model I got from Thomas Kuhn's (1962) notion of paradigm. The idea that the force of such vague ideas arises from our admiring them but not knowing why comes from Morris Weitz's essay (1966).

7. The concept of evaluation involved in the classical model and the only type of evaluation directly relevant to the process of curriculum development is what Michael Scriven (1967) has called *formative* evaluation.

8. Evaluation as the assessment of educational decisions is not a new idea. This conception gets its earliest clear treatment in Lee Cronbach's (1963) article.

9. Scriven (1967, pp. 68-69) has suggested a similar procedure for obtaining

a valid control "treatment" for comparison with exposure to a curriculum produced by a project. He suggests that cut-rate "new curricula" be created, whereas I suggest here that one design element be improvised in this way.

REFERENCES

Atkin, J. Myron. "Some Evaluation Problems in a Course Content Improvement Project," *Journal of Research in Science Teaching* 1: 1 (1963): 129–32.

Bruner, Jerome. *Toward a Theory of Instruction*. Cambridge, Mass.: Belknap Press, 1966.

Cronbach, Lee. "Course Improvement through Evaluation," *Teachers College Record* (May 1963): 672–86.

Eisner, Elliot W. "Educational Objectives: Help or Hindrance?" *School Review* 75: 3 (1967): 250–60.

Gauthier, David P. *Practical Reasoning*. New York: Oxford University Press, 1963.

Grobman, Arnold. *The Changing Classroom*. BSCS, Bulletin no. 4. Garden City, N.Y.: Doubleday and Co., 1969.

Herrick, Virgil E. "The Concept of Curriculum Design." In Virgil E. Herrick and Ralph W. Tyler (eds.), *Toward Improved Curriculum Theory*. Chicago: University of Chicago Press, 1950.

Jackson, Phillip W., and Elizabeth Belford. "Educational Objectives and the Joys of Teaching," *School Review* 73: 3 (Autumn 1965): 267–91.

Kuhn, Thomas. *The Structure of Scientific Revolutions*. Chicago: University of Chicago Press, 1962.

Macdonald, James B. "The Person in the Curriculum." In Helen F. Robison (ed.), *Precedents and Promise in the Curriculum Field*. New York: Teachers College Press, 1966.

Merrill, Richard J., and David Ridgway. *CHEM Study: The Story of a Successful Curriculum Project*. San Francisco: W.H. Freeman & Sons, 1969.

Scheffler, Israel. "Justifying Curriculum Decisions," *School Review* 66: 4 (Winter 1958): 461–72.

Schwab, Joseph J. "The Practical: A Language for Curriculum," *School Review* 78: 1 (November 1969): 1–23.

Scriven, Michael. "The Methodology of Evaluation." In R.W. Tyler (ed.), *Perspectives of Curriculum Evaluation*. Chicago: Rand McNally & Co., 1967.

Walker, Decker F. "A Case Study of the Process of Curriculum Development." Mimeo. Stanford University, July 1969.

Walker, Decker F. "Toward More Effective Curriculum Development Projects in Art," *Studies in Art Education* (Winter 1970).

Weitz, Morris. "The Nature of Art." In Elliott W. Eisner and D.W. Ecker (eds.), *Readings in Art Education*. Waltham, Mass.: Blaisdell Publishing Co., 1966.

Wooton, William. *SMSG: The Making of Curriculum*. New Haven, Conn.: Yale University Press, 1965.

Selection 3.3

Difficulties to Be Met in Local Curriculum Making

Franklin Bobbitt

In the matter of curriculum making American cities are relatively autonomous. For the most part, each arranges its own courses.

There appears to be a general realization throughout the country that the education of the past is inadequate for the new conditions of a greatly changed society and that we must critically re-examine, reformulate, and extend our educational program. As a consequence, cities and villages from coast to coast are diligently working on this problem.

There is a rapidly growing realization that curriculum making is not the simple perfunctory thing it used to be when a superintendent or a committee in a relatively short time could prepare a syllabus of subject matter and drill exercises, largely in terms of the textbooks to be used. The tendency in any school system at present is to organize general committees for the different levels of instruction—elementary school, junior high school, and senior high school—and then at each level a working committee for each department. More and more, committees are organized with the expectation that the work will continue for several years before it is completed.

It is the belief of the writer that this method of procedure is in conformity with good principles of democratic school administration.

SOURCE. *Elementary School Journal* 25 (May 1925), pp. 653-63. Published by The University of Chicago Press.

Courses of study employed in a given city should not be handed down from some distant centralized agency. Neither should the school systems accept and adopt the pronouncements of the experts in the several fields. With the exception of a very few cases, pronouncements of an authoritative character do not yet exist, whatever may be said in favor of accepting them when they are formulated. Even if we had such authoritative advice, it would have to be applied to the practical conditions of the local situations.

The responsibility rests upon each city to educate its own children. This involves responsibility for the planning of the education as well as responsibility for the conduct of the education. The educational plans will not be properly appreciated and understood if they are merely taken over from some outside source. Those responsible for the work come to realize the nature and intent of the plans through formulating them. Local curriculum making, therefore, should be the method of arriving at the curriculum for any community.

It has been the observation and experience of the writer in his contacts with curriculum committees that they meet with many serious difficulties when they set to work. It is the purpose of this article to enumerate the outstanding obstacles and to present certain suggestions for overcoming them.

1. *Uncertainty as to the function of the school.* Elementary schools appear to have been established originally for the purpose of aiding the pupils in acquiring a command of the tools of thought and communication—reading, writing, spelling, computation, and oral and written expression. Even now, in authoritative pronouncements of the twentieth century, these are called the "fundamental processes." At the other extreme, there is the conception that education has to do with guiding and conditioning the all-sided growth and development of the individual in his personal qualities, disposition, attitudes, habits, powers of judgment, vision of reality, and competence in discharging all of the responsibilities of efficient adulthood.

For the most part, the educational profession is between these two extremes. It is moving from the one toward the other. The different members of the profession, however, have been moving forward at different rates. Some have made but little advance, while others have gone far. If teachers and supervisory officers were all of one mind as to the general function of the school, it would greatly facilitate all of the labors.

2. *Traditions as to the aims or objectives.* Tradition says that education consists of teaching the textbooks. For the content sub-

jects, it is a storing of the facts in memory. For the skill subjects, it is a matter of artificial academic drill in relative, or more often complete, isolation from practical applications. It is coming to appear that, in an improved type of education, information-mastery of the cold-storage, textbook type is to be a minor matter and that academic skills, not currently functioning in life itself, are likewise to play a diminishing part. Education is more and more to be accomplished through a carefully conditioned and carefully guided series of normal life-experiences. Some of these will be at school and some of them elsewhere. They will aim not at mere stores of inert information and unapplied academic skills of vanishing types but rather at abilities to do the things well which are involved in a proper type of human living. *To live as one ought to live* at each successive age-level is the *one* sure way of learning to live as one ought to live at the mature level of adulthood.

Teachers have long been accustomed to thinking in terms of subjects, textbooks, recitations, examinations, etc., all of which belong to the older traditional conception. Most of our educational machinery likewise tends to reinforce and maintain the traditional attitudes and valuations.

So long as the members of a curriculum-making committee have this attitude, the usual one, it is practically impossible for them to understand that specific abilities and activities are the aims and that the actual living of life as it ought to be lived is the way to learn to live it. Such suggestions seem so irrelevant and fantastic that curriculum committees cannot believe that a person is talking seriously when he urges such objectives and procedures for their consideration. They do not *refuse* to take it seriously; they are simply unable to do so. Their minds are tradition-bound. It seems utterly preposterous to them that any sane person can mean that education is anything other than the usual academic teaching of the familiar subjects. Only a few rare teachers, it appears, have achieved the necessary intellectual liberation.

3. *The primitive character of educational science with regard to educational objectives.* Even the fundamentals of educational science are woefully undeveloped. This science does not yet tell us what the objectives of human education are. Neither does it tell us with authority what method is to be employed in order to discover these objectives with certainty.

The consequence of this situation is that each committee has to start at the beginnings of things and establish objectives without sufficient help from education science. Lacking guidance, their thought naturally tends to fall into the familiar grooves of habit.

They find themselves unable to conceive of objectives other than the usual academic objectives. Consequently, they tend merely to formulate the same old-type curriculum. It will differ from previous formulations in date but scarcely in spirit or in content.

When science as it pertains to the objectives is developed, we shall probably discover that the objectives of education are the innumerable specific activities which constitute human life. At present, a curriculum-making committee in any city must make its own survey and analysis of community activities in discovering what these are. It is very laborious work, and the observation and experience of the writer indicate that it is very difficult for a curriculum committee to secure any clear idea of the kinds of abilities and activities which should be classified as objectives. Lacking the science, they lack even the basic concepts in terms of which to consider the problems.

It will not be possible for teacher committees to make any great progress until they can have the intellectual guidance of a well-developed and well-understood educational science pertaining to objectives.

4. *Uncertainty as to educational methods or procedures.* The nature of the educational methods to be employed is determined by the character of the ends to be achieved. If we conceive the end of the process to be the accumulation of textbook information, we shall employ the familiar methods of storing the memory with inert information. On the other hand, if we conceive the end to be right living in all of its manifestations, then we shall seek to organize opportunities for right living as the appropriate means of training. So long as there is uncertainty as to the goals, there must necessarily be uncertainty with regard to the steps to be taken, day by day, in attaining those goals. It is these steps which make up the curriculum.

5. *Traditions relative to the methods or procedures.* While there is doubt in the minds of the relatively few who are really thinking about the problems, the large majority of the teachers employ the methods dictated by tradition. They accept the subject-teaching objectives without question and then adopt the subject-teaching methods as a matter of course. Everything as it has been is assumed to be the right thing. Here and there, of course, even the blindest traditionalist will discover possibilities of improving his methods or devices in detail, but for him the fundamental assumptions remain unchanged. The weight of this tradition and the professional inertness of the great body of teachers who are controlled by it constitute a major obstacle in the way of rational curriculum making. They cannot yet see the specific methods to be employed where living as

one ought to live is the plan of learning to live as one ought to live. They must see this before they can formulate a modern curriculum.

6. *The subject-teaching fallacy.* The subject-teaching fallacy is covered in the preceding paragraph, since it is one of the traditions that education consists merely in teaching the academic subjects. We must call special attention to this difficulty, however, since it is one of the central obstacles which, if dislodged, will remove many of the other obstacles.

So long as the members of a curriculum committee conceive their responsibility to be merely teaching a particular subject in academic isolation, they are unfitted for curriculum making of the modern type. They cannot enter upon the labor of organizing their own departments until they can see human life and human activity as both the objectives of education and the means of education. Until the committee is prepared to see its problems without reference to traditional subjects, it is not prepared to formulate a curriculum of the functional or behavioristic type.

7. *The isolation of the school from the life of the community.* More and more we are coming to see that education results from the pupil's right living, wherever he may be and whatever he may be doing. Subject-teaching education can ignore everything except study and recitation of the subjects. These are almost wholly school activities. Even when there is "home work," this home work is merely a device for extending the school work by using an hour or two of the pupil's time at home. It is "school work" in the sense that it is preparation for academic exercises and has no relation to the pupil's normal home activities.

Both in theory and in practice, education is discarding this academic tradition. It is coming to be believed, for example, that health education results from 168 hours of healthful living each week, that training in practical home arts results from practicing the home arts under the conditions of home responsibilities, that the ability to read comes from doing much reading under normal conditions with normal reading motives, that training for healthful leisure occupations results from participating in normal healthful recreations wherever these may be found within the community, that civic training is the result of living the life of the good citizen wherever one may be, and, in general, that competence in the performance of activities results from the proper performance of these activities under normal conditions. When this becomes our education, quite obviously the school cannot exist in isolation from the community life. It will be engaged in assisting the community to provide the conditions of right living for its children. Some will be provided at the school; but where social conditions are favorable, possibly more of them should be provided elsewhere.

Where schools are thoroughly traditional and isolated from community living, this doctrine is meaningless, and a curriculum committee is relatively helpless, except, of course, to do the traditional thing.

8. *Community habits, attitudes, and traditions.* When any home function—for example, education—is institutionalized and taken over by a specialized agency, the latter, it appears, usually tries to expand its functions in order to assume responsibility as completely as possible. In the nature of the case, it seems that a specialized agency tends toward aggrandizement of function. On the other hand, in giving over the functions to the specialized agency, the home feels a sense of relief in transferring perplexing and laborious responsibilities. It is glad to see the functions taken over as fully and as completely as the special agency wishes.

As a consequence of the operation of this general tendency, schools have been taking over home functions very completely in the case of matters that can be managed at the school, and parents have been more than content to be relieved of their burdens. One's thinking consists largely of transforming wishes into rationalizations, and parents have generously indulged in the process. Where wishes provide the motive power, it does not take long to build up strongly intrenched traditions. The community is content, therefore, to have education managed for them and their children in complete isolation from the general community life. They would like to believe that it can be done in that way, and, as a consequence of their wishes, they readily decide that it can be so done. In attempting even functional curriculum making, therefore, the community will insist that the school do its work on the school premises and leave the home with no responsibility in the case. The curriculum-making committee which would employ normal living as a means of education will find this the most difficult and the most baffling of all of its problems. The community can scarcely be brought to consider the matter, as wishes are among the most potent of inhibitors to thought.

9. *The influence of the material facilities.* Education has agreed that the basic teaching instrument shall be the textbook. During recent years it has had to concede that certain supplementary helps are desirable. But the very term "supplementary" carries with it the assumption that the textbook constitutes the basic instrument. The presence of these traditionally sanctioned and legislatively authorized

teaching bases practically enforces the ancient subject-teaching conception. Professional progress, in the main, will have to be led by those cities which have retained their freedom to use the teaching helps which, in their professional judgment, appear to be the best.

Textbooks are not the only hindrances. The presence of manual-training shops equipped only for a stereotyped series of bench exercises in wood is an obstacle to the development of a functioning course in practical arts actually appropriate for the boys of today. The presence of an elaborately equipped domestic-science "laboratory" is an obstacle to the development of training for home cooking in the kitchens–not laboratories–of the community. The presence of the gymnasium suggests that the muscular exercise needed by the children can be provided for indoors at the school; it is a serious obstacle, therefore, to the realization of the fact that two or three hours of outdoor physical activity is needed every day in the year by every child and quite obviously cannot be provided for by the school. In the same way, other portions of the material equipment enforce in subtle fashion the ancient traditions and stand as obstacles to curriculum-making committees in their consideration of the problems.

10. *The overspecialization of the teaching and supervisory personnel.* Specialization on the part of teachers and supervisors takes a number of forms. To begin with, teachers and supervisors have a specialized understanding of the school and its functions in isolation from the community life. They know the school, but they do not know, in the same detailed way, the community life and the relation of the juvenile generation to the adult generation within this community life. They have specialized in the academic procedures of education but not in the social processes which are even more fundamental in the actual upbringing of children.

There is a strong tendency also to see even the scholastic education not as a whole but as a series of fragments. One who has specialized in intermediate-grade education has little or no interest in, or understanding of, the levels below and above. Likewise, on each of the levels from the kindergarten to the university, there is a group of specialists who know little and care little about the other levels. Furthermore, at any given level, more particularly in the later grades of the elementary school and at all of the higher levels, there is specialization in a single subject or department. The result is that the specialists at a given level are neither interested nor informed with regard to the totality of education at that level. Their professional vision is very restricted, indeed. They are specialists in subject matter but not really specialists in *education*—the full, well-rounded upbringing of human beings.

A clear vision of functional education as a whole or in any of its parts is possible only to one who can view human life along its various lines and on its various levels *in its totality*. One needs this generalized vision of the life processes in order properly to see the educational processes, for the two are one. Under the present conditions of intensive specialization, however, it is practically impossible to secure curriculum-making committees who have this generalized vision as a foundation for their judgments in performing their specific portions of the total task and in co-ordinating their labors with those of other committees. To develop a generalized vision of education is a long, slow process. For those who have become crystallized through habit, it is impossible. This condition within the teaching and supervisory personnel stands as an almost insurmountable barrier to progress. This, more than anything else, is the key obstacle that holds everything else tightly locked.

We need specialization, of course—intensive specialization—but it should be specialization in the right growth and development of human beings, which is quite different from the usual type.

11. *The members of curriculum committees lack the necessary time and energy for the work.* Curriculum committees are made up of teachers, principals, and special supervisors. After the teacher's regular work is completed, there is neither time nor energy, under present conditions, for the long and virile thinking necessary for grappling with these problems of almost interminable complexity. A proper type of curriculum can never be made by those who have only remnants of time and energy to devote to it. This is to demand superhuman powers on the part of very human individuals.

When at the close of a day or a week or a term a committee of tired teachers comes together to work on their portion of the curriculum, it is practically inevitable that their thought will follow the easier grooves of habit. They are not in a mood for intellectual exploration. Ordinarily there is nothing within the situation to motivate non-habitual activities. The whole mental "set" of the tired individual takes the attitude and method of self-protection, and this is to drift along the easy channels of habit.

12. *Those who are in the position of general professional leadership are, for the most part, primarily directors of routine and only secondarily directors of professional thought and labor.* In the operation of a building or of a school system as a whole, there is a large amount of necessary routine administrative labor. In the main, the

principal or superintendent is expected to care for this routine. It is *hoped* that such general officials will perform their purely professional functions with great efficiency, but rarely is there any careful study of the situation to see whether the conditions make it possible for them to take charge of the routine and at the same time give adequate attention to matters of professional leadership and direction. As a matter of fact, rarely do these officials find conditions such that they can attend *primarily* to their purely professional functions. This situation leaves the curriculum-making committees without that generalized leadership which is indispensable. Were they less specialized and less bound by habit and tradition, they might make a respectable contribution without such leadership. They are, however, greatly overspecialized–in part, wrongly specialized–and they are very completely bound by habit.

13. *The hesitation of institutions of professional research and training to take the lead.* Within our teachers' colleges and schools of education there are obstacles to progress which are analogous to those existing within the public-school systems. At this level, too, there is uncertainty as to the general function of the school and as to the specific objectives at which it should aim. As a consequence, there is uncertainty as to procedures. There is confusion and diversity of thinking relative to the place of the various subjects in the curriculum and to the effectiveness of the usual subject-teaching. The professional institutions tend to think of the school in a specialized way and as isolated from the life of the community. The instructors are also intensively specialized and frequently have neither a vision of education in its totality nor interest in it. In large degree, they see education not as a social process but rather as schooling in relative isolation from the social processes. A considerable amount of authoritative work has been done along certain educational lines, such as spelling, arithmetic, handwriting, and reading. The institutions of educational research are able in these subjects to provide an intellectual leadership to working committees which is entirely authoritative. For the great bulk of the training, however, these institutions are as yet unprepared to provide curriculum committees with reliable leadership. This leaves the committees without a type of assistance which is almost indispensable, since the local community is not so situated as to be able to carry on the necessary research. They need a kind of help from experts which the latter are not yet prepared to give.

In presenting these many obstacles to successful curriculum making, it is not the intention of the writer to discourage local workers but rather to assist them in overcoming the difficulties. One must see clearly what the difficulties are and how serious they are before one is prepared to overcome them. Not one of the difficulties is insurmountable.

It is the belief of the writer that those responsible for education in the local community should plan educational labors for the local community. They should not take their plans and their thinking—or their substitutes for thought—as handed down from above, whether from experts or from centralized governmental agencies. They should bear the full responsibility of planning their own work in the light of their own conditions. Naturally, if they are wise, they will secure every possible suggestion from experts and central agencies and utilize them in solving their own practical problems. They will adapt all such suggestions to their special situation as they find it, and they will make their own decisions.

One practical suggestion may be made concerning the mode of attack on these difficulties. The key obstacle, upon which all of the other obstacles depend, is the outworn concept of the nature of education, which is held in some degree by those who bear responsibility, original or derived, for the right upbringing of children. This ancient conception is to be removed, not by attacking it, but rather by showing the modern behavioristic conception with all possible clearness. The latter does not have to be argued; it needs only to be clearly seen and understood.

Let the profession on all of its levels, from the kindergarten to the college, specialize intensively in *education*—that is, *the right upbringing of human beings*—rather than in subjects and the mere thoughtless teaching of subjects. Let it give its vision over to the alert laymen of the community, who need only to see in order to be convinced. Then, when lay and professional men have modernized their conception of the objectives and procedures of education, the key obstacle to progress will have vanished as darkness before light. With this obstacle removed, the other obstacles can be speedily dislodged.

Selection 3.4

The Taxonomy of Educational Objectives—Its Uses in Curriculum Building

David R. Krathwohl

When was the last time that you sat through a staff meeting devoted to curriculum revision? Was much time at that meeting, or the previous one, consumed by discussing the meanings of the terms involved? The phrases in our curriculum statements and objectives often have a political platform style in order to sound convincing and appropriate, but as a result their value for guiding us in the selection of learning experiences is markedly reduced. When we try to exchange ideas about them, we spend too much time trying to find out what is "really meant" by even such a universally desirable goal as critical thinking. On examination it turns out to mean many different things to many people. If you need further convincing, no example is perhaps more obvious than the common use of such a term as "understand."

When teachers say they want their students to "really understand" the principle of acceleration, what do they mean? Is it that the student recall a formula about acceleration? Should he be able to understand an article written about it? Should he be able to apply the formula to a new situation? Should he be able to think up new situations to which the formula is relevant? Any or all of these are possible interpretations of the term "really understand." Do you think two teachers, both of whom agreed that they wanted their

---

SOURCE. In *Defining Educational Objectives,* ed. C. M. Lindvall (Pittsburgh, Penn.: University of Pittsburgh Press, 1964), pp. 19-36.

students to "really understand this principle," would independently select the same aspects from among those just mentioned? It seems unlikely. Yet, rarely do our curriculum meetings get this specific. But only as one becomes this specific can one decide which among the possible learning experiences to use in the classroom. Usually it is not until the curriculum is translated into learning experiences that this becomes apparent.

The state of communication with respect to a term like "really understand" is nothing compared to the confusion that surrounds objectives dealing with attitudes, interests and appreciation. When we say that we want a child to "appreciate" art, do we mean that he should be aware of artwork? Should he be willing to give it some attention when it is around? Do we mean that he should seek it out—go to the museum on his own, for instance? Do we mean that he should regard artwork as having positive values? Should he experience an emotional kick or thrill when he sees artwork? Should he be able to evaluate it and to know why and how it is effective? Should he be able to compare its esthetic impact with that of other art forms?

We could extend this list, but it is enough to suggest that the term "appreciation" covers a wide variety of meanings. And worse—not all of these are distinct from the terms "attitude" and "interest." Thus, if appreciation has the meaning that we want him to like artwork well enough to seek it out, how would we distinguish such behavior from an interest in art—or are interests and appreciations, as we use these words, the same thing?

If the student *values* art, does he have a favorable *attitude* toward it? Are our appreciation objectives the same as, overlapping with, or in some respects distinct from our attitude objectives? Most of us would argue that there are distinctions in the way we use the terms "appreciation," "attitude" and "interest." It is, however, much less certain that when we use these terms in our discussions of curriculum that we are using them in ways that do not differ from one person to another person. When we delve deep enough to determine which meaning we are using, we get into lengthy discussions—and many of our meetings turn out to be just that.

These kinds of problems which exist for curriculum builders are equally serious for those who have the responsibility of evaluating the success of the teacher in meeting the curriculum's objectives. For them there is the problem of very specific communication between curriculum builder and evaluator. In addition, if there are any similarities among different curriculums, similarities that can be meaningfully and precisely communicated, one could compare programs, trade evaluation instruments, and compare the effectiveness of learning devices, materials and curricular organizations. It was with this in mind that a group of college and university examiners, under the leadership of Dr. Benjamin S. Bloom, attempted to devise some means which would permit greater precision of communication with respect to educational objectives. The taxonomy is this means.

What is a taxonomy? You've undoubtedly heard of the biological taxonomies which permit classification into the categories of phylum, class, order, family, genus, species and variety. Ours is also a classification scheme, but the objectives being classified are not plants or animals but educational objectives, and the categories are terms descriptive of the kinds of behavior that we seek from students in educational institutions.

The taxonomy is based on the assumption that the educational program can be conceived as an attempt to change the behavior of students with respect to some subject matter. When we describe the behavior and the subject matter, we construct an educational objective. For instance: the student should be able to recall the major features of Chinese culture; he should be able to recognize form and pattern in literary and art works. The two parts of the objective, the subject matter and what is to be done with respect to the subject matter by the student, are both categorizable. It is, however, the latter, what is to be *done* with the subject matter, which constitutes the categories of the taxonomy. The categorization of subject matter we leave to the librarian.

The taxonomy is divided into three domains: cognitive, affective, and psychomotor. The cognitive includes those objectives having to do with thinking, knowing, and problem solving. The affective includes those objectives dealing with attitudes, values, interests and appreciation. The psychomotor covers objectives having to do with manual and motor skills and has yet to be developed. Our Handbook (Bloom et al., 1956) on the cognitive domain has been published for some time, and has been developed in the most detail. The affective domain, on the other hand, is going through its second and, we hope, final draft. Let us look at the cognitive study first.

Similar to the distinctions most teachers make, this domain is divided into the acquisition of knowledge, and the development of those skills and abilities necessary to use knowledge. Under the heading "Knowledge," which is the first major category of the cognitive domain, one finds a series of sub-categories, each describing the recall of a different category of knowledge. Each of the subheadings is accompanied by a definition of the behavior classified there and by illustrative objectives taken from the educational literature. In addition, there is a summary of the kinds of test items that may be used to test for each category, a discussion of the problems which beset the individual attempting to evaluate behavior in the category, and a large number of examples of test items—mainly multiple choice, but some essay type. These illustrate how items may be built to measure each of the categories.

The classification scheme is hierarchical in nature, that is, each category is assumed to involve behavior which is more complex and abstract than the previous category. Thus the categories are arranged from simple to more complex behavior, and from concrete to more abstract behavior.

Perhaps the idea of the continuum is most easily gained from looking at the major headings of the cognitive domain, which include knowledge, comprehension (ability to restate knowledge in new words), application (understanding it well enough to apply it), analysis (understanding it well enough to break it apart into its parts and make the relations among ideas explicit), synthesis (the ability to produce wholes from parts, to produce a plan of operation, to derive a set of abstracts relations) and evaluation (be able to judge the value of material for given purposes). An objective may include many elementary behaviors, but it is properly classified at the highest level of behavior involved.

There are a number of subheads which lend a specificity and precision to the main headings and help to further define them.

Basically the taxonomy is an educational-logical-psychological classification system. The terms in this order reflect the emphasis given to the organizing principles upon which it is built. It makes educational distinctions in the sense that the boundaries between categories reflect the decisions that teachers make among student behaviors in their development of curriculums, and in choosing learning situations. It is a logical system in the sense that its terms are defined precisely and are used consistently. In addition, each category permits logical subdivisions which can be clearly defined and further subdivided as necessary and useful. Finally the taxonomy seems to be consistent with our present understanding of psychological phenomena, though it does not rest on any single theory.

The scheme is intended to be purely descriptive so that every type of educational goal can be represented. It does not indicate the value or quality of one class as compared to another. It is impartial with respect to views of education. One of the tests of the taxonomy has been that of inclusiveness—could one classify all kinds of educational objectives (if stated as student behaviors) in the framework. In general we have been satisfied that it has met this test.

THE COGNITIVE DOMAIN

The categories of the cognitive domain and some illustrative objectives follow (Bloom et al., 1956, pp. 201-207):

KNOWLEDGE

1.00 KNOWLEDGE

Knowledge, as defined here, involves the recall of specifics and universals, the recall of methods and processes, or the recall of a pattern, structure or setting. For measurement purposes, the recall situation involved little more than bringing to mind the appropriate material. Although some alteration of the material may be required, this is a relatively minor part of the task. The knowledge objectives emphasize most the psychological processes of remembering. The process of relating is also involved in that a knowledge test situation requires the organization and reorganization of a problem such that it will furnish the appropriate signals and cues for the information and knowledge the individual possesses. To use an analogy, if one thinks of the mind as a file, the problem in a knowledge test situation is that of finding in the problem or task the appropriate signals, cues and clues which will most effectively bring out whatever knowledge is filed or stored.

1.10 *Knowledge of Specifics*

The recall of specific and isolable bits of information. The emphasis is on symbols with concrete referents. This material, which is at a very low level of abstraction, may be thought of as the elements from which more complex and abstract forms of knowledge are built.

1.11 *Knowledge of Terminology*

Knowledge of the referents for specific symbols (verbal and non-verbal). This may include knowledge of the most generally accepted symbol referent, knowledge of the variety of symbols which may be used for a single referent, or knowledge of the referent most appropriate to a given use of a symbol.

*To define technical terms by giving their attributes, properties or relations.

*Familiarity with a large number of words in their common range of meanings.

1.12 *Knowledge of Specific Facts*

Knowledge of dates, events, persons, places, etc. This may include very precise and specific information such as the specific date or exact magnitude of a phenomenon. It may also include approximate or relative information such as an approximate time period or the general order of magnitude of a phenomenon.

*The recall of major facts about particular cultures.

*The possession of a minimum knowledge about the organisms studied in the laboratory.

1.20 *Knowledge of Ways and Means of Dealing with Specifics*

Knowledge of the ways of organizing, studying, judging and criticizing. This includes the methods of inquiry, the chronological sequences and the standards of judgment within a field as well as the patterns of organization

---

*Illustrative educational objectives selected from the literature.

through which the areas of the fields themselves are determined and internally organized. This knowledge is at an intermediate level of abstraction between specific knowledge on the one hand and knowledge of universals on the other. It does not so much demand the activity of the student in using the materials as it does a more passive awareness of their nature.

1.21 *Knowledge of Conventions*

Knowledge of characteristic ways of treating and presenting ideas and phenomena. For purposes of communication and consistency, workers in a field employ usages, styles, practices and forms which best suit their purposes and/or which appear to suit best the phenomena with which they deal. It should be recognized that although these forms and conventions are likely to be set up on arbitrary, accidental, or authoritative bases, they are retained because of the general agreement of concurrence of individuals concerned with the subject, phenomena or problem.

*Familiarity with the forms and conventions of the major types of works, e.g., verse, plays, scientific papers, etc.

*To make pupils conscious of correct form and usage in speech and writing.

1.22 *Knowledge of Trends and Sequences*

Knowledge of the processes, directions and movement of phenomena with respect to time.

*Understanding of the continuity and development of American culture as exemplified in American life.

*Knowledge of the basic trends underlying the development of public assistance programs.

1.23 *Knowledge of Classifications and Categories*

Knowledge of the classes, sets, divisions and arrangements which are regarded as fundamental for a given subject field, purpose, argument or problem.

*To recognize the area encompassed by various kinds of problems or materials.

*Becoming familiar with a range of types of literature.

1.24 *Knowledge of Criteria*

Knowledge of the criteria by which facts, principles, opinions and conduct are tested or judged.

*Familiarity with criteria for judgment appropriate to the type of work and the purpose for which it is read.

*Knowledge of criteria for the evaluation of recreational activities.

1.25 *Knowledge of Methodology*

Knowledge of the methods of inquiry, techniques and procedures employed in a particular subject field as well as those employed in investigating particular problems and phenomena. The emphasis here is on the individual's knowledge of the method rather than his ability to use the method.

*Knowledge of scientific methods for evaluating health concepts.

*The student shall know the methods of attack relevant to the kinds of problems of concern to the social sciences.

---

*Illustrative educational objectives selected from the literature.

1.30 *Knowledge of the Universals and Abstractions in a Field*

Knowledge of the major schemes and patterns by which phenomena and ideas are organized. These are the large structures, theories and generalizations which dominate a subject field or which are quite generally used in studying phenomena or solving problems. These are at the highest levels of abstraction and complexity.

1.31 *Knowledge of Principles and Generalizations*

Knowledge of particular abstractions which summarize observations of phenomena. These are the abstractions which are of value in explaining, describing, predicting or in determining the most appropriate and relevant action or direction to be taken.

*Knowledge of the important principles by which our experience with biological phenomena is summarized.

*The recall of major generalizations about particular cultures.

1.32 *Knowledge of Theories and Structures*

Knowledge of the body of principles and generalizations together with their interrelations which present a clear, rounded and systematic view of a complex phenomenon, problem or field. These are the most abstract formulations, and they can be used to show the interrelation and organization of a great range of specifics.

*The recall of major theories about particular cultures.

*Knowledge of a relatively complete formulation of the theory of evolution.

INTELLECTUAL SKILLS AND ABILITIES

Abilities and skills refer to organized modes of operation and generalized techniques for dealing with materials and problems. The materials and problems may be of such a nature that little or no specialized and technical information is required. Such information as is required can be assumed to be part of the individual's general fund of knowledge. Other problems may require specialized and technical information at a rather high level such that specific knowledge and skill in dealing with the problem and the materials are required. The ability and skill objectives emphasize the mental processes of organizing and reorganizing material to achieve a particular purpose. The materials may be given or remembered.

2.00 COMPREHENSION

This represents the lowest level of understanding. It refers to a type of understanding or apprehension such that the individual knows what is being communicated and can make use of the material or idea being communicated without necessarily relating it to other material or seeing its fullest implications.

---

*Illustrative educational objectives selected from the literature.

2.10 *Translation*

Comprehension as evidenced by the care and accuracy with which the communication is paraphrased or rendered from one language or form of communication to another. Translation is judged on the basis of faithfulness and accuracy, that is, on the extent to which the material in the original communication is preserved although the form of the communication has been altered.

*The ability to understand non-literal statements (metaphor, symbolism, irony, exaggeration).

*Skill in translating mathematical verbal material into symbolic statements and vice versa.

2.20 *Interpretation*

The explanation or summarization of a communication. Whereas translation involves an objective part-for-part rendering of a communication, interpretation involves a reordering, rearrangement or a new view of the material.

*The ability to grasp the thought of the work as a whole at any desired level of generality.

*The ability to interpret various types of social data.

2.30 *Extrapolation*

The extension of trends or tendencies beyond the given data to determine implications, consequences, corollaries, effects, etc., which are in accordance with the condition described in the original communication.

*The ability to deal with the conclusions of a work in terms of the immediate inference made from the explicit statements.

*Skill in predicting continuation of trends.

3.00 APPLICATION

The use of abstractions in particular and concrete situations. The abstractions may be in the form of general ideas, rules of procedures, or generalized methods. The abstractions may also be technical principles, ideas and theories which must be remembered and applied.

*Application to the phenomena discussed in one part of the scientific terms or concepts used in other papers.

*The ability to predict the probable effect of a change in a factor on a biological situation previously at equilibrium.

4.00 ANALYSIS

The breakdown of a communication into its constituent elements or parts such that the relative hierarchy of ideas is made clear and/or the relations between the ideas expressed are made explicit. Such analyses are intended to clarify the communication, to indicate how the communication is organized, and the way in which it manages to convey its effects, as well as its basis and arrangement.

4.10 *Analysis of Elements*

Identification of the elements included in a communication.

*The ability to recognize unstated assumptions.

*Skill in distinguishing facts from hypotheses.

4.20 *Analyses of Relationships*

The connections and interactions between elements and parts of a communication.

---

*Illustrative educational objectives selected from the literature.

*The ability to check the consistency of hypotheses with given information and assumptions.

*Skill in comprehending the interrelationships among the ideas in a passage.

4.30 *Analysis of Organizational Principles*

The organization, systematic arrangement and structure which holds the communication together. This includes the "explicit" as well as "implicit" structure. It includes the bases, necessary arrangement and the mechanics which made the communication a unit.

*The ability to recognize form and pattern in literary or artistic works as a means of understanding their meaning.

*Ability to recognize the general techniques used in persuasive materials, such as advertising, propaganda, etc.

5.00 SYNTHESIS

The putting together of elements and parts so as to form a whole. This involves the process of working with pieces, parts, elements, etc., and arranging and combining them in such a way as to constitute a pattern or structure not clearly there before.

5.10 *Production of a Unique Communication*

The development of a communication in which the writer or speaker attempts to convey ideas, feelings and/or experiences to others.

*Skill in writing, using an excellent organization of ideas and statements.

*Ability to tell a personal experience effectively.

5.20 *Production of a Plan, or Proposed Set of Operations*

The development of a plan of work or the proposal of a plan of operations. The plan should satisfy requirements of the task which may be given to the student or which he may develop for himself.

*Ability to propose ways of testing hypotheses.

*Ability to plan a unit of instruction for a particular teaching situation.

5.30 *Derivation of a Set of Abstract Relations*

The development of a set of abstract relations either to classify or explain particular data or phenomena, or the deduction of propositions and relations from a set of basic propositions or symbolic representations.

*Ability to formulate appropriate hypotheses based upon an analysis of factors involved, and to modify such hypotheses in the light of new factors and considerations.

*Ability to make mathematical discoveries and generalizations.

6.00 EVALUATION

Judgments about the value of material and methods for given purposes. Quantitative and qualitative judgments about the extent to which material and methods satisfy criteria. Use of a standard of appraisal. The criteria may be those determined by the student or those which are given to him.

6.10 *Judgments in Terms of Internal Evidence*

Evaluation of the accuracy of a communication from such evidence as logical accuracy, consistency and other internal criteria.

*Judging by internal standards, the ability to assess general probability of accuracy in reporting facts from the care given to exactness of statement, documentation, proof, etc.

---

*Illustrative educational objectives selected from the literature.

*The ability to indicate logical fallacies in arguments.

6.20 *Judgments in Terms of External Criteria*

Evaluation of material with reference to selected or remembered criteria.

*The comparison of major theories, generalizations and facts about particular cultures.

*Judging by external standards, the ability to compare a work with the highest known standards in its field—especially with other works of recognized excellence.

THE AFFECTIVE DOMAIN

The cognitive domain was developed first since it was expected to be the most useful of the three domains. Work on the affective domain was begun immediately but has proceeded much more slowly (Krathwohl et al., 1964). It presented some special problems. For example, the hierarchical structure has been most difficult to find in the affective part of the taxonomy. We found the principles of simple to complex and concrete to abstract were not sufficient for developing the affective domain. Something additional was needed.

We hoped that in seeking the unique characteristics of the affective domain we would discover the additional principles needed to structure an affective continuum. Analysis of affective objectives showed the following characteristics which the continuum should embody: the emotional quality which is an important distinguishing feature of an affective response at certain levels of the continuum, the increasing automaticity as one progresses upon the continuum, the increasing willingness to attend to a specified stimulus or stimulus type as one ascends the continuum, and the developing integration of a value pattern at the upper levels of the continuum.

We had at first hoped that somehow we could derive a structure by attaching certain meanings to the terms "attitude," "value," "appreciation" and "interest." But the multitude of meanings which these terms encompassed, as we observed their use in educational objectives, showed that this was impossible. After trying a number of schemes and organizing principles, the one which appeared best to account for the affective phenomena and which best described the process of learning and growth in the affective field was the process of internalization.

The term internalization is perhaps best defined by the descriptions of the categories of the affective domain. Generally speaking, however, it refers to the inner growth that occurs as the individual

---

*Illustrative educational objectives selected from the literature.

becomes aware of and then adopts the attitudes, principles, codes and sanctions that become a part of him in forming value judgments and in guiding his conduct. It has many elements in common with the term socialization. At its lowest level we have:

1.0 RECEIVING (*Attending*)

At this level we are concerned that the learner be sensitized to the existence of certain phenomena and stimula—that is, that he be willing to receive or to attend to them. To the uninitiated, Bach is repetitive and boring. To those who know what to listen for, his music is intricate and complex; but even the unsophisticated can understand that in some of his works he has written "rounds" if they are made aware of it. The teacher who makes the student aware of such a characteristic in Bach's work is accomplishing the lowest level of behavior in this category.

1.1 *Awareness*

Though it is the bottom rung of the affective domain, "Awareness" is almost a cognitive behavior. But unlike "Knowledge," the lowest level of the cognitive domain, we are not so much concerned with a memory of, or ability to recall, an item or fact as we are that, given an appropriate opportunity, the learner will merely be conscious of something; that he takes into account a situation, phenomenon, object or state of affairs.

*Develops awareness of asthetic factors in dress, furnishings, architecture, city design and the like.

*Observes with increasing differentiation the sights and sounds of the city.

1.2 *Willingness to Receive*

In this category we have come a step up the ladder, but are still dealing with apparently cognitive behavior. At a minimum level, we are describing the behavior of being willing to tolerate a given stimulus, not to avoid it. Like "awareness" it involves neutrality or suspended judgment toward the stimulus. This is a frequently used category of teachers of the arts since we are prone to reject and avoid some of the newer art forms.

*Develops a tolerance for a variety of types of music.

*Accepts differences of race and culture, among one's acquaintances.

1.3 *Controlled or Selected Attention*

At a somewhat higher level we are concerned with a new phenomenon, the differentiation of a given stimulus into figure and ground at a conscious or perhaps semi-conscious level, the differentiation of aspects of a stimulus which are perceived as clearly marked off from adjacent impressions. The perception is still without tension or assessment, and the student may not know the technical terms or symbols with which to correctly or precisely describe it to others.

*Listens to music with some discrimination as to its mood and meaning and with some recognition of the contributions of various musical elements and instruments to the total effect.

*Listens for rhythm in poetry or prose read aloud.

---

*Illustrative educational objectives selected from the literature.

2.0 RESPONDING

At this level we are concerned with responses which go beyond merely attending to the phenomenon. The student is sufficiently motivated that he is not just "willing to attend" but perhaps it is correct to say that he is actively attending. As a first stage in a "learning by doing" process, the student is committing himself in some small measure to the phenomena involved. This is a very low level of commitment, and we would not at this level say that this was "a value of his" or that he had "such and such an attitude." These terms belong to the next higher level that we will describe. But we could say that he is doing something with or about the phenomena beside merely perceiving it as was true at the level previously described—of "selected or controlled attention." An example of such "responding" would be the compliance with rules of good health or safety, or obedience to rules of conduct.

The category of "responding" has been subdivided into three subcategories to describe the continuum of responding as the learner becomes more fully committed to the practice and phenomena of the objective. The lowest stage is illustrated in the preceding paragraph and is named "acquiescence in responding." As the name implies, there is the element of compliance or obedience at this level which distinguishes it from the next level, that of "willingness to respond." Finally, at a still higher level of internalization, there is found a "satisfaction in response" not reached at the previous level of willingness or assent to respond. When there is an emotional response of pleasure, zest, or enjoyment, we have reached this third level.

2.1 *Acquiescence in Responding*

*Willingness to comply with health regulations.

*Observes traffic rules on foot and on a bicycle at intersections and elsewhere.

2.2 *Willingness to Respond*

*Engages, on his own, in a variety of constructive hobbies and recreational activities.

*Keeps still when the occasion or the situation calls for silence. (Situation must be clearly defined.)

*Contributes to group discussion by asking thought-provoking questions.

2.3 *Satisfaction in Response*

*Finds pleasure in reading for recreation.

*Enjoys listening to a variety of human voices, with wide variations in pitch, voice quality and regional accents.

3.0 VALUING

This is the only category headed by a term which is in common use among the expressions of objectives by teachers. Further, it is employed in its usual sense—namely, that a thing, phenomenon or behavior has worth. This abstract concept of worth is not so much the result of the individual's own valuing or assessment as it is a social product that has been slowly internalized or accepted and come to be used by the student as his own criterion of worth.

Behavior categorized at this level is sufficiently consistent and stable that it has come to have the characteristics of a belief or an attitude. The learner displays this behavior with sufficient consistency in appropriate situations that he comes to be perceived as holding a value. At the lowest level of valuing, he is at least willing to permit himself to be so perceived, and at the higher level, he may behave so as to actively further this impression.

---

*Illustrative educational objectives selected from the literature.

3.1 *Acceptance of a Value*

*A sense of responsibility for listening to and participating in a discussion.

3.2 *Preference for a Value*

*Draws reticent members of a group into conversation.

*Interest in enabling other persons to attain satisfaction of basic common needs.

*Willingness to work for improvement of health regulations.

3.3 *Commitment*

*Firm loyalty to the various groups in which one holds membership.

*Practices religion actively in his personal and family living.

*Faith in the power of reason and in the methods of experiment and discussion.

4.0 ORGANIZATION

As the learner successively internalizes values, he encounters situations for which more than one value is relevant. Thus necessity arises for (a) organizing the values into a system, (b) determining the interrelationships among them, (c) finding which will be the dominant and pervasive ones.

4.1 *Conceptualization of a Value*

*Desire to evaluate the thing appreciated.

*Finding and crystallizing the basic assumptions which underlie codes of ethics and are the basis of faith.

4.2 *Organization of a Value System*

*Weigh alternative social policies and practices against the standards of the public welfare rather than the advantage of specialized and narrow interest groups.

5.0 CHARACTERIZATION BY A VALUE OR VALUE CONCEPT

At this level of internalization the values already have a place in the individual's value hierarchy, are organized into some kind of internally consistent system, have controlled the behavior of the individual for a sufficient time so that he has adapted to behaving this way, and an evocation of the behavior is no longer regularly accompanied by emotion or affect.

The individual consistently acts in accord with the values he has internalized at this level, and our concern is to indicate two things—(a) the generalization of this control to so much of the individual's behavior that he is described and characterized as a person by these pervasive controlling tendencies, (b) the integration of these beliefs, ideas and attitudes into a total philosophy or world view. These two aspects constitute the subcategories.

5.1 *Generalized Set*

*Readiness to revise judgments and to change behavior in the light of evidence.

*Acceptance of objectivity and systematic planning as basic methods in arriving at satisfying choices.

5.2 *Characterization*

*Develop for regulation of one's personal and civic life a code of behavior based on ethical principles consistent with democratic ideals.

*Develop a consistent philosophy of life.

*Develop a conscience.

---

*Illustrative educational objectives selected from the literature.

USE OF THE TAXONOMY

You now know what the taxonomy is. Of what value is it? Earlier in discussing some of the problems of curriculum construction we hinted at some of its potential uses.

As you now realize, it focuses on the student's behavior as it is expressed in educational objectives. While objectives are by no means foreign to the elementary and secondary school, not all objectives specify these goals in terms of student behavior. Often they are in terms of teacher behavior—on the assumption that student behavior changes follow certain teacher actions—surely not an airtight assumption! We have found that stating objectives as student behavior puts the focus where it belongs, on the change to be made in the student. It leaves the way open to experimentation with different teacher behaviors to attain most effectively and efficiently the desired goal. Stated this way, the taxonomy provides a basis for working with objectives with a specificity and a precision that is not generally typical of such statements. Further, this specificity and precision in the description of a student behavior makes it much easier to choose the kinds of learning experiences that are appropriate to developing the desired behavior and to building evaluation instruments.

No longer is a teacher faced with an objective like this: "The student should understand the taxonomy of educational objectives." Rather the teacher now specifies whether this would be at the lowest level of Comprehension where he would at least expect the student to be able to translate the term "taxonomy" into something like "a classification system of educational goals," or perhaps at a deeper level of understanding, classified as Interpretation, where the student could restate the ideas of the taxonomy in his own words. In short, you should find the taxonomy a relatively concise model for the analysis of education objectives.

In building a curriculum you have undoubtedly paused to consider, "Are there things left out—behaviors I'd have included if I'd thought of them?" The taxonomy, like the period table of elements or a "check-off" shopping list, provides the panorama of objectives. Comparing the range of the present curriculum with the range of possible outcomes may suggest additional goals that might be included. Further, the illustrative objectives may suggest wordings that might be adapted to the area you are exploring.

Frequently when we are searching for ideas in building a curriculum we turn to the work of others who have preceded us. Where both your work and that of others are built in terms of the taxonomy categories, comparison is markedly facilitated. Translation of objectives into the taxonomy framework can provide a basis for precise comparison. Further, where similarities exist, it becomes possible to trade experiences regarding the values of certain learning experiences with confidence that there is a firm basis for comparison and that the other person's experience will be truly relevant.

It is perhaps also important to note the implication of the hierarchical nature of the taxonomy for curriculum building. If our analysis of the cognitive and affective areas is correct, then a hierarchy of objectives dealing with the same subject matter concepts suggests a readiness relationship that exists between those objectives lower in the hierarchy and those higher in it. While we regularly give some attention to this kind of sequential relation for objectives in the cognitive domain, it is less a prominent feature of the affective—a point to which we shall return.

How might the taxonomy be useful in better evaluating teaching? For one thing, teachers rarely analyze standardized tests. They have the feeling that these were put together by experts who know more than they do and, though they may feel a vague discontent with the test, too often they do not analyze the content of these tests against their objectives to determine how well they match. Here again, by using the taxonomy as a translating framework one can compare the test with the teacher's goals. In its simplest form this may be a determination of the proportion of items in each of the major taxonomy categories. This alone is often enough information to help a teacher determine a test's relevance. Such an analysis is particularly useful where one test must be selected from several considered for adoption. For instance, the taxonomy could be used as a common framework for comparing the Iowa Tests of Basic Skills with the revised Stanford Achievement Test.

A similar analysis of the items of the tests the teacher constructs himself checked against his own objectives may be revealing of over- or under-emphasis on particular objectives.

As has already been indicated, the Handbook's (Bloom et al., 1956) sample items and discussions of how to build test items at each of the taxonomy levels may be quite helpful to a teacher. But above and beyond this, the teacher will find the taxonomy is a key to increasing numbers of item collections. Dressel and Nelson (1956) have published an 805-page folio of test items in science keyed to the taxonomy and subject matter. A teacher can use such a folio to select the items needed for a test, modifying them to fit the class level.

A related use of the taxonomy is its role in facilitating evaluation of a school's educational experiments. The most frequent type of school experimentation is the comparison of teaching methods, devices or curricula. In all of these comparisons, use of the taxonomy facilitates better communications and comparisons between experiments and between experimenters and adds to the precision of the operational definitions of the variables involved. Thus some television experimentation has resorted to taxonomic classifications to determine the instructor's competence in teaching abilities and skills as well as in conveying knowledge via this medium.

The emphasis in programmed learning on a complete and detailed analysis of the behaviors to be taught immediately suggests a possible role for the taxonomy. Recent literature on programming (Fry, 1963; Mager, 1962) has recognized the taxonomy as a tool for the analysis of curriculums as the first step in programming. Because of its heirarchical structure, analysis by means of the taxonomy assists programming in still another way. The level of categorization aids in placing the material in the program sequence and in planning the overall sequential development of the skill or ability.

So far, we have been discussing largely those uses of the taxonomy which stem from the cognitive domain. Curricula trends seem to show a move away from emphasis in the affective area. Indeed, schools have been attacked because of their concern with these kinds of objectives. But even though teachers continue to think affective goals are important, in comparison with the emphasis on cognitive objectives, there is little direct attack on these goals. There are occasional sociometric tests, group work, and some class elections, but the bulk of learning in this area is incidental learning. Partly this is a matter of confusion about what goals we are seeking. Partly it is a matter of not knowing how best to seek the goal even if the confusion were resolved.

The analytic framework which the taxonomy brings to the affective area should aid in the clarification of what goals are being sought. Guidance and counseling personnel using instruments dealing with the affective domain may find it useful to categorize the measures yielded by their instruments and, to the extent possible, compare this information with that needed by the teachers to reach their goals. The qualification "to the extent possible" is necessary because the taxonomy does not provide categories for all behavior, but only that which is desirable behavior, such as would be sought in a school curriculum. Psychological tests frequently include measures of undesirable behavior. In general, however, it is hoped that the affective domain categories will prove a useful framework for clarification of terminology and relating counselor data to teacher goals.

Along these same lines, an analysis of existing instruments demonstrates that the bulk of our measurement is concentrated at the very top levels—at the most complex behaviors. Use of this framework to analyze the Edwards Personnel Preference Schedule or the California Test of Personality, for instance, shows no measures of the lower levels of the affective area. This suggests that increased concentration on measurement instruments for the lower levels of the affective area might be helpful.

If our analysis of the affective domain is correct, we have a developmental picture of the way in which these goals are reached, from simple receiving and responding through characterization. It makes clear the beginnings of complex objectives such as appreciations, interests and attitudes. It focuses the teachers attention on the development of these simple behaviors which are the building blocks out of which the more complex objectives grow—simple behaviors which rarely are now deliberately taught.

You can, no doubt, now think of additional implications of the taxonomy for your school situation. This material may be enough to help you "understand" the taxonomy a little better. By "understand" we mean that you have some knowledge of the taxonomy, that you have been able to comprehend what it is about—that is, be able to describe it in your own words. Hopefully, you are at least at the level of application and can see some possible uses. Perhaps in the discussion of this material it will be time for some evaluation to see how well my objectives were achieved.

REFERENCES

Bloom, Benjamin S., et al. *A Taxonomy of Educational Objectives*. Handbook I: *The Cognitive Domain*. New York: Longmans, Green, 1956.

Dressel, Paul L., and Clarence Nelson. *Questions and Problems in Science*. Test Folio No. 1. Princeton, N.J.: Educational Testing Service, 1956.

Fry, Edmond. *Teaching Machine and Programmed Instruction*. New York: McGraw Hill, 1963.

Krathwohl, David R., Benjamin S. Bloom, and Bertram Masia. *A Taxonomy of Educational Objectives*. Handbook II: *The Affective Domain*. New York: David McKay, 1964.

Mager, Robert F. *Preparing Objectives for Programmed Instruction*. Palo Alto, Calif.: Fearon, 1962.

Selection 3.5

A Conceptual Framework for Curriculum Design

Hilda Taba

Any enterprise as complex as curriculum development requires some kind of theoretical or conceptual framework of thinking to guide it. To be sure, theoretical considerations are, and have been, applied in making decisions about curriculum, and possibly more theoretical ideas are available than have been applied in practice. What is lacking is a coherent and consistent conceptual framework.

In recent literature there have been signs that this lack has been recognized. Evidently an awareness is growing that an advance in practice cannot continue without some advance in the consolidation of the theory of curriculum development. Bayles points out that today educational theory is "in the state of suspended animation," for until the early 1940s the whole twentieth century had witnessed a flood of energetically fostered proposals for improvement of the educational process, and since then, little of note seemingly has been added. He feels that to improve our theory we must do two things: clarify our thinking about democracy and what it means for keeping school, and reconsider our assumptions regarding the nature of learners and the learning process (1959, p. 5).

SOURCE. In *Curriculum Development: Theory and Practice* (New York: Harcourt, Brace, and World, 1962), pp. 413-44.

Caswell points out further that such curriculum theories as exist are beset with confusion, are at odds with each other, and seem to have relatively little effect on practice. There is failure to recognize clearly "the foundations upon which curriculum theory must rest" and a failure to draw from the basic sciences "a consistent body of basic principles, to interpret these principles as they apply to education, and to extend their application so that a clear guide to practice is provided." There is, further, too great a reliance on a particular principle in curriculum designs, as is illustrated by the juxtaposition of the child-centered and subject-centered basis for organizing curricula. Other principles are interpreted too narrowly, such as interpreting experience—the stuff of which curriculum is made—as being its own justification and therefore not subject to adult planning and guidance. Inappropriate theories are applied, as when theories which apply to general education are used in making decisions about vocational education (1950, pp. 110-13). He further outlines the issues in curriculum which, though raised decades ago, are no nearer resolution or even clearer now that they were then, such as how to determine the values which should guide curriculum development, how curriculum is to be related to persistent problems of American life, and how one should go about developing curriculum (Caswell, 1952, pp. 208-9).

DEFICIENCIES IN THE RATIONALE OF CURRICULUM DESIGNS

Some light may be thrown on the nature of needed conceptual framework by an examination of the deficiencies and gaps in the rationale of the current curriculum designs. . . . These designs and the rationale on which they seem to rest involve many difficulties and leave many gaps.

. . . One important characteristic of adequate curriculum development is that the decisions made in the course of planning rest on multiple criteria and consider a multiplicity of factors. In contrast, one common characteristic of the designs described in chap. 21 of *Curriculum Development* is their tendency to center their rationale in some single criterion or principle. The controversy over the child-centered and the subject-centered curriculum is an illustration of such an elevation of a single principle into the sole foundation for the entire "approach" to curriculum. Since obviously a curriculum has to do with teaching something to somebody, it can be neither entirely content centered nor child centered in the sense of neglecting either the nature of the learner or the nature of content. A more or less fundamental choice between the two may be involved in decisions as to whether the interests and activities of children or the content topics shall serve as organizing centers for teaching-learning units. But even here, considerations other than mere juxtaposition of children's needs and interests and the logic of content enter.

A similar tendency is illustrated by the way the principle of integration of knowledge is applied in discussions of the core curriculum. According to theoretical statements, the chief principle of the core curriculum is supposed to be integration of knowledge. Yet trouble brews if this principle overrides the consideration of the unique requirements of the various areas of knowledge and if integration is effected without sufficiently considering what the appropriate threads of integration might be and what aspects of the content of various disciplines can appropriately be brought together.

This tendency to rationalize a curriculum pattern in terms of a single principle, at least in theoretical statements, while overlooking the relevance of other equally important considerations is in effect a gross oversimplication which has many undesirable consequences. One is a kind of myopia in developing and implementing curriculum designs. The patterns for the scope and sequence appropriate for social studies have been discussed as if they were equally appropriate for all subjects. The designs which have been tested only on the elementary level have been extended into high school without testing their appropriateness on that level.

This limitation in rationale has also produced a somewhat doctrinaire position regarding the particular patterns of organizing curricula and rigid concepts of what each pattern entails. These doctrinaire positions resulted not only in a proliferation of "approaches," but each position also tended to rule out, or to allocate an incidental role to, certain types of learning experiences which make perfectly good sense, such as excluding the possibility of studying organized subject matter in some "approaches" and of creative activities or the pursuit of projects animated by individual interests in others. It is interesting to note that while the practice has moved away from these doctrinaire positions to a more balanced perspective regarding the role of the learner and of the subject matter, the argument persists. Except for the fact that the shoe is on the other foot, the arguments in the 1930s, when the battle was to introduce sufficient consideration of the learners, are duplicated today, when the battle is to reintroduce disciplined content. The problem of balance is unresolved. Only the stakes have changed.

The writer argued for a policy of balance between the requirements of content and of the psychological demands thirty years ago:

> The conflict of policies regarding the central principles of the organization of educational processes and content is a comparatively old one. The discussion of it has taken the form of a conflict between the psychological and the logical organization of the subject matter of instruction.
>
> The general position of those standing for the priority of the logic of the subject matter as a basis for organization of educational materials . . . is that there are binding principles of thought, leading ideas and compelling generalizing concepts . . . which are . . . necessary for a consistent and intelligent way of looking at the phenomena of life. . . . To a certain extent this position is a correct one, especially when viewed in the light of the present prevailing attempts toward the psychological organization. The present practice of using the individual as . . . unit, around which and according to the demands of which, the educational process is to be organized are frequently based on a narrow and one-sided concept of that individual. [Taba, 1932, pp. 224-25]

Another series of problems and difficulties is introduced by the confusion about which principles or considerations apply at which points of curriculum development. Such principles and criteria as have been articulated are often misapplied: considerations which are relevant to selection are applied to organization, principles relevant to organization of learning experiences are applied to organization of content, and vice versa. While the basic principles and criteria for good curricula apply in some measure across all decisions regarding curricula, certain considerations are logically central to certain aspects of it. Different criteria are logically central to making decisions about objectives, the selection and organization of content, and the selection and organization of learning experiences. In selecting content, for example, its validity and significance are the primary criteria, while principles of learning are more central to organizing it. The principle of using primary experience is misapplied when primary experience is used as a center for organizing content rather than as a first step in a cumulative learning sequence.

The "doctrine" of interest has been subject to the same type of misapplication. The principle that the curriculum should meet the interests of the students is appropriate in selecting from a larger body of material a specific sample of content detail which is equally potent in elucidating the basic ideas. It is misapplied when used as a criterion for selecting the entire range of content and, worse still, as a center for organizing content on all levels.

A clearer analysis of the points at which curriculum decisions are being made, and of the principles and considerations that apply to each, should open a way to a more comprehensive approach to curriculum development as well as to identifying more precisely the fundamental differences and agreements among the various theories. It is possible, for example, that there is a genuine difference between educators who insist that intellectual development is the exclusive center to educational effort and those who maintain that it is only one of the many powers to be developed and that cognitive aspects of development in turn depend on other facets of growth. But it is impossible to discover what the difference is as long as one group defines intellectual power as erudition and another as capacity to handle cognitive processes, and as long as both positions mask additional assumptions behind the facade of their chief point of argument, such as assumptions regarding the ways in which intellectual powers develop, whether they are an automatic byproduct of the mastery of "disciplines" or require special provisions for ways of learning them. One cannot get far in arguments about the importance of integrated learning as against the virtues of pursuing isolated disciplines as long as there is no clarity about precisely what is being integrated or what the integrating threads are, or can be.

But perhaps the greatest deficiency in the current curriculum theories are the gaps they leave in conceptualizing curriculum development and hence also in implementing it. In most of the designs some important components are missing; the relationships between these elements are not clearly enough stated, or there are no provisions for moving from one point to another. Goodlad illustrates this deficiency by analyzing a document pertaining to curriculum development as follows:

> The document identifies the basic values of democracy and the functions of the school in a democratic society. Apparently, the functions of the school should in some way follow or depend on the values presumed for life in democracy. But the nature of that relationship and the method of deriving school functions from societal values are not made clear. The document goes on to list the demands imposed by a democratic society and to pose goals for education. Of necessity value-judgments are involved in moving from an analysis of society to an elaboration of desirable educational objectives. Do we educate individuals to adjust to a particular characteristic of society, or do we educate individuals to revise society? Value-theory is involved, but just how and where, the document does not make clear.

> Next, the report examines the needs of the individual. The purpose of the examination is to set up methods of teaching. Yet, in the introduction to the section, the authors state that instructional goals are clarified by examining characteristics of the human personality. If the principle is sound, should not the school examine learners to determine what, as well as how to teach? Should not an analysis of learners precede as well as follow the stating of educational objectives? And should not the purpose of examining learners before the formulation of objectives be quite different from the purpose of examining learners after the objectives have been formulated? [1958, p. 393]

As was indicated in the chapter on evaluation, the lack of relationship among objectives, the content outline, and the evaluation program has often been noted. Objectives tend to be more ambitious than the provisions for learning experience warrant. Evidently, the conceptual framework of the newer curriculum designs does not provide adequately for moving from objectives to content or the instructional pattern and from both to the methods and the manner of evaluation.

While the newer curriculum patterns extended vastly the concept of desirable objectives, they failed to provide corresponding ways of translating these objectives into appropriate learning experiences. No theoretical distinctions regarding the types of learning experiences required by various types of objectives are made to differentiate the instructional techniques necessary to implement these objectives. The result is that the curriculum guides based on these patterns present somewhat arbitrary and unrealistic expectations. They ask teachers to achieve objectives but provide no foundation for making the necessary practical provisions. No matter how high-sounding the claims for the importance of such objectives as critical thinking and democratic loyalties are, one cannot regard them as anything but pious hopes as long as there is no clear plan for appropriate learning experiences.

A theoretical vacuum seems also to exist between the requirements of a curriculum design and the administrative arrangements necessary to its effective implementation. To be effective, a given curriculum plan, such as a broad field curriculum or a core program, requires a certain type of scheduling, certain instructional materials, and certain ways of using staff talents. One can kill a potentially promising curriculum design by poor scheduling, insufficient materials, inappropriate grouping of students, or an ineffective staff organization. The potentialities of the core curriculum have never been really explored because the conditions under which it was tried seldom lived up to requirements for its success. Neither the staffing nor the accounting for credits accommodated this curriculum pattern. When a transition was made from the rigidly prescribed curriculum sequence to greater freedom for classroom teachers to select and organize the content of the curriculum, there was no corresponding arrangement for communication among teachers to ensure proper sequence and to avoid repetition and overlapping. The current experiments in mass mediums fail to consider such consequences of a shift from small-group to large-group organization as the elimination of the nurturing contacts in small groups. These omissions not only reflect deficiencies of implementation, they also reflect gaps in theoretical thinking and incomplete conceptualization of the relationships among the total outcomes, curriculum, learning, and the conditions under which learning takes place. Therefore, it is possible to propose shifts in grouping and in group sizes without considering any other effects except those on achievement of information.[1]

The designs described in chapter 21 of *Curriculum Development* also show too meager a consideration of the nature and pacing of the transition from knowledge organized around children's experience to a systematically organized study of a discipline or an area as the maturity of students increases. As understanding matures, a greater emphasis on systematic study is both possible and needed. There is little discussion in curriculum treatises of just how and when this transformation takes place, with the result that, in some designs, the systematic study is rather generally shunned and, in others, specialized subjects may be pushed too far down the age level.

To this array of difficulties one must add the difficulties arising from insufficient analysis of the elements themselves. The treatment of content is one example. The difficulties which flow from treating school subjects and their content without differentiation of the levels of knowledge has already been dealt with. . . . This unanalytic attitude toward content could be summarized by paraphrasing the famous phrase of Gertrude Stein: "A subject is a subject is a subject." This view of school subjects creates an illusory conflict over the functions of content which vanishes when confusion is cleared by examining the different levels of knowledge, and the special function which each serves in the educational process. Such an analysis should also make it possible to differentiate the role that each of these levels plays in organizing content. While subjects conceived and taught as collections of facts might be poor centers of organization, the basic ideas of a discipline, or of a series of disciplines, could be so used without the dangers and difficulties pointed out about the subject of organization. The same difficulty appears in determining the scope and sequence. If the content is seen as consisting of (a) specific facts, (b) basic principles or ideas, and (c) overarching concepts and systems of thinking, the decisions about what to use for determining the scope, sequence, and integration would be less subject to confusion.

All of the above are traps in curriculum thinking and planning which arise out of ineffective or insufficient conceptualization and in turn contribute to unscientific attitudes toward curriculum development. The doctrinaire positions lead the protagonists of a particular design to defend that design as a credo or a doctrine instead of as a hypothesis and a possibility. Consequently, the problems of curriculum design are argued in an atmosphere of partisanship, and ideas are debated in terms of protagonist and antagonist positions and not in a climate of honest scientific inquiry. Issues which should be subject to scientific research or to the test of experimental evidence are treated as matters of personal beliefs. One "school" believes in correlation of subject matter, and the next one thinks it is a degradation of education. This doctrinaire approach has prevented the systematizing of the perception of the entire complex of factors that need to be considered in curriculum development. Some essential considerations are played down because they do not support the basic beliefs and preferences, and others assume a more dominating role than their contribution warrants.

Under these conditions, it is not surprising that active research and experimentation in the area of comprehensive curriculum development is as meager as it is, and that changes in curricula are introduced on a wide scale without sufficient logical analysis or testing under experimental conditions prior to their adoption. Witness the current avalanche of special programs for the gifted which are being introduced without even settling what the meaning of "gifted" is, or where one draws the line between those who are and those who are not, let alone considering the possible psychological and social consequences of this move.[2] By settling on the administrative devices of grouping and acceleration as a means for dealing with heterogeneity in ability, the schools are refusing to meet the problems of heterogeneity by making qualitative changes in the curriculum, such as an open-ended curriculum organization which offers more varied opportunities for dealing with the fundamentals of curriculum on several levels of depth.

This doctrinaire and unscientific attitude is also reflected in the manner in which changes are made. When some one aspect of an approach is discredited or found wanting, the entire scheme is discarded in favor of something different, rather than retaining what is useful and correcting what was faulty. This happened when the atomistic and sterile "subject" curriculum provoked an opposition to any planned content in the early progressive movement. It occurred in the reaction to the Herbartian order of five steps in learning, which no doubt were sterile when they were first introduced in this country but which make a good deal of sense when underpinned with a more dynamic interpretation of learning. And today, in the name of excellence, we are supposed to go "back to the fundamentals," to the "hard subjects," in spite of what has been learned in the meanwhile about the role of experience, motivation, and active inquiry in enhancing learning and in producing intellectual excellence. Whether we want to produce scientists and mathematicians or simply responsible human beings and enlightened citizens for democracy, the curriculum still needs to be child-centered in the sense that a productive learning sequence cannot be constructed apart from starting from where the child is and proceeding developmentally. An effective curriculum still needs to make connection with individual needs and concerns and to build bridges from here to there.

A scientific attitude toward curriculum making should at least cultivate a greater respect for the task and a greater humility in the face of it, to prevent such thoughtless and wild swings of the pendulum as seem to be characteristic of American curriculum development. It would also require a greater investment in careful study and research than is now common in curriculum development or change.

. . .

THE ELEMENTS OF THE CURRICULUM

In order to develop a design for a curriculum it is necessary to identify its basic elements. Tyler, for example, points out that "it is important as a part of a comprehensive theory of organization to indicate just what kinds of elements will serve satisfactorily as organizing elements. And in a given curriculum it is important to identify the particular elements that shall be used" (Herrick and Tyler, 1950, p. 64).

But even among the meager statements about these elements,

there is no consensus as to how to categorize them. Tyler identifies three, which seem to be pertinent mostly to establishing a sequence of learning experiences and are rather similar to the threads of integration discussed [elsewhere]. These are the concepts which recur in the sequence of learning experiences, skills which take a long time to master, and values and ideas (Herrick and Tyler, 1950, pp. 63-64).

Perhaps one way of identifying these elements is to consider the major points about which decisions need to be made in the process of curriculum development, as described above, including such considerations as the principles of learning and ideas about the nature of learners and of knowledge. The points of these decisions—the aims and objectives, the content and learning experiences, and evaluation—then become macroscopic elements of the curriculum.

Most curriculum designs contain these elements, but many have them in defective balance, mostly because these elements are poorly identified or have an inadequate theoretical rationale. For example, the subject design usually pays relatively little attention to objectives, or defines them in too narrow a scope. The core curricula stress learning experiences but are often defective in describing their content, or else the scope of the content is defective. Many curriculum designs eventuate in a program which is inappropriate to the students for whom it is intended, either because it is based on an inadequate concept of the learning process or because a greater uniformity of learning is assumed than is warranted. Few curriculum designs postulate and provide for the upper and lower limits in achieving objectives according to student backgrounds or for different qualities of depth according to differences in ability. Such defects in design usually pose difficulties in implementation.

An analysis of the curriculum designs described either in books on curriculum or in curriculum guides also reveals that, while each involves something of all elements, these elements are inadequately related to the stated central emphasis. For example, an integrated curriculum will usually contain some provisions for specialized knowledge. An experience curriculum usually includes organized subject-matter content, and a subject curriculum will employ first-hand experiences. Either these "extras" are bootlegged, or else what are supposed to be black and white differences in the central emphasis are nothing more than an accentuation of one element over others. The main difference among these designs lies more in how the various elements are balanced than in the complete absence of attention to any one element.

With a greater clarity about the structure of curriculum and about its elements, these black and white differences among the various designs should increasingly disappear. This is noticeable in the curricula for mathematics proposed recently. There is a definite emphasis on content, but its development is related, even though not always consciously, to such objectives as understanding mathematical principles and developing a method of thinking, creativity, and discovery. This is a far cry from the older "content" emphasis which was characterized by sheer mastery of content and manipulative skills with practically no attention to the principles of learning intellectual processes.

An effective design also makes clear what the bases of the selection and the emphases on the various elements are, as well as the sources from which these criteria are derived. It should, furthermore, distinguish which criteria apply to which element. For example, a design should make clear whether its objectives are derived from consideration of the social needs as revealed in the analysis of society, the needs of individual development as revealed by the analysis of the nature of learners and their needs as individuals, or both. In a similar manner, both the choice of content and its organization need to be accounted for by an analysis of the unique characteristics of the learning process. When this rationale is not clear, distortions occur in the manner in which content is organized, or else the content is organized in a manner which makes it "unlearnable." Some current designs pay too little attention to the needs of society, or the perspective on these needs is derived from an inadequate analysis of the data on culture and society. This results in objectives of narrowed scope, or objectives which are removed from social realities. Still other designs are based on analysis or the content of the disciplines only, with little or no attention to the characteristics of learners or of the learning process. Many curriculum guides involve all these bases implicitly but fail to state them explicitly. This makes it difficult to establish priorities in applying criteria and principles or their combinations.

Designs with no rationale, or a confusing one, result in a curriculum framework with a high overtone of prescription because the requirements regarding content or the nature of learning experiences are difficult to explain and seem to demand a docile acceptance of directives by those who implement the curriculum in the classroom. As a matter of fact, much of the distance between theory and practice may be caused by just such lack of rationale. Such a curriculum also tends to remain inflexible. An implied rationale is not easily subject to examination and revision according to changes in any of the bases on which it was founded. New data which become available on learning or on changes in the cultural needs, in the nature of student population, or of the content are not easily translated into the curriculum. Such a curriculum can be changed only by what could be called an earthquake method of curriculum revision: a periodic reshuffling of the entire scheme instead of a continuous readaptation.

RELATIONSHIPS AMONG THE ELEMENTS

It is especially important for a curriculum design to make clear how the various elements and the criteria or considerations connected with them are related to each other. A decision made about any one element out of relationship to others is bound to be faulty, because each element of curriculum acquires meaning and substance in reference to other elements and by its place in the pattern that encompasses all others. For example, the specific objectives derive their meaning from the larger aims of the school. If the main aim of the school is to develop intelligent citizenship, then the development of the ability to think critically becomes important. The fact that critical thinking is an important objective imposes certain requirements on the selection and organization of learning experiences, and this, in turn, makes it necessary to include the evaluation of thinking in the program of evaluation. The type of content organization adopted sets limits on the learning experiences which are possible. The consideration of the nature of the students and their backgrounds determines what approaches to the content and to establishing the sequences of learning experiences are effective. The way in which the content of a subject is organized for curriculum purposes is, in a similar manner, controlled by the structure of the discipline which the subject represents.

If the essence of learning mathematics is the capacity to handle abstract symbols and a system of ideas, then the learning experiences in mathematics need to be designed to develop this capacity. If the essence of literature is to develop empathy and capacity to identify with human values, problems, and dilemmas, then the experiences in learning literature must include activities designed to develop this empathy and not be limited to intellectual analysis of forms of literature, the quality of expression, or information about characters. Often inadequate decisions are made at points involving such relationships partly because of lack of clarity about the nature of the elements, or a failure to see the relationship between the criteria which apply to each of them. We tend to apply first one and then another criterion individually instead of thinking of these criteria as a constellation, in which each has a bearing on the others.

Herrick illustrates the necessity for examining the relationships among the elements of the curriculum by analyzing schematic models for curriculum designs (Herrick and Tyler, 1950, p. 41). One of these is a diagram of the elements of a curriculum and their relationships as seen by the curriculum consultants in the Eight Year Study (Giles, McCutcheon, and Zechiel, 1942, p. i).

This design describes four elements: objectives, subject matter, method and organization, and evaluation. In essence, it suggests for the curriculum maker four questions: What is to be done? What subject matter is to be used? What methods and what organization are to be employed? How are the results to be appraised? The design also indicates that each of these elements is related to the others and that, therefore, decisions regarding any of them are dependent on decisions made on others.

However, this design fails to indicate the bases on which the decisions regarding these elements are to be made: the sources from which objectives are derived, which criteria, in addition to objectives, govern the selection and organization of content, and what relationships exist among these criteria.

A design also needs to make explicit its relationship to the factors in school organization and the instructional resources which are necessary to implement it. B. O. Smith, Stanley, and Shores include these considerations in their discussion of the various types of

FIGURE 3.5-1. Elements of a Curriculum

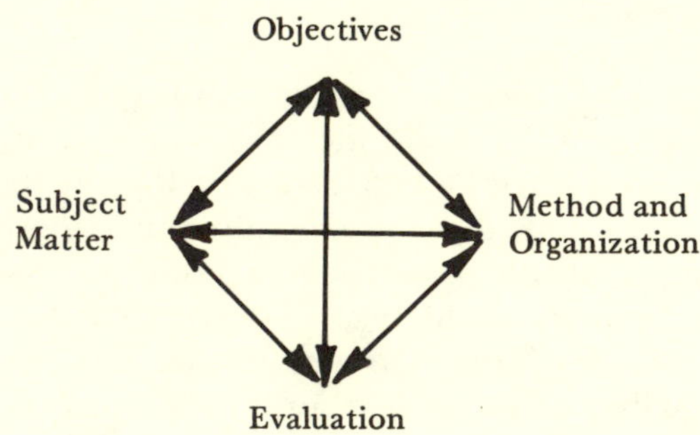

curriculum patterns. They point out, for example, that the subject curriculum requires teachers with intensive training in one subject field, that the best training for teachers for the activity curriculum is one which combines broad general training in content fields with "specialized training in child and adolescent development, guidance and project methods of teaching." Flexibility of scheduling and in grouping of students is a special requirement of the core curriculum (1957, pp. 239, 324).

While the organization of the school and its institutional facilities should be shaped to implement the curriculum, the reverse is usually the case. The functioning curriculum is fitted into the existing arrangements and shaped by the limitations in these conditions. When the conditions necessary for implementing a curriculum design are not fulfilled, a discrepancy between the intended and the actual curriculum is naturally created. It has already been pointed out that a fully integrated curriculum remains an impossibility as long as evaluation and accounting of the program for college entrance is in terms of separate subject areas, as long as teachers are trained along specific subject-matter lines, and as long as the patterns of team teaching are ineffectively developed. When teaching materials are limited to texts, a curriculum design centered on problem solving and calling for sophistication in handling a variety of resources is somewhat unrealistic. The failure to assess realistically the effect of existing conditions has often led to the discrediting of a given curriculum design when the difficulty may not have been in the design but in the discrepancy between the requirements of the design and the conditions for implementing it.

Further, a good design describes the elements and the relationships among them and their supporting principles in such a fashion as to indicate priorities among the factors and principles to be considered. Not all criteria and principles have equal significance in developing an adequate design, or even as norms for a good curriculum. At present there is little analysis of the priorities of these considerations, with the result that often criteria of least significance have a priority over those of greatest consequence. For example, the criterion of efficiency and economy seems to be the major consideration in such proposals regarding curriculum change as team teaching and the use of television. One wonders also whether the advantage to the development of talent in the few gifted is worth the disadvantage accruing from the ability grouping in the form of social and psychological consequences of such a grouping.

Some curriculum analysts consider the decisions about the

centers around which to organize curriculum central to the whole business of curriculum development. Herrick, for example, proposes that a curriculum design becomes more usable in improving educational programs if its major focus is on problems of selecting and organizing the teaching-learning experiences of children and youth (Herrick and Tyler, 1950, p. 44). There are many reasons for allocating a central role to decisions regarding the selection and organization of the curriculum. Certainly, in practice, this is the central task around which decisions regarding selection of objectives revolve. All other decisions, and the criteria and considerations pertaining to them, come into focus in relation to this central decision.

THE PROBLEMS AND PRINCIPLES OF ORGANIZATION

The problems of organization are central to a design of curriculum. A design should, and usually does, convey an idea of how it deals with the major issues of organization: what centers are used for organizing curriculum experiences, what the concept of scope is and how to determine an adequate scope, what provisions are made for sequence of content and of learning experiences, and how to handle integration of knowledge.

The Centers for Organizing the Curriculum

In curriculum development, decisions about what centers to use for organizing curriculum experiences are rather crucial. As indicated . . ., many other decisions regarding selection and organization come to focus around the problems of centering. The merits and disadvantages of the different centers for organizing curriculum have already been discussed. Here only some general points about the role of centering or focusing need to be made.

First, the decisions connected with focusing, such as those involved in planning a unit, bring all other decisions into perspective and organize the ideas relevant to these decisions. For example, it is around the task of formulating a unit that it is possible to perceive and to examine the relationships among objectives, content, learning experiences, and evaluation. The development of organized teaching units also brings home the extent to which all curriculum decisions need to be made in the light of consciously understood criteria and relationships. It is impossible to make good decisions about the method of learning and teaching apart from considering the objectives that students should attain, or apart from concepts regarding the nature of the learners and the principles of learning. The decisions faced regarding organization of content bring into play the necessity of analyzing the functions of the various levels of content as well as the nature of learners and thus demonstrate a way of applying multiple considerations in making curriculum decisions which curriculum makers cannot learn abstractly.

How the nature of organizing centers influences the selection of the content and learning experiences and vice versa becomes clear also. For example, if the basic ideas are the centers for organizing the unit, these ideas then determine which specific details of information are relevant and which particular learning experiences are useful to develop these concepts and ideas and to achieve other non-content-related objectives.

The organizing focuses are also crucial to the manner of dealing with the problems of scope, sequence, and integration. For example, the kind of centers used in organizing each unit of social studies determines the kind of sequence which can be built into the entire social-science curriculum as well as the relationships which can exist between social sciences and other subjects, such as literature. In reverse, once the scope and sequence are established they determine to a certain extent how the specific areas of curriculum can be organized, such as which centers of organization can be employed or which sequence of learning experiences can be used. It becomes clear that decisions regarding the focusing centers of specific units and those pertaining to scope and sequence as indicated in the framework of the curriculum are interdependent. The decisions about focusing of specific units cannot be made out of context of the total design without the danger of discontinuity and inconsistency.

This means, of course, that the two types of activities, analysis of the various elements of the curriculum and organization, represent two separate but interrelated steps, and this interrelationship needs to be maintained on both the specific and the general level of curriculum organization. The description of ways for dealing with the elements of the curriculum may outline the objectives and set criteria for selection of content and of learning activities in general. These essential aspects of curriculum planning and thinking are faced only at the point of putting these elements together into a functioning unit. A method of curriculum development which devotes a long time to the analysis of objectives and philosophy, and which then omits the organizing of teaching units, usually results in guides on paper which do not function in classrooms.

The general analysis only furnishes the bricks from which to compound a functioning curriculum. But the general analysis is insufficient without the subsequent step of translating general objectives into specific ones and without a methodology of translating into a functioning curriculum the criteria which apply to these decisions severally and collectively. One qualification for the focus or center of curriculum organization, then, is that the organization which it produces lives up to such criteria as adaptability to the ability levels of students, the varied conditions in schools, the resources of the teachers, and the interests of children.[3]

Scope, Sequence, and Integration

A design should indicate clearly the bases and provisions for the scope and continuity of learning. Scope is a way of describing what is covered, or what is learned. As was pointed out earlier, one needs to determine what is learned in two different dimensions: what content is mastered and what mental processes are acquired (or what noncontent objectives are achieved). The failure to see scope as a two-dimensional problem has created the dilemma of breadth and depth. When scope is seen solely as the breadths of content covered, the demands of coverage are in conflict with demands arising out of requirements of depth. The wider the coverage, the less time there is to develop depth of understanding and a high level of conceptualization, to incorporate ideas into a personal system of thinking, and so on. Often these two dimensions are confused and a more extensive coverage of the subject is identified with depth. The continuity of learning has two aspects: that of a vertical progress from one level to another, and that of a relationship between the learnings in various areas of the curriculum which take place at the same time. The first of these is associated with the term *sequence,* the other with the term *integration.* The problem of providing continuity of learning also presents itself on two different levels: the level of organizing specific units of teaching and learning, and the level of the design for the entire curriculum.

Much of the confusion and difficulty in developing cumulative and continuous learning comes from the fact that in setting up sequences in curriculum designs, only the sequence of content is considered, while the sequence of the powers and competencies is largely overlooked. The result is that the curriculum sequence reflects growth in the mental powers only to the extent that the level of content requires it, and not because of a clear plan for the developmental sequence of these powers, competencies, and skills. Out of this confusion grow all sorts of difficulties: poor articulation between the levels of schooling, the perennial complaints by each level of lack of preparation on the preceding level, misplaced expectations, and a lowered amount of growth. The attempts to "cure" these difficulties by changing the content and setting standards of excellence in the light of content achievement alone are bound to be less successful than addressing the standards of excellence to the formulation of developmental sequences in either intellectual or other types of performance.

When the problems of both scope and sequence are seen in two dimensions—one which sketches out the pattern of the content to be covered, and the other which indicates the kinds of powers or capacities to be developed and a sequence of developing them—the dilemma of scope and depth can be put into a more balanced perspective. This perspective would aid in deciding when the extension of the scope of content interferes with the development of the scope of mental powers and how the sequence of content could assure a sequence in levels of mental powers, or vice versa.

This double pattern of scope and sequence makes certain requirements on the centers of organization. Centers of organization need to combine most advantageously the requirements for advancing both the level of content and the level of mental operations. Using the basic ideas as focusing centers has several advantages in this respect. First, if the basic ideas are clearly outlined, it is also easier to see which intellectual powers and operations are necessary to deal with them. If units are organized around ideas, it is, for example, easier to determine what levels of abstraction may be required and what type of relationships between various ideas are possible and necessary than it is when only the topics and their dimensions are available for analysis.

This organization also makes it possible to examine more precisely both the sequence of content that is being employed and the sequence in the powers and capacities that are developed in the successive levels of curriculum. The units on different grade levels can be examined to see what ideas have been added and which are extended, and whether the contexts in which these additions are being made add up to sufficient scope of understanding. It will also be possible to determine whether there is an increment in such powers as the capacity to analyze data, to organize ideas, to respond to feelings and values, to appreciate aesthetic qualities, or to express feelings and ideas.

Below is an attempt to analyze for the elementary social studies the sequence in content and the cumulative maturation of the concept of difference, which is a recurring concept from one grade level to another.

TABLE 3.5-1. Sequence of the Concept of Difference

Grade level	Areas in which the concept is developed	Sequency of the concept of "differences"
I	Home, family, school	Difference in families in: 1. Family composition 2. Occupation 3. Income
II	Work in community: farm, transportation, and supermarket	People do different things to meet life's needs.
III	Comparative communities	People do things in different ways today than long ago, and differently in different cultures.
IV	California—now and before	Differences in reasons for people coming to California, for different kinds of occupations here, etc. Differences in ways of life according to geographic and historical conditions.
V	Life in the United States	Extension of IV. Different feelings about coming to or moving about the U.S. Different patterns of life. Effects of different environments.
VI	The Western Hemisphere—how the various functions of life are carried on, such as economy, education, government	The functions of life are met in different ways as determined by climate, topography, history, type of people.
VII	World trade	Different ways the various countries process, use, or distribute the natural resources of the earth.
VIII	United Nations	Different ways in which the various cultures can be helped to meet life's needs.*

*From the minutes of a curriculum planning session, Contra Costa County Schools, Pleasant Hill, California.

Content organized around large central ideas is also amenable to analysis of the ideas drawn from various disciplines in order to check validity and significance. For example, the units in the areas described above were analyzed to see what ideas they contained that might be classified as history, sociology, geography, economics, and anthropology. An example of the sociological ideas in social studies from Grades 1-3 (Contra Costa Schools, June 1961) is given in Table 3.5-2.

TABLE 3.5-2. Sample Content Analysis of Sociological Ideas in Units, Grades 1-3

Central Ideas	Grade 1	Grade 2	Grade 3
Groups, Society, and Communication	As students at school we expect to learn certain things and we expect to behave in a particular way. Children feel differently about what schools expect of them. A family group may differ in structure, *i.e.*, one-parent home, foster home, etc. A child has two sets of relatives—his mother's relatives and father's relatives. Families have different rules for their children. The teacher is also a member of a family.	The clerk in the supermarket is also a member of a family and a consumer. The farmer is an employer, a consumer, and a member of a family A supermarket needs the newspaper for advertising.	A Zulu child and a nomadic Arab child are members of a tribe as well as of a family. A Chinese child has an extended family. A Swiss child has a family structure more nearly like ours. People who have no written language pass along their knowledge and tradition by word of mouth. Our form of writing was first evolved among the Arab people. The Chinese have a pictograph form of writing. Music, dance, and ceremonies can be used to communicate with others. The primitive of Africa, the Arab, the Chinese, and our communities have each developed a certain kind of music. Among the Chinese celebrations are held for the entire family.

TABLE 3.5-2. Continued

Central Ideas	Grade 1	Grade 2	Grade 3
Human Ecology	Homes in cities may differ from homes in small towns or on a farm. Schools in the country may be different from schools in town or city. Some "grandparents" receive checks from "the county."	People live in different kinds of communities. When a community grows larger more services, such as schools, churches, libraries, etc., are needed. A commuting community needs many roads and filling stations. A small community may have a volunteer fire service; larger communities have full-time firemen. A community may not meet all the needs of the people who live there—employment, hospitalization, etc. Some services (school, fire, etc.) are provided by taxes, some are provided by individuals (TV repairs, barber), and some by companies (banking, electricity). Irrigation canals are built by the government to bring water to farms. The farmer needs schools, recreation, etc., just as people in large communities do.	Primitive people (Zulu or rain-forest primitives) use the plants and animals of their environment to provide food, clothing, and shelter. Modern communities (Swiss people or our community) are less dependent on their environment for food, clothing, and shelter. Where there is water in the hot, dry lands we find farms. The farmers live in permanent homes. The nomad of the hot, dry land and the people who live on boats in Hong Kong harbor must trade to meet their basic needs. The people of Switzerland are concerned with the tourist trade as a result of their natural scenery. The family and tribe of the primitive community provide religion, recreation, teaching of the young, and enforcement of tribal rules. Our community has schools, churches, and government to do this. Each community celebrates occasions in a traditional manner.

			Modern transportation helps the Swiss people secure chocolate beans from another country and deliver the Swiss chocolate to far-away markets.
Personality and Socialization Processes	At school where there are many children we have rules for the sake of safety. Family living demands that we share space, parents' time, etc., with other members. Families teach their children to behave a certain way. They may punish them for not obeying the rules. In some families the role of the "bread-winner" is carried by someone other than or in addition to the father. Father's work is very important to the family. Some jobs, such as shopping, fixing things, etc., may be done by different family members.		Zulu children are taught to accept the ways of their people. Arab, Chinese, and Swiss children are each taught a particular way of behaving. Each of the four cultures teaches girls to behave in a special way and boys to behave in a special way. Among the Zulu the oldest son of the chief will inherit the position of chief. Among the Arabs the male has a special position. In the Chinese culture age is given great respect.
Social Processes	Families carry on many work and play activities together. Parents who commute to work have little time to spend with children in the evening.	We have laws related to keeping milk clean and cows free from disease. We have laws related to keeping food markets clean and free from disease.	

TABLE 3.5-2.

Central Ideas	Grade 1	Grade 2	Grade 3
	Fathers who travel have time with their families only on certain days.	All businesses need fire and police protection.	
Social Relations and Culture			Traders and missionaries have brought changes to primitive people. The United Nations and WHO are bringing many changes among primitives and underdeveloped peoples. People do not always like the changes that are brought to them.
Social Control			The Zulu have certain rules the members must follow, such as obedience to the chief on a hunt. Brave behavior is rewarded by the chief. In our communities there are laws related to trade—a limit on how much a tourist may bring back into this country.

A Sequence of Mental Operations

A chart of learning activities makes possible a similar analysis of the mental operations represented by the learning experiences. If the learning activities in the various units are clearly stated, they can be examined to determine the scope and range they represent and the cumulative growth they provide in powers other than the understanding of content—thinking, academic and group skills, attitudes, values, and sensitivities. A sequence in developing sensitivity to differences starts in the first grade by reading about a new child in the school and then discussing what it feels like to be one and what the ways are of making a new child feel at home (Contra Costa County Schools, 1959, p. 13). The second-grade unit on the farm inducts the students into feelings about farm life and ends with writing a story, "The Farmer Who Would Not Move Away" (Contra Costa County Schools, 1959, pp. 39 and 41). In the third grade the children have the task of projecting themselves into the life in many cultures, and they begin to explore how the various kinds of people—the primitives in the rain forest, the Hong Kong boat dwellers, the Sahara nomads—feel about their culture. They are asked to write on themes such as, "If I were a primitive child I would like to. . . ." (Contra Costa County Schools, 1961, p. 13).

Such an analysis permits a projection upwards. What other aspects of cultural sensitivity can be built on this particular one, and how can an increasing capacity to put oneself in other people's shoes be cumulatively developed? What additional dimensions are necessary to develop the degree of cosmopolitan cultural sensitivity needed and which particular contexts are especially appropriate?

A cumulative sequence is observable also in logical and critical thinking. After observing and analyzing what the teacher, principal, custodian, and cafeteria workers do, the first graders develop chart stories on the theme, "We have many helpers at school." They begin to differentiate such things as what must be done for the baby, what is fun to do and what is troublesome, what people might like and dislike about different types of houses, or what responsibilities are carried by different family members. The burden of differentiation and abstraction increases in the second grade, where the children are asked to differentiate the services needed and provided in different types of communities and the ways in which these services are paid for. They now write on topics such as, "This is the day when the electricity failed." In the third grade, the students are asked to analyze a film on the idea of what is primitive by developing a list of qualities and activities which are evidences of a primitive way of life. Subsequently they read a story about life in the rain forest and are then asked to determine which statements in the list are true of the family described in the story and in which way that family shows evidence of being primitive. This requires a degree of abstraction, of logical inference, of contrasting and comparing.

What should be the expectation on the next level of children who have mastered these intellectual processes? In other words, what is the sequence in the processes of thinking? If students in one unit have learned to classify simple ideas, is the next attempt at classification more demanding? If they have learned to derive simple generalizations from fairly simple facts, are they challenged in the next unit to move on to a higher and a more complex level? Do students who have learned to compare and contrast a simple set of conditions have an opportunity next to do the same on a more abstract or complex level? Do those who have learned to state simple sequences of events next learn to state and to discover sequences in argumentation?

As the students return to the same central idea or concept, it is possible to determine whether they only add to its content and meaning or whether these additions also increasingly demand higher levels of mental operations, such as an increasingly higher level of abstraction and an increasingly wider radius of application. In other words, it is necessary to plot a developmental sequence of cumulative growth both in power and in content in order to determine whether the subsequent contexts merely yield new information while requiring the same powers of comprehension and the same level of thinking, or whether there is an increment in both.

Advantages of a Double Sequence

Such a double scheme of composing scope and sequence by ideas and concepts treated and by the behaviors expected has several advantages. Both the behavior reactions and the content are accessible to an objective analysis of their cumulative effect. The scheme of scope and sequence is not jeopardized by a varied type of organization, and, in reverse, no one single type of organization needs to be imposed for the sake of a coherent scope and sequence. It is equally possible to apply such a scheme to a curriculum organized by subjects, by topics which cut across disciplines, or by problems. And it would also be possible to vary the schemes of organization from area to area, such as using problems as the main approach in one and a topical organization in the next. If ideas serve as centers of organization, variety in approaches does not destroy the comparability of the threads.

Such a scheme would also open up the possibility of developing a single consistent pattern of scope and sequence from the elementary through the high school, and across all subjects, which the current curriculum designs do not provide. None of them encompasses all grade levels or everything that the curriculum contains.

The same would be true of establishing and examining the integration or the horizontal relationship among disciplines or subjects. If ideas are used as the basic threads for establishing these relationships, integration can be achieved on several levels and in several ways, and not limited to the combining of particular subjects. For some ideas a crossing of historical, sociological, and anthropological material may be necessary to give proper dimension. Integration of scientific and social facts may be most relevant for others. Still others may require a combination of practical life situations with theoretical principles. In other words, it would not seem necessary to apply a single pattern of integration in all subjects or at every step in their study.

Another advantage of structuring the scope, sequence, and integration by ideas and behaviors rather than by subjects and content topics is that such a scheme has a flexibility which permits adjustments to the nature of student population and to the local conditions in particular schools. As was pointed out, units structured around ideas and developed by dimensions of topics and sampling of content permit a variety of adjustments. Each dimension can be extended or contracted according to the limits in students' perception and their level of understanding. These extensions and contractions can be made at any point: in the depth required, by developing an idea only on a certain level; in the extent of comparisons required, by limiting comparison only to certain aspects of culture or carrying it only to a certain level of exactitude; in the number of the concrete samples used, by using a larger number of concrete examples with the less able. One can require more or less exacting types of analysis, abstracting, and generalizing. Alternatives can be substituted either in specific ideas to be pursued or in specific samples of content, provided these alternatives are equally relevant to the main ideas. Coverage and level of expectation are thus brought into a rational control, and changes in each can be effected without revising the entire scheme.

This makes it possible to have a *common* curriculum pattern without necessitating a uniform curriculum. Teachers can be free to give adequate attention to content without having to submit to the tyranny of uniform, fixed, and static content. While the same threads

FIGURE 3.5-2. A Model for Curriculum Design*

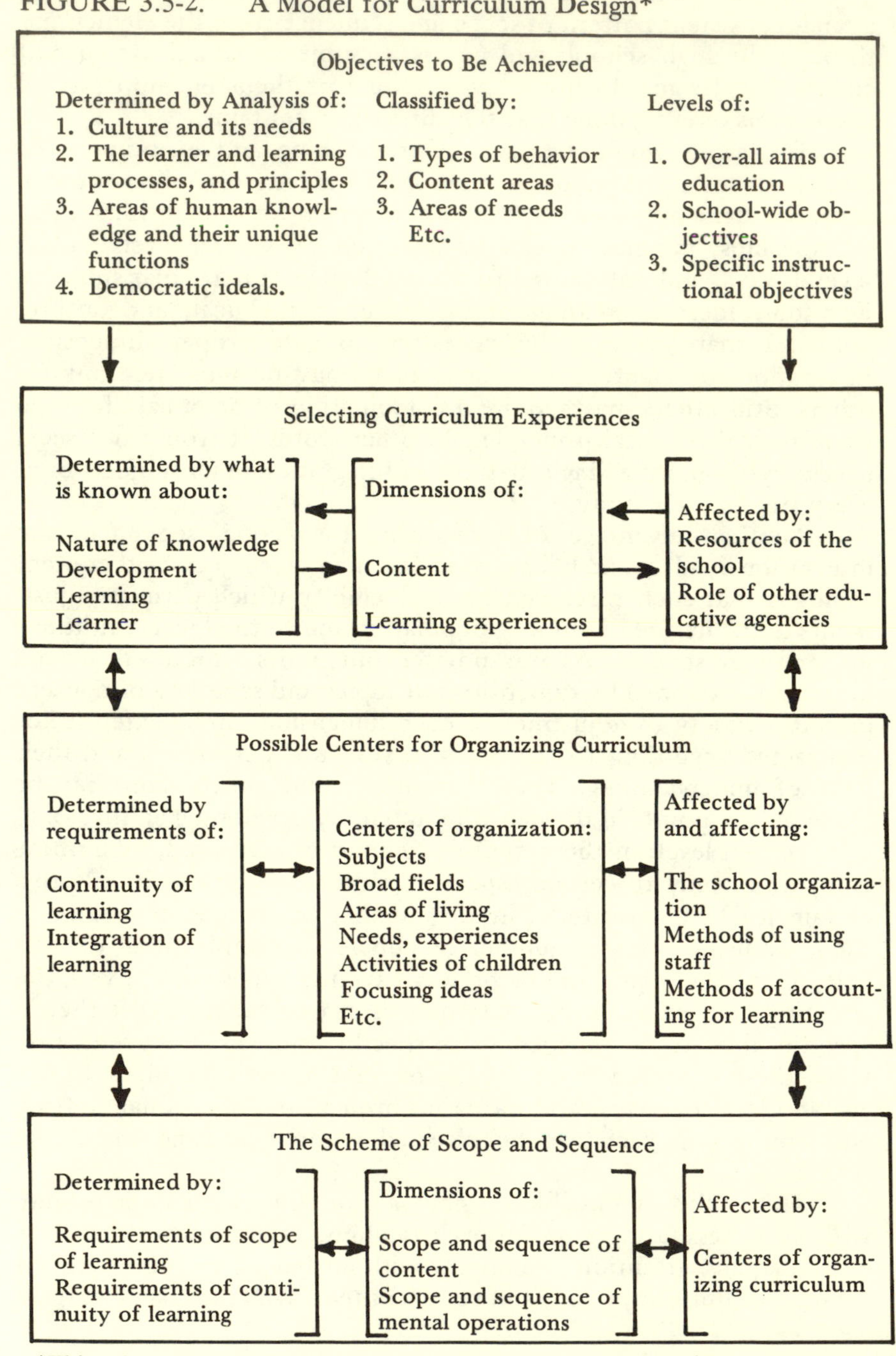

*This scheme is an extension of the one presented by Herrick (Herrick and Tyler, 1950, p. 43)

go through all grade levels and all areas, these threads may be developed with different student groups in different ways.

This type sequence of scope requires careful experimentation and research. The elements that compose them are not strangers. The idea of teaching for concepts and ideas is older than Mark Hopkins' log, and most people know what is meant by behavioral objectives. What is new and requires new study is the cumulative sequence in achieving them. This would require longitudinal studies of the curriculum and its outcomes, similar to the longitudinal studies of physical growth and development. No such studies have as yet been made.

The schematic model of a curriculum design (Figure 3.5-2) attempts to organize the considerations presented above: the chief points at which curriculum decisions are made, the considerations that apply to each, the relationships that should exist among these points, and the criteria.[4]

NOTES

1. Ward traces the deficiencies in the program for the gifted to the shortcomings in theoretical thinking (1961).
2. Getzels and Jackson point out, for example, that the current concept of giftedness tends to be limited not only exclusively to cognitive qualities but even simply to a high IQ (1962, p. 2).
3. Goodlad presents this problem in the form of outlining a three-dimensional planning which takes place on the pre-classroom level and a three-dimensional synthesis which is necessary "if children are to experience a series of dynamic learning-teaching acts" (1956, pp. 11-22).
4. This scheme is an extension of one presented by Herrick (1950, p. 43).

REFERENCES

Bayles, E. "Present Status of Education Theory in the U.S.," *School and Society* 87 (January 1959).

Caswell, Hollis L. "Sources of Confusion in Curriculum Theory." In V.E. Herrick and R.W. Tyler (eds.), *Toward Improved Curriculum Theory*. Supplementary Education Monograph No. 71. Chicago: University of Chicago Press, 1950.

Caswell, Hollis L. "Significant Curriculum Issues," *Educational Leadership* 9 (January 1952): 207–14.

Contra Costa County Schools, *Social Studies, Grades 1–6*. Pleasant Hill, Calif.: Contra Costa County Schools, 1959.

Contra Costa County Schools. "A Content Analysis of the Contra Costa County Social Studies Curriculum." Pleasant Hill, Calif.: Contra Costa County Schools, June 1961. Mimeo.

Getzels, J.W., and Jackson, P. *Creativity and Intelligence: Explorations with Gifted Children*. New York: Wiley, 1962.

Giles, H.H., S.P. McCutcheon, and A.N. Zechiel. *Exploring the Curriculum*. New York: Harper and Row, 1942.

Goodlad, John I. "Three Dimensions for Organizing the Curriculum for Learning and Teaching." In Vincent Glennon (ed.), *Frontiers of Elementary Education III*. Proceedings of a Conference on Elementary Education. Syracuse, N.Y.: Syracuse University Press, 1956.

Goodlad, John I. "The School Scene in Review," *School Review* 66 (Winter 1958): 391–401.

Herrick, Virgil I., and Ralph W. Tyler (eds.) *Toward Improved Curriculum Theory*. Supplemental Educational Monograph No. 71. Chicago: University of Chicago Press, 1950.

Smith, B. Othanel, William O. Stanley, and J. Harlan Shores. *Fundamentals of Curriculum Development*. Yonkers-on-Hudson, N.Y.: World Book Co., 1950.

Taba, Hilda. *Dynamics of Education*. New York: Harcourt, Brace, and World, 1932.

Ward, V.S. "The Function of Theory in Programs for the Gifted," *Teachers College Record* 62 (April 1961): 532–36.

Selection 3.6

Curriculum and Planning: Visions and Metaphors

James B. Macdonald and David E. Purpel

PREFACE

Sometime in 1981, Jim Macdonald and I agreed to write an article on the history and current status of curriculum planning for a book to be published in Israel and edited by Zvi Lamm of the Hebrew University of Jerusalem. The original idea was that this book would first be published in Hebrew and later in an English translation. We wrote the article, and it was translated into Hebrew and published in 1983 as part of a book. As far as I know, no English edition of this book has appeared (Lamm, 1983).

Jim and I had planned to present the article for publication in America, and in 1982 we received permission to do so by the publisher. We have presented much of the material in the article to our classes, and many students urged us to get it into print. We never did get around to it.

Following Jim Macdonald's death in 1983, I decided that it was important to share this work with our colleagues in the field. I have made some modest changes in the article in response to helpful criticisms from colleagues, but I believe that its essence is unchanged from the original. Some people have asked me to indicate which part of the paper is Mac-

---

SOURCE. From *Journal of Curriculum and Supervision* 2 (Winter 1987): 178–92. Reprinted with permission of the Association for Supervision and Curriculum Development.

donald and which is Purpel. I doubt I could answer this accurately even if I were convinced that it was necessary. Some passages are surely his and others surely mine, but much of it emerged from our joint effort.

However, aspects of this paper do evoke the significant legacy of Jim Macdonald's contribution to education. Most broadly, and probably most fundamentally, Jim saw this paper as meeting the need to explore and to do serious rethinking about curriculum. He saw it as advancing new modes of analysis and expression and as a venture into largely uncharted realms of discourse. Second, I believe he was expressing his love of and commitment to the field of curriculum and was intent on breathing new life into a field pronounced by some to be deceased. Third, he wanted very much in this paper to emphasize the enormous importance of the fact that the language and processes of curriculum and curriculum planning are embedded in metaphysical, philosophical, and moral concerns. Fourth, the article can be seen as an extension of the ideas on religion and curriculum that he presented in "A Transcendental Developmental Ideology of Education" (Macdonald, 1974, pp. 85–116).

Naturally, I hesitate to speculate on what he would have wanted or would have said on these matters. However, I do know that while we were writing this piece, he was particularly eager to encourage colleagues to present their own larger visions and thereby to stimulate debate and discussion on what as educators we can and should affirm. His life's work was dedicated to that task of affirmation, a task to which he continues to make an enduring contribution.

— David E. Purpel

THEORETICAL PERSPECTIVES

Curriculum planning both as fact and theory is so pervasive in education that it approaches a sense of inevitability. However, the field of curriculum planning, as well as curriculum itself, is a twentieth-century development. Certainly there have existed for centuries courses of study, programs, and categories of knowledge and skill, but the emergence of curriculum and curriculum planning as distinct enterprises with specialized knowledge and functions is a recent event. It is also clear that this field, like other professional fields, exists within a particular historical and cultural context. Thus, not surprisingly, curriculum planning is dominated by the main currents of technological, linear, and positivistic thinking of our contemporary culture. Its mode of thinking employs such basic metaphors as machine, engineering, utility, and quality control.

In curriculum planning, we have come to use the term "the Tyler rationale" as a shorthand way of referring to this overall conception of curriculum and curriculum planning (Tyler, 1949). The Tyler rationale is essential to understanding today's curriculum-planning process, since it remains the foundational and functional paradigm for the profession. The rationale is related to classical economic decision-making theory and carries in it the ethos of our technical and engineering culture. The rationale further complements the general climate of cost accounting, efficiency, and accountability with its focus on student and teacher competency, and fits perfectly with metaphors of school as business or factory, and which requires quality control of the presumed product of schooling: student achievement. The rationale also lends itself well to certain political dimensions of schooling, inasmuch as it clearly communicates a simple and logical process to nonprofessionals, and so it functions to serve the status quo by focusing on how, not why, making sure that what "is" is taught more efficiently and effectively.

We believe, however, that the Tyler rationale has outworn its usefulness as the major paradigm for curriculum planning. It is proposed as an essentially neutral rational process where values, when they appear, are separated and treated as separate data in a rational decision-making process. There are many reasons for raising critical questions about the Tyler rationale, reasons that arise from a number of critiques of modernism.

Curriculum planning in Tyler's rationale accepts without question the existing political and social setting—status quo as a basis for planning. Social reality is what it appears to be, and so the existing authority relations and social hierarchy are assumed to be positive and acceptable in the surround of the curriculum planning process. With this acceptance there comes an aura of expert elitism, which permeates the planning context.

From an intellectual point of view there are two critical concepts of the Tyler rationale that must be considered: (1) the centrality of the process of rational decision making and (2) the identification of specific behaviors to be selected, elicited, organized, and evaluated. Individual behavior becomes the focus of the planning process, which is a clear example of the philosophical liberal paradigm that sees each individual's acts as separate and autonomous from the world around them and more or less meritorious in terms of the general success criteria of school and society. There is little or no mention of the impact of the students' background and culture; hence context is not seen to be relational, but merely as facilitative. This lack of sensitivity to cultural diversity flies in the face of numerous studies of student behavior that dramatically indicate the impact of sociocultural factors that provide contextual and relational influences far transcending the simplistic rational, linear decisions of the

Tyler model. Thus, the Tyler rationale may be said to fit easily in a hierarchical society with the use of an expert or elite group to create school learning settings that reflect the interests of those dominant groups of society. There is no clear statement of who plans, under what conditions, and in whose interest!

Systematic critiques of the Tyler rationale have come from several sources, including neo-Marxist, sociology of knowledge, aesthetic, and religious perspectives. The neo-Marxist critiques have taken place in the context of critiques of the function of schooling in capitalist society. Their basic assertion is that schools function to preserve the class system by reproducing the status quo via the differential distribution of knowledge to children of different social classes. The curriculum of the school is treated here as cultural capital. Those entering with more capital accumulate more capital in proportionately greater degrees than those entering with less. Further, those entering with less capital are often tracked into special classes or special curriculum tracks—thus effectively cutting off access to kinds of learning (capital) that others have. From this perspective, the dominant thought process and techniques of curriculum planning simply provide an efficient and effective reproduction of a class system, with its privileges and power.

Up to this point, the neo-Marxist critique makes a decidedly deep cut in ordinary views of schooling. Nevertheless, it is not clear either historically or critically whether the rejection of a Tylerism is based on its essential character or on the fact that it serves the wrong master. Historical examples and the materialistic basis of Marxist philosophy lead us to think that it is the latter. Marxism, we suspect, is embedded in the same general culture as capitalism, and the assumptive base of each allows them to use Tyler's or Skinner's behaviorism with equal facility. We find the Marxist critique flawed on this basis: its acceptance of materialistic opportunism in the service of different ends. It is surely clear that Marx, like Machiavelli, searched for a base other than values for human action. If human beings are a random accidental occurrence in the cosmos and create themselves and their own destiny through the obtaining and justification of power by small groups of elites, then the Tyler model is a useful control mechanism to bring about desired ends. It seems clear that both capitalistic and communistic ideologies are embedded in the common dominant technological, materialistic culture.

Fortunately, we are not without other insights into the human condition. Though they may lack the grandeur of thorough systematic frameworks, they have appeared consistently and meaningfully on the human scene. We refer here to three such frameworks: (1) methodological anarchism, (2) aesthetics, and (3) religion.

Feyerabend has presented an *anarchistic* theory of knowledge. His basic premise is that science is essentially an anarchistic enterprise and that "theoretical anarchism is more humanitarian and more likely to encourage progress than its law-and-order alternatives" (1975, p. 17). He is referring primarily to scientific methodology for inquiry and suggests science is best served by a methodological motto—"anything goes." Feyerabend supports this position with a quote from Einstein:

> The external conditions which are set for [the scientist] by the facts of experience do not permit him to let himself be too much restricted, in the construction of his conceptual world, by the adherence to an epistemological system. He, therefore, must appear to the systematic epistemologist as a type of unscrupulous opportunist. . . . [P. 18]

This perspective is not far removed from our position here in relation to planning processes. The dominant planning paradigm, just as empirical experimental methodology, has preempted the thought processes of the profession. Feyerabend maintains that "a complex medium containing surprising and unforseen developments demands complex procedures and defies analysis on the basis of rules that have been set up in advance and without regard to the ever-changing conditions of history" (p. 18). Surely the same may be said in the perspective of a monolithic planning paradigm like the Tyler rationale. The educational enterprise is too complex and holds too many unforeseen developments in the ever-changing conditions of planning to be restricted to one linear, rational, simplistic planning mode.

The critique from an *aesthetic* point of view addresses the basic problem of the separation of means from ends inherent in the technical planning approach. Thus, ends are stated and means are then emphasized. In many instances, the means become another sort of ends in themselves. Aesthetically many activities are worth doing for the sake of engagement in them, and the value of such activity lies in the dynamics of participation. The outcomes of such pursuits are neither known nor relevant to the justification for doing them. Thus, inherent in an aesthetic concern is the realization that outcomes of any tangible sort are unknowable until after the fact.

This view has been developed in depth in relation to evaluation by Elliot Eisner, who suggests that the concepts of connoisseurship and educational criticism lead to a qualitative form of educational inquiry (1985, pp. 216–52). J. Steven Mann, in his work on curriculum criticism, also calls for a basic transformation from a technological to an aesthetic mode: "from a framework in which the curriculum is input in a production system to one in which [curriculum] is regarded as an envisionary work of art that conveys meaning" (1968–69, p. 8). Thus from an aesthetic viewpoint, curriculum planning is planning for living environments, not productive outcomes of some larger system; and the planning activity itself should reflect the same qualitative concern for the personal and meaningful engagement with others in the process. The activity of the planning process must be to some extent self-justifying in human terms, not merely justified by some efficient and effective outcome.

Religious critique focuses on beliefs that correlate patterns in human experiences. Its purpose is to project interpretive models reflecting unitary wholes that share similarities with the aesthetic, especially those models that focus on a moral and ethical critique of human relationships. However, critique from a transcendentalist viewpoint is especially instructive and useful for the purposes here, because it previews the platform proposal that follows later.

An illustration of the meaning of transcendence here is the work of Peter Berger (1969). Addressing religion from the orientation of "natural theology," Berger points out the existence of "signals of transcendence" in common human activity, that is, phenomena in our experience that appear to point beyond an everyday reality, a literal going beyond the normal, everyday world. The prototypical human gestures that constitute these signals are: (1) the human trait for *order*, (2) the basic human experience of *play*, (3) the capacity to extend into the future through *hope*, (4) the universal phenomena of *damnation*, and (5) the existence of *humor*.

All these experiences take us beyond the everyday, normal world, the world of Tyler's behavioral objectives. Technical curriculum planning does not respond to this human potential. From a moral and ethical perspective, the Tyler rationale can be said to be amoral, which in itself is good reason for its rejection, since education is a moral enterprise. The curriculum as planned is a series of "shoulds," mastery of which will purportedly lead students to be "good" persons, to live a "good" life, and to make a "good" society. These are moral promises to the young, which lead to moral ends. However, there is no moral grounding for the Tyler rationale — no affirmation of basic beliefs, no reverence for life, no concern for compassion, or worrying about justice.

Moreover, this planning procedure is bankrupt in terms of nourishing a democratic community. If we assume that democracy means participation and community means people in communication and communion, then the Tyler rationale does not recognize the existence of a true democratic community. It is, indeed, most clearly an elitist planning procedure, from the top down, which is most effectively used to specify and isolate bits of culture and persons rather than build community. In this sense, the procedure is alienating. As a paradigm that deals with human affairs, the Tyler rationale is set in a view of humanity as infinitely perfectible and human society as characterized by progress. Each human being, if we are to believe Bloom, can be taught anything in his or her own time (1971, pp. 17–49). The hubris and arrogance of such a controlling and manipulative approach are clear to see. It is, in fact, this very epitome of the linear rational planning approach that leads to the division and isolation of the individual to be manipulated for "learning" purposes around specific objectives, expert-selected and defined.

The linear rational planning approach is almost entirely technical talk, though some scientific talk is inherent in the early part of the Tyler rationale (needs assessment, etc.). There is, however, no built-in way to recognize the political, aesthetic, or moral aspects of life in the dominant language systems. Further, the recognition and the concern for qualities of humanness that are necessary for any full view of human nature are excluded in Tylerism. There is no opportunity for intellectual play, creativity, or expression of our essentially subjective nature; the reflection of compassion, or love and justice, joy, awe, or wonder goes unrecognized. No suggestion of the need for critical consciousness or a just community resides in this paradigm. What we have is a planning process that denies by omission and intention the essentially spiritual quality of human existence and the essential "sovereignty of the Good" (Murdock, 1970) where development of environments for living and learning are concerned.

PLATFORMS AND CURRICULUM PLANNING

We propose that curriculum planning as process must embody the transcendent, both in its cultural and spiritual meanings. The process must facilitate transcendence of the status quo through cultural consciousness and active subjectivity (art, play, etc.); it must embody the recognition of the essential spiritual qualities of human existence. In order to generate a model for such a process, we believe it necessary to articulate a platform for curriculum planning. Whatever platform exists for the technical approach is neither clear nor stated. The need for a platform is, however, a critical part of any planning procedure. Thus, as Michael Polanyi has clearly stated, our thinking and perceiving always proceed in a "from–to" relationship (Polanyi and Prosch, 1975, p. 71). There is, in other words, a necessary tacit platform from which we project a planning procedure.

The importance of "platform" has been discussed at length by hermeneutic philosophers. The work of Hans Gadamer (1976) is especially instructive. Each situation represents a standpoint that limits the possibility of vision. Thus, the concept of a "horizon" is an essential part of each situation, and many thinkers have used the word to characterize the way in which thought is tied to a platform. It is this platform that allows us to see beyond what is nearest to us. Without such a platform we are limited to and overvalue what seems to have a sense of immediacy to us. We must be concerned with both the limiting and liberating power of the metaphors that shape our ideas on what education is to be.

Technical rationales have not explicitly presented their horizons. They do in part proceed in a manner described by Gadamer as "overvaluing what is nearest to them." Partly this is due to the ahistorical quality of technical thinking. We propose that a platform is a critical part of any planning process, and its historical and transcendent metaphysical qualities as well as its moral, ethical, political, and aesthetic characteristics are fundamental to understanding and evaluating any planning procedure. And in this spirit we address the problem of platform.

The use of the term platform in curriculum talk appears in Walker's (1971) work. Walker posited and described a model of the process of curriculum development that consisted of three elements: (1) platform, (2) design, and (3) deliberation. Concerning platform, Walker says:

> The curriculum developer does not begin with a blank slate. He could not begin without some notion of what is possible and desirable educationally. The system of beliefs and values that the curriculum developer brings to his task and that guides the development of the curriculum is what I call the curriculum's *platform*. The word "platform" is meant to suggest both a political platform and something to stand on. The platform includes an idea of what is and a vision of what ought to be, and these guide the curriculum developer in determining what he should do to realize his vision. [P. 52]

The platform for our proposed model of curriculum planning to a very considerable extent relies on the use of religious metaphors because we believe they help to focus attention on the scientific, political, moral, aesthetic, as well as the religious, contents. Ian Barbour (1974) contrasts models in science and religion, both of which he believes make use of analogy and metaphor. Each should be taken seriously, but not literally, for neither are literal pictures of reality. Religious models, however, serve a diversity of functions that differ from scientific or technical models.

Religious models often recommend a way of life or are an endorsement of a set of moral principles. They may express and evoke a distinctive self-commitment to a communal creed that often engenders a characteristic set of attitudes toward human existence. But beyond these noncognitive uses, a religious model can provide a cognitive perspective that directs our attention to particular patterns in events, a perspective that allows us to interpret history and human experience.

Barbour describes certain distinctive types of experience that are addressed in a religious framework: (1) awe and reverence, which remind us of our dependence, finitude, limitation, and contingency; (2) mystical union as expression of the unity of all things; (3) moral obligation in the form of ethical decisions and assumption of responsibility and sometimes subordination of our own inclinations; (4) reorientation and reconciliation related to acknowledgment of guilt and repentance, which may be followed by the experience of forgiveness; (5) interpersonal relationships as experience of dialogue between persons characterized by directness, immediacy, and mutuality; (6) key historical events of the corporate experience of the community, which help us understand ourselves and what has happened to us; and (7) order and creativity in the world, the intricate complexity and interdependence of forms. Religious models also go beyond the interpretation of experience. According to Barbour, they have the capacity to express attitudes, to disclose realities that lead to harmonizing whatever events are at hand, and to contribute to constructing metaphysical systems (pp. 49–70).

A PROPOSED PLATFORM

In constructing our platform, we believe it is imperative that we first try to make clear that which has been traditionally tacit in models of curriculum planning, namely, those assumptions about ultimate meaning and about the relationships between humanity and the universe. In so doing, some of our language will perforce be quite different from the conventional curriculum rhetoric, which tends to be technical, neutral, and detailed in tone. Largely because of the enormous dominance of the technical model of thought, educators typically find themselves uncomfortable with the language and metaphors of personal belief and religious affirmation. Many equate "religion" with denominationalism and organized religion. A good many educators have a great deal of antipathy toward organized religion for a variety of reasons, such as painful personal experiences, matters relating to the separation of church and state, and historical considerations including organized religion's stance toward civil liberties, human rights, and social justice. For many, the term religion evokes sanctimony, excess piety, rigid tolerance, sentimentality, and the like.

Our view is that, however legitimate these concerns may be, and we certainly share some of them, they constitute an unnecessary barrier to the basic impulse to search for ultimate meaning and purpose that is common to us all. We must not allow this impulse and the language of this impulse to become the sole property of a separate and distinct group of clergy, theology professors, or churchgoers. We must recover the language of religion and metaphysics as integral parts of our individual and communal searches for meaning, even though this can and will continue to create discomfort for those of us educated to be skeptical if not scornful of religious inquiry.

We have ourselves experienced this discomfort in writing this paper, as our hope has been to place curriculum within a framework that speaks to basic personal, social, and spiritual values. Our fear has been that our language might seem sentimental, fuzzy, and pious, thereby repelling many of our readers. Our conviction, as we have said, is that these concerns are common to all even though there are obviously enormous differences in the way we relate to them. Our decision is to accept the risk based on the faith that our readers would resonate with the spirit and intentionality if not the specifics of our effort. We therefore present some of our basic beliefs not as an attempt to demonstrate their superiority but to indicate what lies beneath our proposed model and to broaden the nature of the dialogue on curriculum planning. We believe that the metaphors of control, certainty, and elitism implicit in the Tyler rationale are not appropriate for questing for our highest human aspirations. We believe that the use of religious metaphors can help us in the continuing efforts to understand the process of curriculum planning and, more particularly, can help to develop a model that goes beyond technology, control, and alienation.

We choose to view the world as part of a larger transcendent reality, and our task as humans to be that of being in harmony with it. We believe that much is already known about these divine intentions, though we still have much to learn about them and much to do before they are fulfilled. We believe that humans are intended to be participants in the development of a world in which justice, love, dignity, freedom, joy, and community flourish. We believe that we are meant to pursue a path of truth, beauty, and goodness. We believe that the world exists in an imperfect and incomplete state but that man and woman possess the aesthetic and intellectual sensibilities to re-create themselves and the world in unity with the divine; the wholeness of body, mind, and spirit; earth and cosmos; and humanity and nature. It is well to remind ourselves of the common derivation of these words — whole, holy, and heal — so that we may see education as a sacred process that can lead us to be whole again and heal the wounds of history.

We also know that the path to that unity has been filled with uncertainties and obstacles and that our education must be conducted in recognition of that uncertainty and resistance. Although we have faith that humanity has developed and will continue to develop morally and spiritually, we must be mindful of the continuing presence of such evils as injustice, war, disease, greed, violence, oppression, ignorance, fear, prejudice, and alienation. It is evils such as these that provide the barriers to personal and cultural fulfillment; that is, the ability to live a life of aesthetic and moral excellence, a life of joy, creativity, abundance, and meaning. The most fundamental and highest goal of education then becomes human liberation, in both a negative and positive sense. Negatively, liberation means being free from unnecessary constraints and barriers to human dignity and potential such as those that come from being poor, frightened, misguided, ignorant, and unaffirmed — in a word, controlled. Human liberation in a positive sense refers to the capacity for full consciousness, fulfillment, joy, integration — in a word, freedom. Harvey Cox makes reference to two categories of liberation as reflected in the Exodus-Easter metaphor. The Exodus story reflects the deep human impulse for political and economic freedom and escape from human subjugation and hence becomes a metaphor for social liberation. Easter to Cox " . . . celebrates the liberation of all men and women from 'sin and death.' 'Sin' is understood as whatever chains people to the past, and 'death' as whatever terrifies them about the future" (1973, p. 152). It is in this sense that Easter becomes a metaphor for personal liberation. We believe that education should help in the process of re-creating and celebrating both Exodus and Easter, or as Cox puts it, "I suggest that Exodus and Easter add up to a vision of 'God' as whatever it is within the vast spectacle of cosmic evolution which inspires and supports the endless struggle for liberation, not just from tyranny but from all bondages. 'God' is that power which despite all setbacks never admits to final defeat" (p. 153).

We add our affirmation to the millions of others who have been and continue to be in touch with that awesome inspiration, support, and determination. We believe that mankind is also endowed with two incredible, albeit not fully realized, capacities that are the signal requirements for the struggle, that is, both a critical and an imaginative consciousness. As Michael Polanyi (1966) says, what is common to all thought and inquiry is human imagination and intuition. It is our faith that humanity will be liberated only when these consciousnesses are fully developed. We must be fully and keenly aware about how and what our lives and environment are and what they mean as the bases for guiding our imagination and intuition in the development of ever closer approximations of cosmic unity.

We are, therefore, clear on liberation as the goal for education, mindful, of course, that there are other very important and closely related educational goals such as skill mastery, informative knowledge, and explanation. However, we are also clear that in our present condition, we experience much of life as paradoxical and confusing. We are always confronting dilemmas, uncertainties, and ambiguities as we try to unravel mystery and as we seek deeper and broader understanding of the meaning of life. More specifically, professional educators continually confront such paradoxes, uncertainties, and dilemmas as they try to develop educational experiences that resonate with their values. Compulsory education to teach freedom? A prescribed curriculum as a way of promoting creativity? Can we have equality and excellence? Community and efficiency? Socialization and liberation? Control and freedom? Moreover, adding to the difficulty is the reality of a pluralism and diversity among educators and the lay public about the nature of the educational process. Indeed, this is still another paradox, that of recognizing and celebrating diversity while at the same time pursuing unity and integration.

A MODEL FOR CURRICULUM PLANNING

Curriculum planning of the logical sort is not inevitable, nor is it necessarily desirable, since there are valid situatons in which significant curriculum planning is not appropriate. For example, in an educational orientation that stresses a student-centered curriculum, planning would seem to be limited to arranging for instruction appropriate to students' expressed interests. It has been said that the single most critical question for curriculum planners is "What should be left to chance?" If and when there is some positive response to that question, curriculum planning becomes appropriate; that is, when there is a need for considered and informed organization of learning activities. Curriculum planning becomes a modest task if we use "interesting" as a criterion for content selection, since the major task is simply to find out what students consider to be interesting. However, if we decide also, or instead, to teach what is "important," we are faced with a much more problematic situation, one that requires experience, dialogue, and a decision-making process. We have already indicated in our framework that education should be something more than responding to student interests, in that education involves the most important questions of human existence. We therefore accept the importance of curriculum planning and present an alternative model, one informed by the educational framework described and the exercise of reason.

Three critically important points must be made initially as background for our model. First, we see our curriculum process as being an important educative opportunity for the participants. The hope is that this curriculum-planning process will provide liberating experiences that will promote the personal and social development of the curriculum planners. Second, the process is not to be seen as prescriptive except in the sense that it is designed to be in harmony with the educational framework. A key element in this model is that it provides a diversity, pluralism, and most importantly is intended to allow for openness. This model definitely does not assume or posit any particular curricular form such as the teaching of disciplines or any specific instructional format such as homogenous grouping. The model assumes that major questions will cut across settings but that there will be a wide variety of local response to these questions. Third, curriculum planning is seen here as more than a problem-solving process in that we see it as having an important critical function as well. Curriculum planners are not technicians only, although there are technical aspects involved; they are also inquirers and critics of education responsible for conceptualizing and posing problems and issues. We assume that this process is a continuous and ongoing one; it is characterized by constant reexamination, research, and reevaluation.

Given our framework of assumptions and values and given the three initial aspects of the model, we need to address three additional related issues: What is the nature of the process? Who is to be involved in it? and How are decisions to be made?

In *Seduction of the Spirit*, Harvey Cox (1973, pp. 144–68) describes techniques that he used in learning about different religious groups and forms, techniques he calls "participatory hermeneutics" and "experimental liturgy." We have blended and adapted aspects of these techniques to serve as the basis for our suggested process of curriculum planning. We offer three elements of the process:

1. *Data gathering and analysis*. In this phase, curriculum planners need to gain perspective on the particular issue. They will need to know the history and background of the larger issues and how they are manifested in the particular setting. It is also the stage where the issues are analyzed against the basic frameworks, that is, how the particulars relate to matters of liberation, personal and social development, and the rest of the fundamental values. The planners will need to review the research field, become aware of the various conceptual orientations, and be able to make and produce connections between the field in general and the specific in particular situations. This phase provides an opportunity to gain historical and theoretical perspectives, thereby providing the planners with a background on the meaning and significance of what is involved.

2. *Participation observation*. In this phase, curriculum planners actually become involved in the issue by actively participating in related activities. The planners can do this in a context of ongoing, related programs in their own setting or in other settings. They can also perform this function by developing and participating in experimental, pilot programs. The essential aspect of this stage is that planners have the opportun-

ity to gain insight from being directly involved with practice and their own experience of it. Although valuable insight can be gained from being involved with the programs in place, more creative planning is likely to emerge from involvement in highly imaginative, far out, even daring experiments, some of which could be specifically designed for this purpose. One effect of this phase would be to temper the detachment of planners from educational activities and other colleagues. The data gathering and the participation set the stage for a dialectic of theory and practice as well as between the abstract and the concrete.

3. *Interpretation*. At this stage, the curriculum planners share the individual meanings each has derived from the process. It is not a time to "compute pros and cons" and grind out a "solution" but an opportunity to deal honestly with individual interpretations. Curriculum planners will need here to indicate part of their own biographies — their own values, assumptions, backgrounds, orientations, and life-views. Out of a thorough and open sharing process will emerge the decision and recommendations. Our faith is that this decision is likely to be a wiser one, since it will reflect at least some degree of the diversity of human feelings, ideas, and judgments.

Cutting through these three elements of the process, of course, will be considerable dialogue. We do not wish to prescribe the nature of the dialogue except to indicate some general criteria for its form and substance.

The tone of the dialogues will need to reflect the major values expressed in our framework; they will be personally nonjudgmental and characterized by a celebration of diversity with a sensitivity to personal dignity. They will require intellectual rigor, aesthetic sensibility, and free-flowing imagination. They will very likely be conducted in a context of inadequate information, insufficient understanding, differing interpretations, that is, with uncertainty. The substance of the dialogues will deal with the dialectical quality of the issues involved. Discussions will deal with the abstract and the concrete, with the individual and the group, with understanding and meaning, with the relationship between the educational setting and larger units including society and culture, between the ideals and the actual. Nothing in this description of the dialogue should be interpreted as meaning that we intend to prescribe anything except as we urge a congruence between the values of the framework and the dialogues. We reiterate that our framework posits openness, experimentation, diversity, variety, and freedom.

The matter of who is to be involved in the dialogue is best determined within the context of each setting and the particular issue. However, a few guidelines are appropriate. Clearly the decision of who should be involved ought to be made within a framework of democratic principles, professional requirements, and efficiency. There needs to be representation of those who are directly involved and affected by the issue; the process certainly requires the use of talent — expertise, experience, imagination, and knowledge. Since curriculum planning is in part a task-oriented process, attention must be paid to logistical concerns such as the size of the group and the extent of involvement of its members, for such concrns affect the group's ability to meet its responsibilities.[1]

Finally, there is the question of how decisions are to be made. Within the framework, decisions will need to be made with full regard for the legitimacy of each person's orientations and for the need to affirm each one's dignity and at the same time in awareness of both the importance of making a decision and the significance of making no decision. We favor an approach that is directed at achieving as much consensus as is possible, though we are aware that in some situations achieving full consensus may seem unnecessary or unreachable. However, we are very much taken by the commitment to and success within a consensus approach by such groups as the Society of Friends. Such groups extend their principles of individual affirmation and trust in the process of open and honest sharing to the ultimate test of requiring decisions to be made through consensus rather than the more prevalent democratic forms of vote-taking. The difficulty with vote-taking, as a Quaker collegue once indicated, is that "it fails to take intensity of feeling into account."

THE SIGNIFICANCE OF CURRICULUM PLANNING

We are very much aware that our orientation is not, and cannot be, the last word in the development of a conception of curriculum planning. An enormous amount of critical and imaginative work must be done in order to forge powerful and compelling alternatives to the existing technical orientation. It is not just that this work would be a useful and interesting task but that we see such efforts as a metaphor for the urgent and critical task of freeing ourselves from the narrowness of the existing mechanistic and control-oriented paradigm that shapes so much of our culture.

We have argued that any model of curriculum planning is rooted in a cluster of visions — a vision of humanity, of the universe, of human potential, and of our relationships to the cosmos. These visions, though dimly viewed and rarely articulated, nonetheless have a profound impact on our day-to-day educational practices and on our more theoretical formulations. It is for this fundamental reason that we are so troubled when we encounter the notion that curriculum planning is a separate function divorced from its human, social, economic, political, and religious context. Curriculum planning is but an index, a reflection, an aspect, an activity that emerges from an orientation and vision of who and what we are, where we come from, and where we are going.

What is of the most extraordinary import, of course, is which particular vision we decide to choose, for the choosing of a vision allows us to become that vision. The vision implicit in the Tyler rationale is a needlessly limited and distorted one, a vision that posits the status quo, the necessity for control, and the possibility of objectivity and neutrality. We believe that we as a species do indeed search and yearn for profound meaning, that we aspire to freedom and are endowed with the genius that will make this possible. It is to this vision that curriculum planning and all other educational processes should be directed.

NOTES

1. We are assuming that curriculum planning will occur in groups, but this is not to preclude the possibility that in certain circumstances it would be appropriate for one person to do the curriculum planning. Of course, in this situation the basic framework could and would apply.

REFERENCES

Barbour, Ian G. *Myths, Models and Paradigms: A Comparative Study in Science and Religion*. New York: Harper and Row, 1974.

Berger, Peter. *A Rumor of Angels*. Garden City, N.Y.: Doubleday and Co., Anchor Books, 1969.

Bloom, Benjamin. "Mastery Learning and Its Implications for Curriculum Development." In Elliot W. Eisner (ed.), *Confronting Curriculum Reform*. Boston: Little, Brown and Co., 1971.

Cox, Harvey. *The Seduction of the Spirit*. New York: Simon and Schuster, 1973.

Eisner, Elliot W. *The Educational Imagination*. New York: Macmillan, 1985.

Feyerabend, Paul. *Against Method*. Atlantic Highlands, N.J.: Humanities Press, 1975.

Gadamer, Hans-George. "The Historicity of Understanding." In Paul Connenton (ed.), *Critical Sociology*. New York: Penguin Books, 1976.

Lamm, Zvi (ed.). *New Trends in Education*. Trans. into Hebrew by Dov Porat. Tel Aviv: Yachdav, 1983.

Macdonald, James B. "A Transcendental Developmental Ideology of Education." In William F. Pinar (ed.), *Heightened Consciousness, Cultural Revolution, and Curriculum Theory*, pp. 85–116. Berkeley, Calif.: McCutchan Publishing Corp., 1974.

Mann, J. Steven. "Curriculum Criticism," *Curriculum Theory Network* 2 (Winter 1968–69).

Murdock, Iris. *The Sovereignty of the Good*. New York: Schocken Books, 1970.

Polanyi, Michael. *The Tacit Dimension*. Garden City, N.Y.: Doubleday and Co., Anchor Books, 1966.

Polanyi, Michael, and Harry Prosch. *Meaning*. Chicago: University of Chicago Press, 1975.

Tyler, Ralph. *Principles of Curriculum and Instruction*. Chicago: University of Chicago Press, 1949.

Walker, Decker F. "A Naturalistic Model for Curriculum Development," *School Review* 80 (November 1971): 51–65.

PART FOUR

The Hidden Curriculum

Part One identified an important distinction in the field of curriculum, namely, a distinction between school curriculum as planned experiences, on the one hand, and as actual experiences of students, on the other.

This distinction is important not only in understanding differences in curriculum definition but also in examining differences in curriculum reality. Differences in curriculum reality examined by Glatthorn (1987, pp. 3–4) illustrate a continuum and are identified as "the recommended curriculum, the written curriculum, the taught curriculum, the supported curriculum, the tested curriculum, and the learned curriculum." Table 4.1 summarizes Glatthorn's types of curriculums. The differences reflect a necessity to give attention to all the "types" of curriculum. The differences also reflect the fact that the several types identified in Table 4.1 are neither mutually exclusive nor identical but may, in any particular time or place, give rise to discrepancy.

Some analyses of school curriculum have focused on a discrepancy between what a curriculum says *ought* to be taking place in schools and what first-hand observation reveals actually *does* take place. This discrepancy underlies the concept of hidden curriculum, an issue of much recent attention in the field. The hidden curriculum usually refers to formal schooling that is inconsistent with, indeed, may be detrimental to, what is prescribed by the written curriculum. In addition, the hidden curriculum may refer to the attitudes and values

Table 4.1 **Definition of Curriculum**

Glatthorn Type	*Definition*	*Some Questions*
Recommended	The ideal curriculum — what some scholar or committee thinks the curriculum should be.	What constitutes scholarship in the curriculum field? Who should be included on such committees? What criteria determine what curriculum is "the ideal?"
Written	The curriculum embodied in your district's documents — its scope-and-sequence charts, its curriculum guides, its program of studies booklets . . . the "official" curriculum.	How are such documents identified? Do they include any besides those identified here? What makes a curriculum "official"?
Taught	What teachers actually teach in the classroom . . . (What) you would observe if you could sit there every day of the school year.	How is teaching defined? Is teaching related only to what teachers say and do or also to what they do not say or do?
Supported	The resources you provide to support the curriculum—the staff, the time, the tests, the space, the training.	Is curriculum resources themselves or the priority given written curriculum, or reflect in taught curriculum, as resources are allocated? How is resource allocation determined? Are some resources more useful than others for supporting curriculum?

Glatthorn Type	*Definition*	*Some Questions*
Tested	The curriculum you see when you look at unit tests and final examinations . . . the measured curriculum.	Is test dictated by curriculum or vice versa? What is the relationship between curriculum and standardized tests?
Learned	The "bottom line" . . . what the students actually learn . . . the most important curriculum.	What are the relationships among recommended, written, taught, supported, tested, and learned curriculum?

Source: Based on Alan A. Glatthorn (ed.), *Curriculum Renewal* (Alexandria, Va.: ASCD, 198n, pp. 3-4.

embedded in school experiences and relationships. These attitudes and values may be the result of lack of awareness, what Silberman (1970) called mindlessness. These attitudes and values may also be the effects of deliberate deception.

In setting the stage for his analysis of the hidden curriculum, Jackson (1968, p. 33) begins:

> The crowds, the praise, and the power that combine to give a distinctive flavor to classroom life collectively form a hidden curriculum which each student (and teacher) must master if he is to make his way satisfactorily through the school.

Jackson examines elements of institutional expectations of schooling, their impact on learning, and the personality traits of successful students in formulating understanding of hidden curriculums. His work examined actual learner experiences in classrooms and led to a variety of interpretations both of the nature of the hidden curriculums and of the sociopolitical dynamic it manifests. Works by Braun (1970), Snyder (1970), and, especially, Overly (1970) pursued various lines of thinking in this regard.

Snyder's (1970) description of a hidden curriculum in higher education is couched in terms of what the institutional experience teaches students, faculty, and administrators to do in order to survive within a value structure perhaps markedly different from the one made explicit in the formal curriculum. The litany of abuses is all too familiar: good teaching is talked about but sacrificed to other interests; testing one's intellectual limits becomes less important than being best; the curriculum values free inquiry, but the institution values conformity.

Others (e.g., Freidenberg, 1963; Hentoff, 1966) have noted similar discrepancies at all levels of schooling. Indeed, discrepancies between what much of the curriculum literature purports to be the nature and the purpose of learning in schools and what the school's critics have described in various ways have been a major thesis of much popular as well as professional literature beginning in the 1960s (e.g., Gross and Gross, 1969).

Tanner and Tanner (1980, pp. 38–40) treat the hidden curriculum as collateral learning, a phenomenon identified by Dewey (1938) a half-century ago. Collateral learning, for Dewey, is the development of attitudes and values among students that is often more important than subject matter. Tanner and Tanner reinforce a point made in Selection 1.1 by Oliver, namely, that "extracurricular activities" is a misnomer inasmuch as school activities *in toto* is part of the curriculum. These authors also point out that, for many, the hidden curriculum refers to unintended and negative learning.

In Selection 4.1, Goodlad reports selected findings of "A Study of Schooling," which he directed.* Goodlad's study was undertaken to increase understanding of schools in order to improve them. His study of elementary-junior-senior high triples in seven states utilized interviews, questionnaires, school observations, and document analyses to examine a variety of curriculum phenomena from several perspectives. Goodlad recognizes both an explicit and an implicit curriculum, the latter a hidden curriculum, in formulating two questions: "What are schools asked to do?" and "What do schools do?" In Selection 4.1, Goodlad addresses these two questions and a third, "What should schools do?"

Beginning by illustrating a great deal of state-to-state consensus, Goodlad identifies basic skills, traditional subjects, vocational education, citizenship, and personal development as curriculum goals most frequently addressed. School data reflect these overall priorities but reveal considerable school-to-school variation in time allocations. The study finds a lack of attention to other stated goals, including communicating through writing and speaking, evaluating knowledge,

---

*Other reports of the study are contained in the April, 1983, issue of *Educational Leadership* and the March, 1983, issue of *Phi Delta Kappan*, as well as in Goodlad (1984).

and developing positive attitudes toward learning. However, the study also finds high levels of satisfaction with the schools' actual priorities among both parents and students. What begins to emerge is a hidden curriculum reinforced, if not dictated, by consumer expectations.

Goodlad provides extensive illustration of curriculum content in various subject areas and from grade level to grade level. He concludes that norms for teaching and learning tend to be set in the teaching of basic skill areas, the areas of highest congruence between state goals and school practice, and the areas of highest student and parent satisfaction. In concluding, Goodlad wonders whether we want to pursue curriculum commitments embodied in the explicit curriculum of the schools or those embodied in the implicit, hidden curriculum.

Review of the Goodlad study reveals at least two things: (1) schools tend to meet the highest curriculum priorities identified in state documents, such as teaching of basic skills and coverage of the traditional subjects with varying amounts of attention and (2) schools vary greatly in the ways they address other stated curriculum goals.

Sviotnik (1983) also presents a great amount of tabulated data from "A Study of Schooling." These data reveal averages in behavior from which he generalizes about the teaching behaviors in classrooms. He concludes:

> It is but a short inferential leap to suggest that we are implicitly teaching dependence on authority, linear thinking, social apathy, passive involvement, and hands-off learning. This so-called "hidden" curriculum is disturbingly apparent. [P. 29]

Whatever the specific lessons of a hidden curriculum, it has become increasingly apparent that what we teach in schools is an expression of values, at least implicitly. It seems desirable, then, to examine a curriculum's implicit values to determine their nature and whether or not they coincide with those values intended.

In Selection 4.2, Purpel and Ryan explore the nature and relationships between values and the content of the school's curriculum, specifically, in moral education. They argue that moral education is implicit in the curriculum either because of the nature of problems being explored by students, whatever the subject area, or because of the kind of instructional activities in which students are involved. The authors also explore manifestations of moral education in the hidden curriculum of student classroom and school culture. They point to numerous specific examples of moral education implicit in both the formal and the hidden curriculum.

Purpel and Ryan argue that moral education is an inevitable

dimension of the school's curriculum. They argue, further, that students and school staff should raise levels of awareness about the values content of the curriculum and explore its consistency with their own values and their intent. The authors conclude that these groups then need to affirm or modify the curriculum in accord with their heightened awareness of social, economic, and political realities. For these authors, relationships between school curriculum and the distribution of wealth and power, for example, need to be understood and addressed. All groups responsible for school curriculum need to ensure that school curriculum is consistent with moral intent.

CURRICULUM AND SOCIAL CRITIQUE

In envisioning a system of universal education, Horace Mann and his contemporaries attempted to address two problems: the growing manpower needs brought on by the industrial revolution and the poverty rampant in industrial towns. "Thus, while the curriculum was made up of reading, writing, and arithmetic, these studies were couched in lessons that stressed hard work, perseverance, self-denial, and promptness" (Stevens and Wood, 1987, p. 153). Further, because "industrial production necessitated that work be governed by the clock, and that workers become accustomed to artificial, man-made time divisions . . . (one) component of the hidden curriculum was the organization of the school" (p. 154).

Anyon's work in Selection 4.3 provides both a conceptual framework and an empirical basis for understanding the hidden curriculum and the significance of its relationship with the world of work. Within the framework of a sociology of knowledge, she describes ways in which different curriculum knowledge is made available, or not, to students in different social classes. According to this work, school curriculum supports the socioeconomic status quo and, in the view of many, an unjust pattern of power and domination in society at large.

She begins with a conceptual framework that defines social class in terms of relationships one has with (1) the system of ownership or capital, (2) others in the workplace and society, and (3) one's own work activity. On these bases, she identifies capitalist, working, and middle classes. Anyon argues that differences in adult social class roles, that is, in the relationships identified, account for differences in curriculum knowledge made available to students.

The sample of schools used to collect data included five elementary schools in one state. Anyon identifies these schools in four social classes: (1) working class, (2) (lower) middle class, (3) affluent professional (upper middle class), and (4) capitalist. After noting obvious similarities among all five schools, such as school rules, textbooks, tests, students, and teachers, Anyon goes on to report differences among them. In each case, she defines the nature of student work and the criteria used for student performance evaluation. Although tabulated data are not included in the report, Anyon presents extensive illustration of differences in the schools in various curriculum areas and in classroom control. Table 4.2 summarizes characteristics of social class relationships and differences in school curriculum.

Interested readers may find one or more of the physical, educational, and interpersonal characteristics of school environment useful in explaining how and why a hidden curriculum manifests itself. Social class background of teachers, school expectations, and school-community cultural congruence may be particularly inviting explanatory variables given the extent of research related to each. However, Anyon's point is a prior one—to illustrate what actually happens in school, regardless of why.

Perhaps the earliest treatment of the hidden curriculum was ASCD's *The Unstudied Curriculum* (1963). According to Schubert (1986, p. 184), the ASCD treatment of curriculum side effects was part of a broader look at alternative views of curriculum organization.

Study of the hidden curriculum is also associated with critical theory in the field of curriculum. A study by Apple and King (1977) illustrates a reconceptualist analysis of hidden curriculum. Investigating documented differences in standardized test performance among groups of primary grade students who had, and had not, attended kindergarten, Apple used classroom observation techniques to gather a variety of student and teacher behavior data in kindergarten classrooms. Apple concludes that differences in test performance in the primary years were not, as many assume, necessarily tied to differences in academic preparation attributable to kindergarten experiences. Rather, differences were linked to the kindergarteners' having learned "to go to school," a real, if unintended learning.

Selection 4.4 by Apple also offers empirical data for establishing how knowledge is made available to students in schools. Apple points out that "the statement that school knowledge has some connections to the larger political economy merely restates the issue" (Apple, 1985, p. 148).

To address the Spencerian query examined in Part Two, Apple points out in Selection 4.4 that the knowledge of most worth may be the cultural capital of the dominant social class. The focus of Apple's

Table 4.2 **Social Class and School Curriculum Elements**

			Curriculum		
Social Class	*Relationship to Social Production*	*School*	*Definition of Schoolwork*	*Evaluation Criteria*	*Teacher Control*
Capitalist	Owns virtually all real and symbolic property Controls work enterprise directly, that is, determines investments and profits Assumes role of conceptualization, that is, planning and management	Executive, elite	Develop analytical powers; produce quality intellectual products; problem solving	Conceptual skill levels	Tight during lesson presentations; otherwise none
Middle classes	Owns some property Given degrees of autonomy in work roles	Affluent, professional	Independent creative activity carried out independently; expression	Individuality; appropriateness to conceptual-ization	Ongoing negotiation between teacher and students
	Assigned roles for creativity and some decision making	Lower middle class	Getting correct answers; some choice and decision making	Correctness; neatness	Based on known criteria
Working class	No ownership No control Routine, mechanical tasks	Working class	Following rules; rote behavior	Correctness and following rules	Arbitrary, unexplained

Source: Based on J. Anyon, "Social Class and the Hidden Curriculum of Work," *Journal of Education* 162:67–92, Winter, 1980.

attention is the school textbook, the vehicle of curriculum that dominates classroom activities and school homework. Apple's premise is that the set of sociopolitical relationships that determines the content and form of published textbooks has significant explanatory power in examining the dynamics of the school's hidden curriculum. Apple focuses on the elhi market, that is, the elementary and secondary textbook series, and the college survey market. Apple describes, in detail, the conditions of the publishing marketplace, the biodemographics of editorial personnel in the major publishing houses, and the dynamics of in-house decision making. Some of his findings parallel those of Kirst and Walker (1971).

While acknowledging the danger of economic reductionism inherent in the reconceptualist view of curriculum, Apple points out the lack of large-scale and detailed investigations of the hidden curriculum. It is interesting to note that, although Apple focuses investigation of the hidden curriculum on the textbook, Anyon points out in Selection 4.2 that textbooks may not differ from school to school regardless of social class. The relative value of textbooks and other school variables in explaining differences in school learning needs to be clarified. Clearly, more study in this area is needed.

One of Apple's findings is the sexist relationships among editorial staffs in many textbook publishing houses (Apple, 1985, pp. 153–54). A more fundamental source of sexism in school curriculum is examined by Martin in Selection 4.5. Martin argues that scholarship in the foundations of education has ignored important sexist bias in the work of Rousseau and, as a result, has not only failed to recognize the historical roots of bias but also misinterpreted the work of an important educational philospher.

Martin examines Book V of Rousseau's *Emile*, demonstrating that, unlike the developmental model of education traditionally attributed to Rousseau in his plan for Emile, the model of curriculum Rousseau prescribes for Sophie is a production model. Martin investigates parallels between key assumptions in the philosophical discourses of Rousseau and Plato. She demonstrates that, unlike Plato, Rousseau's emphasis on the family and the substantive differences of gender lead him to differences in views about the education of men and women.

Martin then presents two accounts of the apparent sexist discrepancy in the prescriptions in Books I–IV of *Emile* and those in Book V. One account is that Rousseau prescribed different educational models for men and women. Another account is that educationists have, in fact, misinterpreted Books I–IV and that Rousseau's educational prescriptions for men and women are both based on a production model rather than a developmental one. Martin argues the second account.

She also points out the role of teacher as manipulator in Rousseau's work.

In Martin's treatment, the sex bias manifested in the school's hidden curriculum, indeed, in American culture, is traced to the foundations of education. Martin's findings reject a deliberate intent on the part of educational historians to hide a sexist treatment in Rousseau's work. Nevertheless, her findings do illustrate the power of attitudes and values implicit in the school's hidden curriculum, even to the point of misleading scholarly inquiry itself.

The power of expectations as a determinant of school learning is widely recognized. *Pygmalion in the Classroom* (Rosenthal and Jacobson, 1968) documented the power of teacher expectations in the classroom, and it demonstrated that learning could be affected by manipulating expectations. It is now more widely understood, as well, that the social systems both inside and outside the classroom control what is learned.

In another view of hidden curriculum, Giroux and Penna (1979) have developed strategies for counteracting, or replacing, elements of a hidden curriculum that are found to be undesirable. Highlighted in Giroux's work is the point of view that the hidden curriculum is, in fact, not only unintended but can also be at odds with the formal curriculum. The formal school curriculum, for example, intends to foster democratic decision making, but the hidden curriculum of teacher-student interaction in the classroom often teaches autocracy. An important point here, in addition, is that educators and students need to recognize ways in which the school itself reinforces sociopolitical phenomena that are inconsistent with social ideals. According to Giroux, educators and students also need to develop strategies for change.

In Selection 4.6, Giroux examines how various curriculum discourses fail to meet Freire's criterion of study, a "systematic critical attitude and intellectual discipline" (Freire, 1985, p. 1). Concerned with the cultural politics of curriculum discourse, Giroux examines or, as he puts it, interrogates both the conservative curriculum vision (a discourse of management and control) and the developmental-romantic curriculum visions (discourses of relevance and integration). In his analyses of the various curriculum discourse models, Giroux focuses attention on the interaction (intersection) of politics, schooling, and language.

Much of Giroux's analysis also centers around the concept of differences among students and the implications of those differences for curriculum design. Selection 1.3 in Part One describes a debate between Charles W. Eliot and G. Stanley Hall that is also about differences in ability among students and the implications of these differences for curriculum tracking in high schools. Giroux believes that discourse of management and control produces a hidden curriculum of inequality and injustice among students even though its formal rationale may uphold values of equality and justice. Further evidence of the discourse of inequality called equality can be found in the recent *Paideia Proposal* (Adler, 1982).

The discourses of relevance and integration also differ in the ways in which school curriculum can respond to differences in student abilities and needs. In both cases, however, Giroux argues that these discourses fail the Freire criterion. In Giroux's view, a new discourse of cultural politics and critical pedagogy is needed, one that recognizes how the school itself reproduces dominant social discourse and offers teachers and students opportunities to "construct political strategies . . . to fight for schools as democratic public spheres" (Giroux, 1985, p. 36). Giroux is concerned, therefore, not only with understanding the political dynamic of school discourse, the hidden curriculum, but also with transforming it.

Among the most recent treatments of the hidden curriculum is the analysis and selection of readings by Stevens and Wood (1987). In their volume, the editors examine relationships among schooling, justice, preparation for work, ideology, politics, and social change. Although their work is not an examination of the hidden curriculum per se, it synthesizes some of the avenues of thought and investigation associated with the hidden curriculum. The work provides historical, social, and political foundations for the concerns expressed by a wide range of scholars studying the hidden curriculum.

CONCLUSION

What conclusion to draw? Perhaps several conclusions can be enumerated that can then be a basis for further inquiry about the hidden curriculum, indeed, about the curriculum itself.

A reading of the selections in this part of the text reveals:

1. The hidden curriculum and the questions it raises about relationships between intent and actuality in school learning are related to the oldest questions in the field and to fundamental distinctions of definition of the curriculum and its relationship to society.
2. The hidden curriculum seems to be revealed in a matrix for which

one axis represents the significance of identified differences among students, indeed, among human beings, and for which the other axis is differences in school curriculum.

3. Untangling the dynamic of the hidden curriculum is tantamount to untangling the dialectic of school and society, a challenge that the field of curriculum has addressed continuously.
4. The antecedents of the hidden curriculum can be identified both in current and past school practice as well as in the accumulated record of educational thought itself.
5. The hidden curriculum manifests itself both in curriculum materials and in the school experiences of students and teachers.
6. The hidden curriculum is embodied in the very discourse we use to interrogate it, in the conceptual and syntactical structures of the field of curriculum itself.

It is to these latter structures that we turn our final attention.

REFERENCES

Adler, Mortimer J. *The Paideia Proposal*. New York: Macmillan, 1982.

Anyon, Jean. "Social Class and the Hidden Curriculum of Work," *Journal of Education* 162:67–92, Winter, 1980.

Apple, Michael W. "The Culture and Commerce of the Textbook," *Journal of Curriculum Studies* 17: 147–62, April–June, 1985.

Apple, Michael W., and N. R. King. "What Do the Schools Teach?" *Curriculum Inquiry* 6:341–58, 1977.

Association for Supervision and Curriculum Development. *The Unstudied Curriculum*. Alexandria, Va.: ASCD, 1963.

Dewey, John. *Experience and Education*. New York: Macmillan, 1938.

Freire, Paulo. *The Politics of Education, Culture, Power and Liberation*. South Hadley, Mass.: Bergin and Garvey, 1985.

Friedenberg, Edgar Z. *Coming of Age in America*. New York:Random House, 1963.

Giroux, Henry. "Critical Pedagogy, Cultural Politics and the Discourse of Experience," *Journal of Education* 167:22–41, 1985.

Giroux, Henry, and Anthony Penna. "Social Education in the Classroom: The Dynamics of the Hidden Curriculum," *Theory and Research in Social Education* 7:21–42, Spring, 1979.

Glatthorn, Alan A. (ed.). *Curriculum Renewal*. Alexandria, Va.:Association for Supervision and Curriculum Development, 1987.

Goodlad, John I. "A Study of Schooling," *Phi Delta Kappan* 64:552–59, April, 1983.

Goodlad, John I. "What Some Schools and Classrooms Teach," *Educational Leadership* 40:8–19, April, 1983.

Goodlad, John I. "A Place Called School," *Phi Delta Kappan* 64:462–65, March, 1983.

Goodlad, John I. *A Place Called School*. New York: McGraw-Hill, 1984.

Gross, Beatrice, and Ronald Gross (eds.). *Radical School Reform*. New York: Simon and Shuster, 1969.

Hentoff, Nat. *Our Children Are Dying*. New York: Viking Press, 1966.

Jackson, Phillip B. *Life in Classrooms*. New York: Holt, Rinehart and Winston, 1968.

Kirst, Michael W., and Decker F. Walker. "An Analysis of Curriculum Policy Making," *Review of Educational Research* 41:479–509, June, 1971.

Kliebard, Herbert M. "The Drive for Curriculum Change in the United States, 1890–1958: I—The Ideological Roots of Curriculum as a Field of Specialization," *Journal of Curriculum Studies* 4:91–202, July–September, 1979.

Martin, James Roland. "Sophie and Emile: A Case Study of Sex Bias in the History of Educational Thought," *Harvard Educational Review* 51:357–72, August, 1981.

Oliver, Albert I. *Curriculum Improvement: A Guide to Problems, Principles and Procedures*. New York: Dodd, Mead, 1965.

Overly, Norman V. (ed.). *The Unstudied Curriculum*. Alexandria, Va.: Association for Supervision and Curriculum Development, 1970.

Purpel, David E., and Kevin Ryan (eds.). *Moral Education...It Comes with the Territory*. Berkeley: McCutchan, 1976.

Rosenthal, R., and L. Jacobson. *Pygmalion in the Classroom*. New York: Holt, Rinehart and Winston, 1968.

Schubert, William H. *Curriculum: Perspective, Paradigm and Possibility*. New York: Macmillan, 1986.

Silberman, Charles E. *Crisis in the Classroom*. New York:Random House, 1970.

Snyder, B. R. *The Hidden Curriculum*. New York: Knopf, 1970.

Stevens, Edward, and George H. Wood. *Justice, Ideology and Education*. New York: Random House, 1987.

Sviotnik, Kenneth A. "What You See Is What You Get: Consistency, Persistency, and Mediocrity in Classrooms," *Harvard Educational Review* 53:16–31, September, 1983.

Tanner, Daniel, and Laurel N. Tanner. *Curriculum Development: Theory into Practice*. New York: Macmillan, 1975; 1980.

Selection 4.1

What Some Schools and Classrooms Teach

John I. Goodlad

My interest is, has been, and will continue to be in improving education, especially in schools. I am interested in understanding schools so that others and I might use whatever insight is gained in order to improve schools. Any measure of success one has in improving something depends heavily on understanding it.

It was in this spirit that my colleagues and I launched "A Study of Schooling." We have have described the sample and the methodology elsewhere (Goodlad, Sirotnik, and Overman, 1979). In brief, "A Study of Schooling" is an inquiry into school "triples" — elementary schools connecting with junior highs and junor highs connecting with senior highs — in seven widely scattered states. The method is an amalgam of traditional techniques: interviews, questionnaires, observations, and, particularly in the curriculum domain, collections of documents.

A few characteristics make the study unique. First, it endeavors to examine more or less simultaneously a great many of the commonplaces of schooling: goals, teaching practices, curricular content, school and classroom organization, materials used, problems and issues, rules and regulations, and so on. Second, we sought to view these commonplaces from the perspectives of students, teachers, parents, principals, and others. Third,

---

SOURCE. From *Educational Leadership* 40 (April 1983): 8–19. Reprinted with permission of the Association for Supervision and Curriculum Development.

we sought not only to see these commonplaces through the eyes of these groups but also to gain some insight into the satisfactions, dissatisfactions, values, and attitudes of our respondents. Fourth, as a result of this approach, we gathered an extraordinary volume of data about each school in the sample. For example, we have detailed observations of 129 elementary, 362 junior high, and 525 senior high classes, the largest number of classes ever observed in one study, I believe. The resulting data bank provides an opportunity to study not only the actors and things pertaining to schools but also the fascinating relationships among them.

The findings in any one of the many elements of schooling we examined are not markedly different from the findings of those who previously have studied these elements separately. The usefulness of the study, then, is not so much what it contributes to such commonly studied phenomena as classroom teaching but what it adds to our insight into the relationships among these elements and into the functioning of schools as social institutions.

We are prone to regard schools as goal-oriented factories engaged in processing human materials. But no matter how much we seek to reduce goals to specific operations and to redesign the programs of instruction to emphasize these operations, the most important thing about school for the children and youth who go there is the living out of their daily personal and social lives, not academics. There is not one set of goals; there are many. The curriculum and the methods of teaching from class to class may be virtually uniform, but the ambience of each class differs. Indeed, the ambience of each school differs. These differences appear to have more to do with the quality of life and, indeed, the quality of education in schools than do the explicit curriculum and the methods of teaching.

If we can only understand schools clearly in our minds, we might be more successful in improving them. We might then understand why changing the method of teaching reading, for example, accounts for so little in the variance of reading scores. We might then understand why helping teachers better use their present methods of teaching produces such modest outcomes. Substituting a cultural model of schooling for the prevailing production model profoundly changes how we think about schools and significantly influences how we study and seek to improve them. Such a model turns our attention to what schools do and leads us to wonder why.

WHAT SCHOOLS ARE FOR

Let me turn, now, to two questions: What are schools asked to do and what do schools do? Comparing the answers to these two questions inevitably raises a third: What should schools do?

We sought to answer the first of these questions by examining the goals stated or implied in documents produced by the fifty states and the districts in which the schools we studied were located. We sought to study the second of these questions — that is, what schools do — by examining the materials used by teachers, the tests and quizzes they gave, as well as by observing hour after hour in the classrooms of our sample. In addition, we obtained some useful insights from some of the questions we asked on questionnaires and in interviews.

I confine myself here almost exclusively to the formal and operational curricula — that is, the curricula of artifacts and the curricula we observed — but we derived some useful insights also from data on teachers' stated intentions and students' perceptions. The conceptual framework for analyzing these several curricula is described elsewhere (Goodlad, Klein, and Tye, 1979). We recognized, however, that there is both an explicit and an implicit curriculum. The latter sometimes is referred to as the "hidden curriculum" but this term is, I think, misleading. It is little more hidden than is the explicit curriculum of textbooks and workbooks. Describing the implicit curriculum is tricky in that it is largely inferred from the handling of the explicit curriculum and from expectations, rules, and regulations that are not always made explicit.

Clearly, what children and youth learn from the implicit curriculum is derived, in large part, from teaching procedures and techniques in use. I shall make a few generalizations about teaching for purposes of rounding out the picture, but my colleague, Kenneth Sirotnik, has provided a more comprehensive picture in a report on our findings in this area (Sirotnik, 1981).

WHAT SCHOOLS ARE ASKED TO DO

Our analysis of state documents unearthed the broadest and most idealistic expectations for schools as well as high-level agreement among the states at a general level. The goals fit into four broad categories: academic, social and citizenship, vocational, and personal. The intent for each of these areas is defined with considerable clarity in a series of subcategories on which there also is considerable state-to-state agreement.

Most of the state documents, following some philosophical preamble, began with statements such as "develop the ability to read, write, and handle basic arithmetical operations." Consistent with this stated goal priority, most states then went on to identify the subject fields or learnings through which these goals were to be developed. The most frequently listed were language skills, mathematics, science, social sudies, interpersonal skills and topics derived from civics and the behavioral sciences, and the arts — in this order. One would expect these priorities to be reflected in school curricula. This tended to be the case for the schools of our sample.

Most of the state documents we examined mentioned with considerable and almost equal frequency goals pertaining to vocational or career education, citizenship, and emotional and physical well-being. Our data reveal substantial allocation of time and teachers to subjects presumably related to such goals, particularly at the junior and senior high school levels.

We begin to see, then, a degree of parallelism between the states' commitments to academic, vocational, social and citizenship, and personal goals and the average distribution of time and teachers to the subject fields in our sample. However, school-to-school variation, especially in regard to science, social studies, and the arts at the elementary level and to vocational education at the secondary, was substantial.

But a careful analysis of the states' goals for education raises in one's mind some serious questions about the parallelism between what many of these statements convey and what goes on in schools and classrooms. The second statement commonly appearing under academic goals is worded somewhat as follows: "Develop the ability to communicate ideas through writing and speaking." Further down the list we find these statements: "Develop the ability to use and evaluate knowledge" and "develop positive attitudes toward intellectual activity, including intellectual curiosity and a desire for further learning."

These goals convey to me an image of students writing essays and narratives, engaging in dialogue with one another and with their teachers, initiating inquiry into questions not resolved by teachers or in their own minds, and so on. But this is not the picture that emerges from our data. Indeed, the picture is of students passively listening, reading textbooks, completing assignments, and rarely initiating anything — at least in the academic subjects.

Under social, civic, and cultural goals, there is much mention of skill in communicating effectively in groups, advancing the goals and concerns of others, and developing the ability to form productive and satisfying relations with others. But my impressions from the data on the schools we studied are quite opposite. I see, rather, students working alone, although in group settings, in competition with one another, and rarely engaging in anything likely to advance the school goals and concerns of their peers.

The state goals include a highly idealistic array pertaining to democratic processes, enculturation, truth and values, moral integrity, effective use of leisure time, personal flexibility, creativity and aesthetic expression, self-confidence, and the setting of life goals, particularly pertaining to continued learning. My general conclusion from our data is that the schools we studied did not place a high premium on experiencing democratic processes, independent thinking, creativity, personal autonomy, and learning for the sake of learning. Indeed, I wonder how serious we are in stating such expectations in the first place. Independent, autonomous individuals can be annoying when young and infuriatingly deviant as adults. Are we seriously interested in developing such individuals? If we are, then it appears that profound changes in the conduct of schooling are required. One must raise questions as to whether these changes are feasible.

WHAT SCHOOLS DO

Our real priorities for education in schools are best revealed in schools' allocation of time and teachers. Our data suggest four generalizations, among others.

First, the priority given to the ability to read, write, and handle basic arithmetical operations and the subjects presumed to develop these abilities is reflected in the schools of our sample, when the data for our schools are averaged. They devoted, according to the teachers surveyed, approximately 54 percent of the weekly instructional time to reading, language arts, and mathematics at the elementary level. On the average, the junior highs allocated a total of 39 percent of the courses and teachers to English and mathematics; the senior highs an average total of 31 percent. There was a relatively high relationship between parents' satisfaction with their school (as revealed by the grade they gave it) and their satisfaction with the curricula in these two subject areas. And the students of our sample ranked both subjects high in importance.

Second, the rather high importance given to vocational goals in the state documents appears to be paralleled by considerable attention to vocational education at the junior high level and much more attention in the senior high programs. In senior high, this emphasis appears to be somewhat at the expense of academic subjects and the intellectual emphasis desired by many parents of teenage students.

Third, the fluctuation in attention to subjects such as science and social studies, as compared with considerable constancy in language arts and mathematics, particularly at the elementary level, suggests that the schools do not perceive themselves as having an unequivocal mandate regarding science and social studies. The arts and especially foreign languages rank somewhat farther down in the list of curricular priorities. Indeed, if the teaching of foreign languages is to be taken as a major indicator of our interest in other cultures, then it becomes clear that this interest is low. If our sample of schools is at all representative, then those persons who believe foreign languages occupy only a small place in secondary school curriculum are correct.

Fourth, the allocation of time and teachers to the subject fields varies so much from one school to another in our sample that it becomes exceedingly difficult to generalize about the curricular opportunities available to students in our schools. Time available limits the attention given to subjects such as social studies, science, and the arts, especially in elementary schools. Teachers available limit the courses offered in secondary schools. One wonders about teachers in some academic subjects being spread thinly over the three years in some of our senior high schools while, simultaneously, these schools were sufficiently staffed in vocational education to offer a rich array of courses.

The next important determinant of the education schools provide is the activities in the various subject fields and the topics, materials, and evaluation procedures making up these activities. Space prevents me from even summarizing our analysis of topics, materials, quizzes, and the like in the eight subject fields we studied in depth. However, I think it is important to provide some taste of what we found and so I present brief summaries in three fields: English/language arts, social studies, and the arts.

English/Language Arts

Language arts/English formed the backbone of the curriculum in the classes we studied, especially at the elementary level. The various subjects and activities falling under this rubric — reading, composition, handwriting, speaking, listening, spelling, grammar (especially studying the parts of speech), letter writing, literature, using the dictionary — occupied more time at the elementary level and more teachers at the secondary level than any other subject (when junior and senior high data are combined).

The dominant emphasis throughout was that of teaching basic language use skills and mastering mechanics: capitalization, punctuation, paragraphs, syllabication, synonyms, homonyms, antonyms, parts of speech, and so on. These were repeated in successive grades of the elementary years, were reviewed in the junior high years, and reappeared in the low-track classes of the senior high schools. Scattered among these basics were activities suggesting more self-expression and creative thought: story writing, role playing, reading poems, book reports, storytelling, interviews, and the like. To the list of mechanics, teachers at the junior and senior high levels added biography, fiction, nonfiction, poetry, folk tales, short stories, creative writing, keeping a journal, writing original poetry, and short stories. But, at some schools, teachers reported very few of these things.

Reading instruction in the junior and senior highs appeared to be a matter of remediation involving the mechanics of word recognition, phonics, and vocabulary development. In English, there was still a substantial emphasis on the basics of grammar and composition: punctuation, capitalization, sentence structure, paragraph organization, word analysis, parts of speech. The lower-track classes tended to emphasize the mechanics of English usage, whereas the high-track classes were more likely to stress intellectual skills of analysis, evaluation, and judgment, especially through literature. The low-track classes were unlikely to encounter the high-status knowledge dealt with in the upper tracks and normally considered essential for college admission. These classes tended to spend less time on instruction and homework and to experience less teacher enthusiasm and clarity of presentation. There were fewer similarities between tracks within schools than across tracks from school to school.

The most commonly offered courses in English at the high school level were those combining mechanics with some literature, courses only in literature, and those in grammar and composition — in that order. These appeared to form the core of the required English. Beyond this core were electives in journalism, speech, and creative writing.

Teachers in all schools and at all grade levels apparently used a wide array of commercially prepared materials in their teaching of the language arts subjects, especially such things as ditto masters for the preparation of student worksheets. . . .

Textbooks and workbooks appeared with great frequency at the junior and senior high levels, repeating and extending the language usage skills of the elementary grades. Junior high teachers listed some literature commonly studied in their classes. An impression coming through is that students encountered major American and European authors primarily through anthologies of short pieces rather than through entire novels demanding extensive time and effort, particularly during the time available outside of the classroom.

Notable in the materials gathered from teachers was an emphasis on expository, to the neglect of creative, fictional writing. There was an absence of references to studying the historical development of words and language meanings. Also missing at the secondary school level was an emphasis on developing listening skills — although we note from other data that students at all levels were called on to listen a great deal of the time.

Remember the Friday morning spelling test? It's still there. Most of the elementary teachers in our sample listed it. Tests and quizzes increased in frequency of use with progression upward through the levels of schooling. Standardized tests were used at both junior and senior high levels for placing students in classes. Teacher-made tests at these levels appeared to be designed and used, not for diagnosis, but for assessing and marking students' achievement as well as for controlling students' behavior. At all levels, these tests called almost exclusively for short answers and recall of information. Worksheets, often a part of daily instruction, were used cumulatively by many teachers as a basis of marking pupil progress and achievement. These frequently were duplicated from commercial materials. The directions given for this activity often were "copy the sentence" or "circle each verb" or "combine two sentences into one" or "add correct punctuation." If teachers gave tests involving paragraphs or essays, they seldom so indicated.

. . .

Social Studies

Just as our data suggest a firm place in the curriculum for English/language arts and mathematics, they also suggest considerable agreement on a common body of topics and skills to be taught — and these tended to be repeated, with slight increases in difficulty, through the junior high schools and, for the low tracks, into the senior high schools. But there appears to be much less certainty about either the importance of the social studies subjects or what should be taught in them. Students considered the social studies to be less important than English/language arts and mathematics; more important than foreign languages and the arts; and of about equal importance to science, physical education, and vocational educaion. Junior and senior high students viewed the social studies to be among the least useful subjects in relation to their present and future needs.

The curriculum at the elemenary level was amorphous, particularly in the lower grades. Many first- and second-grade classes put together the themes of understanding self and others with discussion of the family and the community. There were more field trips — to community resources and facilities — that occurred later. The intent, apparently, was to begin close at hand, with oneself, and to expand one's understanding of the immediate environment. By the third grade, children frequently were studying community needs such as health care and problems such as conservation of water.

Some classes experienced forays into other cultures (Eskimo or Maori) or the dependence of their community on other communities for certain foods, raw materials, and manufactured goods. The fourth grade often involved study of early colonization and exploration of America, with accompanying use of maps and globes. By the fifth and sixth grades, the themes of history, geography, and civics made their strong appearance:

mostly pertaining to the growth and development of the United States, but frequently with some attention to other countries.

Asked to identify what they were endeavoring to teach, the teachers surveyed listed map skills quite consistently. Commonly, too, they listed such things as acquiring the ability to work in groups, skill in oral expression, facility in library use, understanding similarities among cultures, and an array of the more complex intellectual processes: forming hypotheses, making comparisons, understanding sequences, formulating generalizations and conclusions, and using imagination.

The varied amorphous character of the elementary school social studies program gave way to much greater school-to-school uniformity at the junior high level: United States history, world history, world geography, and commonly, a course in the history of the state in which the school studied was located. There appeared to be high-level agreement on teaching United States history in the eighth grade.

Teachers noted the expectation that their students would learn map skills, the ability to take notes, proficiency in the use of dictionaries and encyclopedias, and the skills of oral and written expression. As did elementary school teachers, junior high teachers listed an array of critical thinking skills: understanding relationships, drawing inferences and conclusions, understanding cause and effect, and so on.

According to our sample, "the basics" of social studies at the senior high level are American history and government. These appeared in some form for all schools. Beyond these courses, all schools but one offered electives, which included economics, sociology, law, anthropology, psychology, world history, the history of the state, world cultures, human relations, current events, and the history and/or geography of a variety of other countries. Except for American history and government, on which there was quite common agreement, the schools offered a rather wide range of courses and topics on some of these electives. The skills most commonly sought, according to the teachers, were in map reading, library use, taking tests, and writing and thinking skills.

We can assume that the tests teachers give reflect what they believe to be important and, in turn, convey to students the kinds of things they are expected to learn. Following this assumption, it appears that teachers in the primary grades of our sample tended not to view social studies as a significant subject in the evaluation of their students. (It will be recalled that classes varied widely in the amount of time devoted to social studies instruction.) Either they gave no tests or they depended on appraising students' understanding through oral questioning. Written testing began in the three upper grades of the elementary school and increased in frequency in junior and senior high schools.

Social studies, as a field of learning, appears to be particularly conducive to the development of reasoning: deriving concepts from related events, testing in a new setting hypotheses derived from another set of circumstances, exploring causal relationships, drawing conclusions from an array of data, and so on. Teachers at all levels listed these and more as intended learnings. Their tests reflected quite different priorities. The tests we examined rarely required other than the recall and feedback of memorized information: multiple choice, true or false, matching like things, and filling in the missing words or phrases. Some essay-type questions were used in the upper elementary grades and reappeared in the secondary schools. But these were not the dominant pattern.

One obvious generalization from our data is that all of the children and youth enrolled in the schools we studied encountered the history, geography, and government of the United States. For most, the initial encounters in the upper elementary grades were renewed in both the junior and the senior high schools. . . .

One puzzling question is why elementary school students liked the social studies less than any other subject. . . . Students were asked to rate their interest in a list of topics selected from several subjects, including the social studies. Topics from the social studies were rated high, but social studies as a subject was rated relatively low in interest among the several curricular fields (Jersild and Tasch, 1949).

The comparative study of cultures does not emerge as a basic in the curricula we examined. Nor did we find much inclusion of global or international content. Over half of all the students in our sample believed that foreign countries and their ideas are dangerous to American government. The emphasis on this nation and the relative lack of understanding of the rest of the globe showed up as well in other questions we asked these students. . . . In many ways, instruction and learning in the social studies look more like instruction and learning in the language arts (without the emphasis on mechanics) than in the social sciences. It appears that we cannot assume the cultivation of goals most appropriate to the social sciences even when social studies courses appear in the curriculum.

The Arts

Clearly, the visual arts and music dominated the arts curriculum of the elementary schools we studied. Children were taught the rudiments of using crayons, watercolor paints, and clay. They used these tools to draw and paint pictures of things around them and stories read; they colored — oh, how they colored! — shapes, animals, and scenes depicted in workbooks; they painted simple still lifes; and, occasionally, they created their own pictorial images.

Music included sight reading, singing a variety of songs (many of them songs that have survived successions of school-goers), and appreciation, including music from other lands. Patriotic songs were learned and repeated. Most schools offered some kind of children's performance during the year in which music was the dominant theme.

Beyond these commonly found programs in music and the visual arts, there were scattered evidences of dance, pantomime, puppetry, performing plays, acting out, embroidery, hooking rugs, and, in one school, film-making. Also, beyond the usual activities in the two customary subjects were making collages, learning about the different musical instruments and sometimes learning to play one or more, studying different careers in music, and learning about famous composers. Most classes paid heed to the advent of seasons and holidays in their sequences and emphases on activities.

Most junior highs offered the visual arts as Art 7, 8, or 9 and music as either Music or Vocal Music 7, 8, and 9. Other offerings included Crafts, Band, Chorus, Graphic Arts, Designcraft, Orchestra, Drama, Cinema, Ensemble, Girls' Chorus, Boys' Chorus, Concert Band, Cadet Band, Glee Club, Guitar, and more. The topics listed by teachers were almost invariably tied to the technical aspects of the art form: techniques of using different media in the visual arts, "proper playing habits," rhythm, melody, harmony, line, texture, pattern.

To Art I, Art II, and Art III in the senior high schools were added a wide array of arts and crafts and especially specialized music courses. Chorus and band courses were relatively common across schools, but courses in Jazz Music, Ceramics, Photography, Sculpture, and Consumer Music — all offered somewhere — were not. As for the junior highs, the topics listed stressed learning to use the media of the visual arts and learning the "performance and rehearsal disciplines" of music. Although teachers stressed goals intrinsic to the arts, they also listed goals that transcend them: power to see beyond the surface of things; a positive attitude toward experimentation; pride in work; appreciation of human dignity and values. However, my impression of the arts, as of other subjects, is that these transcendent goals took secondary position — a remote secondary position — to emphasis on the use of tools and on performance. Students in music classes at the secondary level spent an inordinate amount of class time on rehearsals — for performance at the upcoming football game or some other event.

At the elementary level, the visual arts joined physical education as the only subjects not oriented to textbooks. None was used, if the teachers reporting to us were accurate and complete in their provision of information. Teachers used the arts tools, paints, and paper as their primary materials of instruction. . . . We must not assume, however, that arts classes were dominated exclusively by student activity. Teachers still talked a lot, even in these classes.

Teachers in the junior and senior high visual arts classes used books extensively in planning their classes — that is, books for teachers — but did not use textbooks for students. . . . An array of books on the arts and textbooks for students were used in visual arts classes but not as whole-class resources. There was little overlap, apparently, in the use of these sources for teaching and learning.

At all levels, paper-and-pencil tests were used less in the arts than in other subjects, with the exception of physical education. More often, evaluation was based on participation, performance, or a finished product. Tests, conventionally perceived, were used more often in music than in the other art forms. Tests at all levels usually were teacher made. Tests and quizzes increased in frequency with increase in grade level.

Consistently at all levels, students rated the arts as most interesting and enjoyable among the subject fields and also as relatively unimportant and easy. Although they did not participate a great deal in selecting learning materials and activities, students did this more in the arts than in the academic subjects. Both principals and teachers in our sample viewed the arts as providing students with unique opportunities for personal development, for the provision of aesthetic experiences. It appears that the arts programs of these schools, more than other programs, captured the personal interest of students.

. . .

SOME DISCREPANCIES: DO WE LIKE THEM?

The allocation of time and teaching resources to the elementary and secondary schools in the sample reflected those goals most commonly articulated and most likely to appear first in documents prepared by the states. Our data, whatever the source, reveal not only the curricular dominance of English/language arts and mathematics but also the consistent and repetitive attention to basic facts and skills. Developing "the ability to read, write, and handle basic arithmetic operations" pervades instruction from the first through the ninth grades and the lower tracks of courses beyond. These are the fundamental operations on which schools have concentrated from the beginning. They appear still to be today. Back to the basics is where we always have been.

What the schools in our sample did not appear to be doing was developing all those abilities commonly listed under "intellectual development": the ability to think rationally, to use and evaluate knowledge, intellectual curiosity, and a desire for further learning. Only *rarely* did we find evidence to suggest instruction likely to go much beyond mere possession of information to a level of understanding the implications of that information and either applying it or exploring its possible applications. Nor did we see in subjects generally taken by most students activities likely to arouse students' curiosity or to involve them in seeking solutions to some problem not already laid bare by teacher or textbook.

That traditional image of a teacher possessing the knowledge standing at the front of the classroom imparting it to students in a listening mode accurately portrays the largest portion of what we observed. To what degree does this prevailing stereotype condition what teachers do, reinforcing the subtle and perhaps convenient ways the kinds of teaching and learning practices that most neatly fit the circumstances of the classroom? And why should we expect teachers to teach otherwise? This is the way they were taught in school and college.

. . .

There appears not to be in relation to social studies and science the kind of social pressure for the basics brought to bear for English/language arts and mathematics. Indeed, there is among many adults a disposition to deride the tendency of schools to teach relatively inert facts while largely ignoring deeper insights and higher-order intellectual skills. Why, then, does the teaching of these subjects not rise to these expectations? One reasonably plausible explanation is that the norms tend to be set by the teaching of English/language arts and mathematics. These are the most dominant subjects: students regard them as of high importance and, relatively, of considerable use later in life. The teaching of them probably helps to set the norms from which most teachers hesitate to stray.

Another explanation lies in the circumstances of schooling. Effective teaching in social studies and science calls for visits to governmental bodies in session, fields and ponds, industrial laboratories, and the like. Teaching such subjects well calls for departing from textbooks and workbooks in seeking to use multiple resources: films, an array of source books, perhaps construction materials, and small conference rooms. Field trips, deviant ways of teaching, small rooms, and the like call for different schedules and arrangements not conveniently and, therefore, not usually available in schools. Publishing companies attempting to cater to the cutting edge of instructional practice usually lose money. It is more profitable to market textbooks, in spite of the competition. Teachers may start out "fighting the system," but it is much easier, ulimately, to settle down into conventional ways of teaching. And one tends to look more "normal" by doing so. The cards are stacked against deviation and innovation.

Two major deficiencies stand out in all aspects of the curricula we studied, from state and district guides to the most important learnings perceived by students. The first is a failure to differentiate and see the relationships between facts and the more important concepts facts help us to understand. The second, closely related to the first, is a general failure to view subjects and subject matter as merely turf on which to experience the struggles and satisfactions of personal development.

Some evidence to suggest teachers' comprehensions of these important differentiations is found in their statements of what they wanted students to learn. But the mixing together of topics (magnets, for instance) and concepts (energy) in single lists reveals that the use of the former to develop understanding of the latter was not at all clear in the minds of these teachers. There was scarcely any evidence of some awareness of this distinction being operationalized in the classroom. The emphasis on facts and the recall of facts in quizzes demonstrate not just the difficulty of teaching and testing for more fundamental understanding but the probability, supported by our data, that most teachers simply do not know how to teach for higher levels of thinking (such as applying and evaluating scientific principles). This should not surprise us. Their own teachers, for the most part, probably did not know how to do this either.

Regarding the second point, primary teachers frequently appeared to teach, at least part of the time, with some awareness that the topics they introduced were merely instrumental to personal development. But the subject as both end and means clearly dominated in grades above the fourth. We know from other inquiries that school staffs tend not to engage in dialogue about larger goals than those pertaining to acquiring the knowledge and skills embedded in school subjects. Consequently, not often in schools is everything that goes on there viewed and treated as though contributing to traits of mind and character. Rather, one teaches or "takes" algebra and the goal of learning algebra is reinforced by tests and marks in algebra.

There is a place on the report card for marking citizenship, too, but this is something one possesses, presumably, at least to some degree. It is not something to which the activities of school are deliberately directed. Teachers are oriented to teaching particular things — the particular things they were taught in school. Relating these particular things to some larger purpose is not something they think about very much or have been prepared to do. And the professional literature on such matters available to teachers is long on philosophy and short on pedagogical operations.

Conversely, the literature on the teaching of school subjects is long on operations and devoid of theoretical justification. Once again, teachers are reinforced in teaching the facts and skills of the school subjects as though these are primarly what school-based education is all about. And, in practice, it is.

. . .

Although instruction in the arts, physical education, and vocational education emphasized "doing" and performance, there still was a surprising amount of student listening. It is difficult to justify the amount of teacher lecturing in many of the arts classes we observed. Only occasionally is there a need for a teacher to lecture to a class in painting. Essential points are better made, even if frequently repeated to individuals, in the context of a student's ongoing performance. And far too much of the performance we observed was teacher — rather than student — determined. The arts are expected to provide opportunities for creative problem solving and disciplined performance. One fears that teachers in the arts behave all too frequently like teachers in academic subjects because of the prevailing view — among other teachers, not just lay citizens — that the arts are soft and on the edges of importance. Arts teachers should boldly demonstrate the potentiality for doing through the arts what cannot be done readily through the other fields.

. . .

We eat, play, work, and react with others as total persons — everywhere except in the classroom, it appears. Here, we pretend, the mind floats suspended from the rest of the human system, at least temporarily. But the pretense serves poorly the aims of education and comes close to revealing what is most wrong with our schools.

The goals set for schools are particulary idealistic in the social, civic, cultural, and personal domains. It is here that we find the most altruistic expectations for understanding differing value systems; developing productive and satisfying relations with others based on respect, trust, cooperation, and caring; developing a concern for humanity; developing the ability to apply the basic principles and concepts of the sciences, fine arts, and humanities to the appreciation of aesthetic matters; and developing an understanding of the necessity for moral integrity. And, it is here that we find statements about developing the ability to use leisure time effectively, to perceive self positively, to deal with new problems in original ways, and to enjoy and be willing to experience a range of imaginative alternatives.

I conclude that the schools in our sample were contributing minimally to the attainment of such goals. With respect to some, they were rather neutral. With respect to others, they contributed negatively. And, as is the case with other goals, they contributed differentially to individual students and groups of students.

. . .

Learning in school begins and continues primarily as individual activity in a group setting. The total class group is largely a circumstance necessitated economically, not a vehicle for teaching the requirements of cooperative endeavor. Students rarely set group goals, the attainment of which depends on a division of labor and the successful orchestration of the pieces. There is very little in our data to suggest the possibility of "developing productive and satisfying relations with others based on respect, trust, cooperation and caring." There is little to convey the legitimacy of students helping each other with their individual assignments. Rather, to seek help is to run the risk of "cheating." And to give help is to give away some of whatever competitive edge one enjoys. The most charitable view one could have of this is that schools do not deliberately seek to promote antisocial behavior. On the other hand, they appear to do little to promote the prosocial behavior many of our goals for schools espouse.

In the personal domain, our goals speak to the school's role in preparing for the wise and creative use of leisure time. The schools I attended provided for my participation in soccer, basketball, football, and volleyball. These required minimal provision of equipment — a ball, a bat, a net. Neither schools nor households could afford the costs of the skis, racquets, and other equipment required for individual sports. Once having left school, I lost the groups of five, nine, or eleven required for the pursuit of these recreational activities. I was not prepared in the skills required for participation in golf, tennis, skiing, badminton, and the like. Our data suggest that schools have not changed much in their neglect of the physical skills and abilities relevant to the sports most played by adults.

Presumably, children and youth learn something of teamwork in the group sports dominating physical education classes and the extracurricular side of school. But, as in the academic domain, the ambience is one of competition. In the analysis of the physical education programs, we noted that activities were pervaded by competition. My argument is not against competition. It is against the near absence of anything designed to deliberately cultivate the values and skills of constructive social interaction and group accomplishment that we extol as a characeristic of our people but neglect in the breach.

The gap between the rhetoric of individual flexibility, originality, and creativity in our statements of educational goals and the cultivation of these in our schools reveals a monstrous hypocrisy. From the beginning, students experience school and classroom environments that condition them in precisely opposite behaviors — seeking "right" answers, conforming, and reproducing the known. These behaviors are reinforced daily by the physical restraints of the group and classroom, by the kinds of questions teachers ask, by the nature of the seatwork exercises assigned, and by the format of tests and quizzes. They are further reinforced by the nature of the rewards — particularly the subtleties of implicitly accepting "right" answers and behaviors while ignoring or otherwise rejecting "wrong" or deviant answers. Only in the "less important" subjects and the advanced sections of academic courses are there evidences of some significant cultivation and reinforcement of more creative or intellectually independent behaviors.

It is difficult to be sanguine about the moral and ethical learnings accompanying many of the experiences of schooling. My perception is that the emphasis on individual performance and achievement would be more conducive to cheating than to the development of moral integrity. I have difficulty seeing how much of what goes on in classrooms would contribute to understanding and appreciating the contributions of others. I see little in the curriculum, explicit or implicit, likely to promote keen awareness of humanity. . . .

One need not speculate abstractly on the cultivation of goals of self-realization in schools. In general, students doing well feel good about themselves; those performing poorly do not. I wonder about the values in feelings of success derived primarily from personal performance compared with the performance of others. There are not in our data findings to imply stress on seeking to outdo one's previous performance. And I wonder, conversely, about failure that leads individuals to feel that they are not good at all. What are schools doing to "develop the ability to assess realistically and live with one's limitations and strengths?" A small percentage of students receive a large percentage of the failing grades, year after year. It is difficult to perceive this as useful failure. Schools would be markedly different if their ongoing function was to ensure successful performance and not failure. We would not put up for long with a physician who sent our child home with an F for health but no assistance in becoming healthy.

Finally, I wonder about the impact of the flat, neutral emotional ambience of most of the classes we studied. Many observers of modern life have noted our preoccupation with coping. Boredom is a disease of epidemic proportions. Many of the escapes from boredom leave people unsatisfied, unfulfilled, and fretful. For millions, television is a sedative;

for others, drugs and alcohol provide a temporary escape. The secondary students in our sample chose drugs and alcohol, above all others, as their school's worst problem.

. . .

A quite natural and understandable reaction to all of this is to blame those "incompetent, uncaring teachers." But such a response is both simplistic and, largely, unjust. For years, schools and teachers have been criticized for their neglect of the fundamentals. But if our sample is at all representative, it appears that teachers are very preoccupied with trying to teach children and youth precisely what we blame them for not teaching. Then, when we put what they are doing under a microscope and compare it to our most idealistic statements regarding what schools are for, we don't like what we see.

Which way do we want it? Do we want schools and teachers to respond to the messages they most probably hear, the messages telling them to work particularly on children's ability to read, write, and handle arithmetical operations? If so, we should not anticipate much change in what schools do now. English/language arts and mathematics will continue to dominate the curriculum. The other subjects, with the exception of vocational education in the high schools, will continue to have an uncertain, uneven place in the curriculum. The methods of lecturing, questioning, monitoring seatwork, and testing, together with the present materials of instruction, will continue to prevail. About 15 percent of those in attendance will do very well, another 15 to 25 percent will do reasonably well, and minority students will slowly increase their membership in these groups. From 15 to 25 percent will not complete high school, and minority students will continue to be overrepresented in this group. Standardized achievement test scores probably will rise enough to be acceptable and, since a larger percentage of students coming into the major universities will write and spell somewhat better, the pressure to improve schools will diminish somewhat, at least for a few years.

But, the quality of educating in schools will not have improved. Indeed, quite conceivably it could be worse: more boring, less fun, more repetitious, still fewer encounters with significant intellectual problems, even more siphoning of nonacademic students into vocational training, and fewer experiences with the arts. Nonetheless, the nation's teachers will have responded to what they think they hear. This is what they have heard all along, except in occasional periods of serious effort at reform such as in the decade beginning about 1957 and ending about 1967 — and the messages heard then confused teachers. What teachers now hear and have heard may be, for many, what they prefer to hear. It is the message for which they are best prepared to respond.

Or, do we seriously believe in and want for our schools at least some of what is implied in all those goals statements coming after the one about reading, writing, and figuring? If so, the Phoenix rising before us is, indeed, an unfamiliar bird — and perhaps an unlikely one, too. Because now we are confronted with the need to involve students in a variety of ways of thinking, to introduce students to concepts and not just facts, to provide situations that provoke and evoke curiosity, to develop personal standards of work and ensure the satisfaction of meeting them, to develop appreciation of others through cooperative endeavors, to be concerned about the traits of mind and character fostered in schools, and on and on. No longer is it sufficient to teach some facts of geography, a little algebra, or the mechanics of language. The school subjects become means for learnings that transcend them.

Do the preceding sentences provide a glimpse of what we want? I am not at all sure that they do. The educational activities implied reflect what states proclaim the school to be for and what most of the parents in our sample appeared to want. But we have not fully considered the implications of the grand phrases. How many creative thinkers do businesses need? What kind of nation is one awash with autonomous individuals? How many painters and museums can we afford? We are a nation predominantly oriented to the instrumental values of education. If more schooling does not ensure a better job, what good is it?

Still, we keep on repeating our idealistic expectations for schools. We must have some belief in the relevance and worth. Either we must come to terms with unrealistic expectations and settle for schools just a little better than what we now have or put our money where our mouths are. So far, we have designed and supported schools capable of doing only the simplest parts of the whole.

. . .

REFERENCES

Goodlad, John I., M. Frances Klein, and Kenneth A. Tye. "The Domains of Curriculum and Their Study." In John I. Goodlad and associates (eds.), *Curriculum Inquiry: The Study of Curriculum Practice*, pp. 43–76. New York: McGraw-Hill, 1979.

Goodlad, John I., Kenneth A. Sirotnik, and Bette C. Overman. "An Overview of 'A Study of Schooling'," *Phi Delta Kappan* 61: 3 (November 1979): 174–78.

Jersild, Arthur, and Ruth J. Tasch. *Children's Interests and What They Suggest for Education*. New York: Bureau of Publications, Teachers College, Columbia University, 1949.

Sirotnik, Kenneth A. *What You See is What You Get: A Summary of Observations in Over 1000 Elementary and Secondary Classrooms*. A Study of Schooling Technical Report No. 29. Los Angeles: Laboratory in School and Community Education, Graduate School of Education, University of California, 1981.

Selection 4.2

It Comes with the Territory: The Inevitability of Moral Education in the Schools

David E. Purpel and Kevin Ryan

. . . Public schools are actively, continuously, and heavily involved in moral education. We will try in this chapter to support this assumption by specifying the various ways in which moral concerns and viewpoints are expressed in the schools. The great bulk of these moral education experiences and activities are very likely *not* considered to be moral education by those involved. However, we are including in our concept of moral education those events and activities that carry with them some explicit or implicit moral concern, position, or orientation. We are convinced that on any given day anyone sensitive to moral issues will find a great deal of moral education going on in any public school in the nation. There is in effect really no point in debating whether there should be moral education in the schools. What needs to be debated is what form this education should take, since we believe that moral education, in fact, "comes with the territory."

An important disclaimer needs to be made. To our knowledge there is not very much in the way of systematic, precise data on just how much and in what ways moral issues are presented in the schools. We are basing this description on our own personal impressions, observations, and experiences as well as on those of others. The field very much needs much

SOURCE. From *Moral Education . . . It Comes With the Territory*, ed. David Purpel and Kevin Ryan. © 1976 by McCutchan Publishing Corporation.

more precise and detailed information on the moral life of schools, even though we are confident that our impressions have significant bases in reality.

In lieu of hard data, we invite our readers to join us in an imaginary visit to some imaginary schools. As we journey together, we feel confident that some of our observations will seem familiar and that some will not. We urge our readers to augment, correct, or revise our analyses. We are less concerned with convincing our readers that any particular practice does or does not have moral significance than with increasing general sensitivity and understanding of the moral implications of current school experiences.

We will begin our visit by examining and observing the most obvious and most accessible instances, namely those found in the formal curriculum and in the day to day instructional programs.

MORAL EDUCATION IN THE VISIBLE CURRICULUM

An increasing number of schools (no one really knows how many) are involved in curriculum programs that openly and directly deal with moral education. . . . Our analysis will deal *not* with formal programs in moral education but rather with morally laden curriculum that emerges from traditional school practices.

When one visits a school and concentrates on the program of study and the instructional content of classroom activities, he is very likely to encounter a great many instances of morally loaded content in virtually every aspect of the curriculum:

1. A debate on abortion in a biology class raises questions on the value and definition of life.
2. A discussion on the radical nature of the American Revolution in a history class deals with the question of when insurrection and disloyalty are justified.
3. A critical analysis of the values implicit in Huckleberry Finn's relationship to Jim, the runaway slave, in an English class raises questions of the conflict between law and human dignity.
4. A mock trial of Daniel Ellsberg in a civics class raises questions on the meaning of the First Amendment.
5. Any number of moral issues are embedded in the discussions of any number of current events, for example, Watergate, the My Lai massacre, the morality of terrorism.

These activities and others like them can be conducted with explicit and conscious attention to moral issues, but often the moral issues inevitably intrude even when not invited. Naturally, there is immense variation among teachers as to how these issues are handled, but one thing is evident — moral considerations are involved and moral messages are inevitably conveyed about them, deliberately or not.

What our visitors might note is that this kind of moral education goes on in most schools routinely and unchallenged, as accepted and legitimate elements of the formal curriculum.

As we walk through the school corridors we might come across some less traditional settings where moral issues arise easily and naturally. There are, for example, programs in career education and personal development that provide opportunities for students to directly and systematically reflect on their lives so as to help make more informed decisions. Stress is put on self-knowledge and realistic appraisal of self in relation to society, which inevitably involves a whole host of moral questions. For example, students are often asked to deal with such questions as:

1. Should one work for a career that pays well or one that pays not so well but involves considerable opportunities for public service?

2. Should one defer immediate concerns (for example, playing varsity football) for ones with longer range considerations (for example, studying for exams)?

3. Should one plan for a career that will increase the possibility of family alienation? For example, a student under pressure from home to work in the family hardware store contemplates a career in marine biology.

We might also chance to visit other discussion activities having such names as town meeting, class gathering, and show-and-tell that center on personal concerns. What these groups all have in common is an opportunity for students to express and examine personal concerns, many of which have significant moral implications. For example, a child's complaint of feeling friendless and rejected can lead to a discussion of the responsibilities of other class members to respond to the child's needs.

Or we might visit a class where an incident or event is being used as a learning situation, such as a death in the school community, any number of school disciplinary actions, a field trip, petty thievery, or a plagiarism case.

Or we might see a number of other classroom events in which moral issues either intrude themselves or arise but are apparently not stressed. For example, many stories, myths, and folk tales are told and retold in the schools and they inevitably reveal some moral emphasis or another:

1. George Washington and his fallen cherry tree are often used to extol the virtues of honesty and facing the music.

2. "Three Little Pigs" is often used to point up the value of careful planning and industry.

3. Bible readings (in some schools) are used to illuminate a variety of subjects including the divine bases of authority and goodness.

4. Cinderella is presumably rewarded for her patience, forebearance, modesty, and obedience — or is it because she's good looking?

5. "The Man Without a Country" finds that to reject one's nation is to invite despair and emptiness.

6. The little Dutch boy who saved his community from disaster by plugging up a hole in the dike certainly demonstrates the importance of social responsibility and how every little thing helps.

An extended visit would probably give us an opportunity to hear (and see) a great number of exhortations, proverbs, mottos, homilies, and epigrams carrying with them some moral imperatives:

1. Waste not, want not.
2. Love thy neighbor.
3. You reap what you sow.
4. If at first you don't succeed, try, try, again.
5. Patience is a virtue.
6. Think!
7. Make love not war.
8. To thine own self be true.
9. Have a nice day.
10. Busy hands are happy hands. Idle minds are the devil's playground.
11. Fight for dear old P.S. 162.
12. Happiness is anyone or anything at all loved by you.

It's fun (and what's important, very easy) to make such lists. We urge our readers to make their own list of favorite and persistent memories of moral messages received in schools. Here's ours:

1. Patriotic songs like "God Bless America," "America the Beautiful," and "The Battle Hymn of the Republic" said something to us about God's special relationship with the U.S.A.

2. We still remember the Alamo, the Maine, and Pearl Harbor — lest foreign treachery and American bravery and steadfastness be forgotten.

3. King Arthur set on his round table for us a number of vivid instances of loyalty, persistence, dedication, and devotion to God, women,

and a set of rules. (Usually *not* included, we found out later, were Arthur's marital difficulties.)

4. We were often reminded of the long-run advantages of the steady persistent pace of the turtle over the erratically brilliant lope of the easily distracted rabbit.

5. Robin Hood shot holes through the notion that stealing is categorically wrong.

6. Abraham Lincoln's childhood of poverty, honesty, and determination seemed to provide the necessary ingredients for a political career of emancipation, charity for all, and martyrdom.

7. The little engine that could proved that stubbornness and willfulness can overcome humility and modesty.

8. Squanto and his fellow Indians' assistance to the Pilgrims in 1620 became early models of: (a) giving technical assistance to underdeveloped nations, (b) assisting the culturally disadvantaged, and (c) Brotherhood Week.

MORAL EDUCATION IN THE HIDDEN CURRICULUM

Our imaginary visit so far has been mostly limited to an examination of the formal curriculum and to classroom observations. We now need to widen our horizons and to examine those activities that have been labeled the "hidden curriculum." The hidden curriculum has been defined as what students learn that is not in the formal curriculum. It has to do with the relationships among students, teachers, administrators, and staff particularly as they relate to authority, rules, and the quality of interpersonal relations. We will use the term to include some aspects of school that are not really hidden, such as formal rules, as well as to designate the more subtle and informal activities. We shall divide this analysis into four parts: the classroom culture, other formal school activities, the student culture, and the school culture.

The Classroom Culture

In our visit we need to be mindful of how students, teachers, staff, and administrators relate to each other. Lots of very powerful things happen in classrooms that go beyond the formal course of study. Many verbal transactions inevitably involve moral issues. Students, like all institutional citizens, derive notions of fair play, justice, and morality from how they are treated by the institution, its representatives, and fellow constituents. Schools certainly do "teach" about authority, about justice, about what is right and wrong, and about priorities in the myriad of school policies and practices ranging from the trivial to the significant. Think of the moral implications of these school events:

1. An entire class of children is punished because one or a small group has misbehaved.
2. A teacher sets up groups of children to work collaboratively on projects.
3. A pregnant unmarried student is not allowed to attend school.
4. An applicant for the cheerleader squad is blackballed because of "poor citizenship."
5. A student is not allowed to make up an exam because he went on a family trip on the day of the exam.
6. A teacher apologized to a class for having insulted a student during an argument.
7. Some students with a history of trouble making are not allowed to go on a field trip.
8. Some students volunteer to tutor younger children with reading problems.
9. A teacher taunts a child for not being nearly as productive as another sibling.
10. A teacher allows a student fight to continue as a way of settling an issue "once and for all."
11. A civics class decides to work on Saturdays to clean up a local playground.

Further observation might reveal certain patterns that express certain moral views:

1. Teachers hugging, patting heads, and showing affection to kids who have been "good."
2. Students who "misbehave" are chastised, exiled, humiliated, or even beaten.
3. Students who achieve at a certain level are given special privileges like being eligible to participate in varsity sports, work on the school paper, or go on special trips.
4. Students who fight or cheat or argue are, by the same token, often deprived of certain privileges.
5. Students who get all their math problems right often get gold or blue stars on their papers.
6. Students who "try hard" are often singled out and recognized, a policy that often extends to passing any student who shows sufficient effort. In this value system, high achievement/low effort is not as appreciated as low achievement/high effort.

OTHER FORMAL SCHOOL ACTIVITIES

The school, obviously, formally provides opportunities for learning other than courses and subject matter. There are such functions as the counseling and guidance program, athletic programs, various extracurricular activities such as dramatics, band, or debating society. Any one of these programs provides opportunities for issues with strong moral overtones to be developed (for example, winning and losing in a program of competitive athletics; or deciding who gets the lead in the major school production, the talented but uncooperative or the modestly talented but even tempered). And just what would be an appropriate topic for the debating society? "Resolved. All Holidays Should be Celebrated on Mondays" or "Resolved. Marijuana Sales Should be Made Legal"?

We could very well see assemblies and pep rallies that attempt to involve students emotionally and experientially in issues with moral content. For example, the purpose of some Memorial Day exercises seems to be to involve participants in grieving for fallen warriors and for reaffirming the validity and majesty of giving one's life for one's country. Pep rallies are designed to generate the kind of enthusiasm, fervor, and identification that will produce deep and abiding support for athletic teams. If our visit were at Christmas time, we might see a pageant in which students can be expected to experience piety, awe, and reverence.

Student Culture

The observant visitor will see how students themselves (unwittingly or not) become agents of moral education. Teachers very often cite certain youngsters as models to be emulated and admired for their character. (Within this category is the more specific and for some more vivid phenomenon of comparing a student with a sibling.) In addition, students by themselves and without prompting are affected and influenced by other students and are apt to derive notions of good behavior from those they admire. This is an area where subtle combinations of peer and teacher approval provide powerful reinforcements for modeling certain behaviors. Some examples are:

1. Kids beating up "tattletales."
2. Social cliques ostracizing individuals.
3. Kids taunting "show-offs" or "teacher's pets."
4. Kids developing and enforcing rules in playground games.
5. Kids threatening unruly peers lest all are punished.

The strength and power of the student culture is reflected in the increasing tendency of many teachers, particularly student and beginning teachers, to identify with their students. Many teachers find themselves torn between the traditions and forms of the school and the inclination to respond to students' needs and feelings. Students as a group do affect the quality of school life, and their values, be they hedonistic or pietistic, represent another important strand in the moral fabric of the school.

Teachers and administrators often face the opposing values of the school as an institution and the needs of students, individually or collectively. The increasing stress on personal and civil rights has sharply strengthened sensitivity to student concerns and indeed has led to situations where students significantly share decision-making responsibilities. This by itself represents a particular set of values, that is, the values of shared decision making and affording the individual an increased sense of self-worth.

School Culture

The individual school or school system as a whole conveys certain beliefs, attitudes, and tenets that represent moral positions. It is therefore important that we become aware of the operational principles of the school. We can do this by reading official publications like bulletins, codes, and regulations as well as becoming sensitive to the implicit mores of the school. Some examples:

1. Good "conduct" is as important as good achievement.
2. Punctuality and neatness are good.
3. Cheating is bad.
4. Regular attendance is good.
5. School loyalty is good.
6. Informing on misbehavior is good.
7. Respect for adults is good.
8. Overt aggression is bad.
9. Damaging books is bad.

Although there is no question that moral issues and responses are involved in these policies and practices, there is still considerable disagreement and confusion over whether a school ought to represent or stand for a particular moral orientation. It is one thing to say that moral issues are involved in what the schools do and another to maintain that schools ought to deliberately act as moral institutions, that is, to indicate their conception of moral behavior and to proceed accordingly. Should the school deliberately set up moral criteria and judge conduct by those criteria?

For example, one sometimes hears teachers and administrators characterize a particular class or subgroup as having unusual attributes. We have in mind such statements as, "this third grade is a particularly rambunctious group" or "this year's graduating class seems more interested in personal rather than school matters." Are such observations expressions of legitimate school concerns? Should the school intervene in such areas? For example, what should teachers do if a graduating class seems to be on the verge of not following the tradition of making a gift to the school?

CONCLUSION

We have tried here to accomplish two basic tasks: (1) to make a case for the extensive and pervasive ways in which moral education is willy-nilly going on in our public schools, and (2) to try to increase our sensitivities to moral concerns as expressed in school life. Our intention was not to take any particular position on the policies and practices used as examples but only to point up the inevitability of moral education in the schools. We are not criticizing the schools for being moral agents but rather are asking that they be more aware, systematic, and informed about their moral influence.

. . . There is, of course, the prior question of whether any intervention is appropriate, since the argument exists that intervention in the realm of values constitutes manipulation and control of a personal and profound nature. However, we have tried to demonstrate that moral education does in fact go on in schools, and that it inevitably goes on even when not desired or intended. It is our view that the professional must look at the issue not as "should we have moral education in the schools?" but rather as "to what degree and in what dimensions and areas should we deal with moral education in the schools?" We need to become more aware of the implicit techniques and goals that are used, not so as to eliminate them but so as to provide us with a basis for making reasonable judgements no matter how complex and painful they may be.

The basic professional decisions, then, are in the realm of choosing an approach that approximates general school and community policy on moral education. Obviously, professionals need to participate in this policy-making since it is really not possible to separate goals from techniques. However, broad school policy on moral education should emerge from discussions with parents, students, and community representatives. We say this with full knowledge that it creates difficulties, controversies, and conflicts. Professionals, however, have a vital role to play in informing the public on the nature of the issues and the nature of the options.

The age, ability and background of students affects the nature of the program, and many moral education programs stress verbal and intellectual abilities not found in younger children. Some programs require certain levels of emotional and personal maturity. Some goals of moral education can be reached through teaching specific skills; others may be more a matter of developmental growth and maturity. Some programs will require special understanding or training for teachers. . . .

Selection 4.3

Social Class and the Hidden Curriculum of Work

Jean Anyon

Scholars in political economy and the sociology of knowledge have recently argued that public schools in complex industrial societies like our own make available different types of educational experience and curriculum knowledge to students in different social classes. Bowles and Gintis (1976), for example, have argued that students from different social-class backgrounds are rewarded for claassroom behaviors that correspond to personality traits allegedly rewarded in the different occupational strata — the working classes for docility and obedience, the managerial classes for initiative and personal assertiveness. Basil Bernstein (1977), Pierre Bourdieu (Bourdieu and Passeron, 1977), and Michael W. Apple (1979), focusing on school knowledge, have argued that knowledge and skills leading to social power and reward (for example, medical, legal, managerial) are made available to the advantaged social groups but are withheld from the working classes, to whom a more "practical" curriculum is offered (for example, manual skills, clerical knowledge). While there has been considerable argumentation of these points regarding education in England, France, and North America, there has been little or no attempt to investigate these ideas empirically in elementary or secondary schools and classrooms in this country.[1]

This selection offers tentative empirical support (and qualification) of

---

SOURCE. Reprinted, with permission, from *Journal of Education* 162 (Winter 1980): 67–92.

the above arguments by providing illustrative examples of differences in student *work* in classrooms in contrasting social-class communities. The examples were gathered as part of an ethnographical study of curricular, pedagogical, and pupil evaluation practices in five elementary schools.* The article attempts a theoretical contribution as well, and assesses student work in the light of a theoretical approach to social-class analysis. The organization is as follows: the methodology of the ethnographical study is briefly described; a theoretical approach to the definition of social class is offered; income and other characteristics of the parents in each school are provided, and examples from the study that illustrate work tasks and interaction in each school are presented; then the concepts used to define social class are applied to the examples in order to assess the theoretical meaning of classroom events. It will be suggested that there is a "hidden curriculum" in school work that has profound implication for the theory — and consequence — of everyday activity in education.

METHODOLOGY

The methods used to gather data were classroom observation; interviews of students, teachers, principals, and district administrative staff; and assessment of curriculum and other materials in each classroom and school. All classroom events to be discussed here involve the fifth grade in each school. All schools but one departmentalize at the fifth-grade level. Except for that school where only one fifth-grade teacher could be observed, all the fifth-grade teachers (that is, two or three) were observed as the children moved from subject to subject. In all schools the art, music, and gym teachers were also observed and interviewed. All teachers in the study were described as "good" or "excellent" by their principals. All except one new teacher had taught for more than four years. The fifth grade in each school was observed by the investigator for ten three-hour periods between September 15, 1978, and June 20, 1979.

Before providing the occupations, incomes, and other relevant social characteristics of the parents of the children in each school, I will offer a theoretical approach to defining social class.

SOCIAL CLASS

One's occupation and income level contribute significantly to one's social class, but they do not define it. Rather, social class is a series of

---

*The research was funded by Rutgers University Research Council and will be reported in detail elsewhere.

relationships. A person's social class is defined here by the way that person relates to the process in society by which goods, services, and culture are produced.[2] One relates to several aspects of the production process primarily through one's work. One has a relationship to the system of ownership to other people (at work and in society) and to the content and process of one's own productive activity. One's relationship to all three of these aspects of production determines one's social class; that is, all three relationships are necessary and none is sufficient for determining a person's relation to the process of production in society.

Ownership relations

In a capitalist society, a person has a relation to the system of private ownership of capital. Capital is usually thought of as being derived from physical property. In this sense capital is property that is used to produced profit, interest, or rent in sufficient quantity so that the result can be used to produced more profit, interest, or rent, that is, more capital. Physical capital may be derived from money, stocks, machines, land, or the labor of workers (whose labor, for instance, may produce products that are sold by others for profit). Capital, however, can also be symbolic. It can be the socially legitimated knowledge of how the production process works, its financial, managerial, technical, or other "secrets." Symbolic capital can also be socially legitimated skills — cognitive (for example, analytical), linguistic, or technical skills that provide the ability to, say, produce the dominant scientific, artistic, and other culture, or to manage the systems of industrial and cultural production. Skillful application of symbolic capital may yield social and cultural power, and perhaps physical capital as well.

The ownership relation that is definitive for social class is one's relation to physical capital. The first such relationship is that of capitalist. To be a member of the capitalist class in the present-day United States, one must participate in the ownership of the apparatus of production in society. The number of such persons is relatively small: while one person in ten owns some stock, for example, a mere 1.6 percent of the population owns 82.2 percent of all stock, and the wealthiest one-fifth owns almost all the rest (see New York Stock Exchange, 1975; Smith and Franklin, 1974; Lampman, 1962).

At the opposite pole of this relationship is the worker. To be in the United States working class a person will not ordinarily own physical capital; to the contrary, his or her work will be wage or salaried labor that is either a source of profit (that is, capital) to others, or that makes it possible for others to realize profit. Examples of the latter are white-collar clerical workers in industry and distribution (office and sales) as well as the wage and salaried workers in the institutions of social and economic legitimation and service (for example, in state education and welfare institutions).[3] According to the criteria to be developed here, the number of persons who presently comprise the working class in the United States is between 50 percent and 60 percent of the population (see also Wright, 1978; Braverman, 1974;Levison, 1974).

In between the defining relationship of capitalist and worker are the middle classes, whose relationship to the process of production is less clear, and whose relationship may indeed exhibit contradictory characteristics. For example, social service employees have a somewhat contradictory relationship to the process of production because, although their income may be at middle-class levels, some characteristics of their work are working-class (for example, they may have very little control over their work). Analogously, there are persons at the upper-income end of the middle class, such as upper-middle-class professionals, who may own quantities of stocks and will therefore share characteristics of the capitalist class. As the next criterion to be discussed makes clear, however, to be a member of the present-day capitalist in the United States, one must also participate in the social *control* of this capital.

Relationships Between People

The second relationship that contributes to one's social class is the relation one has to authority and control at work and in society.[4] One characteristic of most working-class jobs is that there is no built-in mechanism by which the worker can control the content, process, or speed of work. Legitimate decision making is vested in personnel supervisors, in middle or upper management, or, as in an increasing number of white-collar working-class (and most middle-class) jobs, by bureaucratic rule and regulation. For upper-middle-class professional groups there is an increased amount of autonomy regarding work. Moreover, in middle- and upper-middle-class positions there is an increasing chance that one's work will also involve supervising the work of others. A capitalist is defined within these relations of control in an enterprise by having a position that participates in the direct control of the entire enterprise. Capitalists do not directly control workers in physical production and do not directly control ideas in the sphere of cultural production. However, more crucial to control, capitalists make the decisions over how resources are used (for example, where money is invested) and how profit is allocated.

Relations Between People and Their Work

The third criterion that contributes to a person's social class is the relationship between that person and his or her own productive activity —

the type of activity that constitutes his or her work. A working-class job is often characterized by work that is routine and mechanical and that is a small, fragmented part of a larger process with which workers are not usually acquainted. These working-class jobs are usually blue-collar, manual labor. A few skilled jobs such as plumbing and printing are not mechanical, however, and an increasing number of working-class jobs are *white*-collar. These white-collar jobs, such as clerical work, may involve work that necessitates a measure of planning and decision making, but one still has no built-in control over the content. The work of some middle- and most upper-middle-class managerial and professional groups is likely to involve the need for conceptualization and creativity, with many professional jobs demanding one's full creative capacities. Finally, the work that characterizes the capitalist position is that this work is almost entirely a matter of conceptualization (for example, planning and laying out) that has as its object management and control of the enterprise.

One's social class, then, is a result of the relationships one has, largely through one's work, to physical capital and its power, to other people at work and in society, and to one's own productive activity. Social class is a lived, developing process. It is not an abstract category, and it is not a fixed, inherited position (although one's family background is, of course, important). Social class is perceived as a complex of social relations that one develops as one grows up — as one acquires and develops certain bodies of knowledge, skills, abilities, and traits, and as one has contract and opportunity in the world.[5] In sum, social class describes relationships that we as adults have developed, may attempt to maintain, and participate in every working day. These relationships in a real sense define our material ties to the world. An important concern here is whether these relationships are developing in children in schools within particular social class contexts.

THE SAMPLE OF SCHOOLS

With the above discussion as a theoretical backdrop, the social-class designation of each of the five schools will be identified, and the income, occupation, and other relevant available social characteristics of the students and their parents will be described. The first three schools are in a medium-sized city district in northern New Jersey, and the other two are in a nearby New Jersey suburb.

The first two schools I will call Working-class Schools. Most of the parents have blue-collar jobs. Less than a third of the fathers are skilled, while the majority are in unskilled or semiskilled jobs. During the period of the study (1978–1979) approximately 15 percent of the fathers were unemployed. The large majority (85 percent) of the families are white. The following occupations are typical: platform, storeroom, and stockroom workers; foundrymen, pipe welders, and boilermakers; semiskilled and unskilled assembly-line operatives; gas station attendants, auto mechanics, maintenance workers, and security guards. Less than 30 percent of the women work, some part-time and some full-time, on assembly lines, in storerooms and stockrooms, as waitresses, barmaids, or sales clerks. Of the fifth-grade parents, none of the wives of the skilled workers had jobs. Approximately 15 percent of the families in each school are at or below the federal "poverty" level[6]; most of the rest of the family incomes are at or below $12,000, except some of the skilled workers whose incomes are higher. The incomes of the majority of the families in these two schools (that is, at or below $12,000) are typical of 38.6 percent of the families in the United States (U.S. Bureau of the Census, 1979, p. 2, table A).

The third school is called the Middle-class School,although because of neighborhood residence patterns, the population is a mixture of several social classes. The parents' occupations can be divided into three groups: a small-group of blue-collar "rich," who are skilled, well-paid workers such as printers, carpenters, plumbers, and construction workers. The second group is composed of parents in working-class and middle-class white-collar jobs: women in office jobs, technicians, supervisors in industry, and parents employed by the city (such as firemen, policemen, and several of the school's teachers). The third group is composed of occupations such as personnel directors in local firms, accountants, "middle management," and a few small capitalists (owners of shops in the area). The children of several local doctors attend this school. Most family incomes are between $13,000 and $25,000, with a few higher. This income range is typical of 38.9 percent of the families in the United States (U.S. Bureau of the Census, 1979, p. 2, table A).

The fourth school has a parent population that is at the upper income level of the upper-middle class, and is predominantly professional. This school will be called the Affluent Professional School. Typical jobs are: cardiologist, interior designer, corporate lawyer or engineer, executive in advertising or television. There are some families who are not as affluent as the majority (for example, the family of the superintendent of the district's schools, and the one or two families in which the fathers are skilled workers). In addition, a few of the families are more affluent than the majority, and can be classified in the capitalist class (for example, a partner in a prestigious Wall Street stock brokerage firm). Approximately 90 percent of the children in this school are white. Most family incomes are between $40,000 and $80,000. This income span represents approximately 7 percent of the families in the United States.[7]

In the fifth school the majority of the families belong to the capitalist class. This school will be called the Executive Elite School because most of the fathers are top executives, (for example, presidents and vice presidents) in major U.S.-based multinational corporations—for example, ATT, RCA, City Bank, American Express, U.S. Steel. A sizable group of fathers are top executives in financial firms on Wall Street. There are also a number of fathers who list their occupations as "general counsel" to a particular corporation, and these corporations are also among the large multinationals. Many of the mothers do volunteer work in the Junior League, Junior Fortnightly, or other service groups; some are intricately involved in town politics; and some are themselves in well-paid occupations. There are no minority children in the school. Almost all family incomes are over $100,000 with some in the $500,000 range. The incomes in this school represent less than 1 percent of the families in the United States (see Smith and Franklin, 1974).

Since each of the five schools is only one instance of elementary education in a particular social class context, I will not generalize beyond the sample. However, the examples of school work that follow will suggest characteristics of education in each social setting that appear to have theoretical and social significance and to be worth investigation in a larger number of schools.

SOCIAL CLASS AND SCHOOL WORK

There are obvious similarities among United States schools and classrooms. There are school and classroom rules, teachers who ask questions and attempt to exercise control and who give work and homework. There are textbooks and tests. All of these were found in the five schools. Indeed, there were other curricular similarities as well: all schools and fifth grades used the same math book and series (*Mathematics Around Us*, Scott Foresman, 1978); all fifth grades had at least one boxed set of an individualized reading program available in the room (although the variety and amounts of teaching materials in the classrooms increased as the social class of the school population increased); and all fifth-grade language arts curricula included aspects of grammar, punctuation, and capitalization.[8]

This section provides examples of work and work-related activites in each school that bear on the categories used to define social class. Thus, examples will be provided concerning students' relation to capital (for example, as manifest in any symbolic capital that might be acquired through school work); students' relation to persons and types of authority regarding school work; and students' relations to their own productive activity. The section first offers the investigator's interpretation of what school work *is* for children in each setting, and then presents events and interactions that illustrate that assessment.

The Working-class Schools

In the two working-class schools, work is following the steps of a procedure. The procedure is usually mechanical, involving rote behavior and very little decision making or choice. The teachers rarely explain why the work is being assigned, how it might connect to other assignments, or what the idea is that lies behind the procedure or gives it coherence and perhaps meaning or significance. Available textbooks are not always used, and the teachers often prepare their own dittoes or put work examples on the board. Most of the rules regarding work are designations of what the children are to do; the rules are steps to follow. These steps are told to the children by the teachers and often written on the board. The children are usually told to copy the steps as notes. These notes are to be studied. Work is often evaluated not according to whether it is right or wrong, but according to whether the children followed the right steps.

The following examples illustrate these points. In math, when two-digit division was introduced, the teacher in one school gave a four-minute lecture on what the terms are called (that is, which number is the divisor, dividend, quotient, and remainder). The children were told to copy these names in their notebooks. Then the teacher told them the steps to follow to do the problems, saying,"This is how you do them." The teacher listed the steps on the board, and they appeared several days later as a chart hung in the middle of the front wall: "Divide; Multiply; Subtract; Bring Down." The children often did examples of two-digit division. When the teacher went over the examples with them, he told them for each problem what the procedure was, rarely asking them to conceptualize or explain it themselves:"3 into 22 is 7; do your subtraction and one is left over." During the week that two-digit division was introduced (or at any other time), the investigator did not observe any discussion of the idea of grouping involved in division, any use of manipulables, or any attempt to relate two-digit division to any other mathematical process. Nor was there any attempt to relate the steps to an actual or possible thought process of the children. The observer did not hear the terms dividend, quotient, and so on used again. The math teacher in the other working-class school followed similar procedures regarding two-digit division, and at one point her class seemed confused. She said, "You're confusing yourselves. You're tensing up. Remember, when you do this, it's the same steps over and over again — and that's the way division always is." Several weeks later, after a test, a group of her children "still didn't get it," and she made no attempt to explain the concept of dividing things into groups, or to give them manipulables for their own investigation. Rather, she went over the steps with them again and told them that they "needed more practice."

. . .

In both working-class schools, work in language arts is mechanics of punctuation (commas, periods, question marks, exclamation points), capitalization, and the four kinds of sentences. One teacher explained to me, "Simple punctuation is all they'll ever use." Regarding punctuation, either a teacher or a ditto stated the rules for where, for example, to put commas. The investigator heard no classroom discussion of the aural context of punctuation (which, of course, is what gives each mark its meaning). Nor did the investigator hear any statement or inference that placing a punctuation mark could be a decision-making process, depending, for example, on one's intended meaning. Rather, the children were told to follow the rules. Language arts did not involve creative writing. There were several writing assignments throughout the year, but in each instance the children were given a ditto, and they wrote answers to questions on the sheet. For example, they wrote their "autobiography" by answering such questions as "Where were you born?" "What is your favorite animal?" on a sheet entitled, "All About Me."

In one of the working-class schools, the class had a science period several times a week. On the three occasions observed, the children were not called on to set up experiments or to give explanations for facts or concepts. Rather, on each occasion, the teacher told them in his own words what the book said. The children copied the teacher's sentences from the board. Each day that preceded the day they were to do a science experiment, the teacher told them to copy the directions from the book for the procedure they would carry out the next day, and to study the list at home that night. The day after each experiment, the teacher went over what they had "found" (they did the experiments as a class, and each was actually a class demonstration led by the teacher). Then the teacher wrote what they "found" on the board, and the children copied that in their notebooks. Once or twice a year there are science projects. The project is chosen and assigned by the teacher from a box of three-by-five-inch cards. On the card, the teacher has written the question to be answered, the books to use, and how much to write. Explaining the cards to the observer, the teacher said, "It tells them exactly what to do, or they couldn't do it."

Social studies in the working-class schools is also largely mechanical, rote work that was given little explanation or connection to larger contexts. In one school, for example, although there was a book available, social studies work was to copy the teacher's notes from the board. Several times a week for a period of several months, the children copied these notes. The fifth grades in the district were to study U.S. history. The teacher used a booklet she had purchased called "The Fabulous Fifty States." Each day she put information from the booklet in outline form on the board, and the children copied it. The type of information did not vary: the name of the state, its abbreviation, state capital, nickname of the state, its main products, main business, and a "Fabulous Fact" (for example, "Idaho grew 27 billion potatoes in one year. That's enough potatoes for each man, woman and . . . "). As the children finished copying the sentences, the teacher erased them and wrote more. Children would occasionally go to the front to pull down the wall map in order to locate the states they were copying, and the teacher did not dissuade them. But the observer never saw her refer to the map; nor did the observer ever hear her make other than perfunctory remarks concerning the information the children were copying. Occasionally the children colored in a ditto and cut it out to make a stand-up figure (representing, for example, a man roping a cow in the Southwest). These were referred to by the teacher as their social studies "projects."

Rote behavior was often called for in classroom oral work. When going over math and language arts skills sheets, for example, as the teacher asked for the answer to each problem, he fired the questions rapidly, staccato, and the scene reminded the observer of a sergeant drilling recruits: above all, the questions demanded that you stay at attention: "The next one? What do I put here? . . . Here? Give us the next." Or "How many commas in this sentence? Where do I put them . . . The next one?"

The (four) fifth-grade teachers observed in the working-class schools attempted to control classroom time and space by making decisions without consulting the children and without explaining the basis for their decisions. The teacher's control thus often seemed capricious. Teachers, for instance, very often ignored the bells to switch classes — deciding among themselves to keep the children after the period was officially over, to continue with the work, or for disciplinary reasons, or so they (the teachers) could stand in the hall and talk. There were no clocks in the rooms in either school, and the children often asked, "What period is this?" "When do we go to gym?" The children had no access to materials. These were handed out by teachers and closely guarded. Things in the room "belonged" to the teacher: "Bob, bring me my garbage can." The teachers continually gave the children orders. Only three times did the investigator hear a teacher in either working-class school preface a directive with an unsarcastic "please," or "let's" or "would you." Instead, the teachers said, "Shut up," "Shut your mouth," "Open your books," "Throw your *gum* away — if you want to rot your teeth, do it on your *own* time." Teachers made every effort to control the movement of the children, and often shouted, "Why are you out of your *seat*??!!" If the children got permission to leave the room, they had to take a written pass with the date and time.

. . .

The children are successful enough in their struggle against work that there are long periods where they are not asked to do any work, but just to sit and be quiet.[9] Very often the work that the teachers assign is "easy," that is, not demanding, and thus receives less resistance. Sometimes a compromise is reached where, although the teachers insist that the children continue to work, there is a constant murmur of talk. The children will be doing arithmetic examples, copying social studies notes, or doing punctuation or other dittoes, and all the while there is muted but spirited conversation — about somebody's broken arm, an afterschool disturbance of the day before, and so on. Sometimes the teachers themselves join in the conversation because, as one teacher explained to me, "It's a relief from the routine."

Middle-class School

In the middle-class school, work is getting the right answer. If one accumulates enough right answers, one gets a good grade. One must follow the directions in order to get the right answers, but the directions often call for some figuring, some choice, some decision making. For example, the children must often figure out by themselves what the directions ask them to do, and how to get the answer: what do you do first, second, and perhaps third? Answers are usually found in books or by listening to the teacher. Answers are usually words, sentences, numbers, or facts and dates; one writes them on paper, and one should be neat. Answers must be in the right order, and one can not make them up.

The following activities are illustrative. Math involves some choice: one may do two-digit division the long way, or the short way, and there are some math problems that can be done "in your head." When the teacher explains how to do two-digit division, there is recognition that a cognitive process is involved; she gives several ways, and says, "I want to make sure you understand what you're doing — so you get it right"; and, when they go over the homework, she asks the *children* to tell how they did the problem and what answer they got.

In social studies, the daily work is to read the assigned pages in the textbook and to answer the teacher's questions. The questions are almost always designed to check on whether the students have read the assignment and understood it: who did so-and-so; what happened after that; when did it happen, where, and, sometimes, why did it happen? The answers are in the book and in one's understanding of the book; the teacher's hints when one doesn't know the answer are to "read it again," or to look at the picture or at the rest of the paragraph. One is to search for the answer in the "context," in what is given.

Language arts is "simple grammar, what they need for everyday life." The language arts teacher says, "They should learn to speak properly, to write business letters and thank-you letters, and to understand what nouns and verbs and simple subjects are." Here, as well, the actual work is to choose the right answers, to understand what is given. The teacher often says, "Please read the next sentence and then I'll question you about it." One teacher said in some exasperation to a boy who was fooling around in class, "If you don't know the answers to the questions I ask, then you can't stay in this *class*! (pause) You *never* know the answers to the questions I ask, and it's not fair to me — and certainly not to you!"

Most lessons are based on the textbook. This does not involve a critical perspective on what is given there. For example, a critical perspective in social studies is perceived as dangerous by these teachers because it may lead to controversial topics; the parents might complain. The children, however, are often curious, especially in social studies. Their questions are tolerated, and usually answered perfunctorily. But after a few minutes the teacher will say,"All right, we're not going any farther. Please open your social studies workbook." While the teachers spend a lot of time explaining and expanding on what the textbooks say, there is little attempt to analyze how or why things happen, or to give thought to how pieces of a culture, or, say, a system of numbers or elements of a language fit together or can be analyzed. What has happened in the past, and what exists now may not be equitable or fair, but (shrug) that is the way things are and one does not confront such matters in school.

. . .

Creativity is not often requested. . . . Social studies projects, for example, are given with directions to "find information on your topic," and write it up. The children are not supposed to copy, but to "put it in your own words." Although a number of the projects subsequently went beyond the teacher's direction to find information and had quite expressive covers and inside illustrations, the teacher's evaluative comments had to do with the amount of information, whether they had "copied," and if their work was neat.

The style of control of the three fifth-grade teachers observed in this school varied from somewhat easygoing to strict, but in contrast to the working-class schools, the teachers' decisions were usually based on external rules and regulations, for example, on criteria that were known or available to the children. Thus, the teachers always honor the bells for changing classes, and they usually evaluate children's work by what is in the textbooks and answer booklets.

There is little excitement in school work for the children, and the assignments are perceived as having little to do with their interests and feelings. As one child said, what you do is "store facts in your head like cold storage — until you need it later for a test, or your job." Thus, doing well is important because there are thought to be *other* likely rewards: a good job, or college.[10]

Affluent Professional School

In the affluent professional school, work is creative activity carried out independently. The students are continually asked to express and apply ideas and concepts. Work involves individual thought and expressiveness, expansion and illustration of ideas, and choice of appropriate method and material. (The class is not considered an open classroom, and the principal explained that because of the large number of discipline problems in the fifth grade this year they did not departmentalize. The teacher who agreed to take part in the study said she is "more structured" this year than she usually is.) The products of work in this class are often written stories, editorials and essays, or representations of ideas in mural, graph, or craft form. The products of work should not be like everybody else's and should show individuality. They should exhibit good design, and (this is important), they must also fit empirical reality. Moreover, one's work should attempt to intepret or "make sense" of reality. The relatively few rules to be followed regarding work are usually criteria for, or limits on, individual activity. One's product is usually evaluated for the quality of its expression and for the appropriateness of its conception to the task. In many cases one's own satisfaction with the product is an important criterion for its evaluation. When right answers are called for, as in commercial materials like SRA (Science Research Associates) and math, it is important that the children decide on an answer as a result of thinking about the idea involved in what they're being asked to do. Teacher's hints are to "think about it some more."

The following activities are illustrative. The class takes home a sheet requesting each child's parents to fill in the number of cars they have, the number of television sets, refrigerators, games, or rooms in the house, and the like. Each child is to figure the average number of a type of possession owned by the fifth grade. Each child must compile the "data" from all the sheets. A calculator is available in the classroom to do the mechanics of finding the average. Some children decide to send sheets to the fourth-grade families for comparison. Their work should be "verified" by a classmate before it is handed in.

Each child and his or her family has made a geoboard. The teacher asks the class to get their geoboards from the side cabinet, to take a handful of rubber bands, and then to listen to what she would like them to do. She says, "I would like you to design a figure and then find the perimeter and area. When you have it, check with your neighbor. After you've done that, please transfer it to graph paper and tomorrow I'll ask you to make up a question about it for someone. When you hand it in, please let me know whose it is, and who verified it. Then I have something else for you to do that's really fun. (pause) Find the average number of chocolate chips in three cookies. I'll give you three cookies, and you'll have to eat your way through, I'm afraid!" Then she goes around the room and gives help, suggestions, praise, and admonitions that they are getting noisy. They work sitting, or standing up at their desks, at benches in the back, or on the floor. A child hands the teacher his paper and she comments, "I'm not accepting this paper. Do a better design." To another child she says, "That's fantastic! But you'll never find the area. Why don't you draw a figure inside (the big one) and subtract to get the area?"

The school district requires the fifth grades to study ancient civilizations (in particular, Egypt, Athens, and Sumer.) In this classroom, the emphasis is on illustrating and re-creating the culture of the people of ancient times. The following are typical activities: The children made an 8mm film on Egypt, which one of the parents edited. A girl in the class wrote the script, and the class acted it out. They put the sound on themselves. They read stories of those days. They wrote essays and stories depicting the lives of the people and the societal and occupational divisions. They chose from a list of projects, all of which involved graphic representations of ideas: for example, "Make a mural depicting the division of labor in Egyptian society."

Each child wrote and exchanged a letter in hieroglyphics with a fifth grader in another class, and they also exchanged stories they wrote in cuneiform. They made a scroll and singed the edges so it looked authentic. They each chose an occupation and made an Egyptian plaque representing that occupation, simulating the appropriate Egyptian design. They carved their design on a cylinder of wax, pressed the wax into clay, and then baked the clay. Although one girl did not choose an occupation, but carved instead a series of gods and slaves, the teacher said, " That's all right, Amber, it's beautiful." As they were working the teacher said,"Don't cut into your clay until you're satisfied with your design."

Social studies also involves almost daily presentation by the children of some event from the news. The teacher's questions ask the children to expand what they say, to give more details, and to be more specific. Occasionally she adds some remarks to help them see connections between events.

The emphasis on expressing and illustrating ideas in social studies is accompanied in language arts by an emphasis on creative writing. Each child wrote a rebus story for a first grader whom they had interviewed to see what kind of story the child liked best. They wrote editorials on pending decisions by the school board, and radio plays, some of which were read over the school intercom from the office, and one of which was performed in the auditorium. There is no language arts textbook because, the teacher said, "The principal wants us to be creative." There is not much grammar, but there is punctuation. One morning when the observer arrived, the class was doing a punctuation ditto. The teacher later apologized for using the ditto. "It's just for review," she said. "I don't teach punctuation that way. We use their language." The ditto had three unambiguous rules for where to put commas in a sentence. As the teacher was going around to help the children with the ditto, she repeated several times, "Where you put commas depends on how you say the sentence; it depends on the situation and what you want to say." Several weeks later the observer saw another punctuation activity. The teacher had printed a five-paragraph story on an oak tag and then cut it into phrases. She read the whole story to the class from the book, then passed out the phrases. The group had to decide how the phrases could best be put together again. (They arranged the phrases on the floor.) The point was not to replicate the story, although that was not irrelevant, but to "decide what you think the best way is." Punctuation marks on cardboard pieces were then handed out, and the children discussed, and then decided, what mark was best at each place they thought one was needed. At the end of each paragraph the teacher asked, "Are you satisfied with the way the paragraphs are now? Read it to yourself and see how it sounds," Then she read the original story again, and they compared the two.

Describing her goals in science to the investigator, the teacher said, "We use ESS (Elementary Science Study). It's very good because it gives a hands-on experience — so they can make *sense* out of it. It doesn't matter whether it (what they find) is right or wrong. I bring them together and there's value in discussing their ideas."

The products of work in this class are often highly valued by the children and the teacher. In fact, this was the only school in which the investigator was not allowed to take original pieces of the children's work for her files. If the work was small enough, however, and was on paper, the investigator could duplicate it on the copying machine in the office.

The teacher's attempt to control the class involves constant negotiation. She does not give direct orders unless she is angry because the children have been too noisy. Normally, she tries to get them to foresee the consequences of their actions and to decide accordingly. For example, lining them up to go see a play written by the sixth graders, she says,"I presume you're lined up by someone with whom you want to sit. I hope you're lined up by someone you won't get in trouble with."

. . .

One of the few rules governing the children's movement is that no more than three children may be out of the room at once. There is a school rule that anyone can go to the library at any time to get a book. In the fifth grade I observed, they sign their name on the chalkboard and leave. There are no passes. Finally, the children have a fair amount of officially sanctioned say over what happens in the class. For example, they often negotiate what work is to be done. If the teacher wants to move on to the next subject, but the children say they are not ready, they want to work on their present projects some more, she very often lets them do it.

Executive Elite School

In the executive elite school, work is developing one's analytical intellectual powers. Children are continually asked to reason through a problem, to produce intellectual products that are both logically sound and of top academic quality. A primary goal of thought is to conceptualize rules by which elements may fit together in systems, and then to apply these rules in solving a problem. School work helps one to achieve, to excel, to prepare for life.

The following are illustrative. The math teacher teaches area and perimeter by having the children derive formulae for each. First she helps them, through discussion at the board, to arrive at $A = W \times L$ as a formula (not *the* formula) for area. After discussing several, she says, "Can anyone make up a formula for perimeter? Can you figure that out yourselves? (pause) Knowing what we know, can we think of a formula?" She works out three children's suggestions at the board, saying to two, "Yes, that's a good one," and then asks the class if they can think of any more. No one volunteers. To prod them, she says, "If you use rules and good reasoning, you get many ways. Chris, can you think up a formula?"

She discusses two-digit division with the children as a decision-making process. Presenting a new type of problem to them, she asks, "What's the first decision you'd make if presented with this kind of example? What is the first thing you'd think? Craig?" Craig says, "To find my first partial quotient." She responds, "Yes, that would be your first decision. How would you do that?" Craig explains, and then the teacher says, "OK, we'll see how that works for you." The class tries his way. Subsequently, she comments on the merits and shortcomings of several other children's decisions. Later, she tells the investigator that her goals in math are to develop their reasoning and mathematical thinking and that, unfortunately, "there's no *time* for manipulables."

While right answers are important in math, they are not "given" by the book or by the teacher, but may be challenged by the children. Going over some problems in late September the teacher says, "Raise your hand if you do not agree." A child says, "I don't agree with 64." The teacher responds, "OK, there's a question about 64. (to class) Please check it. Owen, they're disagreeing with you. Kristen, they're checking yours." The teacher emphasized this repeatedly during September and October with statements like, "Don't be afraid to say if you disagree. In the last (math) class, somebody disagreed, and they were right. Before you disagree, check yours, and if you still think we're wrong, then we'll check it out." By thanksgiving, the children did not often speak in terms of right and wrong math problems, but of whether they agreed with the answer that had been given.

There are complicated math mimeos with many word problems. Whenever they go over the examples, they discuss how each child has set up the problem. The children must explain it precisely. On one occasion the teacher said, "I'm more — just as interested in *how* you set up the problem as in what answer you find. If you set up a problem in a good way, the answer is *easy* to find."

Social studies work is most often reading and discussion of concepts and independent research. There are only occasional artistic, expressive, or illustrative projects.

. . .

In social studies — but also in reading, science, and health — the teachers initiate classroom discussions of current social issues and problems. These discussions occurred on every one of the investigator's visits, and a teacher told me, "These children's opinions are important — it's important that they learn to reason things through." The classroom discussions always struck the observer as quite realistic and analytical, dealing with concrete social issues like the following: "Why do workers strike?" "Is that right or wrong?" "Why do we have inflation, and what can be done to stop it?" "Why do companies put chemicals in food when the natural ingredients are available?" and so on. Usually the children did not have to be prodded to give their opinions. In fact, their statements and the interchanges between them struck the observer as quite sophisticated conceptually and verbally, and well informed. . . .

Language arts emphasizes language as a complex system, one that should be mastered. The children are asked to diagram sentences of complex grammatical construction, to memorize irregular verb conjugations (he lay, he has lain, and so on . . .), and to use the proper participles, conjunctions, and interjections, in their speech. The teacher (the same one who teaches social studies) told them, "It is not enough to get these right on tests; you must use what you learn (in grammar classes) in your written and oral work. I will grade you on that."

Most writing assignments are either research reports and essays for social studies, or experiment analyses and write-ups for science. There is only an occasional story or other "creative writing" assignment. . . . The stories they subsequently wrote were, in fact, well structured, but many were also personal and expressive. The teacher's evaluative comments, however, did not refer to the expressiveness or artistry, but were all directed toward whether they had "developed" the story well.

Language arts work also involved a large amount of practice in presentation of the self and in managing situations where the child was expected to be in charge. For example, there was a series of assignments in which each child had to be a " student teacher." The child had to plan a lesson in grammar, outlining, punctuation, or other language arts topic and explain the concept to the class. Each child was to prepare a worksheet or game and a homework assignment as well. After each presentation, the teacher and other children gave a critical appraisal of the "student teacher's" performance. Their criteria were: whether the student spoke clearly; whether the lesson was interesting; whether the student made any mistakes; and whether he or she kept control of the class. On an occasion when a child did not maintain control, the teacher said, "When you're up there, you have authority, and you have to use it. I'll back you up."

The teacher of math and science explained to the observer that she likes the ESS program because "the children can manipulate variables. They generate hypotheses and devise experiments to solve the problem. Then they have to explain what they found."

The executive elite school is the only school where bells do not demarcate the periods of time. The two fifth-grade teachers were very strict about changing classes on schedule, however, as specific plans for each session had been made. The teachers attempted to keep tight control over the children during lessons, and the children were sometimes flippant, boisterous, and occasionally rude. However, the children may be brought into line by reminding them that "it is up to you." "You must control yourself," "you are responsible for your work," you must "set your priorities." One teacher told a child, "You are the only driver of your car

— and only you can regulate your speed." A new teacher complained to the observer that she had thought "these children" would have more control.

While strict attention to the lesson at hand is required, the teachers make relatively little attempt to regulate the movement of the children at other times. For example, except for the kindergartners, the children in this school do not have to wait for the bell to ring in the morning; they may go to their classroom when they arrive at school. Fifth graders often came early to read, to finish work, or to catch up. After the first two months of school the fifth-grade teachers did not line the children up to change classes or to go to gym, and so on, but, when the children were ready and quiet, they were told they could go—sometimes without the teachers.

. . .

DISCUSSION AND CONCLUSION

One could attempt to identify physical, cultural, and interpersonal characteristics of the environment of each school that might contribute to an empirical explanation of the events and interactions. For example, the investigator could introduce evidence to show that the following increased as the social class of the community increased (with the most marked differences occurring between the two districts): increased variety and abundance of teaching materials in the classroom; increased time reported spent by the teachers on preparation; higher social class background and more prestigious educational institutions attended by teachers and administrators; more stringent board of education requirements regarding teaching methods; more frequent and demanding administrative evaluation of teachers; increased teacher support services such as in-service workshops; increased parent expenditure for school equipment over and above district or government funding; higher expectations of student ability on the part of parents, teachers, and administrators; higher expectations and demands regarding student achievement on the part of teachers, parents, and administrators; more positive attitudes on the part of the teachers as to the probable occupational futures of the children; an increase in the children's acceptance of classroom assignments; increased intersubjectivity between students and teachers; and increased cultural congruence between school and community.

All of these—and other—factors may contribute to the character and scope of classroom events. However, what is of primary concern here is not the immediate causes of classroom activity (although these are in themselves quite important). Rather, the concern is to reflect on the deeper social meaning, the wider theoretical significance, of what happens in each social setting. In an attempt to assess the theoretical meaning of the differences among the schools, the work tasks and milieu in each will be discussed in light of the concepts used to define social class.

What potential relationships to the system of ownership of symbolic and physical capital, to authority and control, and to their own productive activity are being developed in children in each school? What economically relevant knowledge, skills, and predispositions are being transmitted in each classroom, and for what future relationship to the system of production are they appropriate? It is of course true that a student's future relationship to the process of production in society is determined by the combined effects of circumstances beyond elementary schooling. However, by examining elementary school activity in its social-class context in the light of our theoretical perspective on social class, we can see certain potential relationships already developing. Moreover, in this structure of developing relationships lies theoretical—and social—significance.

The working class children are developing a potential conflict relationship wih capital. Their present school work is appropriate preparation for future wage labor that is mechanical and routine. Such work, insofar as it denies the human capacities for creativity and planning, is degrading; moreover, when performed in industry, such work is a source of profit to others. This situation produces industrial conflict over wages, working conditions, and control. However, the children in the working-class schools are not learning to be docile and obedient in the face of present or future degrading conditions of financial exploitation. They are developing abilities and skills of resistance. These methods are highly similar to the "slowdown," subtle sabotage, and other modes of indirect resistance carried out by adult workers in the shop, on the department store sales floor, and in some offices.[11] As these types of resistance develop in school, they are highly constrained and limited in their ultimate effectiveness. Just as the children's resistance prevents them from learning socially legitimated knowledge and skills in school and is therefore ultimately debilitating, so is this type of resistance ultimately debilitating in industry. Such resistance in industry does not succeed in producing, nor is it intended to produce, fundamental changes in the relationships of exploitation or control. Thus, the methods of resistance that the working-class children are developing in school are only temporarily, and potentially, liberating.

In the middle-class school, the children are developing somewhat different potential relationships to capital, authority, and work. In this school, the work tasks and relationships are appropriate for a future relation to capital that is bureaucratic. Their school work is appropriate for white-collar working-class and middle-class jobs in the supportive institutions of United States society. In these jobs, one does the paperwork, the technical work, the sales, and the social service in the private and state bureaucracies. Such work does not usually demand that one be creative, and one is not often rewarded for critical analysis of the system. One is rewarded, rather, for knowing the answers to the questions one is asked, for knowing where or how to find the answers, and for knowing which form, regulation, technique, or procedure is correct. While such work does not usually satisfy human needs for engagement and self-expression, one's salary can be exchanged for objects or activities that attempt to meet these needs.

In the affluent professional school, the children are developing a potential relationship to capital that is instrumental and expressive and involves substantial negotiation. In their schooling, these children are acquiring symbolic capital: they are being given the opportunity to develop skills of linguistic, artistic, and scientific expression and creative elaboration of ideas into concrete form. These skills are those needed to produce, for example, culture (artistic, intellectual, and scientific ideas and other "products"). Their schooling is developing in these children skills necessary to become society's successful artists; intellectuals; legal, scientific, and technical experts; and other professionals. The developing relation of the children in this school to their work is creative and relatively autonomous. Although they do not have control over which ideas they develop or express, the creative act in itself affirms and utilizes the human potential for conceptualization and design that is in many cases valued as intrinsically satisfying.

Professional persons in the cultural institutions of society, (in, say, academe, publishing, the nonprint media, the arts, and the legal and state bureaucracies) are in an expressive relationship to the system of ownership in society because the ideas and other products of their work are often an important means by which material relationships of society are given ideological (e.g., artistic, intellectual, legal, and scientific) expression. Through the systems of laws, for example, the ownership relations of private property are elaborated and legitimated in legal form; through individualistic and meritocratic theories in psychology and sociology, these individualistic economic relations are provided scientific "rationality" and "sense." The relationship to physical capital of those in society who create what counts as the dominant culture or ideology also involves substantial negotiation. The producers of symbolic capital often do not control the socially available physical capital nor the cultural uses to which it is put. They must therefore negotiate for money for their own projects. However, skillful application of one's cultural capital may ultimately lead to social (for example, state) power and to financial reward.

The executive elite school gives its children something that none of the other schools does: knowledge of and practice in manipulating the socially legitimated tools of analysis of systems. The children are given the opportunity to learn and to utilize the intellectually and socially prestigious grammatical, mathematical, and other vocabularies and rules by which elements are arranged. They are given the opportunity to use these skills in the analysis of society and in control situations. Such knowledge and skills are a most important kind of *symbolic capital*. They are necessary for control of a production system. The developing relationship of the children in this school to their work affirms and develops in them the human capacities for analysis and planning and helps to prepare them for work in society that would demand these skills. Their schooling is helping them to develop the abilities necessary for ownership and control of physical capital and the means of production in society.

The foregoing analysis of differences in school work in contrasting social-class contexts suggests the following conclusion: the "hidden curriculum" of school work is tacit preparation for relating to the process of production in a particular way. Differing curricular, pedagogical, and pupil evaluation practices emphasize different cognitive and behavioral skills in each social setting and thus contribute to the development in the children of certain potential relationships to physical and symbolic capital, to authority, and to the process of work. School experience, in the sample of schools discussed here, differed qualitatively by social class. These differences not only may contribute to the development in the children in each social class of certain types of economically significant relationships and not others, but would thereby help to *reproduce* this system of relations in society. In the contribution to the reproduction of unequal social relations lies a theoretical meaning, and social consequence, of classroom practice.

The identification of different emphases in classrooms in a sample of contrasting social class contexts implies that further research should be conducted in a large number of schools to investigate the types of work tasks and interactions in each, to see if they differ in the ways discussed here, and to see if similar potential relationships are uncovered. Such research could have as a product the further elucidation of complex but not readily apparent connections between everyday activity in schools and classrooms and the unequal structure of economic relationships in which we work and live.

NOTES

1. But see, in a related vein, Apple and King (1977) and Rist (1973).

2. The definition of social class delineated here is the author's own, but it relies heavily on her interpretation of the work of Eric Olin Wright (1978), Pierre Bourdieu (Bourdieu and Passeron, 1977), and Raymond Williams (1977).

3. For discussions of schools as agencies of social and economic legitimation see Althusser (1971); see also Anyon (1978; 1979).

4. While relationships of control in society will not be discussed here, it can be said that they roughly parallel the relationships of control in the workplace, which will be the focus of this discussion. That is, working-class and many middle-class persons have less control than members of the upper-middle and capitalist classes do, not only over conditions and processes of their work, but over their nonwork lives as well. In addition, it is true that persons from the middle and capitalist classes, rather than workers, are most often those who fill the positions of state and other power in United States society.

5. Occupations may change their relation to the means of production over time, as the expenditure and ownership of capital change, as technology, skills, and the social relations of work change. For example, some jobs that were middle-class, managerial positions in 1900 and that necessitated conceptual laying-out and planning are now working-class and increasingly mechanical: for example, quality control in industry, clerical work, and computer programming (see Braverman, 1974).

6. The U.S. Bureau of the Census defines "poverty" for a nonfarm family of four as a yearly income of $6,191 a year or less U.S. Bureau of the Census, *Statistical Abstract of the United States: 1978* (Washington, D.C.: U.S. Government Printing Office, 1978, p. 465, table 754).

7. This figure is an estimate. According to the Bureau of the Census, only 2.6 percent of families in the United States have money income of $50,000 or over. U.S. Bureau of the Census, *Current Population Reports*, series P-60, no. 118, "Money Income in 1977 of Families and Persons in the United States." (Washington, D.C.: U.S. Government Printing Office, 1979, p. 2, table A). For figures on income at these higher levels, see Smith and Franklin (1974).

8. For other similarities alleged to characterize United States classrooms and schools, but which will not be discussed here, see Dreeben (1968), Jackson (1968), and Sarasan (1971).

9. Indeed, strikingly little teaching occurred in either of the working-class schools; this curtailed the amount that the children were taught. Incidentally, it increased the amount of time that had to be spent by the researcher to collect data on teaching style and interaction.

10. A dominant feeling, expressed directly and indirectly by teachers in this school, was boredom with their work. They did, however, in contrast to the working-class schools, almost always carry out lessons during class times.

11. See, for example, discussions in Levison (1974), Aronowitz (1978), and Benson (1978).

REFERENCES

Althusser, L. "Ideology and Ideological State Apparatuses." In L. Althusser, *Lenin and Philosophy and Other Essays*. Ben Brewster, trans. New York: Monthly Review Press, 1971.

Anyon, J. "Elementary Social Studies Textbooks and Legitimating Knowledge," *Theory and Research in Social Education*, 6 (1978): 40–55.

Anyon, J. "Ideology and United States History Textbooks," *Harvard Educational Review*, 49 (1979): 361–86.

Apple, M.W. *Ideology and Curriculum*. Boston: Routledge and Kegan Paul, 1979.

Apple, M.W., and N. King. "What Do Schools Teach?" *Curriculum Inquiry* 6 (1977): 341–58.

Aronowitz, S. "Marx, Braverman, and the Logic of Capital," *The Insurgent Sociologist* 8 (1978): 126–46.

Benson, S. "The Clerking Sisterhood: Rationalization and the Work Culture of Saleswomen in American Department Stores, 1890–1960," *Radical America* 12 (1978): 41–55.

Bernstein, B. *Class, Codes and Control, Vol. 3. Towards a Theory of Educational Transmission*. (2nd ed.) London: Routledge and Kegan Paul, 1977.

Bourdieu, P., and J. Passeron. *Reproduction in Education, Society, and Culture*. Beverly Hills, Calif.: Sage, 1977.

Bowles, S., and H. Gintis. *Schooling in Capitalist America: Educational Reform and the Contradictions of Economic Life*. New York: Basic Books, 1976.

Braverman, H. *Labor and Monopoly Capital: The Degradation of Work in the Twentieth Century*. New York: Monthly Review Press, 1974.

Dreeben, R. *On What is Learned in School*. Reading, Mass.: Addison-Wesley, 1968.

Jackson, P. *Life in Classrooms*. New York: Holt, Rinehart and Winston, 1968.

Lampman, R.J. *The Share of Top Wealth-Holders in National Wealth, 1922–1956: A Study of the National Bureau of Economic Research*. Princeton, N.J.: Princeton University Press, 1962.

Levison, A. *The Working-Class Majority*. New York: Penguin Books, 1974.

New York Stock Exchange. *Census*. New York: New York Stock Exchange, 1975.

Rist, R.C. *The Urban School: A Factory for Failure*. Cambridge, Mass.: MIT Press, 1973.

Sarasan, S. *The Culture of School and the Problem of Change*. Boston: Allyn and Bacon, 1971.

Smith, J.D., and S. Franklin. "The Concentration of Personal Wealth, 1922–1969," *American Economic Review* 64 (1974): 162–67.

U.S. Bureau of the Census. *Statistical Abstract of the United States: 1978*. Washington, D.C.: U.S. Government Printing Office, 1978.

U.S. Bureau of the Census. *Current Population Reports*. Series P-60, no. 118. Money income in 1977 of families and persons in the United States. Washington, D.C.: U.S. Government Printing Office, 1979.

Williams, R. *Marxism and Literature*. New York: Oxford University Press, 1977.

Wright, E.O. *Class, Crisis and the State*. London: New Left Books, 1978.

Selection 4.4

The Culture and Commerce of the Textbook

Michael W. Apple

I

We can talk about culture in two ways: as a lived process, as what Raymond Williams (1977, p. 19) has called a whole way of life, or as a commodity. (See also Apple and Weis, 1983, esp. chap. 1.) In the first, we focus on culture as a constitutive social process through which we live our daily lives. In the second, we emphasize the products of culture, the very thingness of the commodities we produce and consume. This distinction can of course be maintained only on an analytical level, since most of what seem to us to be things — like lightbulbs, cars, records, and, in the case of this essay, books — are really part of a larger social process. As Marx, for example, spent years trying to demonstrate, every product is an expression of embodied human labor. Goods and services are relations among people, relations of exploitation often, but human relations nevertheless. Turning on a light when you walk into a room is not only using an object, it is also to be involved in an anonymous social relationship with the miner who worked to dig the coal burned to produce the electricity.

This dual nature of culture poses a dilemma for those individuals who are interested in understanding the dynamics of popular and elite culture in

SOURCE. Reprinted, with permission of the author and publisher, from *Journal of Curriculum Studies* (July–September 1979): 191–202.

our society. It makes studying the dominant cultural products — from films to books, to television, to music — decidedly slippery, for there are sets of relations behind each of these "things." And these in turn are situated within the larger web of the social and market relations of capitalism.

While there is a danger of falling into economic reductionism, it is essential that we look more closely at this political economy of culture. How do the dynamics of class, gender, and race "determine" cultural production? How is the organization and distribution of culture "mediated" by economic and social structure (Wolff, 1981, p. 47). What is the relationship between a cultural product — say, a film or a book — and the social relations of its production, accessibility, and consumption? These are not easy questions to deal with. They are not easy in at least two ways. First, the very terms of the language and concepts we use to ask them are notoriously difficult to unpack. That is, words such as "determine," "mediate," "social relations of production," and so on — and the conceptual apparatus that lies behind them — are not at all settled. There is as much contention over their use currently as there has ever been.[1] Thus, it is hard to grapple with the issue of the determination of culture without at the same time being very self-conscious of the tools one is employing to do it with.

Second, and closely related to the first, perhaps because of the theoretical controversies surrounding the topic, there have been fewer detailed and large-scale empirical investigations of these relations recently than is necessary. While we may have interesting ideological or economic analyses of a television show, film, or book,[2] there are really only a few well-designed empirical studies that examine the economics and social relations involved in films and books in general. It is hard to get a global picture because of this.

This lack is a problem in sociological analysis in general; yet it is even more problematic in the field of education. Even though the overt aim of our institutions of schooling has more than a little to do with cultural products and processes, with cultural transmission, it has only been in the last decade or so that the politics and economics of the culture that actually is transmitted in schools has been taken up as a serious research problem. It was almost as if Durkheim and Weber, to say nothing of Marx, had never existed. In the area that has come to be called the sociology of the curriculum, however, steps have been taken to deal with this issue in some very interesting ways. A good deal of progress has in fact been made in understanding whose knowledge is taught and produced in our schools.[3]

While not the only questions with which we should be concerned, it is clear that major curriculum issues are those of content and organization. What should be taught? In what way? Answering these questions is difficult. For not only does the first, for example, involve some very knotty epistemological issues — What should be granted the status of knowledge? — but it is a politically loaded problem as well. To borrow the language of Pierre Bourdieu (Bourdieu and Passeron, 1977) and Basil Bernstein (1977), the "cultural capital" of dominant classes and class segments has been considered the most legitimate knowledge. This knowledge, and one's "ability" to deal with it, have served as one mechanism in a complex process in which the economic and cultural reproduction of class, gender, and race relations is accomplished. Therefore, the choice of a particular content and ways of approaching it in schools is related both to existing relations of domination and to struggles to alter these relations. Not to recognize this is to ignore a wealth of evidence in the United States, England, Australia, France, Sweden, Germany, and elsewhere that links school knowledge — both commodified and lived — to class, gender, and race dynamics outside as well as inside our institutions of education.[4]

Even where there is recognition of the political nature of the curriculum, this does not solve all of our problems. The statement that school knowledge has some (admittedly complex) connections to the larger political economy merely restates the issue. It does not in itself answer how these connections operate. Though the ties that link curricula to the inequalities and social struggles of our social formation are very complicated, occasionally research is available that helps illuminate this nexus, even when it may not be overtly aimed at an educational audience. I want to draw on this research to help us begin to uncover some of the connections between curriculum and the larger political economy. The most interesting of this research is about the culture and commerce of publishing. It sets out to examine the relationship between how publishing operates internally — its social relations and composition — and the cultural and economic market it is situated within. What do the social and eonomic relations within the publishing industry have to do with schools, with the politics of knowledge distribution in education? Perhaps this can be made clearer if we stop and think about the following question.

How is this "legitimate" knowledge made available in schools? By and large it is through something to which we have paid much too little attention — the textbook. Whether we like it or not, the curriculum in most American schools is not defined by courses of study or suggested programs, but by one particular artifact, the standardized, grade-level-specific text in mathematics, reading, social studies, science (when it is even taught), and so on. The impact of this on the social relations of the classroom is also immense. It is estimated, for example, that 75 percent of the time elementary and secondary students are in classrooms and 90 percent of the time they assign to homework is spent with text materials (Goldstein, 1978, p. 1, and Goodlad, 1983). Yet, even given the ubiquitous character of textbooks, it is one of the things we know least about. While the text dominates curricula at the elementary, secondary, and even college levels, very little critical attention has been paid to the ideological, political, and economic sources of its production, distribution, and reception.[5]

In order to make sense out of this, we need to place the production of curricular materials such as texts back into the larger process of the production of cultural commodities, such as books in general. There are approximately 40,000 books published each year in the United States (Coser, Kadushin, and Powell, 1982, p. 3). Obviously, these are quite varied, with only a small portion of them being textbooks. Yet, even with this variety, there are certain constants that act on publishers.

We can identify four "major structural conditions" that by and large currently determine the shape of publishing in the United States.

1. The industry sells its products — like any commodity — in a market, but a market that, in contrast to that for many other products, is fickle and often uncertain.

2. The industry is decentralized among a number of sectors whose operations bear little resemblance to each other.

3. These operations are characterized by a mixture of modern mass-production methods and craftlike procedures.

4. The industry remains perilously poised between the requirements and restraints of commerce and the responsibilities and obligations that it must bear as a prime guardian of the symbolic culture of the nation. Although the tensions between the claims of commerce and culture seem to us always to have been with book publishing, they have become more acute and salient in the last twenty years (Coser, Kadushin, and Powell, 1982, p. 7).

These conditions are not new phenomena by any means. From the time printing began as an industry, books were pieces of merchandise. They were of course often produced for scholarly or humanistic purposes, but before anything else their prime function was to earn their producers a living. Book production, hence, has historically rested on a foundation where from the outset it was necessary to "find enough capital to start work and then to print only those titles which would satisfy a clientele, and that at a price which would withstand competition." Similar to the marketing of other products, then, finance and costing took an immensely important place in the decisions of publishers and book-sellers[6] (Febvre and Martin, 1976, p. 109). Febvre and Martin, in their analysis of the history of book printing in Europe, argue this point exceptionally clearly:

> One fact must not be lost sight of: the printer and the bookseller worked above all and from the beginning for profit. The story of the first joint enterprise, Fust and Schoeffer, proves that. Like their modern counterparts, fifteenth-century publish-

ers only financed the kind of book they felt would sell enough copies to show a profit in a reasonable time. We should not therefore be surprised to find that the immediate effect of printing was merely to further increase the circulation of those works which had already enjoyed success in manuscript, and often to consign other less popular texts to oblivion. By multiplying books by the hundred and then thousand [compared to, say, the laborious copying of manuscripts], the press achieved both increased volume and at the same time more rigorous selection. [P. 109]

Drawing on Pierre Bourdieu's work, we can make a distinction between two types of "capital": symbolic and financial. This enables us to distinguish among the many kinds of publishers one might find. In essence, these two kinds of capital are found in different kinds of markets. Those firms that are more commercial, that are oriented to rapid turnover, quick obsolescence, and the minimization of risks are following a strategy for the accumulation of financial capital. Such a strategy has a strikingly different perspective on time, as well. It has a short-time perspective, one that focuses at the current interests of a particular group of readers. In contradistinction to those publishers whose market embodies the interests of finance capital, those firms whose goal is to maximize the accumulation of symbolic capital operate in such a way that their time perspective is longer. Immediate profit is less important. Higher risks may be taken and experimental content and form will find greater acceptance. These publishers are not uninterested in the "logic of profitability," but long-term accumulation is more important. One example is provided by Beckett's *Waiting for Godot*, which only sold 10,000 copies in the first five years after its publication in 1952, yet then went on to sell 60,000 copies as its rate of sales increased by 20 percent (Febvre and Martin, 1976, p. 44).

This conceptual distinction based on varying kinds of capital does not totally cover the differences among publishers in the kinds of book they publish, however. Coser, Kadushin, and Powell (1982), for example, further classify publishers according to the ways in which editors themselves carry out their work. In so doing, they distinguish among trade, or text, or finally the various scholarly monograph, or university presses. Each of these various labels refers not only to editorial policy. It speaks to a whole array of differences concerning the kind of technology that is employed by the press, the bureaucratic and organizational structures that coordinate and control, the day-to-day work of the company, and the different risks and monetary and marketing policies of each. Each also refers to important differences in relations with authors, in time scheduling, and ultimately in what counts as "success" (Febvre and Martin, 1976, p. 54). Behind the commodity, the book, thus indeed stands a whole set of human relations.

These structural differences in organization, technology, and economic and social relations structure the practices of the people involved in producing books. These include editors, authors, agents, and to a lesser extent, sales and marketing personnel. Digging deeper into these practices also enables us to understand the political economy of culture better. By integrating analyses of internal decision-making processes and external market relations within publishing, we can gain a good deal of insight into how particular aspects of popular and elite culture are presented in published form.

. . .

II

While we may think of book publishing as a relatively large industry, by current standards it is actually rather small when compared to other industries. A comparison may be helpful here. The entire book-publishing industry with its 65,000 or so employees would rank nearly forty to fifty positions below a single one of the highest grossing and largest employing American companies. While its total sales in 1980 were approximately $6 billion, and this does in fact sound impressive, in many ways its market is much less certain and is subject to greater economic, political, and ideological contingencies than these large companies.

Six billion dollars, though, is still definitely not a pittance. Book publishing is an industry, one that is divided up into a variety of markets. Of the total, $1.2 billion was accounted for by reference books, encyclopedias, and professional books; $1.5 billion came from the elementary, secondary, and college text market; $1 billion was taken in from book clubs and direct mail sales; nearly $660 million was accounted for by mass-market paperbacks; and finally books intended for the general public — what are called trade books — had a sales level of $1 billion. With its $1.5 billion sales, it is obvious that the textbook market is no small segment of the industry as a whole (Shatzkin, 1982, pp. 1–2).[7]

The increasing concentration of power in text publishing has been marked. There has been increased competition recently; but this has been among a smaller number of large firms. The competition has also reduced the propensity to take risks. Instead, many publishers now prefer to expend most of their efforts on a smaller selection of "carefully chosen products" (Coser, Kadushin, and Powell, 1982, p. 273).[8]

Perhaps the simplest way to illuminate part of this dynamic is to quote from a major figure in publishing who, after thirty-five years of involvement in the industry, reflected on the question "How competitive is book publishing?" His answer, succint and speaking paragraphs that remained implicit, was only one word — "Very" (Shatzkin, 1982, p. 63).

A picture of the nature of the concentration within text publishing can be gained from a few facts. Seventy-five percent of the total sales of college textbooks was controlled by the ten largest text publishers, with 90 percent accounted for by the top twenty. Prentice-Hall, McGraw-Hill, the CBS Publishing Group, and Scott, Foresman — the top four — accounted for 40 percent of the market (Coser, Kadushin, and Powell, 1982, p. 273). In what is called the "elhi" (elementary and high school) market, the figures are also very revealing. It is estimated that the four largest textbook publishers of these materials account for 32 percent of the market. The eight largest firms control 53 percent. And the twenty largest control over 75 percent of sales (Goldstein, 1978, p. 61). This is no small amount to be sure. Yet concentration does not tell the entire story. Internal qualities concerning who works in these firms, what their backgrounds and characteristics are, and what their working conditions happen to be also play a significant part.

What kind of people make the decisions about college and other texts? Even though many people find their way into publishing in general by accident, as it were, this is even more the case for editors who work in firms that deal with, say, college texts. "Most of them entered publishing simply because they were looking for some sort of a job, and publishing presented itself." (Coser, Kadushin, and Powell, 1982, p. 100) But these people are not all equal. Important divisions exist within the houses themselves.

In fact, one thing that recent research makes strikingly clear is the strength of sex-stereotyping in the division of labor in publishing. Women are often found in subsidiary rights and publicity departments. They are often copy editors. While they outnumber men in employment within publishing as a whole, this does not mean that they are usually a powerful overt force. Rather, they largely tend to be hired as "secretaries, assistants, publicists, advertising managers, and occupants of other low- and mid-level positions." Even though there have been a number of women who have moved into important editorial positions in the past few years, by and large women are still not as evident in positions that actually "exercise control over the goals and policy of publishing." In essence, there is something of a dual labor market in publishing. The lower-paying, replaceable jobs, with less possibility for advancement, are the characteristics of the "female enclaves" (Coser, Kadushin, and Powell, 1982, pp. 154–55).

What does this mean for this particular discussion? Nearly 75 percent of the editors in college text publishing either began their careers as sales personnel or held sales or marketing positions before being promoted to editor (Coser, Kadushin, and Powell, 1982, p. 101). Since there are many fewer women than men who travel around selling college or other level texts, or who hold positions of authority within sales departments that could lead to upward mobility, this will have an interesting effect both on the people who become editors and on the content of editorial decisions as well.

These facts have important implications. They mean that most editorial decisions concerning which texts are to be published — that is, concerning what is to count as legitimate content within particular disciplines and thus what students are to receive as "official knowledge" — are made by individuals who have specific characteristics. These editors are predominantly male, thereby reproducing patriarchal relations within the firm itself. Second, their general background will complement the existing market structure that dominates text production: financial capital, short-term perspectives, and high profit margins will be seen as major goals. A substantial cultural or educational vision, or the concerns associated with strategies based on symbolic capital, will necessarily take a back seat, where they exist at all.

The influence of profit, of the power of that they call commerce, in text production is recognized by Coser, Kadushin, and Powell. As they note about college text publishing, the major emphasis is on the production of books for introductory level courses that have high student enrolments. A good deal of attention is paid to the design of the book itself and to marketing strategies that will cause it to be used in these courses (1982, p. 30). Yet unlike most other kinds of publishing, text publishers define their markets not as the actual reader of the book but as the teacher or professor (p. 56). The purchaser, the student, has little power in this equation, except where it may influence a professor's decision.

Relying on their sense of sales potential and on "regular polling of their markets," a large percentage of college text editors actively search for books. Contacts are made, suggestions given. In essence, it would not be wrong to say that text editors create their own books (p. 135). This is probably cheaper in the long run.

In the United States it is estimated that the production costs of an introductory text for a college-level course is usually between $100,000 and $250,000. Given the fact that text publishers produce a relatively small number of books compared to large publishers of, say, fiction, there is considerable pressure on the editorial staff and others to guarantee that such books sell (pp. 56–57). For the "elhi" market, the sheer amount of money and the risks involved are made visible by the fact that even as of nearly a decade ago, for every $500,000 invested by a publisher in a text, 100,000 copies needed to be sold merely to break even (Goldstein, 1978, p. 56).

These conditions will have ramifications on the social relations within the firm besides the patriarchal structure I noted earlier. Staff meetings, meetings with other editors, meetings with marketing and production staff to coordinate the production of a text, and so on, these kinds of activities tend to dominate the life of the text editor. As Coser and his co-authors (1982, p. 123) so nicely phrase it, "text editors practically live in meetings." Hence, text publishing will be much more bureaucratic and will have more formalized decision-making structures than other publishing. This is partly due to the fact that textbook production is largely a routine process. Formats do not markedly differ from discipline to discipline. And as I mentioned, the focus is primarily on producing a limited number of large sellers at a comparatively high price compared to fiction. Last, the emphasis is often on marketing a text with a standard content, that, with revisions and a little bit of luck, will be used for years to come (Coser, Kadushin, and Powell, 1982, p. 190).

All of these elements are heightened even more in one other aspect of text publishing that contributes to bureaucratization and standardization: the orchestrated production of "managed" texts. These are volumes that are usually written by professional writers, with some "guidance" from graduate students and academics, though such volumes often bear the name of a well-known professor. Written texts and graphics are closely coordinated, as are langauge and reading levels and an instructor's manual. In many ways, these are books without formal authors. Ghostwritten under conditions of stringent cost controls, geared to what will sell and not necessarily to what it is most important to know, managed texts have been taking their place in many college classrooms. While the dreams of some publishers that such texts will solve their financial problems have not been totally realized, the managed text is a significant phenomenon and deserves a good deal of critical attention not only at the college level but in elementary and secondary schools as well, since the managed text is not at all absent in these areas, to say the least (Keith, 1981, p. 12).

Even with the difficulty some managed texts have had in making the anticipated high profits, there will probably be more centralized control over writing and over the entire process of publishing material for classroom use. The effect, according to Coser, Kadushin, and Powell, (1982, p. 366), will be "an even greater homogenization of texts at a college level," something we can expect at the elementary and high school level as well.[10]

These points demonstrate some of the important aspects of day-to-day life within publishing. With all of the meetings, the planning, the growing sampling of markets, the competition, and so forth, one would expect that this would have a profound impact on the content of volumes. This is the case, but perhaps not quite in the way one might think. We need to be very careful here about assuming that there is simple and overt censorship of material. The process is much more complicated than that. Even though existing research does not go into detail about such things within the college text industry specifically, one can infer what happens from its discussion of censorship in the industry at large.

In the increasingly conglomerate-owned publishing field, censorship and ideological control as we commonly think of them are less of a problem than might be anticipated. It is not ideological uniformity or some political agenda that accounts for many of the ideas that are ultimately made or not made available to the larger public. Rather, it is the infamous "bottom line" that counts. "Ultimately . . . if there is any censorship, it concerns profitability. Books that are not profitable, no matter what their subject, are not viewed favorably" (Coser, Kadushin, and Powell, 1982, p. 181).

This is not an inconsequential concern. In the publishing industry as a whole, only three out of every ten books are marginally profitable; only 30 percent manage to break even. The remainder lose money (Compaine, 1978, p. 20). Further, it has become clear that sales of texts in particular have actually been decreasing. If we take as a baseline the years of 1968 to, say, 1976, costs had risen considerably, but sales at a college level had fallen 10 percent. The same is true for the "elhi" text market; coupled with rising costs was a drop in sales of 11.2 percent (Compaine, 1978, pp. 33–34) (though this may have changed for the better given recent sales figures). Thus, issues of profit are in fact part of a rational set of choices within corporate logic.

If this is the case for publishing in general and probably in large part for college text production, is it generalizing to those standardized secondary and, especially, elementary textbooks I pointed to earlier? Are market, profit, and internal relations more important than ideological concerns? Here we must answer that this is so only in part.

The economics and politics of text production is somewhat more complicated when one examines what is produced for sale in our elementary and secondary schools. While there is no official federal government sponsorship of specific curriculum content in the United States in quite the same way as there is in those countries where ministries of education mandate a standard course of study, the structures of a national curriculum are produced by the marketplace and by state intervention in other ways. Perhaps the most important aspect of this is the various models of state adoption now extant.

In many states — most often in the southern tier around to the western sunbelt — textbooks for use in the major subject areas must be approved by state agencies or committees. Or they are reviewed and a limited number are selected as recommended for use in schools. If local school districts select material from such an approved list, they are often reimbursed for a significant portion of the purchase cost. Because of this, even where texts are not mandated, there is a good deal to be gained by local schools in a time of economic crisis if they do in fact ultimately choose an approved volume. The cost savings here are obviously not inconsequential.

Yet it is not only here that the economics of cultural distribution operates. Publishers themselves, simply because of good business practice, must by necessity aim their text publishing practices towards those states with such state adoption policies. The simple fact of getting one's volume on such a list can mean all the difference in a text's profitability. Thus, for instance, sales to California and Texas can account for over 20 percent of the total sales of any particular book, a considerable percentage in the highly competitive world of elementary and secondary school book publishing and selling. Due to this, the writing, editing, promotion, and general orientation and strategy of such production is quite often aimed towards the goal of guaranteeing a place on the list of state-approved material. Since this is the case, the political and ideological climate of these primarily southern states often determines the content and form of the purchased curriculum throughout the rest of the nation. And since a textbook series often takes years to both write and produce and, as I noted earlier, can be very costly when production costs are totaled up, "publishers want assurance of knowing that their school book series will sell before they commit large budgets to these undertakings" (Keith, 1981, p. 8).

Yet even here the situation is considerably complicated, especially by the fact that agencies of the state apparatus are important sites of ideological struggle. These very conflicts may make it very difficult for publishers to determine a simple reading of the needs of "financial capital." Often, for instance, given the uncertainty of a market, publishers may be loath to make decisions based on the political controversies or "needs" of any one state, especially in highly charged curriculum areas. A good example is provided by the California creationism versus evolutionism controversy, where a group of "scientific creationists," supported by the political and ideological right, sought to have all social studies and science texts give equal weight to creationist and evolutionary theories.

Even when California's Board of Education, after much agonizing and debate, recommended "editorial qualifications" that were supposed to meet the objections of creationist critics of the textbooks, the framework for text adoption was still very unclear and subject to many different interpretations. Did it require or merely allow discussion of creation theory? Was a series of editorial changes that qualified the discussions of evolution in the existing texts all that was required? Given this ambiguity and the volatility of the issue in which the "winning position" was unclear, publishers "resisted undertaking the more substantial effort of incorporating new information into their materials" (Goldstein, 1978, p. 47). In the words of one observer of the process: "Faced with an unclear directive, and one that might be reversed at any moment, publishers were reluctant to invest in change. They eventually yielded to the minor editorial adjustments adopted by the board, but staunchly resisted the requirment that they discuss creation in their social science texts" (Goldstein, 1978, pp. 48–49). Both economic and ideological forces enter here in important ways, both between the firms and their markets and undoubtedly within the firms themselves.

Notice what this means if we are to fully understand how specific cultural goods are produced and distributed for our public schools. We would need to unpack the logic of a fairly complicated set of interrelationships. How does the political economy of publishing itself generate particular economic and ideological needs? How and why do publishers respond to the needs of the "public"? Who determines what this "public" is?[11] How do the internal politics of state adoption policies work? What are the processes of selection of people and interests to sit on such committees? How are texts sold at a local level? What is the actual process of text production from the commissioning of a project to revisions and editing to promotion and sales? How and for what reasons are decisions on this made? Only by going into considerable detail on each of these questions can we begin to see how the cultural capital of particular groups is commodified and made available (or not made available) in schools throughout the country.[12]

My discussion of the issues of state adoption policies and my raising of the questions above are not meant to imply that all of the material found in our publich schools will be simply a reflection of existing cultural and economic inequalities. After all, if texts were totally reliable defenders of the existing ideological, political, and economic order, they would not currently be such a contentious area. Industry and conservative groups have made an issue of what knowledge is now taught in schools precisely because there *are* progressive elements within curricula and texts (Apple, 1982c, chap. 5). This is partly due to the fact that the authorship of such material is often done by a particular segment of the new petty bourgeoisie with its own largely liberal ideological interests, its own contradictory consciousness, its own elements of what Gramsci might call "good and bad sense," interests that will not be identical with those embodied in profit maximization or ideological uniformity. To speak theoretically, there will be relatively autonomous interests in specific cultural values within the groups of authors and editors who work for publishers. These values may be a bit more progressive than one might anticipate from the market structure of text production. This will surely have an impact against total standardization and censorship.[13]

These kinds of issues concerning who writes and edits texts, whether they are totally controlled by the complicated market relations and state policies surrounding text publishing, and what the contradictory forces at work are, all clearly need further elaboration. My basic aim has been to demonstrate how recent research on the ways in which culture is commodified can serve as a platform for thinking about some of our own dilemmas as teachers and researchers in education concerned with the dynamics of cultural capital.

III

So far, I have employed some of the research on book publishing to help understand an issue that is of great import to educators — how and by whom the texts that dominate the curriculum come to be the way they are. As I mentioned at the very outset of this essay, however, we need to see such analyses as constituting a serious contribution to a larger theoretical debate about cultural processes and products as well. In this concluding section, let me try to make this part of my argument about the political economy of culture clear.

External economic and political pressures are not somewhere "out there" in some vague abstraction called the economy. As recent commentators have persuasively argued, in our society hegemonic forms are not often imposed from outside by a small group of corporate owners who sit around each day plotting how to do in workers, women, and people of color. Some of this plotting may go on of course. But just as significant are the routine grounds of our daily decisions, in our homes, stores, offices, and factories. To speak somewhat technically, dominant relations are ongoingly reconstituted by the actions we take and the decisions we make in our own local and small areas of life. Rather than an economy being out there, it is right here. We rebuild it routinely in our social interaction. Rather than ideological domination and the relations of cultural capital being something we have imposed on us from above, we reintegrate them within our everday discourse merely by following our commonsense needs and desires as we go about making a living, finding entertainment and sustenance, and so on.[14]

These arguments are abstract, but they are important to the points I want to make. For while a serious theoretical structure is either absent from or is often hidden within the data presented by the research I have drawn on, a good deal of this research does document some of the claims I made in the above paragraph. As the authors of *Books* put in their discussion of why particular decisions are made:

> For the most part, what directly affects an editor's daily routine is not corporate ownership or being one division of a large multi-divisional publishing house.

Instead, on a day-to-day basis, editorial behavior is most strongly influenced by the editorial policies of the house and the relationship among departments and personnel within the publishing house or division. [Coser, Kadushin, and Powell, 1982, p. 185]

This position may not seem overly consequential, yet its theoretic import is great. Encapsulated within a changing set of market relations that set limits on what is considered rational behavior on the part of its participants, editors and other employees have "relative autonomy." They are partly free to pursue the internal need of their craft and to follow the logic of the internal demands within the publishing house itself. The past histories of gender, class, and race relations and the actual "local" political economy of publishing set the boundaries within which these decisions are made and in large part detemine who will make the decisions. To return to my earlier point about text editors usually having their prior roots in sales, we can see that the internal labor market in text publishing, the ladder on which career mobility depends, means that sales will be in the forefront ideologically and economically in these firms. "Finance capital" dominates, not only because the economy out there mandates it, but because of the historical connections among the mobility patterns within firms, rational decision making based on external competition, political dynamics, and internal information, and, because of these things, the kinds of discourse that tend to dominate the meetings and conversations among all the people involved within the organizational structure of the text publishers.[15] This kind of analysis makes it more complicated, of course. But surely it is more elegant and more grounded in reality than some of the more mechanistic theories about the economic control of culture that have been a bit too readily accepted. It manages to preserve the efficacy of the economy while granting some autonomy to the internal bureaucratic and biographical structure of individual publishers, while at the same time recognizing the political economy of gendered labor that exists as well.

Many areas remain that I have not focused on here, of course. Among the most important of these is the alteration in the very technology of publishing. Just as the development and use of print "made possible the growth of literary learning and journals" and thereby helped create the conditions for individual writers and artists to emerge out of the more collective conditions of production that dominated guilds and workshops, so too one would expect that the changes in the technology of text production and the altered social and authorial relations that are evolving from them will also have a serious impact on books. At the very least, given the sexual division of labor in publishing, new technologies can have a large bearing on the deskilling and reskilling of those "female enclaves" I mentioned earlier.[16]

Further, even though I have directed my attention primarily to the "culture and commerce" surrounding the production of one particular cultural commodity — the standardized text used for tertiary and "elhi"-level courses — it still remains an open question as to how exactly the economic and ideological elements I have outlined actually work through some of the largest of all text markets: those found in the elementary and secondary schools. However, in order to go significantly further we clearly need a more adequate theory of the relationship between the political and economic (to say nothing of the cultural) spheres in education. Thus, the state's position as a site for class, race, and gender conflicts, how these struggles are "resolved" within the state apparatus, how publishers respond to these conflicts and resolutions, and ultimately what impact these resolutions or accords have on the questions surrounding officially sponsored texts and knowledge, all of these need considerably more deliberation. (See Apple, 1982c; Dale et al., 1981; Apple, 1982a) Carnoy's and Dale's recent work on the interrelation between education and the state and Offe's analyses of the state's role in negative selection may provide important avenues here.[17]

This points to a significant empirical agenda, as well. What is required now is a long-term *and* theoretically and politically grounded ethnographic investigation that follows a curriculum artifact such as a textbook from its writing to its selling (and then to its use). Not only would this be a major contribution to our understanding of the relationship between culture, politics, and economy, it is also absolutely essential if we are to act in ways that alter the kinds of knowledge considered legitimate for transmission in our schools.[18] As long as the text dominates curricula, to ignore it as simply not worthy of serious attention is to live in a world divorced from reality.

NOTES

1. I have described this in more detail in Apple (1982b). For further analysis of this, see Williams (1977), Sumner (1979), Cohen (1978), and Hirst (1979).

2. See Gitlin (1982). The British journal, *Screen*, has been in the forefront of such analysis. See also Wright (1975). An even greater number of investigations of literature exist, of course. For representative approaches see Eagleton (1976).

3. It is important to realize, however, that educational institutions are *not* merely engaged in transmission or distribution. They are also primary sites for the *production* of technical/administrative knowledge. The contradiction between distribution and production is one of the constitutive tensions educational institutions must try to solve; up till now they have usually been unsuccessful. For arguments about the school's role in the production of cultural capital, see Apple (1982c, esp. chap. 2).

4. For an analysis of recent theoretical and empirical work on the connections between education and cultural, economic, and political power, see Apple (1982c).

5. I do not want to ignore the importance of the massive number of textbook analyses that concern themselves with, say, racism and sexism. These are significant, but are usually limited to the question of balance in content, not the relationship between economic and cultural power. Some of the best analyses of the content and form of educational materials can be found in Apple and Weis (1983). See also Keith (1981).

6. As Febvre and Martin (1976) make clear, however, in the fifteenth and sixteenth centuries, printers and publishers did act as well as "the protectors of literary men," published daring books, and frequently sheltered authors accused of heresy. See p. 150.

7. For estimated figures for years beyond 1980, see Dessauer (1982).

8. While I shall be focusing on text production here, we should not assume that texts are the only books used in elementary, secondary, and college markets. The expanding market of other material can have a strong influence in publishing decisions. In fact, some mass-market paperbacks are clearly prepared with both school and college sales in the forefront of the publishers' decisions. Thus, it is not unusual for publishers to produce a volume with very different covers depending on the audience for which it is aimed. See Compaine (1978).

9. Coser, Kadushin, and Powell (1982, p. 113), however, do report that most editors, no matter what kind of house they work for, tend to be overwhelmingly liberal.

10. I have discussed this at greater length in Apple (1983a).

11. For an interesting discussion of how economic needs help determine what counts as the public for which a specific cultural product is aimed, see the treatment of changes in the radio sponsorship of country music in Peterson (1978). See also DiMaggio and Useem (1982).

12. I have discussed the relationship between the commodification process and the dynamics of cultural capital at greater length in Apple (1982c).

13. A related argument is made in Kellner (1981). See also Wexler (1982).

14. This is discussed in greater detail in Apple (1982b).

15. Wexler's (1982) argument that texts need to be seen as the result of a long process of transformative activity is clearly related here. In essence, what I have been attempting to demonstrate is part of the structure in which such transformations occur and which makes some more likely to occur than others.

16. The relationship between deskilling, reskilling, and the sexual division of labor is treated in more depth in Apple (1983). See also Gordon, Edwards, and Reich (1982).

17. I am indebted to Dan Liston (1982) for documenting the possible power of Offe's work. See also Dale (1982), Carnoy (1982), and Apple (1982b).

18. I do not want to imply that what is "transmitted" in schools is necessarily what is in the text. Nor do I want to claim at all that what is taught is wholly "taken in" by students. For analyses of teacher and student rejection, mediation, or transformation of the form and/or content of curriculum see Willis (1977), Everhart

(1983), Apple (1983), and the chapters by Linda McNeil, Andrew Gitlin, and Lois Weis in Apple and Weis (1983).

REFERENCES

Apple, M. *Ideology and Curriculum*. Boston: Routledge and Kegan Paul, 1979.

Apple, M.W. "Common Curriculum and State Control," *Discourse* 2: 4 (1982): 1–10.(a)

Apple, M.W. (ed.). *Cultural and Economic Reproduction in Education: Essays on Class, Ideology and the State*. Boston: Routledge and Kegan Paul, 1982.(b)

Apple, M.W. *Education and Power*. Boston: Routledge and Kegan Paul, 1982.(c)

Apple, M.W. "Curriculum in the Year 2000: Tensions and Possibilities." *Phi Delta Kappan* 64 (January 1983): 321–26.(a)

Apple, M.W. "Work, Gender and Teaching," *Teachers College Record* 84 (Spring 1983): 611–28.(b)

Apple, M.W., and L. Weis (eds.). *Ideology and Practice in Schooling*. Philadelphia: Temple University Press, 1983.

Bernstein, B. *Class, Codes and Control, Volume 3*. Boston: Routledge and Kegan Paul, 1977.

Bourdieu, P., and J.C. Passeron. *Reproduction in Education, Society and Culture*. Beverly Hills, Calif.: Sage, 1977.

Carnoy, M. "Education, Economy and the State." In M.W. Apple (ed.), *Cultural and Economic Reproduction in Education: Essays on Class, Ideology and the State*. Boston: Routledge and Kegan Paul, 1982.

Cohen, G.A. *Karl Marx's Theory of History: A Defense*. Princeton, N.J.: Princeton University Press, 1978.

Compaine, B.M. *The Book Industry in Transition: An Economic Study of Book Distribution and Marketing*. White Plains, New York: Knowledge Industry Publications, 1978.

Coser, L., C. Kadushin, and W. Powell. *Books: The Culture and Commerce of Publishing*. New York: Basic Books, 1982.

Dale, R. "Education and the Capitalist State: Contributions and Contradictions." In M.W. Apple, *Cultural and Economic Reproduction in Education: Essays on Class, Ideology and the State*. Boston: Routledge and Kegan Paul, 1982.

Dale, R., G. Esland, R. Furguson, and M. MacDonald (eds.). *Education and the State, Volume I*. Barcombe, Eng.: The Falmer Press, 1981.

Dessauer, J.P. *Book Industry Trends, 1982*. New York: Book Industry Study Group, Inc., 1982.

DiMaggio, P., and M. Useem. "The Arts in Class Reproduction." In M. Apple (ed.), *Cultural and Economic Reproduction in Education: Essays on Class, Ideology and the State*. Boston: Routledge and Kegan Paul, 1982.

Eagleton, T. *Marxism and Literary Criticism*. Berkeley, Calif.: University of California Press, 1976.

Everhart, R. *Reading, Writing and Resistance*. Boston: Routledge and Kegan Paul, 1983.

Febvre, L., and H.J. Martin. *The Coming of the Book*. London: New Left Books, 1976.

Gitlin, T. "Television's Screens: Hegemony in Transition." In M.W. Apple (ed.), *Cultural and Economic Reproduction in Education: Essays on Class, Ideology and the State*. Boston: Routledge and Kegan Paul, 1982.

Goldstein, P. *Changing the American Schoolbook*. Lexington, Mass.: D.C. Heath, 1978.

Goodlad, J.I. *A Place Called School*. New York: McGraw-Hill, 1983.

Gordon, D., R. Edwards, and M. Reich. *Segmented Work, Divided Workers: The Historical Transformation of Labor in the United States*. New York: Cambridge University Press, 1982.

Hirst, P. *On Law and Ideology*. London: Macmillan, 1979.

Keith, S. "Politics of Textbook Selection." Institute on Educational Finance and Governance, Stanford University, April 1981.

Kellner, D. "Network Television and American Society," *Theory and Society* 10 (January 1981): 31–62.

Liston, D. "Have We Explained the Relationship Between Curriculum and Capitalism? *Educational Theory* (1982).

Peterson, R.A. "The Production of Cultural Change: The Case of Contemporary Country Music," *Social Research* 45 (Summer 1978): 292–314.

Shatzkin, L. *In Cold Type*. Boston: Houghton and Mifflin, 1982.

Sumner, C. *Reading Ideologies*. New York: Macmillan, 1979.

Wexler, P. "Structure, Text and Subject: A Critical Sociology of School Knowledge." In M.W. Apple (ed.), *Cultural and Economic Reproduction in Education: Essays on Class, Ideology and the State*. Boston: Routledge and Kegan Paul, 1982.

Williams, R. *Marxism and Literature*. New York: Oxford University Press, 1977.

Willis, P. *Learning to Labour*. Westmead, Eng.: Saxon House, 1977.

Wolff, J. *The Social Production of Art*. London: Macmillan, 1981.

Wright, W. *Sixguns and Society*. Berkeley: University of California Press, 1975.

Selection 4.5

Sophie and Emile: A Case Study of Sex Bias in the History of Educational Thought

Jane Roland Martin

Standard texts in the history of educational thought teach that Rousseau's philosophy of education emphasizes the concept of nature (Ulich, 1945, 1948; Brumbaugh and Lawrence, 1963; Rusk, 1965; Nash, Kazamias, and Perkinson, 1965; Price, 1967; Nash, 1968; and Cahn, 1970). These texts tells us that Rousseau proposes an education that follows nature, one that trusts the child's spontaneous impulses and allows for natural development. They tell us that the ideal of the educated person Rousseau embraces is that of natural man, that he stresses the common nature of mankind, and that the objective he sets for education is the liberty and happiness of the individual. Above all, they suggest that Rousseau's guiding metaphor is growth: he conceives of the child as a plant whose course of development is determined by nature, and of the educator as a gardener whose task is to ensure that corrupt society does not interfere with that predetermined pattern of development.

I will argue that Rousseau's many references to nature have misled his interpreters and that the model of education Rousseau adopts is one of production, not growth. In the introduction to his translation of *Emile*, Allan Bloom remarked that of Rousseau's major works *Emile* is the least studied and discussed (1979, p. 4). He is certainly right that *Emile* deserves

---

SOURCE. Reprinted from Harvard Educational Review 51: 3 (August 1981): 357–72.

closer attention than it now receives from philosophers and political theorists. Historians of educational thought, however, have given the first four books of *Emile*, in which Rousseau discusses the education of boys, their due. Their mistake has been to slight Book V of *Emile* containing Rousseau's account of the education of girls. Had interpreters of his educational philosophy taken seriously what he says there, they might have seen through the language of nature.

Although it is much more than a treatise on education, *Emile* sets forth in loving detail what should constitute the education of Emile, who presumably represents Everyboy, from birth to manhood. That it also sets forth the education of Sophie, Emile's "intended" and presumably Everygirl, is something the standard texts in the field scarcely acknowledge. Some of the best-known anthologies of historical philosophers of education present Emile's education as Rousseau's ideal for both sexes, and never mention Book V.[1] The texts that mention the education to be given Sophie do so with embarrassment, stating only that Sophie's education is to be very different from Emile's (See Brumbaugh and Lawrence, 1963; Nash, 1968; Rusk, 1965; and Archer, 1964.)[2]

Sophie causes historians of educational thought acute discomfort because their interpretation of Rousseau cannot handle her. The education of Sophie is an anomaly relative to the standard interpretation of *Emile*: her education cannot be explained by an interpretation that abstracts education from societal influences and constraints and that pictures it as a process of natural growth and development. The fundamental assumptions Rousseau makes in *Emile* V constitute a *production model of education*. What Sophie is to become is determined not by her nature, as the standard growth interpretation of *Emile* requires, but by the role she is to play in society. Small wonder that historians of educational thought ignore Sophie or dismiss her as an aberration. Rousseau's account of Sophie's education raises questions about the interpretation of *Emile* to which they subscribe.

An adequate interpretation of Rousseau must take into account both Emile and Sophie. Since Rousseau says very different things about their education, there are two distinct approaches to take if one acknowledges the importance of *Emile* V. One approach is to attribute to Rousseau two different conflicting conceptions of education — a growth or natural model for Emile and a production model for Sophie. The other is to attribute to Rousseau a single conception of education. I argue that Rousseau makes the same fundamental assumptions about the education of Sophie and Emile, and that the standard interpretation of his educational philosophy is not only unable to explain what he says about Sophie, but is inadequate even as an interpretation of his account of Emile.

In her important book, *Women in Western Political Thought*, Susan

Moller Okin (1979) has devoted several chapters to Rousseau's theories. She claims that Rousseau makes fundamentally different assumptions about the education of Emile and Sophie. Okin exposes the sex bias in Rousseau's account of Sophie, and Lynda Lange (1979b), in her essay, "Rousseau: Women and the General Will," reveals the sex bias in his political philosophy. (See also Christianson, 1972; Wexler, 1976; and Eisenstein, 1981, chap. 4) Rousseau's philosophy of education and his political philosophy are closely connected, and the sex bias to be found in the one is the counterpart of the sex bias in the other. This essay is only indirectly concerned with Rousseau's own sex bias, however; its primary target is the bias exhibited by the discipline of educational thought in its interpretation of Rousseau's masterpiece. When the discipline of the history of educational thought ignores the writings of one of the few truly significant philosophers who have discussed the education of women, one can only conclude that this issue is not considered an integral part of its subject matter. Sophie and Emile constitute a case study of sex bias, not because historians of educational thought have said hostile things about Sophie, and through her about women generally, but because they have not even considered her important enough to be discussed at all.

PLATO'S PRODUCTION MODEL OF EDUCATION

Allan Bloom has çompared *Emile* to Plato's *Republic*, which Rousseau considered "the most beautiful educational treatise ever written" (1979, p. 40). In that work Plato made fundamental assumptions that, taken together, constitute a production model of education. He arrives at his conception of the Just State through a thought experiment in which Socrates and his companions purport to think away existing institutions and imagine the birth of a city. They start with the principle, enunciated by Socrates, that "not one of us is self-sufficient, but needs many things" (Plato, 1974, p. 369b). Implicit in this principle is the assumption that each person is guided by self-interest and that it is in the self-interest of each to share with others (p. 369c). The question that then arises is whether people will specialize — one person, for example, producing enough food for everyone and another making clothes — or whether they will simply help one another when necessary while remaining as self-sufficient as possible (p. 370a).

At this point in the thought experiment, Socrates introduces an assumption about human nature that is basic to his theory of education. Each one of us, Socrates says, is born more apt for one task than another (p. 370b). This "Postulate of Specialized Natures" must not be understood as attributing to each individual at birth the knowledge of how to perform a specific task. We come equipped with an aptitude for one task above all others, but the skill, knowledge, and traits of character required for performing that task must be acquired. While an individual's specific nature can flourish or, alternatively, be stunted, a person cannot in midlife acquire some new aptitude that supplants the original one. Different aptitudes or talents are distributed over the population as a whole, not over an individual's life.

The Postulate of Specialized Natures does not in itself answer the question of whether people will specialize. To it, however, he adds an assumption about efficiency. Both production and quality are improved, he says, when individuals practice the one craft for which they are by nature most suited rather than several (p. 370b–c). Yet even this assumption does not yield the answer Socrates gives to his own question. He chooses specialization as the recommended mode of production in the Just State because it is, in his view, the most efficient and because he values efficiency (Lange, 1979a).

As it stands, the Postulate of Specialized natures is purely formal; it does not specify the aptitudes or talents people have at birth. Socrates gives this postulate substance in his thought experiment, not, as one might expect, through a close inspection of human nature, but rather by examining the needs of society. From the beginning, a city will need farmers, builders, weavers, cobblers and metal workers, cowherds and shepherds, merchants, and sailors. Eventually it will need also warriors and rulers. Socrates builds up in his imagination a city that constitutes Plato's Just State. Socrates discerns the needs of this Just State and then designs human nature so that it fits them.[3] To suppose that he discerns certain natural talents or aptitudes in people and then designs a state that is to fit them is to get things backwards.

Socrates assumes a one-to-one relationship between human nature and societal roles. This "Postulate of Correspondence" is crucial for Plato's theory of the Just State.[4] He identifies three kinds of jobs to be done in the State — artisan (farmer, builder, and so on), auxiliary (warrior), and ruler — and he defines justice as everyone doing precisely that job for which their nature suits them.

Now, since justice requires that each individual perform one and only one job in society and since Socrates assumes that no person is able to do from birth, or simply by maturing, the task for which that person is naturally suited, the role of education in Plato's Just State becomes apparent. Education must equip people with knowledge, skill, and traits of character that will enable them to perform the societal tasks for which nature suits them.

Plato's conception is a production model of education par excellence. Like all raw material, human beings are malleable, but they do have certain fixed talents or aptitudes set by nature. The task of education is to turn this raw material into a finished product — more precisely, into one of three finished products. The particular product is a matter of discovery for the educator rather than a decision, since it is set by nature. The composition of the raw material is a given and so are the specifications for the three kinds of end product. Though Plato recommends that young children be allowed to play (Plato, 1974, p. 337a), this concesson to freedom should not be interpreted as a denial that the educator's role is to produce certain predetermined individuals. Children move about freely and play so that their true natures will reveal themselves. Once their natures are discovered, the production of artisans, auxiliaries, and rulers can begin.

Plato's conception is not a production model *simpliciter*, however. The task of education is not simply to produce three kinds of people, but to produce people who will fill certain necesssary roles in society. There is, in other words, a "Functional Postulate" implicit in the account of education contained in the *Republic*. Education is conceived of as a servant of the state whose function, for justice to prevail, is to equip the individuals born into it to perform their preassigned functions.

While education plays a key role in Plato's Just State, Socrates simplifies the educator's task enormously by assuming that to perform the same task, people must have the same education (the "Postulate of Identity") and that to perform different tasks they must have a different education (the "Postulate of Difference") (p. 452a). He directs educators to ignore individual differences, except for the inborn talents that fit people to one societal role rather than another. These postulates lead to three separate curricula — for artisans, auxiliaries, and rulers — but one, and only one, version of each.

THE EDUCATION OF SOPHIE

"It is not good for a man to be alone. Emile is a man. We have promised him a companion. She has to be given to him. That companion is Sophie. In what place is her abode? Where shall we find her? To find her, it is necessary to know her. Let us first learn what she is; then we shall better judge what places she inhabits" (p. 357). So begins *Emile*, Book V.

"Everything that characterizes the fair sex ought to be respected as established by nature," Rousseau says (p. 363). As Book V proceeds, however, it becomes clear that in attributing traits to Sophie and calling them "natural," Rousseau is selective. What exactly are Sophie's characteristics? She has an agreeable and nimble mind (p. 364), a mind for details rather than general principles (p. 377). She loves adornment (p. 365), guile is a natural talent of hers (p. 370), and the art of coquetry is born with her (p. 385). Rousseau does not envision these or Sophie's other natural characteristics as emerging full-blown at birth, though he says that her love of adornment finds expression almost from birth in an attraction to jewels, mirrors, dresses, and dolls to dress up (p. 367). Like Plato's future guardians (his auxiliaries and rulers), in whom the traits of fierceness and gentleness develop over time, Sophie's natural qualities are simply aptitudes that require training and education so that they will be neither stunted nor abused.

In Sophie's case, Rousseau clearly embraces the Postulate of Specialized Natures: Sophie's nature is for him as inborn, fixed, and specific as the natures of the inhabitants of the Just State are for Plato. Rousseau also embraces the Postulate of Correspondence: Sophie's nature suits her for one and only one role in society, namely, that of wife and mother.[5] Sophie's proper purpose, Rousseau says, is to produce not just a few, but many children (p. 362). If this appears to be a biological, rather than a societal, role for Sophie to play, let it be understood that she must also give the children she bears to her husband; that is to say, she must make it clear to him and the world through her modesty, attentiveness, reserve, and care for his reputation that they are his (p. 361). The unfaithful woman, Rousseau says, "dissolves the family and breaks the bonds of nature. In giving the man children which are not his, she betrays both" (p. 361). Thus Sophie is destined to be not simply the bearer of children, but the preserver of family bonds. She is destined also to govern her husband's household (p. 384), oversee his garden (p. 385), act as his hostess (p. 383), raise his children (p. 361), and, above all, please him (p. 358). In sum, she is to play the traditional female role in the traditional patriarchal family.

Rousseau speaks the language of nature, but his conception of education is, like Plato's, that of production. For Rousseau, Sophie is raw material to be turned by education into a finished product. The basic structure of Rousseau's account of the education of Sophie is identical to that of Plato's account of the education of artisans, auxiliaries, and rulers. The task of Sophie's education is to equip her for her societal role. "Whether I consider the particular purpose of the fair sex, whether I observe its inclinations, whether I consider its duties, all join equally in indicating to me the form of education that suits it" (p. 364). Thus Rousseau embraces the Functional Postulate as well as the Postulates of Specialized Natures and of Correspondence. And when he says, "Once it is demonstrated that man and woman are not and ought not to be constituted in the same way in either character or temperament, it follows that they ought not to have the same education" (p. 363), it becomes quite clear that he also embraces Plato's Postulates of Identity and Difference. Since for

Plato societal roles correspond to people's natures, he ultimately connects educational treatment with people's natures, and that is what Rousseau does when he prescribes different educational treatment for Sophie and Emile.

Rousseau repeatedly refers to nature in Book V of *Emile*, yet if a growth conception of education was implicit in his account of Sophie, he would not devote the attention he does to the possibility of Sophie's acquiring characteristics that he claims are not hers by nature. For one who directs his readers time and again to follow nature, Rousseau is inordinately concerned that Sophie might become something other than the obedient wife and nurturant mother he wants her to be. Will Sophie "be nurse today and warrior tomorrow?" Rousseau asks. "Will she suddenly go from shade, enclosure, and domestic cares to the harshness of the open air, the labors, the fatigues, and the perils of war?" (p. 362). Not if Rousseau has his way, but the very questions acknowledge that she might, were her education not strictly supervised. "To cultivate man's qualities in women and to neglect those which are proper to them is obviously to work their detriment," he continues (p. 364). In Rousseau's concern to tell mothers not to make men out of their daughters, a production interpretation of his theory of education finds its vindication.

As Rousseau conceives of Sophie, she is born with a wide range of capacities. In attributing certain qualities to her nature, he is selective. The traits he calls natural are those that in his view should be developed, but they are certainly not the only ones that could be developed. Because Sophie can acquire any number of traits that Rousseau would rather women not possess, it is not plausible to attribute to him a growth conception of education for women in which the teacher is viewed simply as a gardener. A gardener provides the proper conditions for a plant to flourish. In contrast, Rousseau's educator must attend to every detail of Sophie's education so that the traits inappropriate to the role of wife and mother within a patriarchal context are frustrated. Rousseau appeals to nature, but he does not trust it; on the contrary, he insists that positive steps be taken to shape and form Sophie to meet clearly defined specifications.

THE DIFFERENCE OF SEX

Plato set forth his thoughts on the education of women in Book V of the *Republic*. Rousseau set forth his in Book V of *Emile*. Plato argues that being male or female is like being bald or hairy: it is a difference of no consequence in determining whether or not a person belongs to the guardian class in the Just State, and so it makes no difference in determining the education an individual should receive (p. 454b–e). In *Emile* V

Rousseau argues that being male or female is a difference of consequence in determining a person's place in society (pp. 357ff); indeed, a close reading of Book V suggests that he believes that sex is the only difference that makes a difference. "Sophie ought to be a woman as Emile is a man," Rousseau says. "That is to say, she ought to have everything which suits the constitution of her species and her sex in order to fill her place in the physical and moral order" (p. 357). The implications of this statement are clear: Sophie has one place to fill, Emile another, and their education ought to equip them for their respective places. Since the places of the two sexes are different, it seems evident to Rousseau that the education each is to receive must be different.

The objective of the education Plato would provide women — at least those who by nature are suited to be guardians in his Just State — is to develop reason in order to grasp the most general principles and ultimately discern the Good, so that the individual can rule herself and her fellow citizens. The education Rousseau would provide women could not be more dissimilar. Sophie, the prototype of women, is to be educated not to rule, but to obey. She is to learn to be modest, attentive, and reserved (p. 361); to sew, embroider, and make lace (p. 368). Works of genius are out of her reach, Rousseau says (p. 386), nor does she have the precision and attention to succeed at the exact sciences (p. 387).

The question naturally arises of how such radically different accounts of the education of women could be given by philosophers who make the same fundamental assumptions about education. The answer lies in the fact that the postulates of the model of education that Plato and Rousseau both embrace are purely formal and that they give them different content. Plato posits three distinct societal roles and maps them onto human nature by attributing to people at birth the aptitudes for the traits and skills that he associates with each role. In his account of the education of Sophie, Rousseau does the same thing, but instead of singling out for Sophie one of Plato's three roles, he selects the traditional female role in a patriarchal society and imposes its associated traits and skills on her nature. The education Sophie receives has to be different from that of the future female guardians in Plato's Just State. Their nature suits them to rule the state: Sophie's suits her to obey her husband.

Why do Plato and Rousseau give such radically different content to the postulates of the production model of education? There are two separate, but related, answers to this question. In Book V of the *Republic* Plato abolishes private property and the family and institutes instead communal living and childrearing arrangements (pp. 457d, 458d, 462b–d). Therefore, there is for him no traditional female role of wife and mother to map onto human nature. Second, Plato argues that sex is not a determinant of a person's nature (455e). Rousseau consciously rejects both these elements of Plato's philosophy. He argues that if the family is removed from society, the bonds of love that Plato wants to establish among members of the guardian class, as well as the attachment he wants them to have for the state, cannot develop. It is "by means of the small fatherland which is the family that the heart attaches itself to the large one," Rousseau says (p. 363). He also maintains that sex is the determinant of a person's nature.

THE EDUCATION OF EMILE FOR CITIZENSHIP

One of Okin's major conclusions about Rousseau is that his definition of Emile's nature is an open-ended one while Sophie "is defined in a totally teleological way, in terms of what is perceived to be her purpose in life" (1979, p. 135). She is certainly right about Sophie. Sophie is made to obey Emile: "To please men, to be useful to them, to make herself loved and honored by them, to raise them when young, to care for them when grown, to counsel them, to console them, to make their lives agreeable and sweet — these are the duties of women at all times and they ought to be taught from childhood" (p. 365). Rousseau says that Sophie has a place to fill in the "physical and moral order." In truth, the place he assigns her falls squarely within the social order.

Okin's thesis that Rousseau uses a double standard in defining male and female natures explains what appear to be two separate strands in Rosseau's educational philosophy: a production model for Sophie and a growth model for Emile. She points out that scholars have acknowledged that the education Rousseau proposes for women "is based on principles that are in direct and basic conflict with those that underlie his proposals for the education of men" (1979, p. 135).

A dualistic interpretation enables one to understand why Book V of *Emile* has caused discomfort to historians of educational thought. They have treated Rousseau as an educational monist whose underlying model is one of natural growth and development. In relation to this interpretation, the education of Sophie is anomalous. There is, however, an alternative monistic interpretation of Rousseau's educational thought that explains both Sophie's and Emile's education. It has the advantage of being able to show that the differences Rousseau insists on in the education of males and females are matters of detail rather than conflicting or contradictory principles. The unified interpretation I propose is that the production model of education presupposed by Rousseau in his account of the education of Sophie underlies his account of the education of Emile as well.

At the beginning of Book I of *Emile*, Rousseau says that on leaving his hands the pupil will be neither magistrate nor soldier nor priest; rather he will be a man (pp. 41–42). If we take Rousseau at his word, we must conclude that a narrow, vocational mold is not to be imposed on Emile. It does not follow, however, that Rousseau places no mold on him at all. Despite the imagery of plants and shrubs, Emile's tutor is not to allow each and every aspect of his potential to flourish: Rousseau wants Emile to be a particular sort of man and he would have the tutor arrange every detail of Emile's education toward that end. The person Emile is to be is a morally autonomous individual: a rational man who joins thought and action, whose judgments are objective, and whose beliefs are formed independently of others. Trained early to be as self-sufficient as possible — "Let the child do nothing on anybody's word" (p. 178) — it is no accident that the first book Emile is allowed to read is *Robinson Crusoe* (p. 184).

The mold Rousseau imposes on Emile of the rational, moral, autonomous individual may seem to be quite independent of any role or function Emile is supposed to play in society. In fact, however, it matches Rousseau's definition of the most important role of all, namely that of citizen in his ideal city state. *The Social Contract* enables one to understand how Rousseau solves the problem he posed at the beginning of *Emile* — of educating Emile to be at one and the same time an autonomous man and a citizen. How can a person be free, Rousseau wants to know, if the person is a member of a civil society and hence subject to its laws? Rousseau's solution to this problem is to be found in his concept of the General Will. In contrast to what Rousseau calls the Will of All, which is simply the sum of the private wills of all citizens and as such disregards the common good, the General Will has the common good as its object. It is the result of independent deliberation by citizens who are rational, impartial, and sufficiently informed about the issues (Rousseau, 1947, Book II, ch. 2ff). Individual autonomy and obedience to law are reconciled in Rousseau's ideal state because the laws of that state are expressions of the General Will and because each citizen participates in that Will. The laws that each citizen must obey and that seem to limit individual freedom are enactments of the cool, objective deliberations about the common good. Thus, in obeying the laws of the state, each citizens governs himself. Freedom is therefore preserved even as the state rules its subjects (Rousseau, 1947, p. 19). Moreover, since for Rousseau the General Will is always right, the moral integrity of the individual, as well as the individual's autonomy, is preserved in the state. Small wonder Bloom says that Emile is, in effect, taught *The Social Contract* (Bloom, 1979, p. 27; see also Pamenatz, 1972; p. 326; Masters, 1968, p. 42; Broom, 1963, chap. 5). In educating Emile to be a man, Rousseau is really equipping him with the traits and skills that a citizen in his ideal state must have in order to participate in the General Will.

The function Rousseau assigns to Sophie is that of wife and mother in a partriarchal society; the function he assigns Emile is that of citizen in an ideal state. It is important in reading *Emile* to distinguish between the role of citizen in the actual states Rousseau knew and that same role in his ideal city state. To be sure, Sophie's function, or role, did exist in the states with which Rousseau was acquainted; however, there is no reason to suppose that he intended it to disappear in the ideal city state of *The Social Contract*. Rousseau's arguments against Plato's abolition of the family are enough by themselves to suggest that Sophie would have the same role to play in that state as she would in Rousseau's own France or Geneva. Moreover, in insisting that she is by nature subordinate to Emile's authority, he makes it both necessary for her to remain in the traditional female role and impossible for her to be a citizen in the ideal state.[6] As Okin (1979, p. 119) has said, Emile is educated to be his own man and Sophie is educated to be his own woman. As his own man Emile can be a citizen and participate in the General Will without sacrificing his freedom. As Emile's own woman, Sophie can be neither a citizen in Rousseau's sense nor free in the sense of being an autonomous person.

Upon recognizing that Emile's education is intended to equip him to participate in the General Will, it becomes clear that the fundamental educational assumptions Rousseau makes in regard to Emile are the same ones he makes in regard to Sophie. Like Sophie, Emile is born with certain aptitudes and capacities, but because he is male the capacities and aptitudes he is born with are quite different from those of Sophie. Whereas Sophie is by nature subordinate, Emile at birth has the potential to be his own legislator, which in turn involves the potential to grasp general principles and to reach independent conclusions. Thus his inborn nature, a direct result of his being male, suits him for the role of citizen in Rousseau's ideal city state. Since Emile's natural talents are not fully developed at birth and do not just emerge at maturity, education is necessary. Emile's education is totally different from Sophie's because his role is to be different from hers. Were their roles to be the same, Rousseau would, without a doubt, propose the same upbringing for them.

THE EDUCATION OF EMILE FOR PATRIARCHY

Okin is mistaken when she says that Rousseau's definition of Emile's nature is an open-ended one and that Emile "must be free to become whatever he can and will" (1979, p. 135). Just as Sophie must develop attractiveness, Emile must develop strength (p. 365); just as she must endure injustice, he must revolt against it (p. 369). If Emile were really free to become anything at all, he would not need a tutor to control and manipulate his total environment. Rousseau says to Emile's tutor:

Do you not dispose, with respect to him, of everything which surrounds him? Are you not the master of affecting him as you please? Are not his labors, his games, his pleasures, his pains, all in your hands without his knowing it? Doubtless he ought to do only what he wants: but he ought to want only what you want him to do. He ought not to make a step without your having foreseen it; he ought not to open his mouth without your knowing what he is going to say. [P. 120]

Readers of *Emile* cannot help but notice that Emile's tutor appears to manipulate him. In fact, Rousseau requires the tutor to be a master of that art. It is not that in a corrupt society Emile's nature cannot flourish untended, for he is to be educated in isolation from all society. Manipulation is necessary because Rousseau wants to ensure that only selected aspects of Emile's nature will flourish. A citizen in Rousseau's ideal state is both a person who can transcend private interests and a person of independent judgment who is subservient to none. A range of vices and other weaknesses — from lying (p. 101) to arrogance (p. 86) — are hence denied Emile.[7] The qualities that in Rousseau's view define Sophie's nature also are denied Emile (p. 364). He can no more become a gentle person and acquire Sophie's keen powers of observation than become a thief, for his education must equip him not only to be a participant in the General Will, but to be head of the family Sophie serves. *Emile* ends when, a few months after the marriage of Emile and Sophie, Emile informs his tutor that he will soon be a father. If Sophie is destined to be wife and mother in a patriarchal family, Emile is destined to be the patriarch.

Both Okin (1979) and Lange (1979b) have delineated clearly the societal role Rousseau assigns to Sophie. Neither one, however, has discussed the significance for Rousseau's educational philosophy of his assigning Emile, as Sophie's husband, the societal role of patriarch. Rousseau's definition of Emile's nature is more open-ended than that of Sophie, only insofar as his dual role of patriarch and citizen is more open-ended. Emile is not free to become anything at all: he is the one who exercises authority in the family, who has the ultimate say in decision making, and who represents the family in its dealings with the outside world. He has no choice in these matters.

I emphasize Emile's patriarchal role here, for while Rousseau never explicitly links Emile's education to the role of participant in the General Will, Book V leaves no room for doubt that Emile will play the dominant role in "the small fatherland which is the family" and that his education must equip him for this task. Thus if proponents of the standard interpretation of Emile wish to deny my claim that Emile's tutor is training him to be a citizen in Rousseau's sense of the term, they will still have to contend with Emile's other role as head of family. This role, which they can scarcely deny belongs to Emile, lends credence to a production interpretation of

Rousseau's educational thought. One perceptive commentator has said that if Rousseau's child "is to walk the path of nature, it will not be because there is a natural affinity between the child and this path, but because his tutor has led him along it" (Pekarsky, 1977, p. 356). It is clear that the path along which the tutor leads Emile is defined by Emile's functions; indeed, Rousseau maps Emile's function onto his nature as surely as he maps Sophie's function onto hers.

A UNIFIED INTERPRETATION OF EMILE

Whether one takes Rousseau to be determining Emile's nature or to be discovering it, it is important to understand that although Emile's education differs in its specifics from Sophie's, the principles that govern his education govern hers as well.[8] "If I do not want to push a boy to learn to read, a fortiori I do not want to force girls to before making them well aware of what the use of reading is," Rousseau says (p. 368). The principle that experience should precede verbal studies because books teach one to talk about what one does not know (p. 184) is an important one for Rousseau and he clearly intends it to hold for males and females. The fact that he assigns different natures and roles to males and females will mean that the uses to which reading is put will vary for Emile and Sophie, and this in turn may dictate a different choice of books. One can be sure that *Robinson Crusoe* will not be given to Sophie, but the principle that books should be avoided until an age at which second-hand experience will amplify rather than be a substitute for first-hand experience is not thereby affected.

It has been said that Rousseau discovered childhood. He certainly does tell Emile's tutor to respect childhood (p. 107) and to treat Emile according to his age (p. 91). Rousseau understood what modern psychology now tells us, namely, that children have their own way of seeing, thinking, and feeling (p. 90). The principle that education must respect the child's cognitive structures and emotional states is as central to Rousseau's philosophy of education as is the principle of delayed verbal learning. It is not, however, a principle that governs the education of Emile alone. One must take account of what is suitable to both age and sex, he says in Book V (p. 374). The principle that childhood must be respected is to be applied to Sophie's education, in the light of her particular modes of thinking, feeling, and perceiving the world.

Books I–IV of *Emile* contain any number of important educational principles, many of which will sound familiar to those who are acquainted with the open-classroom movement of the late 1960s and early 1970s and with the writings of radical school reformers of that period. (See Featherstone, 1969, pp. 195-205; Silberman, 1973; Rathbone, 1971; Nyquist and Hawes, 1972.) Rousseau maintains that educators should discard the distinction between work and play, since Emile's games are his business (p. 161); that education comes to us from nature, men, and things (p. 38); that the teacher's first duty is to be humane and to respect childhood (p. 79); that excessive severity and indulgence are to be avoided (p. 86); that the primary instrument of teaching should be well-regulated freedom (p. 92).

These principles all apply to Sophie's education. Sewing is Sophie's work, but it is also her play, for she wants to sew and learn how to do it in order to adorn her doll (pp. 376–68). She is to be subjected early to constraints Emile never knows, because all their lives girls "will be enslaved to the most continual and most severe of constraints — that of the proprieties" (p. 369). Still, she is not to be subjected to undue severity; she ought not to live like her grandmother, Rousseau says, but rather ought to be "lively, playful, and frolicsome, to sing and dance as much as she pleases, and to taste all the innocent pleasures of her age" (p. 374). The real differences between the education Rousseau proposes for Sophie and for Emile are readily accounted for by the differences Rousseau sees in the social roles he assigns them. The order to be humane is not countermanded in Sophie's case: her role simply requires that the humanity of her teachers take particular forms. Even the fact that Emile is to be educated in isolation and Sophie is not can be explained without positing a conflict of principles. The role of citizens exists in society only in corrupted form. To prepare Emile for that role in the ideal state, Rousseau deems it necessary to remove him from society. Sophie's role, however, exists in at least some segments of society in its pure form, and so there is no need to remove her from family and friends.

The elements of Books I–IV of *Emile* that so many educators have found attractive are compatible with the unified interpretation of *Emile* I am presenting here.[9] The principles of teaching and learning that Rousseau sets forth in those books can be understood as specifying the content of the educational treatment ordered by the postulates of Identity and Difference. This interpretation preserves important features of Rousseau's educational philosophy, while making clear their relationship to other elements of his thought. It also explains why manipulation plays the part it does in Rousseau's educational thought. A growth interpretation of *Emile* cannot account for the fact that Emile's tutor is supposed to manipulate and control him, even when he is removed from the corrupting influences of society. Rousseau's manipulative principle, which clearly governs Sophie's education as well as Emile's, constitutes an anomaly for the conception of the educator as gardener.[10] When, however, it is understood that the task of Emile's tutor is to produce an end product along predetermined specifications, the principle that the educator should give the pupil the illusion of freedom—all the while controlling carefully what the pupil learns — is no longer anomalous, but is exactly what one would expect of an educational theory that tells the teacher to be humane but gives that teacher a hidden agenda.

CONCLUDING REMARKS

In *The Language of Education*, Israel Scheffler (1960, p. 37) has said that the metaphor of growth "embodies a modest conception of the teacher's role, which is to study and then indirectly to help the development of the child, rather than to shape him into some preconceived form." Given the total control the tutor exercises over Emile's education, it is difficult to understand how standard texts in the history of educational thought could have attributed to Rousseau a growth conception of education. Scheffler criticizes the growth metaphor for masking the fact that the educator must make choices no gardener ever faces (pp. 50ff). I would add to this the criticism that in drawing attention to the development of the child, the growth metaphor ignores the social and political dimensions of education. The opening pages of *Emile* testify to the fact that Rousseau himself recognized that the educational is the political. He used the language of growth, but he was not fooled by that language. His interpreters have been fooled by it and have done Rousseau the injustice of supposing that the large political concerns with which he wrestled all his life play no role in the education he prescribes for Emile.

A production interpretation of Rousseau's educational thought acknowledges his concern for the political. It enables one to see that even though Emile is to be raised in isolation, from a theoretical standpoint, Rousseau, like Plato, envisions education as an enterprise that is linked closely to political purposes and ideals.[11] While Emile is to be educated for the role of citizen, and hence for the political realm, Sophie is not. Although Rousseau grudgingly acknowledges that she could acquire the rationality, objectivity, and independence he demands of those who participate in the General Will, the education Sophie is to receive will ensure that she will develop none of those attributes. Sophie will inhabit the home; she will not be qualified to venture out of it into the political realm. As head of family, Emile will also inhabit the home: yet his role of patriarch will not exclude him from being a full-fledged member of the political sphere. Indeed, Rousseau says that it is "the good son, the good husband, and the good father who make the good citizen" (p. 363). The personal autonomy that Sophie must have to be a citizen is precluded by being wife and mother. Emile, however, must be an autonomous agent within the family as in the state; indeed, his role of patriarch can be understood as Rousseau's ideal citizen writ small.

Bloom (1979, p. 22) considers the relationship between Emile and Sophie to be a union of complementary equals. (See also Wexler, 1976, p. 274; Broome, 1963, pp. 98–101.) Yet, a union in which one person must always obey the other, as Sophie must obey Emile, is scarcely one of equals. It is true that Rousseau would educate Sophie to wield power over Emile through the judicious use of manipulation and guile. Since he does not grant her the right to make her own decisions, let alone Emile's, one must conclude, against Bloom, that the egalitarian ideal for which Rousseau is famous is to hold in the political — but not the private — domain. Since the political domain is not open to Sophie, the limits to his egalitarianism are clear; equality is a principle intended to govern relations among males, not relations between males and females. That Sophie's place is not the political realm, but the home, is itself, then, a political commitment of Rousseau's.

I have argued that the standard interpretation of Rousseau's educational philosophy cannot explain the education of Sophie because it is based on Rousseau's account of Emile. In this respect it is like those psychological theories of development that have difficulty incorporating findings about females because they are derived from male research data. (See Gilligan, 1977 and 1979.) The response of the psychologists to this difficulty is to impose on their female subjects a masculine mold. The response of historians of educational thought to Sophie is either to banish her from their texts or to acknowledge her existence while making no effort to understand or explain her plight.

It is tempting to say that the standard interpretation of *Emile* ignores Book V because historians of educational thought have wanted to protect Rousseau from the scorn of modern readers who would not share his views about the place of women.[12] This is too facile an explanation, however, for historians also ignore Book V of the *Republic*, in which Plato argues that women as well as men can be suited by nature to be rulers of the Just State, and that future female rulers should receive an education identical to that of future male rulers. The sad truth is that historians of educational thought have ignored not only Rousseau's sex bias, but the whole topic of the education of women. They have neglected Sophie because they have implicitly defined their subject matter as the education of male human beings, rather then the education of all human beings.

When the education of females is excluded from the subject matter of the history of educational thought, we are all losers. Women lose because their experience is neither reflected nor interpreted in the works they are made to study and because they are denied the chance to understand and evaluate the range of ideals — from Sophie to Plato's guardians, which the great educational theorists of the past have held for them. Men lose because they are made to believe that the education of women has never been, and hence must not be, a topic worthy of philosophical discussion, and because they are not given an opportunity to ponder the question of whether sex or gender is a relevant category in educational thought. The loss to the history of educational thought itself is perhaps the greatest, for, as I have tried to show through the example of Rousseau, interpretations that neglect the education of women certainly will be incomplete and may even be thoroughly mistaken.

NOTES

1. For example, see Cahn (1970), Price (1967), and Ulich (1945;1948). Insofar as commentators on Rousseau's general philosophy have discussed his views on education, they, too, have tended to slight Book V of *Emile*. See Masters (1968), Perkins (1974), and Roche (1974). One notable exception to this tendency of Rousseau scholars is Broome (1963).

2. Although Archer contains lengthy selections from Book V of *Emile*, the introduction by S.E. Frost simply says: "*Rousseau's theory of the education of girls*. In this he contradicts all he has advocated for Emile. The girl is educated to please the man and everything she is to learn is relative to men." Excerpts from Book V of *Emile* in *The Emile of Jean Jacques Rousseau*, ed. William Boyd (New York: Teachers College Press, 1956) appear in a chapter entitled "Marriage" although Rousseau himself calls the relevant section of Book V, "Sophie, or the Woman."

3. Some interpreters of Plato would argue that Socrates assumes a parallelism between human nature and societal needs. However, the account of education contained in the *Republic* makes plausible the interpretation given here.

4. Nicholas P. White abstracts from *Republic* II a principal of the Natural Division of Labor that encompasses what I am calling the Postulate of Specialized Natures and the Postulate of Correspondence. For the present purpose, however, it is important to keep these postulates separate. See White (1979).

5. These might well be considered to be two distinct roles, but Rousseau clearly views them as forming a single one.

6. On this point see Lange (1979b). She argues, moreover, that the obvious strategy of eliminating the sexism of Rousseau's theory of the General Will by eliminating the patriarchal family is not feasible. See also Okin (1979, p. 134) and Christianson (1972, p. 292).

7. "The first education ought to be purely negative. It consists not at all in teaching virtue or truth but in securing the heart from vice and the mind from error" (*Emile*, p. 93). Judith N. Shklar argues that this "negative education" is necessary because Emile is to be educated to be his real self. She forgets that since Emile is to be educated apart from society, there is no need for the tutor to protect him to the extent that he does against society. See Shklar (1972, p. 360; 1969, p. 148).

8. This point is compatible with my claim that Rousseau is committed to the Difference Postulate. That Postulate holds that Sophie and Emile must be given different educational treatment, not that the principles governing their treatment must be different. Compare Broome (1963, p. 99).

9. Some may wonder if principles of teaching and learning that were advocated by proponents of open classrooms are compatible with the model of education I am attributing to Rousseau. A production model does not entail the harsh methods of teaching and the rigid structures that radical school reformers rejected. Since the Identity and Difference Postulates are purely formal, the methods to be used in equipping people for a given role or function in society can be harsh, but they can also be humane; moreover, they can be employed in a wide range of contexts, the traditional school being only one.

10. I am assuming here the "naive" conception of gardening spelled out by Israel Scheffler (1960), since it is the one employed in the standard interpretation of *Emile*. Rousseau's manipulative principle might well be compatible with a different conception of that activity.

11. Emile's isolation raises questions, however, about whether he can be educated to fulfill the roles assigned him.

12. Not all modern readers find Rousseau's discussion of Sophie objectionable. See Bloom (1979, p. 23); Broome (1963, pp. 98ff).

REFERENCES

Archer, R.L. (ed.). *Jean-Jacques Rousseau: His Educational Theories Selected from Emile, Julie and Other Writings*. Woodbury, N.Y.: Barron's Educational Series, 1964.

Bloom, Allan (trans.). *Emile*, by Jean-Jacques Roussau. New York: Basic Books, 1979.

Broome, J.H. *Rousseau: A Study of His Thought*. London: Edward Arnold, 1963.

Brumbaugh, Robert S., and Nathaniel M. Lawrence. *Philosophers on Education: Six Essays on the Foundations of Western Thought*. Boston: Houghton Mifflin, 1963.

Cahn, Steven M. *The Philosophical Foundations of Education*. New York: Harper and Row, 1970.

Christianson, Ron. "The Political Theory of Male Chauvinism: J.J. Rousseau's Paradigm," *Midwest Quarterly* 13 (1972): 291–99.

Eisenstein, Zillah. *The Radical Future of Liberal Feminism*. New York: Longman, 1981.

Featherstone, Joseph. "The British Infant Schools." In Ronald and Beatrice (eds.), *Radical School Reform*. New York: Simon and Schuster, 1969.

Gilligan, Carol. "In a Different Voice: Women's Conceptions of Self and Morality," *Harvard Educational Review* 47 (1977): 481–517.

Gilligan, Carol. "Woman's Place in Man's Life Cycle," *Harvard Educational Review* 49 (1979): 431–46.

Lange, Lynda. "The Function of Equal Education in Plato's *Republic* and *Laws*."

In Lorenne M.G. Clark and Lynda Lange (eds.), *The Sexism of Social and Political Theory*. Toronto: University of Toronto Press, 1979. (a)

Lange, Lynda. "Rousseau: Women and the General Will." In Lorenne M.G. Clark and Lynda Lange (eds.), *The Sexism of Social and Political Theory*. Toronto: University of Toronto Press, 1979. (b)

Masters, Roger D. *The Political Philosophy of Rousseau*. Princeton: Princeton University Press, 1968.

Nash, Paul. *Models of Man: Explorations in the Western Educational Tradition*. New York: Wiley, 1968.

Nash, Paul, Andreas M. Kazamias, and Henry J. Perkinson. *The Educated Man: Studies in the History of Educational Thought*. New York: Wiley, 1965.

Nyquist, Ewald B., and Gene R. Hawes (eds.). *Open Education*. New York: Bantam, 1972.

Okin, Susan Moller. *Women in Western Political Thought*. Princeton Universtiy Press, 1979.

Pamenatz, John. "Ce Qui Ne Signifie Autre Chose Sinon Qu'on Le Forcera D'Etre Libre." In Maurice Cranston and R.S. Peters (eds.), *Hobbes and Rousseau*. New York: Doubleday, 1972.

Pekarsky, Daniel. "Education and Manipulation." In Ira S. Steinberg (ed.), *Philosophy of Education 1977: Proceedings of the 33rd Annual Meeting of the Philosophy of Education Society*. Urbana: University of Illinois, 1977.

Perkins, Merle L. *Jean-Jacques Rousseau*. Lexington: University Press of Kentucky, 1974.

Plato. *Republic*. Trans. by G.M.A. Grube. Indianapolis: Hackett, 1974.

Price, Kingsley. *Education and Philosophical Thought*. (2d ed.) Boston: Allyn and Bacon, 1967.

Rathbone, Charles H. (ed.). *Open Education*. New York: Citation Press, 1971.

Roche, Kennedy F. *Rousseau: Stoic and Romantic*. London: Methuen, 1974.

Rousseau, Jean-Jacques. *The Social Contract*. New York: Hafner, 1947.

Rusk, Robert R. *The Doctrines of the Great Educations*. (Rev. 3rd ed.) New York: St. Martin's, 1965.

Scheffler, Israel. *The Language of Education*. Springfield, Ill.: Thomas, 1960.

Shklar, Judith. *Men and Citizens*. Cambridge, Eng.: Cambridge Universty Press, 1969.

Shklar, Judith. "Rousseau's Images of Authority." in Maurice Cranston and R.S. Peters (eds.), *Hobbes and Rousseau*. New York: Doubleday, 1972.

Silberman, Charles E. (ed.). *The Open Classroom Reader*. New York: Vintage, 1973.

Ulich, Robert. *History of Educational Thought*. New York: American Book, 1945.

Ulich, Robert. *Three Thousand Years of Educational Wisdom*. Cambridge, Mass: Harvard University Press, 1948.

Wexler, Victor G. "Made for Man's Delight: Rousseau as Antifeminist," *American Historical Review* 81 (1976): 266–291.

White, Nicholas P. *A Companion to Plato's Republic*. Indianapolis: Hackett, 1979.

Selection 4.6

Critical Pedagogy, Cultural Politics, and the Discourse of Experience

Henry A. Giroux

Writing about the act of studying, the Brazilian educator Paulo Freire (1985) argues that "studying is a difficult task that requires a systematic critical attitude and intellectual discipline acquired only through practice" (p. 1). He further argues that underlying the nature of this practice are two important pedagogical assumptions. First, the reader should assume the role of a subject in the act of studying. Second, the act of studying is not merely a relationship with the immediacy of the text; on the contrary, it is in the broader sense an attitude toward the world. He is worth quoting at length on these issues:

> Studying a text calls for an analysis of the study of the one who, through studying, wrote it. It requires an understanding of the sociological-historical conditioning of knowledge. And it requires an investigation of the content under study and of other dimensions of knowledge. Studying is a form of reinventing, re-creating, rewriting, and this is a subject's, not an object's task. Further, with this approach a reader cannot separate herself or himself from the text because she or he would be renouncing a critical attitude toward the text. . . . Because the act of study is an attitude toward the world, the act of study cannot be reduced to the relationship of reader to book or reader to text. In fact, a [text] reflects its author's confrontation with the world. It expresses this confrontation. . . . One who studies should never

SOURCE. Reprinted, with permission, from *Journal of Education* 167:2 (1985): 22–41.

stop being curious about other people and reality. There are those who ask, those who try to find answers and those who keep on searching. [P. 1]

Freire's comments are an important place to begin this essay, because they make suggestive and problematic the issue of how to theorize and develop a pedadogy that embodies forms of experience in which teachers and students display a sense of critical agency and empowerment. Freire's emphasis on the notion of agency, in this case, is particularly important because it conjures up images both of critique and of possibility. In the first instance, there is an implied demand to understand how experience in schools is accomplished in a manner that actively silences the possibility for critical learning and for critical agency. In the second instance, Freire distinctly employs a language and a challenge for organizing pedagogical experiences within social forms and practices that "speak" to developing more critical, open, explorative, and collective modes of learning.

I will argue that for such a challenge to be met critical educators need to develop a discourse that can be used to interrogate schools as ideological and material embodiments of a complex web of relations of culture and power, on the one hand, and as socially constructed sites of contestation actively involved in the production of lived experiences on the other. Underlying such an approach would be an attempt to define how pedagogical practice represents a particular politics of experience, that is, a cultural field where knowledge, discourse, and power intersect so as to produce historically specific practices of moral and social regulation (Henriques, et al., 1984). Similarly, this problematic points to the need to interrogate how human experiences are produced, contested, and legitimated within the dynamics of everyday classroom life. The theoretical importance of this type of interrogation is directly linked to the need for critical educators to fashion a discourse in which a more comprehensive politics of culture and experience can be developed. At issue here is the recognition that schools are historical and structural embodiments of forms and culture that are ideological in the sense that they signify reality in ways that are often actively contested and experienced differently by various individuals and groups. That is, schools are anything but ideologically innocent; nor are they simply reproductive of dominant social relations and interests. Yet they do exercise forms of political and moral regulation intimately connected with technologies of power that "produce asymmetries in the abilities of individuals and groups to define and realize their needs" (Johnson, 1983, p. 11.). More specifically, schools establish the conditions under which some individuals and groups define the terms by which others live, resist, affirm, and participate in the construction of their own identities and subjectivities.

Within this theoretical perspective, I will argue that power has to be understood as a concrete set of practices that produce social forms through which different sets of experience and modes of subjectivities are constructed [Simon, in press]. Discourse in this equation is both constitutive of and a product of power. It functions to produce and legitimate configurations of time, space, and narrative that position teachers and students so as to privilege particular renderings of ideology, behavior, and the representation of everyday life. Discourse as a technology of power is given concrete expression in forms of knowledge that constitute the formal curricula as well as in the classroom social relations that "impale" themselves on both the body and the mind (Foucault, 1980). Needless to say, these pedagogical practices and forms are "read" in different ways by both teachers and students (McLaren, in press). But nonetheless within these socially constructed sets of pedagogical practices are forces that actively work to produce subjectivites that consciously and unconsciously display a particular "sense" of the world.

In this case, the problem to be analyzed has a dual focus. First, I want to interrogate those forms of educational discourse and practices that produce real injustices and inequities through a particular structuring of pedagogical experiences. Second, I want to move beyond the language of critique and in doing so analyze the possibility for constructing forms of pedagogical practice that allow for teachers and students to assume the thoughtful, critical role of transformative intellectuals. In each instance, I will look at the ways in which schools both embody and reflect social antagonisms through the social relations that are constructed around particular pedagogical views of culture, knowledge, and experience.

EDUCATIONAL PRACTICE AND THE DISCOURSE OF MANAGEMENT AND CONTROL

> Schools should teach you to realize yourself, but they don't. They teach you to be a book. It's easy to become a book, but to become yourself you've got to be given various choices and be helped to look at the choices. You've got to learn that, otherwise you're not prepared for the outside world. [White and Brockington, 1983, p. 21]

The high school student who gave this reply provides both an important "reading" of his own school experiences and an indication that the pedagogical discourse and practices that shaped it were not successful. But to argue that such a pedagogy was not successful demands further elaboration as to how such a discourse and practice characterizes itself, what assumptions inform it, and what particular interests underlie its view of culture, knowledge, and the teacher-student relations it supports.

The set of pedagogical practices I am about to analyze are informed by a discourse that I want to label as the discourse of management and control. Inherent in this discourse is a view of culture and knowledge in which both are often treated as part of a storehouse of artifacts constituted as canon. While this discourse has a number of characteristic expressions, its most recent theoretical defense can be found in Adler's (1982) *The Paideia Proposal*. Adler calls for the schools to implement a core course of subjects in all twelve years of public schooling. His appeal is to forms of pedagogy that enable students to master skills and specific forms of understanding, with respect to predetermined forms of knowledge. In this view, knowledge appears beyond the reach of critical interrogation except at the level of immediate application. In other words, there is no mention of how such knowledge gets chosen, whose interests it represents, or why students might be interested in learning it. In fact, students in this perspective are constituted as a unitary body removed from the ideological and material differences that construct their subjectivities, interests, and concerns in diverse and multiple ways. I would argue that the concept of difference in this instance becomes the negative apparition of the "other." This is particularly clear in Adler's case, since he dismisses the diverse social and cultural differences among students with the simplistic and reductionistic comment that "Despite their manifold individual differences the children are all the same in their human nature" (Adler, 1982, p. 42). In this discourse a predetermined and hierarchically arranged body of knowledge is taken as the cultural currency to be dispensed to all children regardless of their differences and interests. Equally important is the fact that the acquisition of such knowledge becomes the structuring principle around which the school curriculum is organized and particular classroom social relations legitimated. In this case, it is an appeal to school knowledge exclusively that constitutes the measure and worth of what defines the learning experience. That is, the value of both teacher and student experience is premised on the transmission and inculcation of what can be termed "positive knowledge." Consequently, it is in the distribution, management, measurement, and legitimation of such knowledge that this type of pedagogy invests its energies. Cusick (1983), in his ethnographic study of three urban secondary schools, comments on the problematic nature of legitimating and organizing schools' practices around the notion of "positive knowledge."

> By positive knowledge I mean that which is generally accepted as having an empirical or traditional base. . . . The assumption that the acquisition of positive knowledge can be made interesting and appealing in part underlies the laws that compel everyone to attend school, at least until their mid teens. . . . The conventional assumption would have it that the curriculum of a school exists as a body of

knowledge, agreed upon by staff and approved by the general community and by district authorities who have some expertise, and that it reflects the best thinking about what young people need to succeed in our society. But I did not find that. [Pp. 25, 71]

What Cusick did find was that school knowledge organized in these terms was not compelling enough to interest many of the students he observed. Moreover, educators locked into this perspective responded to student disinterest, violence, and resistance by shifting their concerns from actually teaching positive knowledge to maintaining order and control, or as they put it, "keeping the lid on." Cusick (1983) is worth quoting at length:

> Not only did the administrators spend their time on those matters (administration and control), they also tended to evaluate other elements, such as the performance of teachers, according to their ability to maintain order. They tended to arrange other elements of the school according to how they contributed or failed to contribute to the maintenance of order. The outstanding example of that was the implementation in both urban schools of the five-by-five day, wherein the students were brought in early in the morning, given five periods of instruction with a few minutes in between and a fifteen-minute mid-morning break, and released before one o'clock. There were no free periods, study halls, cafeteria sessions, or assemblies. No occasions were allowed in which violence could occur. The importance of maintaining order in those public secondary schools could not be underestimated. [P. 108]

Within this discourse, student experience is reduced to the immediacy of its performance and exists as something to be measured, administered, registered, and controlled. Its distinctiveness, its disjunctions, its lived quality are all dissolved in an ideology of control and management. . . .

This type of discourse not only wages symbolic violence against students in that it devalues the cultural capital they possess as a significant basis for school knowledge and inquiry, it also tends to position teachers within pedagogical models that legitimate their role as "clerks" of the empire. Unfortunately, the technocratic interests that embody the notion of teachers as clerks is part of a long tradition of management models of pedagogy and administration that have dominated American public education (Callahan, 1962). More recent expressions of this logic include a variety of accountability models, management by objectives, teacher-proof curriculum materials, and state-mandated certification requirements. . . . This type of school policy also makes for good public relations in that school adminstrators can provide technical solutions to the complex social, political, and economic problems that plague their schools, while simultaneously invoking the principles of accountability as an indicator of success.

The message to the public is clear: if the problem can be measured, it can be solved. But mainstream educational discourse is not all of one piece: there is another position within mainstream educational discourse that does not ignore the relationship between knowledge and learning, on the one hand, and student experience on the other. It is to this position that I will now turn.

EDUCATIONAL PRACTICE AS THE DISCOURSE OF RELEVANCE AND INTEGRATION

The discourse of relevance in educational theory and practice has a long association with various tenets of what has been loosely called progressive education in the United States. From Dewey to the Free School Movement to the 1960s and 1970s to the present emphasis on multiculturalism, there has been a concern with taking the needs and cultural experiences of students as a starting point from which to develop relevant forms of pedagogy.[1] Since it is impossible to analyze in this essay all of the theoretical twists and turns this movement has taken, I want to focus exclusively on some of its dominant ideological tendencies along with the way in which its discourses structure the experiences of both students and teachers.

In its most commonsense form, the educational discourse of relevance privileges a notion of experience in which the latter is equated either with "fulfilling the needs of kids" or with developing cordial relations with students so as to be able to maintain order and control in the school. In many respects these two discourses represent different sides of the same educational ideology. In the discourse of "need fulfillment," the concept of "need" represents an *absence* of a particular set of experiences. In most cases, what educators determine as missing are either the culturally specific experiences that school authorities believe students must acquire so as to enrich the quality of their lives or, in more instrumental terms, the fundamental skills they "need" in order to get jobs once they leave the public schools. Underlying this view of experience is the logic of cultural deprivation theory, which defines education in terms of cultural enrichment, remediation, and basics.

Within this discourse, there is little recognition that what is legitimated as privileged experience often represents the enforsement of a particular way of life that signifies its superiority with a "revenge" on those who do not share its attributes. More specifically, the experience of the student as "other" is cast within a discourse that often labels it as deviant, underprivileged, or "uncultured." Consequently, not only do students bear the sole responsibility for school failure, but there is also little or no theoretical room for interrogating the ways in which administrators and teachers actually create and sustain the problems they attribute to the students in question. This uncritical view of studens, particularly of those from subordinate groups, is mirrored in a refusal by the discourse of relevance to examine critically how it provides and legitimates forms of experience that embody the logic of domination. One glaring example of this was brought home to me by a secondary school teacher in one of my graduate courses who constantly referred to her working-class students as "low life." In this case, there was no sense of how this language actively constructed her relations with these students, though I am sure the message was not lost on them. . . .

When students refuse to acquiesce to this type of humiliating discourse, teachers and school administrators generally face problems of order and control. One response is the discourse of cordial relations. The classic instance of dealing with students in this discourse is to try to keep them "happy" either by indulging their personal interests through appropriately developed modes of "low status" knowledge or by developing good rapport with them (Cusick, 1983; Sizer, 1984). Defined within a logic that views them as the "other," students now become objects of inquiry in the interest of being understood so as to be more easily controlled. The knowledge, for example, used by teachers with these students is often drawn from cultural forms identified with class-, race-, and gender-specific interests. But relevance, in this instance, has little to do with emancipatory concerns. Instead, it translates into pedagogical practices that attempt to appropriate forms of student and popular culture in the interests of "keeping the lid on." Furthermore, it provides a legitimating ideology for forms of class-, race-, and gender-specific forms of tracking. The tracking at issue here is developed in its most subtle form through an endless series of school electives that appear to legitimate the cultures of subordinated groups while actually incorporating them in a trivial pedagogical fashion. Thus, working-class girls are "advised" by guidance teachers to take "Girl Talk" while middle-class students have no doubts about the importance of taking classes in literary criticism. In the name of relevance and order, working-class boys are encouraged to select "industrial arts" while their middle-class counterparts take courses in advanced chemistry. These practices and social forms along with the divergent interests and pedagogies they produce have been analyzed extensively elsewhere (Giroux and Purpel, 1983) and need not be repeated here.

In its more theoretically argued forms, the discourse of relevance translates into what I will call the discourse of integration, a transition signaled by a more liberal view of student experience and culture. Within this discourse, student experience is defined either through the individualizing psychology of "child centeredness" or the logic of normative pluralism. Understood as part of a "natural" unfolding process, student experience is not tied to the imperatives of rigid disciplinary authority but to the exercise of self-control and self-regulation. The focus of analysis in this discourse is the child as a unitary subject, and the pedagogical practices emphasized are structured around the goal of encouraging healthy expression and harmonious social relations.

Central to the discourse of integration is a problematic that equates freedom with "the bestowal of love" and what Carl Rogers calls "unconditional positive regard" and "empathic understanding" (Rogers, 1969). This pedagogical canon positions teachers within a set of social relations that strongly emphasizes self-directed learning, links knowledge to the personal experiences of students, and attempts to help students to interact with one another in a positive and harmonious fashion. How student experiences get developed within this discourse is, of course, directly related to the larger question of how they are constructed and understood within the multiple discourses that embody and reproduce the social and cultural relations that characterize the larger society. While this issue is generally ignored in the language of child centeredness, it is appropriated as a central concern in another version of the discourse of integration, which employs what can be called the pedagogy of normative pluralism.

In the pedagogy of normative pluralism the analysis and meaning of experience shifts from a concern with the individual child to the student as a part of a specific cultural group. Accordingly, the naming and understanding of experience proceeds through a range of social categories that situates the individual child within a network of diverse cultural connections. Of central theoretical importance is the way in which the concept of culture is defined and interrogated in this perspective. Defined primarily in anthropological terms, culture is viewed as the ways in which human beings make sense of their lives, feelings, beliefs, thoughts, and the wider society (Kluckhorn, 1949). Within this discourse, the notion of difference is stripped of its "otherness" and accommodated to the logic of a "polite civic humanism" (Corrigan, 1985, p. 7). That is, difference no longer symbolizes the threat of disruption. On the contrary, it now signals an invitation for diverse cultural groups to join hands under the democratic banner of an integrative pluralism. It is worth pointing out that the relation between difference and pluralism is central to this perspective; it serves to legitimate the idea that in spite of differences manifested around race, ethnicity, language, values, and life-styles there is an underlying equality among different cultural groups that disavows privileging any one of them. Thus, the notion of difference is subsumed within a discourse and set of practices that promote harmony, equality, and respect within and between diverse cultural groups.

This is not to suggest that conflict is ignored in this approach, nor am

I suggesting that the social and political antagonisms that characterize the relationship between different cultural groups and the larger society are denied. On the contrary, such problems generally are recognized but they are seen as issues to be discussed and overcome in the interest of creating a "happy and co-operative class," which will hopefully play a fundamental role in bringing about a "happy and cooperative world" (Jeffcoate, 1979, p. 122). Within this context, cultural representations of difference as conflict and tension become pedagogically workable only within the language of unity and cooperation. Consequently, the concept of difference turns into its opposite, for difference now becomes meaningful as something to be resolved within *relevant* forms of exchange and class discussions. Lost here is a respect for the autonomy of different cultural logics and any understanding of how such logics operate within asymmetrical relations of power and domination. In other words, the equality that is associated with different forms of culture as lived and embodied experiences serves to displace political considerations regarding the ways in which dominant and subordinate groups are produced, mediated, and expressed within concrete social practices both in and outside schools.

. . .

In its more theoretically sophisticated versions, the pedagogy of normative pluralism recognizes the existence of racial, gender, ethnic, and other types of conflict among different groups but is more ideologically honest about why they should not be emphasized in the curriculum. Appealing to the interests of a "common culture," this position calls for a pedagogical emphasis on the common interests and ideals that characterize the nation. As one of its spokespersons, Nathan Glazer (1977), puts it, the choice of what is taught "must be guided . . . by our conception of a desirable society, of the relationship between what we select to teach and the ability of people to achieve such a society and live together in it" (p. 51). What is troubling in this position is that it lacks any sense of culture as a terrain of struggle; moreover, it does not pay any attention to the relationship between knowledge and power. In fact, underlying Glazer's statement is a facile egalitarianism that assumes but does not demonstrate that all groups can actively participate in the development of such a society.

. . .

The discourse of relevance and integration falls prey to a deeply ingrained ideological tendency in American education as well as the mainstream social sciences to separate culture from the relations of power.

Culture in this view becomes the object of sociological inquiry and is analyzed primarily as an artifact that embodies and expresses the traditions and values of diverse groups. There is no attempt in this view to understand culture as the sacred and lived principles of life, characteristic of different groups and classes as these emerge within asymmetrical relations of power and fields of struggle. In essence, culture as a particular relation between dominant and subordinate groups, expressed in the form of lived antagonistic relations that embody and produce particular forms of meaning and action, remains unexplored in the discourse of relevance and integration. Actually, this discourse excludes the concept of dominant and subordinate culture altogether, and by doing so fails to recognize the importance of wider political and social forces as these affect all aspects of school organization and everyday classroom life.

By refusing to acknowledge the relations between culture and power, the discourse of relevance and integration fails to understand how schools themselves are implicated in reproducing dominating discourses and social practices. In this view it is assumed that schools can analyze problems faced by different cultural groups and out of such analyses students will develop a sense of understanding and mutual respect that will in some way influence the wider society. But schools do more than influence society; they are also shaped by it. That is, schools are inextricably linked to a larger set of political and cultural processes, and they not only reflect the antagonism embodied in such processes but also embody and reproduce them. The question generally ignored in this discourse is how do schools actually work to produce class, race, and gender differentiations along with the fundamental antagonisms that structure them? In other words, in what ways are the wider forms of political, economic, social and ideological domination and subordination invested in the language, texts, and social practices of the schools as well as in the experiences of the teachers and students themselves? Similarly, how is power within schools expressed as a set of relations that privilege some groups while disconfirming others? The important point here is that the discourse of relevance and integration not only lacks an adequate theory of domination and the role that schools play in such a process, but also lacks a critical understanding of how experience is *named, constructed,* and *legitimated* in schools. Understood in these terms, such a discourse fails to analyze how the social relations that students and teachers bring to the classroom get expressed and mediated.

. . .

. . . Another major criticism of the discourse of relevance and integration is that it depoliticizes the notion of language by defining it primarily in technical terms (mastery), or in terms that argue for its communicative value in developing dialogue and transmitting information. In other words, language is privileged as a medium for verbal exchanges and presenting knowledge, and, as such, is abstracted from its constitutive role as an instrument and site of struggle over different meanings, practices, and readings of the world. Within this discourse, there is no sense of how language practices can be used to actively silence some students, or how the privileging of particular forms of language can work to disconfirm the traditions, practices, and values that subordinate language practices embody and reflect. Similarly, there is the failure to develop the important pedagogical task of having teachers learn forms of language literacy, in which one has a critical understanding of the structure of language as well as the theoretical skills needed to help students develop a language in which they can both validate and critically engage their own experiences and cultural milieus (Hymes, 1982; Kress and Hodge, 1979).

It is not surprising that within this discourse questions of cultural difference are generally reduced to a single emphasis on the transmission of curriculum. The learning and understanding of school knowledge become the sole medium through which problems are identified and resolved. Lost here are the ways in which power is invested in institutional and ideological forces that bear down on and shape social practices of schooling in a manner not evident through an analysis of curriculum texts in their isolated moment of classroom usage. There is no clear understanding, for example, of how social relations operate in schools through the organization of time, space, and resources, or the way in which different groups experience these relations via their economic, political, and social locations outside of schools. But this discourse not only fails to understand schooling as a cultural process that is inextricably linked to the inescapable presence of wider social forces; it also appears incapable of recognizing how forms of resistance might emerge in schools (Giroux, 1983).

CRITICAL PEDAGOGY AND THE DISCOURSE OF CULTURAL POLITICS

I now want to shift theoretical gears and return to the assumption, implicit in Paulo Freire's statement made at the beginning of this essay, that learning involves a subject in the act of studying and that the act of studying is constructed out of a broader relationship with the world. I want to begin by making a bold move. I want to argue that for a critical pedagogy to be developed as a form of cultural politics, it is imperative that both teachers and students be viewed as transformative intellectuals (Aronowitz and Giroux, 1985). The category of transformative intellectual is helpful in a number of ways. First, it signifies a form of labor in which thinking and learning are inextricably related, and, as such, offers a counter-ideology to instrumental and management pedagogies that separate conception from execution and ignore the specificity of experiences and subjective forms that shape both teacher and student behavior. Second, the concept of transformative intellectual calls into play the political and normative interests that underlie the social functions that structure and are expressed in teacher and student work. In other words, it serves as a critical referent for educators to make problematic the interests that are inscribed in the institutional forms and everyday practices that are subjectively experienced and reproduced in schools. Finally, viewing teachers and students as intellectuals further demands a critical discourse that analyzes how cultural forms bear down on schools and how such forms are experienced subjectively. This means that critical educators need to understand how lived and material forms of culture are subject to political organizations, that is, how they are produced and regulated.

In effect, I am arguing for a pedagogy of cultural politics that is developed around a critically affirmative language that allows educators as transformative intellectuals to understand how subjectivities are produced within those social forms in which people move but that are often only partially understood (Giroux and Simon, 1984). Such a pedagogy makes problematic how teachers and students sustain, resist, or accommodate those languages, ideologies, social processes, and myths that position them within existing relations of power and dependency. Moreover, it points to the need to develop a theory of politics and culture that analyzes power as an active process — one that is produced as part of a continually shifting balance of resources and practices in the struggle for privileging specific ways of naming, organizing, and experiencing social reality. Power, in this case, becomes a form of cultural production, linking agency and structure through the ways in which public and private representations are concretely organized and structured within schools. Furthermore, power is understood as an embodied and fractured set of experiences that are lived and suffered by individuals and groups within specific contexts and settings. Within this perspective, the concept of experience is linked to the broader issue of how subjectivities are inscribed within cultural processes that develop with regard to the dynamics of production, transformation, and struggle. Understood in these terms, a pedagogy of cultural politics presents a twofold set of tasks for critical educators. First, they need to analyze how cultural production is organized within asymetrical relations of power in schools. Second, they need to construct political strategies for participating in social struggles designed to fight for schools as democratic public spheres.

In order to make these tasks realizable, it is necessary to assess the political limits and pedagogical potentialities of the different but related instances of cultural production that constitute the various processes of schooling. It is important to note that I am calling these social processes instances of cultural production rather than using the dominant left concept of reproduction.[2] The latter, I believe, points adequately to the various economic and political ideologies and interests that get reconstituted within the relations of schooling, but it lacks an understanding of how such interests are mediated, worked on, and subjectively produced, regardless of the interests that finally emerge.

A critical pedagogy that assumes the form of a cultural politics needs to examine how cultural processes are produced and transformed within three particular, though related, fields of discourse. These are: *the discourse of production, the discourse of text analysis*, and *the discourse of lived cultures*. Each of these discourses has a history of theoretical development in various models of left analysis, and each has been subjected to intense discussion and criticism, which need not be repeated here.[3] What I want to do is to look at these discourses in terms of the potentialities they exhibit in their interconnections, particularly as they point to a new set of categories for developing forms of educational practices that empower teachers and students around emancipatory interests.

EDUCATIONAL PRACTICE AND THE DISCOURSES OF PRODUCTION, TEXT ANALYSIS, AND LIVED CULTURES

The discourse of production in educational theory has focused on the ways in which the structural forces outside the immediacy of school life construct the objective conditions within which schools function. Within this discourse are illuminating analyses of the state, the workplace, foundations, publishing companies, and other political interests that directly or indirectly influence school policy. Moreover, schools are understood within a network of larger connections that allow analyses of them as historical and social constructions, embodiments of social forms that always bear a relationship to the wider society. At its best, the discourse of production alerts us to the need to understand the importance of ideological and material structures as particular sets of practices and interests that legitimate specific public representations and ways of life. It is inconceivable to analyze the process of schooling without understanding how these wider forms of production are constructed, manifested, and contested both in and out of schools. An obvious example of this is to analyze the ways in which state policy embodies and promotes particular practices that legitimate and privilege some forms of knowledge over others or some groups over others. Equally significant would be an analysis of how dominant modes of discourse in educational practice are constructed, sustained, and circulated outside schools. For instance, critical educators need to do more than identify the language and values of corporate ideologies as they are manifested in school curricula; they also need to deconstruct the processes through which they are produced and circulated. Another important aspect of the discourse of production is that it points to the way in which labor is objectively constructed; that is, it provides an analysis of the conditions under which people work and the political importance of these conditions in either limiting or enabling what educators can do. This issue is especially important for analyzing the critical possibilities that exist for public school teachers and students within specific conditions of labor to act and be treated as intellectuals. Quite simply, if teachers and students are subject to conditions of overcrowding, lack time to work collectively in a creative fashion, or are subject to rules and regulations that disempower them, the technical and social conditions of labor have to be understood and addressed as part of the discourse of reform and struggle.

At the same time, the discourse of production has to be supplemented with analyses of textual forms. In this case, it is necessary to enlist a discourse that can critically interrogate cultural forms as they are produced and used within specific classrooms. What is significant about this type of discourse is that it provides teachers and students with the critical tools necessary to analyze those socially constructed representations and interests that organize and emphasize particular readings of curricula materials. This is a particularly important mode of analysis because it argues against the idea that the means of representation in texts are merely neutral conveyors of ideas.

It points to the need for careful systematic analyses of the way in which material is used and ordered in school curricula and how its "signifiers" register particular ideological pressures and tendencies. At its best, such a discourse allows teachers and students to deconstruct meanings that are silently built into the structuring principles of the various systems of meaning that organize everyday life in schools. In effect, it adds a new theoretical twist to analyzing how the hidden curriculum works in schools.

This type of textual criticism can be used, for example, to analyze how the technical conventions or images within various forms such as narrative, mode of address, and ideological reference attempt to construct a limited range of positions from which they are to be read. Richard Johnson (1983) is worth quoting on this point:

> The legitimate object of an identification of "positions" is the pressures or tendencies on the reader, the theoretical problematic which produces subjective forms, the directions in which they move in their force — once inhabited. . . . If we add to this the argument that certain kinds of text ("realism") naturalise the means by which positioning is achieved, we have a dual insight of great force. The particular

promise is to render processes hitherto unconsciously suffered (and enjoyed) open to explicit analysis. [Pp. 64–65]

Coupled with traditional forms of ideology critique of the subject content of school materials, the discourse of text analysis provides a valuable insight into how subjectivities and cultural forms work within schools. The value of this kind of work has been exhibited in analysis of the stuctured principles used in the construction of prepackaged curriculum materials, where it has been argued that such principles utilize a mode of address that positions teachers merely as implementers of knowledge (Apple, 1983).

. . .

I want to conclude by arguing that in order to develop a critical pedagogy around a form of cultural politics, it is essential to develop a discourse that does not assume that lived experiences can be inferred automatically from structural determinations. In other words, the complexity of human behavior cannot be reduced to merely identifying the determinants, whether they be economic modes of production or systems of textual signification, in which such behavior is shaped and against which it constitutes itself. The way in which individuals and groups both mediate and inhabit the cultural forms presented by such structural forces is in itself a form of production, and needs to be analyzed through a related but different discourse and mode of analysis. In this case, I want to briefly present the nature and pedagogical implications of what I call the discourse of lived cultures.

Central to the discourse of lived cultures is the need to develop what can be loosely called a theory of self-production (Touraine, 1977). In the most general sense, this would demand an understanding of how teachers and students give meaning to their lives through the complex historical, cultural, and political forms that they both embody and produce. A number of issues need to be developed within a critical pedagogy around this concern. First, it is necessarry to acknowledge the subjective forms of political will and struggle. That is, the discourse of lived cultures needs to interrogate how people create stories, memories, and narratives that posit a sense of determination and agency. This is the cultural "stuff" of mediation, the conscious and unconscious material through which members of dominant and subordinate groups offer accounts of who they are and present different readings of the world. It is also part of those ideologies and practices that allow us to understand the particular social locations, histories, subjective interests, and private worlds that come into play in any classroom pedagody (Johnson, 1983).

If we treat the histories, experiences, and languages of different cultural groups as particularized forms of production, it becomes less difficult to understand the diverse readings, responses, and behaviors that, let's say, students exhibit to the analysis of a particular classroom text. In fact, a cultural politics necessitates that a discourse be developed that is attentive to the histories, dreams, and experiences that such students bring to schools. It is only by beginning with these subjective forms that critical educators can develop a pedagogy that confirms and engages the contradictory forms of cultural capital that constitute how students produce meanings that legitimate particular forms of life.

Searching out and illuminating the elements of self-production that characterize individuals who occupy diverse lived cultures is not merely a pedagogical technique for confirming the experiences of those students who are often silenced by the dominant culture of schooling; it is also part of a discourse that interrogates how power, dependence, and social inequality structure the ideologies and practices that enable and limit students around issues of class, race, and gender. Within this theoretical perspective, the discourse of lived cultures becomes valuable for educators because it can serve to illuminate not only how power and knowledge intersect to disconfirm the cultural capital of students from subordinate groups, but also how it can be translated into a language of possibility. That is, it can also be used to develop a critical pedagogy of the popular, one that engages the knowledge of lived experience through the dual method of confirmation and interrogation. The knowledge of the "other" is engaged not simply to celebrate its presence, but also because it must be interrogated critically with respect to the ideologies it contains, the means of representation it utilizes, and the underlying social practices it confirms. At stake here is the need to develop a link between knowledge and power, one that suggests realizable possibilities for students. That is, knowledge and power intersect in a pedagogy of cultural politics so as to give students the opportunity not only to understand more critically who they are as part of a wider social formation, but also to help them critically appropriate those forms of knowledge that traditionally have been denied to them.

In conclusion, each of the discourses I have briefly presented and analyzed involves a different view of cultural production, pedagogical analysis, and political action. And while each of these forms of production involves a certain degree of autonomy in both form and content, it is important that a critical pedagogy be developed around the inner connections they share within the context of a cultural politics. For it is within these interconnections that a theory of both structure and agency can construct a new language, point to new questions and possibilities, and allow educators as transformative intellectuals to struggle for the development of schools as democratic public spheres.

NOTES

1. I want to make clear that there is a major distinction between the work of John Dewey (1916), in this case, and the hybrid discourses of progressive, educational reform that characterized the late 1960s and 1970s. The discourse of relevance and integration that I am analyzing here bears little resemblance to Dewey's philosophy of experience in that Dewey stressed the relationship between student experience, critical reflection, and learning. In contrast, the call for relevance that abounds today generally surrenders the concept of systematic knowledge acquisition and uncritically privileges an anti-intellectual concept of student experience. For a critique of these positions, see Aronowitz and Giroux (1985) and Giroux (1981).

2. The reproductive thesis in radical educational theory has been developed out of the work of Bowles and Gintis (1976). A critique of this position can be found in Giroux (1983).

3. A major analysis of these discourses and the traditions with which they are generally associated can be found in Johnson (1983). I have drawn freely from Johnson's work in this section of the paper.

REFERENCES

Adler, M. *The Paideia Proposal*. New York: Macmillan, 1982.

Apple, M. *Education and Power*. New York: Routledge and Kegan Paul, 1983.

Aronowitz, S., and H. Giroux. *Education Under Seige*. South Hadley, Mass.: Bergin and Garvey, 1985.

Bowles, S., and H. Gintis. *Schooling in Capitalist America*. New York: Basic Books, 1976.

Callahan, R. *Education and the Cult of Efficiency*. Chicago: University of Chicago Press, 1962.

Corrigan, P. *Race, Ethnicity, Gender, Culture: Embodying Differences Educationally — An Argument*. Unpublished paper, Ontario Institute for Studies in Education, 1985.

Cusick, P. *The Egalitarian Ideal and the American School*. New York: Longman, 1983.

Dewey, J. *Democracy and Education*. New York: The Free Press, 1916.

Foucault, M. *Power and Knowledge: Selected Interviews and Other Writings*. (C. Gordon, ed.) New York: Pantheon, 1980.

Freire, P. *The Politics of Education*. South Hadley, Mass.: Bergin and Garvey, 1985.

Giroux, H. *Ideology, Culture and the Process of Schooling*. Philadelphia: Temple University Press, 1981.

Giroux, H. *Theory and Resistance in Education*. South Hadley, Mass: Bergin and Garvey, 1983.

Giroux, H., and D. Purpel (eds.) *The Hidden Curriculum and Moral Education*. Berkeley, Calif.: McCutchan Publishing, 1983.

Giroux, H., and R. Simon. "Curriculum Study and Cultural Politics," *Journal of Education* 166 (Fall 1984): 226–38.

Glazer, N. "Cultural Pluralism: The Social Aspect." In M. Tumin and W. Plotch (eds.), *Pluralism in a Democratic Society*. New York: Praeger, 1977.

Henriques, J., W. Holloway, C. Urwin, C. Venn, and V. Walkerdine. *Changing the Subject*. New York: Methuen, 1984.

Hymes, D. *Ethnolinguistic Study of Classroom Discourse*. Final Report to the National Institute of Education. Philadelphia: University of Pennsylvania, 1982.

Jeffcoate, R. *Positive Image: Towards a Multicultural Curriculum*. London: Writers and Readers Cooperative, 1979.

Johnson, R. "What is Cultural Studies?" *Anglistica* 26(1–2)(1983): 7–81.

Kluckhorn, C. *Mirror for Man: The Relation of Anthropology to Modern Life*. New York: McGraw-Hill, 1949.

Kress, G., and R. Hodge. *Language as Ideology*. London: Routledge and Kegan Paul, 1979.

McLaren, P. *Schooling as a Ritual Performance*. Boston: Routledge and Kegan Paul, in press.

Rogers, C. *Freedom to Learn*. Columbus, Ohio: Charles Merrill, 1969.

Simon, R. "Work Experience as the Production of Subjectivity." In D. Livingston (ed.), *Critical Pedagogy and Cultural Power*. South Hadley, Mass.: Bergin and Garvey, in press.

Sizer, T. *Horace's Compromise*. Boston: Houghton Mifflin, 1984.

Touraine, A. *The Self-production of Society*. Chicago: University of Chicago Press, 1977.

White, R., and D. Brockington. *Tales Out of School*. Routledge and Kegan Paul, 1983.

PART FIVE

Implementation, Evaluation, and Change

Until relatively recently, nearly all curriculum literature has addressed planning issues, at least for the most part. Little in the literature has addressed curriculum implementation or evaluation issues. Issues related to implementation and evaluation were little noticed in the past, a time in which an established value system would not, or could not, be challenged, and there was little, if any, attempt at curriculum change. Today, however, rapid and significant social change, a wider expression of pluralistic values, the widespread failure to implement newly planned curriculums in the 1960s and 1970s, and the increasing clamor for accountability have focused greater attention on curriculum implementation and evaluation.

In addition, the research and development literature that evolved with the nationally supported curriculum interventions of the last quarter-century documents our understanding of implementation, evaluation, and change. Questions such as "Under what circumstances is curriculum implementation most feasible?" and "What are the relationships between processes of curriculum planning, implementation, and evaluation?" and "What is the nature of the change process in curriculum?" are now documented in that literature. More recent standard curriculum texts include significant attention to issues of curriculum implementation, evaluation, and change (see ASCD, 1983; Doll, 1982; Hunkins, 1980; McNeil, 1985; Miller and Seller, 1985; Pratt, 1980; Schubert, 1986; Wiles and Bondi, 1984). This part of the text surveys the issues and some of the literature related to curriculum implementation and evaluation, and it examines relationships between school curriculum and change.

CURRICULUM IMPLEMENTATION

The lack of specific comprehensive and systematic attention to the issue of curriculum implementation until the 1970s constituted a serious gap in the curriculum literature. A survey of some standard curriculum texts fifteen or twenty years ago would have reinforced the assumption that the major problem in curriculum was planning, or developing, curriculum (see, for example, Anderson, 1965; Doll, 1970; Saylor and Alexander, 1974). At that time, little attention had been given to implementation or evaluation and their relationships to change. This state of affairs may have been related to (1) an implicit assumption in most curriculum planning literature that implementation would be automatic, (2) the field's lack of direct attention to implementation issues, and (3) confusion about the boundaries between curriculum and instruction.

Curriculum implementation is treated only indirectly in the general curriculum literature fifteen years ago. Doll (1970, pp. 339–54), for example, discussed what he called promising strategies of implementation under headings of in-service education and the role of the school supervisor. His conception of in-service education recognized a link between a curriculum, as a plan of action, and what actually happens between teachers and students in instructional situations. However, Doll treated the issue as one of many related to in-service education instead of directly as a matter of curriculum. In a similar way, Doll's view of the school supervisor as a resource in curriculum implementation, among other things, discussed implementation in terms of instructional improvement. The most recent edition of his work (Doll, 1982) evidences significant change in conceptualization of curriculum, with extensive attention to curriculum change and improvement, communication, and leadership, in addition to curriculum evaluation.

Indirect references to issues now seen as curriculum implementation are found in older treatments under a variety of other headings. Hand (1955, pp. 386–89), for example, states that authority and responsibility for curriculum implementation rest with the school building principal because he or she is a leader in curriculum, as well as a key line administrator, in any system of schooling. An indirect focus on curriculum implementation can be seen in older textbook treatments of field testing. However, the trying out of new curriculum elements before widespread adoption is discussed by Caswell and Campbell (1935, pp. 508–11). After objectives, content, materials, activities, or other parts of a curriculum have been designed, a field test may be made to discover optimum conditions for adoption and implementation.

Confusion and ambiguity about the boundaries between curriculum and instruction have resulted in other voids in the treatment of curriculum implementation. For example, Saylor and Alexander (1974, p. 245) at one time made curriculum implementation and classroom instruction synonymous: "Instruction is thus the implementation of the curriclum plan, usually, but not necessarily, involving teaching in the sense of student-teacher interaction in a school setting."

Although instruction is certainly related to curriculum implementation, it is imprecise, at least, to equate the two. Curriculum implementation can include a number of intermediate activities that support translating a curriculum design into intended instructional activity, such as construction of instructional materials or activities, in-service education, and supervisory activity. Therefore, it may be useful to define curriculum implementation as those activities that translate a curriculum design into intended instructional activity. As Patterson and Czajkowski (1979) point out, curriculum implementation has been neglected, both in practice and in theory, because it is related to various components of planning; to change strategies of reason, power, and influence; and to staff development. But implementation is more complex than identification of component parts.

In a more recent treatment of curriculum implementation, Loucks and Lieberman (in ASCD, 1983, pp. 126–41) recognize important political, cultural, and school organization perspectives. In regard to curriculum implementation, they examine concepts of human development and change, teacher participation in change, and support systems. The authors conclude by applying insights to local implementation problems, discussing, in particular, districtwide curriculum implementation of and local response to curriculum mandates of federal and state government.

Some direct attention has been given to curriculum implementation and related variables (Beauchamp, 1981, pp. 171–76). Some authorities have found that optimum conditions for curriculum implementation include commitment of the classroom teacher, his or her participation in curriculum planning, administrative leadership, and appropriateness of perceived school conditions. Michaelis and colleagues (1975, pp. 459–63) reflect conventional thinking that curriculum implementation is related to such variables as teacher preparation, community support, available resources, and the use of support personnel in schools.

Similarly, Schaffarzick and Hampson (1975, pp. 6–10) related implementation to evaluation, dissemination, experimentation, and school staff development. More recently, Hunkins (1980, pp. 275–92) has examined both piloting and final curriculum implementation phases, identifying conditions for feedback and consolidation, support systems, and communication.

Gress (1973; 1980) completed a comprehensive review and analysis of the curriculum implementation literature in this regard. He based his analysis on the Fullan and Pomfret (1977) research review, the Rand (1980) work, and Teacher Corps literature (Smith, 1979). Gress identified five categories of implementation variables: (1) features of the curriculum to be implemented, (2) teacher characteristics, (3) teacher roles in curriculum planning and implementation, (4) school environment variables, and (5) curriculum resources. Table 5.1 specifies variables in each implementation category and displays common findings in the research literature. Among other things, Gress found that curriculum implementation is optimum:

1. For least complex curriculum changes that are most compatible with other curriculum elements;
2. Among experienced and professionally secure teachers;
3. When teachers have been involved in planning, understand role expectations in implementation, and have access to staff development resources as needed;
4. In a noncrisis school district environment with evidence of high priority from school leadership;
5. With three to five years for change and adequate resource appropriation.

Table 5.1 **Curriculum Implementation Variables Identified in Selected Research Literature**

	Literature Source		
	P & F	*Smith*	*Rand*
1 Curriculum features			
11 Match with local mores			
12 Noncontroversial			
13 Explicitness	x		x
14 Response to real problem(s)	x		
15 Noncomplexity	x		

	Literature Source		
	P & F	Smith	Rand
2 Teacher characteristics			
21 Experience, competence, and/or security	x		
22 Relationship to planning and implementation			
221 Recognises need for change	x		
222 Participation in decision making	x		x
223 Positive perception(s) of participation			
224 Materials construction			
225 Understanding of implementation role(s)		x	
226 Inservice participation	x		x
227 Consultant interaction	x		
228 Positive parent contact		x	
229 Positive peer contact			x
3 Teacher roles in implementation			
31 Regular activities, monitoring, communication		x	
32 Relationship to implementation (see 22)			
33 Schoolwide role behaviors			
331 Leadership initiative			x
332 Administrator support	x	x	x
333 Supervisor/consultant support	x		x
334 School staff interaction	x		
335 Peer feedback	x		
336 Competent boundary personnel		x	
4 School environment			
41 Noncrisis community support			x
42 Open, trusting atmosphere	x		
43 Incentives for change	x		
44 Responsive organizational structure		x	
45 School district enthusiasm			x
5 Implementation resources			
51 Two- to five-year timeline	x		
52 Adequate fiscal resources			
53 Adequate curriculum materials	x		
54 School district priority	x		

In a recent ASCD publication, Hord and colleagues (1987) examine curriculum implementation both in terms of the process itself and in terms of the professional role groups involved. In Selection 5.1, from that work, the authors describe implementation as innovation configurations. This work is based on research by Hall and Loucks (1981) to identify components of a curriculum innovation and their variations in use. Components refer to operational features of the innovation as planned, including instructional materials and equipment, teacher diagnosis of students, prescribed record keeping, use of an identified teaching technique, and instructional scheduling. The authors point out that other examples of components might include grouping, program objectives, and the like. Variations of a curriculum innovation in use refer to observable teacher behaviors related to components. The behaviors are conceptualized and described along a continuum of no implementation to full implementation.

Hord and her colleagues provide ample illustrations of innovation components and variations with use of a sample curriculum implementation and sample checklists in Selection 5.1. The authors give fairly extensive directions for gathering and using configuration data. Data gathering might be used in formative or summative curriculum evaluation. The data gathering might also be used for diagnosing teacher, school, and school district implementation of a curriculum innovation that appears to be the principal intent of this work.

In other chapters of their work, Hord and colleagues examine the role of effective facilitators of curriculum implementation. Their emphasis is on leadership functions and on taking charge of change in schools generally. However, other chapters examine curriculum implementation from the individual teacher's perspective and from the perspective of levels of use. The individual teacher's implementation of a curriculum innovation is investigated by considering various profiles. Graphic profiles illustrate different ways in which individual teachers may, or may not, move through identified stages of change in the implementation of an innovation. The stages of implementation are investigated by describing levels of use in specific classroom cases. Brief case summaries identify and illustrate stages of nonuse, use, and disuse.

CURRICULUM EVALUATION

Curriculum evaluation is the final link in the cycle of curriculum processes. According to Beauchamp (1981, pp. 176–81), curriculum evaluation includes both evaluation of a curriculum design, its uses and its outcomes, and evaluation of curriculum processes.

In an early treatment of curriculum and evaluation, Shane and McSwain (1958, pp. 56–67) discussed the nature of educational evaluation generally. In that discussion, the authors noted a whole range of definitions of evaluation that existed even then. They conclude their treatment by insisting that any definition of evaluation must include attention to its external and internal dimensions. These two dimensions distinguish between:

> a continuous process of inquiry, based on criteria cooperatively developed in the school community, which leads to warranted conclusions with respect to how successfully the school is studying, interpreting, and guiding socially desirable changes in human behavior, [and] a process within us, as a result of which we make our interpretations of the environment around us and, accordingly, direct our behavior. [P. 60]

Curriculum evaluation may involve elements of both dimensions.

Our purpose here is to elaborate the nature and scope of curriculum evaluation. In doing so, we recognize that curriculum evaluation is a particular application of a more general process used in schools and elsewhere. The evaluation of a curriculum design may include attention to any or all of its elements—objectives, subject matter, instructional activities, the evaluation schema itself. Evaluation of the outcomes may include attention to any one or more of the dimensions of the instructional process and its consequences. Every aspect of curriculum can be brought under the microscope of evaluation. The choice of curriculum arena, choices made for involvement and organization of people for planning, curriculum-planning procedures, and roles played by leadership personnel are all subject to evaluation. The feedback from evaluation can improve curriculum and provide continuity and growth.

In the relatively extensive treatment of evaluation in Selection 5.2, Kemmis relates evaluation to curriculum development and innovation in Australia. He begins by asserting a mutuality in the relationships between curriculum development and evaluation.

Kemmis states and discusses principles of rationality as reasonableness, autonomy and responsibility, community self-interest, plurality of value perspectives, the self-critical community, propriety in the production and distribution of information, and appropriateness of evaluation. In each case, the author is guided by his initial definition but offers two alternative principles as well (see Table 5.2). The reader

Table 5.2 **Alternative Principles for Curriculum Evaluation**

Principle	*Alternative 1*	*Alternative 2*	*Alternative 3*
1. Rationality as	Reasonableness and autonomy	Rule following	Rational planning
2. Accountability	Based on autonomy and responsibility	Based on truth and justice	Based on contractual obligation
3. Interest as	Community self-interest	Public interest	Sponsor's interest
4. Value perspectives	Plurality	Expert	Sponsor's
5. Arena	Self-critical community	External evaluators	Sponsor's evaluators
6. Propriety	In production and distribution of information	"Impropriety"	Sponsor access to information
7. Perspective	Appropriateness	Methodological "tunnel vision"	Sponsor controlled

Source: Based on S. Kemmis, "Seven Principles for Programme Evaluation," *Journal of Curriculum Studies* 14:221–40, July–September, 1982.

is confronted, in sum, with three sets of curriculum evaluation principles from which choices can be made.

The Kemmis work focuses on issues related to the methodology of evaluation. The Scriven work (in Tyler et al., 1967, pp. 29–83) also examines methodology. There are several other issues related to curriculum evaluation one may want to consider. Perhaps the most comprehensive identification of evaluation models for curriculum is that assembled by Rodgers (in ASCD, 1983, pp. 142–53). Table 5.3 reproduces information about nine approaches to evaluation: (1) student gain by testing, (2) institutional self-study by staff, (3) blue ribbon panel, (4) transaction-observation, (5) management analysis, (6) instructional research, (7) social policy analysis, (8) goal-free evaluation, and (9) adversary evaluation. For each approach, the authors have identified evaluation purpose, key elements, role purview, protagonists, case examples, risks, and payoffs (pp. 148–50). The reader is urged to investigate the work of individual protagonists and the case examples cited in the table.

CURRICULUM AND CHANGE STRATEGIES

Curriculum planning, implementation, and evaluation may be seen as interrelated processes. A major challenge of the school's curriculum processes is to respond to change and, at times, to foster it. It is the ongoing set of curriculum processes that allows the schools to accommodate change. Seguel (1966, pp. 112–14) has pointed out Harold Rugg's contributions to the curriculum field's thinking about social change. She notes that Rugg's contributions may have been motivated in part by his own personal experience with it. Indeed, it is likely that many contributions to the curriculum field may have been related to change issues. In the past three decades, certainly, a renewed interest in issues related to innovation and change has invigorated the field.

In Selection 5.3, Cuban examines determinants both of curriculum change and of curriculum stability. His historical analysis, somewhat abridged, includes 1870–1970, a period marked by enormous growth in numbers of students, in teachers and schools, in bodies of knowledge, in school roles, and in bureaucracy. Cuban links curriculum change to corporate industrialism, progressivism, the cold war and political change, state and federal laws, court decisions, publishers, foundations, college professors, professional associations, and school constituencies. He links change to contributions of educational statesmen, including Dewey, W. T. Harris, Thorndike, Bobbitt, and Tyler; and he links change to blurred organizational goals for schools, unclear technology, uncertain outcomes, and fluid participation in school curriculum.

Cuban examines curriculum change in classrooms in some detail, particularly during the periods 1870–1900, 1910–1930, and 1960–1970. Then he turns attention to determinants of curriculum stability. These include the functions of schooling, accrediting and testing agencies, textbooks, state and federal laws and agencies, organizational rationality in schools, and loose bureaucratic compliance with external mandates.

The historical tenor of Cuban's analysis in Selection 5.3 prompts recall of the complementary analyses of Caswell (Selection 1.2) and Boyd (Selection 1.4). These analyses all underscore awareness of the relatively short life of the field of curriculum in American education. For example, among the change models clarified in the Boyd selection in Part One was disjointed incrementalism. McNeil (1985, pp. 107–8) sees this model as a "nonmodel"; Cuban counts it among the determinants of stability. What is planned change? Why is it necessary? What are the bases for accomplishing it in schools? According to Chin

Table 5.3 **Nine Approaches to Educational Evaluation**

Approach	*Purpose*	*Key Elements*	*Purview Emphasized*	*Protagonists*	*Cases, Examples*	*Risks*	*Payoffs*
Student gain by testing	To measure student performance and progress	Goal statements; test score analysis, discrepancy between goal and actuality	Educational psychologists	Ralph Tyler Ben Bloom Jim Popham Mal Provus	Steele Womer Lindvall-Cox Husen	Oversimplify educational aims; ignore processes	Emphasize, ascertain student progress
Institutional self-study by staff	To review and increase staff effectiveness	Committee work; standards set by staff; discussion; professionalism	Professors, teachers	National Study of School Evaluation Dressel	Boersma-Plawecki Knoll-Brown Carpenter	Alienate some staff; ignore values of outsiders	Increase state of awareness; sense of responsibility
Blue ribbon panel	To resolve crises and preserve the institution	Prestigious panel; the visit; review of existing data & documents	Leading citizens	James Conant Clark Kerr David Henry	Flexner Havighurst House et al. Plowden	Postpone action; overrely on intuition	Gather best insights, judgment
Transaction-observation	To provide understanding of activities and values	Educational issues; classroom observation; case studies; pluralism	Client, audience	Lou Smith Parlett-Hamilton Bob Rippey Bob Stake	Macdonald Smith-Pohland Parlett Lundgren	Overrely on subjective perceptions; ignore causes	Produce broad picture of program; see conflict in values
Management analysis	To increase rationality in	Lists of options; estimates;	Managers, economists	Leon Lessinger Dan	Kraft Doughty-	Overvalue efficiency;	Feedback for decision

	day-to-day decisions	feed-back loops; costs; efficiency		Stufflebeam Marv Alkin Alan Thomas	Stakenas Hemphill	undervalue implicit	making
Instructional research	To generate explanations and tactics of instruction	Controlled conditions, multivariate analysis; bases for generalization	Experimentalists	Lee Cronbach Julian Stanley Don Campbell	Anderson, R. Pella Zdep-Joyce Taba	Artificial conditions; ignore the humanistic	New principles of teaching and material development
Social policy analysis	To aid development of institutional policies	Measures of social conditions and administrative implementation	Sociologists	James Coleman David Cohen Carol Weiss	Coleman Jencks Levitan Trankell	Neglect of educational issues, details	Social choices, constraints clarified
Goal-free evaluation	To assess effects of program	Ignore proponent claims, follow checklist	Consumers, accountants	Michael Scriven	House-Hogben	Overvalue documents & record keeping	Data on effect with little co-option
Adversary evaluation	To resolve a two-option choice	Opposing advocates, cross-examination, the jury	Expert, juristic	Tom Owens Murray Levine Bob Wolf	Owens Stake-Gjerde Reinhard	Personalistic, superficial, time-bound	Information impact good; claims put to test

Source: Association for Supervision and Curriculum Development, *Fundamental Curriculum Decisions* (Alexandria, Va.: ASCD, 1983), pp. 142–53.

Note: These descriptive tags are greatly oversimplified. The approaches overlap. Different proponents and different users have different styles. Each protagonist recognizes that one approach is not ideal for all purposes. Any one study may include several approaches. The grid is intended only to show some typical, gross differences among contemporary evaluation activities.

and Beene: "Planned change is the conscious (...deliberate and intended) utilization and application of knowledge as an instrument or tool for modifying patterns and institutions of practice" (Bennis et al., 1969, p. 33).

In curriculum change, it is necessary both to introduce new knowledge and to deal "with the resistance, anxieties, threats to morale, conflicts, disrupted interpersonal communications, and so on, which prospective changes...evoke in the people affected" (p. 33). The kinds of knowledge used to produce change in schools include behavioral knowledge and knowledge of the nonhuman environment as well as technologies derived from them.

Further analysis by Chin and Beene puts change strategies into one of three genotypes: (1) rational/empirical, (2) normative/reeducative, and (3) power/coercive. Their treatment of the intellectual genesis of change strategies in each of these genotypes focuses, in particular, on basic assumptions common to the models in each. Underlying rational/empirical models is the assumption of Western Enlightenment and classical liberalism that humans are essentially reasonable beings who react to environmental stimuli and assert self-interest rationally. Normative/reeducative models assume an interactive relationship between people and their environment that balances social expectations against individual needs and replaces reason with an intelligence founded on pragmatic principles prominent in the earlier part of this century. Power/coercive models use political and economic means of persuasion as well as moral guilt or shame sentiments to influence behavior and give direction. The curriculum field uses change strategies that correspond to elements of all three of the genotypes described (Bennis, et al., 1969, pp. 34–57).

One basis for choosing a strategy may be the degree of curriculum change sought. McNeil (1977, pp. 116–17) developed five categories of curriculum change for discussion and illustration. As McNeil points out, "anticipation [of category/degree of change]"will facilitate planning of resources to effect the change" (p. 117).

Curriculum can be likened to an ongoing constitutional convention, an arena for the sorting of values and priorities that is the business of public policy-making, that is, politics. Indeed, school curriculum is the most important public policy we make and, thus, among the most competitive.

What makes curriculum political? In response, Wiles and Bondi (1984, p. 344) argue:

> It is competition that makes curriculum political; competition for authority and control, competition for scarce resources, competition for the primacy of values. In two short decades, American education has gone from an era of abundance to an era of scarcity, and such scarcity has bred a new and fierce competition in education which is regularly "played out" in the curriculum arena.

In such an unstable environment, a number of variables mitigate against change, including fear, logical conservatism, prior obligations, high risk, lack of identification with change, and little change in awareness (Wiles and Bondi, 1984, pp. 351–52). Among other things, Wiles and Bondi relate change to values, a central focus of this text.

In a much earlier treatment of innovation and an examination of issues related to curriculum change, Miel (1946, pp. 1–14) begins attempting to understand the forces of curriculum crystallization. Such an understanding was thought to be a necessary first step in the systematic fostering of curriculum change.

In Selection 5.4, Miel describes the manifestations of crystallization in the curriculum of the American schools of her time, that is, the graded school, the textbook, the separate school subjects organization, the activity program, and then current principles of curriculum planning. She identifies a number of invalid assumptions and faulty conceptions in the curriculum field that foster the crystallization of school curriculums. Though her analysis and many of her examples are more than forty years old, Miel's work on this topic is timely nonetheless.

CONCLUSION

In the past, primary attention in the curriculum field was given to the process of curriculum planning. Efforts at curriculum development, improvement, and reform were seen as synonymous with planning. Until relatively recently, little attention had been given to the processes of curriculum implementation and evaluation, either in theory or in practice.

However, the perceived failure of the national curriculum movements of the 1950s and 1960s to have an impact on schools commensurate with their potential resulted in greater attention to curriculum implementation and evaluation. Initial work in these areas has resulted in a better understanding of the nature and dynamics of curriculum change. The renewed emphasis within the curriculum field on the use of change models has forced curriculum to go beyond the simplistic planning of new materials that characterized it in an earlier era.

REFERENCES

Anderson, Vernon E. *Principles and Procedures of Curriculum Improvement* (2nd ed.). New York: Ronald Press, 1965.

Association for Supervision and Curriculum Development. *Readings on Curriculum Implementation*. Alexandria, Va.: ASCD, 1980.

Association for Supervision and Curriculum Development. *Fundamental Curriculum Decisions*. Alexandria, Va.: ASCD, 1983.

Beauchamp, George A. *Curriculum Theory*. Itasca, Ill.: F.E. Peacock, 1961; 1968; 1975; 1981.

Bennis, Warren G., et al. (eds.). *The Planning of Change* (2nd ed.). New York: Holt, Rinehart and Winston, 1969.

Berman, Paul, and Milbrey W. McLaughlin. *An Exploratory Study of School District Cooperation*. Santa Monica, Calif.: Rand, 1979.

Boyd, William L. "The Changing Politics of Curriculum Policy-Making for American Schools," *Review of Educational Research* 48:577–628, Fall, 1978.

Caswell, Hollis L., and Doak S. Campbell. *Curriculum Development*. New York: American Book Company, 1935.

Doll, Ronald C. *Curriculum Improvement*. Boston: Allyn and Bacon, 1964; 1970; 1974; 1978.

Fox, G. Thomas, Jr. *Limitations of a Standard Perspective on Program Evaluation: The Example of Ten Years of Teacher Corps Evaluations*. Madison: University of Wisconsin, 1977.

Fullan, Michael, and Alan Pomfret. "Research on Curriculum and Instruction Implementation," *Review of Educational Research* 47:335–97, Winter, 1977.

Gress, James R. "An Experimental Study of the Effects of Teacher Participation in a Curriculum Engineering Task on Selected Dimensions of Curriculum Implementation," AERA Paper, New Orleans, March, 1973.

Gress, James R. "Managing Curriculum/Program/System Change," *Resources in Education* 15:72, September–October, 1980.

Hall, Gene E., and S. F. Loucks. "Program Definition and Adaptation: Implications for Inservice," *Journal of Research and Development in Education* 14:46–58, October, 1981.

Hand, Harold C. "The Principal as a Leader in Curriculum Revision," *Bulletin of the National Association of Secondary School Principals* 39:386–89, October, 1955.

Hord, Shirley M., et al. *Taking Charge of Change*. Alexandria, Va.: ASCD, 1987.

Hunkins, Francis P. *Curriculum Development*. Columbus, Ohio: Charles E. Merrill, 1980.

Kemmis, Stephen. "Seven Principles for Programme Evaluation in Curriculum Development and Innovation," *Journal of Curriculum Studies* 14:221–40, July–September, 1972.

McNeil, John D. *Curriculum: A Comprehensive Introduction*. Boston: Little, Brown, 1977; 1981; 1985.

Michaelis, John U., et al. *New Designs for Elementary School Curriculum and Instruction* (2nd ed.). New York: McGraw-Hill, 1975.

Miel, Alice. *Changing the Curriculum: A Social Process*. New York: Appleton-Century-Crofts, 1946.

Miller, John P., and Wayne Seller. *Curriculum Perspectives and Practice*. New York: Longman, 1985.

Patterson, Jerry L., and Theodore I. Czajkowski. "Implementation: Neglected Phase in Curriculum Change," *Educational Leadership* 37:204–7, December, 1979.

Pratt, David. *Curriculum Design and Development*. New York, Harcourt, Brace, Jovanovich, 1980.

Robison, Helen F. (ed.). *Precedents and Promise in the Curriculum Field*. New York: Teachers College Press, 1966.

Saylor, J. Galen, and William M. Alexander. *Curriculum Planning for Better Teaching and Learning*. New York: Holt, Rinehart and Winston, 1954; 1966; 1974; 1981.

Schaffarzick, Jon, and Hampson, David H. (eds). *Strategies for Curriculum Development*. Berkeley: McCutchan, 1975.

Schaffarzick, Jon, and Gary Sykes (eds.). *Value Conflicts and Curriculum Issues*. Berkeley: McCutchan, 1979.

Schubert, William H. *Curriculum: Perspective, Paradigm and Possibility*. New York: Macmillan, 1986.

Seguel, Mary Louise. *The Curriculum Field: Its Formative Years*. New York: Teachers College Press, 1966.

Shane, Harold G., and E. T. McSwain. *Evaluation and the Elementary Curriculum* (2nd ed.). New York: Henry Holt, 1958.

Tyler, Ralph W., et al. (eds.). *Perspectives of Curriculum Evaluation*. Chicago: Rand McNally, 1967.

Wiles, Jon, and Joseph C. Bondi. *Curriculum Development, A Guide to Practice*. Columbus, Ohio: Bell and Howell, 1979; 1984.

Selection 5.1

The Various Forms of an Innovation

Shirley M. Hord, William L. Rutherford, Leslie Holing-Austin, and Gene E. Hall

In Springdale, Assistant Superintendent Jenkins believed it important for all administrators to be knowledgeable about the new effective teaching program. For this reason administrators would receive advance training before teachers would be expected to use the program. She arranged to have program trainers come to the district and conduct a training session for the entire central office instructional staff and all principals in the district. Teachers received training during the summer, and began using the program in the fall.

By October, it became clear to Jenkins that many teachers were uncertain about how the program was to be used. Teachers in one elementary school complained that the new approach was too time consuming, that restructuring all their lesson plans into the new format was creating too much paperwork, and that the approach was so structured that it was stifling their creativity. The secondary coordinators reported that many high school teachers had not changed their teaching practice because it was their understanding that they could choose whether to use or not to use the program. Both the elementary and secondary coordinators reported that teachers were upset when they received a classroom visit because they thought only

---

SOURCE. From Shirley M. Hord, William L. Rutherford, Leslie Holing-Austin, and Gene E. Hall, *Taking Charge of Change*. Reprinted with permission of the Association for Supervision and Curriculum Development.

"weak" teachers were being targeted for visits and were expected to use the program.

In fact, several teachers had mentioned that they thought the district was penalizing the group for the shortcomings of a few by requiring everyone to attend the training session. Finally, Jenkins was especially distressed to hear that one principal had told his faculty not to worry about the program, that the teaching approach recommended was mostly common sense, and that good teachers were already doing most of it anyway.

Springdale's situation illustrates the common difficulty in communicating to all teachers clear and consistent information about the specific elements of a new program and expectations for its use. Moreover, even when clear information is shared with teachers, you, the facilitator, will often find extensive variations in how teachers implement a new program in their individual classrooms. For example, a new reading program may consist of a textbook, a set of supplementary materials, a record-keeping system, and a set of assessment tests. One teacher may use all pieces of the program in exactly the ways the in-service trainer suggested they be used. A second teacher may use the textbook but not the supplementary materials, use some of the assessment tests, and modify the record-keeping system. A third teacher may use only the textbook.

It is important for a number of reasons for you as a facilitator to be able to identify the specific ways in which teachers put a program into operation. (You can help yourself in this task, and greatly improve teachers' understanding of their tasks, by always communicating in specific operational terms what the program is to look like in classroom practice.) Once implementation is under way, you must be able to identify exactly what specific teachers are doing with the program in order to determine how best to assist them. For example, in the reading program example described above, the teacher who is using only the textbook needs a completely different type of assistance than the teacher who is using all parts of the program. You will also need detailed information about how the program is being implemented to be able to report with confidence to parents, school board members, and others. Finally, before you can consider student outcome data in an attempt to answer the question of how well a certain program works, you must be certain to what degree the program actually has been implemented. It is impossible to determine whether a program has merit if, in fact, it has been poorly or only partially implemented.

THE CONCEPT OF INNOVATION CONFIGURATIONS

The concept of innovation configurations (Hall and Loucks, 1981) emerged from our research on the change process. In our studies, we often attèmpted to answer the question, "How are teachers using *X* Program?" It soon became obvious that we needed to address a prior question: "What exactly is *X* program?"

Answering this question is not always as straightforward as it might seem. Often educational programs are defined in terms of their attributes, ultimate goals, or implementation requirements. One might describe a new program in general terms such as "It's easy to use," or "It's been shown to increase student achievement," or "It's fun and students enjoy it." Such statements may be helpful in some ways, but they do not help the teacher to know what to do with the program.

Describing a program in terms of its ultimate goals also offers little help with the task of implementation. For example, an art program might be intended to develop stronger relationships between teachers and the local art museum, thus encouraging students to visit the museum and bring their parents. While teachers need to be aware of the purpose of what they are doing, goals alone cannot tell them how to implement the program in the classroom. Implementation requirements are another common, but inadequate, way of describing programs. A computer program might require that teachers attend four days of training and that each classroom be equipped with ten student terminals. Again, these requirements are important, but do little to specify how the program is to be operated.

While attributes, goals, and implementation requirements are important, we believe it is critical to be able to talk about an educational program in clear, operational terms. To be truly helpful to teachers, you must be able to describe how a program will look in actual practice in the classroom. This concern guided our research and led to the development of the concept of innovation configurations.

Innovation configurations (IC) represents the patterns of innovation use that result when different teachers put innovations into operation in their classrooms. In the course of our early work, we noted that individual teachers (and professors) used different parts of an innovation in different ways. When these parts were put together, a number of patterns emerged, each characterizing a different use of the innovation. We called these patterns innovation configurations. We developed a tool, the IC component checklist (Heck, Stiegelbauer, Hall, and Loucks, 1981), for use in identifying the components, or parts, of an innovation and variations in the use of each part. This procedure has helped to answer the question "What is it?" Before we focus our attention on the checklist, however, it is important to explain some of the basic terms we use in talking about IC.

Terminology Related to IC

We use the term *component* to mean the major operational features or parts of any innovation. With instructional innovations, component descriptions are usually based on materials, teacher behaviors, and student activities. A simple example would be a continuous progress math program with three components:

Component 1: Use of instructional materials
Component 2: Grouping of students
Component 3: Testing and use of test results

A language arts program might consist of the following four components:

Component 1: Use of sequenced program objectives
Component 2: Use of program materials
Component 3: Use of prescribed writing process
Component 4: Student recording of writing progress

In some programs, those components that have been determined to be essential to innovation use are designated as *critical*. Other, *related* components are not considered essential to the innovation but are recommended by the developer or facilitator as "nice to have." Designation of a component as critical or related can be done by a developer, change facilitator, user, or evaluator, preferably through a consensus-reaching process involving all these persons. Also, the designations may change during the life cycle of the innovation. For example, in the case of the continuous progress math program, the facilitator may decide that during the first year of use, only component 1 (use of program materials) is critical. In other words, teachers must use the program materials, but they may choose to use or not to use components 2 and 3. As implementation progresses and teachers use component 1 successfully, however, the other two components will be given attention and perhaps be designated as critical.

Within each component, there are a number of possible *variations* that might be observed during implementation. Variations represent the different ways in which a teacher can put a component into operation in the classroom. Note the variatons in each of the three components of the continuous progress math program:

Component 1: Use of instructional materials
a. program materials only
b. program materials plus basic text
c. text only
d. teacher-made materials only

Component 2: Grouping of students
a. large, heterogeneous groups
b. large, homogeneous groups
c. small groups
d. completely individualized

Component 3: Testing and use of test results
a. testing once every six weeks but nothing done with test results
b. testing weekly with test results fed back to students
c. student self-testing upon completing each objective

As we have mentioned, configurations are the operational patterns of an innovation that result from implementation of different component variations. In the example above, one teacher of the continuous progress math program might be teaching students as a large group, using program materials plus the basic text (component 1, variation b), with testing done every six weeks but nothing done with test results (component 3, variation a). "Component 1, variation b; component 2, variation b; and component 3, variation a"; or "bba" represents this teacher's configuration. Other combinations of component variations represent other configurations. When configurations for a large number of teachers have been identified, it is possible to determine the most common ones and to identify the teachers who are using identical or similar configurations and those who are not. Again, this information is helpful in determining what types of assistance are most appropriate for specific teachers.

Another term that often comes up in relation to IC is that of *fidelity*. Often people assume that as developers of the IC concept, we must be proponents of strict fidelity, expecting teachers to use a program exactly as it was envisioned by an innovation developer. Actually, we do not take a stand on the fidelity issue; that is, we do not propose that one particular configuration of use of an innovation is what all teachers should be doing. We do, however, argue for the need for facilitators to be well informed about how teachers are using a program, whatever their use may be. It is up to the facilitators of each specific program to determine what "ideal" practice is and to determine how much variation from that ideal is acceptable.

MORE ABOUT IC COMPONENT CHECKLISTS

As mentioned earlier, the IC component checklist is a tool for identifying specific components or parts of an innovation and the variations that might be expected as the innovation is put into operation in classrooms or schools. An innovation-specific checklist should be developed for each program that is to be the focus of a school improvement effort. Once you have developed the checklist, you can use it to introduce the program and communicate how the components and variations might be phased in for classroom use. Once implementation is under way, you can use the checklist to monitor program progress by interviewing teachers about their use of the program and their typical classroom practice. During or immediately after each interview, you can complete an IC component checklist for each teacher by circling the number or letter of the variation that best describes that teacher's practice within each component.

The IC component checklist can be organized into various formats. The simplest format is to prepare the checklist in list or outline form, much as the continuous progress math program checklist was organized. You can use this checklist by simply placing a check mark by the appropriate variations. Another way of organizing the checklist is a left-to-right format, with the variations of each component organized across the page. Using this format, you can place the variation judged to be the ideal or most acceptable variation of each component in the far left column, with the other variations ranging in order of descending acceptability across the page so that the least desirable variation appears in the far right column. An example of an IC component checklist organized in the left-to-right format is shown in Figure 5.1-1. Note the use of the vertical dotted and solid lines to indicate ideal, acceptable, and unacceptable practice. Variations to the left of the dotted line are considered ideal. Variations located between the dotted and solid vertical lines are acceptable, though not ideal, and variations to the right of the solid line are unacceptable. This format provides a graphic picture of ideal or preferred practice, valuing some variations over others.

In constructing a checklist, you will find that there is no set number of components that an innovation should have and no set number of variations that a component should have. The number of components will be determined by the major parts of the innovation. Most innovations will have between three and eight major parts, although some complex innovations will contain more. Variations within components should represent meaningful differences in classroom practice and yet not be so numerous as to make it difficult to identify patterns of use. Generally, you will find three to five variations, although in some cases only two variations will exist (as

FIGURE 5.1—1 Tutoring Program Checklist

Component	(1)	(2)	(3)
*1. Materials and Equipment	At least 5 different program materials are used with each child each session.	At least 3 different program materials are used with each child each session.	Fewer than 3 different program materials are used with each child each session.
*2. Diagnosis	Children are diagnosed individually using a combination of tests and teacher judgment.	Children are diagnosed individually using teacher judgment only.	Children are diagnosed individually.
3. Record-Keeping	Individual record sheet used to record diagnosis and prescription.	No individual record sheets are used.	
*4. Use of Teaching Technique	Continually readjusts task according to child needs; uses rewards to reinforce success.	Does not continually readjust task according to child needs; does not use rewards.	
5. Grouping	Children are taught in pairs.	Children are not taught in pairs.	
*6. Scheduling	Children are taught for 30 minutes 3 times per week. Each session is equally divided between children.	Children are taught for 30 minutes 3 times per week, time for each child and each task varies slightly when necessary.	Children are not taught for 30 minutes per week 3 times per week, or time for each child and each task varies markedly or is not considered.

CODE: ——— Variations to the right are unacceptable; variations to the left are acceptable.
------- Variations to the left are ideal, as prescribed by the developer.
* Denotes critical components. From: Heck, Stiegelbauer, Hall, and Louck, 1981.

in the case when something is or is not present). Occasionally you may identify more than five variations within a component.

You can identify components of an innovation and variations within components by reviewing written materials on the program and interviewing the developer or some other authority on the program. From this information a preliminary checklist (often in the form of a list or outline) can be developed. This preliminary checklist can be useful in communicating what the program is and clarifying expectations for its use. If implementation is already under way when the preliminary checklist is developed, you can use it to observe and interview a small number of users to verify the initially identified components and variations and to identify others. Using the information gained through this initial data-gathering activity, you (often in collaboration with the developer/program authority) can then revise and expand the checklist to better reflect actual classroom practice. At this time, decisions are usually made about which variations are more desirable than others. The revised checklist then can be used to interview a larger number of users in different adopter sites, and further revisions can be made if necessary.

Constructing checklists is a complex task. One- and two-day workshops are available to train facilitators in developing skills in checklist construction. Our intent here is to introduce you to the concept of IC, the process of checklist development, and the application of the IC component checklist in facilitating the implementation of educational programs.

IC AND THE SPRINGDALE EFFECTIVE TEACHING PROGRAM

When Springdale's Assistant Superintendent Jenkins began to realize that teachers felt uncertain about how the effective teaching program was to be used, she met with the instructional coordinators and later with school principals to discuss the matter. The discussions revealed that while everyone seemed to have a general understanding of the program, few people understood exactly what was expected of teachers in their use of the program in daily classroom practice. Jenkins realized that a large part of the confusion could have been avoided if she had prepared an IC component checklist at the outset. Certainly at this time it was important to develop an IC component checklist in order to communicate expectations about the program and how it was to be implemented.

Working with several of the instructional coordinators and the program trainer who had provided training for the district, Jenkins developed a preliminary checklist. In mid-November, she used the checklist to interview and observe a small sample of teachers. Using information gained from these interviews, she and the instructional coordinators made revisions, developing the checklist shown in Figure 5.1–2. For the first year of implementation, they decided that component 2: selecting and stating objectives, component 3: explaining and modeling, and component 5: providing guided practice, were most important. (Note the asterisk on the checklist by these components, indicating that they are considered critical.) When collecting IC data and doing teacher observations, facilitators would focus most attention on these components. Jenkins and her associates identified variations within each component as ideal, acceptable, or unacceptable, to use as a guideline on which to base their expectations for the first year of implementation. (Note the use of the dotted and solid vertical lines on the checklist indicating ideal, acceptable, and unacceptable variations.) In the second year of implementation they would focus more attention on the remaining three components as well as on the initial three components identified as critical during the first year.

In late November, copies of the checklist were shared with all principals to communicate the district's expectations concerning implementation of the effective teaching program. The principals decided to meet with their teachers before the Christmas break, in departmental and grade-level meetings, to discuss the program and explain the district's expectations and priorities for the first year of implementation. Prior to this meeting, principals were encouraged to collect information about teacher concerns. Principals then structured their meetings around the concerns and issues raised by teachers. The principals reported that teachers found the meeting helpful and asked numerous questions about how much time they would have before they would be expected to begin using the program and how they would be evaluated on its use.

In January and February, instructional coordinators scheduled a series of grade-level and subject-area meetings focused on the specific components of the program identified as critical in year 1: selecting and stating objectives, explaining and modeling, and providing guided practice. In March and April, teachers were provided opportunities to observe "veteran" teachers using the program in a neighboring school district. A schedule was worked out in order to provide release time for each teacher who wanted to participate in this observation activity; substitutes were hired to cover the classes teachers missed while observing. In May, the principals and instructional coordinators completed an IC checklist on each teacher as one part of their assessment of the new program's first year of implementation.

FIGURE 5.1—2 Springdale Effective Teaching Program Checklist

Component 1: Using an Anticipatory Set				
(1)	(2)	(3)	(4)	(5)
Teacher typically uses an anticipatory set including the elements of review, preview, motivation, and direction	Teacher typically uses an anticipatory set that includes one to two appropriate elements	Teacher typically uses an anticipatory set that consists mainly of focusing attention	Teacher seldom uses an anticipatory set	Teacher never uses an anticipatory set
***Component 2: Selecting and Stating Objectives**				
(1)	(2)	(3)	(4)	(5)
Teacher typically uses an objective that is relevant to students and states it in student terms	Teacher typically uses an objective that is relevant to students but seldom states it	Teacher typically states objectives, but not in student terms	Teacher seldom uses an objective	Teacher never uses an objective
***Component 3: Explaining and Modeling**				
(1)	(2)	(3)	(4)	
Teacher typically explains and models so that students see and understand	Teacher typically explains so that students understand but does not model	Teacher typically gives explanations that are not on the student's level	Teacher typically makes assignments with no explanation or modeling	

Component 4: Checking for Understanding

(1)	(2)	(3)	(4)	(5)
Teacher typically checks for understanding and gives immediate feedback after each section of the lesson	Teacher occasionally checks for understanding and gives feedback during the lesson	Teacher typically checks for understanding at the end of the lesson and gives feedback	Teacher occasionally checks for understanding at the end of the lesson	Teacher typically assigns work without checking for understanding

*Component 5: Providing Guided Practice

(1)	(2)	(3)	(4)
Teacher typically checks work as students practice	Teacher occasionally checks work as students practice	Teacher does not check work as students practice	Teacher typically does not provide practice for students

*Component 6: Providing Independent Practice

(1)	(2)	(3)
Teacher typically assigns independent practice that is appropriate for all students in length and difficulty	Teacher typically assigns independent practice that is appropriate for most students, but inappropriate for a few	Teacher typically does not provide for independent practice

CODE: _____ Variations to the right are unacceptable; variations to the left are acceptable.
------- Variations to the left are ideal, as prescribed by the developer.
*Denotes critical component

NOTE: This checklist is an integration of checklists focused on the Madalyn Hunter Effective Teaching Program developed by two North Carolina principals in the "Even Champions Have Coaches Training Program" (Draughon and Hord 1986).

DISPLAY AND INTERPRETATION OF IC DATA

Springdale School District's use of an IC component checklist demonstrates how IC can be used to help clarify a program in the initial phases of implementation. IC can also be helpful in monitoring an implementation effort in progress and in identifying innovation components that may need attention. Depending on the purpose for which the data are to be used, IC data can be organized and displayed in a number of ways. Two ways of organizing data that we have found to be especially useful are by individual user and by innovation component. Let's use the example of The Science Program (TSP) to demonstrate the utility of organizing data in these two ways (Hall, Hord, Rutherford, Loucks, Huling, and Heck, 1982).

TSP is a second-generation science curriculum based on the science curriculums developed in the sixties and the experiences of those who have used them over the years. TSP places equal emphasis on learning the basic principles and theories of science and learning to design, conduct, and interpret scientific investigations. The program emphasizes students' working with materials, with the teacher serving in a tutorial role. The program is divided into a series of units; each unit has a theme that gradually emerges as the activities of the unit are covered. A set of standardized TSP tests have been designed to assess achievement in science content and science process. The IC component checklist for TSP is shown in Figure 5.1–3.

To illustrate our approaches to organizing data, we will examine hypothetical IC data collected from ten teachers in the program midway through the first year of implementation. In Figure 5.1–4, the data from the ten teachers are displayed by individual user. These data indicate that teacher D appears to be the farthest along in use of the program, while teachers E and F show the least degree of implementation. Using this information, a facilitator might ask Teacher D to assist other teachers with their use of the program and investigate why teachers E and F are not using the program more. The facilitator then can provide personalized assistance to help them improve their use of the program. The data also indicate that all teachers except teachers A, B, and D could benefit from assistance in how to balance the content/process emphasis of the program, while teachers B, E, and F need assistance focused on student grouping.

Organizing and displaying IC data by individual user helps to reveal what types of assistance would be most valuable to individual users. Also, with data organized this way, it is possible to identify individuals who are using identical or highly similar configurations of the program. For example, teachers H and J are using the exact same configuration of the program; the configurations of teachers G and I are also identical, and are

FIGURE 5.1—3 (TSP) Science Program Configuration Checklist

	(1)	(2)	(3)	(4)	(5)
*Component 1: Units Taught	All units and most activities are taught	Most units and activities are taught	Some units are taught	A few selected activities are taught	No units or activities are taught
*Component 2: Use of Materials:	Students are constantly manipulating science materials	Only the teacher and selected students handle the materials most of the time	Typically, the teacher does demonstrations and the students watch		
Component 3: Student Grouping:	Students work individually and in small groups	Students are kept in three to five permanent groups	The whole class is taught as a group		
*Component 4: Process/Content Emphasis:	Science content and science processes are emphasized qually	Science content is given major emphasis	The processes of science are given major emphasis	Memorization of facts and reading about science are emphasized	
*Component 5: Assessment	All TSP assessment activities are used	Some TSP assessment activities are used	Teacher-made tests are used on a regular basis	Tests are not given regularly	

CODE: ——— Variations to the right are unacceptable; variations to the left are acceptable.
------- Variations to the left are ideal, as prescribed by the developer.

*Denotes critical components.

FIGURE 5.1—4 Teachers' Use of Each Component by Variation Numbers

Teacher	*Components* 1. Units Taught	2. Use of Materials	3. Student Grouping	4. Process/ Content Emphasis	5. Assess-ment
A	1	2	2	1	3
B	2	3	3	1	3
C	1	1	1	3	2
D	1	1	1	1	1
E	5	3	3	2	3
F	4	2	3	4	4
G	2	2	2	2	3
H	2	2	2	3	3
I	2	2	2	2	3
J	2	2	2	3	3

highly similar to those of teachers H and J. Teachers E and F have configurations highly similar to each other and probably could benefit from similar types of assistance. Additional insights can be gained by examining the IC data by innovation component, as shown in Figure 5.1–5. These data provide a more global overview of the implementation of TSP. The chart indicates that, considering the short time implementation has been under way, teacher use of the program is progressing well. Teachers are teaching many of the units and activities and, in some cases, students are being allowed to manipulate the program materials. Teachers should be congratulated for their rapid progress with these aspects of the program. However, the IC data indicate some problems with the process/content emphasis of the program. There are also variations in how teachers are grouping students. The IC data, reorganized by innovation component, can provide insight into the parts of the program on which facilitators should focus. In this case, it appears that facilitators need to focus on helping teachers begin to use TSP tests and encourage the equal emphasis of content and process. The data indicate that using in-service sessions to reemphasize the use of units, activities, and materials probably would not be the best approach. Rather, teachers E and F, who most need this type of assistance, should receive personalized attention.

FIGURE 5.1—5 Percentage of Teachers Using Each Variation of Each Component

Component 1:	1	2	3	4	5
Units Taught	30%	50%		10%	10%
Component 2:	1	2	3		
Use of Materials	20%	60%	20%		
Component 3:	1	2	3		
Student Grouping	20%	50%	30%		
Component 4:	1	2	3	4	
Process/Content Emphasis	30%	30%	30%	10%	
Component 5:	1	2	3	4	
Assessment	10%	10%	70%	10%	

SUMMARY

In this chapter we have discussed the concept of innovation configurations (IC) and its application in school improvement. IC represents the different ways individual users implement an innovation in their own settings. It is important for you as a change facilitator to be able to identify the specific ways teachers are using a program so that you can make informed decisions about how to offer support and assistance. The concept of IC is particularly useful in helping to clarify and communicate expectations related to the use of an innovation during the initial implementation phase and in monitoring implementation in progress to identify the individuals and parts of the program that require the facilitator's attention.

The IC component checklist is a tool for summarizing the descriptions of identified component parts of an innovation and the variations in how parts are put to use. In some programs some components are considered critical while others are considered related. A critical component is one that must be used if the innovation is to be considered implemented, while a related component is not considered essential to the innovation, but is recommended by the developer or facilitator. Critical components are designated on the checklist with an asterisk (*).

A variety of IC component checklist formats can be used, but organizing the checklist in a left-to-right format, with the variations of each component organized across the page, has the advantage of graphically displaying those variations valued over others. The ideal or more acceptable variation of the component is displayed in the far left column, with the other variations ranging in order of descending acceptability across the page. Ideal or most acceptable practice is placed to the left of a dotted line; a solid vertical line is used to indicate unacceptable practice, placed to the right of the line. Variations located between the dotted and solid vertical lines are acceptable, though not ideal.

IC data can be displayed and used in a number of ways. Two particularly useful ways of organizing data are by individual user and by innovation component. When IC data are organized by individual user, it is possible to identify what types of assistance would be most valuable to specific persons. When IC data are organized by innovation component, it is possible to identify the parts of the program that are being used most successfully and those that require additional time and attention from the facilitator.

IC can be used for purposes of formative evaluation, to help pinpoint areas in need of attention, and to help facilitators decide how best to intervene. IC is also useful in summative evaluation; it addresses the question of how well a program has been implemented and thus helps evaluators decide how much confidence to place in the outcome data. If a program has been implemented to a high degree, facilitators usually can be confident that their outcome measures are a fair reflection of the program's success or failure. On the other hand, if the program has not been implemented acceptably, outcome data cannot fairly reflect a program's potential.

Innovation configurations is a useful concept for change facilitators. Understanding how individuals are implementing a specific program provides the change facilitator with information for designing appropriate support and assistance. Used in combination with the other diagnostic dimensions of the concerns-based adoption model, innovation configurations can make a substantial difference in the school improvement process.

. . .

REFERENCES

Draughon, B.S., and S.M. Hord, "Even Champions Have Coaches: Principals Provide Professional Development for Their Peers," *Journal of Staff Development* 7: 2 (1986): 81-90.

Hall, G.E., and S.F. Loucks. "Program Definition and Adaptation: Implications for Inservice," *Journal of Research and Development in Education* 14, 2 (1981): 46-58.

Hall, G.E., S. Hord, W.L. Rutherford, S.F. Loucks, L.L. Huling and S.A. Heck. *Workshop on Innovation Configurations: The Trainer's Manual.* Austin: Research and Development Center for Teacher Education, University of Texas at Austin, 1982.

Heck, S., S.M. Stiegelbauer, G.E. Hall, and S.F. Loucks. "Measuring Innovation Configurations: Procedures and Applications." Austin: Research and Development Center for Teacher Education, University of Texas at Austin, 1981.

Selection 5.2

Seven Principles for Program Evaluation in Curriculum Development and Innovation

Stephen Kemmis

Different definitions of evaluation abound. The Australian Curriculum Development Centre (CDC) Study Group on curriculum evaluation reviewed a variety of definitions with currency in the evaluation literature and adopted the following one as the most useful guide for the evaluation of CDC's own projects and programs and for curriculum evaluation more generally: "Evaluation is the process of delineating, obtaining and providing information useful for making decisions and judgments about educational programs and curricula (Curriculum Development Centre, 1977, p. 24)".

This definition highlights the function of evaluative information in assisting decision making. It reflects a fairly widespread agreement among evaluation theorists about the role of evaluation in informing action at discrete decision points. (See, e.g., Cronbach, 1963; MacDonald, 1973,; Stufflebeam, 1971.). But it is important to recognize that a curriculum program and its evaluation are highly interactive, not only in "summative" decisions, but throughout the process of curriculum development. In short, the discrete decision points are few and far between and evaluation permeates development: the two processes are not discontinuous. Accord-

---

SOURCE. Reprinted in an abridged form, with the permission of the author and publisher, from Journal of Curriculum Studies 14 (July–September 1982): 221–40.

ingly, a desirable definition of evaluation will acknowledge the mutuality of the relationship between evaluation and curriculum development.

. . .

It is critical in deciding on a definition to guide evaluation efforts to give due importance to the pervasiveness of the evaluation dimension of all human activity, and to the fact that it is present in a range of individual and public judgment processes that exist whether or not an evaluation is formally commissioned or expected of project and program participants. Indeed, when evaluations of particular programs *are* commissioned, they should approximate (and focus and sharpen) these informal critical processes, not ignore or supplant them. Though the formality of commissioning or requiring an evaluation imposes certain obligations to formalize and discipline the individual and public judgment processes that occur naturally in considered activity, formal evaluations should attempt deliberately to preserve something of the conviviality of the informal processes.

Preserving conviviality is no easy task. These principles attempt to provide a framework within which conviviality can be preserved by emphasizing the continuity and mutuality of concern between program participants, a program sponsor, an evaluation sponsor, and an evaluator. They also attempt to emphasize that evaluation forms a natural part of the critical thinking that guides the development process. This is not to say that formal evaluations can lack rigor, discipline, or honesty; rather, it is to assert that their critical edge should be tempered with humane values rather than narrowly technocratic or bureaucratic concerns.

Accordingly, the definition of evaluation that has informed and guided the development of these principles is this: *Evaluation is the process of marshalling information and arguments that enable interested individuals and groups to participate in the critical debate about a specific program.* So construed, evaluation consists in harnessing and refining the ubiquitous processes of individual and public judgment, not in resolving or replacing them with a technology of judgment.

. . .

1. THE PRINCIPLE OF RATIONALITY AS REASONABLENESS

Program participants act reasonably in the light of their circumstances and opportunities. It is the task of an evaluation to illuminate the reasoning that guides program development and evolution, to identify the contextual and historal factors that influence it, and to facilitate critical examination of these matters in and around the program community.

Evaluation is always guided by the impulse to understand and to act on the basis of understanding. It thus has a major role to play in articulating justifications of action. Properly speaking, the justification of action is not merely a backward-looking enterprise, to be equated with post-rationalization. On the contrary, it is concerned with demonstrating both *how* things have come to be as they are (that is, with illuminating the reasoning that has guided the activities of those associated with a program and identifying the circumstances that shaped and constrained them) and with providing information and arguments that can justify contemplated action.

. . .

The implication of the principle of rationality as reasonableness is that evaluators will attend to a wide variety of perspectives on a program, to the diverse claims made about it, to its context, and to its history. They will thus be in a position to harness and refine the individual and public judgment processes by which the program comes to be understood and by which its value is determined. The quality of the evaluation may be judged by the quality of its contribution to informing and improving the critical debate about the program.

Evaluation should thus aim to contribute to program improvement both directly and indirectly: by its direct interaction with program participants and by feeding and refining the interaction between program participants and their audiences.

An alternative principle to the principle of rationality as reasonableness, and one that is not advocated here, is that of "rationality as rule-following." Stake's (1975) label of "preordinate" fits evaluation approaches that have prior rules for judging a program and do not respond to immediate value-perspectives, information needs, and circumstances. For example, some evaluation approaches are based on the notion of rational consumption and set out criteria and standards that must be met before a program can be considered a "good buy." Scriven's (1974) "product evaluation checklist" is perhaps the best example of this. It lists thirteen considerations in the evaluation of products, producers, and proposals, and sets standards of adequacy for each. They are: (1) need; (2) market; (3) performance: true field trials; (4) performance: true consumer; (5) performance: critical comparisons; (6) performance: long term; (7) performance: side effects; (8) performance: process; (9) performance: causation; (10) performance: statistical significance; (11) performance: educational significance; (12) cost effectiveness; and (13) extended support.

These are powerful considerations, and the model provides a useful set of questions to be asked of a program or product. But the criteria are subject to interpretation in application and they do not respond sufficiently to the nature of the critical debate that actually attends a program. . . .

A second alternative principle, also not advocated here, is the view of rationality implied in "rational planning." This view sees justification as based on the notion of satisfaction of needs. If a need can be identified and regarded as an urgent one, then programs can be designed to satisfy it. Relatively few educational programs can be said to satisfy urgent needs, though education as a whole responds to a general social need. But the rational planning approach tends also to take a contractual view of programs: to see them in terms of the obligations imposed on those brave or foolish enough to accept grants to develop programs. Within such a view, measurements of need-reduction or aims-achievement, coupled with fulfillment of contractual obligations, are sufficient to demonstrate that a program is successful.

Potential grantees exploit the invitation this approach suggests, "manufacturing" needs, overpromising, and using limited or biased measures. The exploitations are not always deliberate; rather, they are inspired by a cultural tendency towards legalism and concepts of exchange rooted in economics. Such values have their place, of course, and program evaluations that do not attend to the contractual obligations of grantees may fail to take account of important aspects of the programs

. . .

To adopt the principle of rationality as reasonableness is thus to take the view that social truths are socially negotiated and historically and culturally relative. It is to reject the notion that any discrete set of rules can be formulated that will provide universal criteria of program adequacy. Similarly, it is to reject the notion that programs can be justified solely by reference to their own goals, objectives, and obligations or by reference solely to needs reduction. Evaluations based on either of these alternative perspectives are likely to be limited and partial, providing an inadequate basis of information and argument for those who want to enter the critical debate about a program.

2. THE PRINCIPLE OF AUTONOMY AND RESPONSIBILITY

Moral responsibility for an outcome can only be ascribed to a person to the degree that his or her free choice of action as an autonomous moral agent was a cause of that outcome. Curriculum development projects and programs are co-operative enterprises. Evaluators must illuminate the interactive character of accountability for a program.

Just as the evaluator may assume that those involved with a program act rationally in the sense that they are open to arguments based on reason, so it may be assumed that those involved with the program are autonomous and responsible moral agents. This has implications for the way program participants, evaluators, evaluation sponsors, and program sponsors view accountability issues in evaluation.

Most program sponsors use or distribute public funds for program development and implementation. They are publicly accountable for their use of these funds; program participants must also account for their use of the resources allocated to them. Financial and management procedures usually accompany development project fundings to ensure that accountability demands are met. A "maximalist" view of accountability requires program participants to justify every decision about the use of resources by reference to program goals, social needs, and the consequences of each decision (especially in terms of program outcomes for students and teachers). But it is sufficient to adopt a "minimalist" view of accountability as keeping financial and other records that show that programs have operated within their budgets and according to their terms of reference, and to make these records open to view. (See Stake, 1973, pp. 1–3).

More generally, the minimalist view of accountability is based on the principle of autonomy and responsibility. According to this principle, moral responsibility for an outcome can be ascribed to a person only to the degree that his or her free choice of action as an autonomous moral agent was a cause of that outcome. To the degree that the person's choices were constrained by others, or by circumstances outside his control, then to that degree the person cannot be held responsible (or at least not solely responsible) for the outcomes.

. . .

One alternative principle concerning accountability not advocated here would be one based on ideals of truth and justice. According to such a principle, an evaluator or program sponsor might adopt some view of what constituted true and just work, perhaps spelling out criteria for truth and justice. These would then constitute a view of what "the good" (or best) in curriculum development might be. Program participants could be held accountable for deviations from this ideal.

This sort of principle is clearly unsuitable given the commitment already declared to the notion that social truths are socially negotiated. And it is unsuitable in a pluralist society where different value-perspectives, with different patterns of coherence and legitimacy, coexist. Curriculum development always expresses social and educational values, and it is proper that they be critically analyzed and examined in each case. Far from asserting what values are proper for a program and then judging it according to those values alone, evaluations should attempt to explore the diverse values and value perspectives expressed in a program and the work of those involved in developing it, setting these in a context of the diverse values of the wider society beyond the development group.

. . .

A second alternative view of accountability, likewise not advocated here, might be one based on the notion of contractual obligation. Such a view would seem to be based more on notions of prudence and expedience than on principle. Nevertheless, it is worth exploring briefly. The accountability issue as it has been aired in education has frequently been discussed in these terms. According to this view, there is a chain of obligations from the classroom teacher through education systems to ministers of education and ultimately through parliaments to the people. Each superordinate agency is seen as totally responsible for the actions of all subordinates. This view is based on a notion of management that might be described as highly positivistic, that is, the notion that management causes events to occur. This managerialism is contrary to the facts of development, of course: subordinates are not mere operators whose every action is determined by job specification. It is also contrary to the values of professionalism in education: teachers are not operatives but relatively autonomous professionals. (This value reaches its peak in the notion of academic freedom; it is moderated by notions of social responsibility.)

. . .

Ideals for action as a basis for accountability are thus inadequate as are purely contractual views. There is merit in both alternatives: the one puts a premium on the value commitments of program sponsors; the other puts a premium on the responsibility of program staff to meet their contractual obligations. But each is insufficient, failing to recognize value plurality and the co-operative character of development work (a program sponsor is not simply an initiator of development activity; it negotiates the character and amount of development activity in planning and executing its programs).

3. THE PRINCIPLE OF COMMUNITY SELF-INTEREST

When a curriculum development project is formed, it is a community of self-interests — it represents the self-interests of all participants within its terms of reference. The evaluator has a responsibility to illuminate the extent of commonality and conflict among the values and interests of participants in this community.

When a program sponsor enters relations with other agencies (education systems or individual officers who work on its projects, for example) and negotiates the terms of reference that set up a project or program, it forms a community of self-interests with them. Within the terms of reference of the program, the (self-) interests of the sponsor and these other individuals or groups coincide. Program organization always has this co-operative character. A program sponsor is thus always only one among a number of participants in the communities of self-interests formed by its projects and programs.

Individual self-interests, which exist outside the terms of reference of the co-operative, are irrelevant to it unless conflicts of interest prejudice the interests of the co-operative itself.

When a program sponsor commissions a project or sets up a program, it establishes a community of self-interests. Similarly, when a program sponsor commissions an evaluation study, it should recognize that the role of the sponsor is a critical aspect of the program to be evaluated. Sponsorship of development and evaluation confers no exclusive right to have the interests of the sponsor served at the expense of other participants in the community of self-interests. With respect to both programs and their evaluations, the actions of program sponsors may be examined in terms of their fairness in agreeing on terms of reference and negotiating contracts. House and Care (1977) set out conditions indicative of fair agreement, one of which is community self-interestedness. The conditions are: noncoercion; rationality; acceptance of terms; joint agreement; disinterestedness; universality; community self-interestedness; equal and full information; nonriskiness; possibility; "counting all votes"; participation.

. . .

Once a community of self-interests has been formed, however, a program sponsor's particular interests must be considered in an evaluation study alongside the interests of other participants. A sponsoring agency cannot expect to withdraw from the co-operative enterprise at the point of judgment in the guise of "disinterested observer" (disavowing involvement). It is relevant to note that the concept of the interests of a sponsoring agency is a slippery one, at least in the case of government agencies, charitable foundations, and the like. As institutions, these agencies are themselves communities of interests bound together by the common goals of their enterprise and the organization of their common work. They may be defined by an act, charter, or constitution; governed by a council; responsible to a minister; and express a variety of interests in their staff. Within them, a variety of individuals bring their interests to bear in shaping the overall common interest. At the same time, these diverse individuals are capable of disinterest, suspending their own values and interests as they try to understand and develop the common work. The notion of a community of self-interests is an important one simply because it emphasizes these "internal" and "external" negotiations. Programs are co-operative efforts among participants and thus sponsors cannot disavow their involvement when commissioning evaluation studies.

. . .

Two alternative principles to the principle of community self-interest could be proposed, based on the one hand on the notion of "the public interest" (defined outside the interests of participating individuals and agencies), or, on the other, on the notion of the sponsor's self-interest. The first might depend on some definition of what is supposed to be in the public good and specify criteria by which programs might be judged; the second might assert a narrow definition of value according to the sponsor's own perspectives. For reasons already outlined in the discussion of earlier principles (social negotiation of social truths, pluralism, the importance of contributing the critical debate about a program), neither of these approaches is a reasonable option. Since the sponsoring agency is a participant in the development process along with other groups and agencies, it is interested in improving the quality of critical debate about curriculum. To do so, it requires evaluations that share information among those involved in the process (with due regard for the protection of the rights of individuals) rather than evaluations that serve only its own purposes or only those of other particular groups within the co-operative. (Equally, it is not interested in evaluations that serve only the purposes of those outside the communities of self-interests it forms.)

4. THE PRINCIPLE OF PLURALITY OF VALUE PERSPECTIVES

A range of different value perspectives becomes relevant in judging a program. An evaluation should identify these different perspectives and be responsive to the different concerns they imply.

Program participants' values and interests are served by their participation in curriculum development. The particular individuals and agencies cooperating in a project or program have their own values and interests that may be independently justified. Other audiences for the work of a project or program will likewise judge it by reference to their own values and interests. A program sponsor can claim no monopoly on the values or criteria by which a program is to be evaluated.

According to the principle of plurality of value perspectives, program evaluators should recognize that a range of perspectives may be relevant in making a judgment of it. Any judgment of the value of a project or program will be made in the light of the value commitments of the judge; program evaluators should therefore inform themselves and their audiences about the value perspectives of relevant judges, be responsive to their concerns, and provide information that is appropriate (and valued most highly) as evidence according to their criteria of judgment. If the information and arguments collected in the course of the evaluative study are relevant and significant to the audiences of the evaluation, there is a greater likelihood that they will be used in the critical debate about the program.

As an alternative to this principle, the view could be taken that judgments of a program should be the prerogative of those best equipped to judge: for example, competent authorities in curriculum as a field, curriculum development processes, the subject matter of the program, or teaching and learning processes. While these specialists may well be able to provide valuable information and insights into the program, they are not the only ones entitled to judge it. An evaluation should embrace such perspectives but should go beyond them to take into account the perspectives of other interested parties (for example, students, parents, community groups, or employers). The mature judgment of specialists may be of great value to audiences less familiar with specialist debates about the nature and worth of a program, but lay concerns demand attention too: as clients or observers of the program, laymen must have their questions treated seriously in an evaluation study, have specialist issues made accessible to them, and see how these specialist issues fit into the broader context of the issues concerning the program as a whole.

Still another principle that could be adopted would concern a sponsor's own right to judge, and the primacy of its right as a sponsor of development to have its own questions answered. To be sure, a program evaluation should address questions that the sponsor regards as important. But such a principle, pursued single-mindedly, would have a conservative and defensive effect. It would make the evaluation a service for the sponsor at the expense of other audiences with legitimate rights to be heard. In order to feed the critical debate about the program and to refine it, an evaluation must engage the perspectives of a variety of audiences.

5. THE PRINCIPLE OF THE SELF-CRITICAL COMMUNITY: INTERNAL EVALUATION, EVALUATION CONSULTANCY, META-EVALUATION, EXTERNAL AND INDEPENDENT EVALUATION

Critical debate about the nature and worth of a program already exists within and around its program community. It is the task of program evaluation to refine this debate and improve its bearing on program action. Evaluation consultancy may provide additional tools for this purpose. Meta-evaluation efforts may help to improve the quality of the contribution of program evaluation. An external evaluation may contribute to the criticial debate by increasing awareness of a particular set of values and interests relevant to a program; it should not be thought of as an alternative to the self-critical process. An independent evaluation may help to harness program self-criticism where the program community is diffuse or divided by controversy. Self-criticism by the program community is the primary basis for program evaluation; other evaluation efforts extend it in different ways but do not supplant it.

The community of self-interests formed by a curriculum project or program is likely to embrace a variety of value perspectives that, through their interaction in its life and work, create a continuing conversation about its nature and worth. This conversation provides a basis for systematic self-criticism within the community; it is nourished by contact with perspectives from the wider social and educational communities outside.

A major task for program evaluation is to harness this self-critical conversation: to collect the perspectives and judgments of those associated with a program, to reclaim meanings and concerns from the flux of program experience, and to make this store of understandings available to participants and other audiences. Describing the program, formulating issues regarded as significant by those associated with it, collecting judgments and portraying these in ways that are accessible to evaluation audiences — these are activities through which the evaluator can contribute to the critical debate about a program and improve the quality of the critique.

. . .

The implication for evaluators is that evaluations should be responsive to audience concerns and the real, experienced issues that surround a program. The evaluation task is thus an educative one, informing and developing the understandings of those associated with the program. The evaluation may accept as its primary task the formulation of program issues in ways that clarify them for program participants and audiences. It may report frequently rather than just towards the end of the evaluation, so that the perspectives of participants and audiences can be engaged more or less continually rather than in a single confrontation of perspectives.

. . .

Regarding the program as a self-critical community does not mean that it is an insular group feeding only on its own perspectives; using the self-critical debate within the program as a basis for the evaluation does not mean that the evaluation becomes simply a kind of self-report. Through the evaluation (as well as through program initiatives), participants should be brought into contact with the perspectives of other relevant judges and audiences, some of whom may be quite distant from the program. The self-critical community of the program can incorporate the perspectives of "outsiders" by creating a conversation with them through which both sides can learn each other's perspectives. This can occur if the program and the evaluation create opportunities for outsiders to see the work (or portrayals of the work), to consider it, to judge it, and to explain their judgments.

The principle of the self-critical community establishes self-criticism as the cornerstone of program evaluation. All participants in the community of self-interests formed by the program have a right to be heard in the critical process. As already indicated, the value of self-criticism does not preclude external judgment; rather, it attempts to create mechanisms whereby external judgments can be incorporated into project or program thinking. To emphasize the value of self-criticism is not to advocate program insularity; on the contrary, it is to emphasize the value of authentic knowledge as a basis for development and debate and to encourage participants to take a broad, critical view of the program in its wider historical context. But it is also to stress that once a program surrenders self-knowledge to external authority as a basis for development, it loses its autonomy as an intellectual community.

As a corollary to this principle, it follows that each participant agency in the co-operative enterprise of a program regards itself as a self-critical community, and evaluates its own activities in a spirit of self-criticism. The primary implication of the principle of the self-critical community is that curriculum projects and programs should establish "internal" evaluation mechanisms that can systematically record and develop the critical debate about their work.

. . .

The principle of the self-critical community is a recognition of the natural existence of self-reflection within a program, on the one hand, and the natural critical debate around it, on the other. Such a principle may encourage those involved in project and program evaluation to be "responsive" in the sense that Stake (1975) uses the term. He says:

> An educational evaluation is *responsive evaluation* if it orients more directly to program activities than to program intents; responds to audience requirements of information; and if the different value perspectives present are referred to in reporting the success and failure of the program. [P. 14]

But in addition to this, such a principle may encourage evaluators to see their work as part of a naturally occurring process of evaluative activity in a program, not distinct from it.

It would be possible to adopt alternative principles to this one. On the one hand, curriculum programs could be evaluated solely by teams of expert external evaluators, thus putting the validation function of evaluation before all others. Or program sponsors could adopt a form of evaluative activity based on their own perspectives of what projects and programs should be, thus establishing the primacy of their own value frameworks (as seals of approval) in every program evaluation. But neither of these principles will suffice. The co-operative nature of curriculum development and the diffuse control of educational organizations (with different participants having different sources of legitimacy — teachers' professionalism, schools' autonomy, ministerial responsibility for state systems, parents' and community roles in school councils, students' rights, etc.)

mean that curriculum evaluations must encompass wider views than those of substantive experts or program sponsors' particular predilections. Program evaluators simply cannot afford to ignore the wider debate about a program in its social and educational context.

Current trends in the history of evaluation have been significantly influenced by the demands of project evaluation, where outside groups of evaluators have been called in to observe and evaluate curriculum development work in order to provide external validation of the quality of development. As a consequence, much recent evaluation literature reflects an expectation that evaluations will be "objective," disinterested, expert, and validatory. But external evaluation cannot provide unilateral validation. There is an older trend in evaluation based on school accreditation, inspection, and appraisal that is more organically related to school curriculum work. But the techniques these purposes generated are not well suited to the evaluation of innovative curriculum projects or programs. The older tradition stabilized itself around the organization of a school rather than around the organization of a new curricular activity or product.

Project or program evaluation must be able to negotiate between the demands for curriculum validation and the conditions of schooling in different systems. Program evaluation cannot treat curricula as discrete products, to be considered as if they existed independently of their contexts of application, nor can it focus all its attention on the conditions in schools adopting particular innovations. The principle of self-critical community recognizes that innovations enter adopting systems by a process of negotiation; evaluation should facilitate negotiation by refining the critical debate.

The people who work on, use, and sponsor a particular program form a natural focus for its evaluation activities; their work provides a natural forum for critical thinking about it. The principle of the self-critical community may encourage those associated with innovative programs to regard their natural evaluative work as a primary, not a secondary, evaluation function; accordingly, it is proper to expect that "internal," self-critical evaluations will provide the primary basis for judgments about the nature and worth of programs. Evaluation should not be regarded as a specialist activity tagged on to development to monitor and observe from a position of privilege (the outside observer) as if the interests that guided evaluation work were unrelated to the interests of those that guide the developers (that is, that there are no confluences or conflicts among their values and interests). Evaluation is interactive and reactive; it should not be construed as "objective" and outside the whole system of social relationships that constitute curriculum development programs in practice.

6. THE PRINCIPLE OF PROPRIETY IN THE PRODUCTION AND DISTRIBUTION OF INFORMATION

Evaluation processes inevitably affect the political economy of information in a program (the production and distribution of information about it). Because information and arguments justify or legitimize decisions, evaluation affects the distribution of power and resources in program situations. Program participants and interested observers live with the consequences of the use and abuse of evaluation information. An evaluation should have explicit principles of procedure that govern its conduct and its processes of information production and distribution.

As suggested in the introduction to these principles, evaluation is often defined as "delineating, obtaining, and providing information for making decisions and judgments about educational programs." Indeed, formal evaluation efforts may well be included among the management and decision-making processes of a project or program. Though it has been an explicit purpose of these principles to widen the definition, it would be naïve to assert that evaluation was not normally regarded as an important management and decision-making tool. Evaluation processes thus link the generation of information and arguments about a program with the power to decide: those responsible for deciding the shape and conduct of a program, whether it should be implemented, or even whether it should be continued or discontinued will look to evaluation studies as sources of information and arguments when they make their decisions. Evaluation is thus inevitably a political process, affecting the flows of information in a situation and having life consequences for those who inhabit it.

. . .

The production and distribution of information about people, projects, and programs through evaluation must be regulated according to a principle of propriety capable of taking into account the moral, social, and political consequences of information use and abuse. The evaluator must find procedures appropriate to each context by which he or she can negotiate the disputed territory between the public's "right to know," management's "right to relevant information," and the individual's "right to discretion." Even in cases where innovators are anxious to have their work more widely known, or where teachers regard their work as exemplary, there may be consequences of the release of information that may jeopardize their future opportunities. Evaluators must treat seriously the problems raised by the political economy of information production and distribution — the role of evaluation in the distribution of power in particular settings and in the support or denial of already existing power structures. It is not sufficient to take a moralistic stance on open information, on privacy, or on the rights of sponsors: the production and distribution of information inevitably affects the politics of the program situation, and it is up to the evaluator to find procedures that are defensible within the particular context and technically feasible given the constraints of time and resources.

. . .

Alternative principles can hardly be framed in terms of "impropriety": no one could accept the notion that an evaluation should use information improperly. The principle of propriety presented here does specify the rights of participants in a program to know how the information is to be used and controlled. It attempts to set up a model of equitable distribution of information based on the rights and obligations of all those involved in an evaluation study. Evaluations would operate in a spirit contrary to the present principle if they were an exclusive information service for evaluation sponsors rather than a service to a range of audiences associated with the program, if they used secret reporting, if they failed to take into account the diverse perspectives and interpretations of participants and evaluation audiences, or if they published reports in forms suitable only for research audiences. The principle thus establishes a view of evaluation opposed both to the view that evaluation is an arm of the educational research industry serving some general ideal of truth or "the public interest," and to the view that it is a tool to be used in the service of bureaucratic responsibility. (See MacDonald, 1976.)

Furthermore, the principle of propriety in the production and distribution of information establishes the view that evaluators have the responsibility to be aware of the consequences of information production and distribution and to respond in defensible ways by developing appropriate procedures for information control.

7. THE PRINCIPLE OF APPROPRIATENESS

Evaluation design is a practical matter. An evaluation must be appropriate to the program setting, responsive to program issues, and relevant to the program community and interested observers. An evaluation design must be renegotiated as the study progresses in the light of changing circumstances, issues and interests, and in the light of its own consequences (as they become apparent).

The contemporary scene in evaluation theory and research abounds with evaluation models and approaches with a bewildering variety of foci and employing a diversity of specific techniques. While this variety and diversity must be acknowledged, evaluators and evaluation sponsors should not adopt an unconstrained eclecticism with respect to evaluation just because no dominant orthodoxy has emerged in the field. These principles, and the value commitments they embody, identify some forms of evaluation as unacceptable. To be acceptable, particular evaluations should embody the six principles previously presented, but they must also be appropriate to their objects. That is to say, evaluation studies must suit the curriculum projects, programs, processes, or products to be evaluated and the contexts in which they appear. The design of an evaluation is a practical matter, depending on considerations of purposes; audiences; substantive issues raised by program theory, aspirations, organization, and practice; resources; issues of information control in the particular political economy of the program and its evaluation; relevant evidence; methods for data collection; issues and approaches to analysis and interpretation; and modes of reporting.

Evaluators and participants in curriculum projects and programs must take all of these topics into account in designing or commissioning evaluation studies. The appropriateness of evaluation designs is a practical matter, not a technical or theorectical one. Decisions about the form an evaluation should take cannot be made by reference to the "internal logics" of evaluation models and approaches alone; such decisions must take into account the needs, preferences, obligations, circumstances, and opportunities of those who will be most closely involved in the evaluation process (as evaluators, program participants, sponsors, evaluation audiences).

As in the case of the sixth principle, it is hardly possible to propose an alternative principle of "inappropriateness." But inappropriate evaluation designs are often proposed for the evaluation of curriculum projects and programs. Such designs are ones that suffer from "methodological tunnel vision," employing evaluation models dogmatically or inflexibly when more sensitive attention to the critical debate about a program or the circumstances of its operation would suggest a different approach. Evaluation designs are also inappropriate when they fail to serve those most closely involved in the work of a program, reporting instead only to sponsors or research audiences. These audiences have a legitimate claim for evaluative information, to be sure, but evaluations frequently fail to serve the needs and interests of those most directly affected by the work.

If the evaluators of curriculum projects and programs take seriously the thrust of the definition of evaluation proposed at the beginning of this paper — that it is the process of marshalling information and arguments that enable interested individuals and groups to participate in the critical debate about a specific program — then it is less likely that they will err on the side of inappropriateness. Appropriate evaluations will take into account the social and contextual conditions under which educational programs operate and include a meta-evaluation component: the evaluation will thus include an element of self-reflection that allows those involved with the evaluation and the program to monitor its effects on program development and evolution and on the social life of the program as a community. The aim of this self-reflection is to treat the appropriateness of the evaluation as problematic and dynamic, not as something that can be decided once and for all at the design stage. It is to recognize that evaluation programs, like curriculum programs, are negotiated between interested individuals in the light of their consequences.

. . .

REFERENCES

Cronbach, L.J. "Course Improvement Through Evaluation," *Teachers College Record* 64 (1963): 672–93.

Curriculum Development Centre. *Curriculum Evaluation: A CDC Study Group Report*. Canberra, Australia: CDC Professional Series, Curriculum Development Centre, 1977.

House, R.E., and R.S. Care. "Fair Evaluation Agreement." Center for Instructional Research and Curriculum Evaluation, University of Illinois at Urbana-Champaign, mimeographed, 1977.

MacDonald, B. "Briefing Decision-Makers." In E.R. House (ed.), *School Evaluation: The Politics and Process*. Berkeley, Calif.: McCutchan, 1973.

MacDonald, B. "Evaluation and the Control of Education." In D.A. Tawney (ed.), *Curriculum Evaluation Today: Trends and Implications* (London: Schools Council Research Studies, Macmillan, 1976).

Scriven, M. "Evaluation Perspectives and Procedures." In W.J. Popham (ed.), *Evaluation in Education: Current Applications*. Berkeley, Calif.: McCutchan, 1974.

Stake, R.E. "School Accountability Laws," *Evaluation Comment* 4 (1973): 1–3.

Stake, R.E. "To Evaluate an Arts Program." In R.E. Stake (ed.), *Evaluating the Arts in Education: A Responsive Approach*. Columbus, Ohio: Charles E. Merrill, 1975.

Stufflebeam, D.L., et al. *Educational Evaluation and Decision Making in Education*. Itasca, Ill.: Peacock, 1971.

Selection 5.3

Determinants of Curriculum Change and Stability, 1870-1970

Larry Cuban

The notion of change fascinates educational researchers and practitioners. The spicy tang of power, buried within the idea of intentional change, has lured many writers into searching out how it occurs, why it seldom turns out as anticipated, and what can be done to improve the process. Curriculum, one version of planned school change, has been no exception to that lure. This chaper analyzes forces, planned and unplanned, external and internal to school systems, that influence curriculum.

. . .

In this analysis, curriculum will refer to intentional experiences within the school planned for students. This includes what is taught (embracing, as well, theories that determine the content); how knowledge, skills, and attitudes are taught; and the materials teachers and students use. This narrow definition excludes the hidden curriculum, school culture, home, and community influences; it sharply limits the scope and potential of changes within schools, but does so realistically, in my judgment. This definition, of course, should not imply that what is taught is necessarily learned.

SOURCE. From *Value Conflicts and Curriculum Issues*, eds. Jon Schaffarzick and Gary Sykes.

. . .

This restricted meaning of the term permits mapping, albeit crudely, the levels of impact that external and internal forces have on curriculum change and stability. Distinctions can be drawn between different degrees of influence on theory, content, instruction, and materials. Moreover, distinctions can be made between forces that require much or little change in teacher behavior.

. . .

Forces affecting and determining both change and stability in curriculum over the last century, as defined here, including the different levels of impact, will be scrutinized.

THE SETTING: 1870–1970

By the 1870s, the structure of corporate school boards, superintendents as experts, principals as administrators, and teachers as all-purpose agents of society was in place. Nailed-down desks, box-like classrooms off main corridors, separate grade levels, textbooks, and blackboards were familiar landmarks on the schoolkeeper's horizon. In David Tyack's (1974, p. 39) phrase, the "one best system" had been installed. Polishing, refining, and sharpening would, of course, occur; but the key structures of the modern school system that we know today had been installed sufficiently in cities by the closing decades of the nineteenth century to capture popular belief and developing professional pride as the ways schools ought to be.

Familiar as these elements were then and now, the century has seen enormous changes in, to list only a few, numbers of children who go to school, how long they attend, dollars spent, varied curricula, increase in special personnel and buildings, and, probably most influential, the expansion of the school's role as an institution. (See Folger and Nam, 1967; Grant and Lind, 1975)

Remember these were the years when waves of immigrant children spilled over classrooms, when state compulsory attendance laws were enacted, when two world wars, a depression, and a crusade against poverty penetrated schools' daily operations. Nor can the post-World War II, massive rural-to-urban migrations that inundated unprepared northern and western schools be omitted. For school practitioners, it was a century of enormous growth and change.

. . .

From the antebellum, narrowly defined role of inculcating minimal literacy, basic values, and an appreciation of God and country, successive waves of lay and professional reformers expanded that role to one of the schools as a child welfare agency (Cremin, 1961, pp. viii, ix; Cohen, 1964, p. 78). "Are we to have the schools ignore the larger work of education and remain . . . an inflexible missionary of the three R's?" asked one early twentieth-century reformer. "Or is it," he continued, "to take, as its responsibility, the entire problem of child life and master it?" (Cohen, 1964, p. 64)

In subsequent decades, answers to these questions were found in school play areas for the cramped child, school-distributed clothes for the ragged, hot food for the hungry, school-provided medical care for the sick, vocational training for the unskilled, patriotism for the foreigner, and driver and sex education and antidrug, alcohol, and tobacco instruction for the unwary teenager (Cremin, 1961, pp. 58–89). The school was now to integrate all the splintered functions urban life and industrialization previously had shaved off from family, work, and neighborhood. Both the growth in the school's role and the facts of physical growth resulted from forces inside and ouside the school.

. . .

I do have a perspective; but it is drawn from various theories anchored—I hope by data—in how schools function both internally and as part of larger organizations. My affection for those theories, based on experience and research, colored the choices I made. Readers should know the perspective offered here: The organizational traits of schools as independent units and as members of a larger system; the traditional nature of schooling as a compulsory process; the nature of classroom instruction, including teacher characteristics, largely explain, I feel, the curricular change and stability that have marked schools over the last century. . . .

DETERMINANTS OF CURRICULAR CHANGE

Broad Social, Economic, and Political Movements

Over the last century, the nation has experienced a number of events and movements that have altered the fabric of our culture. Because schools are culturally bound in our society, logic dictates that they were affected by these forces. More than logic, however, is needed; evidence helps. I have selected just a few of the movements that have had profound national impact to illustrate their influence upon curriculum (Berman et al., 1975).[1]

Corporate Industrialism. A number of writers have documented the impact of post-Civil War industrialization, especially the growth of the corporate organizational model, on schooling in the late nineteenth and early twentieth centuries (Tyack, 1974; Cremin, 1961; Katz, 1971; Spring, 1972; Krug, 1964). While these writers disagree over why schools were so easily influenced, effects were, nonetheless, observable.

What about influence on various levels of curriculum? The image of the factory and the related values of efficiency, order, worker obedience, and standardization of a finished product often surfaced in curriculum. School administrators, for example, spent much time preparing uniform guides for teachers. After working an entire year, Superintendent Luther Short proposed the first graded course of study for the Franklin County (Indiana) schools in 1883. This 231-page volume detailed what each teacher and class were to do each fifteen minutes between 9 a.m. and 4 p.m. (Graham, 1974).

Illustrative of the concern for uniformity and efficiency, school administrators eagerly embraced the then magic words of "scientific management." Callahan has richly documented turn-of-the-century educators with stopwatches determining which amount of time for spelling achieves more. Superintendents were telling school boards that the "increase of 1.7 recitations per week per teacher reduced the annual cost per pupil by $3.10." The savings were enough to "pay for nearly 13,000 pupil-recitations in expensive Greek." Professors taught that breaking down curriculum into its tiniest parts would establish standards for improved instruction. Or, in John Franklin Bobbitt's words, "the ability to add at a speed of 65 combinations per minute, with an accuracy of 94 percent is as definite a specification as can be set up for any aspect of the work of the steel plant" (Callahan, 1962, pp. 75, 81). . . .

Progressivism. Here also an extensive literature on political and social reforms between 1890 and 1920 impacting schools is available. The cold water dousing of America by the consequences of immigration, unrestrained industrialism, and urban growth awakened lay and professional reformers to slums, poverty, and ignorance. They needed tools to attack problems. City, state, and federal governments offered some levers for change, as did schools. They were accessible. They influenced the next generation. Cadres of reformers imbued wih a religious faith in science, knowledge, and civic morality saw the school as a splendid tool of reform (Tyack, 1974; Krug, 1964; Katz, 1971).

. . .

The cutting edge of change was various, overlapping groups of professionals and practitioners who, for lack of a better word, could be labeled "progressives." Through school surveys, Tyack (1974) identified two groups of professors, superintendents, and other educators as "educational scientists and administrative progressives" who exerted great influence on what school systems adopted in curriculum. By 1927, over 181 surveys had been done. In one study of fifty cities, almost 50 percent of the school systems reported that revision of curriculum occurred as a direct result of these surveys.

. . .

Another group, called "pedagogical progressives," affected instruction and curriculum. Frances W. Parker, John Dewey, William Wirt, and others developed in public and private schools different conceptions of teacher, child, and curriculum. While writers differ about the results of these reformers' efforts, that they recast traditional teacher roles and captured the imagination of succeeding generations of educators is well documented. Their thrust was to move the child to the center of the learning process. To make children active participants and to develop learning communities of children and teachers where continuity between home and school existed was their direction. To link up various portions of the curriculum that had for years been taught separately without much effort to make such connections was a way of realizing this thrust. These views required much of the teacher.

. . .

Whether these progressives influenced the daily classroom routine in most public schools is uncertain. Their efforts seem to have had more currency in classrooms of suburban and private schools. What these reformers did, however, was influence what people said and talked about; curriculum, theory, the language of practitioners and professors, and curriculum guides shifted to a more child-centered and experience-linked vocabulary. To that degree they influenced curriculum.

. . .

Cold War and National Defense. The most recent surge of curriculum reform, spanning the decade between the mid 1950s and mid 1960s, has been amply documented. (See Silberman, 1971, pp. 158–206; Black, 1967, pp. 162–85; Goodlad et al., 1966; Wirt and Quick, 1977.) Origins of the privately and federally funded efforts to toughen up what was taught in public schools were traced to the defensive, hostile, and insecure military position of the United States vis-à-vis Russia in the early 1950s. . . . The security gap was linked to deficiencies in technical and scientific schooling youth received (Silberman, 1971, p. 169). That this linkage coincided with attacks by public figures and academicians on the alleged softness and intellectual decay in schools made possible a vocal and prestigious coalition of critics.

In the early and mid 1950s, the National Science Foundation and private groups underwrote several curriculum development projects headed by well-known academics such as Jerrold Zacharias and James Killens. These professors were persuaded that the science taught in schools was anemic and outdated. Sputnik triggered further critical outbursts at schools and mobilized far more intensely these forces already at work. The passage of the National Defense Education Act marked the capstone of a movement to inject new scientific content and academic vigor into the classroom (Black, 1967, pp. 162–85).

By the mid 1960s, private and public funding of new biology, chemistry, and physics courses based on notions of the structure of a discipline and inquiry methods of teaching had been developed by scholars and, in a few instances, teachers. In a survey completed in 1964–1965, 20 percent of the students taking introductory physics were using new curriculum materials; among the ablest college-bound teenagers, the totals reached 40 percent for physics, 25 percent for biology, and 20 percent for chemistry (Silberman, 1971, p. 171).

While disappointing to many of its advocates, the figures demonstrate a filter-down effect into classrooms. By the end of the decade, over $200 million in federal funds had been invested in curriculum. Publishers were bidding on curriculum packages emerging from projects. The new physics, for example, was released to D.C. Heath, who by 1967 sold over a quarter million copies. Under federal grants, teachers attended summer and yearlong sessions on university campuses, taking notes from scholars about what to teach when they returned to their classrooms. School systems began adopting the new curricula and texts. Teachers, unevenly and slowly, began using the materials in classes (Kirst and Wirt, 1972, p. 213; Black, 1967, p. 167).

While only a few social movements have been briefly cited, it is easy to document their impact on schools and curriculum; it is, however, far more difficult to prove that a movement led directly to consequences observed in schools. . . .

Based upon such a frail foundation and recognizing that whatever is written here will be tainted by the possibility that only a correlation exists, it does seem reasonable to say in view of the folklore, observations, and available evidence that these movements helped determine curricular change.

Political-Legal Decisions

Another force for change that helps determine curriculum are state and federal laws and court decisions. . . .

State and Federal Laws. Whether the result of lobbying by special interests or sweeping social changes that produced potent political coalitions, state and federal laws have either mandated specific courses for students or produced changes in what content was taught. Consider just a few examples:

1. A 1966 survey revealed that a majority of states require courses in the dangers of alcohol and narcotics; half of the states mandate U.S. history and physical education. More recent entries into the curriculum, such as driver education and vocational-technical training, have often been lobbied into state mandates to local districts. While strong-willed districts can get around weak enforcement machinery, such laws have the effect of introducing courses where none or few existed (Kirst and Wirt, 1972, p. 210).

2. Federal laws impacting directly on curriculum have a long history. Vocational legislation dates back to the Smith-Hughes Act (1917), with subsequent revisions over the next half-century. In 1972, almost $1 billion was authorized for buildings, teacher training, and support of industrial subjects, home economics, trades, technical occupations, and a host of related areas. The National Defense Education Act (1958) supported science, math, and foreign languages; in 1964, the law was extended to English, reading, history, and geography. The Economic Opportunity Act (1964) influenced preschool curricula with its Head Start programs; the Elementary and Secondary Education Act (ESEA) (1965), targeted on the disadvantaged, touched over 90 percent of the nation's school districts with classes for talented and underachieving youth, enrichment programs, and scores of other activities; the Juvenile Deliquency and Youth Offenses Act (1961), Civil Rights Act (1964), International Education Act (1966), and Ethnic Heritage Act (1972) all contained positions that touched existing courses of study or stimulated curriculum development (Tiedt, 1972, pp. 123–24, 129–30).

. . .

3. In addition to these laws, federal agencies have spent funds to improve curriculum, particularly the National Science Foundation and Office of Education. Over $250 million has been spent by these agencies to develop new biology, math, physics, social studies, and English. Impact of such massive funding ventures has been cited before in course adoption and new textbook content.[2]

Court Decisions. While there have been a number of court decisions involving teacher rights, student rights, religious instruction, and other related issues, the instances of judicial intervention into the school curriculum, as defined here, remain modest but are, nonetheless, growing. . . .

In the decade following the *Brown* decision, many desegregated school districts changed ability groups, teacher practices, and texts and integrated the curriculum. A number of studies document the ripple of changes that ebbed and flowed through schools undergoing desegregation (Orfield, 1975; Sullivan, 1969; Mack, 1968).

In *Hobson v. Hansen* (1967), federal Judge Skelly Wright ruled that the four-track system designed by Superintendent Carl Hansen in Washington, D.C., had been a conscious effort to segregate white from black sudents and must therefore be dismantled. In Washington and those other school districts that were either ordered to or chose to end tracking, the impact on teachers was felt in subsequent years. "College-bound," "general," "business," and "basic" courses of study gave way to classes where "ability," as one teacher put it, "is too widespread." Or, as another said, "it takes about three times as much time to cover materials." According to partisans of tracking, standards, grades, and what was covered in class deteriorated. As a result of these changes, more stress was placed upon a new list of educational buzz words: flexible grouping, individualized instruction, and diagnostic and prescriptive teaching. Most of these translated unevenly into classroom practice (Orfield, 1975, p. 325).

. . . With desegregation, revised curriculum guides soon emerged from school districts that altered their lily-white history, English, and other content areas. By the 1970s, textbook publishers had cranked out schoolbooks and pamphlets that one critic of history texts felt moved to "praise what the American-history textbooks have . . . achieved in their treatment of black Americans" (Orfield, 1975, p. 69). New courses, especially in the high schools, were introduced that dealt separately with blacks, Hispanic Americans, human relations, and other combinations. . . .

Influential Groups

If one were to map out who influences curriculum at various levels, the dispersal of the decision-making process would probably surprise readers. External groups, such as publishers, foundations, professors and researchers, and professional associations, and groups internal to the school community, such as students, teachers, curriculum workers, superintendent, school board, and citizens, are many, but not all, of the participants in this decision-making process. The splintering of control over curriculum undercuts the notion that school boards and superintendents make curricular decisions. Another fact that would jump out at the reader of that map is the incredible complexity of interrelationships. It is a messy map. Yet messy as it would appear, some of these groups act as top sergeants of social change in schools.

Many of these groups mediate between the sharp probes of social change in schools, softening jagged points, smoothing rough edges, and selecting what is important that needs doing. Many of these groups lobby social impulses into legislation and many translate national hopes into local practice. Many of these groups sell change. . . .

Publishers. Students spend a great deal of time reading and memorizing texts. Each child, according to Hillel Black (1967), reads at least thirty-two thousand textbook pages in his or her twelve years of public schooling. The Texas Governor's Commission on Public Education estimated in 1969 that 75 percent of a child's classroom and 90 percent of his or her homework time was spent in using schoolbooks. Observer after observer has reported teacher reliance on textbooks at both elementary and secondary levels. What gets into books, then, has a captive audience. Yet most publishers, especially the larger, corporately owned ones, seldom initiate or take many risks in charting new directions in content. As one major publishing editor-in-chief put it: "In our business, the customer chooses" (Black, 1967, pp. 3, 120; see also Kirst and Wirt, 1972; Goodlad et al., 1974; Broudy, 1975; Wirt and Quick, 1977).

As uninnovative as that remark sounds, publishers responding to the marketplace do, indeed, change what students read, memorize, and forget. Already referred to have been the new science and mathematics texts that have replaced older, outdated ones. New inquiry approaches, softbound books, cassettes, and a basketful of new instructional materials and devices have penetrated the nation's classrooms. Publishers are responsible for translating many of the national curriculum efforts into marketable products that textbook sales representatives (the real footsoldiers of change) sell to teachers.

Foundations. The Ford, Rockefeller, Carnegie, and Kettering foundations over the last two decades have filled gaps left from federal support of curriculum development in such areas as the arts and social sciences. Ford's well-known Fund for the Advancement of Education spent $50 million, for example, over a fifteen-year period in team teaching, masters of arts teaching programs, teacher use of instructional technology, and other innovations. It was followed by a $30 million, decade-long, Comprehensive School Improvement Program that focused on new staffing patterns, new curriculum materials, and technology. Here, too, impact, according to the foundation's report, was most uneven and temporary (Kirst and Wirt, 1972; Kiger, 1972).

Professors. Money from external groups is not the only prod for change. Professors in liberal arts and in schools of education, through their writings, research, and students, have had impact on school curriculum . . .

Professional Associations. During the surge of curriculum change in the 1950s and 1960s, the American Association for Advancement of Science and the American Institute for Biological Sciences fought for the concept of evolution in biology books. The American Mathematical Society sponsored the new math effort until federal funds picked up the tab. Similarly, the American Council of Learned Societies helped revise social studies (Kiger, 1972, pp. 539–54).

Because local school boards lack money to mount major curriculum revision, develop sophisticated instructional materials, or carry on even modest research, these external groups play an important role in generating curricular choices from which schools can distribute new content to staff and help prepare teachers for change.

Internal Groups. Internal groups such as students, teachers, specialists, superintendents, and principals carry potent vetoes over change and do initiate curricular change by choosing among the alternatives. One group, however, that can determine curricular change by itself is aroused, angry parents. No superintendent or school board can safely ignore the sporadic flash flood of hot anger that sweeps over a school system when particular community values are stung to their core. The 1974 textbook furor in West Virginia's Kanawha County is only one instance. Many school systems have had their Kanawhas over sex education, obscene library books, subversive content, and so forth. While these are examples of negative (yet quite potent) change, for the most part parents view curriculum as technical matters best left to professionals, save for those instances where basic values are ruffled. There have been other cases, of course, when parent-teacher associations (PTAs) and lay groups have campaigned quietly but persistently for curricular change and gotten them—over time. The Progressive Education Association's Commission on the Relation of School and College, for example, helped get the remarkable Eight-Year Study underway in 1933 (Cremin, 1961, pp. 253–56). . . .

Influential Individuals

Ask ten historians of education which five persons have determined curricular change in the last century and my guess is that only a few names would turn up on all ten lists. . . .

Consider five people who might or might not appear on historians' lists: teacher and philosopher John Dewey, superintendent and philosopher William T. Harris, Professor Edward Thorndike, Professor John Franklin Bobbitt, and professor and writer Ralph Tyler. These five men—and there could just as well be another five names—affected theory, content, materials, and instruction through their writings and teaching. Most were professors and thereby exerted much influence on students—many of whom subsequently became professors. Most were prolific writers, producing articles, textbooks, and essays. They were translators of social change; they mediated between movements and school practice. Here, again, were valuable top sergeants of social change. Because they wrote and taught, however, their direct effect on each level of curriculum is most difficult to sort out.

. . .

Evidence suggests that these five persons had much more impact on theory and development than on other levels of curriculum. They affected ideas. Intellectual histories are made of such stuff. It was Dewey who captured the imagination of a generation of teachers, administrators, and reformers with the possibilities of a new teaching role. What remains to be mapped out are the intellectual threads that can be traced into content, materials, and classroom instruction. . . .

These, then, are the primary forces that determined change in curriculum over the last century. Social, political, and economic changes exerted the most impact while the rest of the determinants acted as second- and third-level mediators softening, selecting, modifying, and promoting different, less potent, versions of movements jolting the culture. Vulnerable to each wave of social change, laws and court decisions, political lobbies, publishers, and a host of other groups, the schools were easily penetrated.

. . .

Organizational Traits

The perspective on schools' vulnerability to social change that I offer has been suggested by others. It is found in the organizational traits of schools and school systems. It may help to explain in a slightly different way why social forces, groups, and individuals penetrate schools so easily. The four organizational characteristics that may explain this vulnerability are blurred goals, unclear technology, uncertain outcomes, and fluid participation (Bidwell, 1965; March and Cohen, 1974; Wayland, 1972; Sieber, 1968; Sarason, 1971).

Blurred Goals. Periodically over the last century the National Education Association, White House Conferences, blue-ribbon commissions, and, closer to home, PTA committees of the neighborhood elementary school have produced formal listings of goals. In 1874, a group of college presidents and school superintendents agreed that the school is "obliged to train the pupils into habits of prompt obedience to teachers and the practices of self-control in its various forms" (Tyack, 1967a, pp. 324–26).

In 1918, The National Education Association's Commission on Secondary Education produced seven "main objectives" for schooling. Among them were health, "worthy home membership," vocation, citizenship, "worthy use of leisure," and ethical character. Moreover, each child should develop "his personality primarily through the activities designed for the well-being of his fellow members and of society as a whole." Across the country, school systems rapidly adopted these goals (U.S. Bureau of Education, 1918, p. 12).

Successive redefinition of what the goals should be occurred in each subsequent decade. By 1956, the White House Conference on Education looked back and concluded:

> The basic responsibility of the schools is the development of the skills of the mind, but the over-all mission has been enlarged. Schools are now asked to help each child become as good and as capable in every way as native endowment permits. The schools are asked to help children to acquire any skill or characteristic which a majority of the community deems worthwhile. The order given by the American people to the schools is grand in its simplicity; in addition to intellectual achievement, foster morality, happiness, any useful ability. [Quoted in Campbell, 1958, p. 17]

Not only do goals change over time, but few formal goal statements are sufficiently clear to guide public school administrators or board members to make policy and evaluate outcomes.

Unfocused goals mirror, in part, a lack of consensus among participants over what schools are for. Because of erratic and inconsistent entry, flow, and exit of participants in making school decisions, it is most difficult to gain a broad, stable agreement upon what schools should do.

Unclear Technology. Teacher, books, and a chalkboard sum up the basic technology used with children in virtually all public school classrooms. Add an overhead projector, a record player, tape recorder, and TV console in the corner, and the technological advances of the past century that have entered classrooms have been almost exhausted. But technology is more than hardware. It is educational engineering through systematic analysis to help teachers and administrators go where they wish and get there successfully.

Yet, after two decades of claims for programmed instruction, closed-circuit television, computer-assisted instruction, and behavioral objectives, changes have been meager.

For the fifty million pupils who attend class in elementary and secondary schools five hours every day, the Commission on Instructional Technology concluded that not more than 5 (but probably closer to 1) percent of the time "involves media of instruction other than the teacher, the book, the blackboard, and pictures, charts and maps hung on the wall." After two decades of the claims for the advantages of instructional TV, less than 3 percent of total classroom hours in the sixteen largest school systems involve television (Tieckton, 1970, pp. 68–69).

Advanced school technology, be it hardware, software, or system analysis, remains unimplemented for a number of reasons; but one obvious reason is that basic questions about learning and teaching still remain unanswered. How does a child learn? What makes an effective teacher? Can a school shape values? Without reliable answers to these and other fundamental questions, the level of technology will remain where it currently is.

Uncertain Outcomes. Most school goals are intangible, as are results of schooling. If schools were in the business of building bridges, landing airplanes, or producing winning football teams, goal achievement would be concrete. After all, bridges stand or fall; planes land safely or not; teams win, tie, or lose. Moreover, there are blueprints, flight plans, and game plans plugged into well-known traditional and developed technologies. Some cause-effect relationship exists between a craft and a product. Not so for schooling.

Schools are expected, for example, to produce youth who are "worthy" citizens. There is simply no way of clearly determining whether a school has achieved its goal when a student graduates from high school. Even if "worthy" citizenship could be reduced to a set of behavioral objectives—and when it is, how trivial they appear—the achievement of those specific targets would seldom convince a reasonable person that individual youths in a graduating class were good citizens. For the most part, this commonly expressed goal has not been reduced to specific, measurable terms but has remained at the general level where the phrase means different things to parents, taxpayers, teachers, and students.

What compounds the inherent ambiguities of school goals is the uncertainty of existing teacher technology. We know very little about exactly how a teacher's verbal and decision-making skills, personality, text, and other tools impact either groups of children or individuals over the course of a half-hour, a day, or a year. The mysterious interplay among teacher, skills, tools, children, and time continues to elude researchers. Without much basic understanding of the technology of teaching, no solid linkage can be made between what is done and what happens. Cause and effect continue to play hide and seek with one another. And without that linkage, uncertain outcomes will often frustrate observers and practitioners.

. . .

Fluid Participation. I use "participation" to mean who gets involved in making decisions and the amount of attention given to problems as they arise and disappear. Public schools are under lay control. Lay control explains to a great degree why there is much traffic in and out of school systems. Contrary to popular belief that the board of education makes policy and the superintendent implements it, there are few clean lines of separation of authority or amount of time spent by each on making decisions. While at no point are the board and superintendent far from the process, they do not totally dominate it. The number of part-time participants in school system decision making stretches a long way. Beyond board members, superintendent, and central administration, there are principal, teacher, and student organizations, municipal officials, parental and civic groups, as well as cranky and fired-up individuals. Many of these participants enter, make noise, and exit at different points with varying volume and amount of time spent, again depending on the issue and the school district. Because there are thousands of school districts varying in size and governance, observers often need a scorecard to figure out who is where, doing what, and for how long (See Gittell, 1967; Cuban, 1975).

. . .

Any number of studies on school systems during a crisis underscore the broad spectrum of entry-noise-exit participation as well as the part-time attention paid to particular problems. Apart from crisis situations, board and superintendent remin central; but, depending on issue and district, participation remains fluid. Such participation accounts, in part, for blurred goals. Varied coalitions of participants form; bargaining between coalitions produces both multiple and compromise goal; coalitions splinter, disappear, reappear, and reshape previous goals, adding new ones—some of which clash with others, producing a slightly different but undeniably long list of unclear goals. Loose, shifting, part-time participation also reveals the vulnerability of school systems to either criticism or pressure. Kanawha is practitioners' shorthand for curriculum vulnerability. Boundaries of public school systems are soft, easily penetrated by both individuals and groups determined to participate in decision making.

. . .

CURRICULUM CHANGE IN CLASSROOMS

By change, I refer to three levels. When an idea, a practice, or a program is begun, that is one level of change. If what is initiated is then implemented, that is, not only undertaken but what was expected to be done was, indeed, done, then this is a second level of change. A third level is when the idea, practice, or program is incorporated into existing subject matter and instruction. A number of instances already cited demonstrate that curriculum change occurred at the first two levels. In a few cases, there were third-level changes.[3] It is the last level of change that can be the most enduring and have the most impact upon children. . . .

There is a problem, however. How do you find out whether the abundant and diverse wealth of curriculum changes penetrated classrooms over the last century? One way is to find out what was going on in classrooms before and after these changes. But how? What sources of historical data on classrooms exist?

We have photographs of children in class, their teachers, activities, and the physical layout of schools. We have books teachers taught from. We have students' work and later recollections of their experiences as students, although these sources, along with those drawn from parents, remain largely untapped. We also have teachers' reports. Next, we have the largest source of data—although, here again, much mining has to be done—drawn from people who visited classrooms, that is, reporters, parents, social scientists, administrators, and professors.

. . .

I shall examine briefly three different time periods: post–Civil War to about 1900, the two decades after the progressive movement, and the years after Sputnik, 1960s–1970s. The purpose of examining the three periods is to look at classrooms before massive reform waves swept across the educational landscapes and then examine classrooms in two separate time periods after waves of curriculum change to see what had occurred.

1870s–1900s

. . .

In looking at classroom photographs and the art of those years, what strikes an observer immediately is class size, student behavior uniformity, and teacher dominance. Images of the military jump out at a viewer. Classes over fifty were common in these photos; children sitting in rows, hands clasped, or standing at attention show up repeatedly. Invariably, children's eyes are on the teacher. Tight discipline, strict obedience, and fear are inferences one can reasonably make about those classrooms. Photos probably showed the ideal superintendents, principals, and teachers wished to capture. Turning to written accounts confirms that the photos were more than suggestive.[4]

Barbara Finkelstein (1974, p. 81; 1970, pp. 35, 316) mined the writings of participants—teachers and students recalling their experiences—and observers—jounalists and foreign travelers—to describe classrooms across the country in diverse settings from before the Civil War until 1890. "We find," she concluded, "that teachers assigned lessons, asked questions, and created standards of achievement designed to compel students to assimilate knowledge and practice skills in a particular fashion." In all accounts she examined, she found only three instances of teaching situations in which teachers "engaged students in discussions designed to elicit student ideas, . . . and no descriptions of discussions which required students to interpret or criticize textbook material." The task of the teacher, as one Oregonian recalled, was "keeping order and hearing recitation." Teachers had classes chant, repeat, and memorize text selections. Even some students "who never learned to read or write could," as one North Carolina teacher remarked, "spell by heart every word in Webster's Spelling Book."

Drillmasters, as Finkelstein calls them, teachers were also moral overseers. They demanded from students obedience, cleanliness, patriotism, diligence, and respect. To drill and oversee morality, teachers were disciplinarians who used rod, cane, ruler, hand, ridicule, and other assorted tools in the Lord's work of teaching children to act right. In exercising these various roles, teachers often looked on "academic failure as evidence of moral sloth" (Finkelstein, 1970, chap. 4; 1974, p. 84).

Repeatedly, observers and former students recall how textbooks were the sole sources of information. Ruth Elson's study of nineteenth-century textbooks demonstrates the kinds of knowledge memorized while underscoring the moral content of these materials. That texts were sole sources should not surprise anyone since in the late nineteenth century, most teachers had little more than grammar school or perhaps high school training. They needed something to lean on (Elson, 1964, chaps. 3, 5, 6, 9).

Moreover, superintendents, school boards, and teachers used text content as the basis of evaluating student performance. In Portland, Oregon, under the close supervision of Superintendent Samuel King, teachers drilled students on the material covered on tests, With few exceptions, text questions required definitions, facts, and recall of textbook explanations (Tyack, 1967b).

. . .

1910s–1930s

After its birth in the 1890s, progressivism blossomed in the initial decades of the twentieth century. Embracing the ideology, superintendents, principals, and professors helped differentiate curriculum, spread the use of mental tests, stressed ability grouping, and helped focus on the child's interests.

The curriculum expanded and specialists joined teachers in working with children. Play entered the primary classroom and laboratories and extracurricular activities became part of secondary schools. Teachers now were expected to do more than teach the 3Rs and oversee the moral development of their charges; they were to be warm, caring individuals seeking out children's interests and designing learning activities jointly with students. It was "an age of reform," Cremin concluded, "as thousands of local districts adopted one or another of the elements in the Progressive program" (Cremin, 1961, p. 291).

. . .

John Dewey visited public and private schools and in collaboration with his eldest daughter, Evelyn, wrote *Schools for Tomorrow*. They cited examples of curriculum tailored to children's interests. The photos they illustrated their book with were strikingly different from the traditional classroom photos of activities before 1900. Many pictures did not even have a teacher in them—an unforgivable omission two decades earlier. Photos often showed children doing things rather than sitting and listening. Most photos had children outside schools in playgrounds, gardens, and meadows.

The programs and teachers the Deweys described had children and teachers working together on various activities. While they described, for the most part, private, university-linked, and small public elementary schools, they did observe an all-black public school in Indianapolis and gave rave notices to Superintendent William Wirt's Gary school system (Dewey and Dewey, 1962).

A few years later, however, a team of evaluators was invited to assess Gary's progressive school plan. In many ways, they concluded, the new school organization and the way children conducted themselves were decided advances over previous schooling in Gary. But classroom instruction in history, mathematics, language arts, and geography were found to be still traditional and formal. Having a new philosophy is one thing; having the bulk of a teaching staff committed to it, they felt, is another (Cremin, 1961, p. 160).

Were one to have moved to another Indiana city in the mid twenties, as two sociologists did, when progressivism had become the conventional wisdom of schoolkeepers, another picture of classroom life would emerge. In Muncie, Indiana, as Cremin reminds us, schools may have been more typical of what happened in the country than the Winnetkas and Denvers, small private schools that progressive promoters pointed to in their writings.

"The school," the husband and wife team of sociologists concluded after living in Muncie for eighteen months, "like the factory, is a thoroughly regimented world." They compared the curriculum and activities of Muncie schools in 1890 and 1924. There were, in 1924, more courses; more practical, job-oriented activities; more emphasis on physical education; more electives, sports, clubs, and dances now were a far more important segment of students' lives in school (Lynd and Lynd, 1924). . . .

According to the Lynds, more than a few traces remain of the nineteenth-century drillmaster. There was much less overt evidence of the moral overseer on teaching in what the Lynds observed, although they saw the local "Y" teaching Bible classes in all elementary schools and giving a course for credit at the high school. Yet the secular morality of teaching for patriotism, support for group solidarity, and local values were evident to the Lynds in student responses to surveys they administered. . . .

Ten years later when the Lynds returned to Muncie, there was much more evidence of the administrative progressives having reached top school positions than any real impact of Deweyan ideas on classrooms. Education, the Lynds observed, had become "scientific with a vengeance." Administration had become a series of specialists. Planning, personnel, and reorganization were the new magic words of administrators in the 1930s (Lynd and Lynd, 1937, p. 205).

Had changes occurred in classrooms? The Lynds do not describe classroom life as clearly in their second study as they did in their first. They pointed to the loosening of the grip of lecture and recitation and more emphasis on thinking and development of individual students. How much of that went on is uncertain, especially in the face of successive school budget cuts in the depression, which drove elementary class size over fifty and high school class size to over thirty-five.

Data dealing with classroom observation in the 1920s and 1930s are hard to uncover and have yet to be synthesized. Inferences, however, can be drawn from the launching of the Eight-Year Study. In the depression decade, when progressive ideology dominated educators' thinking, the Commmission on the Relation of School and College report on high schools indicted current (1931) practice on drilling students, ignoring the gifted, sticking to a lifeless curriculum, and enduring ineffectual instruction. Similarly, Hollingshead's (1949) study of Elmtown's youth suggests a school with a suffocating network of rules and a rigidly divided class structure reinforced by separate courses of study for college-bound, business, and other students. And, if the case studies artfully used by Willard Waller in his 1932 text, *The Sociology of Teaching*, reveal anything, it is that in rural and small town America, teaching had yet to be revolutionized by progressive pedagogy. The drillmaster, moral overseer, and disciplinarian roles are all there beating loudly as young teachers marched to the imperatives of the age-old process of teaching.

While the evidence is spotty, by the 1930s, Cremin's verdict was that Muncie's conservative progressivism (a phrase that probably meant minimal impact of progressive pedagogy at the classroom level) "typifies the influence of progressive education on the pedagogical mainstream during the interbellum era." Having conceded that for every Winnetka there were probably many more schools that taught McGuffey well into the 1930s, he concluded that progressivism left its unmistakable imprint on the formal curriculum through expansion and reorganization and on the elementary classroom instruction, as "students and teachers alike tended to be more active, more mobile, and more informal in their relationships with one another" (Cremin, 1961, p. 305).

. . .

1960s–1970s

Much has already been made of the surge of curriculum reform in the decade spanning the Eisenhower, Kennedy, and Johnson administrations. Course content changed; new courses appeared; old ones disappeared. Textbooks got flashier, softer, and more expensive as they embraced eye-catching graphics. New instructional materials produced by national curriculum groups showed up in classrooms. Innovative instructional tactics, inquiry learning, and so forth dominated professional journals and convention programs and caused spasms of irritation from school boards and superintendents anxious to catch on to whatever bandwagon was passing. The same question remains, however: Was there impact on the classroom?

. . .

In the early 1970s, university researcher John Goodlad and a team of veteran practitioners observed 150 primary grade classrooms, including kindergartens, in almost seventy different schools in metropolitan areas of thirteen states (Goodlad et al., 1974). The observers expected to find those highly publicized innovations in content, classroom organization, and instruction that sprang from the reform surge of the 1960s being implemented by teachers. Individualized instruction, team teaching, ungraded classrooms, inquiry learning, new materials and equipment, and a host of other changes spurred by outside and inside forces were objects of the search. What they found surprised them. "Many of the changes we have believed to be taking place in schooling," they concluded, "have not been getting into classrooms." After a decade and a half of widely endorsed changes, innovations "were blunted on school and classroom door." Most schools, they found, were "marked by sameness regardless of location, student enrollment," or label given to them by administrators (p. 97).

. . .

Journalist Charles Silberman spent four years studying schools in the late 1960s. He and a small staff visited scores of classrooms in different settings around the country. His conclusions mirror Goodlad's, although Silberman is far more critical. His "items" from the classroom are devastating cases that document his charges of "mindlessness" in schools and tedium in classrooms. On mathematics and science curriculum reforms, Silberman minces no words. If one visits classes as he did, one "will discover that the great bulk of students' time is still devoted to detail, most of it trivial, much of it factually incorrect, and almost all of it unrelated to any concept, structure, cognitive strategy, or indeed anything other than the lesson plan" (Silberman, 1971, p. 172). His conclusion: After the great surge of curriculum and instructional reform between 1957 and 1967 "things are much the same as they had been twenty years ago, and in some respects not as good as they were forty years ago" (p. 159). . . .

Just a sampling from that classroom observation literature in the 1960s is striking in its similarity. Ned Flanders, one of the more active and prolific investigators, summed up the situation in 1970 by saying, "Teachers usually tell pupils what to do, how to do it, when to start, when to stop, and how well they did whatever they did." Other studies, both large- and small-scale, involving elementary through high school, urban and suburban, reach virtually the same conclusions in classrooms being teacher centered, group oriented, and adult dominated (Flanders, 1970; see also Good and Brophy, 1973; Jackson, 1968; Smith and Geoffrey, 1968; Bellack et al., 1966; Cicourel et al., 1974; Mehan, 1978). . . . Classrooms seem resistant to reformers' intentions. This is not to say that what happened in classrooms in 1870 is exactly what is happening a century later. It is to say that there seems to be a puzzling structural continuity between classrooms a century apart. . . .

DETERMINANTS OF CURRICULAR STABILITY

. . .

There are at least two main forces that help determine stability in curriculum.[5] Since so much focus in educational literature has been on change and so little has been written of forces that bring continuity to curriculum, I will try to show relationships, explain linkages, and, wherever possible, show evidence of a cause-effect connection.

External Forces

Anyone familiar with American schools and the tradition of local control is often amazed at the similarities in curriculum across the nation. . . . The primary determinant for that similarity and also for stability in curriculum is the socializing functions of schooling.

Functions of Schooling. Invariably, the history of the modern school returns to progressive beliefs in schooling. The core of progressive ideology was that the school was the prime instrument in making wise adults out of children.

The family, especially if it was poor, immigrant, or black, was not up to the complex job of preparing children for adulthood in an industrial society, reformers said. In a turn-of-the-century society where crime, poverty, class conflict, and unassimilated foreigners faced fervent reformers, the school, in their view, should be a paragon of order, punctuality, good citizenship, morality, obedience, and loyalty. The first step was to get children into the school. Reformers' successful drive for compulsory attendance laws matured by the end of World War I into an elaborate machinery of truant officers, supervisors, and clerks who counted heads and made sure children were in school.

Before, but especially since, the progressive years, social, political, and economic functions have driven much of what we recognize as modern compulsory schooling. John Dewey, Willard Waller, the Lynds, and, more recently, Robert Dreeben (1968), Herb Gintis (1972), Samuel Bowles (1972), Alex Inkeles (1966), and many others have mapped out core functions inherent to compulsory schooling in preparing children for work, a stratified society, citizenship, and, in Inkeles' phrase, "social competence." While writers differ significantly in explaining why these functions have arisen and persist, they generally agree that the school is a powerful agent in socializing children into adult roles.

Teachers and administrators have absorbed the socializing functions into both their ideology and behavior. Casual observations of schools and classrooms, especially elementary, yield many instances of teachers and schools inculcating and reinforcing in a conscious manner regularity, proper work habits, patriotism, and other adult expectations. Moral, political, and work socialization, embedded in class and school rules, students as helpers, and rhetoric, is taken seriously. (See Lortie, 1975, chap. 5; Finkelstein, 1975; Waller, 1965, pt. 4; Jackson, 1968.)

Parents and citizens expect children to be socialized by the schools. Gallup polls on what schools should do, episodic citizen anger at controversial texts, and fired-up parents at school board meetings, furious over an untraditional teacher, are only outward evidence of loyalty to the school's function of socialization; and, needless to add, potent reminders to the stewards of children about what the community expects.

How do these socializing functions help determine stability in the curriculum? At the simplest level, since the 1900s, many of these functions have been incorporated into courses of study, individual courses, and companion texts, for example, vocational and technical education, civics, and American history. Much teacher activity, such as homework, classroom helpers, and emphasis on punctuality, neatness, and following rules, has been directed at preparing students for adult roles. By integrating socialization for adult roles into their ideology and behavior, teachers and administrators expect to build children into fine citizens, consumers, and employees (Elson, 1964; Black, 1967).

These profoundly conservative functions are interwoven daily throughout the formal curriculum and teachers' activities. Curricular innovations, particularly those that challenge socialization functions, get short shrift by practitioners. Try to drop American history or vocational education from the curriculum, for example, or try to stop teachers from teaching little boys and girls the values of honesty, cleanliness, neatness, punctuality, and how little people should work, play, and learn. Reformers have found such efforts to be dead-end roads. Because such functions are so much a part of who teachers are, what they do, and the organization of the school day and the formal curriculum, they account for much of the stubborn continuity in course content and instruction over the decades.

. . .

Accrediting and Testing Agencies. Accreditation is viewed as an educational life or death issue. High school graduates, for example, from a nonaccredited school find college admission officers most reluctant even to consider them. Formal curriculum requirements of the Southern Association of Schools and Colleges and the North Central Association, for instance, set local standards that are pursued religiously. While these agencies seldom levy sanctions, the threat of withdrawal is ever present, reinforcing their minimum requirements. Drastic or unusual curriculum changes become most difficult to undertake in the face of these requirements.

National tests devised by the College Entrance Examination Board and standardized ability and achievement tests such as the Stanford and the Iowa are commonly given across the nation. Over one million students take the College Boards and over seven hundred colleges require it. Local school districts gear portions of their curriculum to the tests; pressures easily build within school districts to standardize instructional and curricular practices in order to cut down on variations between schools (Wayland, 1972, pp. 601–02; Kirst and Wirt, 1972, pp. 208–09).

Since most of these tests and standard-setting groups originated in the early decades of the twentieth century, they have given a solid durability to particular courses of study, content, and instruction over the years. Both accrediting associations and national tests have helped smooth out regional differences and brought a degree of uniformity to curriculum. It was precisely against the tyranny of college tests and entrance requirements that the Eight-Year Study was launched in the 1930s, completed in the 1940s, and ultimately forgotten by the 1970s.

Textbooks. In the late nineteenth century, McGuffey readers were a common school experience. Nowadays, with a publishing industry national in scope, most school systems hold onto texts three to five years, although with revisions a popular text can last for a decade. In the elementary schools, basal readers and series that span the grades can give continuity to a reading program and prove most durable (resistant to change). In secondary schools, texts are plugged into particular course offerings, especially at the high school, thus creating interlocking pressure between books and formal courses for maintaining existing arrangements (Wirt and Quick, 1977; Kirst and Wirt, 1972, p. 212).

State and Federal Laws and Agencies. New legislation affecting curriculum acts as a change agent, upsetting existing situations. However, once enacted, state-mandated courses, for instance, are virtually impossible to abolish (in effect, once in, always in). Testing programs and court decisions combine to introduce initial changes, but in time these changes often ossify and become resistant to modification.

. . .

Internal Forces

. . .

School systems and schools as organizations are rational and irrational, bureaucratic and unbureaucratic, loosely structured and tightly structured, open to change and closed to change, and vulnerable and invulnerable. These dualities often occur at the same time. We know, for example, of bureaucratic resistance to certain curriculum change in the very organization that receives with open arms curriculum proposals from foundations or influential educators. Some of these organizational traits account for change; some account for stability. For some traits, relationships have yet to be figured out. . . .

Organizational Rationality. School systems are organized bureaucratically, yet they are unlike corporate, military, or industrial bureaucracies. Schools do have a division of labor, ranks of offices, rules, and an elaborate record-keeping apparatus. They do emphasize lines of authority, equitable application of rules, uniformity in practice, and impartiality. Yet differences between bureaucracies exist, as will be pointed out shortly.

Bureaucracy is rooted in rationality. Goals, objectives, planning, problem solving, and evaluation are simply outward bureaucratic signs of an inward embrace of rationality. The notion of rationality and the organization's continuing hunt for it have had a strong impact on stability in curriculum.

When curriculum is considered, bureaucracy and rationality have prevailed. Coordinating committees, periodic reviews of courses and texts, and curriculum planning are only a few attempts at rationalizing curriculum making. Where did this rational model of curriculum development come from?

Lawrence Cremin located the origin of rational curriculum making in the late nineteenth century, when schools themselves were being bureaucratized. W. T. Harris, according to Cremin, came up with the model. The child comes in contact with the course of study, which is developed by educators, who are concerned about what is important to study, where it should appear, and how much should be digested. The teacher, through a text, teaches the details of that course of study and tests students to assess whether the curriculum has been learned. "All the pieces were present for the game of curriculum making that would be played over the next half-century," Cremin says, "only the particular combinations and the players would change" (Cremin, 1979, p. 210).

He argues that progressives and every subsequent generation of curriculum reformers down through the 1950s, for all their reports, pronouncements, conferences, and journal articles announcing curriculum revolutions, accepted the rational model of curriculum making laid down by Harris. Cremin graciously and admirably admits he erred in previous writings by accepting reformers' pronouncements. He found that, regardless of which "pedagogical revolution" he analyzed, "the Puritans remained in the curriculum" (Cremin, 1979, p. 212).

. . .

Loose Coupling. To begin with, school bureaucracies are not machines. Administrative directives to teachers on how instruction should occur are not instantly received, acted on, and the requested results produced. The contents of a curiculum guide may or may not turn up in a classroom. What the teacher teaches may or may not be what the student learns. Each of these examples shows a relationship that is coupled (attached yet only mildly responsive to one another, all the while retaining a separate identity) (Weick, 1976).

Loose coupling, such as between principal, teacher, curriculum, and pupil, is an organizational trait that may explain both curricular change and stability. For example, earlier reference to dispersed decision making in curriculum, that is, students, teachers, principals, and so forth, was a variant of a loosely coupled decision-making system. Modest, gradual changes can penetrate schools slowly in a fragmented, disjointed fashion. Given a certain context, change could occur. Loosely coupled systems, however, seem to nourish continuity more persistently than change.

. . .

Teachers and Teaching . . . Consider two basic facts that teachers, unlike doctors, lawyers, or plumbers, have had to cope with over the last half-century: They teach groups; and their clients are drafted. From such facts have flowed a series of organizational responses: self-contained classrooms, deep concern for motivating children to learn, an equally deep concern for maintaining order, and a limited instructional technology of textbooks and recitation (Lortie, 1975; Jackson, 1968; Dreeben, 1968).

Most classrooms today have one teacher, about thirty children in a crowded space, and a course of study that has to be completed by a certain time. To get students, some of whom would prefer to be elsewhere, to work in the time and space available requires the teacher to create activities that keep students attentive. The fear of chaos breaking out is strong and abiding among teachers. But to design activities and maintain order for groups of conscripted children in a small space, knowing full well that with thirty personalities and energetic bodies the unpredictable will occur, is a tough set of demanding tasks.

Teachers' prime responses have been to keep children busy, talk a lot, and keep them in groups. This is not necessarily the only response, or the best or worst one; but it is one that has been steadfast. . . .

Teachers talk a lot, keep children and themselves busy, and teach in groups. One study found that at least three-quarters of classroom student time was occupied by the teacher instructing a group of more than half the class, with the remainder working in small groups or independently. Classrooms consisting of several small groups and individuals were in the minority. In the secondary schools, most instructional time is spent by teachers in front of groups (Dreeben, 1973, p. 465).

. . .

The teacher's universe is that classroom. That is what counts to each teacher. The few psychic rewards teachers get are from instruction, erratic evidences of student learning, and relating to children. Moreover, because, as Philip Jackson put it, "the path of educational progress could be more easily traced by a butterfly than a bullet," much uncertainty haunts teachers in assessing whether they are effective day to day or over the course of a year. Groups test results are useful but less persuasive than former students returning to say how much they learned from that teacher (Jackson, 1966, p. 4).

Teachers teach groups but try to reach individuals — a wrenching frustration, given the constraints under which they work. Teachers resent deeply interruptions or any chipping away of instructional time. Clerical tasks, noninstructional duties, and sudden administrative demands annoy them. They feel strongly that the best change that could happen is to give them more time and resources to work with students uninterruptedly.

Because the teacher's universe is the classroom and because teachers treasure the freedom they have once they close their door to the outside world, they are also isolated from one another. That form of isolation reinforces conservative responses toward change efforts. Group approaches to problem solving and sustained cooperation are missing from teacher culture. Reluctance to share instructional ideas and problems beyond an immediate partner or team member is common; the drive by individual teachers to reinvent the wheel in their classrooms when constructing solutions to curricular problems is just as common. Moreover, the teacher's day is locked into working with children with little time, save lunch or perhaps a planning period, for adult exchange. When stress on the classroom teacher as an autonomous decision maker and the legal and moral authority for children are added, isolation is further encouraged and group instructional ventures are discouraged. From the self-contained classroom as teacher's universe flow intellectual isolation, painful uncertainty over solving problems, and very little opportunity to analyze one's behavior (Lortie, 1975, Chaps. 6 and 7; Cuban, 1972). . . .

As the classroom helps to shape what teachers do, how they do it, and what they value, we must also look at how teachers are recruited and socialized to see what impact these have on teacher attitudes and behavior. Dan Lortie's recent study on teaching as an occupation has opened up rich areas of investigation. Using large samples of teachers, he found that who entered the classroom and how they learned to teach developed among teachers a conservative, highly individual, and present-oriented outlook toward the job (Lortie, 1975, p. 106).

. . .

Also learned quickly, according to Lortie, is that the present is more important than the future. Generally, teacher salary schedules load up increases in the first decade and a half. After that, there are few subtantial raises. Teachers call it "being buried." Moreover, a career in teaching means you teach until you retire — an ideal that fewer beginning teachers aspire to. When combined with the "endemic uncertainties" of teaching effectiveness, concern for the present — epitomized in daily rather than monthly or annual lesson plans —becomes understandable (Lortie, 1975, pp. 83–86).

. . .

CONCLUSION

. . .

Vulnerable to each wave of social change over the last century, schools were easily penetrated. What made schools involuntarily receptive to entry were a set of organizational traits (blurred goals, uncertain technology, and so forth) that made schools vulnerable to every gust of change that blew against the classroom door. These primary and secondary determinants of change appeared formidable. . . .

. . .

The primary determinant that might explain puzzling continuities in curriculum was the socializing functions of schools. In addition, there were a number of external instruments, such as accrediting agencies, national tests, and legislation that reinforced school socialization and thereby strengthened curriculum continuity.

There were also internal forces that stabilized curriculum. Such school organizational traits as rationality, loosely coupled structures, teaching as an occupation, and the classroom as a workplace help explain those stubborn continuities and classrooms' seeming invulnerability to change.

. . .

I have tried to show that schools are vulnerable to social change; social change, softened by mediating forces, turns into governance, organizational, and curricular changes; curriculum change impacts far more on theory, courses of study, and content than on instruction and classroom life; and basic processes at work in classrooms, including teacher instruction and student responses, have a potent stability that resists intrusion, especially if the teacher is uncertain or skeptical of the change.

. . .

The teacher, and I wince that it still has to be said, is the source of both curricular change and stability. If anything more constuctive and positive is to happen with children and schools, policymakers must have far more dependable knowledge about what goes on in schools and classrooms. There is a small body of research that points to the limited nature of change that can be introduced into classrooms and the pivotal influence of the teacher in determining the pace and extent of that change. My experience and that of thousands of other teachers taught me that years ago. Perhaps research and policy making can catch up with folk wisdom. . . .

NOTES

1. By change, I paraphrase the degrees of change sketched out by Berman et al. (1975). Initiative to make a change is one level; implementation of that change is another level, and the degree the change is incorporated into subject matter and instruction is a third level. If a change occurs at any one of these levels, it is included here.

2. Kirst and Wirt (1972, p. 213) and Wirt and Quick (1977) examine in depth the impact of federal involvement in subsidizing curriculum reform.

To add some further detail to how state and federal legislation spurs curricular change, I was a master teacher in, and later director of, a federally funded program aimed at training returned Peace Corps volunteers to teach and develop curriculum materials in three innercity schools in Washington, D.C., between 1963 and 1967. In those four years, our funding came from the Juvenille Deliquency Youth Offenses Control Act and the Economic Opportunity Act, neither of which deals explicitly with reforming local school curricula; yet the project did have a modest impact upon what individual teachers chose to teach and how they taught it. As a superintendent since 1974 in Arlington, Virginia, I have seen other instances of state and federal influences upon curriculum. A recent state law followed by federal legislation holding school districts responsible for educating all handicapped children between the ages of two and twenty-one has affected how schools are organized, what is taught, and how instruction takes place, especially in elementary clasrooms.

In the last two years, we have sought out a number of federal grants in order to deal with specific problems that seemed beyond available local resources, specifically, development of multiethnic materials and bilingual instruction. These federal funds crystalized our impulses into concrete programs. Coincindentally, shortly after we had begun our search for bilingual funds, the Office of Civil Rights in the Department of Health, Education and Welfare threatened withdrawal of other federal funds if we did not initiate certain kinds of bilingual programs acceptable to the federal agency as they interpreted the *Lau v. Nichols* decision. The threats, in my judgment, were of marginal influence compared to the incentives of federal funds. Finally, Title IX guidelines on sex discrimination led our school board to set as policy a series of directives to the professional staff on what is appropriate content for instructional materials, texts, and other sources.

3. These three levels of change are drawn from Berman et al. (1975).

4. In Tyack (1974), a rich collection is displayed; also in the museum of the city of New York's Jacob Riis collection and in *American Education*, June, 1974, and August-September, 1975, issues (Washington, D.C.: U.S. Office of Education).

5. The determinants I searched for are those constant over time rather than those that appear temporarily. The forces of stability, in my judgment, are more closely related to structures, organizations, and basic processes of schooling than to passing events or shifting public moods.

REFERENCES

Bellack, Arno, et al. *The Language of the Classroom*. New York: Teachers College Press, 1966.

Berman, Paul, et al. *Federal Programs Supporting Educational Change*, vol. 5, Executive Summary. Santa Monica, Calif.: Rand Corporation, 1975.

Bidwell, Charles. "The School as a Formal Organization." In James March (ed.), *The Handbook of Organizations*. New York: Rand McNally, 1965.

Black, Hillel. *The American School Book*. New York: William Morrow, 1967.

Bowles, Samuel. "Unequal Education and the Reproduction of Social Division of Labor." In Martin Carnoy (ed.), *Schooling in a Corporate Society*. New York: David McKay, 1972.

Broudy, Eric. "The Trouble with Textbooks," *Teachers College Record* 77 (September 1975): 13–34.

Callahan, Raymond E. *Education and the Cult of Efficiency*. Chicago: University of Chicago Press, 1962.

Campbell, Roald F. "What Peculiarities in Educational Administration Make It a Special Case." In Andrew Halpin (ed.), *Administrative Theory in Education*. Chicago: Midwest Administrative Center, 1958.

Cicourel, A.V., et al. *Language Use and School Performance*. New York: Academic Press, 1974.

Cohen, Sol. *Progressives and Urban School Reform*. New York: Bureau of Publications, Teachers College, Columbia University, 1964.

Cremin, Lawrence A. *The Transformation of the School*, New York: Random House, 1961.

Cremin, Lawrence. "Curriculum-Making in the United States." *Teachers College Record* 73 (December 1979): 207–20.

Cuban, Larry. "The Death of Intellect; or How to Change Teachers Into Cretins Without Really Trying." In Harry Passow (ed.), *Opening Opportunities for Disadvantaged Learners*. New York: Teachers College Press, 1972.

Cuban, Larry. "*Hobson v. Hansen*: A Study in Organizational Response," *Educational Administration Quarterly* 2 (Spring 1975): 15–37.

Dewey, John, and Evelyn Dewey. *Schools of Tomorrow*. New York: E.P. Dutton, 1962.

Dreeben, Robert. *On What Is Learned in Schools*. Reading, Mass.: Addison-Wesley, 1968.

Dreeben, Robert, "The School as a Workplace." In Robert M.W. Travers (ed.), *Second Handbook of Research on Teaching*. Chicago: Rand McNally, 1973.

Elson, Ruth. *Guardians of Traditions*. Lincoln: University of Nebraska Press, 1964.

Finkelstein, Barbara J. "Governing the Young: Teacher Behavior in American Primary Schools, 1820–1880; A Documentary History." Ed.D. diss. Teachers College, Columbia University, 1970.

Finkelstein, Barbara J. "The Moral Dimensions of Pedagogy," *American Studies* (Fall 1974).

Finkelstein, Barbara J. "Pedagogy as Intrusion. Teaching Values in Popular Primary Schools in Nineteenth-Century America," *History of Childhood Quarterly* (Winter 1975).

Flanders, Ned. *Analyzing Teacher Behavior*. Reading, Mass.: Addison-Wesley, 1970.

Folger, John K., and Charles B. Nam. *Education of the American Population*. Washington, D.C.: GPO, 1967.

Gintis, Herbert. "Toward a Political Economy of Education." *Harvard Educational Review* 42 (February 1972).

Gittell, Marilyn. *Participants and Participation*. New York: Center for Urban Education, 1967.

Good, Thomas L., and Jere E. Brophy. *Looking in Classrooms*. New York: Harper and Row, 1973.

Goodlad, John I., et al. *The Changing School Curriculum*. New York: Fund for Advancement of Education, 1966.

Goodlad, John, et al. *Looking Behind the Classroom Door*. Worthington, Ohio: Charles A. Jones, 1974.

Graham, Patricia A. *Community and Class in American Education, 1865–1918*. New York: John Wiley, 1974.

Grant, W. Vance, and C. George Lind. *Digest of Educational Statistics, 1974 Edition*. Washington, D.C.: GPO, 1975.

Hollingshead, August B. *Elmtown's Youth*. New York: John Wiley, 1949.

Inkeles, Alex. "The Socialization of Competence," *Harvard Educational Review* 36 (Summer 1966).

Jackson, Philip. "The Way Teaching Is." In *The Way Teaching Is*. Washington, D.C.: National Education Assoc., 1966.

Jackson, Philip. *Life in Classrooms*. New York: Holt, Rinehart and Winston, 1968.

Katz, Michael B. *Class, Bureaucracy, and Schools*. New York: Praeger, 1971.

Kiger, Joseph C. "Foundation Support of Educational Innovation by Learned Societies, Councils, and Institutes." In Matthew Miles (ed.), *Innovation in Education: A Foundation Goes to School*. New York: Ford Foundation, 1972.

Kirst, Michael W., and Frederick M. Wirt. *The Political Web of American Schools*. Boston: Little, Brown, 1972.

Krug, Edward A. *The Shaping of the American High School*. New York: Harper and Row, 1964.

Lortie, Dan. *School Teacher*. Chicago: University of Chicago Press, 1975.

Lynd, Robert S., and Helen M. Lynd. *Middletown*. New York: Harcourt, Brace and Co., 1924.

Lynd, Robert S., and Helen M. Lynd. *Middletown in Transition*. New York: Harcourt, Brace and Co., 1937.

Mack, Raymond. *Our Children's Burden*. New York: Random House, 1968.

March, James, and Michael Cohen. *Leadership and Ambiguity*. New York: McGraw-Hill, 1974.

Mehan, Hugh. "Structuring School Structure," *Harvard Educational Review* 48 (February 1978).

Orfield, Gary. "How to Make Desegregration Work: The Adaptation of Schools to Their Newly-Integrated Student Bodies," *Law and Contemporary Problems, Part II* 39 (Spring 1975): 314–40.

Sarason, Seymour B. *The Culture of the School and the Problem of Change*. Boston: Allyn and Bacon, 1971.

Sieber, Sam. "Organizational Influences on Innovative Rules." In Terry L. Eidell and Joanne M. Kitchell (eds.), *Knowledge Production and Utilization in Educational Administration*. Portland, Ore.: Center for the Advanced Study of Educational Administration, 1968.

Silberman, Charles. *Crisis in the Classroom*. New York: Random House, 1971.

Smith, Louis, and William Geoffrey. *The Complexities of an Urban Classroom*. New York: Holt, Rinehart and Winston, 1968.

Spring, Joel. *Education and the Rise of the Corporate State*. Boston: Beacon Press, 1972.

Sullivan, Neil. *Now Is the Time: Integration in the Berkeley Schools*. Bloomington: University of Indiana Press, 1969.

Tickton, Sidney. *To Improve Learning*. Vol. 1. New York: R.R. Bowker, 1970.

Tiedt, Sidney. "Historical Development of Federal Aid Program." In *What Should Be the Policy Toward Financing Elementary and Secondary Education in the United States?* U.S. Senate. Washington, D.C.: GPO, 1972.

Tyack, David (ed.) "Statement of the Theory of Education in the United States of America as Approved by Leading Educators." In *Turning Points in American Educational History*. Waltham, Mass.: Blaisdell, 1967(a).

Tyack, David. "Bureaucracy and the Common School: The Example of Portland, Oregon, 1851–1913," *American Quarterly* (Fall 1967): 4. (b)

Tyack, David. *The One Best System*. Cambridge, Mass.: Harvard University Press, 1974.

U.S. Bureau of Education. "Cardinal Principles of Secondary Education." Bulletin No. 35. Washington, D.C.: U.S. Goverment, 1918.

Waller, Willard. *The Sociology of Teaching*. New York: John Wiley, 1965.

Wayland, Sloan. "Structural Features of American Education as Basic Factors in Innovation." In Matthew Miles (ed.), *Innovation in Education: A Foundation Goes to School*. New York: Ford Foundation, 1972.

Weick, Karl E. "Educational Organizations as Loosely-Coupled Systems," *Administrative Science Quarterly* 21 (March 1976): 3–4.

Wirt, John G., and Suzanne K. Quick. "National Curriculum Projects and Development in Education." Unpublished Report. Washington, D.C.: Rand Corporation, 1977.

Selection 5.4

Crystallization in Education

Alice Miel

Somewhere in South America there is a tribe of primitive people who, though living on perfectly dry ground today, nevertheless persist in building pile dwellings for themselves.

It has been the problem always of those who would help to bring about curriculum change to persuade people to give up their pile-dwellings-on-dry-ground. This clinging to what was once a good arrangement long after it has ceased to serve any useful purpose whatsoever is the commonest form of *crystallization*. Crystallization has been described as a good beginning that has turned in upon itself. Or it may be defined as the point reached when an idea or habit is accepted uncritically so that it limits the integrity, autonomy, and opportunities for self-expression of individuals and groups.

Crystallization of curriculum practice is a recurrent phenomenon in American education. It is also a complex one. It is not always easy to determine when a constellation of habits in an educational institution is making for a desirable economy of effort and providing a useful basis of continuity to individual and group living, or when it represents an area concerning which all thinking has stopped and which is serving as a deterrent to constructive

---

SOURCE. In *Changing the Curriculum: A Social Process* (New York: Appleton-Century Co., 1946), pp. 1-14.

action. Therefore, it should be rewarding to students of curriculum change to learn something of the nature of this phenomenon of crystallization in order to gain the ability to deal with it. In this chapter, accordingly, we shall examine some of the manifestations of crystallization in the curriculum of American schools.

THE GRADED SCHOOL AS A CONTRIBUTOR TO CRYSTALLIZATION

One good example of the way in which crystallization works in education is the development of the graded school. Before the Civil War, education was expanding at a rapid rate. As schools began having to accommodate large numbers of children, various systems of classification were experimented with. Finally the scheme of grading the school was discovered. It spread rapidly, not only among city schools where such a plan was a real boon in the early days of organizing mass education, but also to one-room rural schools where it could never have been appropriate. This method of classification started a whole chain of events, each of which helped to fix the pattern more securely than before. Textbooks began to be graded, and there appeared first readers, fourth-grade arithmetics, eighth-grade spellers, and so on. At first by trial and error, later by "scientific experimentation," "proper" grade placement of subjects and subject matter was determined. The college relieved its crowded curriculum by forcing some subjects into the high-school curriculum; congestion at that level was reduced by passing on a number of courses to the elementary school. Algebra became fixed in the ninth grade, long division in the fourth grade, beginning reading in the first.

Since the system began with grade one, the kindergarten had a hard time establishing a place for itself in the free public school. As the elementary school terminated traditionally with grade eight, rural schools still find it difficult to make what should be a simple reform, the sending of seventh and eighth graders to a central secondary school. The 8-4 plan was finally broken in many city schools by the junior-high-school movement. But that change had chiefly the disappointing result of moving departmentalization farther down into the grades.

With the grade pattern so firmly established, most attempts at curriculum change have been at the level of juggling within the system. Few persons have had the vision to try to break the pattern itself, much less had success in doing so.

This one example illustrates the chief characteristics of crystallization: (1) a commendable beginning turned inward; (2) the shutting off of thinking in a certain area; (3) the tendency to spread to all kinds of schools; (4) the tendency to become interlocked with other aspects of the curriculum; (5) the tendency to persist stubbornly (especially if written into state laws); and (6) the tendency, if once broken, to be replaced rapidly by another crystallization (in this case, departmentalization).

CRYSTALLIZATION THROUGH THE TEXTBOOK AND SCHOOL SUBJECTS

Another interesting illustration of the operation of crystallization in curriculum matters is the development of the American textbook and the related development of school subjects during the nineteenth century. New instructional materials were badly needed at that time, for the curriculum was being enriched by the rapid addition of new courses.

Rugg (1926, pp. 20-21) gives some interesting figures in this connection. Between the years 1787 and 1870 no fewer than 149 new titles of subjects of courses found their way into the printed programs of the secondary schools, 75 of them being interposed in the three years between 1825 and 1828. Three hundred and sixty different histories had been published in America before 1860.

From the middle of the century on, textbooks were prepared largely by college professors who were narrowly specialized. Gradually the curriculum became oriented around those subjects of specialization. "Furthermore," says Rugg (1926, p. 31) in commenting on this development, "the professors because of their . . . grounding in cautious research methods . . . tended to concentrate their attention upon the past. . . . Having a fear of unsound generalization, hence a fear of the contemporary in history, the new, the unauthenticated in science, they more and more neglected the vital affairs of current life."

Even though some of those weaknesses of textbook writing have been corrected in more recent years, the subjects which textbooks helped to entrench in the curriculum remain with us. It is only in the past two decades that any considerable number of persons have been able to think outside the subject frame at all. Another result of the "textbook movement" is a group of publishing houses and authors with large financial interests in curriculum.

THE ACTIVITY PROGRAM AS A MANIFESTATION OF CRYSTALLIZATION

A third example from our own day is perhaps the best illustration to be found of the replacement of one crystallization by another. It all came about when educators began to take seriously the principle that children learn by doing. Pioneer individuals and groups started to experiment with ways of utilizing this principle in curriculum-building. Many of the experiments were so successful that numbers of other educators became convinced that here was something they should be trying out in their own schools. Gradually a new pattern crystallized. It went by different names, but in the early 1930s *the activity program* was the current favorite.

A whole dictionary full of new terms and a great body of educational literature grew up around the *unit of work* as the central feature of the activity program. Things reached the point where an elementary teacher viewed the playground as the place where children might learn a colonial dance when they were studying their "Colonial Unit"; a music teacher offered, as her contribution to the children's study of the city water supply, to teach "Row, Row, Row Your Boat" and "Flow Gently, Sweet Afton"; while a third teacher claimed room on the bandwagon because she used the activity, flashcards.[1]

Distortions and counterfeits of the original idea behind the activity movement made thoughtful people everywhere begin to question some of the newly crystallized practices. Heads of certain large city school systems, however, saw in the procedures, now routinized and mechanized almost beyond recognition, hope of accomplishing the prodigious task of modernizing their elementary curriculum in a relatively short time. In some cases the activity program was installed at once by administrative *fiat.* In others, it was tried out experimentally in selected schools for a time, then installed in all schools with exact procedures indicated to teachers for beginning specified units of work and carrying them through to a "culminating activity." Of course, the new program met with resistance at first. Innovations are difficult to accept when people have been finding their security by operating in habitual ways. But it is almost certain that, ten and twenty years from now, those who were hardest to convince in the beginning will be the staunchest supporters of the activity program when word comes that it is time to revise the curriculum once more.

To gain some idea of the extent to which schools are encrusted with crystallizations large and small, one has only to start listing the obvious phenomena that the school and only the school exhibits. One might start with the orders given to children—"Stay out until the bell rings," "Don't come in after the bell rings," "No talking," "Don't leave your seat without permission," "Don't help anyone else," "Sit still," "Wait until recess." Then one might list school marks, grade norms, the eight-, nine-, or ten-month term, schooling from ages five to seventeen, school open from eight to four, boys' lines and girls' lines, readers, "schoolhouse" brown, and so on with a long list.

CRYSTALLIZED PROCEDURES FOR CURRICULUM-MAKING

Perhaps the most important form of crystallization in curriculum development has been the standardization of procedure for making changes in the curriculum which began to take shape in the 1920s. That was the period when local school systems such as those of Los Angeles, Winnetka, Denver, Detroit, St. Louis, and Baltimore were commencing to give serious attention to problems of curriculum change.

Toward the end of that decade books and studies dealing with principles and techniques for curriculum-making commenced to appear. A glance at the table of contents of a representative work published in 1929 reveals the nature of the pattern that was emerging. The author promises to consider such questions as:

> How should the curriculum organization be set up?
> How should the duties of the aims committee be performed?
> What procedure should production committees follow?
> How should a new course of study be installed?

Following the publication of such books came almost a frenzy of curriculum activity in the '30s. A study made by the United States Office of Education in 1936 revealed organized curriculum-development programs under way in more than seven-tenths of the cities over 25,000 in population (see Harap, 1937). A great many such enterprises were being carried on in smaller centers also. Most of those programs had been initiated since 1932.

By 1934 the pattern for curriculum-making that is most familiar today had become fixed and widespread. Evidence of the fact that curriculum development had been reduced to a formula calculated to work in any school system of size is a study by Trillingham (1934), who set about to learn how curriculum programs were organized and administered at that time in a number of large cities throughout the country. This, in brief, is the pattern he discovered and which he then recommended for general use in sizable school systems:

1. The superintendent of schools initiates the curriculum program and is ultimately responsible for the curriculum.
2. In direct charge is a curriculum director, assisted by a curriculum specialist or consultant who is "to aid and stimulate teacher groups" and "critically evaluate the progress of the curriculum program."
3. A curriculum council or cabinet is chosen by the superintendent to determine the philosophy of the school and general guiding principles, "to set up general objectives of the program," to serve as a clearing house, and, finally, to approve work submitted by various committees.
4. An aims committee has the job of formulating the aims of education and determining the program of studies to be offered.
5. A production committee for each subject and each division becoming active determines subject aims, subject content, pupil activities, materials, and so on.
6. A course-appraisal committee for each new course of study oversees the try-outs of new materials.
7. A course-installation committee sees to it that the course is properly installed after study by the principals and teachers who are to use it.
8. A continuous course-improvement committee keeps bringing the course up to date.

WEAKNESSES IN PROCEDURES AS CRYSTALLIZED

This plan for organizing and administering curriculum programs deserves careful study, for it represents perhaps the most dangerous type of crystallization in the whole curriculum picture today. The most obvious weakness of the procedure recommended by Trillingham is its underlying assumption that the curriculum is a series of documents periodically to be added to, revised, brought up to date. In other words, at the time of Trillingham's study, *curriculum* was still synonymous with *course of study,* in the realm of operation if not in the realm of theory.[2]

In the second place it is taken for granted that superintendents of schools, curriculum directors, and curriculum specialists shall launch all curriculum programs, selecting the personnel of working committees, evaluating the progress of those committees, and taking full responsibility for the results. This method of work violates the fundamental principles of democratic participation. It looks, indeed, as if here were the type of curriculum program which Saylor (1941, p. 2) characterizes thus: a program "planned in terms of course of study preparation, but organized so as to promote acceptance of the completed course by teachers through participation of representative teachers in its preparation."

A third observation regarding Trillingham's proposals is that there is an unquestioned assumption that curriculum revision in the sense here employed must be a system-wide activity. The possibility of autonomy for individual schools within the system is given no consideration.

A fourth observation has to do with the recommended first steps in curriculum revision. First a philosophy must be written down by one small group; next it must be broken down into principles or objectives; at this point new groups take over to break objectives into smaller bits called "aims." These are worked out for different subjects and grade levels of the school system. The whole procedure is based on connectionism in psychology—reduce the desired response of the pupil to a convenient unit of behavior, then set a stimulus situation to produce and fix that response—an additive rather than a developmental approach.

A final observation is that two groups of persons seem to have been entirely ignored in this master plan of participation in curriculum development. Those groups are the learners themselves and their parents and other adults in the community who have a stake in educational undertakings.

FAULTY CONCEPTION OF CURRICULUM UNDERLIES CRYSTALLIZED PROCEDURES

This whole formula for organizing and administering curriculum programs, which is still in common use today,[3] is based on a faulty definition of the curriculum. A year after Trillingham's report came the publication of Caswell and Campbell's influential work, *Curriculum Development* (1935). This book set forth a broad conception of the curriculum which cleared the air with regard to conflicting definitions of that term and should have freed curriculum workers from the limitations of mere course-of-study preparation. As refined in a later book by Caswell (1943, p. 188), this now generally accepted definition of the curriculum reads: "The curriculum is . . . composed of the actual experiences which children undergo under the guidance of the school."[4]

The fact that course-of-study preparation is still the most common activity in the field of curriculum development shows that the full implications of the newer definition of the curriculum are not as yet grasped by any great number of people. If it is true that the curriculum is composed of the experiences children undergo, it follows as a corollary that *the curriculum is the result of interaction of a complex of factors, including the physical environment and the desires, beliefs, knowledge, attitudes, and skills of the persons served by and serving the school;* namely, the learners, community adults, and educators (not forgetting the custodians, clerks, secretaries, and other "non-teaching" employees of the school).

If this corollary is studied carefully it will be seen that curriculum change is something much more subtle than revising statements written down on paper. To change the curriculum of the school is to change the factors interacting to shape that curriculum. In each instance this means bringing about changes in people—in their desires, beliefs, and attitudes, in their knowledge and skill. Even changes in the physical environment, to the extent that they can be made at all, are dependent upon changes in the persons who have some control over that environment. In short, the nature of curriculum change should be seen for what it really is—a type of social change, change in people, not mere change on paper.

INSIGNIFICANT RESULTS FROM CRYSTALLIZED PROCEDURES

The faulty conception of the curriculum that underlies most of the curriculum programs to date is one reason for reexamining current procedures in curriculum-making at this time. A further reason for reexamination of the pattern of curriculum development as it has crystallized in our day is that this pattern has produced such insignificant results. In spite of all the attention and energy that has been directed toward solution of curriculum problems during the last two decades, it is rather generally agreed that there has been relatively little fundamental change in the curriculum of American schools in the years when rapid advances in technology have been making drastic changes in the whole culture surrounding the schools. When careful study was made of 1,175 selected courses of study produced by representative school systems during the years 1930 to

1940, one of the major findings was that "there is a great dearth of the kind of new content which is needed for our times" (Bruner *et al.,* 1941, p. 207). Although certain favorable trends were discovered, the following facts were considered significant (p. 209):

1. There is a persistent attempt in the majority of courses to utilize traditional subject matter to satisfy new needs.
2. Part of the new content that has been introduced is in many instances not significant. It is as academic as is the remainder of the course. . . .
3. Some of the new material does not provide for a sufficiently thorough analysis of the problem involved. Like many other innovations, some of the material seems to have been introduced merely because it was novel.
4. There are glaring shortages in content in certain fields. For example . . . in social studies there is little or no mention of advertising and its widespread influence, art, child labor, housing, insurance, installment buying and consumer education, social security, dictatorships and many other vital problems today. . . .
5. The underlying philosophy of many of the courses prevents the content from assuming full significance. For example, the idea that science should remain "pure" stultifies the social emphasis that might otherwise be present. . . .

In short, existing courses have been overhauled slightly and a few new courses have been added to the curriculum as a result of all the curriculum activity that has been in vogue. In view of the need, however, changes have been superficial indeed.

A still more recent study by Hopkins, Stratemeyer, and Woodring (1945) shows that not even did a second world war succeed in bringing great reality into the school curriculum, if one may judge by representative curriculum materials produced during that period. In the introduction to a *List of Outstanding Teaching and Learning Materials 1942-1945* these observations, among others, are made:

Two major concerns of school people seemed to stand out. They were minimum essentials and character education. Frequently they were referred to under different names but the intent was the same. There was more discussion than agreement. There were vague feelings that the subject essentials were not adequate and the character was more than the overtones of a traditional program. Yet there was little attempt to clarify and implement these feelings. The old essentials still prevail.

Experiences and needs of children were generously suggested as a means to orient them to the subject matter of the courses of study. Such experiences and needs were rarely used as a basis around which to build a curriculum.

The use of community resources was suggested in many instances as desirable in teaching and learning. The emphasis in general, however, was upon books as the normal and desirable resource and upon book learning as the basic essential for educational achievement.

The effects of the war period appeared in two ways: first, in the new areas of study such as aviation and meteorology, and second, in the new emphasis given to old subjects, especially health and physical education, mathematics, and science.

Again there is evidence that changes in the curriculum are too few and too insignificant.

Read in the light of the foregoing comments on courses of study prepared in the decade of the '30s and since, Rugg's summary of methods of curriculum-making current in 1926 has a familiar ring:

Partial, superficial, and timorous "revision" rather than general, fundamental, and courageous reconstruction characterizes curriculum-making in the public schools . . . the existing program is always taken as the point of departure. . . . Thus curriculum-making becomes a process of accretion and elimination. There is little, indeed almost no movement under way in public schools to initiate curriculum-making from the starting point either of child learning or of the institutions and problems of American life. For over fifty years, tinkering has characterized the attack on the curriculum. In most centers the situation remains essentially unchanged. [P. 427]

If such are the results of mechanical curriculum procedures, efficient as they may appear to be on paper, it is evident that the process of curriculum change needs study.

FAILURE TO BENEFIT WIDELY FROM INNOVATING PRACTICE

Parallel with the development of the standardized curriculum program as just described has been experimentation on the part of pioneering individuals and groups in an effort to improve the experiences which children have under the guidance of the school. There is a growing number of schools employing a more functional approach to curriculum change. Not a few of them have arrived at some rather creative solutions to persistent educational problems. Their experience is valuable to others, and there are available many accounts of the changes such schools have made. Elsie Ripley Clapp's *Community Schools in Action* (1939) is a good example. There are also *The Community School,* edited by Samuel Everett (1938), and *Youth Serves the Community,* edited by Paul Hanna (1936), as well as recent yearbooks of the Department of Supervision and Curriculum Development of the National Education Association and issues of *Progressive Education,* particularly those for the years 1939-41.

Such accounts of promising practices are stimulating and worth while. But, in most cases, the innovators have failed to record for the benefit of others the detailed steps they took in making basic curriculum change possible in their schools. Since there has been a dearth of careful analyses of how fundamental changes have been brought about in people and in their ways of working, schools have borrowed from those who have blazed the trail whatever they could most easily lay hands on—often the outer shell only. Thus another impulse toward crystallization of curriculum practice has resulted.

It is recognized that out of experimentation by pioneers in education and dissemination of their findings through imitation considerable progress has been made. Indeed, it would be quite wasteful for each individual or group to pioneer for itself in all aspects of living. The question is whether or not crystallization is an inevitable result of trying to profit from the experience of others. Is there not some way in which the value of human experience may be transferred to others without the stultifying effect of borrowing ready-made solutions?

The writer is convinced that there are better ways of bringing about curriculum change than have yet been widely employed in American education. There has long been a need to discover those better ways and to bring them together into a form that would be useful to curriculum workers. There is need to learn both how to break down undesirable crystallization in education and how to prevent new crystallizations from setting in.

. . . As was pointed out earlier in this chapter, the changes involved when the school curriculum is really modified are actually changes in the attitude and behavior of persons. The changes in those persons must be in the direction of greater flexibility and greater awareness of fundamental issues. . . .

NOTES

1. To be fair to a commendable curriculum innovation and to the many educators who made creative use of the newly popular curriculum principle, it should be stated that thereby a number of promising changes have been effected in the program of many schools. In fact, the activity concept as analyzed by Lois Coffey Mossman in *The Activity Concept* (The Macmillan Company, 1939) and others continues to provoke thoughtful reexamination of practice and to contribute to desirable changes in the school curriculum. It is against mechanization and distortion of a valid curriculum principle that this discussion is directed. It is a wasteful procedure to replace an older crystallization merely with a newer, fresher one.

2. That some shift in thinking has occurred in the decade since Trillingham's work is attested by the following report in the *Curriculum Journal*, Feb.,

1942, p. 53: "Some of the most important curriculum developments in the Bakersfield (California) city schools are those that do not ordinarily receive attention. For instance, workshop facilities have been developed where supervisors have adequate room to hold meetings within their offices and space where projects may be assembled and work in various types of art, poetry, and so forth may be carried on right in the workshop by teachers. . . . The supervisors of music and art, the material for the testing program, the circulating library, the central library for circulating books for children, as well as the Audio-Visual Aids Department are all housed in one place where the teachers may come and go into either of the laboratories for assistance."

3. For evidence of the truth of this statement one has only to consult the department "News from the Field" in the *Curriculum Journal* during its last year of publication (1942-1943).

4. This definition is essentially the one accepted for the purposes of this discussion. The writer is aware that some educators have begun in recent years to regard the curriculum as all of the experiences children have under any circumstances. The latter definition is the result of a belief that curriculum workers, in selecting and organizing learning experiences for and with children, have tended to ignore the influences of the child's out-of-school living. Those advancing the idea hope that a definition of the curriculum so broad as to erase the lines between the child's school experiences and those outside the tutelage of the school will guarantee wiser planning of those experiences.

The writer is in entire sympathy with the point of view that all of each child's experiences must be taken into account in curriculum-planning. But it should be quite possible to do so without blurring the word *curriculum* until it loses its root character. As a word that meant in the original Latin "a racetrack" and as a word that has for centuries been associated with schooling, it must, to be true to itself, it seems, connote something planned and planned for, a somewhat limited segment of life, not all of it.

The definition here accepted does not limit the curriculum to experiences which children have within the four walls of the school or within school hours. It does mean, however, that a quarrel between a mother and a father on Saturday night will not be considered as part of their child's curriculum, important as that quarrel is in its *implications for that curriculum.* The curriculum is here limited to those experiences for which the school has some opportunity of affecting.

REFERENCES

Bruner, Herbert, et al. *What Our Schools Are Teaching*. New York: Teachers College, Columbia University, 1941.

Caswell, Hollis L. *Education in the Elementary School*. New York: American Book Co., 1943.

Caswell, Hollis L., and Campbell, Doak S. *Curriculum Development*. New York: American Book Co., 1935.

Clapp, Elsie Ripley. *Community Schools in Action*. New York: Viking, 1939.

Everett, Samuel (ed.). *The Community School*. New York: D. Appleton-Century, 1938.

Hanna, Paul (ed.). *Youth Serves the Community*. New York: D. Appleton-Century, 1936.

Harap, Henry (ed.). *The Changing Curriculum*. New York: D. Appleton-Century, 1937.

Hopkins, L. Thomas, Florence Stratemeyer, and Maxie N. Woodring. *List of Outstanding Teaching and Learning Materials 1942–1945*. Washington, D.C.: NEA Department of Supervision and Curriculum Development, 1945.

Rugg, Harold. *Curriculum-Making: Past and Present*. Twenty-sixth Yearbook of the National Society for the Study of Education. Part I, pp. 20–21. Bloomington, Ill.: Public School Publishing, 1926.

Saylor, J. Galen. *Factors Associated with Participation in Cooperative Programs of Curriculum Development*. New York: Teachers College, Columbia University, 1941.

PART SIX

Theory and Research

Previous parts of this text have identified major issues and illustrated alternative curriculum perspectives. The issues and perspectives presented undoubtedly will provoke further inquiry. A final issue to be investigated here is the structure of curriculum inquiry, the kinds of questions to be raised, and the ways in which they may be addressed. What is the nature of curriculum theory? What are its conceptual and syntactical structures? What are the directions of research in the field?

Curriculum theory addresses a range of issues. The contents of the triennial summaries of curriculum in the *Review of Educational Research* between 1930 and 1969 indicate a broad range of professional interests: curriculum planning and development; philosophical, social, and psychological foundations of curriculum; elements and design of curriculums; teaching and learning materials, resources, and activities; history and status of the curriculum field; research and evaluation; and curriculum change. In recent years, the same broad range of interests may be found in specialized publications like *The Journal of Curriculum Studies, Journal of Curriculum Theory,* and *Curriculum Inquiry* and in the more general *Educational Researcher, Harvard Educational Review, and Educational Theory*. The two ASCD publications, *Educational Leadership* and the newer *Journal of Curriculum and Supervision*, are also valuable sources of perspective on curriculum theory and research.

Over a decade ago, Huebner (1976, p. 14) addressed curriculum theorists and researchers and argued that increasing diversity of interest had been fatal to the curriculum field and that the prospect of revitalization was limited:

> There can be no renascence, because the field as it now constitutes itself, has no unity or integrity. We might speak of a possible reincarnation if we discover some interests that now have autonomy or can be readily associated with other practical interests, and return to our roots.

Huebner also argued for a singular curriculum focus on "the identification and making present of content to persons," that is, developing "an awareness of how content is related to culture . . . [and] making content . . . accessible to students" (pp. 9–15). His argument notwithstanding, the field of inquiry has renewed itself, as shown by Huebner's own work and that of other curriculum reconceptualists, the evolution of critical praxis in the field, and the work of a new generation espousing traditional curriculum theory.

PROBLEMS OF THEORY BUILDING

As a beginning, it will be useful to point to two initial problems that emerge in discussions of curriculum theory and research. A first problem recalls definitional dissonance. Is a curriculum a prescription for teaching or is it a description of learning in schools? Clearly, it can be either. But it must be one or the other, at least in pursuit of a particular line of research. For theory building and research to proceed systematically in a field, its conceptual and syntactical focuses must be clear and consistent, and clearly and consistently elaborated.

In the field of curriculum, the existence of several focuses results in the pursuit of several lines of theory building and various kinds of research. Beauchamp (1981, p. 82) argues, for example, that curriculum theory should concern itself with clarifying value bases, with characteristics of curriculum design, and with curriculum processes. Willis (1971, p. 41) suggests that "we might expect to find curriculum theory attempting to develop some comprehensive conception about the nature of experience."

A second problem emerges from diversity of perspective within the field of curriculum (Macdonald, 1971). Diversity gives rise to additional varieties of theory building and research. In addition to differences in orientation arising from varying definitions of curriculum, then, there are differences in perspective that result in differences in theory as well as practice. The perspective of most practitioners is the development of curriculums and the ultimate improvement of classroom instruction. There has been less emphasis on understanding curriculum phenomena and the generation of new knowledge in curriculum. But theorists in the field have pursued both lines of research.

In Selection 6.1, Beauchamp explores what he calls communication problems in curriculum writing by analyzing the scope of the field. Writing in curriculum includes five general areas: (1) definitional structures, (2) foundations, (3) curriculum planning, (4) subject matters to be included in curriculum, and (5) curriculum theory.

Additional exploration of the curriculum field results from Beauchamp's discussion of textbooks, state and federal laws prescribing curriculum, administrative and conceptual levels of curriculum development, the meanings of terms, and alternative curriculum designs.

In discussing textbooks viewed primarily as curriculum theory, Beauchamp identifies his own work (1981) as well as the work of Johnson (1967), Goodlad (1979), and Unruh (1975). In his examination of curriculum writing, Walker (ASCD, 1980, pp. 78–80) describes writing about curriculum writing, a category of curriculum literature that includes metatheory and criticism. Illustrative works include Apple (1971), Young (1971), Pinar (1975), Eisner and Vallance (1974), Eisner (1970), Goodlad (1968), Huebner (in ASCD, 1966), and Schwab (1969). We would suggest, in addition, that more recent work by Tanner and Tanner (1980), Schubert (1986), and McNeil (1985) are helpful in overviewing the curriculum field *qua* field. Walker (in ASCD, 1980, p. 8) concludes:

> Curriculum writing seems to me to be a slice of public life itself. It is as rich and varied as that life, and as confused and confusing.... A rich confusion is the right state for curriculum writing. I don't know how it could do better.

The remainder of Part Six illustrates this conclusion.

PARADIGMS FOR THEORY

A number of curriculum experts have reviewed and categorized paradigms for curriculum theory, such as Beauchamp, 1981; McNeil, 1985; Schubert, 1986; and Tanner and Tanner, 1980. For Schubert (1986, p. 170), a paradigm is "loosely connected set(s) of ideas, values, and rules that govern(s) the conduct of inquiry, the ways in which data are interpreted, and the way the world may be viewed."

A paradigm prescribes both conceptual and syntactical structures of research, that is, it identifies both phenomena to be studied and the method of research to be employed. Paradigms for curriculum research may be classified as rational, practical, and reconceptualist. Rational paradigms focus on technical processes in attempts to develop general principles for curriculum planning, implementation, and evaluation. Practical paradigms focus on problems that are situationally specific, involving social interaction. Reconceptualist paradigms focus on critiques of individual emancipation within a power structure.

Traditional Paradigms

In Selection 6.2, Johnson links paradigms to definition. For Johnson (1967, p. 130), a "curriculum is a *structured series of intended learning outcomes*." Johnson then identifies selected contributions to traditional curriculum research and attempts to distinguish among several important conceptual elements. He concludes by offering a scheme for classifying elements of curriculum, instruction, and teaching. His formulations illustrate a traditional approach.

A reading of Johnson's presentation can offer at least two insights. First, curriculum concerns itself with a complex of interrelated phenomena. Second, some systematic attention to conceptual structure in the field, together with an evolution of consensus about the validity and usefulness of that structure, seems a necessary condition for fruitful theory building and research.

Almost twenty years ago, Goodlad (1969, p. 374) concluded:

> As far as the major questions to be answered in developing a curriculum are concerned, most of the authors in the 1960 and 1969 issues [of *The Review of Educational Research*] assume those set forth in 1950 by Ralph Tyler. . . . No other scheme has served in a similar way.

Although some new questions have been raised, and new lines of theoretical development intitiated in the field's most recent decades, the Tyler questions continue to dominate traditional curriculum inquiry.

In a well-known work, Goodlad and Richter (1966) directed further attention at the development of a curriculum conceptual system to elaborate Tyler. Their work elaborated a system for relating values, educational aims, and learning opportunities. They underscored the need for specialized expertise in deriving aims from values and, in turn, opportunities from aims.

In a reappraisal of the Tyler model, Kliebard (1970) identifies limitations that may provide a critical perspective of traditional curriculum paradigms generally. Kliebard asserts that an ideological framework is implicit in Tyler's work and that the philosophical screen Tyler uses for selecting curriculum objectives is Tyler's own framework disguised in technical language. Kliebard also takes issue with the rationality of Tyler, a rationality that oversimplifies human decision-making. Apple (1972) has proposed that the roots of traditional curriculum thinking be investigated in order to trace the development of its implicit value structure, which he characterizes as quasi-scientific. He describes the evolution of curriculum thought as "caught up in a process by which complex ethical and political concerns are progressively transformed into technical problems...[so that] basic human dilemmas are made into puzzles for which easy solutions can be found" (Apple, 1972, pp. 11–12).

An important aspect of curriculum theory and research is methodological. The nature of the phenomena under study and the purpose for that study provide methodological direction in any field. Nonetheless, the *method* of research is itself an issue that, if treated as a prior question, can suggest or dictate the kinds of questions and phenomena to be investigated.

The professional literature reveals that research in the field of curriculum pursues different meanings and conceptions, on one hand, and different methodologies, on another. In traditional curriculum inquiry, research is generally synonymous with philosophical inquiry that results in prescriptions for curriculum design. The inquiry seeks to discover what the curriculum *ought* to be.

Some curriculum specialists see research in curriculum as the building of empirical theory describing what is and not what ought to be. Beauchamp (1981), the most consistent curriculum authority in this regard, finds an empirical approach to curriculum inquiry useful for developing and understanding phenomena and relationships in the field. He stresses the descriptive, explanatory, and predictive functions of theory and the methods of scientific inquiry in his comprehensive work on curriculum theory.

According to Schubert (1986, p. 181), empirical inquiry posits principles of control and certainty, operates in the interest of lawlike propositions that are testable, assumes knowledge to be value-free and objectified, values efficiency and parsimony, and accepts social reality as it is. In an assessment of the fruitfulness of an empirical approach in curriculum, McNeil (1977, p. 308) notes that "there is great disenchantment with the notion that the curriculum field will amass empirical generalizations, put them into general laws, and weld these laws into a coherent theory." Nevertheless, there are methodological alternatives.

A Practical Paradigm

In Selection 6.3, Schwab begins with illustrations of a theory crisis in curriculum. Apparently dismayed at simplistic attempts to ground curriculum theory in sweeping and exclusive generalizations about knowledge and mind, social purpose and direction, or human personality, Schwab calls for an ecletic approach to theory building in the field. He recognizes that social scientists are not likely to produce an all-encompassing theory in the foreseeable future and that no theory can account for the nuances and idiosyncrasies of particular curriculum situations. Therefore, Schwab calls on curriculum specialists to utilize the practical arts of problem solving, and his discussion of these arts illustrates how their use differs from traditional theory building. Schwab thus suggests how activity in the curriculum field would change as a result of the focus he advocates here.

It may be useful to recall that Schwab's proposals were made in a social context larger than the field of curriculum itself. His call for a return to the practical arts, which "begin with the requirement that existing institutions and existing practices [including a school's curriculum] be preserved and altered piecemeal, not dismantled and replaced" (Schwab, 1969, p. 14) coincided with the so-called Romantic critics' demands for radical school reform. Besides bringing about needed changes, the practical arts require attention to specific problems in individual schools and the anticipation of the effects of new solutions to existing problems. Schwab's proposal might be seen as a call for the calm deliberation of the school administrator as an alternative both to the wholesale reforms of social critics and the detached inquiry of the theoretician. To be sure, such a proposal in the field of curriculum probably continues to have much appeal.

In a critique of Schwab's proposal, however, Starratt (in Pinar, 1974, pp. 16–35) offers a number of salient insights that may be useful for clarifying further the nature of the curriculum field. First, he suggests that:

> the one-dimensional and fragmented theory we suffer with at present seems to require a much larger effort to develop a comprehensive theory, rather than a need to flee the task of theory in despair and immerse ourselves in the perhaps more satisfying but shortsighted tasks of solving immediate problems.

Starratt uses traditional argument between behaviorist and humanist, between individual freedom and social adaptation advocate, between academician and moralist, to point out that each has something to say to the other. "The last word has not been said on ways of striking balance" (p. 22). Starratt sees the theoretician's task to be an eclectic and synthesizing one, though nonetheless crucial. Both Starratt and Macdonald (1967) point out that curriculum theory building has been one-sided. Starratt refers to the constraints of logical positivism; Macdonald calls it the problem of rationality. Both see a need for a more inclusive perspective in theory building.

Second, Starratt (in Pinar, 1974, p. 25) points out that "the political negotiation and management of educational problems is the job of teachers, administrators, and central office supervisors, not of curriculum theorists." Without denying the importance of practical problem solving, Starratt suggests that exclusive attention to it in the curriculum field confuses the role of the theorist with that of the practitioner and benefits neither.

Starratt objects to Schwab's focus on present educational institutions. He agrees that "in so far as curriculum theory is involved with utopian proposals, with little appreciation of the policy arena, . . . he [Schwab] is right on target" (Starratt, in Pinar, 1974, p. 27). However, Starratt points out, third, that abandoning farsighted speculation altogether would be a fatal risk for the field of curriculum, especially in its early stages of theory-building activity.

Further use of the practical paradigm, however, may suggest an alternative perspective. Having illustrated ways in which the eclectic arts can be used in thinking about teachers, learners, subject matter, and milieu, so-called curricular commonplaces, Schubert (1986, pp. 301–5) uses an interactive model to suggest sixteen categories of questions to direct inquiry.

In a lengthy report of application of Schwab's practical model of curriculum inquiry, Fox (1985, p. 82) reported development and use of two simulations:

> Simulation I has often revealed that we are not as yet prepared to undertake the curriculum project that we are considering. Simulation II has helped us develop specifications and timetables that are realistic. These simulations are much more than a convenient checklist or rehearsal of possibilities. Their importance lies mainly in their role as tools for the curriculum team's considerations and practical alternatives in the light of the real costs.

Fox concludes that use of Schwab's principles has led to a further distinction between simulation and curriculum research. This distinction appears to have both theoretical and, appropriately, practical implications.

Reconceptualist Paradigms

Recent attention in the field has turned to existential dimensions of curriculum problems, among others. An early proposal to draw on concepts and methods of psychoanalytic theory to address curriculum issues such as the purpose and nature of learning experience was made by Louise Tyler (1958). Her initial investigations in this area probably uncover some roots for curriculum theory and research that have blossomed in the work of the reconceptualists.

The work of the reconceptualists begins as a critical antithesis of the traditional work in the field of curriculum. Pinar's (1974) early work brings together some of this critique. In his preface to a collection of conference essays, Pinar (1974, pp. x–xii) cites at least four issues that provide a unifying reconceptualist theme: (1) confidence in schools as liberating institutions, (2) the shape of future reform, (3) commitment to public education, and (4) the future of scientism in the field of education.

The last of these issues refers to a conflict within the curriculum field between the previously discussed empiricism, on the one hand, and the critical approaches of the reconceptualists, on the other hand. All the issues can also be seen in the context of the broader heightened consciousness and cultural revolution in American society, a useful backdrop for understanding the work of reconceptualization in curriculum.

In identifying critical theorists in curriculum, Schubert (1986, pp. 320–26) identifies two groups: reconstructionists and reconceptualists. The first group includes scholars such as Dewey, Counts and Rugg, and Hopkins. The second includes contemporaries like Pinar, Phenix, Greene, Macdonald, Huebner, and Kliebard. Reconceptualization has also been postcritical. Engaged in critical praxis, this group includes Giroux, Apple, and Pinar, among others. This third reconceptualist group may be neo-Deweyan in its emphasis on the importance of experience in individual development and neo-Counts in its emphasis on changing social phenomena through the school's curriculum.

Klohr (1980) has characterized reconceptualists in terms of organic and holistic views of man, individuals as agents in the construction of knowledge, emphasis on experience including both personal and public knowledge, importance of preconscious knowledge, emphasis on the humanities, value of personal liberty and higher levels of consciousness, diversity and pluralism as means and end, reconstruction of sociopolitical processes, and invention of new language. Schubert, and Willis (1982), characterize the earlier reconstructionists in similar ways.

Pinar's attention in Selection 6.4 is directed to what some reconceptualists see as an imbalance in the curriculum field, namely, in favoring general versus particular understanding in the conduct of inquiry. Pinar notes that the imbalance is evident not only in the work of empirical/analytic theorists but also in the work of some reconceptualists engaged in critical praxis. He also notes, "It was precisely this flight from particularity which Schwab attacked . . . " (Pinar, 1981, p. 175).

After suggesting a rationale for the imbalanced emphasis on general understanding, Pinar examines distinctions between simple description of particular experience and what he calls lived experience, and he points to limitations of some ethnography in this regard. Pinar then suggests criteria for particular inquiry, including empathy, specification of criteria for judgment, identification of domain assumptions, social negotiation, working oneself through experience, and attunement. Pinar concludes by arguing the consequent merits of qualitative research and autobiographical method in the conduct of particular inquiry in curriculum.

In a field where theory and practice have preferred rational conceptualizations and empirical method historically, Pinar offers alternatives. Indeed, he not only argues the validity of the alternatives but disputes the feasibility of traditional preferences. Conceptualizing knowledge as a dialectic of individual self in a particular situation, Pinar advances a curriculum perspective that gives the learner exclusive control of his or her own learning and warns about a danger in attempting to control others. Pinar focuses on the inevitability of lack of one's working through stages of knowing and argues that to do otherwise is to become developmentally arrested. In this selection, the author also uses qualitative theory and autobiographical method to identify tools for curriculum theory.

Methodology is as important an aspect of curriculum theory and research in reconceptualist paradigms as it is in the traditional paradigms already discussed. As before, the nature of phenomena under study may suggest methodological direction. In many cases, the study of personal experience and the meaning of language, often themes in reconceptualist work, lend themselves to artistic versus scientific methodologies.

Eisner (1981) uses differences between scientific and artistic approaches to illustrate a range of research emphases. He begins by pointing out that the term "qualitative" is misleading, should not be understood as distinct from nonqualitative, and refers to research to describe, understand, predict, and control qualities. He also points out that both scientific and artistic are broadly interpreted as used in his analysis.

Table 6.1 identifies nine dimensions in which scientific and artistic approaches to research may differ, and it summarizes differences in the two approaches. Artistic method focuses on the investigator's experience and elicits meaning versus truth. The method often uses language figuratively and seeks to illustrate rather than generalize. Eisner gives attention to qualitative research not because he believes that scientific approaches should be rejected in favor of artistic approaches but because he values diversity in inquiry, a central feature of the curriculum field.

Artistic method, like scientific method, is not value-free. Art values credibility; science values reliability and validity. Art is idiosyncratic; science is inferential. Art values license; science values control. The traditional and practical curriculum paradigms express implicit value structures. The same is true for the reconceptualist paradigm.

Table 6.1 **Dimensions of Scientific and Artistic Research Methods**

Dimension	*Scientific Method*	*Artistic Method*
Form of representation	Formal statements; literal use of language	Figurative use of language; nonverbal expression
Appraisal criteria	Reliability and validity	Credibility
Points of focus	Observable behavior	Experience; personal meaning
Nature of generalization	Sampling procedure; inferential statistics	Illustration; idiosyncratic
Role of form	Interchangeable methods of data presentation; standardized report format	Form is part and parcel of the content . . . medium as message
Degree of license	Relatively limited	Relatively unlimited
Sources of data	Other persons, places, and things	The investigator's experience
Basis of knowing	Formal propositions	Multisensory data
Ultimate aims	Discovery of truth	Creation of meaning

Source: Based on E.W. Eisner, "On the Differences Between Scientific and Artistic Approaches to Qualitative Reason," *Educational Research*: 5–9, April, 1981.

THEORY AND PRACTICE

Some curriculum specialists have found it useful to explore the nature of relationships between the theoretical and the practical, that is, to investigate the research-into-practice problem. Short (1973, pp. 242–43) has made an initial foray into this area and states, "the relationship of research to practice is not a one-to-one relationship; rather it appears to be a series of complexly interrelated steps, . . . a problem . . . of knowledge production and utilization." Short identified dimensions of both knowledge production and utilization, especially with respect to curriculum, and examined the nature of relationships between the two. Pursuit of this kind of problem in curriculum may prove useful for creating greater cohesiveness and integrity in the field.

Curriculum theorists and practitioners tend to be divided not only in professional focus but also in institutional allegiances. Theorists include college and university faculty, mostly, though not entirely, within the field of education whose work, although applicable, is rarely used within the university itself. Practitioners include elementary and secondary school administrators and teachers, almost entirely, who have little direct interest in the university. In addition, many theorists spend little time in, indeed, seem averse to, real elementary and secondary schools. Many practitioners spend little time at theory. Probably overstated, this problem is nonetheless real.

In Selection 6.5, Connelly and Ben-Peretz examine teachers' traditional roles in curriculum. They offer rationale to discount past focuses on action research and research as implementation strategy. Instead, they propose an interactive model of researchers, curriculum developers, and teachers.

Connelly and Ben-Peretz offer a collaborative model to even pursuit of theory and practice in the field of curriculum. In a similar way, McCutcheon (ASCD, 1983) offers collaboration as one way of addressing communication problems identified by Beauchamp in Selection 6.1.

Developments in curriculum theory and research rely, to a great extent, on conceptual and methodological structures and on the substantive inputs of constituent groups. The future direction of the curriculum field is, of course, unknown. The weight of tradition is great, but some new directions or at least new perspectives loom large. How the enterprises of theory and practice in the field can be coordinated may not be clear at this time. However, that they must be related is very clear.

CONCLUSION

Continuing inquiry is the basis for vitality in any field. Theory-building and research activities afford new insights and suggest alternative solutions for continuing problems. Which questions to ask and how to set about looking for answers is the final set of issues explored in this introduction to the curriculum field.

A review of theory and research in curriculum reveals four persistent themes that reflect problems in the field: (1) fundamental differences with respect to definitions of curriculum, (2) theoretical versus practical pursuits, (3) the relative youth of the field itself, and (4) the inevitability of the interpenetration of curriculum and society.

Some curriculum authorities agree on the need for structure for theory and research activities, but they do not agree on either the focus or the method of inquiry. With respect to focus, alternative emphases parallel a continuum of definitions of curriculum explored earlier. This continuum includes focuses on a plan for learning as well as on individual learning experiences. With respect to method, the alternatives include traditional philosophical inquiry, empiricism, and existentialist approaches.

Some curriculum authorities, convinced of the inappropriateness of the theoretical, have concentrated on solving immediate curriculum problems. Another group concerns itself with the important problem of knowledge production and utilization—relating theory and practice in the field.

Curriculum is a young field. Its attention to systematic theory building is scarcely thirty years old. In that light, its accomplishments thus far hold much promise for the future.

REFERENCES

Apple, Michael W. "The Hidden Curriculum and the Nature of Conflict," *Interchange* 2:27–40, 1971.

Apple, Michael W. "Curriculum Scholarship and Historical Awareness," Paper presented at the annual meeting of the Professors of Curriculum, Philadelphia, March, 1972.

Association for Supervision and Curriculum Development. *Language and Meaning*, Alexandria, Va.: ASCD, 1966.

Association for Supervision and Curriculum Development. *Considered Action for Curriculum Improvement*. Alexandria, Va.: ASCD, 1980.

Association for Supervision and Curriculum Development. *Fundamental Curriculum Decisions*. Alexandria, Va.: ASCD, 1983.

Association for Supervision and Curriculum Development. *Current Thought on Curriculum*. Alexandria, Va.: The Association, 1985.

Beauchamp, George A. *Curriculum Theory*. Itasca, Ill.: F.E. Peacock, 1961; 1968; 1975; 1981.

Connelly, F. Michael, and Miriam Ben-Peretz. "Teachers' Role in the Using and Doing of Research and Curriculum Development," *Journal of Curriculum Studies* 12:95–107, April–June, 1980.

Eisner, Elliott W. "Curriculum Development: Sources for a Foundation for the Field of Curriculum," *Curriculum Theory Network* 5:3–15, Spring, 1970.

Eisner, E. W. "On the Differences Between Scientific and Artistic Approaches to Qualitative Reason," *Educational Researcher* 81:5–9, April, 1981.

Eisner, Elliott W., and Elizabeth Vallance (eds.). *Conflicting Conceptions of Curriculum*. Berkeley: McCutchan, 1974.

Fox, Seymour. "The Vitality of Theory in Schwab's Conceptualization of the Practical," *Curriculum Inquiry* 15:63–89, September, 1985.

Goodlad, John I. "The Curriculum: A Janus Look," *The Record* 70:95–107, 1968.

Goodlad, John I. "Curriculum: State of the Field," *Review of Educational Research* 39:367–88, June, 1969.

Goodlad, John I., and Maurice N. Richter, Jr. *The Development of a Conceptual System for Dealing with Problems of Curriculum and Instruction*. Los Angeles: Institute for Development of Educational Activities, University of California, 1966.

Goodlad, John I., et al. *Curriculum Inquiry*. New York: McGraw-Hill, 1979.

Huebner, Dwayne. "The Moribund Curriculum Field: Its Wake and Our Work," AERA invited address, San Francisco, April, 1976.

Johnson, Mauritz, Jr. "Definitions and Models in Curriculum Theory," *Educational Theory* 17:127–40, Spring, 1967.

Kliebard, Herbert M. "Reappraisal: The Tyler Rationale," *School Review* 78:259–72, February, 1970.

Klohr, Paul. "The Curriculum Field—Gritty and Ragged?" *Curriculum Perspectives* 1:1–7, September, 1980.

Macdonald, James B. "An Example of Disciplined Curriculum Thinking," *Theory Into Practice* 6:166–71, October, 1967.

Macdonald, James B. "Curriculum Theory," *Journal of Educational Research* 64:196–200, January, 1971.

McNeil, John D. *Curriculum: A Comprehensive Introduction*. Boston: Little, Brown, 1977; 1981; 1985.

Pinar, William (ed.). *Heightened Consciousness, Cultural Revolution and Curriculum Theory*. Berkeley: McCutchan, 1974.

Pinar, William (ed.). *Curriculum Theorizing: The Reconceptualists*. Berkeley: McCutchan, 1975.

Pinar, William F. "Whole, Bright, Deep with Understanding: Issues in Qualitative Research and Autobiographic Method," *Journal of Curriculum Studies* 13:173–88, September, 1981.

Schubert, William H. *Curriculum: Perspective, Paradigm and Possibility*. New York: Macmillan, 1986.

Schwab, Joseph I. "The Practical: A Language for Curriculum," *School Review* 77:1–23, November, 1969.

Short, Edmund C. "Knowledge Production and Utilization in Curriculum," *Review of Educational Research* 43:237–301, Summer, 1973.

Tanner, Daniel, and Laurel N. Tanner. *Curriculum Development: Theory into Practice*. New York: Macmillan, 1975; 1980.

Tyler, Louise. "Psychoanalysis and Curriculum Theory," *School Review* 66:446–60, Winter, 1958.

Unruh, Glenys G. *Responsive Curriculum Development*. Berkeley: McCutchan 1975.

Willis, George. "Curriculum Theory and the Context of Curriculum," *Curriculum Theory Network* 6:41–59, Winter, 1971.

Willis, George. In Edmund Short (ed.), *Conceptions of Curriculum Knowledge*. University Park: Pennsylvania State University Press, 1982, pp. 45–49.

Young, M.F.D. (ed.). *Knowledge and Control: New Directions for the Sociology of Education*. London: Collier-Macmillan, 1971.

Selection 6.1

Curriculum Thinking

George A. Beauchamp

The curriculum field is fraught with communication problems. There are both communication problems among curriculum scholars as well as problems in communication between curriculum scholars and curriculum practitioners. These are the result of thinking differently about curriculum or of using language that is ambiguous or confusing in the curriculum field.

This selection will explore communication problems by analyzing the scope of the field as revealed through principal writings on curriculum as presented in curriculum texts, by looking at curriculum influences and substitutes, by distinguishing between administrative and conceptual levels of curriculum development, and by examining some of the language of explanation and persuasion commonly used in the literature. Finally some of the problems and issues raised for curriculum developers will be mentioned.

THE SCOPE OF THE FIELD

One way to look at the scope of the curriculum field is to observe the contents of textbooks written on the subject of curriculum. It will not

---

SOURCE. From *Fundamental Curriculum Decisions*. The 1983 ASCD Yearbook. Reprinted with permission of the Association for Supervision and Curriculum Development.

be possible here to give a complete and specific analysis of textbook contents, but we can illustrate certain categories of content and comment about their significance in communicating about curriculum matters.

Most textbook writers present definitional structures for the word *curriculum*. For example, Smith, Stanley, and Shores (1957) defined the curriculum as follows: "A sequence of potential experiences is set up in the school for the purpose of disciplining children and youth in group ways of thinking and acting. This set of experiences is referred to as the curriculum" (p. 3). Ragan and Shepherd (1977) viewed "the elementary school curriculum as including *all the experiences of children for which the school accepts responsibility*" (p. 2). Johnson (1977) referred to curriculum "as a structured series of intended learning outcomes" (p. 6). Saylor and Alexander (1974) defined curriculum as "a plan for providing sets of learning opportunities to achieve broad goals and related specific objectives for an identifiable population served by a single school center" (p. 6).

In their analysis of various curriculum conceptions, Saylor and Alexander observed that the term is used in two distinct ways. One is as something intended, and the other is as something actualized (p. 3). This distinction in definition is interesting because it points up vividly a sore spot among curriculum writers; namely, whether we should distinguish between curriculum and instruction in our thinking. So much of this hinges upon the use of the word *experience*. The most commonly used definition of curriculum states something to the effect that the curriculum consists of all of the experiences of children and youth under the auspices of the school. For some, the experiences are planned for in the form of educational opportunities or intended cultural structures. These elements are planned by organized groups prior to instruction. For others, the experiences are meant to be learning experiences that may take place at any time including during periods of instruction. This distinction poses a real dilemma in curriculum communication.

There are really only three legitimate uses of the word "curriculum." One is to speak of a *curriculum*. This is the substantive, or content, dimension of curriculum. A second is to speak of *a curriculum system*. A curriculum system encompasses the activities of curriculum planning, implementing, and evaluating; these constitute the process dimension of curriculum. A third use is to speak of *curriculum as a field of study*. The latter, of course, consists of study of the first two plus associated research and theory-building activities. It should be noted that all curriculum meanings hinge upon what one refers to when speaking of *a curriculum*.

A second rather consistent body of content included in curriculum textbooks is a discussion of topics emanating from philosophical, social and cultural, historical, and psychological foundations of education. The purpose for including these topics is to draw from those areas basic data, or principles, for determining educational goals, the selection of culture content for the curriculum, and the organization of that content. Three things appear to dominate that process. One is to establish the role of the school in society as background for determining what to teach. The second is to make clear basic information about the characteristics and habits of potential school students. A third is to help with the complicated process of content selection and organization in light of the first two plus information about past experience in curriculum affairs. Although virtually all curriculum textbooks contain such information in one form or another, some deal with the subjects to a greater extent than others. For example, the books by Smith, Stanley, and Shores (1957), Zais (1976), and Taba (1962) contain extended discussions of the import of educational foundations for curriculum work. In many respects, some of the best knowledge in the curriculum field is derived from these foundations.

Techniques for curriculum planning are a third area of discussion in curriculum textbooks. Here writers tender advice to those who would plan curricula. A good way to illustrate this type of advice is to cite the scheme outlined by Taba (1962):

Step 1: Diagnosis of needs
Step 2: Formulation of objectives
Step 3: Selection of content
Step 4: Organization of content
Step 5: Selection of learning experiences
Step 6: Organization of learning experiences
Step 7: Determination of what to evaluate and of ways and means of doing it (p. 12).

Most such advice is reasonable and can be followed by curriculum planners if they wish to do so. We have had a geat deal of experience with the process of curriculum planning in the United States, and most of it has been done at the school or school district level. Curriculum planning along with implementation and evaluation may be thought of as the process dimension of the curriculum field.

A fourth substantive area discussed by curriculum textbook writers is the subject matters to be included in curricula. Authors who address themselves to this area of curriculum usually divide according to whether they are writing books about elementary or secondary school curricula, and these are quite different from books principally addressed to techniques of curriculum planning or curriculum foundations and principles. Although some space may be allocated to foundations or planning techniques, sizable amount of space is devoted to chapters on individual school subjects.

For example, Ragan and Shepherd (1977) devote six of their 14 chapters to subjects taught in the elementary school. Tanner (1971) devoted eight of 11 chapters to secondary school subjects. The purpose of such writing is to convey to readers the trends in content selection and organization as these writers see them. Although the subjects undertaken by writers as discussed here are unique, their purpose in writing is quite consistent (and perhaps complementary) with those writers who spend most of their time and space on techniques of curriculum planning. They render advice about what to do once curriculum planners get around to the task of writing the curricula, but concerns about curriculum content and orgnization are more appropriately thought of as the substantive dimension of the curriculum field.

A few books that may be viewed as textbooks are devoted to the subject of curriculum theory. Writers in this area of curriculum are concerned predominately with the development of rational explanation for curriculum phenomena. So far, writers have not come up with formulations that might be labeled as curriculum theories but, nonetheless, the area is being explored. Two authors have spoken of their works as the development of conceptual systems rather than theories even though much theoretical effort must have gone into their development. Johnson (1977) developed a conceptual model for curricular and instructional planning and evaluation. A distinguishing feature of Johnson's writing about curriculum has been his insistence upon distinguishing between curricular and instructional planning and products. Goodlad (1979) has developed a conceptual system for guiding curriculum practice and inquiry. The heart of Goodlad's conceptualization consists of four decision levels or domains: societal, institutional, instructional, and personal/experiential. Unruh (1975) developed a series of propositions and constructs as theoretical bases for the direction of curriculum development. Beauchamp (1981) presented an analysis of the conditions and circumstances under which curriculum theory might be built, reviewed past developments in curriculum theory, and pointed up need for further advancements in this area.

The scope of the basic literature of the field then may be described as consisting of meanings attached to basic concepts and constructs, curriculum foundations, the process dimension of curriculum (including planning, implementing, and evaluating), the substantive dimension of curriculum (including content and design), and theory development. Diversity of opinion among writers in each of these areas abounds. Such diversity supports the contention that there are few areas of substantive agreement among curriculum scholars, which means they have failed to generate an appreciable amount of knowledge that may be said to be indigenous to the curriculum field.

Curriculum research as well has to produce results that would help alleviate the above conditions. Repeatedly, curriculum research has been criticized for dealing with inconsequential problems, for inappropriate designs and techniques, and for not being theory-oriented. The paucity of theory-oriented research is a major contributor to the failure to develop substantive knowledge in the field.

CURRICULUM INFLUENCES AND SUBSTITUTES

The contents of school curricula are often influenced by circumstances and conditions external to the curricula. In some cases, they actually are substituted for the curriculum. The latter is particularly true with the case of textboks for students in the various school subjects. In many schools and school districts in the United States, the cluster of adopted student textbooks is the closest thing to a curriculum available in those schools. The subjects are chosen, the subject matters are already organized, and the schools thereby have an educational program without further effort.

From time to time, state and federal goverments pass laws that either influence or prescribe curriculum content, and curriculum content may be influenced by decisions made in our courts. Since education is a function of the states, more influence ensues from state goverments than from the federal goverment. In any case, when laws prescribe curriculum content, curriculum planners have no option other than to include the content in the curriculum being planned. This constitutes the most direct and demanding influence upon curriculum content that originates outside the system.

Federal acts and titles have had a great influence in recent years upon curriculum content and organization. The National Defense Education Act of 1958 (NDEA) is an outstanding illustration. Under funding provided by that act, a plethora of projects were launched, most of which were designed to improve the character of the contents of various school subjects. Familiar examples were the Elementary School Science Project (ESSP), the Science Curriculum Impovement Study (SCIS), and the School Mathematics Study Group (SMSG). It is interesting to note that most science and mathematics projects were concerned more with the syntactics (skills and processes) of these disciplines than with fixed bodies of content. Bilingual education is another example of curriculum content added in most states because of federal funding. These are simply a few examples of another way in which the content and organization of school curricula may be influenced by federal acts and titles. Despite the fact that education is a function of the state and despite the fact that individual school systems do involve their personnel in curriculum planning activities, the federal goverment has exerted considerable influence upon the content and organization of school curricula in recent years.

ADMINISTRATIVE AND CONCEPTUAL LEVELS OF CURRICULUM DEVELOPMENT

Curriculum development is often thought of at two different levels. One level may be termed an administrative level; the other is more a conceptual level. I use curriculum development and curriculum plannning as one and the same notion. I see no real distinction between the two.

Adminstrative Levels

By administrative level of curriculum development, I mean simply those political or organizatonal groups or agencies that may influence directly or indirectly the curricula of our schools. The influences of the federal goverment have already been discussed. Since education is a function of the state, however, State Departments of Education may issue curriculum materials in the form of guides. Usually those are suggested rather than mandatory guidelines, but the states have the legal right to make them mandatory if they choose to do so. States may require that certain subjects and/or topics be taught in the schools and occasionally they specify the amount of time that must be allocated to that subject or topic. In a few states, county education offices act similarly except they may also add supervisory services.

Most curriculum planning (that is, most efforts that produce curriculum documents intended to be used in the schools) is done at the school district or individual school level. If one were to look through the curriculum documents displayed at the annual ASCD conference, it would become clear that the sources of virtually all of those documents were schools or school districts. In fact, the history of curriculum planning is really a recounting of the efforts of people in schools and school districts to develop their own curricula.

The fact that ideas appropriate for school curricula are generated by various social, political, and professional groups contributes to the confusion within the curriculum field. Writers often speak of the different levels at which curriculum decisions are made, which raises the question of when an idea for curriculum content actually becomes a part of a curriculum. This brings the discussion back to the problem of defining a curriculum. In other words, when in the course of events of selecting from our total culture are those portions of our culture chosen to be included in a curriculum for specific schools? Normally, that selection is made by people working for a board of education and subject to the policy acceptance of that board. These people may be teachers, supervisors, principals, or curriculum directors. If this can be a criterion for determining the production of a curriculum, then the decisions or suggestions of other groups or agencies can only be considered influences upon the decisions of those actually engaged in curriculum planning.

Conceptual Levels

At least four conceptual levels of curriculum planning are easily identifiable. They are in order of increasing complexity: textbook adoption, simple curriculum modification, broader curriculum review and overhaul, and a complete curriculum analysis.

Textbook adoption has become an almost universal task confronting schools and school districts. To the extent that the culture content to be taught in schools is a major consideration in textbook adoption and to the extent that the subjects are chosen in the process, it may be said that many curriculum-type decisions are made by those selecting textbooks. But to the extent that no document that may be called a curriculum is produced, textbook selection cannot legitimately be referred to as a process of curriculum planning.

A second level of curriculum planning may be termed a simple curriculum modification. This level of curriculum work can occur only if a curriculum (a document, that is) exists. The process is usually simple, involving minor changes in language, or changes in sequence due to past experience with the curriculum, or the addition of new ideas that have emerged from the teachers. This level of curriculum change frequently takes place when the existing curriculum is relatively new, and the planning group deems that substantial modifications are not warranted.

A third level may be termed a broader curriculum. Here again the assumption is that a curriculum exists, but it has been used for a sufficient length of time that the time has come to systematicallly revise the entire curriculum. Most of the action here is to update the curriculum content in light of new developments resulting from research and other sources, and/or to change the curriculum format in light of the experience of teachers. This level may involve such actions as review of curriculum materials from other school areas, use of consultants on problem areas, review of curriculum literature on contemporary curriculum concerns, and so forth. The most probable activity would be the mustering of and discussion of problems raised by teachers as a result of their experience in using the "old" curriculum.

The fourth level may be termed a complete curriculum analysis and development. Normally, this level is undertaken in a situation in which no policy document called a curriculum exists, or in situations where a curriculum is very old and not currently in use. The total process may take place in a series of phases or steps. First, a leadership group or a curriculum council may be needed to organize the work phases and to coordinate various subgroup efforts. A second step might be to conduct a listing and appraisal of the current curriculum practices in the school(s) as a focus for further deliberation. A third phase may be termed a study phase. Here, the curriculum planners investigate curriculum ideas and practices not present in the analysis of their own practices. This phase is essential for bringing in new curriculum ideas and is the most time consuming of all of the phases. A fourth phase may be the formulation of criteria for the selection of curriculum ideas to be included in the new curriculum. A fifth phase is the actual writing of the new curriculum. A sixth step is sometimes recommended, and that is to follow the writing phase with a testing period before the curriculum is officially implemented. Not all of these phases are recommended by all curriculum writers, and different labels may be used.

THE LANGUAGE OF EXPLANATION AND PERSUASION

In curriculum writing several terms are used to explain or persuade. These terms often are used interchangeably and occasionally inappropriately. I refer here to such terms as philosophy, ideology, theory, model, scheme, and rationale. The following discussion of these concepts is not an attempt to establish definitions for these terms, but rather is an attempt to clarify some of their more appropriate uses in the field of curriculum.

Philosophy

From a dictionary perspective, the term *philosophy* refers to the study or science of the search for truth and principles underlying knowledge and human nature and conduct. Thus, the philosopher is free to study the whole gamut of human affairs. It is extremely doubtful that anyone should propose a philosophy of curriculum even though the study of philosophy of education has been around for a long while. Theory and philosophy are often confused because a full-blown philosophy may be undergirded by related but specific theories. For example, philosophers are concerned with epistemology, which is referred to as the theory of knowledge. John Dewey (1916) stated: "If we are willing to conceive education as the process of forming fundamental dispositions, intellectual and emotional, toward nature and fellow men, philosophy may even be defined *as the general theory of education*" (p. 383). If one accepts Dewey's conclusion, it becomes obvious that many theories are possible within the general area of philosophy to account for the dimensions of education and, within the sphere of education, there are possible theories to explain the specific dimensions of education such as theory of instruction, curriculum theory, administrative theory, and so forth. This does not mean, however, that the process used by philosophers may not be used in theory development. Theorists must use logic and critical analysis, for example, in their theoretical endeavors.

Ideology

Closely related to the usage of the word philosophy is the term *ideology*. In general, ideology refers to a system of ideas derived from sensation and composed of a body of doctrine, myth, and symbols of a social movement, institution, class, or large group. Eastman (1967) exemplified the notion of ideology in relation to philosophy when he developed the idea that Dewey's educational theory (philosophy) remained in a reasonably stable state, but that it was gradually ideologized by the progressive education movement. In writing about ideology and the curriculum, Apple (1979) spoke of the hidden curriculum as an avenue through which ideological configurations of dominant interests in society are tacitly taught to students in schools.

Theory

The term *theory* frequently is used mistakenly for such notions as a point of view, an attitude, a hypothesis, or an opinion. Theory, however, is a much more vigorous concept, especially in terms of the modes of theory building. In general, theory is an explanation for an identified set of events. Variation in definition of theory hinges on interpretation of the word *explanation*.

Two definitions of theory will illustrate sufficiently. Rose (1953) defined theory as "an integrated body of definitions, assumptions, and general propositions covering a given subject matter from which a comprehensive set of specific and testable hypotheses can be deduced logically" (p. 52). Kerlinger (1973) defined theory as "a set of interrelated constructs (concepts), definitions, and propositions that present a systematic view of phenomena by specifying relations among variables, with the purpose of explaining and predicting the phenomena" (p. 10). Theory may be classed into two types: scientific and nonscientific. Theories are developed by the techniques of science, or they are developed by careful use of logic, or both, utilizing fairly stringent rules. Theories are essential to the development of knowledge.

A great deal of attention has been given in recent years to the idea of developing theory in the curriculum field. If we translate the spirit of the definitions of theory identified in the paragraph above, a curriculum theory may be defined as "a set of related statements that give meaning to a school's curriculum by pointing up the relationships among its elements and by directing its development, its use, and its evaluation" (Beauchamp, 1981, p. 60). It is interesting to note that, within the total group of curriculum writers who have addressed themselves to theory, people can be identified who advocate and use a major scientific approach to theory as well as people who are committed to a more philosophic approach. It is sad to say that, despite the hundreds of pages that have been written on the subject, there appears to be no well-developed curriculum theory. Development of curriculum theory appears to be shackled by problems of concept and definition, lack of recognized knowledge in the field, and the paucity of theory-oriented research.

Model

Model is a term that is frequently used interchangeably with theory. A model is an analogy. The construction of a model is a way of representing given phenomena and their relationships, but the model is not phenomena. A model of an airplane is not the airplane. A set of blueprints is not a building. Models may be used to represent events and event interactions in a compact and illustrative manner. Models are useful tools, and theorists use them extensively. But a model is not a theory, and theorists should use them as means to ends.

Scheme

The word s*cheme* is properly used to refer to a systematic plan or program for something to be done. The word is not used frequently in curriculum discourse, but it does fit certain categories of curriculum proposal. Two examples will illustrate my meaning. Earlier in the chapter, I outlined five phases or steps that might be used in the process of complex curriculum planning. Those suggested phases are a scheme for that kind of undertaking. English (1980) proposed curriculum mapping as a technique in curriculum development. The procedure involves having teachers note what they have been teaching in terms of concepts, skills, and attitudes under a general subject heading such as geography or mathematics plus the amount of time spent on each subject. Both of these illustrations are schemes or systematic plans for a specific practice.

Rationale

A *rationale* is a reasoned exposition intended to give an underlying or rational foundation for some phenomena. Sometimes the word is used as an alternative for theory, but theory is the more complicated of the two conceptually. We hear the term used in curriculum, but mostly in terms of reasons for performing certain curriculum activities. The most frequently cited rationale in curriculum literature is the Tyler rationale (Tyler, 1950, pp. 1-2).

IMPLICATION FOR CURRICULUM DEVELOPERS

The purpose in discussing the language concepts in the preceding pages is to help potential curriculum planners in the process of ordering their own language and behavior as they launch and carry out their projects. Where choices in language interpretation confront them, curriculum planning groups will simply have to make their own choices in meaning or interpretation. Only in this way can communication be facilitated among the members of the planning group. But in order to discuss the consequences of the foregoing problems in communication for curriculum developers, certain assumption will have to be made. It is assumed that: (1) most curriculum developers will be people who are involved in a school or a school district, (2) people who intend to plan curricula will be concerned principally with responding to the question of what shall be taught in their schools, (3) curriculum developers are serious about their business to the extent that the results of their deliberations ultimately will become the official policy of their board of education.

One can set aside most of the considerations discussed in this chapter under curriculum inputs and substitutes with the admonition that these will be considered by the curriculum planners. One can also set aside the problems inherent in theory building because that is not the work of the curriculum developer. Some of the schemes, rationales, and conceptual systems may, however, be of help as advice to curriculum developers on procedural matters.

Clearly, the first decision that must be made by potential curriculum developers is at the administrative level. This is a simple decision for school people because they only have to choose between the planning arena of the school district and the individual school. Most will choose the district in all probability. In large urban areas, the region or subdistrict may be the choice. The second decision will have to be a choice in conceptual level of curriculum development, and the choice here is conditioned by the curriculum status within the district. The most sophisticated of the choices is the complete curriculum analysis. These two decisions will probably be tentatively reached by leadership personnel in the district, but the decisions must be tentative until the next cluster of decisions is made.

The next cluster of decisions consists of the choice of personnel to be involved, their organization for work, and their tasks. Most curriculum writers who address themselves to the techniques of curriculum planning come close to agreeing that the personnel who perform the tasks of curriculum planning ought to be involved in making decisions about what to do, why it should be done, and how to do it. . . . Generally, it is perceived that teachers will constitute the majority of those involved, but it is not generally agreed that all teachers should be involved. Decisions about involvement of personnel really are part of the planning for the planning activity.

The procedures or steps to be followed are really a free choice. Most all of the schemes offered by curriculum writers would be helpful, but curriculum developers should feel very comfortable if they develop their own scheme of work.

Before launching a curriculum development project, it is most important that administrative personnel ensure time and resources for the proposed project. Curriculum literature is not helpful on this point. The history of curriculum development projects in school districts is that they are either done piecemeal periodically, such as during paid work in summer vacations, or they are carried out after school hours without additional compensation for those involved. Curriculum development is important enough to deserve better consideration.

In addition to time, other resources must be available to those expected to do the planning. Curriculum literature, curriculum plans from other school districts, and consultants are among the possible sources to be needed by planners. Serious curriculum development can be expensive for boards of education to undertake; therefore, time and resource considerations are most important at the outset of a project. Furthermore, the magnitude of the project should be guided by the resources available.

Finally, a word should be said about the design of the curriculum to be planned. Basically, the design of most curricula will be subject-centered. Curriculum literature contains accounts or decriptions of proposals for other types of design, but in most schools, such proposals have had little effect. Therefore, it is predictable that the culture content portion of new curricula will be organized around the recognized school subjects. For help with that organization, curriculum developers may wish to turn to people who specialize in the individual school subjects for guidance.

Within the organization of the subjects there are three curriculum concepts that warrant attention by the curriculum developers. Those concepts are: scope, sequence, and articulation. Scope refers to the breadth or total amount of subject content that may be planned for any group of students at any grade level or for the total school. Sequence is a matter of intentionally ordering topics or subjects. Articulation refers to intended relationships among the subjects. Articulation is particularly important in a subject-centered design.

Other concerns about curriculum design depend upon the desires of the planners. It is commonly suggested that a curriculum should contain a set of intended goals and/or objectives to be followed by the culture content referred to in the paragraph above. . . . To the extent that the curriculum planners wish to influence the planning for instruction, they may wish to include suggested activities for students to perform. Curriculum planners may wish to ensure the proper implementation of their curriculum; if so, a set of such intentions may be included in the curriculum. The same may be said for intentions for evaluation and replanning. The total format decision really rests upon the shoulders of the curriculum developers. It is to be their curriculum, and they are the ones who must live with it once the job is completed.

REFERENCES

Apple, Michael W. *Ideology and Curriculum*. Boston: Routledge and Kegan Paul, 1979.

Beuchamp, George A. *Curriculum Theory*. (4th ed.) Itasca, Ill: Peacock, 1981.

Dewey, John. *Democracy and Education*. New York: Macmillan, 1916.

Eastman, George, "The Ideologizing of Theories: John Dewey's Educational Theory, A Case in Point," *Educational Theory* 17 (April 1967): 103–19.

English, Fenwick W. "Curriculum Mapping," *Educational Leadership* 37 (April 1980): 558–60.

Goodlad, John I., and associates. *Curriculum Inquiry*. New York: McGraw-Hill, 1979.

Johnson, Mauritz. *Intentionality in Education*. Albany, N.Y.: Center for Curriculum Research and Services, 1977.

Kerlinger, Fred N. *Foundation of Behavioral Research*. (2nd ed.) New York: Holt, Rinehart, and Winston, 1973.

Ragan, William B., and Gene D. Shepherd. *Modern Elementary Curriculum*. (5th ed.) New York: Holt, Rinehart and Winston, 1977.

Rose, Arnold M. "Generalizations in the Social Sciences," *American Journal of Sociology* 59 (August 1953): 49–58.

Saylor, J. Galen, and William M. Alexander. *Planning Curriculum for Schools*. New York: Holt, Rinehart and Winston, 1974.

Smith, B. Othanel, William O. Stanley, and J. Harlan Shores. *Fundamentals of Curriculum Development* (2nd ed.) New York: World Book Company, 1957.

Taba, Hilda. *Curriculum Development: Theory and Practice*. New York: Harcourt, Brace and World, 1962.

Tanner, Daniel T. *Secondary Curriculum*. New York: Macmillan, 1971.

Tyler, Ralph W. *Basic Principles of Curriculum and Instruction*. Chicago: University of Chicago Press, 1950.

Unruh, Glenys G. *Responsive Curriculum Development*. Berkeley, Calif.: McCutchan, 1975.

Zais, Robert S. *Curriculum: Foundations and Principles*. New York: Crowell, 1976.

Selection 6.2

Definitions and Models in Curriculum Theory

Mauritz Johnson

Educational researchers have traditionally been more concerned with improving education than with understanding it. This observation by Lazarsfeld and Sieber (1964, p. 33) seems valid for educationists in general, whether engaged in research or some other endeavor, such as "curriculum development." And, indeed, the noneducationist scholars who have of late interested themselves in curriculum reform projects also are more concerned with *improving* school programs than with gaining increased insight into the nature of curriculum. As scholars, all of them are, of course, interested in some kind of theory, but not in *curriculum* theory. Their views regarding curriculum may be sound, but they are no more firmly grounded in theory than those of education professors.

At the same time, educational practitioners—teachers, administrators, and even those with titles indicating specific responsibility for curriculum development—while interested in curriculum, are not particularly concerned with curriculum *theory*. After all, they feel, their concern is the practical one of improving the curriculum, not studying it. A perusal of the curriculum literature of the past twenty years will reveal, moreover, that the professors of education who have achieved reputations as "curriculum specialists" have chiefly been experts on *how* to organize and direct professional and lay groups effectively for curriculum improvement by applying princi-

SOURCE. *Educational Theory* 17, no. 2 (Spring 1967), pp. 127-40.

ples of group-dynamics and human-relations. These specialists have seemed more concerned with improving the *process* of curriculum development than with any specific improvement in the curriculum itself, and whatever interest they may have had in *organizational* theory and the psychology of groups, they have evidenced little concern for curriculum theory.

Thus the majority of educationists, educational practitioners, and scholars active in curriculum reform are oriented toward improvement rather than understanding, action and results rather than inquiry. Nevertheless, a small but increasing number of students of education are directing their attention to questions of curriculum theory for no other immediate purpose than to increase understanding of curricular phenomena. The theoretical clarification they bring about may ultimately benefit both scholars and practitioners in their efforts to improve curriculum, but this possibility is not the immediate motive for attempting to construct a curriculum theory. The theorist cannot allow himself to be forced into justifying his inquiry solely on the basis of its immediate utility.

THEORIES AND PLATFORMS

Current theoretical work on curriculum is of two types—programmatic (doctrinal) and analytic. Phenix (1964), who subtitled his book "A Philosophy of the Curriculum for General Education," engaged in both analysis and prescription. He analyzed various disciplines and built a taxonomy of meanings. He also proposed certain criteria for curriculum selection and organization. But at the same time he advocated a specific program of general education.

Similarly, Broudy, Smith, and Burnett (1964) subtitled their work "A Study in Curriculum Theory," and while they, too, examined criteria and classified the uses of knowledge, they also delineated a program of general education for the secondary schools. Beauchamp, likewise, explored in some detail the problems of formulating a theory, but his own illustrative model of a curriculum theory was programmatic with respect to process (planning), rather than substance or structure. He acknowledged that his own "curriculum position was imposed upon the field of curriculum theory as organized in the classification scheme. . ." (1961, p. 116).

All of these current scholars are well aware of the difference between a curriculum position and curriculum theory. In the past, however, even the "giants" of the profession seemed not to note this distinction. One of the most remarkable collaborations of eminent educational thinkers occurred in 1924-26 when Bagley, Bobbitt,

Bonser, Charters, Counts, Courtis, Horn, Judd, F. J. Kelly, Kilpatrick, H. Rugg, and Works joined in preparing a composite statement on "The Foundations of Curriculum-Making" (Rugg, 1926). Despite the fact that every member felt obliged to append his own reservations about the report, the Committee's 58 "principles" represented a consensual *position*, rather than a curriculum theory. That the Committee considered it to be a theory is evident, however, from an announcement in the introductory section (p. 11) that "each member . . . has not insisted upon the acceptance of his own curriculum theory . . . ." On the other hand, it had been stated previously that the group was explicitly concerned with ". . . writing a platform of *practical forward steps* in curriculum-making . . ." (p. 6). In this same paragraph the confusion is increased by Rugg's reference to ". . . this platform of curriculum theory . . . ."

Clearly, platforms and theories are two different things. Platforms propose policies, theories provide explanations. Included among the "principles" proposed by the 1926 Committee were many normative statements. Not until the 28th item was any definition of curriculum provided, and that was clearly "programmatic," as Scheffler (1970, p. 19) uses the term. "The curriculum," stated the Committee, "should be conceived . . . in terms of a succession of experiences and enterprises having a maximum of lifelikeness for the learner" (Rugg, 1926, p. 18). By considering "experiences and enterprises" to be the essential elements of curriculum, the Committee obscured the distinction between curriculum and instruction; by qualifying these elements with "lifelikeness," it engaged in exhortation instead of explanation.

But the Committee was aware of the problem of terminology. "From the beginning of our discussion," Rugg reported, "it was apparent that we did not understand each other. The chief task which we confronted was the erection of a common vocabulary" (p. 4). Vocabulary is still one of the chief problems in curriculum theory. Note, for example, the confusion evidenced as late as 1962 in the ASCD pamphlet, "What are the Sources of the Curriculum?," in which "curriculum" is confused with "curriculum development" and "source" is confused with "determinant."

CURRICULUM AND INSTRUCTION AS SYSTEMS

Some current theorists (Macdonald, 1964; Faix, 1966) favor a "systems" or process model for curriculum, in which the elements are inputs, processes, outputs, and feedbacks. They recognize the necessity of explicating the relation between curriculum and instruction, but in viewing curriculum cybernetically, they, too, confuse curriculum *per se* with the curriculum development process. Macdonald (1964) has included both content and process in his "curriculum system," but since the system ". . . is made up of people as its basic units . . ." (p. 6) and its output is "transmitted . . . to the instructional setting (also a separate social system)" (p. 12), one finds it difficult to identify the curriculum itself, either *as* or *in* the system. Surely curriculum does not consist of people.

In Macdonald's model some of the variables conventionally labelled as "sources" are considered to be "inputs."[1] This only makes sense if the system in question is construed as the "curriculum development system." To consider these variables "inputs" into the curriculum itself makes no more sense than to consider them "sources" of the curriculum.

Maccia and Macdonald disagree on the relationship of curriculum to instruction. To Macdonald these are separate concepts (systems?) that overlap to some extent. Maccia, on the other hand, holds that curriculum is a component of instruction by virtue of being a variable in "teacher behavior."[2] Thus, she sees curriculum not as a system but as "instructional content." This content consists of "rules." Rules are conceived as "structures," which, in sets, constitute "disciplines" (1965, p. 8; 1963, p. 6).

The role of curriculum in instruction is implicit in Maccia's definition of instruction as "influence toward rule-governed behavior." Since curriculum equals rules,[3] its function must be to *govern,* i.e., regulate, behavior. But there are two levels of discourse here. Whose behavior does curriculum govern? Is curriculum the set of rules that *learners* are influenced through instruction to govern their behavior by, or does curriculum, as rules, govern the *teacher's* behavior in instruction? By Maccia's formula, $B_t = I_c R M_c$ (the only one in which curriculum, I_c, appears), it seems to be the teacher's behavior that curriculum governs. But the teacher's behavior in instruction influences students' behavior toward governance by rules. Are these the same rules that constitute curriculum? What *is* a curriculum?

THE CONCEPT OF CURRICULUM

Accepted usage identifies curriculum with "planned learning experiences." This definition is unsatisfactory, however, if "curriculum" is to be distinguished from "instruction." Whether experiences are viewed subjectively in terms of the sensibility of the experiencing individual or objectively in terms of his actions in a particular setting, there is in either case no experience until an interaction between the individual and his environment actually occurs. Clearly, such interaction characterizes *instruction*, not curriculum.

A concept of curriculum that limits it to a *post hoc* account of instruction is of little value. Surely curriculum must play some role in *guiding* instruction. If so, it must be viewed as anticipatory, not reportorial. Curriculum implies intent.

Surely, too, a useful concept of curriculum must leave some room for creativity and individual style in instruction. In other words, decisions regarding the learning experiences to be provided are the result of instructional planning, not of curriculum development. The curriculum, though it may limit the range of possible experiences, cannot specify them. Curriculum must be defined in other terms.

In view of the shortcomings of the currently popular definition, it is here stipulated that curriculum is a *structured series of intended learning outcomes.* Curriculum prescribes (or at least anticipates) the *results* of instruction. It does not prescribe the *means*, i.e., the activities, materials, or even the instructional content, to be used in achieving the results. In specifying outcomes to be sought, curriculum is concerned with *ends*, but at the level of attainable learning products, not at the more remote level at which these ends are justified. In other words, curriculum indicates *what* is to be learned, not *why* it should be learned.

This view of curriculum seems to be in substantial accord with that of Gagné (1966, p. 6) who defines curriculum as ". . . a series of content units . . . ," a content unit being ". . . a capability to be acquired under a single set of learning conditions. . . ." Eisner, too, appears to endorse this view when he states that a teacher is engaged in curriculum building when he decides ". . . what to teach and how to order what he teaches" (1965, p. 156), but then appears to depart from it when he stipulates later that ". . . the basic unit of the curriculum is an activity" (1965, p. 158). The central thesis of the present paper is that curriculum has reference to what it is intended that students *learn*, not what is intended that they *do*.

There seems to be rather general agreement as to what *can* be learned, i.e., what the categories of learning outcomes are. Three "domains" are commonly recognized: the cognitive (Bloom, 1956), the affective (Krathwohl, 1964), and the psychomotor. Other classification schemes may be preferred, but the component types of outcomes are well recognized and accepted. They include factual knowledge, symbolic equivalents, concepts, generalizations, intellectual skills, manipulative skills, attitudes, interests, values, and appreciations.

The nature of a particular intended learning outcome limits the range of possible appropriate learning experiences and thus guides instructional planning. A learning experience has an activity component and a content component, i.e., it involves some kind of activity with some kind of content. A curriculum item that deals with a skill-type outcome restricts the range of appropriate activities, but may or may not impose any limitations on the content. On the other hand, an item which concerns facts, concepts or generalizations specifies content, but leaves considerable option with respect to activity. When an affective outcome is specified, neither content nor activity may be greatly restricted, although most affects have fairly definite referents (implying content) and schools are concerned that most affective outcomes be intellectually grounded (implying activity).

No curriculum item fully defines instructional *content*. Instructional content includes not only that which is implied or specified in the curriculum, but also a large body of *instrumental* content selected by the teacher, not to be learned, but to facilitate the desired learning. Concepts and generalizations are not learned directly but rather through numerous encounters with specific manifestations, the selection of which is an instructional, rather than curricular, function.

Every curriculum item defines instructional *activity* to some degree. Although there are many ways of developing a concept or a skill, the accepted approaches to each kind of outcome are finite. When the intended outcome is specified, therefore, certain possible activities are ruled out and others favored.

The *order* of learning experiences also is influenced by curriculum. A curriculum is not a random series of items, but a *structured* one, even if only to the extent of indicating that the order in which certain outcomes are achieved is immaterial. Insofar as the sequence of development is not considered to be a matter of indifference, the curriculum must be specific about the proper order. But structure is not merely a matter of temporal sequence. It also refers to hierarchical relations among items.

CURRICULUM STRUCTURE

That curriculum implies such ordering is obviously the assumption underlying the widespread current attention to the structure of knowledge, especially of that knowledge derived from inquiry which constitutes the disciplines. It is implicit in the analysis by Phenix (1962) and explicit in that of Schwab (1964a, b) that disciplines are structured both conceptually and syntactically (methodologically). Presumably, therefore, curriculum items assume their significance and meaning from their relationship to one another and to the mode of inquiry on the basis of which this relationship was derived or verified.

Thus, if a and b are appropriate curricular items, then aRb is likely to be appropriate also. If a and b are concepts, aRb is a generalization. It may be classificatory (e.g., Addition and multiplication are binary operations), correlational (e.g., Men tend to be taller than women), a function (e.g., F = ma), a definition of another concept (e.g., Density is mass per unit of volume), or in some other way relate two concepts within some structure.

Curriculum must indicate such relationships. Concepts and generalizations do not occur singly. They form clusters, and a decision to include one of them is often tantamount to a decision to include a whole cluster. A teacher or curriculum developer is not free to include a concept such as "capillarity" and to exclude, for example, "surface tension." These clusters are not equivalent, however, to "instructional units." The curriculum does not specify what organizational units are to be used in instruction, but it does indicate organizational relationships among the intended outcomes. In this sense, curriculum is a *structured* series of intended learning outcomes.

SOURCE OF CURRICULUM

It is necessary to account for the source of these intended outcomes. In most discussions of this question the sources of the curriculum are regarded to be (1) the needs and interests of the learners, (2) the values and problems of the society and (3) the disciplines or organized subject matter. All three of these may indeed impose criteria for the selection of curriculum items, but only the third can be considered a *source* of them. At that, it is only a partial source, since it ignores the body of unorganized knowledge and related skills and attitudes that lie outside of the recognized disciplines. The source of curriculum—the only possible source—is the total available culture. This was recognized by Bellack in 1956 (p. 99) when he identified ". . . the expanding content of the culture as the source of curriculum content," which he defined, in turn, as ". . . those elements of the content of the culture which are considered appropriate or relevant to the instructional aims of the school." This is not to say what the curriculum *should* be, but what it *is*. When Rugg and Withers (1955, p. 669) say that the curriculum *should be* "culture-centered," they mean something quite different from the present assertion that the curriculum is *necessarily* "culture-derived."

Not all cultural content is of a sort that could be incorporated into the curriculum. Only that which is teachable and available is eligible for inclusion. Artifacts and social institutions are components of a culture, but they are not teachable. Even some knowledge and skills, though teachable and very much a part of the culture, are not available for curriculum, since they are kept secrets by families, craft groups, corporations, or governments.

SELECTION OF CURRICULUM ITEMS

It is obvious that all that is available and teachable in the culture cannot be included in a given curriculum. Selection is essential. Although who does the selecting is an important educational policy question, it is not a concern of curriculum theory. What is of concern, however, is that whatever criteria are used be made explicit.

There are many possible criteria, some sensible, others silly, depending on one's ideology. Some factions insist that curriculum items bear upon persistent problems of living or current social problems; others emphasize the significance of items to the understanding of an organized field of study; still others favor selection on the basis of the experiences and interests of the potential learners. Some of these preferences are more applicable to instructional organization than to curriculum selection. Those who insist on applying them to selection are, of course, free to do so, but the notion of curriculum clusters restricts their freedom to select items at will without regard for structural considerations.

Moreover, a distinction can be made between curriculum selection for training and for education. Training implies learning for use in a predictable situation; education implies learning for use in unpredictable situations. The development of a training curriculum begins with a job analysis in which the tasks to be performed and the knowledge, skills, and attitudes needed to perform them are identified. The uses of training are, in the terminology of Broudy, Smith, and Burnett (1964, pp. 46-55) replicative and applicative. The uses of education are associative and interpretative.

Man's systematic efforts to interpret his experiences are represented by those organized bodies of knowledge, skills, and attitudes known as disciplines. An educational curriculum is developed by selecting among and within these disciplines those elements which analysis identifies as having the greatest potential interpretive value. Once the disciplines considered most relevant in the interpretation of experience have been identified, internal selection criteria become dominant. Which specific curriculum items are selected depends on how fundamental and crucial they are to the discipline, how well they explicate its structure, how powerful they are in furthering its characteristic thought processes and modes of inquiry. Phenix has called attention to the simplifying, coordinating, and generative features of disciplines. Appropriate selection criteria would maximize the probability of retaining these features in the curriculum and, hence, in instruction. Phenix (1962, p. 58) holds that "a discipline is knowledge organized for instruction."

CURRICULUM AND INSTRUCTION

Although curriculum is not a system, it may be viewed as the output of a "curriculum-development system" and as an input into an "instructional system." (See Figure 6.2-1.)

FIGURE 6.2-1. A Model Showing Curriculum as an Output of One System and an Input of Another

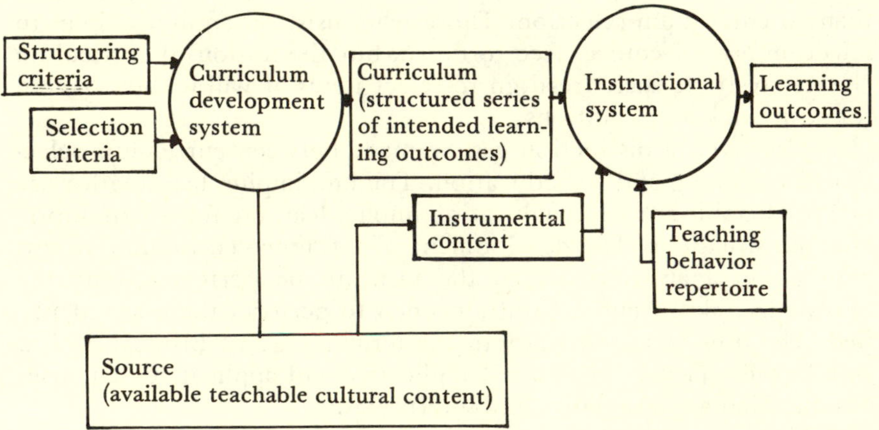

The instructional system has three components: planning, execution (instruction), and evaluation. Instructional planning occurs at various levels, varying in their temporal proximity to the actual instruction. Most remote is that strategic planning which results in the design of "courses" and "instructional units" within courses. Here an appropriate number of curriculum items (intended learning outcomes) are selected and organized for instructional purposes. Course and unit planners have considerable freedom in their selection and organization, so long as they do not violate curriculum stipulations with respect to hierarchy (clusters) and order. In a graded school organization, several versions of each course and unit may have to be planned to take into account differences in students' ability and readiness. Actually, each version is a different course and should be so designated, though this is seldom the case. In a nongraded instructional program, the curriculum can be arranged into a single series of courses through which students pass at varying rates.

Individual teachers continue the process of instructional planning up to and throughout the execution stage. It is they who make the final choice of learning activities and instrumental content in terms of the characteristics of the students, the availability of resources, and the exigencies of the ongoing instructional process. Even at this point, decisions must be governed by the intended outcomes stipulated by the curriculum and incorporated into the course and unit plans.

The evaluation aspect of instruction obviously involves a comparison of actual learning outcomes with the intended learning outcomes. For purposes of such comparison it is necessary to create a situation in which the student can exhibit behavior indicative that he has learned, i.e., has achieved the intended learning outcome. It is in this evaluation context that Mager's (1961, p. 12) injunction to specify objectives operationally as terminal behaviors at defined levels of performance under defined conditions applies. This is not to say, however, that learning consists of a change in behavior or that learning has not occurred if a behavioral change cannot be demonstrated. Nor is it the case that there has been no teaching where learning cannot be shown to have occurred. Teaching occurs whenever appropriate actions intended to produce learning are taken. Because the intentions are not fulfilled or no evidence of their being fulfilled is available does not in any way disqualify the actions as teaching.

Instruction consists of two sets of interaction. One is Dewey's "transaction" between the student and the environment manipulated by the teacher. As indicated earlier, both the content of the environment and the activities of the student are governed by the curriculum. The second interaction is the interpersonal one between the teacher and students. Flanders and Amidon (1963) have developed a procedure for analyzing this interaction, and Bellack (in Bellack and Davitz, 1963), Smith (1961), Ryans (1965), and others have examined the linguistic, logical, and information-processing characteristics of the classroom discourse that facilitates the interaction. Maccia (1964) has pointed out that the interaction has both motivational and content bases. The content base is clearly either derived from or inspired by curriculum, and unless the motivational base is entirely nonrational (sentimental, hedonistic, or magisterial), it, too, is curriculum-relevant.

It seems evident that many, if not most, of the so-called "curriculum reform" projects of the past decade have been concerned with instruction far more than with curriculum. Indeed, some of them have never made their curriculum explicit, whereas they have trespassed heavily in the instructional planning domain, going as far as to specify not only the learning activities to be provided but the instructional materials to be used, as well. These suggestions may well be excellent ones, so long as it is not assumed that alternative activities and materials could not possibly be devised to carry out the same curriculum as well or better. It seems probable that some of these projects have encroached upon instructional planning in a deliberate, if cynical, effort to make the curriculum "teacher-proof." On the other hand, syllabuses, courses of study, and curriculum guides have for years been freighted with lengthy compilations of suggested activities, materials, evaluation procedures, and other instructional advice, whereas, aside from an extensive list of vague objectives and an expository outline of so-called "content," they have seldom presented any curriculum at all, in the sense the term has been used in this paper.

CURRICULUM EVALUATION AND RESEARCH

Macdonald (1965) has correctly pointed out that curriculum evaluation is all too often conducted at the output point of instruction rather than at the input position. Thus curriculum evaluation is confounded with instructional evaluation. Curriculum serves as the criterion for instructional evaluation; variations in instruction cannot be permitted to enter into the evaluation of curriculum. If curriculum is to be evaluated empirically on the basis of instructional outputs, then differences in instructional effectiveness must be controlled, randomized, or partialed out. Gagné has suggested a scaling method whereby instructional output data may be used "... to provide information about the sequence of a curriculum," but notes that it "... does not provide an *evaluation* of a curriculum." "It does *not* tell us how good the curriculum is." To determine the effectiveness of an entire curriculum-instruction system, Gagné suggests that "one must actually put the curriculum into use, and then measure the results in terms of student achievement, or some other specified criterion" (1966, p. 14).

It is probable that feedback from instruction can furnish evidence regarding the *structural* validity of a curriculum. On the basis of instructional experience, curriculum items might be found to be incorrectly ordered or hierarchical clusters might be found to be incomplete or contain superfluities. But the validity of curriculum *selection,* i.e., the omission of significant items and the inclusion of insignificant ones, must rest on some criterion other than instructional results. Cronbach (1964a, b) and Stake (1966) have explored this problem at some length, and it may be expected that further progress will be made on it at the Center for Instructional Research and Curriculum Evaluation at the University of Illinois. Essential, however, to such progress is a clear delineation of curriculum and instruction.

Similarly, research on curriculum can only be conducted on the basis of some theoretical framework. As Ryans has observed, "... the chief function of theory is *not* to describe once and for all how certain kinds of phenomena ... operate, but rather to provide a framework for observation and analysis" (1965, p. 38). Whether the formulation of curriculum presented here will serve this purpose remains to be seen.

A schema in which curriculum is viewed as something other than "learning experiences" preserves the autonomy of creative instructional planning, free of remote prescription under the guise of curriculum development. It also clarifies the curricular research domain. Immediately susceptible to competent investigation are such questions as:

What are the rules relating intended outcomes and more general educational and training objectives?

What are the rules for selection of curriculum items within the contexts of education and training?

What are the rules for ordering curriculum items and for determining when order is unimportant?

What are the rules by which hierarchical clusters of curriculum items are identified?

What are the architectonics of nondisciplined cultural content?

What standard system of symbols would be most useful in communicating a curriculum?

SUMMARY

Some problems in current efforts at theorizing about curriculum have been discussed. Little interest in curriculum theory has been manifest by educational practitioners, academic scholars, or curriculum specialists. Curriculum theory has been confused with valuative positions regarding curriculum. The conventional definition of curriculum in terms of "planned learning experiences" has prevented a clear distinction between curriculum and instruction. Consequently, many alleged curriculum documents are primarily prescriptions or suggestions for instruction.

Recent considerations of curriculum theory have focused attention on disciplinary structures, but curriculum has been confused with the curriculum-development system of which it is an output, or it has been considered a part of the instructional system of which it is an input. An attempt was made, therefore, to develop a schema in which curriculum was defined as a structured series of intended learning outcomes. For purposes of clarity and convenience, this schema is summarized below.

A Schema for Curriculum

1. A curriculum is a structured series of intended learning outcomes.
   Corollary. Curriculum does not consist of planned learning experiences.
   Corollary. Curriculum is not a system but the output of one system and an input into another.
   - 1.1 Learning outcomes consist of three classes:
     - 1.11 Knowledge
       - 1.111 Facts: items of verifiable information
       - 1.112 Concepts: Mental constructs epitomizing facts about particular referents
       - 1.113 Generalizations (including laws, principles, rules): statements of relationship among two or more concepts
     - 1.12 Techniques (processes, skills, abilities)
       - 1.121 Cognitive: methods of operating on knowledge intellectually
       - 1.122 Psycho-motor: methods of manipulating the body and material things effectively with respect to purposes
     - 1.13 Values (affects)

1.131 Norms: societal prescriptions and preferences regarding belief and conduct

1.132 Predilections: individual preferential dispositions (attitudes, interests, appreciations, aversions)

1.2 Whenever a curriculum is used in instruction, the intention (to achieve the outcomes) is implicit regardless of the curriculum's origin or sanction.

2. *Selection* is an essential aspect of curriculum formulation.

2.1 The *source* from which curriculum is selected is the available culture.

Corollary. Societal problems and the needs and interests of children are not sources of curriculum.

2.11 Modern communication makes available cultural content that is not indigenous to the society in which the curriculum is formulated.

2.12 Some indigenous cultural content may be unavailable due to the secrecy of those in possession of it.

2.2 Cultural content available for curriculum is of two types: disciplinary and nondisciplinary.

2.21 The *content* embodied in organized *disciplines* is derived from systematic inquiry conducted within a framework of assumptions and procedures accepted by scholars competent to conduct such inquiry.

2.22 *Nondisciplinary content* is derived empirically from experience other than deliberate inquiry.

2.3 Various *criteria* may govern the selection of curriculum from available cultural content.

2.31 The only *necessary*, albeit insufficient, criterion for curriculum selection is that the content be *teachable.*

2.311 Teachability implies learnability, but the converse does not necessarily hold.

2.312 Cultural content is *teachable* if the learning of it by one person can be facilitated by direct or remote interaction with another person.

2.313 *Teaching* is the process by which one person interacts with another with the *intention* of influencing his learning.

2.3131 There can be teaching where there is no learning.

2.3132 There can be learning without teaching.

2.314 Learning is the process by which an individual invests cultural content with *meaning,* thereby becoming capable of acting differently toward that item, or another item, of cultural content.

Corollary. Learning does not necessarily change behavior, but it changes the potential for behavior.

2.3141 Learning can be detected only by contriving a situation in which a change in behavior can be manifested.

2.3142 Learning is independent of any demonstration of its occurrence.

2.315 Cultural content is *learnable* if meaning can be perceived in it.

2.3151 Cultural content has *meaning* for an individual to the extent that he recognizes appropriate rules by which his actions toward it may be governed.

2.3152 Meanings may be symbolic, empiric, esthetic, ethic, synoetic, or synoptic (Phenix, 1964).

2.32 *Ideology* determines what additional criteria are imposed in curriculum selection.

2.321 A given society may demand that curriculum be selected in conformity with a specified set of political, social, economic, or moral *values.*

2.322 Curriculum content may be selected with regard to its *utility* in the social order or in the present or anticipated life situations of learners.

2.323 Curriculum content may be selected with regard to its *significance* in the structure of intellectual disciplines.

2.33 The basis of curriculum selection differs for *training* and for *education.*

2.331 *Training* is the process of preparing an individual to perform defined functions in a predictable situation.

2.332 *Education* is the process of equipping an individual to perform undefined functions in unpredictable situations.

2.333 The selection of curriculum content for training is based on an *analysis* of the specific functions to be performed and the specific situations in which they are to be performed.

2.334 The selection of curriculum content for education is based on its having the widest possible *significance* and greatest possible *explanatory* power.

2.34 The selection of some curriculum items necessitates the selection of related items.

2.341 A set of closely related items is a curriculum *cluster.*

2.342 A curriculum cluster may consist of one type or mixed types of curriculum items.

3. *Structure* is an essential characteristic of curriculum.

3.1 Curriculum structure reveals orderings that are mandatory for instruction.

3.11 The ordering of some curriculum items is indifferent.

3.12 The ordering of some curriculum clusters determines the gross ordering of constituent items, but not their internal order.

3.13 Some curriculum clusters are ordered internally.

3.14 Curriculum ordering disregards instructional temporal spacing (grade or age placement).

3.2 Curriculum structure reveals taxonomic (hierarchical) relationships, whether or not order of items is significant.

4. Curriculum guides instruction.

4.1 Instruction is the interaction between a teaching agent and one or more individuals intending to learn.

4.2 Instruction engages intended learners in activities with cultural content.

4.21 The teaching agent influences the activities of those intending to learn.

4.22 The range of appropriate instructional activities is limited by the *type* of curriculum item.

4.23 Instructional content includes both curricular and instrumental content.

4.231 Curricular content is that cultural content explicitly intended to be learned.

4.232 Instrumental content is optional cultural content introduced into the instructional situation, not to be learned but to facilitate the intended learning.

4.24 Instructional planning consists of the selection and ordering of instructional activities and instrumental content on the basis of curriculum.

4.25 A *learning experience* is the subjective concomitant of activities with instructional content on the part of an individual engaging in them.

4.3 Instruction is episodic.

4.31 An instructional episode consists of a series of teaching cycles relevant to one or more curriculum items.

4.311 A teaching cycle involves perception, diagnosis, and action or reaction by a teaching agent and intended learners (Smith, 1961).

4.312 Teaching cycles are initiated by structuring or soliciting moves (Bellack and Davitz, 1963).

4.313 Teaching cycles include reflexive response or reaction moves (Bellack and Davitz, 1963).

4.314 Actions and reactions in teaching cycles are linguistic, performative, or expressive (Smith, 1961).

4.32 Several instructional episodes may relate to the same curriculum item, just as a given instructional episode may relate to a number of curriculum items.

5. Curriculum evaluation involves validation of both selection and structure.

5.1 Empirical evidence based on instruction can identify structural errors and omissions in selection (Gagné, 1966).

5.2 Judgmental and consensual methods are required to validate priorities and identify superfluities in selection.

6. Curriculum is the criterion for instructional evaluation.

6.1 The effectiveness of instruction is represented by the extent to which actual outcomes correspond with intended outcomes.

6.2 Comparisons among instructional plans and among instructors using the same instructional plan can be made only in terms of a given curriculum.

NOTES

1. His inputs include "Cultural Heritage," "Social Pressures," "Behavioral Knowledge," and "Professional Knowledge" (Macdonald, 1964, p. 5). See similar terminology with respect to sources in Association for Supervision and Curriculum Development, "What are the Sources of the Curriculum?" (1962).

2. $I=f(B_tRB_s)$ $B_t=I_cRM_c$ where I denotes instruction; B_t, teacher behavior; B_s, student behavior; I_c, instructional content or curriculum; and M_c, motivational content (Maccia, 1965, p. 8).

3. "A rule is a reason or criterion which leads to one behavior rather than another. It is a way of behaving. . . ," ". . . a way of solving problems. . . ." "In an individual a rule is a cognitive structure" (Maccia, 1964, p. 14).

REFERENCES

Amidon, Edmund J., and Ned A. Flanders. *The Role of the Teacher in the Classroom*. Amidon and Associates, 1963.

Bellack, Arno. "Selection and Organization of Curriculum Content: An Analysis." In *What shall the High School Teach*? Association for Supervision and Curriculum Development Yearbook. Washington, D.C.: The Association, 1956.

Bellack, Arno, and Joel R. Davitz. *The Language of the Classroom*. New York: Institute of Psychological Research, Teachers College, Columbia University, 1963.

Bloom, Benjamin S. (ed.). *Taxonomy of Educational Objectives*. Handbook I: *Cognitive Domain*. New York: Longmans, Green, 1956.

Broudy, Harry S., B. Othanel Smith, and Joe R. Burnett. *Democracy and Excellence in American Secondary Education*. Chicago: Rand McNally, 1964.

Cronbach, Lee J. "Evaluation for Course Improvement." In Robert W. Heath (ed)., *New Curricula*, pp. 231–48. New York: Harper and Row, 1964.

Cronbach, Lee J. "The Psychological Background for Curriculum Experimentation." In Paul C. Rosenbloom (ed.), *Modern Viewpoints in the Curriculum*, pp. 19–35. New York: McGraw-Hill, 1964.

Eisner, Elliot W. "Levels of Curriculum and Curriculum Research," *Elementary School Journal* 66 (December 1965).

Faix, Thomas L. "Structural-Functional Analysis as a Conceptual System for Curriculum Theory and Research." Paper presented at the American Educational Research Association meeting, February 1966. Mimeo.

Gagné, Robert M. "Curriculum Research and the Promotion of Learning." Invited address to AERA meeting, February 1966. Mimeo.

Krathwohl, David R., Benjamin S. Bloom, and Bertram Masia. *Taxonomy of Educational Objectives*. Handbook II: *Affective Domain*. New York: David McKay, 1964.

Lazarsfeld, Paul, and Sam Sieber. *Organizing Educational Research*. Englewood Cliffs, N.J.: Prentice-Hall, 1964.

Maccia, Elizabeth S. "Instruction as Influence Toward Rule-Governed Behavior." Educational Theory Center, Occasional Paper 64–155, Ohio State University, 1964. Mimeo.

Maccia, Elizabeth S. "Curriculum Theory and Policy." Educational Theory Center and Social Studies Curriculum Center, Occasional paper 65–176, Ohio State University, 1965. Mimeo.

Macdonald, James B. "Curriculum Theory: Problems and a Prospectus." Paper presented at Professors of Curriculum meeting, Miami Beach, April 3, 1964. Mimeo.

Macdonald, James B. "Researching Curriculum Output: The Use of a General Systems Theory to Identify Appropriate Curriculum Outputs and Research

Hypotheses." Paper present at the American Educational Research Association meeting, February 1965.

Mager, Robert F. *Preparing Objectives for Programmed Instruction*. Belmont, Calif.: Fearon, 1961.

Phenix, Philip. "The Disciplines as Curriculum Content." In A.H. Passow (ed.), *Curriculum Crossroads*, pp. 57–65. New York: Teachers College Press, 1962.

Phenix, Philip. *Realms of Meaning*. New York: McGraw-Hill, 1964.

Rugg, Harold (ed.). *Foundations of Curriculum-Making*. Twenty-sixth Yearbook of the National Society for the Study of Education. Part II. Bloomington, Ill.: Public School Publishing, 1926.

Rugg, Harold, and William Withers. *Social Foundations of Education*. Englewood Cliffs, N.J.: Prentice-Hall, 1955.

Ryans, David G. "A Model of Instruction Based on Information System Concepts." In James B. Macdonald and Robert L. Leeper (eds.), *Theories of Instruction*, pp. 36–61. Washington, D.C.: Association for Supervision and Curriculum Development, 1965.

Scheffler, Israel. *The Language of Education*. Springfield, Ill.: Charles C. Thomas, 1970.

Schwab, Joseph J. "Problems, Topics and Issues." In Stanley Elam (ed.), *Education and the Structure of Knowledge*, pp. 4–42. Chicago: Rand McNally, 1964.

Schwab, Joseph J. "Structure of the Disciplines: Meanings and Significance." In G.W. Ford and Lawrence Pugno (eds.), *The Stricter of Knowledge and the Curriculum*, pp. 6–30. Chicago: Rand McNally, 1964.

Smith, B. Othanel. "A Concept of Teaching." In B.O. Smith and Robert H. Ennis (eds.), *Language and Concepts of Education*. Chicago: Rand McNally, 1961.

Stake, Robert E. "The Countenance of Educational Evaluation." Center for Instructional Research and Curriculum Evaluation, University of Illinois, 1966. Mimeo.

Selection 6.3

The Practical: A Language for Curriculum

Joseph J. Schwab

I shall have three points. The first is this: that the field of curriculum is moribund, unable by its present methods and principles to continue its work and desperately in search of new and more effective principles and methods.

The second point: the curriculum field has reached this unhappy state by inveterate and unexamined reliance on theory in an area where theory is partly inappropriate in the first place and where the theories extant, even where appropriate, are inadequate to the tasks which the curriculum field sets them. There are honorable exceptions to this rule but too few (and too little honored) to alter the state of affairs.

The third point, which constitutes my thesis: there will be a renaissance of the field of curriculum, a renewed capacity to contribute to the quality of American education, only if the bulk of curriculum energies are diverted from the theoretic to the practical, to the quasi-practical and to the eclectic. By "eclectic" I mean the arts by which unsystematic, uneasy, but usable focus on a body of problems is effected among diverse theories, each relevant to the problems in a

---

SOURCE. *School Review* 77 (November 1969), pp. 1-23.

different way. By the "practical" I do *not* mean the curbstone practicality of the mediocre administrator and the man on the street, for whom the practical means the easily achieved, familiar goals which can be reached by familiar means. I refer, rather, to a complex discipline, relatively unfamiliar to the academic and differing radically from the disciplines of the theoretic. It is the discipline concerned with choice and action, in contrast with the theoretic, which is concerned with knowledge. Its methods lead to defensible decisions, where the methods of the theoretic lead to warranted conclusions, and differ radically from the methods and competences entailed in the theoretic. I shall sketch some of the defining aspects of practical discipline at the appropriate time.

A CRISIS OF PRINCIPLE

The frustrated state of the field of curriculum is not an idiopathology and not a condition which warrants guilt or shame on the part of its practitioners. All fields of systematic intellectual activity are liable to such crises. They are so because any intellectual discipline must begin its endeavors with untested principles. In its beginnings, its subject matter is relatively unknown, its problems unsolved, indeed, unidentified. It does not know what questions to ask, what other knowledge to rest upon, what data to seek or what to make of them once they are elicited. It requires a preliminary and necessarily untested guide to its enquiries. It finds this guide by borrowing, by invention, or by analogy, in the shape of a hazardous commitment to the character of its problems or its subject matter and a commitment to untried canons of evidence and rules of enquiry. What follows these commitments is years of their application, pursuit of the mode of enquiry demanded by the principles to which the field has committed itself. To the majority of practitioners of any field, these years of enquiry appear only as pursuit of knowledge of its subject matter or solution of its problems. They take the guiding principles of the enquiry as givens. These years of enquiry, however, are something more than pursuit of knowledge or solution of problems. They are also tests, reflexive and pragmatic, of the principles which guide the enquiries. They determine whether, in fact, the data demanded by the principles can be elicited and whether, if elicited, they can be made to constitute knowledge adequate to the complexity of the subject matter, or solutions which, in fact, do solve the problems with which the enquiry began.

In the nature of the case, these reflexive tests of the principles of enquiry are, more often than not, partially or wholly negative, for, after all, the commitment to these principles was made before there was well-tested fruit of enquiry by which to guide the commitment. The inadequacies of principles begin to show, in the case of theoretical enquiries, by failures of the subject matter to respond to the questions put to it, by incoherencies and contradictions in data and in conclusions which cannot be resolved, or by clear disparities between the knowledge yielded by the enquiries and the behaviors of the subject matter which the knowledge purports to represent. In the case of practical enquiries, inadequacies begin to show by incapacity to arrive at solutions to the problems, by inability to realize the solutions proposed, by mutual frustrations and cancellings out as solutions are put into effect.

Although these exhaustions and failures of principles may go unnoted by practitioners in the field, at least at the conscious level, what may not be represented in consciousness is nevertheless evidenced by behavior and appears in the literature and the activities of the field as signs of the onset of a crisis of principle. These signs consist of a large increase in the frequency of published papers and colloquia marked by *a flight from the subject of the field.* There are usually six signs of this flight or directions in which the flight occurs.

SIGNS OF CRISIS

The first and most important, though often least conspicuous, sign is a flight of the field itself, a translocation of its problems and the solving of them from the nominal practitioners of the field to other men. Thus one crucial frustration of the science of genetics was resolved by a single contribution from an insurance actuary. The recent desuetude of academic physiology has been marked by a conspicuous increase in the frequency of published solutions to physiological problems by medical researchers. In similar fashion, the increasing depletion of psychoanalytic principles and methods in recent years was marked by the onset of contributions to its lore by internists, biochemists, and anthropologists.

A second flight is a flight upward, from discourse about the subject of the field to discourse about the discourse of the field, from *use* of principles and methods to *talk* about them, from grounded conclusions to the construction of models, from theory to metatheory and from metatheory to metametatheory.

A third flight is downard, an attempt by practitioners to return to the subject matter in a state of innocence, shorn not only of current principles but of all principles, in an effort to take a new, a pristine and unmediated look at the subject matter. For example, one conspicuous reaction to the warfare of numerous inadequate principles in experimental psychology has been the resurgence of ethology, which begins as an attempt to return to a pure natural history of behavior, to intensive observation and recording of the behavior of animals undisturbed in their natural habitat, by observers, equally undisturbed by mediating conceptions, attempting to record anything and everything they see before them.

A fourth flight is to the sidelines, to the role of observer, commentator, historian, and critic of the contributions of others to the field.

A fifth sign consists of marked perseveration, a repetition of old and familiar knowledge in new languages which add little or nothing to the old meanings as embodied in the older and familiar language, or repetition of old and familiar formulations by way of criticisms or minor additions and modifications.

The sixth is a marked increase in eristic, contentious, and *ad hominem* debate.

I hasten to remark that these signs of crisis are not all or equally reprehensible. There is little excuse for the increase in contentiousness nor much value in the flight to the sidelines or in perseveration, but the others, in one way or another, can contribute to resolution of the crisis. The flight of the field itself is one of the more fruitful ways by which analogical principles are disclosed, modified, and adapted to the field in crisis. The flight upward, to models and metatheory, if done responsibly, which means with a steady eye on the actual problems and conditions of the field for which the models are ostensibly constructed, becomes, in fact, the proposal and test of possible new principles for the field. The flight backward, to a state of innocence, is at least an effort to break the grip of old habits of thought and thus leave space for needed new ones, though it is clear that in the matter of enquiry, as elsewhere, virginity, once lost, cannot be regained.

In the present context, however, the virtue or vice of these various flights is beside the point. We are concerned with them as signs of collapse of principles in a field, and it is my contention, based on a study not yet complete, that most of these signs may now be seen in the field of curriculum. I shall only suggest, not cite, my evidence.

THE CASE OF CURRICULUM

With respect to flight of the field itself, there can be little doubt. Of the five substantial high school science curricula, four of them—PSSC, BSCS, Chems and CBA—were instituted and managed by subject-matter specialists; the contribution of educators was small and that of curriculum specialists near vanishing point. Only Harvard Project Physics, at this writing not yet available, appears to be an exception. To one of two elementary science projects, a psychologist appears to have made a substantial contribution but curriculum specialists very little. The other—the Elementary Science Study—appears to have been substantially affected (to its advantage) by educators with one or both feet in curriculum. The efforts of the Commission on Undergraduate Education in the Biological Sciences have been carried on almost entirely by subject-matter specialists. The English Curriculum Study Centers appear to be in much the same state as the high school science curricula: overwhelmingly centered on subject specialists. Educators contribute expertise only in the area of test construction and evaluation, with here and there a contribution by a psychologist. Educators, including curriculum specialists, were massively unprepared to cope with the problem of integrated education and only by little, and late, and by trial and error, put together the halting solutions currently known as Head Start. The problems posed by the current drives toward ethnicity in education find curriculum specialists even more massively oblivious and unprepared. And I so far find myself very much alone with respect to the curriculum problems immanent in the phenomena of student protest and student revolt. (Of the social studies curriculum efforts, I shall say nothing at this time.)

On the second flight—upward—I need hardly comment. The models, the metatheory, and the metametatheory are all over the place. Many of them, moreover, are irresponsible—concerned less with the barriers to continued productivity in the field of curriculum than with exploitation of the exotic and the fashionable among forms and models of theory and metatheory: systems theory, symbolic logic, language analysis. Many others, including responsible ones, are irreversible flights upward or sideways. That is, they are models or metatheories concerned not with the judgment, the reasoned construction, or reconstruction of curriculums but with other matters—for example, how curriculum changes occur or how changes can be managed.

The flight downward, the attempt at return to a pristine, unmediated look at the subject matter, is, for some reason, a missing symptom in the case of curriculum. There are returns—to the classroom, if not to other levels or aspects of curriculum—with a measure of effort to avoid preconceptions (e.g., Smith, Bellack, and studies of communication nets and lines), but the frequency of such studies has not markedly increased. The absence of this symptom may have significance. In general, however, it is characteristic of diseases that the whole syndrome does not appear in all cases. Hence, pending further study and thought, I do not count this negative instance as weakening the diagnosis of a crisis of principle.

The fourth flight—to the sidelines—is again a marked symptom of the field of curriculum. Histories, anthologies, commentaries, criticisms, and proposals of curriculums multiply.

Perseveration is also marked. I recoil from counting the persons and books whose lives are made possible by continuing restatement of the Tyler rationale, of the character and case for behavioral objectives, of the virtues and vices of John Dewey.

The rise in frequency and intensity of the eristic and *ad hominem* is also marked. Thus one author climaxes a series of petulances by the remark that what he takes to be his own forte "has always been rare—and shows up in proper perspective the happy breed of educational reformer who can concoct a brand new, rabble-rousing theory of educational reform while waiting for the water to fill the bathtub."

There is little doubt, in short, that the field of curriculum is in a crisis of principle.

A crisis of principle arises, as I have suggested, when principles are exhausted—when the questions they permit have all been asked and answered—or when the efforts at enquiry instigated by the principles have at least exhibited their inadequacy to the subject matter and the problems which they were designed to attack. My second point is that the latter holds in the case of curriculum: the curriculum movement has been inveterately theoretic, and its theoretic bent has let it down. A brief conspectus of instances will suggest the extent of this theoretic bent and what is meant by "theoretic."

CHARACTERISTICS OF THEORY

Consider first the early, allegedly Herbartian efforts (recently revived by Bruner). These efforts took the view that ideas were formed by children out of received notions and experiences of things, and that these ideas functioned thereafter as discriminators and organizers of what was later learned. Given this view, the aim of curriculum was to discriminate the right ideas (by way of analysis of extant bodies of knowledge), determine the order in which they could be learned by children as they developed, and thereafter present these ideas at the right times with clarity, associations, organization, and application. A theory of mind and knowledge thus solves by one mighty coup the problem of what to teach, when, and how; and what is fatally theoretic here is not the presence of a theory of mind and a theory of knowledge, though their presence is part of the story, but the dispatch, the sweeping appearance of success, the vast simplicity which grounds this purported solution to the problem of curriculum. And lest we think that this faith in the possibility of successful neatness, dispatch, and sweeping generality is a mark of the past, consider the concern of the National Science Teachers Association only four years ago "with identifying the broad principles that can apply to any and all curriculum development efforts in science," a concern crystallized in just seven "conceptual schemes" held to underlie all science. With less ambitious sweepingness but with the same steadfast concern for a single factor—in this case, a supposed fixed structure of knowledge—one finds similar efforts arising from the Association of College Teachers of Education, from historians, even from teachers of literature.

Consider, now, some of the numerous efforts to ground curriculum in derived objectives. One effort seeks the ground of its objectives in social need and finds its social needs in just those facts about its culture which are sought and found under the aegis of a single conception of culture. Another grounds its objectives in the social needs identified by a single theory of history and of political evolution.

A third group of searches for objectives are grounded in theories of personality. The persuasive coherence and plausibility of Freudianism persuaded its followers to aim to supply children with adequate channels of sublimation of surplus libido, appropriate objects and occasions for aggressions, a properly undemanding ego ideal, and an intelligent minimum of taboos. Interpersonal theories direct their adherents to aim for development of abilities to relate to peers, "in-feers," and "supeers," in relations nurturant and receiving, adaptive, vying, approving and disapproving. Theories of actualization instruct their adherents to determine the salient potentialities of each child and to see individually to the development of each.

Still other searches for objectives seek their aims in the knowledge needed to "live in the modern world," in the attitudes and habits which minimize dissonance with the prevailing mores of one's community or social class, in the skills required for success in a trade or vocation, in the ability to participate effectively as member of a group. Still others are grounded in some quasi-ethics, some view of the array of goods which are good for man.

Three features of these typical efforts at curriculum making are significant here, each of which has its own lesson to teach us. First, each is grounded in a theory as such. We shall return to this point in a moment. Second, each is grounded in a theory from the social or behavioral sciences: psychology, psychiatry, politics, sociology, history. Even the ethical bases and theories of "mind" are behavioral. To this point, too, we shall return in a moment. Third, they are theories concerning *different* subject matters. One curriculum effort is grounded in concern for the individual, another in concern for groups, others in concern for cultures, communities, societies, minds, or the extant bodies of knowledge.[2]

NEED FOR AN ECLECTIC

The significance of this third feature is patent to the point of embarrassment: no curriculum grounded in but one of these subjects can possibly be adequate, defensible. A curriculum based on theory about individual personality, which thrusts society, its demands and its structure, far into the background or ignores them entirely, can be nothing but incomplete and doctrinaire, for the individuals in question are in fact members of a society and must meet its demands to some minimum degree since their existence and prosperity as individuals depend on the functioning of their society. In the same way, a curriculum grounded only in a view of social need or social change must be equally doctrinaire and incomplete, for societies do not exist only for their own sakes but for the prosperity of their members as individuals as well. In the same way, learners are not only minds or knowers but bundles of affects, individuals, personalities, earners of livings. They are not only group interactors but possessors of private lives.

It is clear, I submit, that a defensible curriculum or plan of curriculum must be one which somehow takes account of all these sub-subjects which pertain to man. It cannot take only one and ignore the others; it cannot even take account of many of them and ignore one. Not only is each of them a constituent and a condition for decent human existence but each interpenetrates the others. That is, the character of human personalities is a determiner of human society and the behavior of human groups. Conversely, the conditions of group behavior and the character of societies determine in some large part the personalities which their members develop, the way their minds work, and what they can learn and use by way of knowledge and competence. These various "things" (individuals, societies, cultures, patterns of enquiry, "structures" of knowledge or of enquiries, apperceptive masses, problem solving), though discriminable as separate subjects of differing modes of enquiry, are nevertheless parts or affectors of one another, or coactors. (Their very separation for purposes of enquiry is what marks the outcomes of such enquiries as "theoretic" and consequently incomplete.) In practice, they constitute one complex, organic agency. Hence, a focus on only one not only ignores the others but vitiates the quality and completeness with which the selected one is viewed.

It is equally clear, however, that there is not, and will not be in the foreseeable future, one theory of this complex whole which is other than a collection of unusable generalities. Nor is it true that the lack of a theory of the whole is due to the narrowness, stubbornness, or merely habitual specialism of social and behavioral scientists. Rather, their specialism and the restricted purview of their theories are functions of their subject, its enormous complexity, its vast capacity for difference and change. Man's competence at the construction of theoretical knowledge is so far most inadequate when applied to the subject of man. There have been efforts to conceive principles of enquiry which would encompass the whole variety and complexity of humanity, but they have fallen far short of adequacy to the subject matter or have demanded the acquisition of data and modes of interpretation of data beyond our capabilities. There *are* continuing efforts to find bridging terms which would relate the principles of enquiry of one subfield of the social sciences to another and thus begin to effect connections among our knowledges of each, but successful bridges are so far few and narrow and permit but a trickle of connection. As far, then, as theoretical knowledge is concerned, we must wrestle as best we can with numerous, largely unconnected, separate theories of these many, artificially discriminated subsubjects of man.

I remarked in the beginning that renewal of the field of curriculum would require diversion of the bulk of its energies from theory to the practical, the quasi-practical, and the eclectic. The state of affairs just described, the existence and the necessarily continuing existence of separate theories of separate subsubjects distributed among the social sciences, constitutes the case for one of these modes, the necessity of an eclectic, of arts by which a usable focus on a common body of problems is effected among theories which lack theoretical connection. The argument can be simply summarized. A curriculum grounded in but one or a few subsubjects of the social sciences is indefensible; contributions from all are required. There is no foreseeable hope of a unified theory in the immediate or middle future, nor of a metatheory which will tell us how to put those subsubjects together or order them in a fixed hierarchy of importance to the problems of curriculum. What remains as a viable alternative is the unsystematic, uneasy, pragmatic, and uncertain unions and connections which can be effected in an eclectic. And I must add, anticipating our discussion of the practical, that *changing* connections and *differing* orderings at different times of these separate theories, will characterize a sound eclectic.

The character of eclectic arts and procedures must be left for discussion on another occasion. Let it suffice for the moment that witness of the high effectiveness of eclectic methods and of their accessibility is borne by at least one field familiar to us all—Western medicine. It has been enormously effective, and the growth of its competence dates from its disavowal of a single doctrine and its turn to eclecticism.

THE PLACE OF THE PRACTICAL

I turn now, from the fact that the theories which ground curriculum plans pertain to different subsubjects of a common field, to the second of the three features which characterize our typical instances of curriculum planning—the fact that the ground of each plan is a theory, a theory as such.

The significance of the existence of theory as such at the base of curricular planning consists of what it is that theory does not and cannot encompass. All theories, even the best of them in the simplest sciences, necessarily neglect some aspects and facets of the facts of the case. A theory covers and formulates the *regularities* among the things and events it subsumes. It abstracts a general or ideal case. It leaves behind the nonuniformities, the particularities, which characterize each concrete instance of the facts subsumed. Moreover, in the process of idealization, theoretical enquiry may often leave out of consideration conspicuous facets of *all* cases because its substantive principles of enquiry or its methods cannot handle them. Thus the constantly accelerating body of classical mechanics was the acceleration of a body in "free" fall, fall in a perfect vacuum, and the general or theoretical rule formulated in classical mechanics is far from describing the fall of actual bodies in actual mediums—the only kinds of fall then known. The force equation of classical dynamics applied to bodies of visible magnitudes ignores friction. The rule that light varies inversely as the square of the distance holds exactly only for an imaginary point source of light. For real light sources of increasing expanse, the so-called law holds more and more approximately, and for very large sources it affords little or no usable information. And what is true of the best of theories in the simplest sciences is true a fortiori in the social sciences. Their subject matters are apparently so much more variable, and clearly so much more complex, that their theories encompass much less of their subjects than do the theories of the physical and biological sciences.

Yet curriculum is brought to bear not on ideal or abstract representatives but on the real thing, on the concrete case in all its completeness and with all its differences from all other concrete cases on which the theoretic abstraction is silent. The materials of a concrete curriculum will not consist merely of portions of "science," of "literature," of "process." On the contrary, their constituents will be particular assertions about selected matters couched in a particular vocabulary, syntax, and rhetoric. They will be particular novels, short stories, or lyric poems, each, for better or for worse, with its own flavor. They will be particular acts upon particular matters in a given sequence. The curriculum will be brought to bear not in some archetypical classroom but in a particular locus in time and space with smells, shadows, seats, and conditions outside its walls which may have much to do with what is achieved inside. Above all, the supposed beneficiary is not the generic child, not even a class or kind of child out of the psychological or sociological literature pertaining to the child. The beneficiaries will consist of very local kinds of children and, within the local kinds, individual children. The same diversity holds with respect to teachers and what they do. the generalities about science, about literature, about children in general, about children or teachers of some specified class or kind, may be true. But they attain this status in virtue of what they leave out, and the omissions affect what remains. A Guernsey cow is not only something more than cow, having specific features omitted from description of the genus; it is also cowy in ways differing from the cowiness of a Texas longhorn. The specific not only adds to the generic; it also modulates it.

These ineluctable characteristics of theory and the consequent ineluctable disparities between real things and their representation in theory constitute one argument for my thesis, that a large bulk of curriculum energies must be diverted from the theoretic, not only to the eclectic but to the practical and the quasi-practical. The argument, again, can be briefly summarized. The stuff of theory is abstract or idealized representations of real things. But curriculum in action treats real things: real acts, real teachers, real children, things richer and different from their theoretical representations. Curriculum will deal badly with its real things if it treats them merely as replicas of their theoretic representations. If, then, theory is to be used well in the determination of curricular practice, it requires a supplement. It requires arts which bring a theory to its application: first, arts which identify the disparities between real thing and theoretic representation; second, arts which modify the theory in the course of its application, in the light of the discrepancies; and, third, arts which devise ways of taking account of the many aspects of the real thing which the theory does not take into account. These are some of the arts of the practical.

THEORIES FROM SOCIAL SCIENCES

The significance of the third feature of our typical instances of curriculum work—that their theories are mainly theories from the social and behavioral sciences—will carry us to the remainder of the argument for the practical. Nearly all theories in all the behavioral sciences are marked by the coexistence of competing theories. There is not one theory of personality but twenty, representing at least six radically different choices of what is relevant and important in human behavior. There is not one theory of groups but several. There is not one theory of learning but half a dozen. All the social and behavioral sciences are marked by "schools," each distinguished by a different choice of principle of enquiry, each of which selects from the intimidating complexities of the subject matter the small fraction of the whole with which it can deal.

The theories which arise from enquiries so directed are, then, radically incomplete, each of them incomplete to the extent that competing theories take hold of different aspects of the subject of enquiry and treat it in a different way. Further, there is perennial invention of new principles which bring to light new facets of the subject matter, new relations among the facets and new ways of treating them. In short, there is every reason to suppose that any one of the extant theories of behavior is a pale and incomplete representation of actual behavior. There is similar reason to suppose that if all the diversities of fact, the different aspects of behavior treated in each theory, were somehow to be brought within the bounds of a single theory, that theory would still fall short of comprehending the whole of human behavior–in two respects. In the first place, it would not comprehend what there may be of human behavior which we do not see by virtue of the restricted light by which we examine behavior. In the second place, such a single theory will necessarily interpret its data in the light of its one set of principles, assigning to these data only one set of significances and establishing among them only one set of relations. It will remain the case, then, that a diversity of theories may tell us more than a single one, even though the "factual" scope of the many and the one are the same.

It follows, then, that such theories are not, and will not be, adequate by themselves to tell us what to do with human beings or how to do it. What they variously suggest and the contrary guidances they afford to choice and action must be mediated and combined by eclectic arts and must be massively supplemented, as well as mediated, by knowledge of some other kind derived from another source.

Some areas of choice and action with respect to human behavior have long since learned this lesson. Government is made possible by a lore of politics derived from immediate experience of the vicissitudes and tangles of legislating and administering. Institution of economic guidances and controls owes as much to unmediated experience of the marketplace as it does to formulas and theories. Even psychotherapy has long since deserted its theories of personality as sole guides to therapy and relies as much or more on the accumulated, explicitly nontheoretic lore accumulated by practitioners, as it does on theory or eclectic combinations of theory. The law has systematized the accumulation of direct experience of actual cases in its machinery for the recording of cases and opinions as precedents which continuously monitor, supplement, and modify the meaning and application of its formal "knowledge," its statutes. It is this recourse to accumulated lore, to experience of actions and their consequences, to action and reaction at the level of the concrete case, which constitutes the heart of the practical. It is high time that curriculum do likewise.

THE PRACTICAL ARTS

The arts of the practical are onerous and complex; hence only a sampling must suffice to indicate the character of this discipline and the changes in educational investigation which would ensue on adoption of the discipline. I shall deal briefly with four aspects of it.

The practical arts begin with the requirement that existing institutions and existing practices be preserved and altered piecemeal, not dismantled and replaced. It is further necessary that changes be so planned and so articulated with what remains unchanged that the functioning of the whole remain coherent and unimpaired. These necessities stem from the very nature of the practical—that it is concerned with the maintenance and improvement of patterns of purposed action, and especially concerned that the effects of the pattern through time shall retain coherence and relevance to one another.

This is well seen in the case of the law. Statutes are repealed or largely rewritten only as a last resort, since to do so creates confusion and diremption between old judgments under the law and judgments to come, confusion which must lead either to weakening of law through disrepute or a painful and costly process of repairing the effects of past judgments so as to bring them into conformity with the new. It is vastly more desirable that changes be instituted in small degrees and in immediate adjustment to the peculiarities of particular new cases which call forth the change.

The consequence, in the case of the law, of these demands of the practical is that the servants of the law must know the law through and through. They must know the statutes themselves, the progression of precedents and interpretations which have effected changes in them, and especially the present state of affairs—the most recent decisions under the law and the calendar of cases which will be most immediately affected by contemplated additions to precedent and interpretation.

The same requirements would hold for a practical program of improvement of education. It, too, would effect its changes in small progressions, in coherence with what remains unchanged, and this would require that we know *what is and has been going on in American schools.*

At present, we do not know. My own incomplete investigations convince me that we have not the faintest reliable knowledge of how literature is taught in the high schools, or what actually goes on in science classrooms. There are a dozen different ways in which the novel can be read. Which ones are used by whom, with whom, and to what effect? What selections from the large accumulation of biological knowledge are made and taught in this school system and that, to what classes and kinds of children, to what effect? To what extent is science taught as verbal formulas, as congeries of unrelated facts, as so-called principles and conceptual structures, as outcomes of enquiry? In what degree and kind of simplification and falsification is scientific enquiry conveyed, if it is conveyed at all?

A count of textbook adoptions will not tell us, for teachers select from textbooks and alter their treatment (often quite properly) and can frustrate and negate the textbook's effort to alter the pattern of instruction. We cannot tell from lists of objectives, since they are usually so vastly ambiguous that almost anything can go on under their aegis or, if they are not ambiguous, reflect pious hopes as much as actual practice. We cannot tell from lists of "principles" and "conceptual structures," since these, in their telegraphic brevity are also ambiguous and say nothing of the shape in which they are taught or the extent.

What is wanted is a totally new and extensive pattern of *empirical* study of classroom action and reaction; a study, not as basis for theoretical concerns about the nature of the teaching or learning process, but as a basis for beginning to know what we are doing, what we are not doing, and to what effect—what changes are needed, which needed changes can be instituted with what costs or economies, and how they can be effected with minimum tearing of the remaining fabric of education effort.

This is an effort which will require new mechanisms of empirical investigation, new methods of reportage, a new class of educational researchers, and much money. It is an effort without which we will continue largely incapable of making defensible decisions about curricular changes, largely unable to put them into effect and ignorant of what real consequences, if any, our efforts have had.

A very large part of such a study would, I repeat, be direct and empirical study of action and reaction in the classroom itself, not merely the testing of student change. But one of the most interesting and visible alterations of present practice which might be involved is a radical change in our pattern of testing students. The common pattern tries to determine the extent to which *intended* changes have been brought about. This would be altered to an effort to find out what changes have occurred, to determine side effects as well as mainline consequences, since the distinction between these two is always in the eye of the intender and side effects may be as great in magnitude and as fatal or healthful for students as the intended effects.

A second facet of the practical: its actions are undertaken with respect to identified frictions and failures in the machine and inadequacies evidenced in felt shortcomings of its products. This origin of its actions leads to two marked differences in operation from that of theory. Under the control of theory, curricular changes have their origin in new notions of person, group or society, mind or knowledge, which give rise to suggestions of new things curriculum might be or do. This is an origin which, by its nature, takes little or no account of the existing effectiveness of the machine or the consequences to this effectiveness of the institution of novelty. If there is concern for what may be displaced by innovation or for the incoherences which may ensue on the insertion of novelty, the concern is gratuitous. It does not arise from the theoretical considerations which commend the novelty. The practical, on the other hand, because it institutes changes to repair frictions and deficiencies, is commanded to determine the whole array of possible effects of proposed change, to determine what new frictions and deficiencies the proposed change may unintentionally produce.

The other effective difference between theoretical and practical origins of deliberate change is patent. Theory, by being concerned with new things to do, is unconcerned with the successes and failures of present doings. Hence present failures, unless they coincide with what is repaired by the proposed innovations, go unnoticed—as do present successes. The practical, on the other hand, is directly and deliberately concerned with the diagnosis of ills of the curriculum.

These concerns of the practical for frictions and failures of the curricular machine would, again, call for a new and extensive pattern of enquiry. The practical requires curriculum study to seek its problems where its problems lie—in the behaviors, misbehaviors, and nonbehaviors of its students as they begin to evince the effects of the training they did and did not get. This means continuing assessment of students as they leave primary grades for the secondary school, leave secondary school for jobs and colleges. It means sensitive and sophisticated assessment by way of impressions, insights, and reactions of the community which sends its children to the school; employers of students, new echelons of teachers of students; the wives, husbands, and cronies of exstudents; the people with whom exstudents work; the people who work under them. Curriculum study will look into the questions of what games exstudents play; what, if anything, they do about politics and crime in the streets; what they read, if they do; what they watch on television and what they make of what they watch, again, if anything. Such studies would be undertaken, furthermore, not as mass study of products of the American school, taken in toto, but as studies of significantly separable schools and school systems–suburban and inner city, Chicago and Los Angeles, South Bend and Michigan City.

I emphasize sensitive and sophisticated assessment because we are concerned here, as in the laying of background knowledge of what goes in schools, not merely with the degree to which avowed objectives are achieved but also with detecting the failures and frictions of the machine: what it has not done or thought of doing, and what side effects its doings have had. Nor are we concerned with successes and failures only as measured in test situations but also as evidenced in life and work. It is this sort of diagnosis which I have tried to exemplify in a recent (Schwab, 1969) treatment of curriculum and student protest.

A third facet of the practical I shall call the anticipatory generation of alternatives. Intimate knowledge of the existing state of affairs, early identification of problem situations, and effective formulation of problems are necessary to effective practical decision but not sufficient. It requires also that there be available to practical deliberation the greatest possible number and fresh diversity of alternative solutions to the problem. The reason for this requirement, in one aspect, is obvious enough: the best choice among poor and shopworn alternatives will still be a poor solution to the problem. Another aspect is less obvious. The problems which arise in an institutional structure which has enjoyed good practical management will be novel problems, arising from changes in the times and circumstances and from the consequences of previous solutions to previous problems. Such problems, with their strong tincture of novelty, cannot be solved by familiar solutions. They cannot be well solved by apparently new solutions arising from old habits of mind and old ways of doing things.

A third aspect of the requirement for anticipatory generation of alternatives is still less obvious. It consists of the fact that practical problems do not present themselves wearing their labels around their necks. Problem situations, to use Dewey's old term, present themselves to consciousness, but the character of the problem, its formulation, does not. This depends on the eye of the beholder. And this eye, unilluminated by possible fresh solutions to problems, new modes of attack, new recognitions of degrees of freedom for change among matters formerly taken to be unalterable, is very likely to miss the novel features of new problems or dismiss them as "impractical." Hence the requirement that the generation of problems be anticipatory and not await the emergence of the problem itself.

To some extent, the *theoretical* bases of curricular change—such items as emphasis on enquiry, on discovery learning, and on structure of the disciplines—contribute to this need but not sufficiently or with the breadth which permits effective deliberation. That is, these theoretic proposals tend to arise in single file, out of connection with other proposals which constitute alternatives or, more important, constitute desiderata or circumstances which affect the choice or rejection of proposals. Consider, in regard to the problem of the "single file," only one relation between the two recent proposals subsumed under "creativity" and "structure of knowledge." If creativity implies some measure of invention, and "structure of knowledge" implies (as it does in one version) the systematic induction of conceptions as soon as children are ready to grasp them, an issue is joined. To the extent that the latter is timely and well done, scope for the former is curtailed. To the extent that children can be identified as more or less creative, "structure of knowledge" would be brought to bear on different children at different times and in different ways.

A single case, taken from possible academic resources of education, will suggest the new kind of enquiry entailed in the need for anticipatory generation of alternatives. Over the years, critical scholarship has generated, as remarked earlier, a dozen different conceptions of the novel, a dozen or more ways in which the novel can be read, each involving its own emphases and its own arts of recovery of meaning in the act of reading. Novels can be read, for example, as bearers of wisdom, insights into vicissitudes of human life and ways of enduring them. Novels can also be read as moral instructors, as sources of vicarious experience, as occasions for esthetic experience. They can be read as models of human creativity, as displays of social problems, as political propaganda, as revelations of diversities of manners and morals among different cultures and classes of people, or as symptoms of their age.

Now what, in fact, is the full parade of such possible uses of the novel? What is required by each in the way of competences of reading, discussion, and thought? What are the rewards, the desirable outcomes, which are likely to ensue for students from each kind of reading or combinations of them? For what kinds or classes of students is each desirable? There are further problems demanding anticipatory consideration. If novels are chosen and read as displays of social problems and depictions of social classes, what effect will such instruction in literature have on instruction in the social studies? What will teachers need to know and be able to do in order to enable students to discriminate and appropriately connect the *aperçus* of artists, the accounts of historians, and the conclusions of social scientists on such matters? How will the mode of instruction in science (e.g., as verified truths) and in literature (as "deep insights" or artistic constructions or matters of opinion) affect the effects of each?

The same kinds of questions could be addressed to history and to the social studies generally. Yet, nowhere, in the case of literature, have we been able to find cogent and energetic work addressed to them. The journals in the field of English teaching are nearly devoid of treatment of them. College and university courses, in English or education, which address such problems with a modicum of intellectual content are as scarce as hen's teeth. We cannot even find an unbiased conspectus of critical theory more complete than *The Pooh Perplex,* and treatments of problems of the second kind (pertaining to interaction of literature instruction with instruction in other fields) are also invisible.

Under a soundly practical dispensation in curriculum the address of such questions would be a high priority and require recruitment to education of philosophers and subject-matter specialists of a quality and critical sophistication which it rarely, if ever, sought.

As the last sampling of the practical, consider its method. It falls under neither of the popular platitudes: it is neither deductive nor inductive. It is deliberative. It cannot be inductive because the target of the method is not a generalization or explanation but a decision about action in a concrete situation. It cannot be deductive because it deals with the concrete case, not abstractions from cases, and the concrete case cannot be settled by mere application of a principle. Almost every concrete case falls under two or more principles, and every concrete case will possess some cogent characteristics which are encompassed in no principle. The problem of selecting an appropriate man for an important post is a case in point. It is not a problem of selecting a representative of the appropriate personality type who exhibits the competences officially required for the job.

The man we hire is more than a type and a bundle of competences. He is a multitude of probable behaviors which escape the net of personality theories and cognitive scales. He is endowed with prejudices, mannerisms, habits, tics, and relatives. And all of these manifold particulars will affect his work and the work of those who work for him. It is deliberation which operates in such cases to select the appropriate man.

COMMITMENT TO DELIBERATION

Deliberation is complex and arduous. It treats both ends and means and must treat them as mutually determining one another. It must try to identify, with respect to both, what facts may be relevant. It must try to ascertain the relevant facts in the concrete case. It must try to identify the desiderata in the case. It must generate alternative solutions. It must make every effort to trace the branching pathways of consequences which may flow from each alternative and affect desiderata. It must then weigh alternatives and their costs and consequences against one another and choose, not the right alternative, for there *is* no such thing, but the best one.

I shall mention only one of the new kinds of activity which would ensue on commitment to deliberation. It will require the formation of a new public and new means of communication among its constituent members. Deliberation requires consideration of the widest possible variety of alternatives if it is to be most effective. Each alternative must be viewed in the widest variety of lights. Ramifying consequences must be traced to all parts of the curriculum. The desirability of each alternative must be felt out, "rehearsed," by a representative variety of all those who must live with the consequences of the chosen action. And a similar variety must deal with the identification of problems as well as with their solution.

This will require penetration of the curtains which now separate educational psychologist from philosopher, sociologist from test constructor, historian from administrator; it will require new channels connecting the series from teacher, supervisor, and school administrator at one end to research specialists at the other. Above all, it will require renunciation of the specious privileges and hegemonies by which we maintain the fiction that problems of science curriculum, for example, have no bearing on problems of English literature or the social studies. The aim here is *not* a dissolving of specialization and special responsibilities. Quite the contrary: if the variety of lights we need are to be obtained, the variety of specialized interests, competences, and habits of mind which characterize education must be cherished and nurtured. The aim, rather, is to bring the members of this variety to bear on curriculum problems by communication with one another.

Concretely, this means the establishment of new journals, and education of educators so that they can write for them and read them. The journals will be forums where possible problems of curriculum will be broached from many sources and their possible importance debated from many points of view. They will be the stage for display of anticipatory solutions to problems, from a similar variety of sources. They will constitute deliberative assemblies in which problems and alternative solutions will be argued by representatives of all for the consideration of all and for the shaping of intelligent consensus.

Needless to say, such journals are not alone sufficient. They stand as only one concrete model of the kind of forum which is required. Similar forums, operating viva voce and in the midst of curriculum operation and curriculum change, are required: of the teachers, supervisors, and administrators of a school; of the supervisors and administrators of a school system; of representatives of teachers, supervisors, and curriculum makers in subject areas and across subject areas; of the same representatives and specialists in curriculum, psychology, sociology, administration, and the subject-matter fields.[3]

The education of educators to participate in this deliberative process will be neither easy nor quickly achieved. The education of the present generation of specialist researchers to speak to the schools and to one another will doubtless be hardest of all, and on this hardest problem I have no suggestion to make. But we could begin within two years to initiate the preparation of teachers, supervisors, curriculum makers, and graduate students of education in the uses and arts of deliberation—and we should.

For graduate students, this should mean that their future enquiries in educational psychology, philosophy of education, educational sociology, and so on, will find more effective focus on enduring problems of education, as against the attractions of the current foci of the parent disciplines. It will begin to exhibit to graduate students what their duties are to the future schoolmen whom they will teach. For teachers, curriculum makers, and others close to the classroom, such training is of special importance. It will not only bring immediate experience of the classroom effectively to bear on problems of curriculum but enhance the quality of that experience, for almost every classroom episode is a stream of situations requiring discrimination of deliberative problems and decision theron.

By means of such journals and such an education, the educational research establishment might at least find a means for channeling its discoveries into sustained improvement of the schools instead of into a procession of ephemeral bandwagons.

NOTES

1. A version of this paper was delivered to Section B of the American Educational Research Association, Los Angeles, February 1969. This paper has been prepared as part of a project supported by a grant from the Ford Foundation.

2. It should be clear by now that "theory" as used in this paper does *not* refer only to grand schemes such as the general theory of relativity, kinetic-molecular theory, the Bohr atom, the Freudian construction of a tripartite psyche. The attempt to give an account of human maturation by the discrimination of definite states (e.g., oral, anal, genital), an effort to aggregate human competences into a small number of primary mental abilities—these too are theoretic. So also are efforts to discriminate a few large classes of persons and to attribute to them defining behaviors: e.g., the socially mobile, the culturally deprived, the creative.

3. It will be clear from these remarks that the conception of curricular method proposed here is immanent in the Tyler rationale. This rationale calls for a diversity of talents and insists on the practical and eclectic treatment of a variety of factors. Its effectiveness in practice is vitiated by two circumstances. Its focus on "objectives," with their massive ambiguity and equivocation, provides far too little of the concrete matter required for deliberation and leads only to delusive consensus. Second, those who use it are not trained for the deliberative procedures it requires.

REFERENCE

Schwab, Joseph J. *College Curriculum and Student Protest.* Chicago: University of Chicago, 1969.

Selection 6.4

"Whole, Bright, Deep with Understanding": Issues in Qualitative Research and Autobiographical Method

William F. Pinar

Qualitative work "aims at particular understanding," in contrast to quantitative research, which "aims at *general* understanding" (Willis, 1978, pp. 7 and 8). Willis's statement echoes one nearly one hundred years earlier: "Understanding has always the particular as its object" (Dilthey, 1978, p. 38). In this essay I will sketch the relation of particularity and understanding, noting its problematic issues. I will conclude with a summary of autobiographical method, thus situating the preceding discussion of issues in qualitative research in a specific form of curriculum research.

GENERAL AND PARTICULAR UNDERSTANDING

The rise of mainstream social science in the twentieth century accompanies increasing control of human life. Lasch (1977) has documented the invasion of the family by the "helping professions" (an extension of the corporate state), Habermas (1973) the rationalizing function of social science in the control of professional life, Marcuse (1978) the influence of media and cultural life in maintaining the individual's alienation from himself and his community. The collapse of epistemology into philosophy

SOURCE. Reprinted, with permission of the author and publisher, from *Journal of Curriculum Studies* 13 (July–September 1981): 173–88.

of science parallels the hegemony of quantification and measurement in the social sciences. One issue is control, knowledge that what holds true in any specific situation will hold true in another. The movement toward increasing political control has its epistemology correlate: Zygmunt Bauman (1978, p. 231) describes the interest in general understanding and the desire for control:

> Only if I can be sure that what I have grasped is from now on immutable and immune to contingencies of fate, can my knowledge give me the feeling of genuine mastery over the object. The real trouble, therefore (the real reason of our anxiety) is not the endemic structure of theoretical understanding, but *the practical lack of control over the life situation* which a most perfect interpretation will still be helpless to redress. *Objective understanding appears, so to speak, as a substitute for practical control over the situation*; as an "intellectual socialization" of the conditions of action which in reality are privately owned. . . .

General understanding is useful as it permits some measure of control over situations that are, as Nietzche noted, in fact in flux. Some control is necessary to carry about our business. It permits goal-directed behavior that is efficient, and thereby more likely effective. One danger is that, relying on rules of conduct and generalization concerning types of situations, one dulls new situations. They become like past ones. That is, of course, the meaning of generalization: looking for in the new what has been seen in the old. One focuses on what is general or common to the situations, not on what is unique to each. In teaching and classroom discourse, this means, as Huebner (1975, pp. 217–36) has pointed out, we have ignored such significant, but difficult to conceptualize and quantify, dimensions of educational activity as the ethical, the aesthetic, and the political. The more exclusively one relies on rules of conduct — such as objectives for one's class to achieve — the more frozen becomes the situation. One is reminded of the "smooth" conversation of some educational researchers, whose projects and achievements slide from their mouths in carefully modulated tones, the conversational equivalent of "muzak." Such individuals may manage new situations and new people predictably and efficiently. However, this routinized behavior comes at the cost of spontaneity and individuality. He becomes a social type that we recognize. His specific self, now to some extent buried behind the mask, is probably as forgotten to him as it is hidden to us. Being with him elicits the social type in us, inhibiting the particular. Developmentally, to the extent one is a type, having regularized one's behavior, and perhaps forgotten one's self-abandonment, one is arrested. One has self-control, often some control of situations, but at the cost of psychological fluidity and movement. This reduction of the individual to the social type numbs him to ethical, aesthetic, and political considerations as these are subservient to and forgotten in this consuming effort to achieve his objectives. In a discipline's effort to achieve objective knowledge, it absolutizes the relative, atemporalizes the historical, and rationalizes the political status quo. In its extreme formulation, fascism is the political correlate to psychological arrest.

To return to our colleague, he has his shadow. This is the person — whom we rarely see at formal meetings — who seems excessively, perhaps compulsively, committed to his individuality, his particularity. Ignoring in situations what is expected or common, he causes awkwardness. When it is appropriate — or so others think — to behave efficiently, he may not. I think we would acknowledge the dangers in each of these caricatures, each of these types. I think we would tend to agree that balance between control and abandon, the common and the idiosyncratic, the particular and the general is desirable. Such balance is of course neither consensually determinable nor timeless. When one observes oneself to be a bit eccentric for one's tastes, then one blends in more with others, forever making appropriate adjustments.

The curriculum field is, in my view, imbalanced toward the general (so is mainstream social science). "Traditionalists" have espoused principles of curriculum and instruction, general guides to development, implementation and evaluation that ignore the specificity of each situation. It was precisely this flight from particularity that Schwab attacked in his *The Practical: A Language for Curriculum* (1970). The traditionalists began to give way to "conceptual–empiricists," social scientists who substituted categorization and quantification for stipulation. Among those whose work functions to reconceptualize the field, the politically and economically oriented curricularists have perpetuated this interest in generalization by utilizing concepts such as "hegemony" and "correspondence theory" to explain the politico-economic functions of curriculum. Autobiographic curriculum theory attempts to redress this imbalance by focusing on concrete individuals in specific situations. Finally, however, work that acknowledges the relation between the general, the abstract, and the specific and concrete, and sketches this relation dialectically, so that each element contributes to the transformation of the other to achieve a higher-order synthesis, must be the objective of us all. But, as Bauman points out, such an ideal requires historical conditions that would make that work unnecessary. It is precisely the exploitation of the working classes by the bourgeoisie, more subtly the oppression of individuals by themselves, the mystification of concrete reality by abstract formulation, and the denial of the importance of the intellect by the philistine who accepts the concrete and everyday as natural and transparent that makes the theoretical agenda enunciated earlier necessary. Because our historical conditions make clear these inhuman practices, we struggle to change them, and it is in the context of this historical struggle that autobiographical work must be situated.

EMPATHY AND EDUCATIONAL CRITICISM

How is understanding of the particular attempted? One view suggests that one begins by reconstructing the intentions of those whose actions are under scrutiny. For instance, the attempt to achieve historical understanding might view the products of past peoples as evidence of the intentions that present-day historians aspire to reconstruct. The object, or end-product of intention, is necessarily a modified, mediated, ambiguous expression of that intention. "The intention is always richer than its tangible traces, as these are invariably residues of its defeats" (Bauman, 1978, p. 25). Labor is in this view a fundamentally artistic expression of spirit; labor is the mediation between the ideal vision of the spirit in us and vicious materiality of this world.[1] To focus solely on the object and its relation to other objects (as in exclusively economic interpretation) truncates the labor process by omitting its psycho-spiritual elements. . . .

At first it seems we have traveled far from this romantic view of objects and actions as deposits, as weaker, thinner sedimentations of richer intentions, of spirit. The focus of mainstream social scientists on the observable does seem to abandon issues of origin and meaning. But the psychoanalytic and Marxian traditions, in ways different from each other and from the romantic view, preserve a sense of manifest and latent, refuse to accept the visible as the final and irreducible. In educational research, aspects of the qualitative tradition suggest an interest in *interpretation*. For instance, Eisner's work on problems in evaluation, while utilizing neither a psychoanalytic nor a Marxian view or method, nonetheless *interprets* classroom practice. The examples of this work in his *The Educational Imagination* (1979) and the essays by Robert Donmoyer (1980), Gail McCutcheon (1979), Elizabeth Vallance (1978), and Thomas Barone, Jr. (1979), escape mere mirroring of what occurs. Such work, while not explicit about its criteria of criticism, contextualizes taken-for-granted educational activity more broadly, in the perspective of the critic. In this way, Eisner's work understands what it studies more penetratingly than does another form of qualitative research, the ethnography, at least as this form is practised by Harry Wolcott (1973) in his study, *The Man in the Principal's Office*, or by Louis Smith (1968) in his study of an urban classroom.

What is praiseworthy in the Smith and Wolcott ethnographies is the effort to describe, and through description understand, the everyday life of those in an urban classroom and of him in a principal's office, respectively. But these examples of qualitative understanding are flawed as they fail to describe *lived* experience. Rather, events, behavior, what is spoken, is recorded. How Ed Bell experienced his schedule, his colleague's intentions, the spirit behind the role, is veiled although not entirely absent. It is a newspaper account of his day, as is Smith's description of the urban classroom. The events of the day are described as "news," from a perspectiveless perspective. In the attempt to be comprehensive and impartial, the qualitativeness of these situations was omitted. What is felt, fantasized, and thought — the reality underneath the words, events, and schedules — is not made explicit. Neither do we sense who the authors are beyond their professional personae, what their immediate experience is, how they were affected by their work. The difficulty with these ethnographies is they collapse onto the surface of what they study, and in so doing, risk triviality.

. . .

In their insensitivity to ethical, aesthetic, political, and poetic aspects of lived experience, ethnographies . . . contribute to the self-alienation and social amnesia that typify the historical present.[2] They have lost a sense of their own motives, adding information that no one has requested because everyone knows it. They originate and end in the mundane, and are here distinguishable from educational criticism formulated by Eisner and practiced by his students. Their accounts also begin in the mundane but do not end there. By permitting the critic to make judgment, such accounts bring to form aspects of the lived experience of the situation. Implicitly, these writers seem to understand that the individual's life history provides the existential conditions for understanding. (I will return to this point later.) This view is indicated in the imagery Eisner employs to describe the work of an educational critic.

Eisner describes this work as "rendering the essentially ineffable qualities constituting works of art into a language that will help others to perceive the work more deeply. In this sense, the critic's task is to function as a midwife to perception" (1979, p. 191). The image of midwife does imply the presence of someone (the unborn child in the image, understanding in the analogy) present yet not visible, encapsulated in the mother's body (or situation not discerned, not yet brought to form). This sense of understanding a present yet not visible is also indicated in the preceding sentence by the use of "ineffable." Strictly speaking, "ineffable" is hyperbole, meaning generally, "indescribable," "incapable of being expressed in words." If this were true, the critic would face a hopeless task. Perhaps Eisner is thinking of a second, less common meaning of the word: "not to be uttered, as in taboo." If so, this use of "ineffable" suggests a particularly important task of the critic, that is, to break the silence maintained by authority, by tradition, the breaking of which represents the piercing of taboo. Such work becomes explicitly political as well as aesthetic, and raises problematic issues concerning the authority of the critic. Are his judgments matters of taste only, of political inclination? How does he legitimate them? As with a midwife, one senses one must have confidence in the critic's work. There would appear to be no criteria outside the critic's past record and reputation. I do not see this reliance on the word of others' as damaging, however. The quantitative critic is in no different position finally. His numbers may disguise his political and aesthetic commitments, but they cannot transcend them.

One next step critical work (in Eisner's sense) might take is the specification of procedure, not in a vulgar, technical way, but in a way that makes explicit how the critic proceeds. It is some, but not sufficient help to say that the "connoisseur"[3] is "to attend to happenings of educational life in a focused, sensitive, and conscious way" (Eisner, 1979, p. 195). How does one achieve such focus, sensitivity, and consciousness? In answering that question, I believe autobiographical method can be of use, and I will suggest how in the final section.

EMPATHY AND EDUCATIONAL UNDERSTANDING

Being "focused, sensitive, and conscious" means, in part, being empathetic. We can observe this, for instance, in Robert Donmoyer's (1979) criticism of Miss Hill's fourth-grade classroom. His view of her as reminiscent of Mary Hartmann is quickly clouded by coming to know her. He sees how her routinized teaching represents her effort to survive a situation organizationally created and maintained. Further, he sees her outside the classroom where she is spontaneous and humane. He describes her, consequently, as a Jekyll-and-Hyde character (p. 232).

Empathy, however, conceals as it reveals. Empathy, a prerequisite for understanding the intentions of others, invites he who empathizes to participate in those intentions, intentions that can function as self-rationalizing, self-forgiving, and obscuring ideas. At least she meant well. She has the highest ideals; it is her situation that prevents their realization. One easily risks complicity with another's delusions and legitimations. In serious autobiographical work, one adopts a critical posture towards one's self-report, scrutinizing one's free-associative account looking for the *functions* of one's explanations of oneself. Similarly, the critic must not abandon his critical task in his empathic effort to understand. He must not only mirror the self-report of the other, as in the ethnographies previously mentioned, as this results in a unidimensional and usually trivial account. Further, in the presence of another — especially when the other characterizes himself as "critic" — one tends to give less free-associative and more defended accounts. The critic, as Eisner suggests with the image of midwife, brings to form what operates underneath the teacher's announced intentions, claimed limitations. The critic's empathy must not make him a political eunuch. As it is for the mother-to-be, bringing to awareness that which is denied, repressed, or simply not known is not a painless procedure. The midwife, for her part, must work to make the process as painless as possible. She must be a trusted colleague who wishes her client well, but in so wishing does not relinquish her independence or critical judgment.

Understanding in this sense is a socially negotiated undertaking. The critic reflects on the report of the other, contextualizing it in his experience and commitments. What Eisner does not (yet) do and what may be part of a next step is the enunciation of a schema that represents a codification of experience and commitments, criteria by which the critic judges, or perhaps a method of judgment and understanding. The schema acts as a kind of sieve through which self-report and observation is poured. Schutz (1978, p. 180) observes:

> Meaning is not a quality of certain lived experiences emerging distinctively in the stream of consciousness. . . . It is rather the result of my explication of past lived experiences which are grasped reflectively from an actual now and from an actual valid reference scheme . . . Lived experiences first become meaningful, then, when they are explicated *post hoc* and become comprehensible to me as well-circumscribed experiences. Thus only those lived experiences are subjectively meaningful which are . . . examined as regards their constitution, and which are explicated in respect to their position in a reference schema that is at hand.

The concept of "valid reference scheme" implies a scientifically derived scheme that obscures problematic political and aesthetic issues. However, Schutz's notion acknowledges the role of the researcher in the determination of meaning. The research does not merely mirror what he observes, as if meaning inhered "out there," in the situation, and the dutiful researcher works to absent himself, and merely reflect back what occurred. This is the error of ethnography, an error that results from the interest in being scientific, from accepting the false dualism of subject and object. It is the researcher's "eye," his capacity to penetrate the surface of situations — the language of the participants, their public intentions, and their observable behavior — to qualities discernible but not yet present, that makes possible understanding. The researcher is a midwife who assists in bringing to birth knowledge not yet born. . . . Gouldner's notion of "domain assumptions" refers to the predispositions of the social theorists and investigators to shape their studies in ways that bias what they discover:

> Domain assumptions about man and society might include, for example, dispositions to believe that men are rational or irrational; that society is precarious or fundamentally stable; that social problems will correct themselves with planned intervention; that human behavior is unpredictable; that man's true humanity resides in his feelings and sentiments. [1970, p. 31]

Erikson (1975) discusses the "motivational dimensions" of the idea. Robert Travers observes: "Knowledge is preconditioned by the forms of our sensibility" (1978). With such words we move from preconscious or unconscious views of the constitution of human life to the psychological life of intellectual interests, to the fully empirical view that true knowledge lies outside the individual and one's sensibility conditions it.

When one is psychologically "present," one can attune oneself to a situation, and one's experience of that situation does indeed depict that situation. We can become conscious of how life-history, commitments, and assumptions operate in our experience of that situation. We become free of them as we become conscious of them. We then attune ourselves to the situation, allowing the problematic — the unknown, the tension — to state itself through us. The situation comes to form through us, and thus our sensibilities do not merely precondition knowledge; they make it possible. By focusing on the "underlife" of the situation, we avoid restatement of the obvious and mundane. Such a focus brings the situation to form; in Dewey's words it becomes an object of articulate thought.

The observer meditates while in situation, keeping explicit his own material. He can later, when he goes over his account, explicate its presence, and delete it as appropriate if the statement is to become public. While in the room, he attempts to include as much as possible. He attunes himself, allowing himself to move through the room visually, emotionally, above all moving as a spirit throughout the room empathically, representing what is experienced though as yet not articulated. He works to sense the unstated problematic, what Dewey also terms "an immediate quality of the whole situation." Through thought and language we convert the unspoken, not-yet-understood "into pertinent and coherent terms." To achieve such understanding a second reading — a reading of the reading — may be necessary in which one applies, in Schutz's terms, a "valid reference scheme" (1978, p. 180).

. . .

Situations exhibit movement[4] to the extent one intuits them accurately, and articulates the intuitive reading so that it is accessible, indeed recognizable to one's students (or colleagues). Through this naming, the situation is brought to form, and becomes mature. Its articulation is its maturity. And as it matures, it disappears as a new situation arises in its place: immature, unnamed, perhaps not yet felt. As time passes, the midwife works, the hidden becomes discernible, and through careful, cautious attunement to qualities, these qualities present themselves as impressions or hunches. One gives this "inner speech" (Vygotsky, 1962) linguistic form, and through conversation, achieves understanding. True, it is possible that one understands more completely before conversation. *But for understanding to have social use, it must be negotiated socially.*

In order to achieve movement, one must be willing to offer up one's "reading." Social negotiation can occur only when the participants are willing to give up aspects of their understanding for the sake of consensual articulation of the disciplinary situation. Further, when one is "caught" in one's own views, one is less likely to accurately read the qualities of the situation, and one is less willing, less able to negotiate a consensual understanding. This is one meaning of "ideological," that one projects, in this case not explicitly psychological material (although political views have their psychological functions and meaning), but unchallengeable, nonnegotiable views of human life. Such views are akin to Gouldner's domain assumptions except they are quite conscious. Mannheim (1960, pp. 86–87) discusses this distortion of understanding and another, more temporally based, distortion:

> Knowledge is distorted and ideological when it fails to take account of the new realities applying to a situation, and when it attempts to conceal them by thinking of them in categories which are inappropriate. . . .
>
> In the same historical epoch and in the same society there may be several distorted types of inner mental structure, some because they have not yet grown up to the present, and others because they are already beyond the present.

In the first paragraph of this passage, we note the ideologue's deforming of the situation by adherence to categories generated and espoused before the situation has presented itself. Such individuals do not attune themselves to the situation, but vice versa. In the second paragraph, two related distortions are noted. The mass of people of a given society are more or less sharing the same — the present — historical moment. Because they are the masses they constitute the present moment. Broadly speaking, they share ideas of what is possible, what is valuable, and so on. But there are always groups and individuals who have yet to reach this historical stage, and the masses view them as "backward." As well, there is always an avant-garde, who have lived through already what the masses live through at the present time. Often the avant-garde forgets that the masses must live through their issues, cannot resolve them by passively accepting the knowledge of the avant-garde. Often the avant-garde forgets what Sartre (1963, p. 248) does not: "Ideas do not change men. Knowing the cause of a passion is not enough to overcome it; one must live it . . . in short one must 'work oneself through'."

Forgetting that historical stages must be lived through, not merely thought through, the avant-garde tends to succumb to smugness and self-superiority. It may offer its understanding of the historical present, but it is obliged to offer up this understanding, to allow the masses to dialectically oppose it in its movement to work through it. Thus each generation discovers anew what was understood before, if in now historically antiquated terms, in terms which do not bring to form the present historical situation. Collingwood (1973) understood this point well. "Every new generation must rewrite history in its own way. . . . The historian himself, together with the here-and-now which forms the total body of evidence available to him, is part of the process he is studying."

Not only specific truths change with each generation, but each generation's interests in those truths changes. Our interests are intimately linked to our interpretation of what is necessary to bring our situation to form, to discern its latent qualities. In this interpretive work, the effort to achieve nomological truth is little help. For interpretation and understanding of human affairs — educational and otherwise — cannot be achieved apart from time, history, and human intention. This fundamental fact some of our quantitative colleagues have evidently forgotten. Part of our task is to remind them. Bauman (1978, p. 70) notes:

> Suppose that somehow an empirical-statistical demonstration of the strictest sense is produced, showing that all men everywhere who have ever been placed in a certain situation have invariably reacted in the same way and to the same extent. Suppose that whenever this situation is reproduced, the same reaction invariably follows. Which is to say: suppose that this reaction is, in the most literal sense of the word, "calculable." Such a demonstration would not bring us a single step closer to the "interpretation" of this reaction. By itself such a demonstration would contribute nothing to the project of "understanding why" this reaction ever occurred and moreover, "why" it invariably occurs in the same way. As long as the "inner," imaginative *reproduction* of the motivation responsible for the reaction remains impossible, we will be unable to acquire that understanding.

Reproduction of motivation is impossible, given its situatedness in time, place, and life history. What quantitative research aspires for is in principle impossible. And, as Winch (1971) has argued, it is undesirable as well.

ATTUNEMENT

To focus more closely upon attunement, and its relation to understanding, I will summarize aspects of Heidegger's work, from which the term "attunement" derives. For Heidegger, understanding is not a methodological problem: it is an ontological one. That is, understanding is a mode of being, not a technical problem for epistemologists or, more narrowly, philosophers of science. Understanding occurs only in the context of being-in-the-world (Bauman, 1978, p. 148). It cannot occur for philosophers who abstract and reduce being-in-the-world to a set of technical problems. Rather, in Bauman's words, understanding occurs only in "our pristine, straightforward, 'prereflexive' being-in-the-world" (p. 149). In this state, if we are attuned, knowledge presents itself. Heidegger writes:

> The essence of being is *physis*. Appearing is the power that emerges. Appearing makes manifest. Already we know then that being, appearings, causes emerge from concealment. Since the essent as such *is*, it places itself in and stands in *unconcealment, aletheia*. We translate, and at the same time thoughtlessly misinterpret, this word as "truth" . . . The essent is true insofar as it is. The true as such is essent. This means: The power that manifests itself stands in unconcealment. In showing itself, the unconcealed as such comes to stand. Truth as unconcealment is not an appendage of being. [Bauman, 1978, p. 150]

Truth is what presents itself to us in situation. History is continually unconcealing. In specific situations, in a classroom for instance, we attune ourselves in order to see that which our everyday eyes do not see. We must close these eyes, listen, and discover what lies concealed. This discovery is not final truth; it is not a logical or methodological exercise. It is not a matter of matching thoughts in me to actions out there. It is a matter of allowing reality, of which I am a spokesman, to speak itself. The original Greek for reality, for the essent, was *physis*. Bauman (1978, pp. 149–50) tells us that it was translated into Latin, through which it was passed on to the present time, as *natura*. Heidegger notes the original meaning:

> What does the word *physis* denote? It denotes self-blossoming emergence (e.g. the blossoming of a rose), opening up, unfolding, that which manifests itself in such unfolding and perseveres and endures in it; in short, the realm of things that emerge and linger on. . . . *Physis* means the power that emerges and the enduring

real under its sway. . . . *Physis* is the process of arising, of emerging from the hidden, whereby the hidden is first made to stand. [Bauman, 1978, p. 150]

Physis as understood by the Greeks derived from lived experience, not from the abstracted generalization associated with natural studies like physics. That *physis* is associated only with natural science, and not at all with the study of experience, underscores the narrowness of the contemporary scientific age (Bauman, 1978, p. 150).

Knowledge occurs in the experience of situation, in the context of daily life. Knowing is not properly a specialized activity practiced by technicians isolated from the mainstream of life. Heidegger:

We know from Heraclitus and Parmenides that the unconcealment of being is not simply given. Unconcealment occurs only when it is achieved by work: the work of the word in poetry, the work of stone in temple and statue, the work of the word in thought, the work of the *polis* as the historical place in which all this is grounded and preserved. [Bauman, 1978, p. 151]

Knowledge is not to be created simply for the sake of its creation, simply to add to "the body of knowledge." This is knowledge divorced from the intentions, needs, and desires of concretely existing individuals. Efforts to understand properly arise in the midst of a *felt* problematic.

AUTOBIOGRAPHICAL METHOD

We are not mere smudges on the mirror. Our life histories are not liabilities to be exorcised but are the very precondition for knowing. It is our individual and collective stories in which present projects are situated, and it is awareness of these stories that is the lamp illumining the dark spots, the rough edges. Dewey's "intuition" and Heidegger's "attunement" both refer to the reflexive grasp of problematic qualities of situations.

This image of grasp captures the unity of self and situation. Molded together, the situation speaks through the self and the self through the situation. Qualitative understanding requires subtle and quiet attention to both. Autobiographical method can be employed to cultivate such attention: to situation as element of the self, to self as situation, and to transformation and reconstitution of both (Pinar, 1979). In such movement, we glimpse dialectical development, the basic structural elements of intellectual and psychosocial development. We glimpse the role of texts and teachers and friends — the role of curriculum — in our movement from the egocentric to the decentred, from provincial to broadminded, from ignorant to knowing human beings. It is a glimpse of this phenomenon previously portrayed in psychological and social theories now situated in the life of a particular individual — oneself.

Autobiographical method offers opportunities to return to our own situations, our "rough edges," to reconstruct our intellectual agendas. The focus in such work is the felt problematic; its method is intuitive. One falls back on oneself — rather than upon the words of others — and must articulate what is yet unspoken, act as midwife to the unborn. One uncovers one's "domain assumptions," one's projections —not in order to clean the slate but in order to understand the slate of which one is the existential basis, the basis that makes knowing possible. William Earle (1977, p. 10) describes what we seek when we work autobiographically:

> And while science and certain theoretical forms of philosophy look for *explanations* of phenomena, "Know thyself" does not enjoin me to find explanations of myself in what lies outside myself, in what is *not* me. "Knowing" is not necessarily explanatory, but it might be regarded as elucidation: that is, raising to explicit, reflexive consciousness that which is already implicitly grasped. It might be an effort to excavate the implicit buried sense of existence of a singular being by that singular being — in a word the "autobiography" of the singular being. "Know thyself" invites me to become explicit as to who I am, what it is for me to exist; what my singular existence has been, where it has been, where it is now, and what lies before me. "Ontological autobiography," we shall call it, with no particular emphasis upon its "graphical" or recorded character; it is a question of a form of consciousness rather than of literature.

What we aspire to when we work autobiographically is not adherence to conventions of a literary form. Nor do we think of audience, of portraying our life to others. We write autobiography for ourselves, in order to cultivate our capacity to see through the outer forms, the habitual explanations of things, the stories we tell in order to keep others at a distance. It is against the taken-for-granted, against routine and ritual we work, for it is the regularized and the habitual that arrest movement — intellectual and otherwise. Arrested, we cannot see movement in others nor contribute to it. In this sense we seek a dialectical self-self relation, which then permits a dialectical relationship between self and work, self and others. Earle (1977, pp. 58–59) describes it as "divestment":

> Divestment may be taken as a "purification" of the soul too much engrossed with what it is not, too much caught up in that deceptively tempting and deceptively rewarding domain of the impurities of existence, where the poor soul futilely sought itself. . . . [Divestment] is a regressive shift of attention from objects or affairs back to the ego that was engrossed with them.

Divestment does not represent retreat from the affairs of the world, from classrooms, politics, and conflicts. It represents reflexive awareness of one's participation in the affairs of the world, a reflexivity that captures the mutual determinancy and mutual creation of both self and situation. Autobiographical method permits such awareness as it reconstructs the past, as it lays bare the relation between self and work, self and others that has prevailed in the past. It portrays, for instance, the ways in which intellectual interests functioned psychologically for us. Such portraits give us an order of information regarding the function of curriculum that we simply have not had before. . . .

To the extent one becomes concious of the dialects of one's intellectual development, one can participate in them. Further, through one's self-understanding one comprehends — from a participant's rather than observer's point of view — the functions of ideas — and texts — in one's intellectual life, and the function of one's intellect in one's own life. "To understand is to rediscover you in me; the spirit retrieves itself on ever higher levels of the configuration; identity of Spirit in me, in you, in every subject of our community, in every system of culture, finally in the totality of spirits and in universal history" (Bauman, 1978, p. 35). Understanding of self is not narcissism; it is a precondition and a concomitant condition to the understanding of others. The process of education is not situated — and cannot be understood — in the observer, but in we who undergo it. In its extreme formulation, truth itself lies in the relation of self to situation, knower to known, in the mode of consciousness that allows the situation to articulate itself, allows the qualitative to surface, the problematic to be resolved. . . .

As scientific understandings of the natural and physical world change, so do understandings of the human world. The quantitative effort to capture, and make static our world derives from an interest to control and predict. Such an effort will continue to fail as long as human beings resist control. Qualitative research is politically progressive, as it is epistemologically sophisticated, because it understands that a basic meaning of human life is movement, conflict, resolution, conflict, resolution, each thesis and antithesis opposing each other in ways give birth to new orders of understanding and life. The task is not to control this movement, nor is it merely to portray it. It is to contribute to it, acting as midwives in the labor that is human history coming to form. This contribution can be made in work with ourselves, as well as work with others. It is work that cultivates the specificity of ourselves, the particularity of self and situation. Autobiographical method is one strategy by which this work can be conducted.

. . .

NOTES

1. See Sartre (1964) for a novelistic portrait of vicosity.
2. For a discussion of this phenomenon see Jacoby (1975).
3. "Connoisseur" is, perhaps, an unfortunate choice of a term: it implies the bourgeois collector of art whose tastes are usually derived from others rather than from his experience as an artist.
4. For a full treatment of this notion see Pinar (1980).

REFERENCES

Barone, T., Jr. "Of Scott and Lisa and Other Friends." In E.W. Eisner (ed.) *The Educational Imagination*. New York: MacMillan, 1979.

Bauman, Z. *Hermeneutics and Social Science*. New York: Columbia University Press, 1978.

Collingwood, R.G. *The Idea of History*. Oxford: Oxford University Press, 1973.

Dilthey, Wilhelm. Quoted in Z. Bauman, *Hermeneutics and Social Science*. New York: Columbia University Press, 1978.

Donmoyer, R. "School and Society Revisited: An Educational Criticism of Mill Hill's Fourth-Grade Classroom." In E. Eisner (ed.), *The Educational Imagination*. New York: MacMillan, 1979.

Donmoyer, R. "The Evaluator as Artist," *Journal of Curriculum Theorizing* 2:2 (Summer 1980).

Earle, W. *Autobiographical Consciousness: A Philosophical Inquiry Into Existence*. Chicago: Quadrangle Books, 1977.

Eisner, E.W. *The Educational Imagination*. New York: MacMillan, 1979.

Erikson, E. *Life History and Historical Moment*. New York: Norton, 1975.

Gouldner, A.W. *The Coming Crisis of Western Sociology*. New York: Basic Books, 1970.

Habermas, J. *Theory and Practice*. Boston: Beacon Press, 1973.

Huebner, D. "Curricular Language and Classroom Meanings." In W. Pinar (ed.), *Curriculum Theorizing: The Reconceptualists*. Berkeley, Calif.: McCutchan, 1975.

Jacoby, R. *Social Amnesia*. Boston: Beacon Press, 1975.

Lasch, C. *Haven in a Heartless World*. New York: Basic Books, 1977.

Mannheim, K. *Ideology and Utopia*. London: Routledge and Kegan Paul, 1960.

Marcuse, H. *The Aesthetic Dimension*. Boston: Beacon Press, 1978.

McCutcheon, G. "Educational Criticism: Methods and Application." *Journal of Curriculum Theorizing* 1:2 (Summer 1979).

Pinar, W.F. "The Voyage Out," *Journal of Curriculum Theorizing* 2:1 (Winter 1979).

Pinar, W.F. "Life History and Educational Experience," *Journal of Curriculum Theorizing* 2:2 (Summer 1980).

Sartre, J.P. *Search for a Method*. New York: Knopf, 1963.

Sartre, J.P. *Nausea*. New York: New Directions, 1964.

Schutz, Alfred. Quoted in Z. Bauman, *Hermeneutics and Social Science*. New York: Columbia University Press, 1978.

Schwab, J.J. *The Practical: A Language for Curriculum*. Washington, D.C.: National Education Association, 1970.

Smith, L.M., and W. Geoffrey. *The Complexities of an Urban Classroom*. New York: Holt, Rinehart and Winston, 1968.

Travers, R.M.W. "Some Comments on Qualitative Approaches to the Development of Scientific Knowledge and the Use of Constructs Derived from Phenomenal Experience." In G. Willis (ed.), *Qualitative Evaluation: Concepts and Cases in Curriculum Criticism*. Berkeley, Calif.: McCutchan, 1978.

Vallance, E. "Scanning Horizons and Looking at Weeds." In G. Willis, (ed.), *Qualitative Evaluation: Concept and Cases in Curriculum Criticism*. Berkeley, Calif.: McCutchan, 1978.

Vygotsky, L.S. *Thought and Language*. Cambridge, Mass.: M.I.T. Press, 1962.

Willis, G. "Qualitative Evaluation as the Aesthetic, Personal, and Political Dimensions of Curriculum Criticism." In G. Willis (ed.), *Qualitative Evaluation: Concepts and Cases in Curriculum Criticism*. Berkeley, Calif.: McCutchan, 1978.

Winch, P. *Ethics and Action*. London: Routledge and Kegan Paul, 1971.

Wolcott, H.F. *The Man in the Principal's Office: An Ethnography*. New York: Holt, Rinehart and Winston, 1973.

Selection 6.5

Teachers' Roles in the Using and Doing of Research and Curriculum Development

F. Michael Connelly and Miriam Ben-Peretz

INTRODUCTION

Periodically there are calls for the schools, and especially for their teachers, to involve themselves in doing research. "Action research," as practitioner-done research is commonly called, was popular in the 1950s and is again receiving attention in the 1970's.[1] The main arguments usually given for such research are that it will yield "realistic" knowledge readily applicable in the classroom, and that doing research is an important change-oriented professional development activity. Neither argument is persuasive, based as they are on a concept of research more appropriate to the social sciences and omitting as they do the action-oriented instructional role of teachers.

Of course, not all appeals and programs for school change show confidence of this kind in teachers. In the 1960s, for example, the massive expansion of centers, laboratories, projects, and heavily funded research was mostly embedded in the notion that school learning could be affected directly from external sources with teachers acting as implementation conduits for research findings and curriculum programmes. . . . McNamara . . . writes that the objective of his article "is to analyse and suggest some *supporting* roles that teachers and students can assume. . . ."

SOURCE. Reprinted in an abridged form, with permission of the authors and publisher, from *Journal of Curriculum Studies* 12:2 (1980): 95–107.

McNamara (1972) acknowledges an active role for both teachers and students in school planning but points out that this might be an answer to the recognized difficulties in implementing external innovations in schools. It is apparent that, for McNamara, action research is primarily an implementation device. Likewise, . . . Fullan (1976) describes a project that is concerned with the difficulties of unlearning old roles and learning new roles in changing social systems. For Fullan, school change would be facilitated by an understanding of role changes. By participating in projects as action researchers, teachers, according to Fullan, would more readily overcome the role-change impediment to successful implementation.

The joining of action research with implementation represents an approach to school change that focuses on the implementation process, with the assumption that if enough were known about teacher involvement in curriculum implementation, research findings and program developments would find their way more directly into the classroom. . . .

GOALS OF ACTION RESEARCH BY TEACHERS

The spirit behind most proposals for action research is captured by Schaeffer's (1967) notion of the school as a centre of inquiry. With Schaeffer and many others we believe that improvement in the quality of educational practices is dependent on an open, investigative, and exploratory attitude on the part of schools and, in particular, their teachers. In our view the most persuasive proposals for school change share this belief in the power of the inquiring teacher mind. However, we also believe that the vision of this end-in-view embedded action-research and action-research implementation is, if not undesirable, at best impractical and contrary to the original spirit of fostering teacher autonomy.

Action Research and Knowledge Production

Popham and Baker's (1970) notion of the "teacher-experimenter" fits the commonly held action-research view of the teacher as a "little researcher." These authors maintain that "through the careful reading of the results of research conducted by others, together with the systematic conduct of small-scale experiments in his own classroom the teacher can be a truly polished professional." Leese, Frasure and Johnson (1965) deal with the subject of the teacher and curriculum research and present guidelines for teachers as experimenters. Such notions tend to reduce inquiry to experimental procedures, surely not the only, or even the most influential form of social-science research. Other forms of research could conceivably be equally useful for teachers. Instead of setting up classroom experiments in order to control phenomena and study them scientifically, teachers could be involved in controlling the way they look at neutral classroom phenomena. The work of the phenomenologisis illustrates this approach (Van Manen, 1979).

More important to our point, however, is the implication that professionalism in teaching depends on an inquiry attitude (with which we agree) oriented to the canons and procedures of scholarly inquiry (with which we disagree). Schools, as Schwab (1969) so convincingly reminds us in his essays on curriculum, are places of action, and teaching is their principal act. Teaching acts may be done more or less well and they may be conducted more or less thoughtfully. To think well, and presumably to teach well, depends on a reflective investigative spirit, and this is the starting place for constructing the means by which defensible instructional actions might be achieved. Following this, we can assert what appears to be self-evident: that the realization of reflective teaching is found in the teacher's attempts to achieve the best instructional acts through consideration of the host of factors in his particular teaching situation. "Small-scale experiments" might, in infrequent cases, be called for in a teacher's consideration of his situation. But these would take their place in a broader deliberative context of teacher planning and decision making about acts of instruction. Such experimentation would *not* have as its aim the production of new knowledge. (Such may, of course, be forthcoming — as Schaeffer (1967) foresaw when he wrote that "Discovering new knowledge about the instructional process is the distinctive contribution which the lower schools may provide." Rather the teacher's investigative attitude, including any experimental work, would be decision-oriented and directed to the immediate improvement of his teaching practice.

One of the most useful formulations of this version of researcher-practitioner relationship known to us is found in Rapoport's (1970) description of the work of the Tavistock Institute where multidisciplinary teams work on problems brought to them by business and other organizations. As Rapoport writes, "the kind of action research suggested here — with its dual agenda, practical and scientific — seeks to resolve the dilemma posed by service requirements on one extreme and academic goals of pure and disinterested knowledge on the other. From this notion of serving both practical and scientific agendas, Rapoport goes on to point out that in "turbulent" fields collaborative and co-operative relationships are needed on the "metaproblems" that are common to both the researcher and the practitioner. Education would surely qualify as a turbulent field and would, if we follow Rapoport's insights, gain from such collaboration.

. . .

Action Research and Policy Implementation

Under what circumstances is it justifiable to treat teachers merely as implementation agents? In our judgment such an approach is *not* justified by the importance of the findings and products of universities and other research and curriculum development teams. Indeed, in our view attention given by R and D to implementation in Europe and North America is both unwarranted and potentially harmful in its fostering of intellectual dependency in teachers. The different functions of research, curriculum development, and teaching combined with the notion that curriculum materials contain potential for diverse ends leads us to the simple point that researchers and developers should do their job and teachers do theirs. There is little justification for researchers and developers stepping beyond their proper functions, as they do in implementation, and attempting to shape the teacher's functions to their perception of what the teacher ought to be doing.

There is, however, one form of curriculum development, curriculum policy formation, where it is appropriate to view teachers as implementers and where it is legitimate to exhibit concern when teachers do not do as they are told. Where curriculum policy clearly reflects public wishes, as it might, for example, in a policy of equal opportunity, teachers *are* obliged to implement. Belize, for example, recently established a policy for agricultural education based on the principle that students should study subjects connected with their lives and their futures.[2] The policy represents an important educational shift in Belize toward curriculum equality and relevance. Furthermore, the policy reflects social changes within the country. The existing government won office, in part at least, on a plan to reform education in directions consistent with their view of social priorities for Belize. In such circumstances the implementation of policy is clearly justifiable. Teachers cannot argue against or otherwise circumvent the policy on the grounds by which research and curriculum development efforts are normally modified and sidetracked. Civil disobedience might, of course, occur, but if it did it would need to be based on an objection to the government's interpretation of social directions and not on pedagogic grounds.

There are, of course, jurisdictions in which curriculum policy takes the form of specific courses of study and other directives for teachers. Under these circumstances we believe that policy has overstepped its function and, quite properly, will be modified and otherwise sidetracked as teachers pursue their instructional function.

. . .

RETHINKING THE RELATIONSHIP OF TEACHERS TO RESEARCH AND CURRICULUM DEVELOPMENT

One of the consequences of the past two decades of enthusiasm for educational research and curriculum development was that teacher education tended to be denigrated. Admittedly, resources were devoted to teacher training, but the overwhelming view was that the education of teachers should follow advances in research and curriculum development. In its least sophisticated version, teacher education throughout this period entailed workshops on how to teach new programs. This practice was not restricted to in-service programs but was, as well, common in preservice programs as methods courses became walk-throughs of modern curricula. Action-research implementation was a different version of this same phenomenon.

Perhaps the most sophisticated reflections of these assumptions occurred in graduate studies programs aimed at closing the infamous gap between research findings and practice. It has been said that some institutions, for example, the Ontario Institute for Studies in Education (OISE), were established with the principal purpose of updating practice by conveying research findings to practitioners (Westbury, 1978). OISE took this notion a step further by establishing field centers throughout the Province of Ontario for the purpose of linking its central research units with local areas. (This purpose, it must be noted, has been significantly modified as field centers have evolved a variety of consultative relationships with local areas.)

. . .

We believe that a rebalancing of teacher education research and curriculum development is needed. Concepts, ideas, and training programs need to be developed that stress the place of teachers in school reform. And redressing the balance is not merely a matter of equalizing effort. Effective plans have to be based on a different notion of the relationship of teachers to research and development: one that recognizes that the work not only of teachers but of researchers as well is justified by the affairs of schools and that the teacher, and others closely connected with teaching, ultimately reinterpret and adopt the findings of research and development. In short, a conceptual partnership of teachers, researchers, and developers revises the relationship of recent years and puts teachers in the lead position. This implies that teacher-education programs need to be developed in their own terms and not in terms of research and curriculum development.

. . .

Functions and Potential of Researchers, Developers, and Teachers

Researchers, developers and teachers may best be seen as supporting each other in curriculum development by virtue of their *different*, but obviously related roles. This relationship, which decisively shifts the teacher's role from implementer to decision maker and independent developer, can be described as follows:

> The strength and major contribution of a developer are that he works with and can translate involved ideas into a form useful for teachers and students. However, the developer cannot imagine, let alone account for, the full range of teaching situations that arise. It is here that the teacher's experience and wisdom enter into curriculum planning in a way that cannot adequately be replaced. The characteristics and needs of the actual classroom situation are the first and final factors determining what should be done in that classroom. The teacher is inescapably the arbitrator between the demands of curriculum materials and of the instructional situation. Only rarely will arbitration lead to a settlement exclusively favouring the developers' intentions. [Connelly, 1972, p. 164]

Consistent with this notion of an effective teacher is the concept of "curriculum potential." The potential of any given set of curriculum materials encompasses developer interpretations as well as the possible uses that might be revealed by external analysts or implementers: "Curricular materials are more complex and richer in educational possibilities than any list of goals or objectives, whether general or specific, and contain more than an expression of the intentions of the writers. If we look upon materials as the end products of a creative process, then any single interpretation yields only a partial picture of the whole" (Ben-Peretz, 1975).

The analysis of curriculum potential for a particular classroom situation offers wide scope for the teacher's exercise of a reflective investigative spirit. Teachers try out various ways of using curriculum materials in concrete classroom situations. Thus the focus of teacher-conducted research becomes one of inquiry into characteristics of classroom situations and materials, generation of alternatives for action and, to use a term of Stake's (1975), "responsive evaluation" of outcomes.

Inquiry, Planning, and Teaching

Consideration of the teacher's function in curriculum development suggests three actions: *inquiry into new research, programs, and policy statements; planning for teaching;* and *teaching*. Each of these activities has characteristic modes of thought. Our interest here is in the first of these activities since it is inquiry that provides the link with research and curriculum development.

There is a choice for those who wish teachers to use new programs and research findings. They can engage teachers in activities designed to implement the new materials or they can engage teachers in an educational inquiry of them. The choice is between implementation and teacher inquiry. It is a choice between engaging teachers in activities designed to overcome their resistance to new ideas versus engaging teachers in an analysis of those ideas and of their potential uses for the teacher's situation. The latter, we believe, will lead to more useful ideas on the teacher's conceptual difficulties when confronted with new curricula and new research. More important, proper study of the program will constitute a genuine educational activity. The risk, of course, is that teachers may then deliberately and on defensible grounds either choose *against* the new program or make major adaptions of it, and they may decide the research is not relevant for their situation.

Teacher Re-education Through Inquiry. Teacher education programs that merely acquaint teachers with new ideas and aim to get teachers thinking along the lines of new material omit the essential intellectual problem at issue. Indeed, the introduction of new courses of study, curriculum guidelines, textbooks, and research findings could become an occasion for profound growth of teachers. The educational problem of introducing teachers to new ideas is one of introducing them to new perspectives. It is not merely a question of teaching teachers more of the same; nor is it merely a question of presenting new content. It is, rather, a question of reorienting teachers toward their subject matter and toward a reason for its place in the curriculum. Educationally, it is both important and difficult to teach and learn at the level of perspective. One-shot workshops and familiarization activities are inadequate to the task. Carefully designed educational settings for teachers are required. Thus new curricula and research findings could serve as the content for teacher-education programs aimed at teacher growth.

Parallelling the two functions of curriculum development described above are two sides to inquiry-oriented teacher-education programs. From the point of view of the instructor there is the hope that with adequate knowledge of the assumptions, strengths, and limitations of new ideas teachers will, indeed, make them their own. This is an appropriate hope since developers and researchers are governed by the same ends as are teachers. Both hope for growth in practice. The difference between the instructor's ambitions in an inquiry program and in a program aimed at implementation is that understanding and knowledge of alternatives replaces implementation activities as the principal instructional purpose. Implementation is a not-too-strongly hoped for by-product.

From the viewpoint of the teacher, inquiry into new ideas is bound up with the practical knowledge used in planning for teaching and in teaching. The teacher's practical knowledge is the background against which the results of inquiry are interpreted, adapted, and chosen for use. Thus the teacher is not interested at all (except, perhaps, for nonpedagogic reasons such as status) in implementation. His concern is to determine the utility of the new ideas consistent with his own practical knowledge.[3] Growth in practical knowledge occurs as the process of inquiry joins with the teacher's personal tests of the ideas through teaching and planning for teaching.

FORMS OF INQUIRY TRAINING PROGRAMS FOR TEACHERS

. . . We divide this variation into three types: the teacher as consumer of research and curriculum development; the teacher as participant in research; and the teacher as partner in research and development.

The Teacher as Consumer of Research

The simplest version of an inquiry program for teachers is where the teacher is thought of as a consumer of research. Teachers are educated in the assumptions, principles, and methods by which new knowledge and new programs were developed. This version of inquiry education for teachers requires no administrative or organizational adjustment in graduate studies and in-service program. All that is required is the abandonment of the notion of implementation and a commitment to fostering the teacher's intellectual independence.

. . .

The Teacher as Participant in Research

A rich problem initiation experience can be found in a graduate practicum by interested practicing teachers. Faculty and full-time students work with the practicing teachers on a problem defined by the teachers. In this way practicing teachers control the problem and the direction of its resolution at the same time as having ready access to scholarly advice and knowledge . . .

On a small scale the doctorate degree for practitioners can constitute an excellent research experience. Practitioners leave the school system for a period of time, develop a proposal connected to their professional careers, and conduct thesis research upon return to their school system. The research is action-oriented in its aim of facilitating the participants' practical life. Such programs amount to an idealized action-research activity where the practitioner is freed of normal duties for a period of time. His work is jointly planned with researchers and is designed so that research results will be useful in his future professional work as decision maker in the educational system.

Teachers as Active Partners in Curriculum Development

Joint Planning. Currently, there appear to be forces for and against joint university-school planning in research and development. The Campbell (1975) report to the U.S. National Institute of Education, for example, calls for less visibility and more autonomy for researchers and developers. On the other hand, as we have analyzed school reform since the 1950s, there seems to be strong support for the joint-planning orientation proposed in this paper. Leithwood's (1976) account of OISE Trent Valley Field Centre's mathematics project with the Peterborough County Board of Education is illustrative. An interesting feature of this project is that the curricular problem was formulated by the local school board prior to the involvement of the Field Centre. Only later did the Centre enter an advisory-working role. Thus, the overall problem and character of the study was set by the board, and the study was aimed at improving board priorities. The Centre, which had mathematics education expertise, saw the board's problem as an opportuity to pursue their own interests. Each partner in the joint project drew on his special expertise in the service of the *common goal*, the development of an innovative new mathematics program, all the while pursuing their different interests. The board wanted to improve the quality of decision making in mathematics education, which it did through a set of products and through personnel involvement in the research and development effort; and the researcher's goal of knowledge-production in the area of school change was achieved.

Joint Curriculum Development. One effective way of involving teachers, albeit in limited numbers, in research and development processes is through their active participation in curriculum development projects, an idea that is different from that of using teachers to provide feedback in the formative stages of curriculum construction or as participating members in a team of external developers. What is suggested here is the setting up of development teams staffed by teachers whose responsibility is the joint planning and construction of a curriculum package from its initial stage up to the final stage of a commercial product.

Such a project was set up at Haifa University as part of the *Man in Nature*[4] curriculum project. The main feature in this project is its focus on teachers as development agents. This is interesting since curriculum projects usually emphasize subject matter, the needs of learners, or society's demands, and tend only as an implementation afterthought to turn to the consideration of teachers. In the Haifa curriculum project carried out by teachers, their needs, preferences, knowledge of school practice and environment, as well as their knowledge of their subject matter served as the starting points for curriculum deliberation.

The project's aims were threefold:

1. Using the teacher as the starting point in curriculum deliberations.
2. Involving teachers in the R and D process as active inquirers and decision makers.
3. Providing a curriculum product for the school system that in itself would be instrumental in teacher involvement in decision making, thus enhancing teacher autonomy.

This meant changing the project in such a way that teachers using it in their classrooms would have to be involved independently in the decision-making process. Thus, instead of publishing one set of materials, several versions of the unit were developed, and teachers chose among them and combined parts of different versions to form their own curriculum. This ties in with the notions of teachers functioning as judges of the requirements of their situation and as partners in the generation of proposals for action.

Joint Research. Jointly planned research is well illustrated by the work of the Institute for Research in Teaching at Michigan State University. The proposal establishing the Institute suggested that teachers collaborate on Institute projects. A recent Institute Report describes the situation as follows:

> During the Institute's planning period, teachers comprised 30 percent of the senior research staff. These teachers (seven in all) collaborated as co-investigators in planning and designing studies. The number of teachers collaborating as senior staff members decreased to 15 percent during the operational years, as teachers were recruited to fill other roles in the research (e.g., as subjects and members of policy boards). Thus teachers participate in various roles in research, (e.g., at the IRT) as subjects, policy makers, data collectors, and more. [Shalway et al., n.d.]

. . .

The various versions of the teachers' role, which emerged from our analysis, are presented diagramatically in Figure 6.5–1. Teachers may be treated as mere transmitters of curricular ideas through "teacher-proof" materials; as active implementers aided by action-research and role-changing strategies; and as adapters in development through the treatment of materials as exhibiting potential for different uses.

There is a growing trend to move away from the image of teachers as neutral transmitters of curricular programs toward a more sophisticated notion of the teacher as an active implementer. This approach is more sensitive to teachers' needs and reflects worthwhile goals, yet still tends to minimize the significance of teachers' possible contributions to the educational enterprise. We have tried to show that teachers can be involved in a wide range of inquiry-oriented activities. Several examples of these activities were presented, ranging from teachers as graduate students to teachers as active curriculum developers. All of our examples permit teachers the opportunity to play a significant role in the complex process of educational decision making.

FIGURE 6.5—1. Possible Interactions Between Teachers' Curricula and Research Results

(a) Teacher-proof curricula	*(b)* Teachers as active implementers	*(c)* Teachers as adapters in development
x	x	x
x′	x′	x′
Materials designed to minimize teacher influence on programs.	Teacher assumed to have impact on implementation of curricular ideas. Action research and implementation oriented strategies aimed at helping teachers understand curricular innovations.	Teacher assumed to be adapters of curriculum and program developers. Teacher inquiry oriented toward discovery of curricular potential, change, and transformation of materials, devising of new alternatives and decision making.
x″	x″	y x″ z

Legend: x—developers' curricular ideas; x′—translation of ideas into curricular materials; x″—implementation of curricular ideas in classroom; y, z—alternative versions of curricular ideas.

NOTES

1. For examples of discussion of research by practitioners, see Best (1970), McNamara (1972), and "Teacher-Researcher" (1970) — for arguments based on the assumption that valid educational research should be based on real-life situations; Krahmer (1967), Odell (1976), Popham and Baker (1970), and Splaine (1975) — for arguments based on the view that teaching functions entail research by their very nature; and Darland (1970), Guisti and Hogg (1973), and Hunter (1973) — for arguments based on the need for enhanced teacher professionalism.

2. See School Farm Project Committee (n.d.). Santos Mahung is currently conducting a dissertation study of the Belize program.

3. For an exploratory account of teachers' practical curriculum knowledge, see Connelly and Elbaz, 1980.

4. *Man in Nature* is a curriculum project in biology for the ninth grade of junior high school in Israel. It is a joint project of the Division of Curriculum Development of the School of Education at Haifa University and the Centre of Curriculum Development of the Israeli Ministry of Education.

REFERENCES

Ben-Peretz, M. "The Concept of Curriculum Potential," *Curriculum Theory Network* 5: 2 (1975).

Best, E.E. "The Classroom Teacher as Educational Researcher," *Independent School Bulletin* 30: 1 (October 1970).

Campbell, R., et al. *R and D Funding Policies of the National Institute of Education: Review and Recommendations*. Final Report of a panel of consultants to the Director of the National Institute of Education and the National Council on Education Research. Washington, D.C.: National Institute of Education, 1975.

Connelly, F.M. "The Functions of Curriculum Development," *Interchange* 3: 2–3 (1972).

Connelly, F.M., and F. Elbaz. "Conceptual Bases for Curriculum Thought," *Yearbook of the Association for Supervision and Curriculum Development 1980*. Washington, D.C.: ASCD, 1980.

Darland, D.D. "The Profession's Quest for Responsibility and Accountability," *Phi Delta Kappan* 52: 1 (September 1970).

Fullan, M., et al. "Action Research in the School: Involving Students and Teachers in Classroom Change." In R.A. Carlton (ed.), *Education, Change and Society: A Sociology of Canadian Education*. Toronto: Gage, 1976.

Guisti, J.P., and J.G. Hogg. "Teacher Status: Practitioner or Professional? *Clearing House* 48: 3 (November 1973).

Hunter, W.A. "Refining and Realizing Teacher as a Profession," *Yearbook of the American Association of College Teachers of Education*. 1973.

Krahmer, E. *Teachers' Lack of Familiarity with Research Techniques as a Problem for Effective Research Dissemination*. Grand Forks: Bureau of Educational Research and Services, University of North Dakota, 1967.

Leese, J., K. Frasure, and M. Johnson. *Excellence, Curriculum and the Teacher*. Albany, N.Y.: Center for Curriculum Research and Services, SUNY-Albany, 1965.

Leithwood, K.A., et al. "Curriculum Change at the System Level: A Four-Year Mathematics Project," *Curriculum Theory Network* 5: 3 (1976).

McNamara, J.F. "Teachers and Students Combine Efforts in Action Research," *Clearing House* 47: 4 (December 1972).

Odell, L. "The Classroom Teacher as a Researcher," *English Journal* 65: 1 (January 1976).

Popham, W.J., and E.L. Baker. *Systematic Instruction*. Englewood Cliffs, N.J.: Prentice-Hall, 1970.

Rapoport, R.N. "Three Dilemmas in Action Research," *Human Relations* 23: 6 (December 1970).

Schaeffer, R.J. *The School as a Center of Inquiry*. New York: Harper and Row, 1967.

School Farm Project Committee. *A Proposed Pilot Project in Agricultural Education*. Belize City, Belize, n.d.

Schwab, J.J. "The Practical: A Language for Curriculum," *School Review* 78: 1 (1969).

Shalway, L., et al. *Teachers Attaining New Roles in Research: A Challenge to the Education Community*. IRT Conference Series, No. 4. East Lansing: Institute for Research on Teaching, Michigan State University, n.d.

Splaine, J. "The Teacher as a Researcher," *Audiovisual Instruction* 20: 1 (January 1975).

Stake, R.E., et al. *Evaluating the Arts in Education: A Responsive Approach*. Columbus, Ohio: Charles E. Merrill, 1975.

"Teacher-Researcher," *Soviet Education* 12: 6–7 (April/May 1970).

Van Manen, M. "The Phenomenology of Pedagogic Observation," *Canadian Journal of Education* 4: 1 (1979).

Westbury, I. "In-service Education: Some Ruminations from the Firing Line." In L. Rubin (ed.), *The In-service Education of Teachers*. Boston: Allyn and Bacon, 1978).